Oracle Press™

OCP Oracle Database 11g: Administration II Exam Guide

(Exam 1Z0-053)

ABOUT THE AUTHOR

Bob Bryla is an Oracle 9*i*, 10*g*, and 11*g* Certified Professional with more than 20 years of experience in database design, database application development, training, and Oracle database administration. He is the primary Internet database designer and an Oracle DBA at Lands' End in Dodgeville, Wisconsin.

In his spare time, he is a technical editor for a number of Oracle Press and Apress books, in addition to authoring several certification study guides for Oracle 10*g* and 11*g*. He has also been known to watch science fiction movies and dabble in videography in his spare time.

About the Technical Editor

Gavin Powell has a BSc. in Computer Science with 20 years of experience in the IT industry. He does Oracle DBA and Internet marketing consulting work, is an accomplished computer technical writer (more than 20 works in print), and is also a semi-professional songwriter, performer, and recording artist. Gavin can be reached at ezpowell@ezpowell.com, gavinpowell@bellsouth.net, or http://oracledba .ezpowell.com.

Oracle Press™

OCP Oracle Database 11g: Administration II Exam Guide

(Exam 1Z0-053)

Bob Bryla

New York   Chicago   San Francisco   Lisbon   London   Madrid
Mexico City   Milan   New Delhi   San Juan   Seoul   Singapore   Sydney   Toronto

The McGraw·Hill Companies

Library of Congress Cataloging-in-Publication Data

Bryla, Bob.
  OCP Oracle database 11g : administration II exam guide (exam 1Z0-053) /
Bob Bryla.
    p. cm.
  Includes index.
  ISBN 978-0-07-159709-8
  1. Electronic data processing personnel—Certification. 2. Database
management—Examinations—Study guides. 3. Oracle (Computer file)
I. Title.
  QA76.3.B8247 2008
  005.75'75—dc22

                                        2008050190

OCP Oracle Database 11g: Administration II Exam Guide (Exam 1Z0-053)

1 2 3 4 5 6 7 8 9 0   FGR FGR   0 1 9 8

ISBN: Book p/n 978-0-07-159712-8 and CD p/n 978-0-07-159713-5
of set 978-0-07-159709-8

MHID: Book p/n 0-07-159712-3 and CD p/n 0-07-159713-1
of set 0-07-159709-3

Sponsoring Editor Tim Green	**Copy Editors** Lisa Theobald Bob Campbell	**Illustration** International Typesetting and Composition
Editorial Supervisor Jody McKenzie	**Proofreader** Bev Weiler	**Art Director, Cover** Jeff Weeks
Project Manager Arushi Chawla, International Typesetting and Composition	**Indexer** Broccoli Information Management	**Cover Designer** Pattie Lee
Acquisitions Coordinator Carly Stapleton	**Production Supervisor** Jim Kussow	
Technical Editor Gavin Powell	**Composition** International Typesetting and Composition	

To the gang at home: I couldn't have done it without you! And the nachos. And Metallica.

CONTENTS AT A GLANCE

CONTENTS

ACKNOWLEDGMENTS

Many technical books need the expertise of more than one person, and this one is no exception. Thanks to John Watson for providing some last-minute materials to help me finish before the very last deadline!

Thanks also go out to the copy editors at International Typesetting and Composition for filling in the gaps in my college English courses, Carly Stapleton and Tim Green for (trying to) keep me on schedule, and Gavin Powell, who gave me good advice when the theoretical met the practical.

Many of my professional colleagues at Lands' End were a source of both inspiration and guidance, especially Brook Swenson, Karen Shelton, and Dan Schwickrath. In this case, the whole is truly greater than the sum of its parts.

If you have any questions or comments about any part of this book, please do not hesitate to contact me at rjbryla@centurytel.net.

INTRODUCTION

I f you're reading this book, you're well on your way to Oracle certification—one of the hottest certifications available for Oracle database professionals. You can achieve several certification tracks and three levels of certification: the Oracle Certified Associate (OCA), Oracle Certified Professional (OCP), and Oracle Certified Master (OCM).

To earn the OCA, you've taken two exams so far and possibly some instructor-led or online courses. The next step, the OCP, requires one instructor-led or online course plus exam 1Z0-053: Oracle Database 11g Administration II. This book covers all the requirements for 1Z0-053 and can be an invaluable supplement to the instructor-led training. The exam questions that appear at the end of each chapter mirror the actual exam's questions; the companion CD contains another sample exam; and after registering on our web site, you can take yet another bonus exam. After you've read this book cover to cover, tried out all of the examples and exercises throughout the book, and passed the included exams, you are another step closer to passing exam 1Z0-053 and obtaining your OCP credential. Oracle Certified Professionals are among the best paid in the IT industry, more than Microsoft-, Sun-, and Cisco-certified professionals. Good luck with your certification journey!

In This Book

This book is organized to serve as an in-depth review for the Oracle Database 11g Administration II exam for professionals who are already certified as OCAs. Each chapter covers a major aspect of the exam, with an emphasis on the *why* as well as the *how to*. All the objectives on the exam are carefully covered in the book.

On the CD

For more information on the CD-ROM, please see the appendix "About the CD-ROM" at the back of the book.

Exam Readiness Checklist

At the end of this introduction you will find an "Exam Readiness Checklist." This table allows you to cross-reference the official exam objectives with the objectives as they are presented and covered in this book. The checklist also allows you to gauge your level of expertise on each objective at the outset of your studies, in order to help you check your progress and make sure you spend the time you need on more difficult or unfamiliar sections. References are provided for each objective exactly as the vendor presents them, along with the section of the study guide that covers that objective and a chapter and page reference.

In Every Chapter

A set of chapter components call your attention to important items, reinforce important points, and provide helpful exam-taking hints. Take a look at what you'll find in every chapter:

- Every chapter begins with **Certification Objectives**—what you need to know to pass the section on the exam dealing with the chapter topic. The objective headings identify the objectives within the chapter, so you'll always know an objective when you see it!

- **Exam Watch** notes call attention to information about, and potential pitfalls in, the exam. These helpful hints are written by authors who have taken the exams and received their certification—who better to tell you what to worry about? They know what you're about to go through!

exam
watch *Remember the precedence of the various points where globalization settings can be specified. On the server side, instance settings take precedence over database settings, but all the server settings can be overridden on the client side: first by the environment, then at the session and statement levels.*

- **Step-by-Step Exercises** are interspersed throughout the chapters. These are typically designed as hands-on exercises that allow you to get a feel for the real-world experience you need in order to pass the exams. They help you master skills that are likely to be an area of focus on the exam. Don't just read through the exercises; they are hands-on practice that you should be comfortable completing. Learning by doing is an effective way to increase your competency with a product.

■ **On the Job** notes describe the issues that come up most often in real-world settings. They provide a valuable perspective on certification- and product-related topics. They point out common mistakes and address questions that have arisen from on-the-job discussions and experience.

■ The **Certification Summary** offers a succinct review of the chapter and a restatement of salient points regarding the exam.

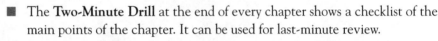

✓ ■ The **Two-Minute Drill** at the end of every chapter shows a checklist of the main points of the chapter. It can be used for last-minute review.

Q&A ■ The **Self Test** offers questions similar to those found on the certification exams. The answers to these questions, as well as explanations of the answers, can be found at the end of each chapter. By taking the Self Test after completing each chapter, you'll reinforce what you've learned from that chapter while becoming familiar with the structure of the exam questions.

Some Pointers

After you've finished reading this book, set aside some time for a thorough review. You might want to return to the book several times and make use of all the methods it offers for reviewing the material:

1. *Reread all the Two-Minute Drills* or have someone quiz you. You also can use the drills for a quick cram before the exam. You might want to make some flash cards out of 3-by-5 index cards with Two-Minute Drill material on them.

2. *Reread all the Exam Watch notes*. Remember that these notes are written by authors who have already passed the exam. They know what you should expect—and what you should be on the lookout for.

3. *Retake the Self Tests*. Taking the tests right after you've read the chapter is a good idea, because the questions help reinforce what you've just learned. However, an even better idea is to go back later and consider all the questions in the book in one sitting. Pretend that you're taking the live exam. When you go through the questions the first time, you should mark your answers on a separate piece of paper. That way, you can run through the questions as many times as you need to until you feel comfortable with the material.

4. *Complete the Exercises.* Did you do the exercises when you read through each chapter? If not, do them! These exercises are designed to cover exam topics, and there's no better way to get to know this material than by practicing. Be sure you understand why you are performing each step in each exercise. If you are not clear on some particular item, reread that section in the chapter.

Exam 1Z0-053

Exam Readiness Checklist

Official Objective	Chapter #	Page #	Beginner	Intermediate	Advanced
Database Architecture and ASM					
Describe ASM	1	18			
Set up initialization parameter files for ASM and database instances	1	26			
Start up and shut down ASM instances	1	36			
Administer ASM disk groups	1	38			
Configuring for Recoverability					
Configure multiple archive log file destinations to increase availability	2	78			
Define, apply, and use a retention policy	2	83			
Configure the flash recovery area	2	85			
Use the flash recovery area	2	89			
Using the RMAN Recovery Catalog					
Identify situations that require RMAN recovery catalog	3	106			
Create and configure a recovery catalog	3	108			
Synchronize the recovery catalog	3	112			
Create and use RMAN stored scripts	3	121			
Back up the recovery catalog	3	125			
Create and use a virtual private catalog	3	129			

Exam Readiness Checklist

Official Objective	Chapter #	Page #	Beginner	Intermediate	Advanced
Configuring Backup Specifications					
Configure backup settings	3	134			
Allocate channels to use in backing up	3	141			
Configure backup optimization	3	141			
Using RMAN to Create Backups					
Create image file backups	4	163			
Create a whole database backup	4	167			
Enable fast incremental backup	4	173			
Create duplex backup and back up backupsets	4	178			
Create an archival backup for long-term retention	4	183			
Create a multisection, compressed, and encrypted backup	4	186			
Report on and maintain backups	4	194			
Using RMAN to Perform Recovery					
Perform complete recovery from a critical or noncritical data file loss using RMAN	5	216			
Perform incomplete recovery using RMAN	5	221			
Recover using incrementally updated backups	5	227			
Switch to image copies for fast recovery	5	229			
Restore a database onto a new host	5	237			
Recover using a backup control file	5	241			
Perform disaster recovery	5	245			
Performing User-Managed Backup and Recovery					
Recover from a lost TEMP file	6	263			
Recover from a lost redo log group	6	265			
Recover from the loss of the password file	6	271			
Perform user-managed complete database recovery	6	276			
Perform user-managed incomplete database recovery	6	284			

Exam Readiness Checklist

Official Objective	Chapter #	Page #	Beginner	Intermediate	Advanced
Perform user-managed and server-managed backups	6	289			
Identify the need for backup mode	6	293			
Back up and recover a control file	6	294			
Using RMAN to Duplicate a Database					
Creating a duplicate database using RMAN	7	312			
Using a duplicate database	7	327			
Performing Tablespace Point-in-Time Recovery					
Identify the situations that require TSPITR	7	330			
Perform automated TSPITR	7	331			
Monitoring and Tuning RMAN					
Monitoring RMAN sessions and jobs	8	345			
Tuning RMAN	8	352			
Configure RMAN for asynchronous I/O	8	358			
Using Flashback Technology					
Restore dropped tables from the recycle bin	9	371			
Perform Flashback Query	9	382			
Use Flashback Transaction	9	389			
Additional Flashback Operations					
Perform Flashback Table operations	9	398			
Configure, monitor Flashback Database and Perform Flashback Database operations	9	406			
Set up and use a Flashback Data Archive	9	401			
Managing Memory					
Implement automatic memory management	10	428			
Manually configure SGA parameters	10	439			
Configure automatic PGA memory management	10	443			

Exam Readiness Checklist

Official Objective	Chapter #	Page #	Beginner	Intermediate	Advanced
Managing Database Performance					
Use the SQL Tuning Advisor	11	459			
Use the SQL Access Advisor to tune a workload	11	470			
Understand Database Replay	11	479			
Space Management					
Manage resumable space allocation	12	493			
Describe the concepts of transportable tablespaces and databases	12	500			
Reclaim wasted space from tables and indexes by using the segment shrink functionality	12	517			
Managing Resources					
Understand the database resource manager	12	529			
Create and use database resource manager components	12	531			
Diagnosing the Database					
Set up Automatic Diagnostic Repository	13	556			
Using Support Workbench	13	562			
Perform block media recovery	13	574			
Automating Tasks with the Scheduler					
Create a job, program, and schedule	14	594			
Use a time-based or event-based schedule for executing Scheduler jobs	14	602			
Create lightweight jobs	14	608			
Use job chains to perform a series of related tasks	14	611			
Administering the Scheduler					
Create windows and job classes	14	615			
Use Advanced Scheduler concepts to prioritize jobs	14	621			
Globalization					
Customize language-dependent behavior for the database and individual sessions	15	636			
Working with database and NLS character sets	15	654			

1
Database Architecture and ASM

Automatic Storage Management (ASM) is a key Oracle Database technology that you should be using in your environment, even if it has only one database and one database instance. The integration of the server file system and a volume manager built specifically for Oracle Database files makes your disk management and tuning task a breeze: Every file object is striped and mirrored to optimize performance. In addition, nearly all ASM volume management tasks can occur while the volume is online. For example, you can expand a volume or even move a volume to another disk while users are accessing it, with minimal impact to performance. The multiplexing features of an ASM cluster minimize the possibility of data loss and are generally more effective than a manual scheme that places critical files and backups on different physical drives. And if that isn't enough, you can use an ASM instance and its disk groups to service more than one database instance, further optimizing your investment in disk hardware.

Before beginning a detailed explanation of how ASM works and how you can leverage it in your environment, this chapter offers a brief overview of the Oracle Database architecture, including instance memory structures, logical database structures, and physical database structures. A thorough understanding of the Oracle Database architecture (if you don't already have this from previous coursework) is required to fully understand and appreciate how ASM works.

After describing how ASM works, the chapter shows you how to set up an ASM instance along with its associated disk groups and required initialization parameters. Starting up and shutting down an ASM instance are similar to that for a database instance, with a few key differences. Finally, you'll be introduced to a few typical ASM administration scenarios that include adding disk groups, dropping disk groups, and rebalancing a disk group.

CERTIFICATION OBJECTIVE 1.01

Understanding Database Architecture and ASM

Before diving into the specifics of ASM, you must have a thorough understanding of Oracle Database and its associated memory and process structures. This section starts with the Oracle physical storage structures, including datafiles, control files, redo log files, and archived redo log files. It also covers the non-database files required to operate Oracle Database, such as initialization files and log files. Next, it reviews the key memory structures in an Oracle instance. Finally, it shows the relationships between the physical storage structures and the memory structures.

Oracle Logical Storage Structures

The datafiles in Oracle Database are grouped together into one or more tablespaces. *Datafiles* are physical structures that are subdivided into *extents* and *blocks*. Each *tablespace* is a little like a logical wrapper for a group of datafiles. Within each tablespace are finer-grained logical database structures, such as *tables* and *indexes*. Another term used is *segments*, which in Oracle Database is used to describe the physical space occupied by a table or an index. The way in which Oracle Database is compartmentalized allows for more efficient control over disk space usage. Figure 1-1 shows the relationship between the logical storage structures in a database.

Tablespaces

An Oracle *tablespace* consists of one or more datafiles; a datafile can be a part of one and only one tablespace. For an installation of Oracle 11*g*, a minimum of two tablespaces are created: the SYSTEM tablespace and the SYSAUX tablespace. A default installation of Oracle 11*g* creates six tablespaces.

Oracle 11*g* (and originally Oracle 10*g*) allows you to create a special kind of tablespace called a *bigfile tablespace*, which can be as large as 128TB (terabytes).

FIGURE 1-1

Logical storage structures

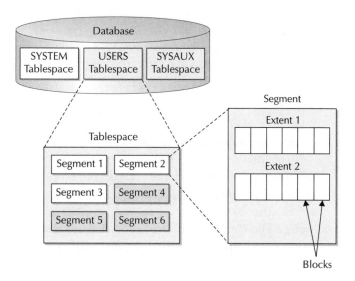

Using bigfiles makes tablespace management completely transparent to the database administrator (DBA); in other words, the DBA can manage the tablespace as a unit without worrying about the size and structure of the underlying datafiles.

Using Oracle Managed Files (OMF) can make tablespace datafile management even easier. With OMF, the DBA specifies one or more locations in the file system where datafiles, control files, and redo log files will reside, and Oracle automatically handles the naming and management of these files.

If a tablespace is *temporary*, only the segments saved in the tablespace are temporary; the tablespace itself is permanent. A temporary tablespace can be used for sorting operations and for tables that exist only for the duration of the user's session. Dedicating a tablespace for these kinds of operations helps to reduce the I/O contention between temporary segments and permanent segments stored in another tablespace, such as tables.

Tablespaces can be either *dictionary managed* or *locally managed*. In a dictionary-managed tablespace, extent management is recorded in data dictionary tables. Therefore, even if all application tables are in the USERS tablespace, the SYSTEM tablespace will still be accessed for managing Data Manipulation Language (DML) on application tables. Because all users and applications must use the SYSTEM tablespace for extent management, this creates a potential bottleneck for write-intensive applications. In a locally managed tablespace, Oracle maintains a bitmap in the header of each datafile (inside a tablespace) to track space availability. Only quotas are managed in the data dictionary, dramatically reducing the contention for data dictionary tables.

As of Oracle 9*i*, if the SYSTEM tablespace is locally managed, then all other tablespaces must be locally managed if both read and write operations are to be performed on them. Dictionary-managed tablespaces must be read-only in databases with a locally managed SYSTEM tablespace.

Blocks

A database *block* is the smallest unit of storage in Oracle. The size of a block is a specific number of bytes of storage within a given tablespace, within the database.

To facilitate efficient disk I/O performance, a block is usually a multiple of the operating system block size. The default block size is specified by the Oracle initialization parameter DB_BLOCK_SIZE. Most operating systems will allow as many as four other block sizes to be defined for other tablespaces in the database. Some high-end operating systems will allow five block sizes. The blocks in the SYSTEM, SYSAUX, and any temporary tablespaces must be of the size DB_BLOCK_SIZE.

Extents

The *extent* is the next level of logical grouping in the database. An extent consists of one or more database blocks. When you enlarge a database object, the space added to the object is allocated as an extent. Extents are managed by Oracle at the datafile level.

Segments

The next level of logical grouping is the *segment*. A segment is a group of extents that form a database object that Oracle treats as a unit, such as a table or index. As a result, this is typically the smallest unit of storage that an end user of the database will deal with. Four types of segments are found in an Oracle database: data segments, index segments, temporary segments, and undo segments.

Every table in a database resides in a single *data segment* consisting of one or more extents; Oracle allocates more than one segment for a table if it is a partitioned table or a clustered table. Data segments include LOB (large object) segments that store LOB data referenced by a LOB locator column in a table segment (if the LOB is not stored inline in the table).

Each index is stored in its own *index segment*. As with partitioned tables, each partition of a partitioned index is stored in its own segment. Included in this category are LOB index segments. A table's non-LOB columns, a table's LOB columns, and the LOB's associated indexes can all reside in their own tablespace (different segments) to improve performance.

When a user's SQL statement needs disk space to complete an operation, such as a sorting operation that cannot fit in memory, Oracle allocates a *temporary segment*. Temporary segments exist only for the duration of the SQL statement.

As of Oracle 10g, manual rollback segments exist only in the SYSTEM tablespace, and typically the DBA does not need to maintain the SYSTEM rollback segment. In previous Oracle releases, a rollback segment was created to save the previous values of a database DML operation in case the transaction was rolled back, and to maintain the "before" image data to provide read-consistent views of table data for other users accessing the table. Rollback segments were also used during database recovery for rolling back uncommitted transactions that were active when the database instance crashed or terminated unexpectedly.

In Oracle 10g, Automatic Undo Management handles the automatic allocation and management of rollback segments within an undo tablespace. Within an undo tablespace, the undo segments are structured similarly to rollback segments, except that the details of how these segments are managed is under control of Oracle, instead of being managed (often inefficiently) by the DBA. Automatic undo segments were available staring with Oracle9i, but manually managed rollback segments are still available in Oracle 10g. However, this functionality is deprecated as of Oracle 10g and will no longer be available in future releases. In Oracle 11g, Automatic Undo Management is enabled by default; in addition, a PL/SQL (Procedural Language/ Structured Query Language) procedure is provided to help you size the UNDO tablespace.

on the
Job
If you're starting out with Oracle Database 11g, all you really need to know is that manual rollback is redundant and will be unavailable in a future release. In addition, automatic undo is standard in Oracle Database 11g.

Oracle Physical Storage Structures

Oracle Database uses a number of physical storage structures on the disk to hold and manage the data from user transactions. Some of these storage structures, such as the datafiles, redo log files, and archived redo log files, hold real user data. Other structures, such as control files, maintain the state of the database objects. Text-based alert and trace files contain logging information for both routine events and error conditions in the database. Figure 1-2 shows the relationship between these physical

FIGURE 1-2

Oracle physical storage structures

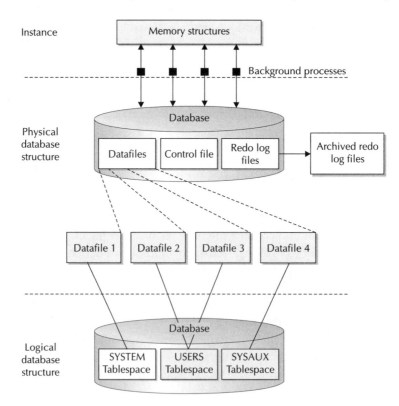

structures and the logical storage structures reviewed in the section "Oracle Logical Storage Structures."

Datafiles

Oracle Database must contain at least one *datafile*. One Oracle datafile corresponds to one physical operating system file on the disk. Each datafile in Oracle Database is a member of one and only one tablespace; a tablespace, however, can consist of many datafiles. The exception is a bigfile tablespace, which consists of exactly one datafile.

An Oracle datafile can automatically expand when it runs out of space, if the DBA created the datafile with the AUTOEXTEND parameter. The DBA can also limit the amount of expansion for a given datafile by using the MAXSIZE parameter. In any case, the size of the datafile is ultimately limited by the disk volume on which it resides.

The datafile is the ultimate resting place for all data in the database. Frequently accessed blocks in a datafile are cached in memory. Similarly, new data blocks are not immediately written out to the datafile but are written to the datafile depending on when the database writer process is active. Before a user's transaction is considered complete, however, the transaction's changes are written to the redo log files.

Redo Log Files

Whenever data is added, removed, or changed in a table, index, or other Oracle object, an entry is written to the current *redo log file*. Oracle Database must have at least two redo log files, because Oracle reuses redo log files in a circular fashion. When one redo log file is filled with redo log entries, the current log file is marked as ACTIVE, if it is still needed for instance recovery, or INACTIVE, if it is not needed for instance recovery. The next log file in the sequence is reused from the beginning of the file and is marked as CURRENT.

Ideally, the information in a redo log file is never used. However, when a power failure occurs or some other server failure causes the Oracle instance to fail, the new or updated data blocks in the database buffer cache might not yet have been written to the datafiles. When the Oracle instance is restarted, the entries in the redo log file are applied to the database datafiles in a *roll-forward* operation to restore the state of the database up to the point at which the failure occurred.

To be able to recover from the loss of one redo log file within a redo log group, multiple copies of a redo log file can exist on different physical disks. Later in this chapter, you will see how redo log files, archived log files, and control files can be *multiplexed* to ensure the availability and data integrity of the Oracle database.

Multiplexing, in a nutshell, means that you have more than one, or many more than one, copies of a structure for performance and availability.

Control Files

Oracle Database has at least one *control file* that maintains the metadata of the database. Metadata is the data about the physical structure of the database itself (the table and field definitions). Among other things, the control file contains the name of the database, when the database was created, and the names and locations of all datafiles and redo log files. In addition, the control file maintains information used by Recovery Manager (RMAN), such as the persistent RMAN settings and the types of backups that have been performed on the database. Whenever any changes are made to the structure of the database, the information about the changes is immediately reflected in the control file.

Because the control file is so critical to the operation of the database, it can also be multiplexed (one or more control files can be copied). However, no matter how many copies of the control file are associated with an instance, only one of the control files is designated as primary for purposes of retrieving database metadata.

The ALTER DATABASE BACKUP CONTROLFILE TO TRACE command is another way to back up the control file. It produces a SQL script that you can use to re-create the database control file in case all multiplexed binary versions of the control file are lost due to a catastrophic failure.

This trace file can also be used, for example, to re-create a control file if the database needs to be renamed or to change various database limits that could not otherwise be changed without re-creating the entire database.

Archived Log Files

Oracle Database can operate in one of two modes: ARCHIVELOG or NOARCHIVELOG mode. When the database is in NOARCHIVELOG mode, the circular reuse of the redo log files (also known as the *online* redo log files) means that redo entries (the contents of previous transactions) are no longer available in case of a failure to a disk drive or another media-related failure. Operating in NOARCHIVELOG mode does protect the integrity of the database in the event of an instance failure or system crash, because all transactions that are committed but not yet written to the datafiles are available in the online redo log files only. So crash recovery is limited to entries currently in online redo logs. If your last backup of datafiles fails before your earliest redo log file, you cannot recover your database.

In contrast, ARCHIVELOG mode sends a filled redo log file to one or more specified destinations and can be available to reconstruct the database at any given point in time in the event that a database media failure occurs. For example, if the disk drive containing the datafiles crashes, the contents of the database can be recovered to a point in time before the crash, given availability of a recent backup of the datafiles, the redo log files, and archived log files that were generated since the backup occurred.

The use of multiple archived log destinations for filled redo log files is critical for one of Oracle's high-availability features known as *Oracle Data Guard*, formerly known as Oracle Standby Database.

Initialization Parameter Files

When a database instance starts, the memory for the Oracle instance is allocated, and one of two types of *initialization parameter files* is opened: either a text-based file called *init<SID>.ora* (known generically as init.ora or a PFILE), or a server parameter file (SPFILE). The instance first looks for an SPFILE in the default location for the operating system ($ORACLE_HOME/dbs on Unix, for example) as either spfile<SID>.ora or spfile.ora. If neither of these files exists, the instance looks for a PFILE with the name init<SID>.ora. Alternatively, the STARTUP command can explicitly specify a PFILE to use for startup of Oracle.

Initialization parameter files, regardless of their format, specify file locations for trace files, control files, filled redo log files, and so forth. They also set limits on the sizes of the various structures in the System Global Area (SGA), as well as how many users can connect to the database simultaneously.

Until Oracle9*i,* using the init.ora file was the only way to specify initialization parameters for the instance. Although it is easy to edit with a text editor, the file has some drawbacks. If a dynamic system parameter is changed at the command line with the ALTER SYSTEM command, the DBA must remember to change the init.ora file so that the new parameter value will be in effect the next time the instance is restarted.

An SPFILE makes parameter management easier and more effective for the DBA. If an SPFILE is in use for the running instance, any ALTER SYSTEM command that changes an initialization parameter can change the initialization parameter automatically in the SPFILE, change it only for the running instance, or both. No editing of the SPFILE is necessary or even possible without corrupting the SPFILE itself.

Although you cannot mirror a parameter file or SPFILE per se, you can back up an SPFILE to an init.ora file. Both the init.ora and the SPFILE for the Oracle instance should be backed up using conventional operating system commands, or in the case of an SPFILE, using Recovery Manager.

When the DBCA (Database Configuration Assistant tool) is used to create a database, an SPFILE is created by default.

Alert and Trace Log Files

When things go wrong, Oracle can and often does write messages to the *alert log*, and in the case of background processes or user sessions, *trace log* files.

The alert log file, located in the directory specified by the initialization parameter BACKGROUND_DUMP_DEST, contains the most significant routine status messages as well as critical error conditions. When the database is started up or shut down, a message is recorded in the alert log, along with a list of initialization parameters that are different from their default values. In addition, any ALTER DATABASE or ALTER SYSTEM commands issued by the DBA are recorded. Operations involving tablespaces and their datafiles are recorded here, too, such as adding a tablespace, dropping a tablespace, and adding a datafile to a tablespace. Error conditions, such as tablespaces running out of space, corrupted redo logs, and so forth, are also recorded here—all critical conditions.

The trace files for the Oracle instance background processes are also located in BACKGROUND_DUMP_DEST. For example, the trace files for PMON (process monitor) and SMON (system monitor) contain an entry when an error occurs or when SMON needs to perform instance recovery; the trace files for QMON (queue monitor) contain informational messages when it spawns a new process.

Trace files are also created for individual user sessions or connections to the database. These trace files are located in the directory specified by the initialization parameter USER_DUMP_DEST. Trace files for user processes are created in two situations: They are created when some type of error occurs in a user session because of a privilege problem, running out of space, and so forth. Or a trace file can be created explicitly with this command:

```
ALTER SESSION SET SQL_TRACE=TRUE;
```

Trace information is generated for each SQL statement that the user executes, which can be helpful when tuning a user's SQL statement.

The alert log file can be deleted or renamed at any time; it is re-created the next time an alert log message is generated. The DBA will often set up a daily batch job (either through an operating system mechanism, the Oracle Database internal scheduling mechanism, or using Oracle Enterprise Manager's scheduler) to rename and archive the alert log on a daily basis.

As of Oracle Database 11g Release 1, the diagnostics for an instance are centralized in a single directory specified by the initialization parameter `DIAGNOSTIC_DEST`; `USER_DUMP_DEST` and `BACKGROUND_DUMP_DEST` are ignored.

Backup Files

Backup files can originate from a number of sources, such as operating system copy commands or Oracle RMAN. If the DBA performs a "cold" backup, the backup files are simply operating system copies of the datafiles, redo log files, control files, archived redo log files, and so forth.

In addition to bit-for-bit image copies of datafiles (the default in RMAN), RMAN can generate full and incremental backups of datafiles, control files, archived redo log files, and SPFILEs that are in a special format, called *backupsets*, readable only by RMAN. RMAN backupset backups are generally smaller than the original datafiles because RMAN does not back up unused blocks. RMAN is the standard for backup and recovery management, except in situations where RMAN backup processing has a detrimental effect on performance.

Oracle Memory Structures

Oracle uses the server's physical memory to hold many things for an Oracle instance: the Oracle executable code itself, session information, individual processes associated with the database, and information shared between processes (such as locks on database objects). In addition, the memory structures contain user and data dictionary SQL statements, along with cached information that is eventually permanently stored on disk, such as data blocks from database segments and information about completed transactions in the database. The data area allocated for an Oracle instance is called the *System Global Area (SGA)*. The Oracle executables reside in the software code area. In addition, an area called the *Program Global Area (PGA)* is private to each server and background process; one PGA is allocated for each user session or server process.

Figure 1-3 shows the relationships between these Oracle memory structures.

System Global Area

The SGA is a group of shared memory structures for an Oracle instance, shared by the users of the database instance. When an Oracle instance is started, memory is allocated for the SGA based on the values specified in the initialization parameter file or hard-coded in the Oracle software. Many of the parameters that control the size of the various parts of the SGA are dynamic; however, if the parameter

FIGURE 1-3   Oracle logical memory structures

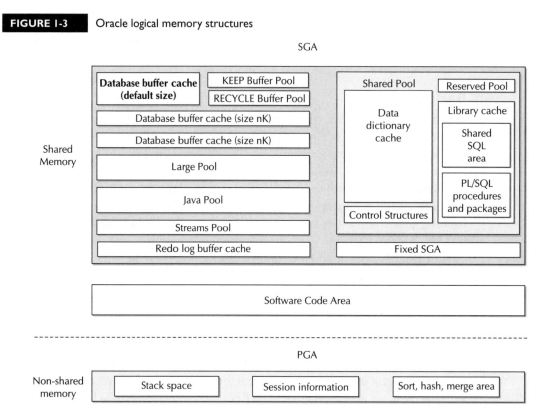

SGA_MAX_SIZE is specified, the total size of all SGA areas must not exceed the value of SGA_MAX_SIZE. If SGA_MAX_SIZE is not specified, but the parameter SGA_TARGET is specified, Oracle automatically adjusts the sizes of the SGA components so that the total amount of memory allocated is equal to SGA_TARGET. SGA_TARGET is a dynamic parameter; it can be changed while the instance is running. The parameter MEMORY_TARGET, new to Oracle 11*g*, balances all memory available to Oracle between the SGA and the PGA to optimize performance.

Memory in the SGA is allocated in units of *granules*. A granule can be either 4MB or 16MB, depending on the total size of the SGA. If the SGA is less than or equal to 128MB, a granule is 4MB; otherwise, it is 16MB. The next few subsections cover the highlights of how Oracle uses each section in the SGA.

Buffer Caches   The database *buffer cache* holds blocks of data from disk that have been recently read to satisfy a SELECT statement or that contain modified blocks that have been changed or added from a DML statement. As of Oracle9*i*, the memory area in the SGA that holds these data blocks is dynamic. This is a good thing, considering that there may be tablespaces in the database with block sizes other than the default block size. Oracle allows for tablespaces with up to five different block sizes (one block size for the default and up to four others). Each block size requires its own buffer cache. As the processing and transactional needs change during the day or during the week, the values of DB_CACHE_SIZE and DB_nK_CACHE_SIZE can be dynamically changed without restarting the instance to enhance performance for a tablespace with a given block size.

Oracle can use two additional caches with the same block size as the default (DB_CACHE_SIZE) block size: the KEEP buffer pool and the RECYCLE buffer pool. As of Oracle9i, both pools allocate memory independently of other caches in the SGA.

When a table is created, you can specify the pool where the table's data blocks will reside by using the BUFFER_POOL_KEEP or BUFFER_POOL_RECYCLE clause in the STORAGE clause. For tables that you use frequently throughout the day, it would be advantageous to place the tables into the KEEP buffer pool to minimize the I/O needed to retrieve blocks in the tables.

Shared Pool   The *shared pool* contains two major subcaches: the library cache and the data dictionary cache. The shared pool is sized by the SHARED_POOL_SIZE initialization parameter. This is another dynamic parameter that can be resized as long as the total SGA size is less than SGA_MAX_SIZE or SGA_TARGET.

The *library cache* holds information about SQL and PL/SQL statements that are run against the database. In the library cache, because it is shared by all users, many different database users can potentially share the same SQL statement.

Along with the SQL statement itself, the execution plan of the SQL statement is stored in the library cache. The second time an identical SQL statement is run, by the same user or a different user, the execution plan is already computed, improving the execution time of the query or DML statement.

If the library cache is sized too small, then frequently used execution plans can be flushed out of the cache, requiring just as frequent reloads of SQL statements into the library cache.

The *data dictionary* is a collection of database tables, owned by the SYS and SYSTEM schemas, which contain the metadata about the database, its structures, and the privileges and roles of database users. The *data dictionary cache* holds a subset of the columns from data dictionary tables after first being read into the buffer cache. Data blocks from tables in the data dictionary are used continually to assist in processing user queries and other DML commands.

If the data dictionary cache is too small, requests for information from the data dictionary will cause extra I/O to occur; these I/O-bound data dictionary requests are called *recursive calls* and should be avoided by sizing the data dictionary cache correctly.

Redo Log Buffer The *redo log buffer* holds the most recent changes to the data blocks in the datafiles. When the redo log buffer is one-third full, or every 3 seconds, Oracle writes redo log records to the redo log files. Additionally, as of Oracle Database 10g, the Log Writer (LGWR) process will write the redo log records to the redo log files when 1MB of redo is stored in the redo log buffer. The entries in the redo log buffer, once written to the redo log files, are critical to database recovery if the instance crashes before the changed data blocks are written from the buffer cache to the datafiles. A user's committed transaction is not considered complete until the redo log entries have been successfully written to the redo log files.

Large Pool The *large pool* is an optional area of the SGA. It is used for transactions that interact with more than one database, message buffers for processes performing parallel queries, and RMAN parallel backup and restore operations. As the name implies, the large pool makes available large blocks of memory for operations that need to allocate large blocks of memory at a time.

The initialization parameter LARGE_POOL_SIZE controls the size of the large pool and is a dynamic parameter as of Oracle9i release 2.

Java Pool The *Java pool* is used by the Oracle JVM (Java Virtual Machine) for all Java code and data within a user session. Storing Java code and data in the Java pool is analogous to SQL and PL/SQL code cached in the shared pool.

Streams Pool New to Oracle 10g, the *streams pool* is sized by using the initialization parameter STREAMS_POOL_SIZE. The streams pool holds data and control structures to support the Oracle Streams feature of Oracle Enterprise Edition. Oracle Streams manages the sharing of data and events in a distributed environment. If the initialization parameter STREAMS_POOL_SIZE is uninitialized or set to zero, the memory used for Streams operations is allocated from the shared pool and can use up to 10 percent of the shared pool.

Program Global Area

The PGA is an area of memory allocating dynamic sections of itself, privately for one set of connection processes. The configuration of the PGA depends on the connection configuration of the Oracle database: either *shared server* or *dedicated server*.

In a shared server configuration, multiple users share a connection to the database, minimizing memory usage on the server but potentially affecting response time for user requests. In a shared server environment, the SGA holds the persistent session information for a user instead of the PGA. Shared server environments are ideal for a large number of simultaneous connections to the database with infrequent or short-lived requests.

In a dedicated server environment, each user process gets its own connection to the database; the PGA contains the session memory for this configuration. The PGA also includes a sort area that is used whenever a user request requires a sort, bitmap merge, or hash join operation.

As of Oracle9i, the PGA_AGGREGATE_TARGET parameter, in conjunction with the WORKAREA_SIZE_POLICY initialization parameter, can ease system administration by allowing the DBA to choose a total size for all work areas and let Oracle manage and allocate the memory between all user processes. As mentioned earlier in this chapter, the parameter MEMORY_TARGET manages the PGA and SGA memory as a whole to optimize performance. The MEMORY_TARGET parameter can help to manage the sizing of PGA and SGA as a whole. In general, PGA was automated in Oracle9i. SGA was automated in 10g. Now that 11g has arrived, the sum of SGA and PGA is now automated as well. Even experienced DBAs find that automated memory structuring is more effective at managing memory allocations.

Software Code Area

Software code areas store the Oracle executable files that are running as part of an Oracle instance. These code areas are static in nature and change only when a new release of the software is installed. Typically, the Oracle software code areas are located in a privileged memory area separate from other user programs.

Oracle software code is strictly read-only and can be installed as either sharable or nonsharable. Installing Oracle software code as sharable saves memory when multiple Oracle instances are running on the same server, at the same software release level.

Background Processes

When an Oracle instance starts, multiple background processes start. A *background process* is a block of executable code designed to perform a specific task. Figure 1-4 shows the relationship between the background processes, the database, and the Oracle SGA. In contrast to a foreground process, such as a SQL*Plus session or a web browser, a background process works behind the scenes. Together, the SGA and the background processes make up an Oracle instance.

FIGURE 1-4

Oracle
background
processes

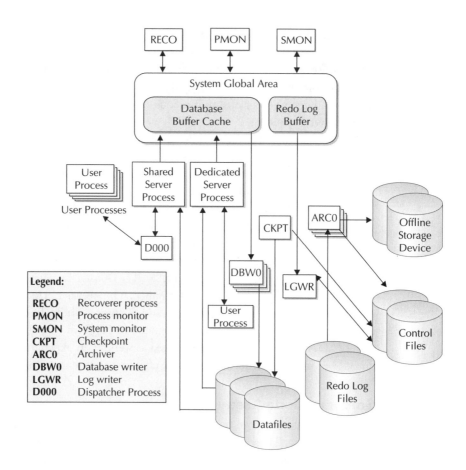

SMON In the case of a system crash or instance failure, due to a power outage or CPU failure, SMON, the *system monitor* process, performs crash recovery by applying the entries in the online redo log files to the datafiles. In addition, temporary segments in all tablespaces are purged during system restart.

One of SMON's routine tasks is to coalesce the free space in tablespaces on a regular basis if the tablespace is dictionary managed (which should be rare or nonexistent in an Oracle 11g database).

PMON If a user connection is dropped or a user process otherwise fails, PMON, the *process monitor*, does the cleanup work. It cleans up the database buffer cache along with any other resources that the user connection was using. For example, suppose a user session is updating some rows in a table, placing a lock on one or more of the rows. A thunderstorm knocks out the power at the user's desk, and the SQL*Plus session disappears when the workstation is powered off. Within milliseconds, PMON will detect that the connection no longer exists and perform the following tasks:

- Roll back the transaction that was in progress when the power went out.
- Mark the transaction's blocks as available in the buffer cache.
- Remove the locks on the affected rows in the table.
- Remove the process ID of the disconnected process from the list of active processes.

PMON will also interact with the listeners by providing information about the status of the instance for incoming connection requests.

DBWn   The *database writer* process, known as DBWR in older versions of Oracle, writes new or changed data blocks (known as *dirty blocks*) in the buffer cache to the datafiles. Using an LRU (Least Recently Used) algorithm, DBWn writes the oldest, least active blocks first. As a result, the most commonly requested blocks, even if they are dirty blocks, are in memory.

Up to 20 DBWn processes can be started, DBW0 through DBW9 and DBWa through DBWj. The number of DBWn processes is controlled by the DB_WRITER_ PROCESSES parameter.

LGWR   LGWR, or *Log Writer,* is in charge of redo log buffer management. LGWR is one of the most active processes in an instance with heavy DML activity. A transaction is not considered complete until LGWR successfully writes the redo information, including the commit record, to the redo log files. In addition, the dirty buffers in the buffer cache cannot be written to the datafiles by DBWn until LGWR has written the redo information.

If the redo log files are grouped, and one of the multiplexed redo log files in a group is damaged, LGWR writes to the remaining members of the group and records an error in the alert log file. If all members of a group are unusable, the LGWR process fails and the entire instance hangs until the problem can be corrected.

ARCn   If the database is in ARCHIVELOG mode, then the *archiver process,* or ARCn, copies redo logs to one or more destination directories, devices, or network locations whenever a redo log fills up and redo information starts to fill the next redo log in sequence. Optimally, the archive process finishes before the filled redo log is needed again; otherwise, serious performance problems occur—users cannot complete their transactions until the entries are written to the redo log files, and the redo log file is not ready to accept new entries because it is still being written to the archive location. At least three potential solutions to this problem exist: make the redo log files larger, increase the number of redo log groups, and increase the number of ARC*n* processes. Up to 10 ARC*n* processes can be started for each instance by increasing the value of the LOG_ARCHIVE_MAX_PROCESSES initialization parameter.

CKPT   The *checkpoint process*, or CKPT, helps to reduce the amount of time required for instance recovery. During a checkpoint, CKPT updates the header of the control file and the datafiles to reflect the last successful *System Change Number* (*SCN*). A checkpoint occurs automatically every time one redo log file fills and Oracle starts to fill the next one in a round-robin sequence.

The DBW*n* processes routinely write dirty buffers to advance the checkpoint from where instance recovery can begin, thus reducing the *Mean Time to Recovery (MTTR)*.

RECO   The *recoverer process*, or RECO, handles failures of distributed transactions (that is, transactions that include changes to tables in more than one database). If a table in the CCTR (contact center) database is changed along with a table in the WHSE (data warehouse) database, and the network connection between the databases fails before the table in the WHSE database can be updated, RECO will roll back the failed transaction.

CERTIFICATION OBJECTIVE 1.02

Describe ASM

ASM is a multiplexing solution that automates the layout of datafiles, control files, and redo log files by distributing them across all available disks. When new disks are added to the ASM cluster, the database files are automatically redistributed across all disk volumes for optimal performance. The multiplexing features of an ASM cluster minimize the possibility of data loss and are generally more effective than a manual scheme that places critical files and backups on different physical drives. One of the key components of an ASM disk is a *disk group*, a collection of disks that ASM manages as a unit.

When creating a new tablespace or other database structure, such as a control file or redo log file, you can specify a disk group as the storage area for the database structure instead of an operating system file. ASM takes the ease of use of OMF and combines it with mirroring and striping features to provide a robust file system and logical volume manager that can even support multiple nodes in an Oracle Real Application Cluster (RAC). ASM eliminates the need to purchase a third-party logical volume manager.

ASM not only enhances performance by automatically spreading out database objects over multiple devices, but it also increases availability by allowing new disk devices to be added to the database without shutting down the database; ASM automatically rebalances the distribution of files with minimal intervention.

The following sections review the ASM architecture, show you how to create a special type of Oracle instance to support ASM, and show how to start up and shut down an ASM instance.

ASM Architecture

ASM divides the datafiles and other database structures into extents, and it divides the extents among all the disks in the disk group to enhance both performance and reliability. Instead of mirroring entire disk volumes, ASM mirrors the database objects to provide the flexibility to mirror or stripe the database objects differently depending on their type. Optionally, the objects may not be striped at all if the underlying disk hardware is already RAID enabled, part of a storage area network (SAN), or part of a network-attached storage (NAS) device.

Automatic rebalancing is another key feature of ASM. When an increase in disk space is needed, additional disk devices can be added to a disk group, and ASM moves a proportional number of files from one or more existing disks to the new disks to maintain the overall I/O balance across all disks. This happens in the background while the database objects contained in the disk files are still online and available to users. If the impact to the I/O subsystem is high during a rebalance operation, the speed at which the rebalance occurs can be reduced using an initialization parameter.

ASM requires a special type of Oracle instance to provide the interface between a traditional Oracle instance and the file system; the ASM software components are shipped with the Oracle Database software and are always available as a selection when you're selecting the storage type for the entire database, when the database is created.

Using ASM does not, however, prevent you from mixing ASM disk groups with manual Oracle datafile management techniques. For example, you might have all of your tablespaces in ASM storage but have one tablespace created on your server's file system to make it easier to transport to another database. Still, the ease of use and performance of ASM makes a strong case for eventually using ASM disk groups for all your storage needs.

Two Oracle background processes introduced in Oracle Database 10g support ASM instances: the rebalancer (RBAL) and ARB*n*. RBAL coordinates the disk activity for disk groups, performing rebalancing when a disk is added or removed. ARB*n*, where *n* can be a number from 0 to 9, performs the actual extent movement between disks in the disk groups.

For databases that use ASM disks, two new background processes exist as of Oracle Database 10g: ASMB and RBAL. ASMB performs the communication between the database and the ASM instance, whereas RBAL performs the opening and closing of the disks in the disk group on behalf of the database. This is the same process as RBAL in an ASM instance, but performs a different, but related, function. In other words, the process behaves differently depending on the type of instance.

<hr>

EXERCISE 1-1

Find New ASM-related Processes in ASM and RDBMS Instances

For this exercise, identify the new background processes on a Linux server for both the RDBMS instance and the ASM instance. On Linux, every Oracle process has its own thread. You can either join the Oracle dynamic performance views V$BGPROCESS and V$SESSION, or use the Linux `ps -ef` command and search for command names containing either the ASM or the RDBMS instance names.

1. Query /etc/oratab for the name of the ASM and RDBMS instances:

```
[oracle@dw ~]$ tail /etc/oratab

#
# Multiple entries with the same $ORACLE_SID are not allowed.
#
#
+ASM:/u01/app/oracle/product/11.1.0/db_1:Y
dw:/u01/app/oracle/product/11.1.0/db_1:Y
[oracle@dw ~]$
```

2. Set the ORACLE_SID environment variable for the RDBMS instance; in this case it is DW:

```
[oracle@dw ~]$ export ORACLE_SID=DW
```

3. Connect to the RDBMS instance and query V$SESSION and V$BGPROCESS to get the list of running processes:

```
[oracle@dw ~]$ sqlplus / as sysdba

SQL*Plus: Release 11.1.0.6.0 - Production on Sun Feb 10 22:22:51 2008

Copyright (c) 1982, 2007, Oracle.  All rights reserved.

Connected to:
Oracle Database 11g Enterprise Edition Release 11.1.0.6.0 - Production
With the Partitioning, OLAP, Data Mining and
 Real Application Testing options

SQL> select sid, serial#, process, name, description
  2>    from v$session join v$bgprocess using(paddr);

       SID    SERIAL# PROCESS     NAME  DESCRIPTION
---------- ---------- ----------  ----- ------------------------------------
       169          1 7113        PMON  process cleanup
       168          1 7117        VKTM  Virtual Keeper of TiMe process
       167          1 7129        DIAG  diagnosibility process
       166          1 7131        DBRM  Resource Manager process
       164          3 7141        PSP0  process spawner 0
       162          1 7157        DSKM  slave DiSKMon process
       165          1 7151        DIA0  diagnosibility process 0
       163          1 7153        MMAN  Memory Manager
       162          1 7157        DBW0  db writer process 0
       148          9 7291        ARC0  Archival Process 0
       146          1 7293        ARC1  Archival Process 1
       147          1 7295        ARC2  Archival Process 2
       145          1 7297        ARC3  Archival Process 3
       160          1 7164        LGWR  Redo etc.
       161          1 7166        CKPT  checkpoint
       141          5 7359        CTWR  Change Tracking Writer
       150          2 7236        RVWR  Recovery Writer
       138          1 7370        FBDA  Flashback Data Archiver Process
       158          1 7170        SMON  System Monitor Process
       136          1 7372        SMCO  Space Manager Process
       159          1 7172        RECO  distributed recovery
       119       1030 7847        CJQ0  Job Queue Coordinator
       140          7 7375        QMNC  AQ Coordinator
       155          1 7174        RBAL  ASM Rebalance master
       157          1 7180        ASMB  ASM Background
```

```
     156            1 7182         MMON  Manageability Monitor Process
     154            1 7184         MMNL  Manageability Monitor Process 2

27 rows selected.
SQL>
```

Note the processes RBAL and ASMB near the end of the list.

4. You can use the `PID` column to identify the Linux process number and query the Linux process directly:

```
SQL> !ps -f -p 7174
UID          PID  PPID  C STIME TTY          TIME CMD
oracle      7174     1  0 21:34 ?        00:00:00 ora_rbal_dw
SQL>
```

5. Next, check for the ASM background processes by setting the `ORACLE_SID` environment variable for the ASM instance (`+ASM`):

```
[oracle@dw ~]$ export ORACLE_SID=+ASM
```

6. Connect to the ASM instance and query `V$SESSION` and `V$BGPROCESS` to get the list of running processes:

```
[oracle@dw ~]$ sqlplus / as sysasm
. . .
SQL> select sid, serial#, process, name, description
  2> from v$session join v$bgprocess using(paddr);
```

SID	SERIAL#	PROCESS	NAME	DESCRIPTION
114	1	6926	PMON	process cleanup
113	1	6928	VKTM	Virtual Keeper of TiMe process
105	1	6950	RBAL	ASM Rebalance master
106	1	6946	CKPT	checkpoint
107	1	6944	LGWR	Redo etc.
109	1	6940	MMAN	Memory Manager
109	1	6940	DSKM	slave DiSKMon process
104	1	6948	SMON	System Monitor Process
103	1	6952	GMON	diskgroup monitor
108	1	6942	DBW0	db writer process 0
111	1	6934	PSP0	process spawner 0
112	1	6932	DIAG	diagnosibility process
110	3	6938	DIA0	diagnosibility process 0
98	36	9858	ASMB	ASM Background

```
14 rows selected.

SQL>
```

Note the new processes RBAL and ASMB in the list. The ARB*n* process starts when a rebalance operation is initiated.

Creating an ASM Instance

ASM requires a dedicated Oracle instance to manage the disk groups. An ASM instance generally has a smaller memory footprint than an RDBMS instance, in the range of 60MB to 120MB. It is automatically configured when ASM is specified as the database's file storage option. When the Oracle software is installed and an existing ASM instance does not already exist, you see the Oracle Universal Installer screen shown in Figure 1-5.

As an example of disk devices used to create ASM disk groups, suppose your Linux server has a number of raw disk devices with the capacities listed in Table 1-1.

You configure the first disk group within the Oracle Universal Installer (OUI), as shown in Figure 1-6.

The name of the first disk group is DATA, and you will be using /dev/raw/raw1 and /dev/raw/raw2 to create the normal redundancy disk group. If an insufficient

FIGURE 1-5

Specifying ASM as the database file storage method

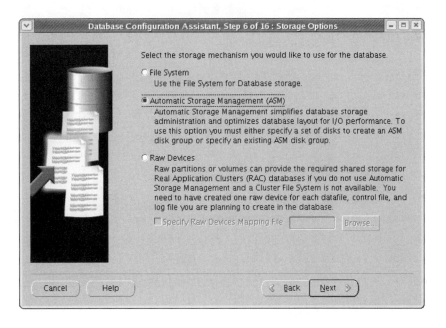

TABLE 1-1	Device Name	Capacity
	/dev/raw/raw1	12GB
Raw Disks for	/dev/raw/raw2	12GB
ASM Disk Groups	/dev/raw/raw3	12GB
	/dev/raw/raw4	12GB
	/dev/raw/raw5	4GB
	/dev/raw/raw6	4GB
	/dev/raw/raw7	4GB
	/dev/raw/raw8	4GB

number of raw disks are selected for the desired redundancy level, OUI generates an error message. After the database is created, both the regular instance and the ASM instance are started.

An ASM instance has a few other unique characteristics. Although it does have an initialization parameter file and a password file, it has no data dictionary,

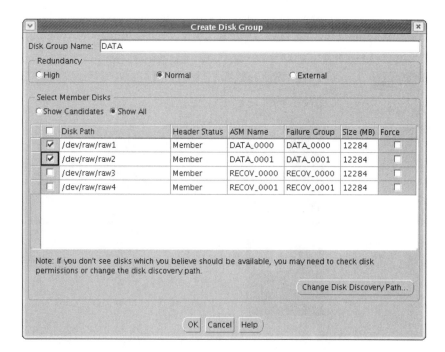

FIGURE 1-6

Configuring the initial ASM disk group with OUI

and therefore all connections to an ASM instance are via SYS and SYSTEM using operating system authentication only. You can only connect to an ASM instance with the CONNECT / AS SYSASM command. Any username/password in the CONNECT command is ignored. Disk group commands such as CREATE DISKGROUP, ALTER DISKGROUP, and DROP DISKGROUP are valid only in an ASM instance. Finally, an ASM instance is either in a NOMOUNT or MOUNT state; it is never in an OPEN state.

As of Oracle Database 11g, a new system privilege called SYSASM separates the SYSDBA database administration privilege from the ASM storage administration privilege. The operating system group OSASM automatically grants the SYSASM privilege to the operating system user; therefore, for an ASM disk group, you use the following commands to connect to an ASM instance with the SYSASM privilege using operating system authentication:

```
export ORACLE_SID=+ASM
sqlplus / as sysasm
```

Although you can still use the SYSDBA privilege in Oracle Database 11g Release 1, Oracle will write a message to the alert log indicating that the SYSDBA privilege is deprecated in the ASM instance for administrative commands and will be removed in a future release.

Here is what you will see in the alert log for the ASM instance:

```
Sun Mar 02 14:57:33 2008
WARNING: Deprecated privilege SYSDBA for command 'CREATE USER'
```

Granting the SYSASM privilege to a database user is identical to granting the SYSDBA or SYSOPER privilege; in this example, you create the user marthag and grant her the SYSASM privilege on the ASM instance, and then connect as marthag:

```
SQL> create user marthag identified by tarese3;
User created.
SQL> grant sysasm to marthag;
Grant succeeded.
SQL> connect marthag as sysasm;
Enter password:
Connected.
SQL>
```

on the **Job**

In Oracle Database 11g Release 1, the operating system group for SYSASM and SYSDBA is the same: dba. Future releases will require separate operating system groups for SYSASM and SYSDBA users.

Because an ASM instance does not have a data dictionary, only the ASM instance's password file is updated with the new user and SYSASM privilege. As you might expect, you can use the REVOKE command to revoke the SYSASM privilege from a user. As with an RDBMS instance, you can query the dynamic performance view V$PWFILE_USERS to see which users have SYSDBA, SYSASM, or SYSOPER privileges in the ASM instance:

```
SQL> select * from v$pwfile_users;

USERNAME                               SYSDBA   SYSOPER  SYSASM
------------------------------------   -------- -------- --------
SYS                                    TRUE     TRUE     TRUE
MARTHAG                                FALSE    FALSE    TRUE
BOBBYB                                 FALSE    FALSE    TRUE

SQL>
```

CERTIFICATION OBJECTIVE 1.03

Set Up Initialization Parameter Files for ASM and Database Instances

The following sections review the new initialization parameters related to ASM and the existing initialization parameters that have new values to support an ASM instance. Starting up and shutting down an ASM instance has a few caveats, the most important of which is that you can't shut down any ASM instance that is managing disks from any active RDBMS instance (you need to shut down the database first). This section also covers the naming conventions Oracle uses for ASM filenames and when you can use an abbreviated ASM filename. No discussion of ASM would be complete without a thorough review of the related dynamic performance views.

ASM Instance Components

ASM instances cannot be accessed using the variety of methods available with a traditional database. This section discusses the privileges available to you that connect with SYSDBA, SYSOPER, and SYSASM privileges. It also distinguish an ASM instance by the new and expanded initialization parameters (introduced in Oracle Database 10*g* and enhanced in Oracle Database 11*g*) available only for an ASM instance. At the end of this section, you'll read about the procedures for starting and stopping an ASM instance, along with the dependencies between ASM instances and the database instances they serve.

Accessing an ASM Instance

As mentioned earlier in the chapter, an ASM instance does not have a data dictionary, so access to the instance is restricted to users who can authenticate with the operating system—in other words, connecting as SYSDBA, SYSASM, or SYSOPER using an operating system user in the dba group.

Users who connect to an ASM instance as SYSDBA or SYSASM (remember that using SYSDBA is deprecated as of Oracle Database 11*g*) can perform all ASM operations, such as creating and deleting disk groups, as well as adding and removing disks from disk groups.

The SYSOPER users have a much more limited set of commands available in an ASM instance. In general, the commands available to SYSOPER users give only enough privileges to perform routine operations for an already configured and stable ASM instance. The following list contains the operations available as SYSOPER:

- Starting up and shutting down an ASM instance
- Mounting or dismounting a disk group
- Altering a disk group's disk status from ONLINE to OFFLINE, or vice versa
- Rebalancing a disk group
- Performing an integrity check of a disk group
- Accessing the V$ASM_* dynamic performance views

ASM Initialization Parameters

A number of initialization parameters are either specific to ASM instances or have new values within an ASM instance. An SPFILE is highly recommended instead of an initialization parameter file for an ASM instance. For example, parameters such as ASM_DISKGROUPS will automatically be maintained when a disk group is added or dropped, potentially freeing you from ever having to change this value manually.

The ASM-related initialization parameters are covered in the following sections.

INSTANCE_TYPE For an ASM instance, the INSTANCE_TYPE parameter has a value of ASM. The default, for a traditional Oracle instance, is RDBMS.

DB_UNIQUE_NAME   The default value for the DB_UNIQUE_NAME parameter is +ASM and is the unique name for a group of ASM instances within a cluster or on a single node.

ASM_POWER_LIMIT   To ensure that rebalancing operations do not interfere with ongoing user I/O, the ASM_POWER_LIMIT parameter controls how fast rebalance operations occur. The values range from 1 to 11, with 11 being the highest possible value. The default value is 1 (low I/O overhead). Because this is a dynamic parameter, you may set this to a low value during the day and set it higher overnight (assuming you're not working a 24-hour shop), whenever a disk-rebalancing operation must occur.

ASM_DISKSTRING   The ASM_DISKSTRING parameter specifies one or more operating system dependent strings to limit the disk devices that can be used to create disk groups. If this value is NULL, all disks visible to the ASM instance are potential candidates for creating disk groups. For the examples in this chapter for the test server, the value of the ASM_DISKSTRING parameter is /dev/raw/*:

```
SQL> select name, type, value from v$parameter
  2      where name = 'asm_diskstring';

NAME                 TYPE VALUE
---------------      ----------  ------------------------
asm_diskstring         2 /dev/raw/*
```

ASM_DISKGROUPS   The ASM_DISKGROUPS parameter specifies a list containing the names of the disk groups to be automatically mounted by the ASM instance at startup or by the ALTER DISKGROUP ALL MOUNT command. Even if this list is empty at instance startup, any existing disk group can be manually mounted.

LARGE_POOL_SIZE   The LARGE_POOL_SIZE parameter is useful for both regular and ASM instances; however, this pool is used differently for an ASM instance. All internal ASM packages are executed from this pool, so this parameter should be set to at least 12MB for a single instance and 16MB for a RAC instance.

ASM_PREFERRED_READ_FAILURE_GROUPS   The ASM_PREFERRED_ READ_FAILURE_GROUPS parameter, new to Oracle Database 11g, contains a list of the preferred failure groups for a given database instance when using clustered ASM instances. This parameter is instance specific: Each instance can specify a failure group that is closest to the instance's node to improve performance—for example, a failure group on the server's local disk.

ASM Dynamic Performance Views

A few new dynamic performance views are associated with ASM instances. Table 1-2 contains the common ASM-related dynamic performance views. Further explanation is provided later in this chapter.

TABLE 1-2   ASM-Related Dynamic Performance Views

View Name	Used in Standard Database?	Description
V$ASM_DISK	Yes	One row for each disk discovered by an ASM instance, used by a disk group or not. For a database instance, one row for each disk group in use by the instance.
V$ASM_DISKGROUP	Yes	For an ASM instance, one row for each disk group containing general characteristics of the disk group. For a database instance, one row for each disk group in use whether mounted or not.
V$ASM_FILE	No	One row for each file in every mounted disk group.
V$ASM_OPERATION	No	One row for each executing long-running operation in the ASM instance.
V$ASM_TEMPLATE	Yes	One row for each template in each mounted disk group in the ASM instance. For a database instance, one row for each template for each mounted disk group.
V$ASM_CLIENT	Yes	One row for each database using disk groups managed by the ASM instance. For a database instance, one row for the ASM instance if any ASM files are open.
V$ASM_ALIAS	No	One row for every alias in every mounted disk group.

Query Disk Groups and Available Raw Devices

In this exercise, you'll find out the disk groups names and their associated underlying devices; then confirm the raw device list on the Linux server.

1. Connect to your database instance (NOT the ASM instance), and query the dynamic performance view V$ASM_DISK:

```
SQL> select group_number, disk_number, mount_status, name, path
  1  from v$asm_disk
  2  order by group_number, disk_number;

GROUP_NUMBER    DISK_NUMBER    MOUNT_STATUS  NAME            PATH
--------------- -------------- ------------- --------------- -------------
0               0              CLOSED                        /dev/raw/raw7
0               1              CLOSED                        /dev/raw/raw8
0               2              CLOSED                        /dev/raw/raw5
0               3              CLOSED                        /dev/raw/raw6
1               0              CACHED        DATA_0000       /dev/raw/raw1
1               1              CACHED        DATA_0001       /dev/raw/raw2
2               0              CACHED        RECOV_0000      /dev/raw/raw3
2               1              CACHED        RECOV_0001      /dev/raw/raw4

8 rows selected
```

Note that four out the eight available raw devices are being used for ASM disk groups.

2. From the Linux command line, query the available raw disk groups with the raw command:

```
[root@dw ~]# raw -qa
/dev/raw/raw1:  bound to major 8, minor 49
/dev/raw/raw2:  bound to major 8, minor 65
/dev/raw/raw3:  bound to major 8, minor 81
/dev/raw/raw4:  bound to major 8, minor 97
/dev/raw/raw5:  bound to major 8, minor 113
/dev/raw/raw6:  bound to major 8, minor 129
/dev/raw/raw7:  bound to major 8, minor 145
/dev/raw/raw8:  bound to major 8, minor 161
[root@dw ~]#
```

ASM Filename Formats

Oracle best practices recommend that ASM files should be created as OMFs, so the details of the actual filename within the disk group are not needed for most administrative functions. When an object in an ASM disk group is dropped, the file is automatically deleted. Certain commands will expose the actual filenames, such as ALTER DATABASE BACKUP CONTROLFILE TO TRACE, as well as some data dictionary and dynamic performance views. For example, the dynamic performance view V$DATAFILE shows the actual filenames within each disk group. Here is an example:

```
SQL> select file#, name, blocks from v$datafile;

    FILE# NAME                                                  BLOCKS
--------- --------------------------------------------- ----------
        1 +DATA/dw/datafile/system.256.627432971            89600
        2 +DATA/dw/datafile/sysaux.257.627432973            77640
        3 +DATA/dw/datafile/undotbs1.258.627432975          12800
        4 +DATA/dw/datafile/users.259.627432977               640
        5 +DATA/dw/datafile/example.265.627433157           12800
        6 /u05/oradata/dmarts.dbf                            32000
        8 /u05/oradata/xport.dbf                             38400

7 rows selected.
```

ASM filenames can be in one of six different formats. In the sections that follow, you'll learn about the different formats and the context in which they can be used—either as a reference to an existing file, during a single-file creation operation, or during a multiple-file creation operation.

Fully Qualified Names

Fully qualified ASM filenames are used only when referencing an existing file. A fully qualified ASM filename has the format

```
+group/dbname/file type/tag.file.incarnation
```

where *group* is the disk group name, *dbname* is the database to which the file belongs, *file type* is the Oracle file type, *tag* is information specific to the file type, and the *file.incarnation* pair ensures uniqueness. Here is an example of an ASM file for the USERS tablespace:

```
+DATA/dw/datafile/users.259.627432977
```

The disk group name is +DATA, the database name is DW, it's a datafile for the USERS tablespace, and the file number/incarnation pair 259.627432977 ensures uniqueness if you decide to create another ASM datafile for the USERS tablespace.

Numeric Names

Numeric names are used only when referencing an existing ASM file. This allows you to refer to an existing ASM file by only the disk group name and the file number/incarnation pair. The numeric name for the ASM file in the preceding section is

```
+DATA.259.627432977
```

Alias Names

An alias can be used when either referencing an existing object or creating a single ASM file. Using the ALTER DISKGROUP ADD ALIAS command, you can create a more readable name for an existing or a new ASM file. The alias is distinguishable from a regular ASM filename because it does not end in a dotted pair of numbers (the file number/incarnation pair), as shown here:

```
SQL> alter diskgroup data
  2      add directory '+data/purch';
Diskgroup altered.

SQL> alter diskgroup data
  2      add alias '+data/purch/users.dbf'
  3      for '+data/dw/datafile/users.259.627432977';
Diskgroup altered.

SQL>
```

Alias with Template Names

An alias with a template can be used only when creating a new ASM file. Templates provide a shorthand for specifying a file type and a tag when creating a new ASM file.

Here's an example of an alias using a template for a new tablespace in the +DATA disk group:

```
SQL> create tablespace users2 datafile '+data(datafile)';
Tablespace created.
```

The template DATAFILE specifies COARSE striping, MIRROR for a normal-redundancy group, and HIGH for a high-redundancy group; it is the default for a datafile. Because the name was not fully qualified, the ASM name for this disk group is as follows:

```
+DATA/dw/datafile/users2.267.627782171
```

You can read more about ASM templates in the section "ASM File Types and Templates" later in this chapter.

Incomplete Names

An incomplete filename format can be used either for single-file or multiple-file creation operations. Only the disk group name is specified, and a default template is used depending on the type of file, as shown here:

```
SQL> create tablespace users5 datafile '+data1';
Tablespace created.
```

Incomplete Names with Template

As with incomplete ASM filenames, an incomplete filename with a template can be used either for single-file or multiple-file creation operations. Regardless of the actual file type, the template name determines the characteristics of the file.

Even though a tablespace is created in the following example, the striping and mirroring characteristics of an online log file (fine striping) are used for the new tablespace instead of the attributes for the datafile (coarse striping):

```
SQL> create tablespace users6 datafile '+data1(onlinelog)';
Tablespace created.
```

ASM File Types and Templates

ASM supports all types of files used by the database except for operating system executables. Table 1-3 contains the complete list of ASM file types; the ASM File Type and Tag columns are those presented previously in the section ASM Filename Formats.

TABLE I-3	ASM File Types

Oracle File Type	ASM File Type	Tag	Default Template
Control files	controlfile	cf (control file) or bcf (backup control file)	CONTROLFILE
Data files	datafile	*tablespace name.file#*	DATAFILE
Online logs	online_log	*log_thread#*	ONLINELOG
Archive logs	archive_log	parameter	ARCHIVELOG
Temp files	temp	*tablespace name.file#*	TEMPFILE
RMAN datafile backup piece	backupset	Client specified	BACKUPSET
RMAN incremental backup piece	backupset	Client specified	BACKUPSET
RMAN archive log backup piece	backupset	Client specified	BACKUPSET
RMAN datafile copy	datafile	*tablespace name.file#*	DATAFILE
Initialization parameters	init	spfile	PARAMETERFILE
Broker config	drc	drc	DATAGUARDCONFIG
Flashback logs	rlog	*thread#_log#*	FLASHBACK
Change tracking bitmap	ctb	bitmap	CHANGETRACKING
Auto backup	autobackup	Client specified	AUTOBACKUP
Data Pump dumpset	dumpset	dump	DUMPSET
Cross-platform data files			XTRANSPORT

The default ASM file templates referenced in the last column of Table 1-3 are presented in Table 1-4.

When a new disk group is created, a set of ASM file templates copied from the default templates in Table 1-4 is saved with the disk group; as a result, individual template characteristics can be changed and apply only to the disk group in which they reside. In other words, the DATAFILE system template in disk group +DATA1 may have the default coarse striping, but the DATAFILE template in disk group

TABLE 1-4	ASM File Template Defaults			

System Template	External Redundancy	Normal Redundancy	High Redundancy	Striping
CONTROLFILE	Unprotected	Two-way mirroring	Three-way mirroring	Fine
DATAFILE	Unprotected	Two-way mirroring	Three-way mirroring	Coarse
ONLINELOG	Unprotected	Two-way mirroring	Three-way mirroring	Fine
ARCHIVELOG	Unprotected	Two-way mirroring	Three-way mirroring	Coarse
TEMPFILE	Unprotected	Two-way mirroring	Three-way mirroring	Coarse
BACKUPSET	Unprotected	Two-way mirroring	Three-way mirroring	Coarse
XTRANSPORT	Unprotected	Two-way mirroring	Three-way mirroring	Coarse
PARAMETERFILE	Unprotected	Two-way mirroring	Three-way mirroring	Coarse
DATAGUARDCONFIG	Unprotected	Two-way mirroring	Three-way mirroring	Coarse
FLASHBACK	Unprotected	Two-way mirroring	Three-way mirroring	Fine
CHANGETRACKING	Unprotected	Two-way mirroring	Three-way mirroring	Coarse
AUTOBACKUP	Unprotected	Two-way mirroring	Three-way mirroring	Coarse
DUMPSET	Unprotected	Two-way mirroring	Three-way mirroring	Coarse

+DATA2 may have fine striping. You can create your own templates in each disk group as needed.

When an ASM datafile is created with the DATAFILE template, by default the datafile is 100MB and autoextensible. The maximum size is 32767MB (32GB).

CERTIFICATION OBJECTIVE 1.04

Start Up and Shut Down ASM Instances

An ASM instance is started much like a database instance, except that the STARTUP command defaults to STARTUP MOUNT. Because there is no control file, database, or data dictionary to mount, the ASM disk groups are mounted instead of a database. The command STARTUP NOMOUNT starts up the instance but does not mount any ASM disks. In addition, you can specify STARTUP RESTRICT to temporarily prevent database instances from connecting to the ASM instance to mount disk groups.

Performing a SHUTDOWN command on an ASM instance will fail if any connected RDBMS instances exist; you need to shut down the dependent RDBMS instances first. The only exception to this is if you use the SHUTDOWN ABORT command on the ASM instance, which eventually forces all dependent databases to perform a SHUTDOWN ABORT after losing the connection with the ASM instance and generating an ORA-15064 error message.

on the
()ob

Use SHUTDOWN ABORT only when you have no other option. A SHUTDOWN ABORT literally kills all processes off at the operating system level. Any pending database change activity will be rolled back on restart. Effectively, the restart will do the work that something like a SHUTDOWN ABORT will do anyway. The only difference is that with SHUTDOWN ABORT you could lose your database. Recovering using RMAN is possible but avoidable. And sometimes you could discover that whoever set up your backups might not have done it quite to the standard most DBAs would hope for.

For multiple ASM instances sharing disk groups, such as in a RAC environment, the failure of an ASM instance does not cause the database instances to fail. Instead, another ASM instance performs a recovery operation for the failed instance. Failures of connected RDBMS instances do not affect ASM instances.

EXERCISE 1-3

Stop ASM Instance with Active Connections

In this exercise, find out what happens when you attempt to stop an ASM instance with active database clients.

1. Query /etc/oratab for the name of the ASM instance:

```
[oracle@dw ~]$ cat /etc/oratab
#
# This file is used by ORACLE utilities.  It is created by root.sh
# and updated by the Database Configuration Assistant when creating
# a database.

# A colon, ':', is used as the field terminator.  A new line terminates
# the entry.  Lines beginning with a pound sign, '#', are comments.
#
# Entries are of the form:
#   $ORACLE_SID:$ORACLE_HOME:<N|Y>:
#
# The first and second fields are the system identifier and home
# directory of the database respectively.  The third filed indicates
# to the dbstart utility that the database should , "Y", or should not,
# "N", be brought up at system boot time.
#
# Multiple entries with the same $ORACLE_SID are not allowed.
#
#
+ASM:/u01/app/oracle/product/11.1.0/db_1:Y
dw:/u01/app/oracle/product/11.1.0/db_1:Y
[oracle@dw ~]$
```

2. Set the ORACLE_SID environment variable for the ASM instance:

```
[oracle@dw ~]$ export ORACLE_SID=+ASM
```

3. Connect to the ASM instance:

```
[oracle@dw ~]$ sqlplus / as sysasm

SQL*Plus: Release 11.1.0.6.0 - Production on Sun Feb 10 22:22:51 2008

Copyright (c) 1982, 2007, Oracle.  All rights reserved.
```

```
Connected to:
Oracle Database 11g Enterprise Edition Release 11.1.0.6.0 - Production
With the Partitioning, OLAP, Data Mining and
 Real Application Testing options
SQL>
```

4. Attempt to shut down the ASM instance:

```
SQL> shutdown immediate
ORA-15097: cannot SHUTDOWN ASM instance with connected RDBMS instance
SQL>
```

Note that using SHUTDOWN ABORT will force the ASM instance to shut down but will eventually force an implicit SHUTDOWN ABORT on each attached database instance.

CERTIFICATION OBJECTIVE 1.05

Administer ASM Disk Groups

Using ASM disk groups benefits you in a number of ways: I/O performance is improved, availability is increased, and the ease with which you can add a disk to a disk group, or add an entirely new disk group, enables you to manage many more databases in the same amount of time. Understanding the components of a disk group as well as correctly configuring a disk group are important goals for a successful DBA.

This section delves more deeply into the details of the structure of a disk group. It also reviews the different types of administrative tasks related to disk groups and shows how disks are assigned to failure groups; how disk groups are mirrored; and how disk groups are created, dropped, and altered. You'll see some raw disk devices used on a Linux server to demonstrate how disk groups are created and maintained in a hands-on lab exercise. You'll also briefly review the EM Database Control interface to ASM; at the command line, you get an introduction to the asmcmd command-line utility that you can use to browse, copy, and manage ASM objects.

Disk Group Architecture

As defined earlier in this chapter, a disk group is a collection of physical disks managed as a unit. Every ASM disk, as part of a disk group, has an ASM disk name that is either assigned by the DBA or automatically assigned when it is assigned to the disk group.

Files in a disk group are striped on the disks using either coarse striping or fine striping. *Coarse striping* spreads files in units of 1MB each across all disks. Coarse striping is appropriate for a system with a high degree of concurrent small I/O requests, such as an Online Transaction Processing (OLTP) environment. Alternatively, *fine striping* spreads files in units of 128KB and is appropriate for traditional data warehouse environments or OLTP systems with low concurrency; it maximizes response time for individual I/O requests.

Disk Group Mirroring and Failure Groups

Before defining the type of mirroring within a disk group, you must group disks into failure groups. A *failure group* is one or more disks within a disk group that share a common resource, such as a disk controller, whose failure would cause the entire set of disks to be unavailable to the group. In most cases, an ASM instance does not know the hardware and software dependencies for a given disk. Therefore, unless you specifically assign a disk to a failure group, each disk in a disk group is assigned to its own failure group.

Once the failure groups have been defined, you can define the mirroring for the disk group; the number of failure groups available within a disk group can restrict the type of mirroring available for the disk group. Three types of mirroring are available: external redundancy, normal redundancy, and high redundancy.

External Redundancy

External redundancy requires only one disk location and assumes that the disk is not critical to the ongoing operation of the database or that the disk is managed externally with high-availability hardware such as a RAID controller.

Normal Redundancy

Normal redundancy provides two-way mirroring and requires at least two failure groups within a disk group. Failure of one of the disks in a failure group does not cause any downtime for the disk group or any data loss other than a slight performance hit for queries against objects in the disk group; when all disks in the failure group are online, read performance is typically improved because the requested data is available on more than one disk.

High Redundancy

High redundancy provides three-way mirroring and requires at least three failure groups within a disk group. The failure of disks in two out of the three failure groups is for the most part transparent to the database users, as in normal redundancy mirroring.

Mirroring is managed at a very low level. Extents, not disks, are mirrored. In addition, each disk will have a mixture of both primary and mirrored (secondary and tertiary) extents on each disk. Although a slight amount of overhead is incurred in managing mirroring at the extent level, it provides the advantage of spreading out the load from the failed disk to all other disks instead of to a single disk.

Disk Group Dynamic Rebalancing

Whenever you change the configuration of a disk group—whether you are adding or removing a failure group or a disk within a failure group—dynamic rebalancing occurs automatically to proportionally reallocate data from other members of the disk group to the new member of the disk group. This rebalance occurs while the database is online and available to users. Any impact to ongoing database I/O can be controlled by adjusting the value of the initialization parameter ASM_POWER_LIMIT to a lower value.

Not only does dynamic rebalancing free you from the tedious and often error-prone task of identifying hot spots in a disk group, it also provides an automatic way to migrate an entire database from a set of slower disks to a set of faster disks while the entire database remains online. Faster disks are added as a new failure group in the existing disk group with the slower disks, and the automatic rebalance occurs. After the rebalance operations complete, the failure groups containing the slower disks are dropped, leaving a disk group with only fast disks. To make this operation even faster, both the ADD and DROP operations can be initiated within the same ALTER DISKGROUP command.

As an example, suppose you want to create a new disk group with high redundancy to hold tablespaces for a new credit card authorization. Using the view V$ASM_DISK, you can view all disks discovered using the initialization parameter ASM_DISKSTRING, along with the status of the disk (in other words, whether it is assigned to an existing disk group or is unassigned). Here is the command:

```
SQL> select group_number, disk_number, name,
  2         failgroup, create_date, path from v$asm_disk;

GROUP_NUMBER DISK_NUMBER NAME        FAILGROUP  CREATE_DA PATH
------------ ----------- ----------  ---------- --------- ------------
           0           0                                  /dev/raw/raw8
           0           1                                  /dev/raw/raw7
           0           2                                  /dev/raw/raw6
           0           3                                  /dev/raw/raw5
           2           1 RECOV_0001  RECOV_0001 08-JUL-07 /dev/raw/raw4
           2           0 RECOV_0000  RECOV_0000 08-JUL-07 /dev/raw/raw3
           1           1 DATA_0001   DATA_0001  08-JUL-07 /dev/raw/raw2
           1           0 DATA_0000   DATA_0000  08-JUL-07 /dev/raw/raw1

8 rows selected.

SQL>
```

Out of the eight disks available for ASM, only four are assigned to two disk groups, DATA and RECOV, each in its own failure group. The disk group name can be obtained from the view V$ASM_DISKGROUP:

```
SQL> select group_number, name, type, total_mb, free_mb
  2         from v$asm_diskgroup;

GROUP_NUMBER NAME        TYPE    TOTAL_MB    FREE_MB
------------ ----------  ------  ---------- ----------
           1 DATA        NORMAL      24568      20798
           2 RECOV       NORMAL      24568      24090

SQL>
```

Note that if you had a number of ASM disks and disk groups, you could have joined the two views on the GROUP_NUMBER column and filtered the query result by GROUP_NUMBER. Also, you see from V$ASM_DISKGROUP that both of the disk groups are normal redundancy groups consisting of two disks each.

Your first step is to create the disk group on the ASM instance:

```
SQL> create diskgroup data2 high redundancy
  2         failgroup fg1 disk '/dev/raw/raw5' name d2a
  3         failgroup fg2 disk '/dev/raw/raw6' name d2b
```

```
4        failgroup fg3 disk '/dev/raw/raw7' name d2c
5        failgroup fg4 disk '/dev/raw/raw8' name d2d;

Diskgroup created.

SQL>
```

Looking at the dynamic performance views, you see the new disk group available in V$ASM_DISKGROUP and the failure groups in V$ASM_DISK:

```
SQL> select group_number, name, type, total_mb, free_mb
  2     from v$asm_diskgroup;
GROUP_NUMBER NAME         TYPE     TOTAL_MB    FREE_MB
------------ ---------- ------ ---------- ----------
           1 DATA         NORMAL      24568      20798
           2 RECOV        NORMAL      24568      24090
           3 DATA2        HIGH        16376      16221

SQL> select group_number, disk_number, name,
  2        failgroup, create_date, path from v$asm_disk;

GROUP_NUMBER DISK_NUMBER NAME         FAILGROUP   CREATE_DA PATH
------------ ----------- ---------- ---------- --------- -------------
           3           3 D2D          FG4         13-JUL-07 /dev/raw/raw8
           3           2 D2C          FG3         13-JUL-07 /dev/raw/raw7
           3           1 D2B          FG2         13-JUL-07 /dev/raw/raw6
           3           0 D2A          FG1         13-JUL-07 /dev/raw/raw5
           2           1 RECOV_0001   RECOV_0001  08-JUL-07 /dev/raw/raw4
           2           0 RECOV_0000   RECOV_0000  08-JUL-07 /dev/raw/raw3
           1           1 DATA_0001    DATA_0001   08-JUL-07 /dev/raw/raw2
           1           0 DATA_0000    DATA_0000   08-JUL-07 /dev/raw/raw1

8 rows selected.

SQL>
```

Now that the configuration of the new disk group has been completed, you can create a tablespace in the new disk group from the database instance:

```
SQL> create tablespace users3 datafile '+DATA2';
Tablespace created.
```

Because ASM files can be OMFs, you don't need to specify any other characteristics when you create the tablespace.

Disk Group Fast Mirror Resync

Mirroring the files in your disk groups improves performance and availability; when a failed disk in a disk group is repaired and brought back online, however, the remirroring of the entire new disk can be time-consuming. There are occasions when a disk in a disk group needs be brought offline because of a disk controller failure; the entire disk does not need remirroring, and only the data changed during the failed disk's downtime needs to be resynced. As a result, you can use the ASM fast mirror resync feature introduced in Oracle Database 11g.

To implement fast mirror resync, you set the time window within which ASM will not automatically drop the disk in the disk group when a transient planned or unplanned failure occurs. During the transient failure, ASM keeps track of all changed data blocks so that when the unavailable disk is brought back online, only the changed blocks need to be remirrored instead of the entire disk.

To set a time window for the DATA disk group, you must first set the compatibility level of the disk group to 11.1 or higher for both the RDBMS instance and the ASM instance (this needs to be done only once for the disk group):

```
SQL> alter diskgroup data set attribute
  2      'compatible.asm' = '11.1.0.0.0';

Diskgroup altered.

SQL> alter diskgroup data set attribute
  2      'compatible.rdbms' = '11.1.0.0.0';

Diskgroup altered.

SQL>
```

The side effect to using a higher compatibility level for the RDBMS and ASM instance is that only other instances with a version number 11.1.0.0.0 or higher can access this disk group. Next, set the disk group attribute DISK_REPAIR_TIME as in this example:

```
SQL> alter diskgroup data set attribute
  2      'disk_repair_time' = '2.5h';

Diskgroup altered.

SQL>
```

The default disk repair time is 3.6 hours, which should be more than adequate for most planned and unplanned (transient) outages. Once the disk is back online, run this command to notify the ASM instance that the disk DATA_0001 is back online:

```
SQL> alter diskgroup data online disk data_0001;

Diskgroup altered.

SQL>
```

This command starts the background procedure to copy all changed extents on the remaining disks in the disk group to the disk DATA_0001 that is now back online.

Altering Disk Groups

Disks can be added and dropped from a disk group; also, most characteristics of a disk group can be altered without re-creating the disk group or impacting user transactions on objects in the disk group.

When a disk is added to a disk group, a rebalance operation is performed in the background after the new disk is formatted for use in the disk group. As mentioned earlier in this chapter, the speed of the rebalance is controlled by the initialization parameter ASM_POWER_LIMIT.

Continuing with our example in the preceding section, suppose you decide to improve the I/O characteristics of the disk group DATA by adding the last available raw disk to the disk group, as follows:

```
SQL> alter diskgroup data
  2      add failgroup d1fg3 disk '/dev/raw/raw8' name d1c;

Diskgroup altered.
```

The command returns immediately and the formatting and rebalancing continue in the background. You then check the status of the rebalance operation by checking the view V$ASM_OPERATION:

```
SQL> select group_number, operation, state, power, actual,
  2      sofar, est_work, est_rate, est_minutes from v$asm_operation;
```

```
GROUP_NUMBER OPERA STAT POWER ACTUA SOFAR EST_WORK EST_RATE EST_MINUTES
------------ ----- ---- ----- ----- ----- -------- -------- -----------
           1 REBAL RUN      1     1     3      964       60          16
```

Because the estimate for completing the rebalance operation is 16 minutes, you decide to allocate more resources to the rebalance operation and change the power limit for this particular rebalance operation:

```
SQL> alter diskgroup data rebalance power 8;
Diskgroup altered.
```

Checking the status of the rebalance operation confirms that the estimated time to completion has been reduced to 4 minutes instead of 16:

```
SQL> select group_number, operation, state, power, actual,
  2     sofar, est_work, est_rate, est_minutes from v$asm_operation;

GROUP_NUMBER OPERA STAT POWER ACTUA SOFAR EST_WORK EST_RATE EST_MINUTES
------------ ----- ---- ----- ----- ----- -------- -------- -----------
           1 REBAL RUN      8     8    16      605      118           4
```

About 4 minutes later, you check the status once more:

```
SQL> /
no rows selected
```

Finally, you can confirm the new disk configuration from the V$ASM_DISK and V$ASM_DISKGROUP views:

```
SQL> select group_number, disk_number, name,
  2     failgroup, create_date, path from v$asm_disk;

GROUP_NUMBER DISK_NUMBER NAME       FAILGROUP   CREATE_DA PATH
------------ ----------- ---------- ----------- --------- ---------------
           1           2 D1C        D1FG3       13-JUL-07 /dev/raw/raw8
           3           2 D2C        FG3         13-JUL-07 /dev/raw/raw7
           3           1 D2B        FG2         13-JUL-07 /dev/raw/raw6
           3           0 D2A        FG1         13-JUL-07 /dev/raw/raw5
           2           1 RECOV_0001 RECOV_0001  08-JUL-07 /dev/raw/raw4
           2           0 RECOV_0000 RECOV_0000  08-JUL-07 /dev/raw/raw3
           1           1 DATA_0001  DATA_0001   08-JUL-07 /dev/raw/raw2
           1           0 DATA_0000  DATA_0000   08-JUL-07 /dev/raw/raw1

8 rows selected.
```

```
SQL> select group_number, name, type, total_mb, free_mb
  2    from v$asm_diskgroup;

GROUP_NUMBER NAME         TYPE     TOTAL_MB    FREE_MB
------------ ---------- ------ ---------- ----------
           1 DATA        NORMAL      28662      24814
           2 RECOV       NORMAL      24568      24090
           3 DATA2       HIGH        12282      11820

SQL>
```

Note that the disk group DATA is still normal redundancy, even though it has three failure groups. However, the I/O performance of SELECT statements against objects in the DATA disk group is improved due to additional copies of extents available in the disk group.

Other disk group ALTER commands are listed in Table 1-5.

Enterprise Manager Database Control and ASM Disk Groups

The Enterprise Manager (EM) Database Control can also be used to administer disk groups. For a database that uses ASM disk groups, the Disk Groups link under the Administration tab brings you to a login page for the ASM instance shown in Figure 1-7. Remember that authentication for an ASM instance uses operating system authentication only. Figure 1-8 shows the home page for the ASM instance.

After authentication with the ASM instance, you can perform the same operations that you performed previously in this chapter at the command line—mounting and dismounting disk groups, adding disk groups, adding or deleting

TABLE 1-5	ALTER DISKGROUP Command	Description
ALTER DISKGROUP Commands	ALTER DISKGROUP ... DROP DISK	Removes a disk from a failure group within a disk group and performs an automatic rebalance
	ALTER DISKGROUP ... DROP ... ADD	Drops a disk from a failure group and adds another disk, all in the same command
	ALTER DISKGROUP ... MOUNT	Makes a disk group available to all instances
	ALTER DISKGROUP ... DISMOUNT	Makes a disk group unavailable to all instances
	ALTER DISKGROUP ... CHECK ALL	Verifies the internal consistency of the disk group

FIGURE 1-7

EM Database
Control ASM
instance login
page

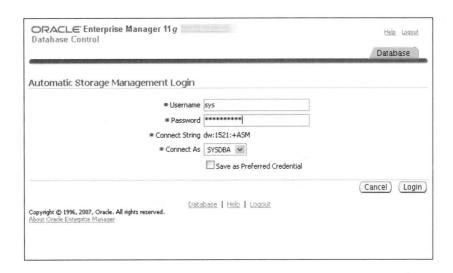

FIGURE 1-8   EM Database Control ASM instance home page

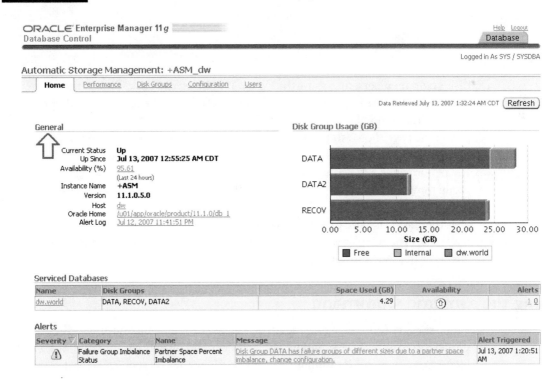

FIGURE 1-9   EM Database Control ASM disk group administration page

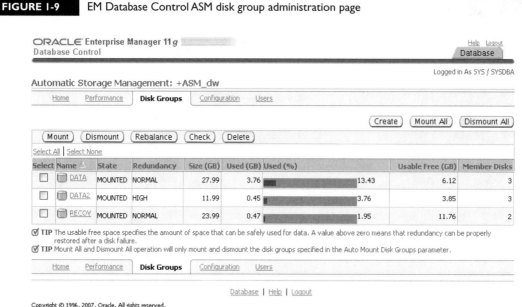

disk group members, and so forth. Figure 1-9 shows the Disk Groups tab of the ASM administration page, whereas Figure 1-10 shows the statistics and options for the disk group DATA.

On the page shown in Figure 1-10 you can see that the new disk in the disk group is significantly smaller than the other disks in the group; this could affect the performance and waste disk space within the disk group. To remove a failure group using EM Database Control, select the member disk's check box and click the Remove button.

Other EM Database Control ASM-related pages show I/O response time for the disk group, the templates defined for the disk group, the initialization parameters in effect for this ASM instance, and more.

Using the asmcmd Command

The asmcmd utility, new to Oracle 10g Release 2, is a command-line utility that provides an easy way for you to browse and maintain objects within ASM disk groups by using a command set similar to Linux shell commands such as ls and mkdir.

FIGURE 1-10 EM Database Control ASM disk group statistics

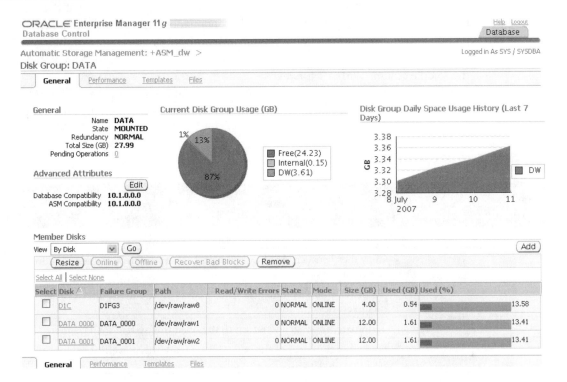

The hierarchical nature of objects maintained by the ASM instance lends itself to a command set similar to what you would use to browse and maintain files in a Linux file system.

Before you can use `asmcmd`, you must ensure that the environment variables `ORACLE_BASE`, `ORACLE_HOME`, and `ORACLE_SID` are set to point to the ASM instance; for the ASM instance used in this chapter, these variables are set as follows:

```
ORACLE_BASE=/u01/app/oracle
ORACLE_HOME=/u01/app/oracle/product/11.1.0/db_1
ORACLE_SID=+ASM
```

In addition, you must be logged into the operating system as a user in the dba group, since the `asmcmd` utility connects to the database with SYSDBA privileges. The operating system user is usually *oracle* but can be any other user in the dba group.

You can use `asmcmd` utility one command at a time by using the format `asmcmd` *command*, or you can start `asmcmd` interactively by typing just `asmcmd` at the Linux shell prompt. To get a list of available commands, type `help` at the `ASMCMD>` prompt. Table 1-6 lists the `asmcmd` commands and a brief description of their purpose; the `asmcmd` commands available only in Oracle Database 11g are noted in the middle column with a Y for yes.

When you start the `asmcmd` utility, you start out at the root node of the ASM instance's file system; unlike in a Linux file system, the root node is designated by

TABLE 1-6 `asmcmd` Command Summary

`asmcmd` Command	11g Only	Description
`cd`		Change the directory to the specified directory.
`cp`	Y	Copy files between ASM disk groups, both in the same instance and in remote instances.
`du`		Recursively display total disk space usage for the current directory and all subdirectories.
`exit`		Terminate `asmcmd` and return to the operating system shell prompt.
`find`		Find all occurrences of the name (using wildcards as well) starting with the specified directory.
`help`		List the `asmcmd` commands.
`ls`		List the contents of the current directory.
`lsct`		List information about current ASM client databases.
`lsdg`		List all disk groups and their attributes.
`lsdsk`	Y	List all disks visible to this ASM instance.
`md_backup`	Y	Create metadata backup script for specified disk groups.
`md_restore`	Y	Restore disk groups from a backup.
`mkalias`		Create an alias for system-generated ASM filenames.
`mkdir`		Create an ASM directory.
`pwd`		Display the current ASM directory.
`remap`	Y	Repair a range of corrupted or damaged physical blocks on a disk.
`rm`		Remove ASM files or directories.
`rmalias`		Remove an ASM alias, but not the target of the alias.

a plus sign (+) instead of a leading forward slash (/), although subsequent directory levels use a forward slash. In this example, you start asmcmd and query the existing disk groups, along with the total disk space used within all disk groups:

```
[oracle@dw ~]$ asmcmd
ASMCMD> ls -l
State     Type     Rebal  Unbal  Name
MOUNTED   NORMAL   N      N      DATA/
MOUNTED   HIGH     N      N      DATA2/
MOUNTED   NORMAL   N      N      RECOV/
ASMCMD> du
Used_MB        Mirror_used_MB
   2143                  4399
ASMCMD> pwd
+
ASMCMD>
```

As with the Linux shell ls command, you can append –l to get a more detailed listing of the objects retrieved by the command. The ls command shows the three disk groups in the ASM instance used throughout this chapter: +DATA, +DATA2, and +RECOV.

Note also that the du command shows only the used disk space and total disk space used across mirrored disk groups; to get the amount of free space in each disk group, use the lsdg command instead.

In this example, you want to find all files that have the string user in the filename:

```
ASMCMD> pwd
+
ASMCMD> find . user*
+DATA/DW/DATAFILE/USERS.259.627432977
+DATA/DW/DATAFILE/USERS2.267.627782171
+DATA/purch/users.dbf
+DATA2/DW/DATAFILE/USERS3.256.627786775
ASMCMD> ls -l +DATA/purch/users.dbf
Type      Redund  Striped  Time     Sys  Name
                                     N    users.dbf =>
                                          +DATA/DW/DATAFILE/
USERS.259.627432977
ASMCMD>
```

Note the line with +DATA/purch/users.dbf: the find command finds all ASM objects; in this case, it finds an alias as well as datafiles that match the pattern.

Use the asmcmd Utility to Create a Backup of the SPFILE

In this exercise, locate the SPFILE in the ASM file hierarchy and make a backup copy to a file system external to the ASM instance. In this exercise, you will use the cp command to back up the database's SPFILE to the /tmp directory on the host's file system.

1. Start at the root of the file system and navigate to the DATA diskgroup for the dw instance:

```
[oracle@dw ~]$ asmcmd
ASMCMD> pwd
+
ASMCMD> ls
DATA/
RECOV/
ASMCMD> cd data/dw
ASMCMD> pwd
+data/DW
ASMCMD> ls
CONTROLFILE/
DATAFILE/
ONLINELOG/
PARAMETERFILE/
TEMPFILE/
spfiledw.ora
```

2. Use the cp command to copy the SPFILE:

```
ASMCMD> cp spfiledw.ora /tmp/BACKUPspfiledw.ora
source +data/DW/spfiledw.ora
target /tmp/BACKUPspfiledw.ora
copying file(s)...
file, /tmp/BACKUPspfiledw.ora, copy committed.
ASMCMD> exit
[oracle@dw ~]$ ls -l /tmp/BACKUP*
-rw-r-----  1 oracle oinstall 2560 Jan 27 09:47
/tmp/BACKUPspfiledw.ora
[oracle@dw ~]$
```

This exercise shows how all database files for the database dw are stored within the ASM file system. It looks like they are stored on a traditional host file system, but instead are managed by ASM, providing built-in performance and redundancy features (optimized for use with Oracle Database 11g), making the DBA's life a bit easier when it comes to datafile management.

CERTIFICATION SUMMARY

This chapter started with a review of the Oracle Database architecture. Some of this material has been covered in previous coursework, but a refresher course is always helpful for day-to-day database administration. More importantly, understanding the basic Oracle tablespace architecture is a prerequisite for understanding how ASM disk groups will store and manage Oracle tablespaces. In addition, understanding the basic Oracle background process architecture will dovetail nicely into a discussion of the ASM-related background processes available in both an ASM instance and an RDBMS instance.

Next, the chapter covered how to create an ASM instance as well as how to set the various ASM-related initialization parameters, preferably stored in an SPFILE. As with an RDBMS instance, a number of dynamic performance views contain information about ASM disk groups, individual disks within disk groups, and files stored within each disk group. The dynamic performance view V$ASM_FILE details the files within a disk group, such as RMAN backupsets, online redo log files, archived redo log files, and datafiles.

The chapter also showed you how to start up and shut down an ASM instance. As a DBA, you must be cognizant of the dependencies between the ASM instance and any RDBMS instances that are connected to disk groups in the ASM instance when you shut down and start up an ASM instance.

Finally, the chapter provided an in-depth overview of ASM disk group administration. These administrative tasks include how to most effectively use the three types of mirroring available in an ASM disk group: external, normal, and high redundancy. In addition, it covered a number of features available starting in Oracle Database 11g, such as disk group fast mirror resync, minimizing the amount of time required to resync a disk group when a disk in a disk group is offline or otherwise unavailable for reasons other than media failure. The command-line utility asmcmd provides a view of the structure of the ASM disk groups using familiar Unix commands such as ls, mkdir, and cp.

✓ TWO-MINUTE DRILL

Understanding Database Architecture and ASM

❑ Oracle database logical structures include tablespaces, segments, extents, and blocks, in order of increasing granularity.

❑ At a minimum, a database must have a SYSTEM and a SYSAUX tablespace.

❑ Oracle database physical structures include datafiles, redo log files, control files, archived log files, initialization parameter files, alert/trace files, and backup files.

❑ Oracle memory structures include the System Global Area (SGA), Program Global Area (PGA), and the software code area.

❑ The primary Oracle background processes are SMON, PMON, DBW*n*, LGWR, ARC*n*, CKPT, and RECO.

❑ The background processes that support ASM instances are RBAL and ARB*n*; databases that use ASM disks have the ASMB and RBAL background processes.

Describe ASM

❑ ASM requires a dedicated instance for managing shared disks, called, not surprisingly, an ASM instance.

❑ Automatic rebalancing of disks in an ASM disk group happens in the background when disks are added or removed from an ASM disk group.

❑ The RBAL background process in an ASM instance coordinates disk activity for disk groups; the ARB*n* processes perform the actual extent movement between the disks in a disk group.

❑ The ASMB background process in an RDBMS instance performs the communication between the database and the ASM instance; the RBAL background process performs the opening and closing of the disks in the disk group for the RDBMS instance.

❑ An ASM instance has an initialization parameter file and a password file, but since there are no datafiles in an ASM instance, there is therefore no data dictionary; all connections to an ASM instance use operating system authentication.

❑ The new SYSASM privilege in an ASM instance facilitates the separation of database administration and storage administration in an ASM instance.

Set Up Initialization Parameter Files for ASM and Database Instances

❑ For an ASM instance, the initialization parameter INSTANCE_TYPE is ASM; for an RDBMS instance, the value is RDBMS.

❑ The DB_UNIQUE_NAME is +ASM for an ASM instance.

❑ ASM_POWER_LIMIT controls the speed of rebalancing operations and ranges from 1 to 11.

❑ ASM_PREFERRED_READ_FAILURE_GROUPS contains a list of preferred failure groups for an RDBMS instance when you use clustered ASM instances.

❑ All ASM-related dynamic performance views are available in both the ASM instance and the RDBMS instance except for VASM_FILE, VASM_OPERATION, and V$ASM_ALIAS.

❑ A fully-qualified ASM filename has the format +*group/dbname/file type/tag* .*file.incarnation*.

❑ Numeric ASM filenames are valid only for existing ASM files.

❑ ASM templates are a shorthand for specifying redundancy types and striping in an ASM disk group.

❑ Redundancy types for an ASM disk group are external, normal, and high.

❑ ASM disk group striping can be fine or coarse.

Start Up and Shut Down ASM Instances

❑ An ASM instance is in the MOUNT state when you use the STARTUP command. An ASM instance cannot be in the OPEN state like an RDBMS instance.

❑ Using STARTUP RESTRICT in an ASM instance prevents database instances from accessing disk groups controlled by the ASM instance.

❑ Performing a SHUTDOWN operation on an ASM instance performs a SHUTDOWN operation on all connected RDBMS instances.

Administer ASM Disk Groups

❑ Coarse striping spreads files in units of 1MB each across all disks; fine striping spreads files in units of 128KB.

❑ Coarse striping is appropriate for environments with a high degree of small I/O requests, such as in an OLTP environment. Fine striping is appropriate for a data warehouse environment and maximizes response time for individual I/O requests.

❏ A failure group is one or more disks in a disk group that share a common resource such as a disk controller.

❏ External redundancy is appropriate for noncritical disk groups or disks that are externally managed by a RAID controller.

❏ Normal redundancy provides two-way mirroring and requires two failure groups within a disk group.

❏ High redundancy provides three-way mirroring with a minimum of three failure groups within a disk group.

❏ Mirroring is managed at a very low level. Extents are mirrored and not the disks.

❏ Each disk in a disk group has a mixture of both primary and mirrored extents.

❏ Dynamic rebalancing occurs automatically within a disk group to proportionally reallocate data from other disk group members to the new disk group member.

❏ ASM files are typically Oracle Managed Files (OMF) but can be manually managed.

❏ Fast mirror resync, available starting in Oracle Database 11g, speeds disk remirroring when a disk fails for reasons such as a controller failure. Only the changed data needs to be resynced when the disk is brought back online.

❏ The default value for disk repair time is 3.6 hours and is controlled by the initialization parameter `DISK_REPAIR_TIME`.

❏ You can monitor disk rebalance operations using the dynamic performance view V$ASM_OPERATION.

❏ You can use the `asmcmd` command-line utility to browse and maintain objects within ASM disk groups.

❏ The `asmcmd` commands new to Oracle Database 11g are cp, lsdsk, md_backup, md_restore, and remap.

SELF TEST

The following questions will help you measure your understanding of the material presented in this chapter. There might be more than one correct answer. Read all the choices carefully. Choose all correct answers for each question:

Understanding Database Architecture and ASM

1. Which of the following tablespaces are required in an installation of Oracle Database 11*g*? (Choose all that apply.)
    A. USERS
    B. SYSTEM
    C. SYSAUX
    D. TEMP
    E. UNDOTBS1
    F. RMAN

2. What is the maximum number of database writer processes (DBWn) in an Oracle database instance?
    A. 1
    B. 10
    C. 20
    D. None; database writer processes exist only in an ASM instance

Describe ASM

3. Which of the following background processes exist in both an ASM instance and an RDBMS instance, and also support ASM disk groups? (Choose all that apply.)
    A. ASMB
    B. RBAL
    C. ARBn
    D. LGWR
    E. ARCn

4. At which level does ASM perform mirroring?

    A. At the database object level

    B. At the tablespace level

    C. At the disk volume level

    D. ASM does not perform mirroring, it only supports disk hardware that is already RAID-enabled

Set Up Initialization Parameter Files for ASM and Database Instances

5. What is the value for `INSTANCE_TYPE` in the init.ora file or SPFILE for an ASM instance?

    A. `RDBMS`

    B. `ASM`

    C. `+ASM`

    D. `NOMOUNT`

    E. There is no such initialization parameter `INSTANCE_TYPE`

6. You connect to an ASM instance with connected RDBMS instances as `SYSOPER` and run this command:

```
SQL> shutdown immediate
```

What happens?

    A. The ASM instance shuts down immediately, and all connected RDBMS instances shut down with the `ABORT` option.

    B. The ASM instance shuts down immediately, and all connected RDBMS instances shut down with the `IMMEDIATE` option.

    C. The command is ignored, since the SYSOPER privilege does not include starting up or shutting down an ASM instance.

    D. The ASM instance is not shut down because there is at least one connected RDBMS instance.

7. The value of the initialization parameter `ASM_DISKGROUPS` on your ASM instance is the following:

```
DATA, RECOV, DATA2
```

What happens when the ASM instance starts? (Choose the best answer.)

    A. Nothing happens until you issue `ALTER DISKGROUP MOUNT` commands.

    B. The ASM instance automatically mounts the disk groups, and you can manually mount any disk groups not in the list.

    C. `ASM_DISKGROUPS` is only valid for RDBMS instances.

    D. The disk devices `DATA`, `RECOV`, and `DATA2` are available to create new disk groups.

8. Which of the following parameters are required for an ASM instance? (Choose all that apply.)

   A. `INSTANCE_NAME`

   B. `INSTANCE_TYPE`

   C. `ASM_DISKGROUPS`

   D. `ASM_POWER_LIMIT`

   E. `ASM_PREFERRED_READ_FAILURE_GROUPS`

Start Up and Shut Down ASM Instances

9. What happens to the state of an ASM instance when a connected RDBMS instance fails?

   A. There is no effect on the ASM instance.

   B. The ASM instance fails.

   C. The ASM instance shuts down automatically.

   D. All other connected RDBMS instances are paused until the failed RDBMS instance restarts.

   E. The ASM instance performs instance recovery on the failed RDBMS instance while continuing to service other RDBMS clients.

10. Which of the following states are valid for an ASM instance? (Choose all that apply.)

    A. `OPEN`

    B. `MOUNT`

    C. `NOMOUNT`

    D. `RESTRICT`

Administer ASM Disk Groups

11. What is the difference between coarse striping and fine striping for files in a disk group?

    A. Coarse striping spreads files in units of 1MB each across all disks, and fine striping spreads files in units of 64KB.

    B. Coarse striping spreads files in units of 1MB each across all disks, and fine striping spreads files in units of 128KB.

    C. Coarse striping spreads files in units of 64MB each across all disks, and fine striping spreads files in units of 1MB.

    D. Coarse striping spreads files in units of 4MB each across all disks, and fine striping spreads files in units of 128KB.

12. In which situation would you use fine striping for an object in an ASM disk group? (Choose all that apply.)

    A. A traditional data warehouse environment

    B. An OLTP system with low concurrency

    C. An OLTP system with high concurrency

    D. A hybrid data warehouse and OLTP environment

    E. An environment with a high degree of concurrent small I/O requests

13. When is it appropriate to use an incomplete ASM filename? (Choose all that apply.)

    A. For single-file creation operations

    B. For multiple-file creation operations

    C. For referencing single database objects

    D. For referencing the same object shared by multiple non-RAC RDBMS instances

14. If you want to use two-way mirroring (normal redundancy) for a new disk group, how many failure groups do you need?

    A. One failure group with two disks on the same controller.

    B. Two failure groups.

    C. Three or more failure groups.

    D. Two-way mirroring is supported only at the operating system level using a RAID hardware or software mirroring solution.

15. Which of the following statements are true about ASM objects and alias names? (Choose all that apply.)

    A. You can use the `ALTER DISKGROUP ADD ALIAS` command to add a more readable alias for an existing object.

    B. You can use an alias to reference an existing object.

    C. You can use an alias to create a new object.

    D. You can use an alias when creating multiple objects.

    E. Alias names typically contain a dotted pair of numbers at the end.

    F. You can use a single alias to reference a group of existing objects.

16. What are the default characteristics of an ASM file created with no options?

    A. The ASM object is striped but not mirrored.

    B. The ASM object is striped and mirrored by default.

    C. The ASM object is mirrored but not striped.

    D. The ASM object is neither striped nor mirrored.

LAB QUESTION

For the disk group DATA2 created earlier in this chapter in the section "Disk Group Dynamic Rebalancing," remove one of the failure groups. Disk space is at a premium and you don't need four-way redundancy for the disk group.

SELF TEST ANSWERS

Understanding Database Architecture and ASM

1. ☑ **B** and **C.** Both the SYSTEM and SYSAUX tablespaces are required.
   ☒ **A, D, E,** and **F** are wrong. While the USERS tablespace is highly desirable for placing application tables in its own tablespace, it is not required; TEMP, USERS, and UNDOTBS1 are created in a default installation of Oracle Database 11g. No RMAN tablespace is created, nor is it required in an installation of Oracle Database 11g.

2. ☑ **C.** The database writer processes are DBW0 through DBW9, and if needed, DBWa through DBWj on most operating system platforms.
   ☒ **A, B,** and **D** are wrong. Database writers exist only in an RDBMS instance.

Describe ASM

3. ☑ **B.** Only the RBAL process exists in both ASM and RDBMS instances for ASM operations. RBAL coordinates the disk activity for disk groups in an ASM instance. RBAL performs the opening and closing of the disks in a disk group in an RDBMS instance, on behalf of the database.
   ☒ **A** is wrong because ASMB exists only in an RDBMS instance that uses ASM disks. **C** is wrong because ARBn only exists in an ASM instance and performs the extent movement between disks in disk groups. **D** is wrong because LGWR only exists in an RDBMS instance and is not ASM related; it writes redo information to the online redo log files. **E** is wrong because ARCn only exists in an RDBMS instance and is not ASM related; it writes online redo log files to archive redo log files when the database is in ARCHIVELOG mode.

4. ☑ **A.** ASM mirrors database objects only.
   ☒ **B, C,** and **D** are wrong. ASM mirrors database objects to provide the flexibility to mirror or stripe each database object differently depending on their type. ASM does not need to mirror a given object if an underlying object is already mirrored by RAID hardware or the operating system.

Set Up Initialization Parameter files for ASM and Database Instances

5. ☑ **B.** As you might expect, INSTANCE_TYPE has a value of ASM for an ASM instance.
   ☒ **A, C, D,** and **E** are wrong. **A** is only valid for an RDBMS (database) instance. **C** is the value for DB_UNIQUE_NAME in an ASM instance. **D** is an option to the STARTUP command.

6. ☑ **D.** All connected RDBMS instances must be shut down before you can shut down an ASM instance with the IMMEDIATE option. If you stop an ASM instance with the ABORT option, all connected RDBMS instances are stopped.

    ☒ **A** is wrong because RDBMS instances shut down with ABORT only if the ASM instance shuts down with the ABORT option or the ASM instance crashes. **B** is wrong because you must explicitly shut down connected RDBMS instances first. **C** is wrong because the SYSOPER privilege, while not as powerful as the SYSDBA or SYSASM privilege, does have the power to start and stop ASM instances.

7. ☑ **B.** The ASM instance automatically mounts the specified disk groups, and you can manually mount any disk groups not in the list.

    ☒ **A** is incorrect, because ASM_DISKGROUPS facilitates automatic mounting of the specified disk groups at startup. **C** is incorrect because ASM_DISKGROUPS is only valid for ASM instances. **D** is incorrect because the parameter ASM_DISKGROUPS contains existing disk groups, not raw devices available for disk groups.

8. ☑ **B.** Only the INSTANCE_TYPE parameter is required, and its value must be ASM.

    ☒ **A, C, D,** and **E** are wrong. ASM_DISKGROUPS can be empty, but then you must mount disk groups manually after starting an ASM instance. ASM_POWER_LIMIT defaults to 1 if it is not set; ASM_PREFERRED_READ_FAILURE_GROUPS, new to Oracle Database 11g, specifies a preferred failure group that is closest to the instance's node to improve performance in a clustered ASM environment.

Start Up and Shut Down ASM Instances

9. ☑ **A.** The ASM instance continues to serve other RDBMS clients. When the failed RDBMS client restarts and recovers, the ASM instance will be ready to service the recovered RDBMS instance.

    ☒ **B, C, D,** and **E** are wrong. The failure of one or more connected RDBMS instances does not affect the status of an ASM instance. An ASM instance does not perform instance recovery for any connected RDBMS instances.

10. ☑ **B, C,** and **D.** You can put the ASM instance into the NOMOUNT mode; the instance is started but no ASM disks are mounted. The MOUNT state mounts all ASM disks in the ASM_DISKGROUPS initialization parameter; you can use STARTUP RESTRICT to temporarily prevent RDBMS instances from accessing mounted disk groups.

    ☒ **A** is wrong. ASM instances cannot be in the OPEN state as an RDBMS instance can.

Administer ASM Disk Groups

11. ☑ **B.** Coarse striping spreads files in units of 1MB each across all disks, and fine striping spreads files in units of 128KB. Remember that striping occurs at the database object level, not at the file or disk failure group level.

☒ **A, C,** and **D** are wrong. None of these striping combinations are available for files in an ASM disk group.

12. ☑ **A** and **B.** Fine striping is appropriate for traditional data warehouse environments or OLTP systems with low concurrency; this maximizes response time for individual I/O requests.

☒ **C, D,** and **E** are wrong. Coarse striping is more appropriate for systems with a high degree of concurrent small I/O requests. A hybrid data warehouse and OLTP environment would indicate a mixture of fine and course striping, depending on the object. Remember that you can individually stripe different object types within the same disk group. For example, you may have a tablespace used for OLTP transactions striped as coarse, and another tablespace used for a data warehouse star schema striped as fine.

13. ☑ **A** and **B.** You can use an incomplete ASM filename when creating single or multiple files. For example, you can create a tablespace and specify only the disk group name; the ASM instance uses OMF to fully qualify the internal name for the tablespace within the disk group.

☒ **C** is wrong because you can't resolve a single database object with an incomplete name such as a disk group name. **D** is wrong because you can share a disk group between RDBMS instances in a RAC environment, but not between standalone RDBMS instances.

14. ☑ **B.** A disk group with two-way mirroring requires two failure groups.

☒ **A** is wrong because two disks on a single controller has a single point of failure and will not support two-way mirroring. **C** is wrong because three or more failure groups is appropriate for high redundancy disk groups. **D** is wrong because you can use operating system RAID solutions for any kind of ASM disk group mirroring solution, although typically you will use operating system or hardware RAID solutions for disk groups defined with external redundancy.

15. ☑ **A, B,** and **C.** You use the `ALTER DISKGROUP ADD ALIAS` command to add an alias for an existing object; you can use an alias to reference an existing object or when you create a new object.

☒ **D** is wrong because you can create an alias only for a single object. **E** is wrong because aliases do not end in a dotted pair of numbers; you will typically create a more readable alias for a fully qualified object name that already contains a dotted pair of numbers at the end. **F** is wrong because a single alias can reference only a single database object within a disk group.

16. ☑ **B.** By default, all ASM objects are striped and mirrored; you cannot disable striping, but you can disable mirroring by using the `EXTERNAL REDUNDANCY` clause when you create a disk group.

☒ **A, C,** and **D** are wrong. You can disable mirroring, but striping always occurs in a disk group for performance.

LAB ANSWER

Disk space is tight so you don't need four members for the DATA2 disk group. Run a query that joins V$ASM_DISKGROUP and V$ASM_DISK to confirm the list of ASM disks that compose the DATA2 disk group:

```
SQL> select dg.name diskgroup, dg.type, d.disk_number,
  2          d.name asmdisk, d.failgroup, d.path
  3  from v$asm_diskgroup dg join v$asm_disk d using(group_number)
  4  where dg.name = 'DATA2';

DISKGROUP    TYPE    DISK_NUMBER ASMDISK     FAILGROUP    PATH
------------ ------  ----------- ----------  ------------ -----------------
DATA2        HIGH              0 D2A         FG1          /dev/raw/raw5
DATA2        HIGH              3 D2D         FG4          /dev/raw/raw8
DATA2        HIGH              2 D2C         FG3          /dev/raw/raw7
DATA2        HIGH              1 D2B         FG2          /dev/raw/raw6

SQL>
```

For a high-redundancy disk group, only three failure groups are necessary, so you drop the disk group and re-create it with only three members:

```
SQL> drop diskgroup data2;
Diskgroup dropped.
```

If the disk group has any database objects other than disk group metadata, you have to specify the INCLUDING CONTENTS clause in the DROP DISKGROUP command. This is an extra safeguard to make sure that disk groups with database objects are not accidentally dropped. Here is the command to re-create the disk group with three disks:

```
SQL> create diskgroup data2 high redundancy
  2      failgroup fg1 disk '/dev/raw/raw5' name d2a
  3      failgroup fg2 disk '/dev/raw/raw6' name d2b
  4      failgroup fg3 disk '/dev/raw/raw7' name d2c;

Diskgroup created.
SQL> select group_number, disk_number, name,
  2          failgroup, create_date, path from v$asm_disk;

GROUP_NUMBER DISK_NUMBER NAME         FAILGROUP    CREATE_DA PATH
------------ ----------- ------------ ------------ --------- ---------------
           0           3                           24-FEB-08 /dev/raw/raw8
           3           2 D2C          FG3          24-FEB-08 /dev/raw/raw7
           3           0 D2A          FG1          24-FEB-08 /dev/raw/raw5
```

```
    3          1 D2B          FG2           24-FEB-08 /dev/raw/raw6
    2          1 RECOV_0001   RECOV_0001    09-AUG-07 /dev/raw/raw4
    2          0 RECOV_0000   RECOV_0000    09-AUG-07 /dev/raw/raw3
    1          1 DATA_0001    DATA_0001     10-AUG-07 /dev/raw/raw2
    1          0 DATA_0000    DATA_0000     10-AUG-07 /dev/raw/raw1

8 rows selected.
SQL>
```

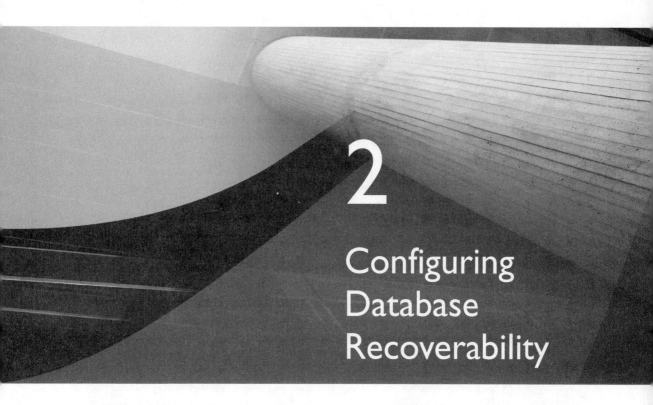

2
Configuring Database Recoverability

Oracle provides a variety of backup procedures and options that help protect an Oracle database. If they are properly implemented, these options will allow you to back up your databases and recover them easily and efficiently. As of Oracle Database 10g, you can use Recovery Manager (RMAN) to execute nearly all of your backup and recovery operations. In situations for which you cannot use RMAN for recovery, such as for a database that is not in ARCHIVELOG mode, user-managed backup and recovery is discussed in Chapter 6.

The first part of this chapter gives you a refresher on both types of backups available to you: *logical* and *physical*. A logical backup backs up individual objects, such as a table or a schema; a physical backup backs up objects with a granularity at the file system level, such as the datafiles that make up a tablespace. A physical backup of a database can occur while the database is either online or offline. You must use RMAN for all online backups except for backing up tablespaces while they are in backup mode (ALTER TABLESPACE BEGIN BACKUP).

This chapter provides a warm-up to RMAN; however, before you can use RMAN to back up or recover a database, you must perform a number of steps: First, your database must be in ARCHIVELOG mode. Then you must ensure that the retention policy and the number of archived log file destinations are appropriate for your environment.

This chapter provides a brief overview of the RMAN commands you'll use on a regular basis. RMAN catalog maintenance, creating RMAN backups, and using RMAN backups for recovery are covered in Chapters 3, 4, and 5, respectively. After covering user-managed backup and recovery in Chapter 6, a discussion of miscellaneous RMAN features occurs in Chapter 7 and RMAN tuning methodologies are covered in Chapter 8.

To wrap up this chapter, you'll learn how to configure and use the flash recovery area both to simplify the location of database backups and automate the disk space allocated for recovery files.

CERTIFICATION OBJECTIVE 2.01

Configuring for Database Recoverability

Oracle offers logical and physical backup capabilities. RMAN can perform both full or incremental logical and physical backups. You should understand the implications and uses of both physical and logical backups to develop the most appropriate solution for your applications.

A robust backup strategy includes both types of backups. In general, production databases rely on physical backups as their primary backup method, while logical backups serve as the secondary method. For development databases and for some small data movement processing, logical backups offer a viable solution.

Your backup and recovery plan should include, at a minimum, these tasks:

- **Configuration**   Define backup destinations, encryption, and retention policies.
- **Scheduling**   Automate backups to minimize human error and manual intervention.
- **Testing**   Perform routine backup and recovery options to ensure that your backup plan works before you experience a real disaster.
- **Monitoring**   Ensure that you minimize the resources used to perform a sufficient backup and minimize the impact to other database users.
- **Restoration**   Restore your database files in the file system (datafiles, archive logs, and so on), from a previous backup.
- **Recovery**   Perform a recovery of the database to the point of failure of the database by applying archived redo log entries to restored database files and rolling forward changes to your restored backup. Know how to recover your database.

Backup and recovery tools such as RMAN can be used in nonemergency situations as well: For example, you can take a snapshot of an entire database at one location and restore it to another location for developers or for testing.

The following sections present information on logical and physical backups, distinguishing between online and offline backups, and focusing on online backups for the rest of this chapter and in the rest of this book. Finally, you'll get a brief overview of RMAN commands. Details of using RMAN for your backup and recovery environment are covered in Chapters 3, 4, 5, 7, and 8.

Logical Backups

A logical backup of a database involves reading a set of database rows and writing them to a file. These records are read independently of their physical location. In Oracle, the Data Pump Export utility performs this type of database backup. To recover using the file generated from a Data Pump Export, you use Data Pump Import.

on the
Job

Oracle's Import and Export utilities, available prior to Oracle Database 10g, are still provided as part of the Oracle 11g installation but are no longer supported. Users of the old Export and Import utilities are encouraged to use Data Pump Export and Data Pump Import instead.

Oracle's Data Pump Export utility queries the database, including the data dictionary, and writes the output to an XML file called an *export dump file*. You can export the full database, specific users or tablespaces, or specific tables. During exports, you can choose whether or not to export the data dictionary information associated with tables, such as grants, indexes, and constraints. The file written by Data Pump Export will contain the commands necessary to completely re-create all the chosen objects and data.

Once data has been exported via Data Pump Export, it can be imported via the Data Pump Import utility. Data Pump Import reads the dump file created by Data Pump Export and executes the commands found there. For example, these commands may include a CREATE TABLE command, followed by an INSERT command to load data into the table.

on the
Job

Data Pump Export and Import can use a network connection for a simultaneous export and import operation, avoiding the use of intermediate operating system files and reducing total export and import time.

The data that has been exported does not have to be imported into the same database, or the same schema, that was used to generate the export dump file. You can use the export dump file to create a duplicate set of the exported objects under a different schema or into a separate database.

You can import either all or part of the exported data. If you import the entire export dump file from a full export, all the database objects, including tablespaces, datafiles, and users, will be created during the import. However, it is often useful to precreate tablespaces and users in order to specify the physical distribution of objects in another database. This is one method of changing the physical structure of a database.

If you want to import part of the data from the export dump file, the tablespaces, datafiles, and users that will own and store that data should be set up prior to the import.

Physical Backups

Physical backups involve copying the files that constitute the database. These backups are also referred to as *file system backups* because they involve using operating system file backup commands. Oracle supports two different types of physical file backups: *offline backups* and *online backups* (also known as *cold* and *hot backups*, respectively). You can use RMAN (covered in this chapter and in Chapters 3, 4, 5, 7, and 8) to perform all physical backups. You can optionally choose to write your own scripts to perform physical backups, but doing so will prevent you from obtaining many of the benefits of the RMAN approach.

Offline Backups

Consistent offline backups occur when the database has been shut down normally (that is, not due to instance failure) using the NORMAL, IMMEDIATE, or TRANSACTIONAL option of the SHUTDOWN command. While the database is offline, the following files should be backed up:

- All datafiles
- All controlfiles
- All archived redo log files
- The init.ora file or server parameter file (SPFILE)
- Text-format files such as the password file and tnsnames.ora

on the **job**
You should never, ever want or need to back up online redo log files. While a slight time savings results from restoring from a cold backup after a clean shutdown, the risk of losing committed transactions outweighs the convenience. Your online redo logs should be mirrored and duplexed so that you more or less eliminate the chances of losing the current online log file.

Having all these files backed up while the database is closed provides a fixed or consistent image or snapshot of the database, as it existed at the time it was closed. The full set of these files could be restored from the backups on disk or tape at a later date, and the database would be able to function simply by restarting the database. It is *not* valid to perform a file system backup of the database while it is open or unless an online backup of tablespace datafiles is being performed with those tablespaces set into backup mode.

A tablespace placed into backup mode switches the tablespace datafiles offline for the purposes of reading and writing data. Any changes made to the tablespace while in backup mode will be wholly written to log files. This gives you datafiles that are static, that can be copied to the file system, and can be used later for recovery and log entry restoration. When a tablespace is switched out of backup mode, all temporary changes made in log files will be applied to (recovered into) the datafile placed online.

Offline backups that occur following database aborts will also be considered inconsistent and can require more effort to use during recoveries—if the backups are usable. A database restarted after a crash needs the online redo log files for crash recovery, but since you do not back up online redo log files, data loss after restoring an inconsistent offline backup is virtually certain.

Online Backups

You can use online backups for any database that is running in ARCHIVELOG mode. In this mode, the online redo logs are archived, creating a log of all transactions within the database.

Oracle writes to the online redo log files in a cyclical fashion: After filling the first log file, it begins writing to the second, until that one fills; then it begins writing to the third, and so on. Once the last online redo log file is filled, the Log Writer (LGWR) background process begins to overwrite the contents of the first redo log file.

When Oracle is running in ARCHIVELOG mode, the ARCn (archiver) background processes makes a copy of each redo log file before overwriting it. These archived redo log files are usually written to a disk device. The files can also be written directly to a tape device, but disk space is cheap enough that the additional cost of archiving to disk is offset by the time and labor savings when a disaster recovery operation must occur.

on the Job

Most production databases, particularly those that support transaction-processing applications, must be run in ARCHIVELOG mode; using RMAN requires that the database be in ARCHIVELOG mode.

You can perform file system backups of a database while that database is open, provided the database is running in ARCHIVELOG mode. An online backup involves setting each tablespace into a backup state, backing up its datafiles, and then restoring the tablespace to its normal state.

on the Job

When using the RMAN utility, you do not have to manually place each tablespace into a backup state. RMAN reads the data blocks in the same manner Oracle uses for queries.

The database can be fully recovered from an online backup, and it can, via the archived redo logs, be rolled forward to any point in time before the failure. When the database is then opened, any committed transactions that were in the database at the time of the failure will have been restored, and any uncommitted transactions recorded in the redo log files and datafiles will be rolled back.

While the database is open, the following files can be backed up:

- All datafiles
- All archived redo log files
- One control file, via the ALTER DATABASE BACKUP CONTROLFILE command
- The SPFILE

Online backup procedures are very powerful for two reasons: First, they provide full point-in-time recovery. Second, they allow the database to remain open during the file system backup. Even databases that cannot be shut down due to user requirements can still have file-system backups. Keeping the database open also keeps the System Global Area (SGA) of the database instance from being cleared when the database is shut down and restarted. Keeping the SGA memory from being cleared will improve the database's performance because it will reduce the number of physical I/Os required by the database on restart.

exam

ⓦatch   *RMAN automatically backs up the control file and SPFILE whenever the entire database or the SYSTEM tablespace are backed up.*

on the

ⓘob   *You can use the FLASHBACK DATABASE option, introduced in Oracle Database 10g, to roll the database back in time without relying on physical backups. To use the FLASHBACK DATABASE command, you must have a flash recovery area defined, be running in ARCHIVELOG mode, and have issued the ALTER DATABASE FLASHBACK ON command while the database was mounted but not open. Logs written to the flash recovery area are used by Oracle during the FLASHBACK DATABASE operation. The configuration and use of the flash recovery area are covered at the end of this chapter.*

RMAN Command Overview

You start RMAN from the operating system command line with, as you might expect, the RMAN command. (See the section entitled "Configure the Flash Recovery Area" later in this chapter for instructions on using Enterprise Manager to perform RMAN operations in a GUI.) In the following sections, you'll learn how to start RMAN from the command line along with a brief overview of the command structure once you are at the RMAN> prompt. Typically, you will script your RMAN commands to avoid typing errors for repetitive operations. Most DBAs run ad-hoc RMAN commands, especially when recovering a database.

Invoking RMAN

Here is a typical and simple invocation of RMAN that connects to a remote recovery catalog (recovery catalogs, schemas in other databases that store backup and structure information for your source database, are covered in Chapter 3):

```
[oracle@dw ~]$ rman target / catalog rman/rman@rac
```

In this example, the target option is used to connect to the database using operating system authentication, and the catalog option is used to connect to a recovery catalog in a different database. RMAN recovery catalog concepts are covered in painful detail in Chapter 3.

Although 13 different RMAN command line options are available when you start RMAN, here are the most common ones:

- **target** Identifies the connect string for the Oracle database you want to back up.
- **catalog** Specifies a recovery catalog database for backup information.
- **nocatalog** Uses the control file for backup information.
- **cmdfile** Specifies an input file containing a list of RMAN commands.
- **log** Sets the name of the log file for RMAN messages.

The cmdfile and log options make it easy to reuse a list of RMAN commands over and over and facilitate running RMAN from a batch process.

RMAN Command Types

The two basic types of RMAN commands are *standalone* commands and *job* commands. Standalone commands are executed only at the RMAN> prompt and are self-contained. Examples of standalone commands are CHANGE, CONNECT, CREATE SCRIPT, and CREATE CATALOG.

In contrast, job commands are usually grouped and run inside of a command block using the RUN command. Within a command block, the failure of any command within the block terminates execution of the block. An example of an RMAN command that can be used only as a job command is ALLOCATE CHANNEL: the channel allocation is valid only for the duration of the command block. (You would use CONFIGURE CHANNEL, a standalone command, to create a default channel.) An RMAN *channel* is one stream of data from the database to a device and corresponds to one database server session.

Here is an example of some commands run within a command block to back up the database, force the archiving of the current online redo log file, and remove obsolete backups:

```
RMAN> run
2> {
3>    backup as compressed backupset database;
4>    sql 'alter system archive log current';
5>    delete noprompt obsolete;
6> }
Starting backup at 15-MAR-08
using channel ORA_DISK_1
channel ORA_DISK_1: starting compressed full datafile backup set
. . .
```

Note that RMAN uses a default channel when you don't explicitly allocate a channel; in this case it's the flash recovery area.

Some commands are both standalone and job commands—in other words, you can use them at the RMAN> command prompt or within a command block. For example, you can use BACKUP DATABASE as a standalone or within a command block; when you run BACKUP DATABASE as a standalone command, RMAN automatically allocates one or more channels based on defaults specified by CONFIGURE CHANNEL and whether or not you're using a flash recovery area.

Table 2-1 provides a list of RMAN commands you'll use on a regular basis, along with some common options and caveats for each command. For the complete list of all RMAN commands and their syntax, see *Oracle Database Backup and Recovery Reference, 11g Release 1*.

TABLE 2-1   Common RMAN Commands

RMAN Command	Description
@	Runs an RMAN command script at the pathname specified after the @. If no path is specified, the path is assumed to be the directory from which RMAN was invoked.
ADVISE FAILURE	Displays repair options for the failure found.
ALLOCATE CHANNEL	Creates a connection between RMAN and a database instance, initiating a database server session that performs the work of backing up, restoring, or recovering an RMAN backup.
BACKUP	Performs an RMAN backup, with or without archived redo logs. Backs up datafiles and datafile copies, or performs an incremental level 0 or level 1 backup. Backs up an entire database or a single tablespace or datafile. Validates the blocks to be backed up with the VALIDATE clause.
CREATE SCRIPT	Creates a stored script in the recovery catalog.
CATALOG	Adds information about file copies and user-managed backups to the repository.
CHANGE	Changes the status of a backup in the RMAN repository. Useful for explicitly excluding a backup from a restore or recovery operation, or to notify RMAN that a backup file was inadvertently or deliberately removed by an operating system command outside of RMAN.
CONFIGURE	Configures the persistent parameters for RMAN. The parameters configured are available during every subsequent RMAN session unless they are explicitly cleared or modified.
CONVERT	Converts datafile formats for transporting tablespaces or entire databases across platforms.
CREATE CATALOG	Creates the repository catalog containing RMAN metadata for one or more target databases. It is strongly recommended that this catalog not be stored in one of the target databases.
CROSSCHECK	Checks the record of backups in the RMAN repository against the actual files on disk or tape. Objects are flagged as EXPIRED, AVAILABLE, UNAVAILABLE, or OBSOLETE. If the object is not available to RMAN, it is marked UNAVAILABLE.
DELETE	Deletes backup files or copies and marks them as DELETED in the target database control file. If a repository is used, the record of the backup file is removed.
DROP DATABASE	Deletes the target database from disk and unregisters it. The target database must be mounted in EXCLUSIVE mode. All datafiles, online redo logs, and control files are deleted. All metadata stored in the recovery catalog is removed.
DUPLICATE	Uses backups of the target database (or use the live database) to create a duplicate database.

| TABLE 2-1 | Common RMAN Commands (*Continued*) |

RMAN Command	Description
FLASHBACK DATABASE	Performs a Flashback Database operation, new to Oracle 10g. The database is restored to a point in the past by System Change Number (SCN) or log sequence number using Flashback logs to undo changes before the SCN or log sequence number, and then archived redo logs are applied to bring the database forward to a consistent state.
LIST	Displays information about backupsets and image copies recorded in the target database's RMAN repository (the catalog). See REPORT for identifying complex relationships between backupsets.
RECOVER	Performs a complete or incomplete recovery on a datafile, a tablespace, or the entire database. Can also apply incremental backups to a datafile image copy to roll it forward in time.
REGISTER DATABASE	Registers a target database in the RMAN repository.
REPAIR FAILURE	Repairs one or more failures recorded in the automated diagnostic repository (ADR).
REPORT	Performs a detailed analysis of the RMAN repository. For example, this command can identify which files need a backup to meet the retention policy or which backup files can be deleted.
RESTORE	Restores files from image copies or backupsets to disk, typically after a media failure. Can be used to validate a restore operation without actually performing the restore by specifying the PREVIEW option.
RUN	Runs a sequence of RMAN statements as a group when those commands are typed out between braces: {*run this stuff*}. The braces form a group of commands, allowing you to override default RMAN parameters for the duration of the execution of the group.
SET	Sets RMAN configuration settings for the duration of the RMAN session, such as allocated disk or tape channels. Persistent settings are assigned with CONFIGURE.
SHOW	Shows all or individual RMAN configured settings.
SHUTDOWN	Shuts down the target database from within RMAN. Identical to the SHUTDOWN command within SQL*Plus.
STARTUP	Starts up the target database. Has the same options and function as the SQL*Plus STARTUP command.
SQL	Runs SQL commands that cannot be accomplished directly or indirectly using standard RMAN commands; for example, it can run SQL 'ALTER TABLESPACE USERS OFFLINE IMMEDIATE'; within RMAN before restoring and recovering the USERS tablespace.
TRANSPORT TABLESPACE	Creates transportable tablespace sets from backup for one or more tablespaces.
VALIDATE	Examines a backup set and reports whether its data is intact and consistent.

Configure Multiple Archive Log File Destinations to Increase Availability

The preparation for using RMAN in your environment consists of two basic steps: change your database to ARCHIVELOG mode (if it is not already), and configure the number and types of archive log destinations to maximize recoverability and availability. In the following two sections, you'll learn how to configure ARCHIVELOG mode and determine the optimal set of archive log destinations.

Configuring ARCHIVELOG Mode

Consistent offline backups can be performed only while the database is shut down. However, you can perform physical file backups of a database while the database is open, provided the database is running in ARCHIVELOG mode and the backup is performed correctly. These backups are referred to as *online backups*.

Oracle writes to the online redo log files in a cyclical fashion: After filling the first log file, it begins writing to the second, until that one fills, and it then writes to the third, and so on. Once the last online redo log file is filled, the LGWR background process begins to overwrite the contents of the first redo log file.

When Oracle is run in ARCHIVELOG mode, the ARC*n* background process makes a copy of each redo log file after the LGWR process finishes writing to it. These archived redo log files are usually written to a disk device. They can instead be written directly to a tape device, but doing this can be very operator intensive and will most likely slow down a busy database while waiting for the LGWR process to finish writing a redo log file to tape. Most likely, you will write your archived redo log files to disk and send the archived log files to tape or delete them once your retention policy is satisfied.

To make use of the ARCHIVELOG capability, you must first place the database in ARCHIVELOG mode. Before starting the database in ARCHIVELOG mode, make sure you are using one of the following configurations, listed from most to least recommended:

■ Enable archiving to the flash recovery area only; use disk mirroring on the disks containing the flash recovery area. The DB_RECOVERY_FILE_DEST parameter specifies the file system location or ASM disk group containing the flash recovery area (see "Configure the Flash Recovery Area" later in this chapter).

- Enable archiving to the flash recovery area and set at least one LOG_ARCHIVE_ DEST_*n* parameter to another location outside of the flash recovery area. (You'll learn how to leverage multiple archive destinations later in the chapter in the section "Leveraging Multiple Archive Destinations.")
- Set at least two LOG_ARCHIVE_DEST_*n* parameters to archive to non-flash recovery area destinations.

The following examples assume that the best configuration, a single mirrored flash recovery area, has been selected. The following listing shows the steps needed to place a database in ARCHIVELOG mode; first, shut down the database, and then issue these commands:

```
SQL> shutdown immediate
SQL> startup mount
SQL> alter database archivelog;
SQL> alter database open;
```

on the
()ob

To see the currently active online redo log and its sequence number, query the V$LOG dynamic view.

If you enable archiving but do not specify any archiving locations, the archived log files reside in a default, platform-dependent location; on Unix and Linux platforms the default location is $ORACLE_HOME/dbs.

Each of the archived redo log files contains the data from a single online redo log. They are numbered sequentially, in the order in which they were created. The size of the archived redo log files varies, but it does not exceed the size of the online redo log files. When an online redo file reaches its specified maximum size, the redo log file is copied to a new archive log file, and the redo log file is then recycled for reuse by new redo log entries.

If the destination directory of the archived redo log files runs out of space, the ARC*n* processes will stop processing the online redo log data and the database will stop until you free up space in the destination directory. Make sure that you have enough space available in the destination directory.

This situation can be resolved by adding more space to the archived redo log file destination disk or by backing up the archived redo log files and then removing them from this directory. If you are using the flash recovery area for your archived redo log files, the database issues a warning alert (via e-mail or on the Enterprise Manager home page) if the available space in the flash recovery area is less than 15 percent, and a critical alert when the available space is less than 3 percent.

Taking action at the 15 percent level, such as increasing the size or changing the location of the flash recovery area, can most likely avoid any service interruptions, assuming that no runaway processes (such as untested SQL code running in production) are consuming space in the flash recovery area.

Leveraging Multiple Archive Destinations

You can use two different sets of archive-related initialization parameters, depending on the edition of the Oracle Database Server software you are using, the number of archived log file destinations you need, and whether the archived log file destinations are only local or both local and remote.

Local-Only Destinations

If you are using only local disk locations (in other words, you're not using a standby database as the destination for archived redo log files) and no more than two local disk locations, you can use the LOG_ARCHIVE_DEST and LOG_ARCHIVE_DUPLEX_DEST parameters. Here is an example of setting these two parameters to an archive location on two different disk drives:

```
LOG_ARCHIVE_DEST = '/u01/app/oracle/arch'
LOG_ARCHIVE_DUPLEX_DEST = '/u03/app/oracle/arch'
```

Note that the disk drives can be local to the server running Oracle Database 11g, or they can be on a network-based storage server hundreds of miles away.

EXERCISE 2-1

Identify the Archive Log File Destinations

In this exercise, you will identify the archived redo log file locations and determine the minimum number of required archive destinations.

1. Connect to your database with SQL*Plus and find the value of the LOG_ARCHIVE_* parameters:

```
SQL> show parameter log_archive_

NAME                                 TYPE          VALUE
------------------------------------ -----------   ----------------
log_archive_config                   string
log_archive_dest                     string
```

```
log_archive_dest_1                    string        SERVICE=RAC1
log_archive_dest_10                   string
log_archive_dest_2                    string
log_archive_dest_3                    string
log_archive_dest_4                    string
log_archive_dest_5                    string
log_archive_dest_6                    string
log_archive_dest_7                    string
log_archive_dest_8                    string
log_archive_dest_9                    string
log_archive_dest_state_1              string        enable
log_archive_dest_state_10             string        enable
log_archive_dest_state_2              string        enable
log_archive_dest_state_3              string        enable
log_archive_dest_state_4              string        enable
log_archive_dest_state_5              string        enable
log_archive_dest_state_6              string        enable
log_archive_dest_state_7              string        enable
log_archive_dest_state_8              string        enable
log_archive_dest_state_9              string        enable
log_archive_duplex_dest               string
log_archive_format                    string        %t_%s_%r.dbf
log_archive_local_first               boolean       TRUE
log_archive_max_processes             integer       4
log_archive_min_succeed_dest          integer       1
log_archive_start                     boolean       FALSE
log_archive_trace                     integer       0
SQL>
```

For this database, there appears to be only one archived log file destination, and it is a remote destination. Only one remote destination must succeed for archiving to be considered successful.

2. A second archived log file destination is available if a flash recovery area is defined. Query the flash recovery area–related parameters:

```
SQL> show parameter db_recov

NAME                                 TYPE        VALUE
------------------------------------ ----------- ---------------
db_recovery_file_dest                string      +RECOV
db_recovery_file_dest_size           big integer 8G
SQL>
```

If you are using Oracle Database 11g Enterprise Edition, LOG_ARCHIVE_DEST and LOG_ARCHIVE_DUPLEX_DEST are deprecated in favor of the newer LOG_ARCHIVE_DEST_n parameters.

Local and Remote Destinations

You can specify up to 10 archive log file destinations, either local or remote. If specified, you must use either the LOCATION parameter for a disk destination or the SERVICE parameter to specify a remote database instance as the destination.

In this example, you have two archived log file destinations on disk, and a third is a standby instance whose service name is STNDBY_CLEVELAND:

```
LOG_ARCHIVE_DEST_1 = 'LOCATION=/u01/app/oracle/arch'
LOG_ARCHIVE_DEST_2 = 'LOCATION=/u03/app/oracle/arch'
LOG_ARCHIVE_DEST_3 = 'SERVICE=STNDBY_CLEVELAND'
```

Defining Minimal Successful Destinations

Regardless of whether you use the LOG_ARCHIVE_DEST or the LOG_ARCHIVE_DEST_n parameter, you can use the LOG_ARCHIVE_MIN_SUCCEED_DEST parameter to specify the number of destinations to which the ARCn processes should successfully copy a redo log file to archive log files, before recycling the online redo log file for reuse. In other words, if you define several destinations, it may be acceptable from a recovery standpoint to have only two destinations available at any given time. Some destinations can temporarily be unavailable due to network issues or a failed standby server. In this case, two available destinations may be sufficient for a potential recovery scenario.

The value of the parameter LOG_ARCHIVE_MIN_SUCCEED_DEST cannot exceed the total number of enabled destinations. In addition, if you are using LOG_ARCHIVE_DEST_n with more destinations designated as MANDATORY than the number of destinations specified by LOG_ARCHIVE_MIN_SUCCEED_DEST, then the parameter LOG_ARCHIVE_MIN_SUCCEED_DEST is ignored.

In addition, if any archive log destination is designated as MANDATORY, a failure of this destination prevents the online log files from being overwritten until the failure is resolved. In this case, parameter LOG_ARCHIVE_MIN_SUCCEED_DEST is also ignored.

Finally, if you're using LOG_ARCHIVE_DEST, Oracle assumes that it is a MANDATORY location. The behavior will be the same as if you specified a destination using LOG_ARCHIVE_DEST_n with the MANDATORY parameter.

CERTIFICATION OBJECTIVE 2.03

Define, Apply, and Use a Retention Policy

Backups can be automatically retained and managed using one of two methods: by a *recovery window* or by *redundancy*. Using a recovery window, RMAN will retain as many backups as necessary to bring the database to any point in time within the recovery window. For example, with a recovery window of seven days, RMAN will maintain enough image copies, incremental backups, and archived redo logs to ensure that the database can be restored and recovered to any point in time within the last seven days. Any backups that are not needed to support this recovery window are marked as OBSOLETE and are automatically removed by RMAN if you are using a flash recovery area and disk space is needed for new backups.

In contrast, a redundancy retention policy directs RMAN to retain the specified number of backups (copies of datafiles and control file). Any extra copies or backups beyond the number specified in the redundancy policy are marked as OBSOLETE. As with a recovery window, obsolete backups are automatically removed if disk space is needed and the flash recovery area is used. Otherwise, you can use the DELETE OBSOLETE command to manually remove backup files and update the catalog.

If the retention policy is set to NONE, no backups or copies are ever considered obsolete, and the DBA must manually remove unneeded backups from the catalog and from disk. By default, the retention policy is a single copy (with the retention policy set to 1). You can set the retention policy to 2 copies using the following RMAN command:

```
RMAN> configure retention policy to redundancy 2;
```

The following example sets the retention policy to a recovery window of 4 days:

```
RMAN> configure retention policy to recovery window of 4 days;
old RMAN configuration parameters:
CONFIGURE RETENTION POLICY TO REDUNDANCY 2;
new RMAN configuration parameters:
CONFIGURE RETENTION POLICY TO RECOVERY WINDOW OF 4 DAYS;
new RMAN configuration parameters are successfully stored
RMAN>
```

Oracle best practices recommends using a recovery window, or a period of time in which it will be possible to uncover any problems with the database, such as an inadvertently dropped table or deleted rows in a table, and be able to perform a point-in-time recovery at just before the error occurred.

In some environments, you may want to disable the retention policy completely. This is useful in an environment where a backup system outside of RMAN stores the disk backups to tape and deletes them. As a result, RMAN does not need to decide when a backup is obsolete and therefore no retention policy is needed. As a result, the details of RMAN backups are maintained up to the time specified by the initialization parameter CONTROL_FILE_RECORD_KEEP_TIME. Here is how you can disable the retention policy:

```
RMAN> configure retention policy to none;
```

EXERCISE 2-2

Query and Change the Retention Policy

In this exercise, you will identify the current RMAN retention policy and change it.

Start RMAN and connect to the recovery catalog (in this example, the recovery catalog is owned by the user RMAN on the database with a system ID (SID) of RAC (if you do not have a recovery catalog configured, you can use NOCATALOG instead):

```
[oracle@dw ~]$ rman target / catalog rman/rman@rac

Recovery Manager: Release 11.1.0.6.0 -
        Production on Mon Mar 17 00:32:38 2008

Copyright (c) 1982, 2007, Oracle.  All rights reserved.

connected to target database: DW (DBID=3048318127)
connected to recovery catalog database
RMAN>
```

1. Show the existing retention policy:

```
RMAN> show retention policy;
RMAN configuration parameters for database
    with db_unique_name DW are:
CONFIGURE RETENTION POLICY TO REDUNDANCY 1;
RMAN>
```

2. Change the retention policy to a recovery window of 10 days:

```
RMAN> configure retention policy to recovery window of 10 days;

old RMAN configuration parameters:
CONFIGURE RETENTION POLICY TO REDUNDANCY 1;
new RMAN configuration parameters:
CONFIGURE RETENTION POLICY TO RECOVERY WINDOW OF 10 DAYS;
new RMAN configuration parameters are successfully stored
starting full resync of recovery catalog
full resync complete
RMAN>
```

CERTIFICATION OBJECTIVE 2.04

Configure the Flash Recovery Area

The flash recovery area, available since Oracle Database 10g, is a unified storage location for all recovery-related files in an Oracle database. As the price of disk space drops, the convenience, increased availability, and decreased recovery times make a completely disk-based backup solution more desirable than tape backup.

The flash recovery area can reside in a single file system directory or as an ASM disk group. In a default installation of Oracle Database 11g, you can easily configure the flash recovery area after you specify the location for the database's datafiles. Figure 2-1 shows the windows where you specify the location of the flash recovery area along with its size. In this example, the flash recovery area will reside in the ASM disk group +RECOV with a maximum size of 8GB.

All the files that you need to recover a database from a media failure or a logical error are contained in the flash recovery area. The files that can reside in the area are divided into two categories: *permanent* or *transient*. Permanent files are actively being used by the database instance and transient files are required only when you need to recover a part of or the entire database.

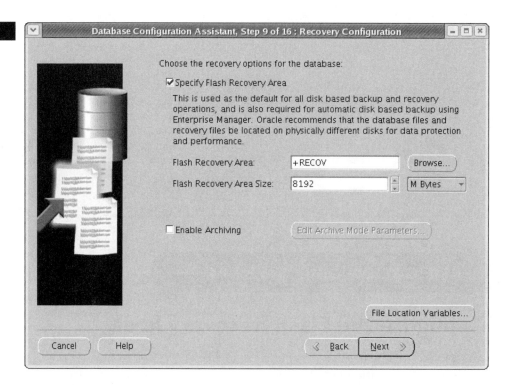

FIGURE 2-1

Database
installation
Recovery
Configuration
and Locations
window

The following permanent items are stored in the flash recovery area:

- **Control file** Oracle stores one copy of the control file in the flash recovery area during an installation.
- **Online redo log files** You can store one mirrored copy from each redo log file group in the flash recovery area.

The following transient items are stored in the flash recovery area:

- **Archived redo log files** When you configure the flash recovery area, one set of archived redo log files is stored in the flash recovery area.
- **Flashback logs** Flashback logs are stored in the flash recovery area when Flashback Database is enabled.

- **Control file automatic backups**   RMAN stores control file automatic backups in the flash recovery area. When RMAN backs up the first datafile, which is part of the SYSTEM tablespace, the control file is automatically included in the RMAN backup.
- **Datafile copies**   When you use the RMAN command BACKUP AS COPY, the datafile copies are stored in the flash recovery area by default.
- **RMAN backupsets**   Files created with the BACKUP AS BACKUPSET command are stored in the flash recovery area.
- **RMAN files**   By default, RMAN uses the flash recovery area as a staging area for backup and recovery of the archive log files from disk or tape.

Three initialization parameters control the default locations for new control files, online redo log files, and data files: DB_CREATE_FILE_DEST, DB_RECOVERY_FILE_DEST, and DB_CREATE_ONLINE_LOG_DEST_n. DB_CREATE_FILE_DEST specifies the default location for Oracle-managed datafiles if you do not explicitly specify a destination. DB_CREATE_ONLINE_LOG_DEST_n specifies up to five locations for online redo log files; if this parameter is not specified, and you create new or additional redo log files, Oracle uses DB_CREATE_FILE_DEST as the destination. Finally, DB_RECOVERY_FILE_DEST specifies the default location for the flash recovery area. If you use DB_RECOVERY_FILE_DEST, you must also specify DB_RECOVERY_FILE_DEST_SIZE. Here is an example of the values of these parameters in a default installation of Oracle Database 11g:

```
SQL> show parameter db_create

NAME                                 TYPE        VALUE
------------------------------------ ----------- ---------------
db_create_file_dest                  string      +DATA
db_create_online_log_dest_1          string
db_create_online_log_dest_2          string
db_create_online_log_dest_3          string
db_create_online_log_dest_4          string
db_create_online_log_dest_5          string

SQL> show parameter db_recovery
```

```
NAME                                         TYPE         VALUE
-------------------------------------------  -----------  ---------------
db_recovery_file_dest                        string       +RECOV
db_recovery_file_dest_size                   big integer  8G
SQL>
```

Notice that none of the DB_CREATE_ONLINE_LOG_DEST_n parameters are specified. As a result, Oracle stores the online redo log files in the location specified by DB_CREATE_FILE_DEST. But there's only one set of online redo log files. You might ask whether this is inviting disaster if a case of media failure occurs. However, if the +DATA disk group is mirrored, you essentially have two or more copies of each online redo log file.

on the **To further optimize the use of disk space for recovery operations, a flash**
Job **recovery area can be shared by more than one database.**

When the flash recovery area is configured, the initialization parameter LOG_ARCHIVE_DEST_10 is automatically set to the flash recovery area location. The corresponding ARC*n* background processes create archived log files in the flash recovery area and any other locations defined by the LOG_ARCHIVE_DEST_*n* initialization parameters.

If you do not specify a flash recovery area during installation, you can use Enterprise Manager Database Control to create or configure the flash recovery area. From the home page, select the Availability tab, and the click the Recovery Settings link to open the window shown in Figure 2-2.

This Recovery Settings window not only allows you to adjust the location and size of the flash recovery area, but it also shows you the flash recovery area disk usage broken down by file type.

The recommended size of the flash recovery area is the sum of the database size, the size of incremental backups, and the size of all archived log files that have not been copied to tape or to another disk location (if they are copied at all). You can keep all of your recovery files in the flash recovery area depending on your recovery window. The minimum size of the flash recovery area should be at least large enough to hold all archived redo log files that have not been copied to tape or another disk location.

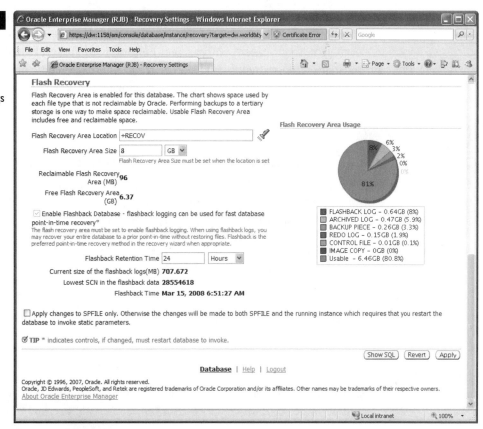

FIGURE 2-2

Configuring the flash recovery area using EM Recovery Settings

---

CERTIFICATION OBJECTIVE 2.05

Use the Flash Recovery Area

The initialization parameter DB_RECOVERY_FILE_DEST_SIZE can also assist in managing the size of the flash recovery area. Its primary purpose is to limit the amount of disk space used by the area on the specified disk group or file system directory. However, it can be temporarily increased once an alert is received to give the DBA additional time to allocate more disk space to the disk group or relocate the flash recovery area.

Short of receiving a warning or critical alert, you can be a bit more proactive in monitoring the size of the flash recovery area. Using the dynamic performance view V$RECOVERY_FILE_DEST, you can see the total used and reclaimable space on the destination file system. In addition, you can use the dynamic performance view V$FLASH_RECOVERY_AREA_USAGE to see a usage breakdown by file type.

EXERCISE 2-3

Query the Location, Contents, and Size of the Flash Recovery Area

In this exercise, use the dynamic performance views V$RECOVERY_FILE_DEST and V$FLASH_RECOVERY_AREA to determine the current size of the flash recovery area. Then reduce the size of the flash recovery area to 4GB.

1. Query the view V$RECOVERY_FILE_DEST from SQL*Plus to see its location and maximum size:

```
SQL> select * from v$recovery_file_dest;

NAME          SPACE_LIMIT SPACE_USED SPACE_RECLAIMABLE NUMBER_OF_FILES
------------  ----------- ---------- ----------------- ---------------
+RECOV         8589934592 1595932672          71303168              13
The flash recovery area is less than 20 percent used.
```

2. Determine the breakdown of file usage within the flash recovery area using V$FLASH_RECOVERY_AREA_USAGE:

```
SQL> select * from v$flash_recovery_area_usage;

FILE_TYPE       PERCENT_SPACE_USED PERCENT_SPACE_RECLAIMABLE
NUMBER_OF_FILES
--------------- ------------------ -------------------------
CONTROL FILE                  .12                         0
1
REDO LOG                     1.87                         0
3
ARCHIVED LOG                  .83                         1
7
BACKUP PIECE                15.75                         0
2
IMAGE COPY                      0                         0
0
FLASHBACK LOG                   0                         0
0
```

```
FOREIGN ARCHIVE                 0                            0
0
D LOG

7 rows selected.

SQL>
```

3. Change the size of the flash recovery area to 4GB:

```
SQL> alter system set db_recovery_file_dest_size = 4g scope=both;
System altered.
SQL>
```

Note that DB_RECOVERY_FILE_DEST_SIZE is a dynamic parameter and therefore takes effect immediately (without a database restart).

Oracle performs some automatic management of the space in the flash recovery area as well. Oracle does this by keeping track of which files are no longer needed for recovery or other flashback functions. If not enough free space exists for new files, Oracle deletes the oldest obsolete files and writes a message to the alert log. When disk space in the flash recovery area is low and insufficient space is free for new files, a message is written to the alert log, an alert is posted on the Enterprise Manager DB Control home page, and a row is added to the data dictionary view DBA_OUTSTANDING_ALERTS. If the available free space is 15 percent or less (85 percent or more used), a warning message is issued. When the available free space reaches 3 percent or less (97 percent or more used), a critical warning is issued.

The column SUGGESTED_ACTION in the data dictionary view DBA_OUTSTANDING_ALERTS provides a possible corrective action for a disk space problem; however, for space pressure in the flash recovery area, your possible corrective actions fall into one of these categories:

- Add additional disk space to the flash recovery area and adjust DB_RECOVERY_FILE_DEST_SIZE.
- Back up files to a tertiary tape or disk device and remove the files from the flash recovery area.
- Review and delete files from the flash recovery area using the RMAN commands REPORT OBSOLETE and DELETE OBSOLETE.
- Change the RMAN retention policy.

Using RMAN with the flash recovery area is covered in more detail in Chapters 4 and 5.

CERTIFICATION SUMMARY

This chapter started with an overview of the types of backups you can and should perform on a regular basis: logical and physical. Physical backups can either be online or offline backups. However, due to the business demands of 100 percent uptime, the luxury of offline backups has given way to online backups, and the Oracle RMAN tool can be used to perform online backups.

Although RMAN is covered in much greater detail later in this book, this chapter presented an overview of how to start RMAN with some basic command line options. RMAN commands fall into two broad categories: standalone and job commands, both of which you can execute at the RMAN command line or as a batch process. It also covered the types of retention policies you can configure within RMAN, depending on your availability and recovery requirements.

Next, you learned about the other prerequisites you need to fulfill before you can run your first RMAN command, such as configuring your database for ARCHIVELOG mode (if not already archived) and specifying the appropriate number and type of archive log file destinations.

Finally, you reviewed the usage and configuration of the flash recovery area, how it automates backup and recovery operations, and how you can monitor the disk space available in the flash recovery area.

TWO-MINUTE DRILL

Configuring for Database Recoverability

❑ A robust backup strategy includes both logical and physical backups.

❑ A logical backup of a database involves reading a set of database rows and writing them to a file.

❑ Oracle's Data Pump Export utility queries the database, including the data dictionary, and writes the output to an XML file called an *export dump file*.

❑ Once data has been exported via Data Pump Export, it can be imported via the Data Pump Import utility.

❑ Physical backups involve copying the files that constitute the database.

❑ Consistent offline backups occur when the database has been shut down normally (that is, not due to instance failure) using the NORMAL, IMMEDIATE, or TRANSACTIONAL option of the SHUTDOWN command.

❑ You can use online backups for any database that is running in ARCHIVELOG mode.

❑ In ARCHIVELOG mode, the online redo logs are archived, creating a log of all transactions within the database.

❑ You can perform file system backups of a database while that database is open, provided the database is running in ARCHIVELOG mode.

❑ The database can be fully recovered from an online backup, and it can, via the archived redo logs, be rolled forward to any point in time before the failure.

❑ The two basic types of RMAN commands are *standalone* commands and *job* commands.

❑ The preparation for using RMAN in your environment consists of two basic steps: change your database to ARCHIVELOG mode (if it is not already), and configure the number and types of archive log destinations to maximize recoverability and availability.

❑ When Oracle is run in ARCHIVELOG mode, the ARCn background process makes a copy of each redo log file after the LGWR process finishes writing to it.

Configure Multiple Archive Log File Destinations to Increase Availability

❑ Changing your database to ARCHIVELOG mode increases recoverability of your database and enables the use of RMAN as a backup and recovery tool for online backups.

❑ The initialization parameter DB_RECOVERY_FILE_DEST specifies the location of the flash recovery area, which can be on a file system or an ASM disk group.

❑ Set at least one LOG_ARCHIVE_DEST_n parameter to a location outside the flash recovery area.

❑ Set at least two LOG_ARCHIVE_DEST_n parameters to archive to non–flash recovery area destinations.

❑ For one or two archived log file destinations, you can use LOG_ARCHIVE_DEST and LOG_ARCHIVE_DUPLEX_DEST.

❑ For more than two archived log file destinations with at least one remote destination, use LOG_ARCHIVE_DEST_n.

❑ Use LOG_ARCHIVE_MIN_SUCCEED_DEST to guarantee that a minimal number of archived log file destinations are accessible by ARCn.

Define, Apply, and Use a Retention Policy

❑ RMAN can retain and manage backups by using either a recovery window or by redundancy.

❑ Using a retention policy of NONE relies on an externally managed recovery window or redundancy.

❑ The default RMAN retention policy is 1 copy.

❑ The initialization parameter CONTROL_FILE_RECORD_KEEP_TIME controls how long RMAN backup information is kept in the target database's control file if a recovery catalog is not used.

Configure the Flash Recovery Area

❑ The flash recovery area is a unified storage location for all recovery-related files in an Oracle database.

❑ All the files that you need in order to recover a database from a media failure or a logical error are contained in the flash recovery area.

❑ The permanent items kept in the flash recovery area are a copy of the control file and mirrored copies of the online redo log files.

❑ The transient items kept in the flash recovery area are the archived redo log files, flashback logs, control file automatic backups, data file copies, and RMAN files used for staging a backup or recovery operation using archived log files.

❑ The initialization parameter `DB_CREATE_FILE_DEST` specifies the default location for database objects that do not explicitly specify a location.

❑ The initialization parameter `DB_CREATE_ONLINE_LOG_DEST_n` specifies a default destination for one set of archived redo log files.

❑ The initialization parameter `DB_RECOVERY_FILE_DEST` specifies the location of the flash recovery area.

❑ The initialization parameter `DB_RECOVERY_FILE_DEST_SIZE` specifies the maximum size of the flash recovery area.

❑ When the flash recovery area is configured, the initialization parameter `LOG_ARCHIVE_DEST_10` is automatically set to the flash recovery area location.

❑ The recommended size of the flash recovery area is the sum of the database size, the size of incremental backups, and the size of all archived log files that have not been copied to tape or to another disk location.

Use the Flash Recovery Area

❑ The initialization parameter `DB_RECOVERY_FILE_DEST_SIZE` can be temporarily increased once an alert is received to give the DBA additional time to allocate more disk space to the disk group or relocate the flash recovery area.

❑ The dynamic performance view `V$RECOVERY_FILE_DEST` shows the total used and reclaimable space on the destination file system or flash recovery area.

❑ Oracle performs some automatic management of the space in the flash recovery area and keeps track of which files are no longer needed for recovery or other flashback functions.

❑ The data dictionary view `DBA_OUTSTANDING_ALERTS` contains a possible corrective action for space pressure in the flash recovery area when the amount of free space in the flash recovery area is 15 percent or less of the total flash recovery area size.

SELF TEST

The following questions will help you measure your understanding of the material presented in this chapter. Read all the choices carefully, because there might be more than one correct answer. Choose all correct answers for each question.

Configuring for Database Recoverability

1. Which of the following statement is not true regarding database backups?

    A. A consistent offline backup occurs after a SHUTDOWN NORMAL, IMMEDIATE, or TRANSACTIONAL.

    B. As of Oracle Database 11g, RMAN supports only online backups.

    C. A physical database backup copies one or more files that constitute the database.

    D. A logical database backup reads a set of database rows and writes them to a file.

    E. A logical database backup reads a set of database rows and writes them to an ASM disk group.

    F. Online backups can occur only when your database is in ARCHIVELOG mode.

2. Which of the following objects can be backed up by RMAN while the database is open? (Choose all that apply.)

    A. Archived redo log files

    B. Online redo log files

    C. Password files

    D. Tablespaces

    E. Tables and indexes

    F. Control files

    G. Server parameter files (SPFILEs)

    H. Datafiles

3. Which of the following are not RMAN standalone commands? (Choose all that apply.)

    A. BACKUP DATABASE

    B. ALLOCATE CHANNEL

    C. CONNECT

    D. CREATE CATALOG

    E. CREATE SCRIPT

Configure Multiple Archive Log File Destinations to Increase Availability

4. Choose the four best commands from the following list that you would use to enable `ARCHIVELOG` mode, and put them in the correct order:

1. `STARUP MOUNT`
2. `SHUTDOWN ABORT`
3. `ALTER DATABASE ARCHIVELOG;`
4. `STARTUP FORCE`
5. `ALTER DATABASE ENABLE ARCHIVELOG;`
6. `ALTER SYSTEM SWITCH LOGFILE;`
7. `SHUTDOWN NORMAL`
8. `ALTER DATABASE OPEN;`
9. `SHUTDOWN IMMEDIATE`

    A. 2, 1, 3, 8

    B. 9, 3, 1, 8

    C. 4, 5, 7, 6

    D. 7, 1, 3, 8

    E. 9, 1, 3, 8

5. Which of the following initialization parameters is not valid?

    A. `LOG_ARCHIVE_DEST_3 = '/rmtdisk/u01/app/oracle/flash'`

    B. `LOG_ARCHIVE_DUPLEX_DEST = '+DATA'`

    C. `LOG_ARCHIVE_DEST = 'SERVICE=RMTDB99'`

    D. `LOG_ARCHIVE_DEST = '/rmtdisk/u01/app/oracle/flash'`

    E. `LOG_ARCHIVE_DEST_10 = 'SERVICE=RMTDB99'`

    F. `LOG_ARCHIVE_DEST_10 = '/rmtdisk/u01/app/oracle/flash'`

6. Your SPFILE contains the following parameter values:

```
LOG_ARCHIVE_DEST_1 = 'LOCATION=/u01/app/oracle/arch'
LOG_ARCHIVE_DEST_2 =
      'LOCATION=/u03/app/oracle/arch MANDATORY'
LOG_ARCHIVE_DEST_3 = 'SERVICE=STNDBY_CLEVELAND MANDATORY'
LOG_ARCHIVE_MIN_SUCCEED_DEST = 1
```

You are not using a flash recovery area. The disk drive containing the directory /u03/app/oracle/arch fails. What happens to the archive processes and the database?

    A. The database pauses because `LOG_ARCHIVE_DEST_2` is `MANDATORY`.

    B. The database continues to run normally with the remaining two archive locations because at least one other destination is marked as `MANDATORY`.

    C. The database continues to run normally with the remaining two archive locations because `LOG_ARCHIVE_MIN_SUCCEED_DEST` is 1.

    D. The database will not start unless `LOG_ARCHIVE_MIN_SUCCEED_DEST` is set to at least the number of `MANDATORY` locations.

Define, Apply, and Use a Retention Policy

7. Which of the following RMAN commands does not correctly configure a retention policy? (Choose the best answer.)

    A. `CONFIGURE RETENTION POLICY TO RECOVERY WINDOW OF 100 DAYS;`

    B. `CONFIGURE RETENTION POLICY TO NONE;`

    C. `CONFIGURE RETENTION POLICY TO REDUNDANCY WINDOW OF 2 DAYS;`

    D. `CONFIGURE RETENTION POLICY TO REDUNDANCY 2;`

8. If you disable the RMAN retention policy, how long are the details of RMAN backups kept?

    A. Until the flash recovery area is full

    B. Up to the time specified by the initialization parameter `CONTROL_FILE_RECORD_KEEP_TIME`

    C. Until the database is shut down

    D. Indefinitely

Configure the Flash Recovery Area

9. Which of the following items are permanent and are stored in the flash recovery area? (Choose all that apply.)

    A. Control file

    B. Archived redo log files

    C. Online redo log files

    D. Control file backup

    E. RMAN backupsets

10. Which of the following items are transient and are stored in the flash recovery area? (Choose all that apply.)

    A. Control file

    B. Archived redo log files

    C. Online redo log files

    D. Control file backup

    E. RMAN backupsets

11. If you specify the initialization parameter DB_RECOVERY_FILE_DEST, what other initialization parameter must be set?

A. DB_CREATE_FILE_DEST

B. DB_CREATE_ONLINE_LOG_DEST_n

C. DB_RECOVERY_FILE_DEST_SIZE

D. No other parameter needs to be set

Use the Flash Recovery Area

12. You have just received a pager alert indicating that the flash recovery area is below 3 percent free space. Which view and column can you query for a possible corrective action for this space condition? (Choose the best answer.)

A. V$FLASH_RECOVERY_AREA_USAGE, PERCENT_SPACE_RECLAIMABLE

B. DBA_OUTSTANDING_ALERT, SUGGESTED_ACTIONS

C. DBA_OUTSTANDING_ALERTS, SUGGESTED_ACTIONS

D. DBA_OUTSTANDING_ALERTS, SUGGESTED_ACTION

LAB QUESTION

Invoke RMAN at the command line; connect to the database using operating system authentication; perform a full compressed backup using a remote catalog; show a list of backups, and delete any obsolete backups.

SELF TEST ANSWERS

Configuring for Database Recoverability

1. ☑ **B.** RMAN can perform both online and offline backups.
    ☒ All other statements about online and offline backups are true.

2. ☑ **A, D, F, G,** and **H.** RMAN can back up archived redo log files, then delete them from the flash recovery area. Tablespaces can be backed up individually by RMAN. Control files are backed up either explicitly during an RMAN backup or implicitly when the SYSTEM tablespace is part of a backup, or by setting RMAN control file autobackup with CONFIGURE CONTROLFILE AUTOBACKUP ON. The SPFILE, but not a static PFILE (text parameter file), can also be included in an RMAN backup. Individual datafiles can be backed up as well.
    ☒ **B** is wrong because you should never back up online redo files, and RMAN will not back them up anyway. **C** is wrong because RMAN will not back up an operating system file such as a password file; you can back up this file manually. **E** is wrong because RMAN cannot back up individual tables and indexes. These types of objects are best backed up by a logical backup using expdp.

3. ☑ **B.** The ALLOCATE CHANNEL command can be used only in a command block; you can define a default channel for a standalone command using the CONFIGURE CHANNEL command.
    ☒ **A, C, D** and **E** are all standalone commands; BACKUP DATABASE can be used as a standalone command or as a job command.

Configure Multiple Archive Log File Destinations to Increase Availability

4. ☑ **E.** The correct commands and sequence for enabling ARCHIVELOG mode are as follows:
    ```
    SHUTDOWN IMMEDIATE
    STARTUP MOUNT
    ALTER DATABASE ARCHIVELOG;
    ALTER DATABASE OPEN;
    ```
    ☒ All other combinations are either in the wrong order or have incorrect or unnecessary steps. You cannot use SHUTDOWN ABORT, as this leaves the database in an unusable state until the database can be recovered (or restarted), thus you cannot enable ARCHIVELOG mode without extra steps. STARTUP FORCE performs a SHUTDOWN ABORT and a STARTUP, which leaves you with the database in OPEN mode, and thus this command is not necessary. ENABLE ARCHIVELOG is not a valid keyword in the ALTER DATABASE command. SHUTDOWN NORMAL is one way to shut down the database gracefully, but then you must wait for all users to disconnect from the database. ALTER SYSTEM SWITCH LOGFILE is a valid command but is not part of the process of switching a database into ARCHIVELOG mode.

5. ☑ **C.** If you use LOG_ARCHIVE_DEST or LOG_ARCHIVE_DUPLEX_DEST, the locations must be a disk device (file system or ASM disk). The destination cannot be another Oracle instance.
☒ **A, B, D, E,** and **F** are incorrect. When you use LOG_ARCHIVE_DEST_n, the destination can be a file system or a database service. By default, if you have a flash recovery area defined, LOG_ARCHIVE_DEST_10 points to the flash recovery area; however, you can override this with any valid disk location or service.

6. ☑ **A.** All archive destinations marked as MANDATORY must be available when ARC*n* attempts to archive a filled redo log.
☒ **B** is wrong because all MANDATORY locations must be available when ARC*n* needs to archive a filled redo log file. **C** is wrong because all MANDATORY locations must be available and the number of available locations must be greater than or equal to the number of locations specified in LOG_ARCHIVE_MIN_SUCCEED_DEST. **D** is wrong because LOG_ARCHIVE_MIN_SUCCEED_DEST can be any integer and is not related to how many LOG_ARCHIVE_DEST_*n* parameters are set to MANDATORY; both parameters work independently to ensure a minimum number of available archive locations.

Define, Apply, and Use a Retention Policy

7. ☑ **C.** REDUNDANCY WINDOW OF 2 DAYS is syntactically incorrect.
☒ **A, B,** and **D** are all valid RMAN commands. You can set the RMAN retention policy to the total number of copies of each database file, to the number of days in the past for which you can restore the database after a logical error, or you can disable the retention policy completely and manage the retention policy externally from RMAN.

8. ☑ **B.** When there is no retention policy, RMAN keeps the details of RMAN backups up to the time specified by the CONTROL_FILE_RECORD_KEEP_TIME initialization parameter.
☒ **A, C,** and **D** are incorrect. The control file or a recovery catalog still contain the information about RMAN backups, and this information is available until CONTROL_FILE_RECORD_KEEP_TIME.

Configure the Flash Recovery Area

9. ☑ **A** and **C.** A mirrored copy of the control file and one mirrored copy of each online redo log file are stored in the flash recovery area.
☒ **B, D,** and **E** aren't considered permanent items.

10. ☑ **B, D,** and **E.** Archived redo log files, backups of the control file, and RMAN backupsets are considered transient and are stored in the flash recovery area.
☒ **A** and **C** aren't considered transient items.

11. ☑ **C.** When you specify the location of the flash recovery area with `DB_RECOVERY_FILE_DEST`, you must also set the parameter `DB_RECOVERY_FILE_DEST_SIZE` to limit the amount of space used by the flash recovery area on the destination file system.

    ☒ **A** is wrong because `DB_CREATE_FILE_DEST` specifies a default location for any database object created without an explicit location. **B** is wrong since `DB_CREATE_ONLINE_LOG_DEST_n` specifies the location for new or additional online redo log files. **D** is wrong since you must specify a size for the flash recovery area.

Use the Flash Recovery Area

12. ☑ **D.** The `REASON` column in `DBA_OUTSTANDING_ALERTS` contains a description for the alert, and the `SUGGESTED_ACTION` provides a recommendation for corrective action. These descriptions also appear in the alerts section of the Enterprise Manager Database Control home page.

    ☒ **A** is wrong since the column `PERCENT_SPACE_RECLAIMABLE` doesn't provide any recommendations, only an amount of disk space that can be reclaimable for objects that may be obsolete in the flash recovery area. **B** and **C** are wrong because there is no such data dictionary view as `DBA_OUTSTANDING_ALERT`, and there is no such column as `SUGGESTED_ACTIONS` in the view `DBA_OUTSTANDING_ALERTS`.

LAB ANSWER

```
[oracle@dw ~]$ rman target / catalog rman/rman@rac

Recovery Manager: Release 11.1.0.6.0 -
          Production on Sat Mar 15 09:56:57 2008
Copyright (c) 1982, 2007, Oracle.  All rights reserved.

connected to target database: DW (DBID=3048318127)
connected to recovery catalog database

RMAN> backup as compressed backupset database;

Starting backup at 15-MAR-08
starting full resync of recovery catalog
full resync complete
allocated channel: ORA_DISK_1
. . .
Starting Control File and SPFILE Autobackup at 15-MAR-08
piece handle=+RECOV/dw/autobackup/2008_03_15/
          s_649418404.388.649418419 comment=NONE
Finished Control File and SPFILE Autobackup at 15-MAR-08

RMAN> list backup;

List of Backup Sets
===================
BS Key  Type LV Size       Device Type Elapsed Time Completion Time
------- ---- -- ---------- ----------- ------------ ---------------
7915    Full    92.09M     DISK        00:00:47     14-MAR-08
        BP Key: 7920   Status: AVAILABLE  Compressed: YES
                   Tag: TAG20080314T234623
. . .

RMAN> delete noprompt obsolete;

RMAN retention policy will be applied to the command
RMAN retention policy is set to redundancy 1
using channel ORA_DISK_1
Deleting the following obsolete backups and copies:
Type                Key    Completion Time    Filename/Handle
```

```
-------------------- ------ ------------------ --------------------
Archive Log          7897    14-MAR-08
             /u01/app/oracle/product/11.1.0/db_1/
             dbs/arch1_1362_630244724.dbf
 . . .
Deleted 9 objects

RMAN>
```

3
Creating
and Maintaining
an RMAN Catalog

I f you're ready to do some backups with RMAN, you'll have to wait until the next chapter. This chapter lays the groundwork for performing RMAN backups by creating the *recovery catalog*. Without a recovery catalog, your backup information is limited to the RMAN information stored in the target database's control file. You'll learn how to do this at the command line and from Oracle Enterprise Manager.

Next, you'll learn how to register and unregister a database from the recovery catalog. Once a database is registered with a recovery catalog, you'll see scenarios for which you might need to resynchronize the RMAN backup information in the target database control file with the recovery catalog. In most cases, RMAN performs the synchronization automatically.

RMAN stored scripts makes your job easier by saving frequently used sequences of commands in a recovery catalog; using stored scripts is one of many advantages of using a recovery catalog for RMAN backups over a target database's control file.

To subdivide the division of labor among several DBAs in your enterprise, the RMAN recovery catalog supports the concept of a *virtual private catalog*; each DBA can view and access only the backup information for which he or she is responsible. This catalog enables a single location for all target database backup information while maintaining a separation of duties, just as Oracle Database Vault can restrict a DBA to accessing only the part of the database for which he or she is responsible.

Next, you'll review the configuration options available in RMAN when you are connected to a target database; each target database has its own set of configurable parameters, such as the compression level, automatic backups of the control file, and channel types.

Finally, the chapter briefly covers a couple of other topics: how to allocate channels for an RMAN backup, and how to skip over files that are identical to those already backed up in previous backup sets (to save on backup time).

CERTIFICATION OBJECTIVE 3.01

Identify Situations that Require RMAN Recovery Catalog

RMAN always stores its *metadata* (information about the database structure, backup sets, and image copies) in the target database's control file. However, there are several advantages, and a few disadvantages, to storing this metadata in a recovery catalog stored in a separate database. The next two sections discuss the pros and cons of using a recovery catalog.

Using the Control File for RMAN Metadata

Oracle strongly recommends using a recovery catalog, but doing so has a few downsides. Whether you use a recovery catalog or not, the RMAN backup information is always stored in the control file of the target database. Although the RMAN information in the control file is aged out based on the value of the initialization parameter CONTROL_FILE_RECORD_KEEP_TIME, this might not be a problem if you use an RMAN retention policy that has a RECOVERY WINDOW that is less than CONTROL_FILE_RECORD_KEEP_TIME. In addition, using your control file as the only repository for RMAN information is easier to manage, because you don't need a second database, which in turn, needs to be backed up. Finally, if you are mirroring your control file in several locations and you create an offsite backup of your control file after every database structure change or RMAN backup, then you will likely never lose your control file and will always be able to restore your database successfully from any media failure, even a complete loss of the database. Using a recovery catalog database also means that you have another database to back up on a regular basis.

Using a Recovery Catalog for RMAN Metadata

If you manage more than one database in your environment, and you want to keep your recovery information for a much longer time, then using a recovery catalog might be justified. A single recovery catalog can store RMAN information for a virtually unlimited number of target databases. In addition, all information in the control file of the target database resides in the RMAN recovery catalog after you perform the first RESYNC CATALOG operation.

Using stored scripts is another reason to use a recovery catalog; you cannot store scripts in the target database's control file. You can save a sequence of commands as a single script to make it easy to run the sequence of commands on demand, or perhaps on a specific schedule. A script can be tied to a specific target database (a local script), or it can be available to all target databases (a global script).

Because you can put the metadata from several databases into a single recovery catalog, you can use the RC_ views, such as RC_ARCHIVED_LOG, RC_BACKUP_FILES, and RC_DATABASE, in the recovery catalog database to retrieve metadata for all target databases. Otherwise, when you're using the target database control file, you must connect to each target database separately and query the V$ views based on the target database's control file.

Finally, using a recovery catalog permits you to use the following RMAN commands:

- BACKUP...KEEP UNTIL TIME   Keep a backup for a period of time that differs from the configured retention policy.
- BACKUP...KEEP FOREVER   Keep a backup indefinitely or until you manually remove it.
- REPORT SCHEMA...AT   Show the structure of the database at a specific time in the past.

CERTIFICATION OBJECTIVE 3.02

Create and Configure a Recovery Catalog

Whether you use a repository for the metadata from one database or a hundred, the repository setup is straightforward and needs to be done only once. The examples that follow assume that you have a default installation of an Oracle 11g database. The repository database itself can be used for other applications if no significant performance degradation occurs when RMAN needs to update metadata in the repository.

on the
job

Using an RMAN target database for the repository is strongly discouraged. Loss of the target database prevents any chance of a successful recovery of the database using RMAN because the repository metadata is lost along with the target database. If both are lost, you will have to maintain manual backups of the target database for recovery of the repository.

The following sequence of commands creates a tablespace and a user to maintain the metadata in the repository database. In this and all subsequent examples, a database with a system ID (SID) of RCAT is used for all repository operations. Three basic steps are required: configure the recovery catalog database, create the recovery catalog owner, and create the recovery catalog itself.

Configure the Recovery Catalog Database

The tablespace that holds the repository database requires at least 125MB to hold recovery catalog entries; here are the minimum *additional* space requirements for the repository, by tablespace:

- 90MB in the SYSTEM tablespace
- 5MB in the TEMP tablespace
- 5MB in the UNDO tablespace
- 15MB in RMAN default tablespace for each database registered in the recovery catalog
- 1MB for each online redo log file

Starting out with available free space of 125MB will in most cases be sufficient for the first year, and enabling automatic extents of 50MB each will be sufficient in the long term depending on how many databases you manage in the recovery catalog. Overall, it's a very small amount of disk space compared to your terabyte data warehouse!

Connect to the repository database with SYSDBA privileges and create the recovery catalog in the RMAN tablespace as follows:

```
[oracle@oc1 ~]$ sqlplus / as sysdba

SQL*Plus: Release 11.1.0.6.0 -
            Production on Tue Aug 28 20:56:24 2007

Copyright (c) 1982, 2007, Oracle.  All rights reserved.

Connected to:
Oracle Database 11g Enterprise Edition Release 11.1.0.6.0 -
    Production
With the Partitioning, Real Application Clusters, OLAP,
    Data Mining and Real Application Testing options

SQL> create tablespace rman datafile '+data'
  2  size 125m autoextend on;

Tablespace created.

SQL>
```

Create the Recovery Catalog Owner

Creating the recovery catalog owner is as easy as creating any database user. In this example, we create the user RMAN to manage the recovery catalog. You could just as easily create a user called FRED to own the recovery catalog. Using RMAN as the catalog owner makes it easier to identify the purpose of the account:

```
SQL> create user rman
  2      identified by rman
  3      default tablespace rman
  4      quota unlimited on rman;

User altered.

SQL> grant recovery_catalog_owner to rman;

Grant succeeded.

SQL>
```

The predefined role RECOVERY_CATALOG_OWNER includes these system privileges:

- ALTER SESSION
- CREATE CLUSTER
- CREATE DATABASE LINK
- CREATE PROCEDURE
- CREATE SEQUENCE
- CREATE SESSION
- CREATE SYNONYM
- CREATE TABLE
- CREATE TRIGGER
- CREATE TYPE
- CREATE VIEW

Later in this chapter, you'll learn how to create virtual catalog owners, each of which will own a virtual private catalog. This enables the division of responsibilities among many DBAs, allowing management of multiple databases using the same RMAN repository.

Create the Recovery Catalog

Now that the RMAN user account exists in the repository database, you can start
RMAN, connect to the catalog, and initialize the repository with the CREATE
CATALOG command:

```
[oracle@dw ~]$ rman catalog rman/rman@rcat

Recovery Manager: Release 11.1.0.6.0 -
    Production on Tue Aug 28 21:24:30 2007
Copyright (c) 1982, 2007, Oracle.  All rights reserved.

connected to recovery catalog database
RMAN> create catalog;
recovery catalog created
RMAN>
```

From this point on, using a repository is as easy as specifying the repository username
and password on the RMAN command line with the CATALOG parameter, or using
the CONNECT CATALOG command in an RMAN session. Within Oracle Enterprise
Manager, you can persist the repository credentials as demonstrated in Figure 3-1.

FIGURE 3-1

Persisting RMAN
repository
credentials

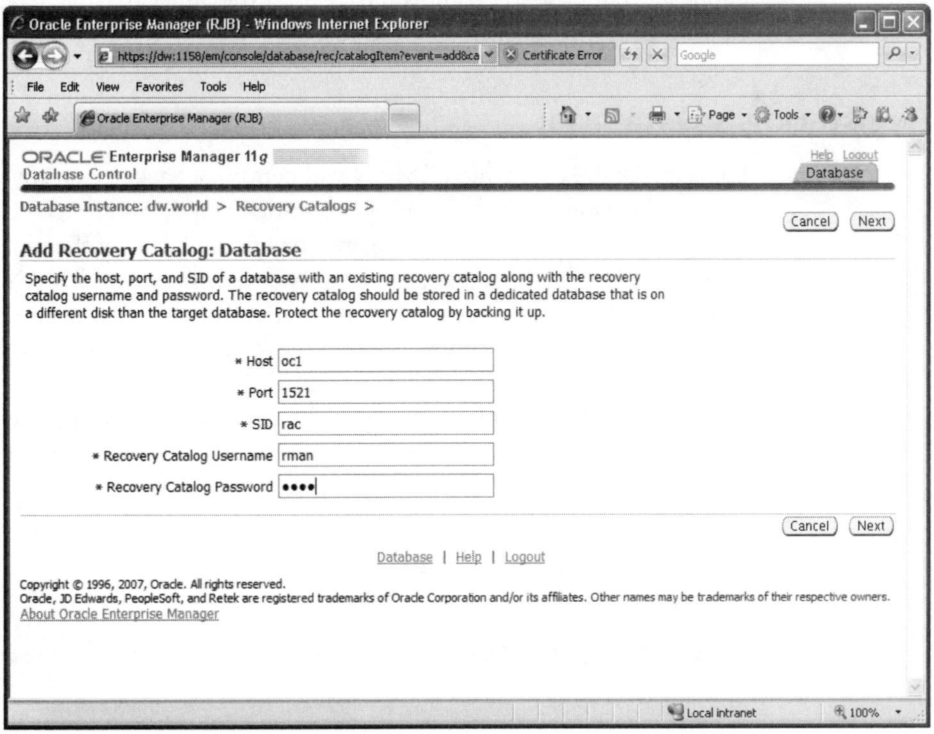

In future EM sessions, any RMAN backup or recovery operations will automatically use the recovery catalog.

CERTIFICATION OBJECTIVE 3.03

Synchronize the Recovery Catalog

Now that you've set up your recovery catalog, you can register one or more of your databases with the recovery catalog. The registration process propagates backup information and the target database structure to the recovery catalog. In general, RMAN saves most information from the control file to the recovery catalog; however, a few operations require you to update the metadata manually in the recovery catalog.

The following sections cover topics related to recovery catalog synchronization: registering a database, unregistering a database, and resynchronizing a recovery catalog. In addition, you'll learn how to change the database identifier (DBID) of a duplicated database to permit you to register the duplicated database in the recovery catalog; the DBID of each database recorded in the recovery catalog must be unique.

Registering a Database

For each database for which RMAN will perform a backup or recovery, you must register the database in the RMAN repository; this operation records information such as the target database schema and the unique DBID of the target database. The target database needs to be registered only once; subsequent RMAN sessions that connect to the target database will automatically reference the correct metadata in the repository. The database must be in the MOUNT or OPEN state to be successfully registered.

The following example connects to the target database using operating system authentication, and to the repository with password authentication:

```
[oracle@dw ~]$ rman target / catalog rman@rcat

Recovery Manager: Release 11.1.0.6.0 -
    Production on Tue Aug 28 21:34:08 2007

Copyright (c) 1982, 2007, Oracle.  All rights reserved.
```

```
connected to target database: DW (DBID=3048318127)
recovery catalog database Password: **********
connected to recovery catalog database

RMAN> register database;

database registered in recovery catalog
starting full resync of recovery catalog
full resync complete

RMAN>
```

All databases registered with the repository must have unique DBIDs; trying to register the database again yields the following error message:

```
RMAN> register database;

RMAN-00571: ========================================================
RMAN-00569: =============== ERROR MESSAGE STACK FOLLOWS ==========
RMAN-00571: ========================================================
RMAN-03009: failure of register command on default channel
    at 03/31/2008 21:38:44
RMAN-20002: target database already registered in recovery catalog

RMAN>
```

As you might expect, you can use Enterprise Manager (EM) to register the database; Figure 3-2 shows the Recovery Catalog Settings page where you can specify a recovery catalog and register the database. If you do not include this step in the registration process, any backups you perform using EM will not be recorded in the recovery catalog.

Changing the DBID of a Database

In the preceding section, you attempted to register the same database in the recovery catalog twice. RMAN prevented the duplicated registration because a database with the same DBID already existed in the recovery catalog. But what if you duplicate a database, and now want to use the same recovery catalog for both databases? You can use the DBNEWID utility, using the `nid` command at the command line prompt.

FIGURE 3-2

Specifying a
repository and
registering a
database using EM

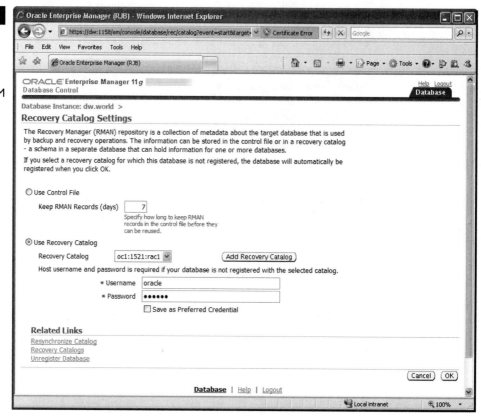

Running `nid` without any parameters shows you the possible parameters:

```
[oracle@oc1 ~]$ nid

DBNEWID: Release 11.1.0.6.0 - Production on Mon Mar 31 23:18:39 2008

Copyright (c) 1982, 2007, Oracle.  All rights reserved.

Keyword     Description                     (Default)
-----------------------------------------------------------
TARGET      Username/Password               (NONE)
DBNAME      New database name               (NONE)
LOGFILE     Output Log                      (NONE)
REVERT      Revert failed change            NO
SETNAME     Set a new database name only    NO
APPEND      Append to output log            NO
HELP        Displays these messages         NO

[oracle@oc1 ~]$
```

TARGET specifies the username and password of the database, as you might expect. You can optionally specify DBNAME to create a new database name in addition to the DBID; if you want to change only the database name, you specify SETNAME=Y.

Here is the DBID for the DW database before you change it:

```
SQL> select dbid, name from v$database;

     DBID NAME
---------- ---------
 423043877 DW

SQL>
```

The database whose name and DBID will be changed must be shut down cleanly and restarted in MOUNT mode, as in this example:

```
SQL> shutdown immediate
Database closed.
Database dismounted.
ORACLE instance shut down.
SQL> startup mount
ORACLE instance started.

Total System Global Area  669581312 bytes
Fixed Size                  1302008 bytes
Variable Size             524288520 bytes
Database Buffers          138412032 bytes
Redo Buffers                5578752 bytes
Database mounted.
SQL> quit
```

Next, you run the nid command at the command line prompt; you want to change only the DBID:

```
[oracle@dw ~]$ nid target=system/syspass@dw

DBNEWID: Release 11.1.0.6.0 - Production on Tue Apr 1 15:15:20 2008

Copyright (c) 1982, 2007, Oracle.  All rights reserved.

Connected to database DW (DBID=423043877)

Connected to server version 11.1.0

Control Files in database:
    +DATA/dw/controlfile/current.276.650894245
    +RECOV/dw/controlfile/current.475.650894245
```

```
Change database ID of database DW? (Y/[N]) => y

Proceeding with operation
Changing database ID from 423043877 to 423071368
    Control File +DATA/dw/controlfile/current.276.650894245 - modified
    Control File +RECOV/dw/controlfile/current.475.650894245 - modified
    Datafile +DATA/dw/datafile/system.272.650894145 - dbid changed
    Datafile +DATA/dw/datafile/sysaux.273.650894147 - dbid changed
    Datafile +DATA/dw/datafile/undotbs1.274.650894147 - dbid changed
    Datafile +DATA/dw/datafile/users.275.650894147 - dbid changed
    Datafile +DATA/dw/datafile/example.281.650894303 - dbid changed
    Datafile +DATA/dw/datafile/rman.283.650895919 - dbid changed
    Datafile +DATA/dw/tempfile/temp.280.650894293 - dbid changed
    Control File +DATA/dw/controlfile/current.276.650894245 - dbid changed
    Control File +RECOV/dw/controlfile/current.475.650894245 - dbid changed
    Instance shut down

Database ID for database DW changed to 423071368.
All previous backups and archived redo logs for this database are unusable.
Database is not aware of previous backups and archived logs
            in Recovery Area.
Database has been shutdown, open database with RESETLOGS option.
Successfully changed database ID.
DBNEWID - Completed successfully.

[oracle@rmanrep ~]$
```

Finally, open the database with the RESETLOGS option:

```
SQL> startup mount
ORACLE instance started.

Total System Global Area   636100608 bytes
Fixed Size                   1301784 bytes
Variable Size              415236840 bytes
Database Buffers           213909504 bytes
Redo Buffers                 5652480 bytes
Database mounted.
SQL> alter database open resetlogs;
Database altered.
SQL>
```

Here is the DW database's DBID after you change it:

```
SQL> select dbid, name from v$database;
```

```
     DBID NAME
---------- ---------
 423071368 DW

SQL>
```

Using the DBNEWID command has at least one downside. Since all backup files contain the old DBID, previous backups are unusable; after you change the DBID, you must open the database for the first time with the RESETLOGS option as shown in the preceding example. In addition, you should perform a full backup of the database, since you now have no usable previous backups.

Unregistering a Database

If you want to migrate your backup information from one recovery catalog to another, either because of space pressure on the existing catalog, or an erroneously registered database, you can unregister a database from a recovery catalog using, as you might expect, the UNREGISTER command. In this example, you connect to the target database and the recovery catalog, and then you execute the UNREGISTER command:

```
[oracle@dw ~]$ rman target / catalog rman/rman@rcat

Recovery Manager: Release 11.1.0.6.0 - Production on Tue Apr 1 16:14:37 2008

Copyright (c) 1982, 2007, Oracle.  All rights reserved.

connected to target database: DW (DBID=3048318127)
connected to recovery catalog database

RMAN> unregister database;

database name is "DW" and DBID is 3048318127

Do you really want to unregister the database (enter YES or NO)? yes
database unregistered from the recovery catalog

RMAN>
```

After you unregister a database, your backup metadata is still stored in the control file for the number of days specified by the initialization parameter CONTROL_FILE_ RECORD_KEEP_TIME. If you reregister the database, Oracle populates the recovery catalog with the backup-related and database structure metadata from the control file. If you wish to add information about any backups not in the control file at the time you reregister the database, you can manually add the backup metadata with the CATALOG command, as you will see in the next section.

Cataloging Additional Backup Files

If you have created backups outside of RMAN, or you have registered your database and RMAN backups have already been aged out of the control file, you can use the CATALOG command to add these backups to the RMAN recovery catalog. The CATALOG command can add the following types of backup files to the recovery catalog with the associated keyword for the CATALOG command:

- **Data file copies**   DATAFILECOPY
- **Backup pieces**   BACKUPPIECE
- **Control file copies**   CONTROLFILECOPY
- **Archived redo log files**   ARCHIVELOG

For example, you might want to record an additional archived log file destination in the recovery catalog, in addition to the archived log files in the flash recovery area that are already recorded. If you want to catalog a number of backup files in a specific Automatic Storage Management (ASM) disk group location or a file system location, you can use the START WITH option. This example uses the START WITH option to catalog all backup files in the ASM disk group +DATA2:

```
RMAN> catalog start with '+DATA2';
```

on the job *The filename or file path specified in the START WITH clause is only a prefix, and no wildcards are allowed.*

EXERCISE 3-1

Cataloging Additional Backup Files

In this exercise, the DW database has an additional archived log destination at /u02/oradata/archivelog, and these archived log files were created before the database was registered with the recovery catalog. Query the file system location using the Unix `ls` command, and add all archived log files in that location to the recovery catalog:

1. Query the file system for a list of backup files:

```
[oracle@dw ~]$ ls -l /u02/oradata/archivelog
total 38020
-rw-r-----  1 oracle oinstall 2012672 Apr  5 12:01 1_1461_630244724.dbf
-rw-r-----  1 oracle oinstall 1712288 Apr  5 12:11 1_1462_630244724.dbf
-rw-r-----  1 oracle oinstall 2115360 Apr  5 12:23 1_1463_630244724.dbf
[oracle@dw ~]$
```

2. Connect to RMAN and use the CATALOG START WITH command to add these archived redo log files to the recovery catalog:

```
[oracle@dw ~]$ rman target / catalog rman/rman@rcat

Recovery Manager: Release 11.1.0.6.0 - Production on Sat Apr 5
12:08:09 2008

Copyright (c) 1982, 2007, Oracle.  All rights reserved.

connected to target database: DW (DBID=3048318127)
connected to recovery catalog database

RMAN> catalog start with '/u02/oradata/archivelog';

searching for all files that match the pattern /u02/oradata/archivelog

List of Files Unknown to the Database
=====================================
File Name: /u02/oradata/archivelog/1_1462_630244724.dbf
File Name: /u02/oradata/archivelog/1_1463_630244724.dbf
File Name: /u02/oradata/archivelog/1_1461_630244724.dbf

Do you really want to catalog the above files (enter YES or NO)? yes
cataloging files...
cataloging done

List of Cataloged Files
=======================
File Name: /u02/oradata/archivelog/1_1462_630244724.dbf
File Name: /u02/oradata/archivelog/1_1463_630244724.dbf
File Name: /u02/oradata/archivelog/1_1461_630244724.dbf
RMAN>
```

If you inadvertently or intentionally unregistered the database, you can reregister the database. However, some of your backup metadata might have been aged out of the control file because reregistration uses metadata from the control file. If you have a flash recovery area, you can easily recatalog all backups in the flash recovery area using the RECOVERY AREA option of the CATALOG command:

```
RMAN> catalog recovery area noprompt;
```

The NOPROMPT keyword, as you might expect, catalogs each backup without confirmation.

Manually Resynchronize the Recovery Catalog

In some situations, you need to resynchronize the metadata in the target database's control file with the recovery catalog. For example, the recovery catalog database might be unavailable for one or more of your backups because of a network problem or because the recovery catalog database is down. In this situation, RMAN records the backup information only in the target database control file. RMAN always records backup information in the control file even when the recovery catalog is unavailable!

ⓌａｔｃＨ   *The RMAN recovery catalog records information about target database structures, archived redo logs, and backups when you run an RMAN BACKUP command or perform a manual resynchronization.*

In addition, you may perform infrequent backups and rely on archived redo log files for a recovery scenario. This is not a problem per se, but the list of recent archived redo log files is not recorded automatically in the recovery catalog.

Finally, you may occasionally make changes to the physical structure of the target database. This information is automatically recorded in the target database control file but not in the recovery catalog.

Manually resynchronizing the recovery catalog is a straightforward process. After you start RMAN (and connect to a recovery catalog, of course), run the RESYNC CATALOG command, as in this example:

```
RMAN> resync catalog;
starting full resync of recovery catalog
full resync complete
RMAN>
```

CERTIFICATION OBJECTIVE 3.04

Create and Use RMAN Stored Scripts

As mentioned earlier in this chapter, RMAN stored scripts helps you automate repetitive groups of RMAN commands, easing the daily grind of being an Oracle DBA. Stored scripts are a good alternative to scripts you store on a traditional file system. Not only is the script stored with the recovery catalog (in other words, you won't lose it when you move the recovery catalog database), you can also control access to stored scripts by restricting a script to a single target database or to all databases managed within the recovery catalog.

Creating RMAN Stored Scripts

You create an RMAN script with the CREATE SCRIPT or CREATE GLOBAL SCRIPT command. The GLOBAL parameter specifies that the script is available to all RMAN target databases sharing this recovery catalog. To create a script as either global or local, you must be connected to the target database and the recovery catalog. This example creates a global script called GLOBAL_BACKUP_DB that creates a full backup including archived log files:

```
RMAN> CREATE GLOBAL SCRIPT
2>       global_backup_db { BACKUP DATABASE PLUS ARCHIVELOG; }

created global script global_backup_db

RMAN>
```

If you wanted the script to be available only to one specific target database, you would omit the GLOBAL keyword. If you already have an RMAN script in a text file on a file system, you can import the script into an RMAN global or local script using this syntax:

```
RMAN> create script global_backup_db from file
2>       '/home/rjb/dbscripts/global_bak.rman';
```

Executing RMAN Stored Scripts

Running a global or local RMAN stored script is straightforward; however, you must execute the script within a RUN block. The syntax is as follows:

```
RUN
{   ...other commands...;
    EXECUTE [GLOBAL] SCRIPT scriptname;
```

```
...other commands...;
}
```

Here is how to run the global script you created in the previous section:

```
RMAN> run { execute script global_backup_db; }
```

You can also use parameters within an RMAN stored script. In other words, if one or two values will change within a script, such as the value for a particular channel or the value of an object to back up, then you can use the & character as a substitution indicator, much as you would in a SQL*Plus script.

EXERCISE 3-2

Creating a Parameterized Stored Script

In this exercise, you'll automate the backup of individual tablespaces. You will create an RMAN global script to accomplish this, with a parameter that will prompt you for a tablespace name.

1. Create a global stored script with the &1 parameter representing a tablespace name:

```
RMAN> create global script backup_ts
2>      {
3>          backup tablespace &1;
Enter value for 1: users
4>      }

created global script backup_ts

RMAN>
```

Notice that the default value for the tablespace parameter is USERS.

2. Run the stored script, and override the default value assigned for the tablespace when you created the script with the SYSTEM tablespace:

```
RMAN> run {execute script backup_ts;}

executing global script: backup_ts

Enter value for 1: system

Starting backup at 19-APR-08
allocated channel: ORA_DISK_1
```

```
channel ORA_DISK_1: SID=127 device type=DISK
channel ORA_DISK_1: starting compressed full datafile backup set
channel ORA_DISK_1: specifying datafile(s) in backup set
input datafile file number=00001 name=+DATA/dw/datafile/
system.256.630244579
channel ORA_DISK_1: starting piece 1 at 19-APR-08
channel ORA_DISK_1: finished piece 1 at 19-APR-08
piece handle=+RECOV/dw/backupset/
      2008_04_19/nnndf0_tag20080419t190155_0.534.65247
925 tag=TAG20080419T190155 comment=NONE
channel ORA_DISK_1: backup set complete, elapsed time: 00:00:25
Finished backup at 19-APR-08

Starting Control File and SPFILE Autobackup at 19-APR-08
piece handle=+RECOV/dw/autobackup/
      2008_04_19/s_652474951.533.652474959 comment=NONE
Finished Control File and SPFILE Autobackup at 19-APR-08
RMAN>
```

Retrieving RMAN Stored Script Metadata

You can retrieve the contents of RMAN stored scripts using the PRINT and LIST commands: the PRINT command shows the contents of an individual script, and the LIST command shows the names of global scripts or both global and local scripts.

This example uses the LIST SCRIPT NAMES command to show both the local and global scripts:

```
RMAN> list script names;

List of Stored Scripts in Recovery Catalog

    Scripts of Target Database DW

        Script Name
        Description
        ------------------------------------------------------------
        local_backup_db

    Global Scripts
```

```
Script Name
Description
----------------------------------------------------------
backup_ts

global_backup_db

RMAN>
```

The LIST GLOBAL SCRIPT NAMES returns only the global script names.

To show the actual contents of a script, use the PRINT command. Because a global script and a local script can have the same name, you qualify the PRINT command with the GLOBAL option if you want to print the global version instead of the local version. This example retrieves the contents of the global_backup_db script:

```
RMAN> print global script global_backup_db;

printing stored global script: global_backup_db
{ BACKUP DATABASE PLUS ARCHIVELOG; }

RMAN>
```

You can spool the contents of a global or local script to a file using the TO FILE option of the PRINT command:

```
RMAN> print global script global_backup_db
2>        to file '/tmp/save_script.rman';

global script global_backup_db written to file /tmp/save_script.rman

RMAN>
```

Managing RMAN Stored Scripts

It's also easy to delete or replace stored scripts. To replace a stored script, use the REPLACE [GLOBAL] SCRIPT command. In this example, you want to modify the global script backup_ts to back up the SYSTEM tablespace in addition to the desired tablespace:

```
RMAN> replace global script backup_ts
2>    {
3>        backup tablespace system, &1;

Enter value for 1: users
```

```
4>      }

replaced global script backup_ts

RMAN>
```

As you might expect, you use the DELETE SCRIPT command to delete a global or local script:

```
RMAN> delete script local_backup_db;

deleted script: local_backup_db

RMAN>
```

CERTIFICATION OBJECTIVE 3.05

Back Up the Recovery Catalog

Since the recovery catalog resides in an Oracle database, it must be backed up and restored just like any other database. You must know how to re-create a recovery catalog when your recovery catalog database backups are incomplete. In addition, you may be required to move the recovery catalog to another database and drop the recovery catalog from a database. These topics, in addition to upgrading a recovery catalog, are covered in the following sections.

Backing Up the Recovery Catalog

Even though this has already been mentioned in this chapter, and in other chapters—and for that matter, in other books—it's worth another reminder: Don't keep your recovery catalog in the same database as your target database. If you lose the target database, you also lose your recovery catalog, and you must rely on a backup or multiplexed copy of the target database control file to re-create the recovery catalog and restore the database, assuming that you have adequate backups and any structural changes to the target database were made within the window of the initialization parameter CONTROL_FILE_RECORD_KEEP_TIME.

Now that you've been reminded to keep the recovery catalog in a separate database, you should also remember to back up the database containing the recovery catalog, using RMAN of course, to ensure that the recovery catalog metadata and backup information are recorded in the recovery catalog database's control file. Here is the Oracle-recommended configuration for ensuring a recoverable recovery catalog database:

1. Configure the database for ARCHIVELOG mode.

2. Set the RMAN parameter RETENTION POLICY to REDUNDANCY greater than 1.

3. Back up the recovery catalog to disk and tape after each target database backup (in other words, two separate media types).

4. Use BACKUP DATABASE PLUS ARCHIVELOG when you back up the recovery catalog.

5. Use CONFIGURE CONTROLFILE AUTOBACKUP ON to ensure that the control file is backed up after every RMAN backup.

This configuration ensures that a complete loss of either a target database or a recovery catalog database is completely recoverable. If you lose both the target database and the recovery catalog database at the same time, it's probably because you are using the target database for the recovery catalog. And, as a final reminder, *do not do that*!

Recovering from a Lost Recovery Catalog

In the event that you lose the recovery catalog database, the recovery operation is much the same as recovering any other database that has adequate backups (using RMAN) and is running in ARCHIVELOG mode. For example, you can restore a control file backup (or use a multiplexed control file), and then restore and perform a complete recovery using RMAN backups of the recovery catalog plus archived redo log files. If you have the luxury of having two recovery catalog databases, you can save the RMAN metadata for one recovery catalog in the database of the other recovery catalog.

If you have no backups of your recovery catalog database, your options are more limited, but not all hope is lost. Here are the steps to follow to retrieve most, if not all, of the metadata for your target database backups:

1. Re-create the recovery catalog database from scratch.

2. Register the target database with the new recovery catalog.

3. Perform a RESYNC CATALOG operation to copy all available backup information from the target database control file.

4. Use the CATALOG START WITH command to add information about any available backups of the target database to the recovery catalog.

Since the previous physical backup files for your target database contain the target DBID, and RMAN identifies each database in its recovery catalog with the DBID, the RMAN CATALOG START WITH command can easily assign each backup to its associated target database in the recovery catalog.

Exporting and Importing the Recovery Catalog

As you can with any database, you can use the Oracle Data Pump export and import utilities expdp and impdp to create logical backups of the recovery catalog. You can use this logical backup to move the recovery catalog to another database. Follow these general steps to move a recovery catalog to another database:

1. Use an export utility to copy the recovery catalog schema to an export dump file.

2. Create the recovery catalog owner on the target catalog database with the appropriate permissions; see "Create the Recovery Catalog Owner" earlier in this chapter.

3. Use the corresponding import utility to copy the recovery catalog schema to the target catalog database.

The next time you launch RMAN, you connect to the same target database but a different recovery catalog database. However, even though the recovery catalog database name is different, the target database's metadata is identical to the metadata in the previous recovery catalog.

on the **job** *You can also use transportable tablespaces to move a recovery catalog schema from one database to another.*

You do not need to run an RMAN CREATE CATALOG command in this scenario; the tables, columns, and views are already in place from the source database.

Dropping a Recovery Catalog

After you have successfully moved the recovery catalog, you can drop the catalog from the previous recovery catalog database. As you might expect, you use the DROP CATALOG command to remove the catalog from the previous recovery catalog database. In fact, you need to run the command twice as a way of confirming your desire to delete, as in this example:

```
RMAN> connect catalog rman/rman@rcat

connected to recovery catalog database

RMAN> drop catalog;

recovery catalog owner is rman
enter DROP CATALOG again to confirm catalog removal

RMAN> drop catalog;

recovery catalog dropped

RMAN>
```

Note that you do not need to connect to a target database to drop a recovery catalog. Also, to ensure that all traces of the recovery catalog owner are removed from the previous recovery catalog database, do not manually remove the recovery catalog owner's schema. Use the DROP CATALOG command instead.

Upgrading the Recovery Catalog

To support a newer RMAN client (for example, your RMAN recovery catalog is at version 10g and a new RMAN client is at version 11g), you use the UPGRADE CATALOG command to update the local packages and schema. As with the DROP CATALOG command, you are prompted twice, and you do not need to be connected to a target database. Here is an example:

```
RMAN> upgrade catalog;

recovery catalog owner is RMAN
enter UPGRADE CATALOG command again to confirm catalog upgrade

RMAN> upgrade catalog;
```

```
recovery catalog upgraded to version 11.01.00.06
DBMS_RCVMAN package upgraded to version 11.01.00.06
DBMS_RCVCAT package upgraded to version 11.01.00.06

RMAN>
```

You receive an error message if you attempt to downgrade the recovery catalog version. However, if the version has not changed, the UPGRADE CATALOG command proceeds in case all required packages are not in place.

CERTIFICATION OBJECTIVE 3.06

Create and Use a Virtual Private Catalog

In many organizations, one DBA cannot manage the RMAN backups for all databases within the organization. In addition, the relatively recent Sarbanes-Oxley mandates require an IT shop to tighten up the security and access to each database so that a DBA can see only the databases and database backups for which they are responsible. As of Oracle Database 11g, you can create an RMAN *virtual private catalog* to facilitate and enforce these separations of duty. In the following sections, you'll get more details about RMAN virtual private catalogs, learn how to create and manage a virtual private catalog, and see a virtual private catalog in action.

Understanding Virtual Private Catalogs

A virtual private catalog is functionally identical to the recovery catalog discussed throughout this chapter; from the perspective of an individual DBA, it appears to be a single catalog containing only his or her databases' metadata and RMAN backup information. From this point on, the recovery catalog discussed earlier in the chapter will be called the *base catalog*. Each virtual private catalog is a logical partition of the base catalog. Each virtual catalog owner relies on a separate Oracle account and several views and synonyms in the recovery catalog database.

As was already done earlier in this chapter, the base recovery catalog owner creates the base catalog and grants the RECOVERY_CATALOG_OWNER role to each Oracle account that will own a virtual private catalog. If databases are already registered in the base recovery catalog, the base catalog owner can grant access to a registered database for a virtual private catalog owner; alternatively, the base

recovery catalog owner can grant the REGISTER privilege to the virtual private catalog owner so he or she can register a new database in the virtual private catalog.

Creating and Managing a Virtual Private Catalog

The following sections show you how to set up a virtual private catalog, create the virtual private catalog owner, and then grant the appropriate privileges to the virtual private catalog owner. Next, the virtual private catalog owner will create a virtual private catalog and register one or more databases. Alternatively, the base catalog owner can grant catalog privileges for an already registered database to a virtual catalog owner.

For the examples in the following sections, the base catalog owner RMAN for the RCAT database will create a virtual private catalog owner VPC1 and grant the RMAN privilege REGISTER DATABASE to VPC1. The DBA of the HR database on the server srv04 will use VPC1 to create a virtual private catalog and register the HR database.

Creating Virtual Private Catalog Owners

On the recovery catalog database, the first step is to create an Oracle account that will own the virtual private catalog:

```
[oracle@rmanrep ~]$ sqlplus / as sysdba

SQL*Plus: Release 11.1.0.6.0 - Production on Tue Apr 22 18:24:39 2008

Copyright (c) 1982, 2007, Oracle.  All rights reserved.

Connected to:
Oracle Database 11g Enterprise Edition Release 11.1.0.6.0 - Production
With the Partitioning, OLAP, Data Mining
        and Real Application Testing options
```

```
SQL> create user vpc1 identified by vpc1
  2  default tablespace users
  3  quota unlimited on users;

User created.
SQL>
```

Granting Permissions to Virtual Private Catalog Owners

Next, you will grant the RECOVERY_CATALOG_OWNER privilege to VPC1, the owner of the new virtual private catalog:

```
SQL> grant recovery_catalog_owner to vpc1;

Grant succeeded.

SQL>
```

Note that the user VPC1 is not the owner of the entire recovery catalog; the role name is a bit misleading. Instead, it means that VPC1 can create his or her own private recovery catalog that is a logical subset of the base recovery catalog.

Optionally, the base recovery catalog owner can now grant permission on existing catalogs using the RMAN GRANT CATALOG command. In this example, the base catalog owner gives permission to VPC1 on the DW database that is already registered in the recovery catalog:

```
RMAN> grant catalog for database dw to vpc1;

Grant succeeded.

RMAN>
```

If the base recovery catalog owner wants the user VPC1 to register his or her own databases, the owner must grant the RMAN privilege REGISTER DATABASE to VPC1, as in this example:

```
RMAN> grant register database to vpc1;

Grant succeeded.

RMAN>
```

Creating a Virtual Private Catalog

Now that the user VPC1 has the appropriate privileges to create and populate a virtual catalog, the next step is to connect to RMAN as the user VPC1 and create the catalog.

For convenience, the user VPC1 connected to the target database HR at the same time that he connected to the recovery catalog. The next step is to create the virtual private catalog itself (this needs to be done only once, just as you need to register a database only once):

```
[oracle@srv04 ~]$ echo $ORACLE_SID
hr
[oracle@srv04 ~]$ rman target / catalog vpc1/vpc1@rcat

Recovery Manager: Release 11.1.0.6.0 -
            Production on Tue Apr 22 18:45:09 2008

Copyright (c) 1982, 2007, Oracle.  All rights reserved.

connected to target database: HR (DBID=3318356692)
connected to recovery catalog database

RMAN> create virtual catalog;

found eligible base catalog owned by RMAN
created virtual catalog against base catalog owned by RMAN

RMAN>
```

If your RMAN client's version is prior to Oracle Database 11g, you must instead use a SQL prompt to execute a stored procedure to create the virtual catalog, as follows:

```
SQL> exec rman.dbms_rcvcat.create_virtual_catalog;
```

Dropping a virtual private catalog is the same as dropping a base catalog; just make sure you do not execute the DROP CATALOG command as the base catalog owner!

Using a Virtual Private Catalog

Now that all the permissions are granted and the virtual catalog has been created, the user VPC1 can register a database:

```
[oracle@srv04 ~]$ rman target / catalog vpc1/vpc1@rcat;

Recovery Manager: Release 11.1.0.6.0 -
            Production on Tue Apr 22 18:57:40 2008
```

```
Copyright (c) 1982, 2007, Oracle.  All rights reserved.

connected to target database: HR (DBID=3318356692)
connected to recovery catalog database

RMAN> register database;

database registered in recovery catalog
starting full resync of recovery catalog
full resync complete

RMAN>
```

To see which databases the user VPC1 can manage via the RMAN virtual private catalog, connect to the recovery catalog database and query the DBINC view:

```
[oracle@srv04 ~]$ sqlplus vpc1/vpc1@rcat

SQL*Plus: Release 11.1.0.6.0 - Production on Tue Apr 22 19:00:30 2008

Copyright (c) 1982, 2007, Oracle.  All rights reserved.


Connected to:
Oracle Database 11g Enterprise Edition Release 11.1.0.6.0 - Production
With the Partitioning, OLAP, Data Mining and
        Real Application Testing options

SQL> select distinct db_name from dbinc;

DB_NAME
--------
DW
HR

SQL>
```

Note that you have to use DISTINCT in the SELECT statement. The DBINC view has one row for each incarnation of a target database; without the use of DISTINCT, more than one row per database will often appear.

CERTIFICATION OBJECTIVE 3.07

Configure Backup Settings

RMAN configuration settings can appear daunting at first, until you realize that the "out-of-the-box" settings for RMAN don't require many configuration changes to perform successful full and incremental backups to disk. The following sections reiterate some key RMAN concepts and capabilities, go into a bit more depth on how to specify alternative backup destinations, cover how to persist some RMAN settings, and show you how to ensure that the control file is backed up with every backup.

Types of RMAN Backups

RMAN supports a number of different backup methods, depending on your availability needs, the desired size of your recovery window, and the amount of downtime you can endure while the database or a part of the database is involved in a recovery operation.

Consistent and Inconsistent Backups

A physical backup can be classified as being a *consistent* or an *inconsistent* backup. In a consistent backup, all datafiles have the same System Change Number (SCN). In other words, all changes in the redo logs have been applied to the datafiles. Because an open database with no uncommitted transactions can have some dirty blocks in the buffer cache, it is rare that an open database backup can be considered consistent. As a result, consistent backups are taken when the database is shut down normally or in a mounted (MOUNT) state.

In contrast, an inconsistent backup is performed while the database is open and users are accessing the database. A recovery operation performed using an inconsistent backup must rely on both archived and online redo log files to bring the database into a consistent state before it is opened. This is because the SCNs of the datafiles typically do not match when an inconsistent backup takes place. As a result, a database must be in ARCHIVELOG mode to use an inconsistent backup method. Apart from that, backup mode tablespaces can produce a lot of redo log entries and recycled log entries could be lost.

Full and Incremental Backups

Full backups include all blocks of every datafile within a tablespace or a database; it is essentially a bit-for-bit copy of one or more datafiles in the database. Either RMAN or an operating system command can be used to perform a full backup, although backups performed outside of RMAN must be cataloged with RMAN before they can be used in an RMAN recovery operation. However, it is possible to recover a database manually without using RMAN.

In Oracle 11g, incremental backups can be level 0 or level 1. A level 0 backup is a full backup of all blocks in the database that can be used in conjunction with differential, incremental, or cumulative incremental level 1 backups in a database recovery operation. A distinct advantage to using an incremental backup in a recovery strategy is that archived and online redo log files may not be necessary to restore a database or tablespace to a consistent state; the incremental backups may have some or all of the blocks needed. Incremental backups can be performed only within RMAN.

Image Copies

Image copies are full backups created by operating system commands or RMAN BACKUP AS COPY commands. Although a full backup created with a Linux cp command can be later registered in the RMAN catalog as a database backup, doing the same image copy backup in RMAN has the advantage of checking for corrupt blocks as they are being read by RMAN and recording the information about the bad blocks in the data dictionary. Image copies are the default backup file format in RMAN.

This is a great feature of Oracle 11g's RMAN for the following reason: If you add another datafile to a tablespace, you also need to remember to add the new datafile to your Linux script cp command. By creating image copies using RMAN, all datafiles will automatically be included in the backup. Forgetting to add the new datafile to a Linux script will make a recovery situation extremely inconvenient at best and a disaster at worst.

Backupsets and Backup Pieces

In contrast to image copies, which can be created in most any backup environment, backupsets can be created and restored only with RMAN. A *backupset* is an RMAN backup of part or all of a database, consisting of one or more *backup pieces*. Each backup piece belongs only to one backupset and can contain backups of one or many datafiles in the database. All backupsets and pieces are recorded in the RMAN repository, the same as any other RMAN-initiated backup.

Compressed Backups

For any Oracle11g RMAN backup creating a backupset, compression is available to reduce the amount of disk space or tape needed to store the backup. Compressed backups are usable only by RMAN, and they need no special processing when used in a recovery operation; RMAN automatically decompresses the backup. Creating compressed backups is as easy as specifying `AS COMPRESSED BACKUPSET` in the `RMAN BACKUP` command.

RMAN Backup Destinations

RMAN backup destinations include a file system disk directory, a tape-based media library, or the flash recovery area. Oracle best practices dictate that you use a flash recovery area for many reasons; Chapter 2 covered the details of configuring and using the flash recovery area and the initialization parameters `DB_RECOVERY_FILE_DEST` and `DB_RECOVERY_FILE_DEST_SIZE`. One of the many benefits of a flash recovery area include automatic file naming for backup files. In addition, RMAN automatically deletes obsolete files in the flash recovery area when it's pressed for space.

To facilitate a completely disk-based recovery scenario, the flash recovery area should be big enough for a copy of all datafiles, incremental backup files, online redo logs, archived redo logs not on tape, control file autobackups, and server parameter file (SPFILE) backups. Using a larger or smaller recovery window or adjusting the redundancy policy will require an adjustment in the size of the flash recovery area. If the area is limited in size due to disk space constraints, at a minimum enough room should be available to hold the archived log files that have not yet been copied to tape. The dynamic performance view `V$RECOVERY_FILE_DEST` displays information about the number of files in the flash recovery area, how much space is currently being used, and the total amount of space available in the area.

The flash recovery area automatically uses Oracle Managed Files (OMF). As part of Oracle 11g's simplified management structure, you do not need to set any of the `LOG_ARCHIVE_DEST_n` initialization parameters explicitly if you need only one location for archived redo log files; if the database is in `ARCHIVELOG` mode, and a flash recovery area is defined, then the initialization parameter `LOG_ARCHIVE_DEST_10` is implicitly defined as the flash recovery area.

As you have seen in many examples, RMAN uses the flash recovery area in a very organized fashion—with separate directories for archived logs, backupsets, image copies, block change tracking files, and automatic backups of the control file and SPFILE. In addition, each subdirectory is named with the date of the backup (for example,

+RECOV/dw/autobackup/2008_09_28), making it easy to find a backupset or image copy when the need arises.

Multiple databases, even a primary and a standby database, can share the same flash recovery area. Even with the same DB_NAME, as long as the DB_UNIQUE_NAME parameter is different, no conflicts will occur. RMAN uses the DB_UNIQUE_NAME to distinguish backups between databases that use the same flash recovery area.

Persisting RMAN Settings

To make the DBA's job easier, a number of RMAN settings can be *persisted*. In other words, these settings will stay in effect between RMAN sessions. In the example that follows, the SHOW ALL command is used to display the default RMAN settings:

```
RMAN> show all;

RMAN configuration parameters for database with db_unique_name DW are:
CONFIGURE RETENTION POLICY TO REDUNDANCY 1;
CONFIGURE BACKUP OPTIMIZATION ON;
CONFIGURE DEFAULT DEVICE TYPE TO DISK; # default
CONFIGURE CONTROLFILE AUTOBACKUP ON;
CONFIGURE CONTROLFILE AUTOBACKUP FORMAT FOR DEVICE TYPE DISK TO '%F';
         # default
CONFIGURE DEVICE TYPE DISK BACKUP TYPE TO
              COMPRESSED BACKUPSET PARALLELISM 1;
CONFIGURE DATAFILE BACKUP COPIES FOR DEVICE TYPE DISK TO 1; # default
CONFIGURE ARCHIVELOG BACKUP COPIES FOR DEVICE TYPE DISK TO 1; # default
CONFIGURE MAXSETSIZE TO UNLIMITED; # default
CONFIGURE ENCRYPTION FOR DATABASE OFF; # default
CONFIGURE ENCRYPTION ALGORITHM 'AES128'; # default
CONFIGURE COMPRESSION ALGORITHM 'BZIP2'; # default
CONFIGURE ARCHIVELOG DELETION POLICY TO NONE; # default
CONFIGURE SNAPSHOT CONTROLFILE NAME TO
   '/u01/app/oracle/product/11.1.0/db_1/dbs/snapcf_dw.f'; # default

RMAN>
```

Any parameters that are set to their default values have # default at the end of the configuration setting. These parameters are easy to review and change using EM, as demonstrated in Figure 3-3.

The next few sections review a few of the more common RMAN persistent settings.

FIGURE 3-3

RMAN persistent
parameters in EM

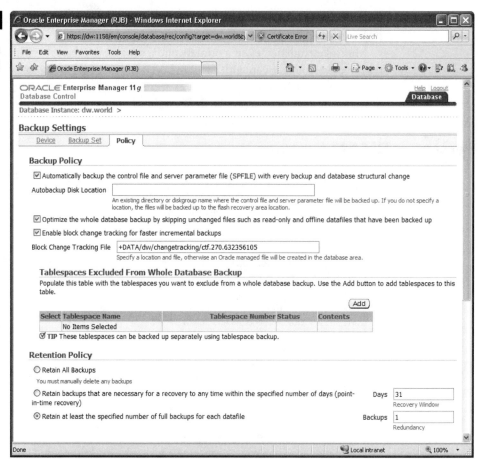

Retention Policy

Backups can be automatically retained and managed using one of two methods: by
a *recovery window* or by *redundancy*. Using a recovery window, RMAN will retain
as many backups as necessary to bring the database to any point in time within
the recovery window. For example, with a recovery window of seven days, RMAN
will maintain enough image copies, incremental backups, and archived redo logs
to ensure that the database can be restored and recovered to any point in time
within the last seven days. Any backups that are not needed to support this recovery
window are marked as OBSOLETE and are automatically removed by RMAN if
a flash recovery area is used and disk space is needed for new backups.

In contrast, a redundancy retention policy directs RMAN to retain the specified number of backups or copies of each datafile and control file. Any extra copies or backups beyond the number specified in the redundancy policy are marked as OBSOLETE. As with a recovery window, obsolete backups are automatically removed if disk space is needed and a flash recovery area is used. Otherwise, you can use the DELETE OBSOLETE command to remove the backup files and update the catalog.

If the retention policy is set to NONE, no backups or copies are ever considered obsolete, and the DBA must manually remove unneeded backups from the catalog and from disk.

The following example sets the retention policy to a recovery window of four days (from a default redundancy policy of one copy):

```
RMAN> configure retention policy to recovery window of 4 days;

new RMAN configuration parameters:
CONFIGURE RETENTION POLICY TO RECOVERY WINDOW OF 4 DAYS;
new RMAN configuration parameters are successfully stored

RMAN>
```

Device Type

If the default device type is set to DISK and no pathname parameter is specified, RMAN uses the flash recovery area for all backups; you can easily override the disk backup location in EM, as you can see in Figure 3-4. As with many of the simplified administration tasks from Oracle 11g, there is no need to allocate or deallocate a specific channel for backups unless you're using a tape device.

Although configuring a tape device is specific to your installation, in general terms you configure a tape device as follows:

```
RMAN> configure channel device type sbt
2>    parms='ENV=(<vendor specific arguments>)';
```

on the **!**
() o b   *sbt is the device type used for any tape backup subsystem, regardless of vendor.*

Although you can use the flash recovery area to restore and recover your database entirely from disk, at some point it becomes inefficient to keep all your backups on disk, especially if you have a large recovery window. As a result, you can make copies of your backup files to tape, and RMAN will dutifully keep track of where the

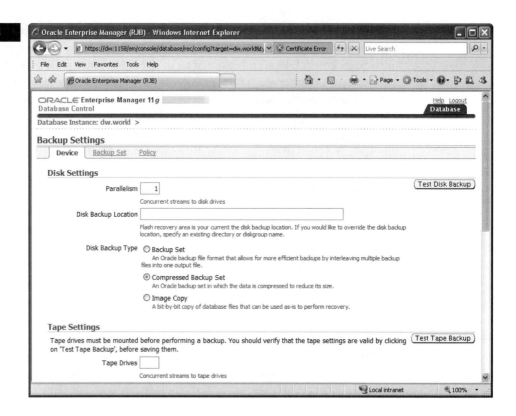

backups are in case you need to restore or recover the database from tape, or restore
archived redo logs to roll forward an image copy in the flash recovery area.

Control File Autobackups

Because of the importance of the control file, you should back it up at least as often
as it changes due to modifications in the structure of the database. By default, the
backup of the control file does not occur automatically. This is a strange default,
considering the importance of the control file and how little disk space it takes to
back it up. Fortunately, RMAN can easily be configured to back up the control file
automatically, either any time a successful backup must be recorded in the repository
or when a structural change affects the contents of the control file (in other words,

cases when a control file backup must occur to ensure a successful recovery if and when a recovery operation is required):

```
RMAN> configure controlfile autobackup on;

new RMAN configuration parameters:
CONFIGURE CONTROLFILE AUTOBACKUP ON;
new RMAN configuration parameters are successfully stored

RMAN>
```

Every RMAN backup from this point on will automatically include a copy of the control file. The control file is also backed up whenever a new tablespace is created or another datafile is added to an existing tablespace.

CERTIFICATION OBJECTIVE 3.08

Allocate Channels to Use in Backing Up

You can allocate channels in two different ways in RMAN: you can set channels with the CONFIGURE command, or you can set them by using the ALLOCATE CHANNEL within a RUN block to override the default channel or if no default channel is defined. As mentioned earlier in the chapter, you don't have to specify any channels if your destination is a disk location.

Here is the line from the SHOW ALL command that specifies the default device type. Note that no default channel is defined since the default device type is DISK:

```
CONFIGURE DEFAULT DEVICE TYPE TO DISK; # default
```

CERTIFICATION OBJECTIVE 3.09

Configure Backup Optimization

In Oracle Database 11g, RMAN supports *backup optimization*. In other words, the RMAN BACKUP command skips backups of one or more files when identical files have already been backed up to the specified device, such as disk or tape. RMAN takes into consideration the retention policy and the backup duplexing capabilities of RMAN to determine whether enough backups of a particular file already exist.

By default, backup optimization is disabled, but you can enable it with this `CONFIGURE` command:

```
RMAN> configure backup optimization on;

new RMAN configuration parameters:
CONFIGURE BACKUP OPTIMIZATION ON;
new RMAN configuration parameters are successfully stored
starting full resync of recovery catalog
full resync complete

RMAN>
```

CERTIFICATION SUMMARY

This chapter started with an overview of the advantages and disadvantages of using an RMAN recovery catalog over using only the control file for backup information. Although there is some extra work to maintain another database to store the recovery catalog information, this disadvantage is relatively minor compared to the advantages of ease of use and more robust recovery capabilities.

Next, assuming that you will eventually need and want a recovery catalog, you stepped through the process of creating a recovery catalog and registering one or more target databases with the recovery catalog. In addition, you learned how to include the metadata for backups created outside of RMAN (in the recovery catalog), further increasing the value of a central backup metadata repository.

Stored scripts, another feature available only with a recovery catalog, helps you automate some routine tasks consisting of many steps or commands, all stored in a single command. Stored scripts can be either local (specific to one database) or available to all databases registered in the catalog.

In the event of a lost or corrupted recovery catalog (which should never happen because you back up your recovery catalog as often as you back up your target database), you reviewed a few different disaster recovery scenarios and learned ways to lessen the potential impact of a full or partial loss of the recovery catalog.

To facilitate the division of labor and responsibility when you have more than one DBA in your organization, you can use the concept of virtual private catalogs. Setting up a virtual private catalog for each DBA in your organization is straightforward and restricts access to only databases for which the DBA is responsible, while at the same time keeping all database backup information in the same recovery catalog.

Finally, you were introduced to RMAN backup types and configuration settings, including how to persist RMAN settings, such as device types and channels, and you also learned how to ensure that the control file is backed up on a regular basis. For those of you wondering when you'll get to start performing some real backups now that the groundwork is laid, the BACKUP command is explored in depth in the next chapter.

✓ TWO-MINUTE DRILL

Identify Situations that Require RMAN Recovery Catalog

❑ If your backups are simple and your database is not mission-critical, the control file is probably sufficient for your RMAN metadata.

❑ If you have several databases to back up, and you want to use stored scripts, then a recovery catalog is highly recommended based on Oracle best practices.

❑ Having a centralized metadata repository permits easy backup reporting because you can use one set of RC_ views in one database to query backup information.

❑ Several useful RMAN commands such as BACKUP ... KEEP FOREVER are available only when you use a recovery catalog.

Create and Configure a Recovery Catalog

❑ The three basic steps for creating a recovery catalog are 1) configure a new or existing database, 2) create the recovery catalog owner, and 3) create the catalog itself.

❑ Only about 125MB of disk space is required for the initial deployment of a recovery catalog.

❑ The predefined role RECOVERY_CATALOG_OWNER includes all privileges necessary to manage a recovery catalog, such as ALTER SESSION, CREATE SESSION, and CREATE TABLE.

❑ You use the CREATE CATALOG command to create the recovery catalog.

❑ You can use Enterprise Manager to persist recovery catalog credentials.

Synchronize the Recovery Catalog

❑ The initial synchronization of the recovery catalog uses the target database control file.

❑ Each database to be backed up needs to be registered with the recovery catalog using the REGISTER DATABASE command.

❑ The target database must be in the MOUNT or OPEN state to register successfully with the recovery catalog.

❑ You can use the DBNEWID utility (enter nid at the command line), to change the value of the DBID for a database. You can also change the database name as an additional option.

❑ After changing the DBID for a database, you must reopen it with RESETLOGS, and then you should perform a full backup of the database.

❑ You can unregister a database from a recovery catalog using the UNREGISTER DATABASE command.

❑ You can catalog several types of backup files with RMAN: data file copies, backup pieces, control file copies, and archived redo log files.

❑ One of many advantages to using a flash recovery area is that it makes it easy for you to recatalog all backup files in the area by using the CATALOG RECOVERY AREA command.

❑ Manual resynchronization of the recovery catalog is required when the recovery catalog is unavailable during an RMAN backup. This applies if you want to catalog archived redo log files or you make physical changes to the target database.

Create and Use RMAN Stored Scripts

❑ You create stored scripts with either the CREATE SCRIPT or CREATE GLOBAL SCRIPT command.

❑ Local scripts are available only for the target database.

❑ Global scripts are available for any target database or even when you are not connected to any target database.

❑ You execute a global or local script within a RUN block.

❑ You execute scripts with the EXECUTE [GLOBAL] SCRIPT command.

❑ The substitution character & permits a default value that can be overridden when the script runs.

❑ The LIST [GLOBAL] SCRIPT NAMES shows a list of the global or global and local scripts in the repository.

❑ The PRINT command shows the contents of a global or local script.

❑ You can use REPLACE [GLOBAL] SCRIPT to replace the contents of a global or local script.

❑ DELETE SCRIPT deletes a script from the recovery catalog.

Back Up the Recovery Catalog

❏ The recovery catalog database is backed up like any other database in your environment.

❏ The recovery catalog should be in ARCHIVELOG mode.

❏ The utilities expdp and impdp can create logical backups of the recovery catalog that can be used in a disaster recovery situation or to move the recovery catalog to another database.

❏ Using transportable tablespaces is another way to move the recovery catalog to another database.

❏ Use the DROP CATALOG command to drop a recovery catalog. Do not manually drop schemas and packages in the recovery catalog database.

❏ You run the UPGRADE CATALOG command to support an RMAN client that is at a later version than the recovery catalog database.

Create and Use a Virtual Private Catalog

❏ A virtual private catalog facilitates the separation of duties among several DBAs.

❏ One or more virtual private catalogs share the same base recovery catalog.

❏ You grant the RECOVERY_CATALOG_OWNER role to each Oracle user account that will own a virtual private catalog.

❏ The base recovery catalog owner can grant permissions on existing registered databases to virtual private catalog owners using the GRANT CATALOG command.

❏ Once you grant a user the RECOVERY_CATALOG_OWNER role, the user creates the virtual catalog with the CREATE VIRTUAL CATALOG command.

❏ The virtual private catalog owner uses REGISTER DATABASE to register a new database, just as a base recovery catalog user would.

❏ You can query the DBINC data dictionary view to determine the databases accessible to the virtual private catalog owner.

Configure Backup Settings

❏ RMAN backups can be full or incremental.

❏ Incremental backups can be level 0 or 1. Level 0 backups are full backups that you can use as part of a differential, incremental, or cumulative incremental level 1 backup strategy.

❑ RMAN image copies are exact copies of datafiles. Using RMAN to make copies of datafiles has the additional advantage of checking for corruption in each block read.

❑ RMAN can use backup compression to save space on the destination device, and RMAN automatically decompresses the backup during a recovery operation.

❑ Using a flash recovery area for RMAN has two advantages: RMAN automatically names backup files in the flash recovery area, and it automatically deletes obsolete backup files when there is space pressure in the flash recovery area.

❑ More than one database can use the flash recovery area.

❑ The RMAN command SHOW ALL lists all persistent RMAN settings.

❑ Use CONFIGURE CONTROLFILE AUTOBACKUP ON to ensure that a backup copy of the target database control file exists after each backup.

Allocate Channels to Use in Backing Up

❑ Channels can be persisted with the CONFIGURE command or assigned within the RUN block using the ALLOCATE CHANNEL command.

❑ Using DISK as the default device type does not require any channel allocation.

Configure Backup Optimization

❑ RMAN uses backup optimization to skip backups of one or more files if identical files have already been backed up to disk or tape.

❑ Backup optimization takes into account duplexing and retention policies before skipping a source file.

❑ You set backup optimization in RMAN with the command CONFIGURE BACKUP OPTIMIZATION ON.

SELF TEST

The following questions will help you measure your understanding of the material presented in this chapter. Read all the choices carefully because there might be more than one correct answer. Choose all correct answers for each question.

Identify Situations that Require RMAN Recovery Catalog

1. Which of the following are good reasons to use a recovery catalog instead of the target database control file? (Choose three.)

   A. You can keep stored scripts in the recovery catalog.

   B. You save space in the control file of the target database used for RMAN backup information.

   C. A recovery catalog is easier to maintain than a control file in each target database.

   D. The recovery catalog can report on the tablespaces and datafiles in the target database at any point in time since the recovery catalog was created.

   E. A recovery catalog can be used to manage RMAN information for more than one database.

2. If you do not use a recovery catalog, what data dictionary or dynamic performance views must you query to retrieve RMAN backup information? (Choose the best answer.)

   A. The V$ views on each target such as V$BACKUP_SET and V$DATAFILE_COPY

   B. The RC_ views on each target

   C. The DBA_ views on each target

   D. V$CONTROLFILE

Create and Configure a Recovery Catalog

3. The net service name of your target database is DW and the net service name of your recovery catalog database is RCAT. The environment variable ORACLE_SID has a value of RCAT. Which of the following sets of commands will successfully create a recovery catalog?

   A. `connect catalog rman/rmanpass`
      `create catalog;`

   B. `connect catalog rman/rmanpass@rcat`
      `create catalog@rcat;`

   C. `connect catalog rman/rmanpass@dw`
      `create catalog;`

   D. `create catalog rman/rmanpass@rcat;`

4. Which of the following roles should you grant to the recovery catalog owner? (Choose the best answer.)
   A. `RECOVERY_CATALOG`
   B. `CATALOG_OWNER`
   C. `RECOVERY_CATALOG_OWNER`
   D. `DBA`

Synchronize the Recovery Catalog

5. Which of the following does not occur when you register a target database with the recovery catalog database using the `REGISTER DATABASE` command?
   A. The recovery catalog is synchronized with the structure of the database from the control file.
   B. Information about manual tablespace backups is registered in the recovery catalog.
   C. Data about recent backups is copied from the control file to the recovery catalog tables.
   D. Metadata rows are created for the target database in the recovery catalog.

6. What is the difference between a partial and a complete recovery catalog resynchronization? (Choose two answers.)
   A. A partial resynchronization occurs when RMAN records have been aged out of the target database's control file because of the value of `CONTROL_FILE_RECORD_KEEP_TIME`.
   B. A partial resynchronization uses the current target database control file and a full resynchronization uses a backup control file.
   C. A full resynchronization uses the current target database control file and a partial resynchronization uses a backup control file.
   D. A full resynchronization includes information about the database structure and not just recent backups.

Create and Use RMAN Stored Scripts

7. What is the difference between an RMAN local script and an RMAN global script?
   A. A local script is available only for a single target database.
   B. A global script references a list of commands in an external file.
   C. A local script references a list of commands in an external file.
   D. A global script can execute commands against many target databases simultaneously.
   E. A local script is available only to the user that created it. A global script is available to all users.

8. You create and execute a stored local script using the following commands:

```
create script full_backup
{
    backup as compressed backupset database;
    delete noprompt obsolete;
}
execute script full_backup;
```

What happens when you run these commands?

A. The script does not run because it must be executed within a RUN block.

B. A full backup occurs and all previous backups and archived redo logs outside of the retention period or retention policy are deleted.

C. The script creation step fails because you must explicitly allocate one or more channels with a stored script.

D. The script does not run because you must specify a target database when you use a local script.

Back Up the Recovery Catalog

9. You have lost the most recent archived redo log files from the recovery catalog database as well as the tablespace containing the RMAN catalog. You can do an incomplete restore of the recovery catalog database to a point in time after the target databases were registered with the recovery catalog. What commands can you use to resynchronize the target database's metadata and backup information with the recovery catalog database?

A. Use the CREATE CATALOG command to re-create the recovery catalog database.

B. Use the REGISTER DATABASE command to reregister the target database control file records.

C. Use the RESYNC CATALOG command to update the recovery catalog with the latest records from the target database's control file and the CATALOG START WITH command to record any additional backups that are no longer in the target database's control file.

D. Use both the CREATE CATALOG and the REGISTER DATABASE commands to resynchronize the target database with the recovery catalog.

10. Under what circumstances would you use the RMAN command UPGRADE CATALOG?

A. When you have made structural changes to the recovery catalog database

B. When you are using a version of the recovery catalog that is older than that required by the RMAN target database client

C. When you are using a version of the RMAN target database client that is older than required by the recovery catalog

D. When you have made structural changes to the target database

Create and Use a Virtual Private Catalog

11. You have created a virtual private catalog to separate your RMAN administration duties among several DBAs for 20 different databases. Which role must you grant to each virtual catalog owner to allow the person to access existing registered databases?

A. `SELECT_CATALOG_ROLE`

B. `REGISTER_CATALOG_OWNER`

C. `VPC_OWNER`

D. `RECOVERY_CATALOG_OWNER`

12. The virtual catalog database owner VPC1 has the `RECOVERY_CATALOG_OWNER` privilege on the database CATDB2 in addition to the RMAN `REGISTER DATABASE` privilege. Which of the following sets of commands will allow an 11g RMAN client to create a virtual catalog, register a new database DW, and create a full database backup?

A.
```
RMAN> connect catalog vpc1/vpc1pwd@dw
RMAN> create virtual catalog;
RMAN> connect target system/syspwd@catdb2;
RMAN> register database;
RMAN> backup database;
```

B.
```
RMAN> connect catalog vpc1/vpc1pwd@catdb2
RMAN> exec
    catowner.dbms_rcvcat.create_virtual_catalog;
RMAN> connect target system/syspwd@dw;
RMAN> register database;
RMAN> backup database;
```

C.
```
RMAN> connect catalog vpc1/vpc1pwd@catdb2
RMAN> create virtual catalog;
RMAN> connect target system/syspwd@dw;
RMAN> grant catalog for database DW to vpc1;
RMAN> backup database;
```

D.
```
RMAN> connect catalog vpc1/vpc1pwd@catdb2
RMAN> create virtual catalog;
RMAN> connect target system/syspwd@dw;
RMAN> register database;
RMAN> backup database;
```

Configure Backup Settings

13. You run the following RMAN command:

```
RMAN> configure controlfile autobackup on;
```

Under what conditions does RMAN back up the control file and the SPFILE? (Choose all that apply.)

A. When an RMAN backup completes

B. When you start RMAN

C. When you connect to a target database

D. When you back up the SYSTEM tablespace

E. When you run the command BACKUP CURRENT CONTROLFILE;

F. When any of the DBA passwords change

G. When you change the size of the flash recovery area

H. When you add a tablespace

14. Which of the following objects cannot be backed up by RMAN using the RMAN BACKUP command? (Choose all that apply.)

A. DATAFILE

B. DATABASE

C. INSTANCE

D. CURRENT CONTROLFILE

E. SPFILE

F. TABLESPACE

G. ARCHIVELOG

H. CONTROLFILE

I. REDOLOG

15. Identify the statements in the following list that are true about managing RMAN persistent settings. (Choose all that apply.)

A. SHOW ALL lists all current settings for the connected target database.

B. You can use the CONFIGURE...CLEAR command to set a configuration value to an empty string.

C. SHOW ALL shows the configuration values that apply to all target databases.

D. You can use the CONFIGURE...CLEAR command to set a configuration value to its default value.

E. SHOW ALL lists all RMAN settings that are different from the default value.

Allocate Channels to Use in Backing Up

16. What happens when you run the following RMAN commands?

```
RMAN> run
{ configure channel ch2 device type disk;
  backup database; }
```

    A. A full database backup is created in the flash recovery area.

    B. The database is backed up to all default channels configured outside of the RUN block plus the additional channel within the RUN block.

    C. The command fails because you cannot use CONFIGURE within a RUN block.

    D. The command fails because you cannot use BACKUP within a RUN block.

Configure Backup Optimization

17. You have configured backup optimization for your database using CONFIGURE BACKUP OPTIMIZATION ON. For which of the following commands will RMAN not skip a backup if the files are identical?

    A. BACKUP DATABASE;

    B. BACKUP TABLESPACE USERS;

    C. BACKUP ARCHIVELOG ALL;

    D. BACKUP BACKUPSET ALL;

SELF TEST ANSWERS

Identify Situations that Require RMAN Recovery Catalog

1. ☑ **A, D,** and **E.** Using a recovery catalog allows you to create and maintain stored scripts. In addition, it keeps a running history of all changes to the database tablespaces and datafiles since the recovery catalog was created. Finally, you can store recovery information for more than one database in a recovery catalog.

   ☒ **B** is not a good reason to use a recovery catalog because the RMAN repository information is always stored in the control file even if you use a recovery catalog. **C** is also not a good reason, because a recovery catalog requires more setup and maintenance in addition to a backup of another database. Also, the control file is simpler to manage, and its size can be controlled with the parameter `CONTROL_FILE_RECORD_KEEP_TIME`. It is much simpler to export a copy of the control file whenever the database structure changes using `ALTER DATABASE BACKUP CONTROLFILE TO TRACE`.

2. ☑ **A.** When you do not use a recovery catalog, information about RMAN backups is available on each individual target in dynamic performance views such as `V$BACKUP_SET` and `V$DATAFILE_COPY`. These views are sourced from the target database control file.

   ☒ **B** is wrong because the `RC_` views exist only in the database containing the recovery catalog. **C** is wrong because the `DBA_` views do not maintain RMAN information. **D** is wrong because `V$CONTROLFILE` contains only the locations of each copy of the target database's control file.

Create and Configure a Recovery Catalog

3. ☑ **A.** The environment variable `ORACLE_SID` is set. Thus, the RMAN command `CONNECT` automatically uses the value of `ORACLE_SID` to connect to the recovery catalog.

   ☒ **B** is wrong because you do not need to specify the name of the recovery catalog database in the `CREATE CATALOG` command. **C** is wrong because it creates the recovery catalog in the target database. **D** is wrong because you cannot combine the `CONNECT CATALOG` and the `CREATE CATALOG` commands.

4. ☑ **C.** The predefined role `RECOVERY_CATALOG_OWNER` includes the system privileges `ALTER SESSION, CREATE CLUSTER, CREATE DATABASE LINK, CREATE PROCEDURE, CREATE SEQUENCE, CREATE SESSION, CREATE SYNONYM, CREATE TABLE, CREATE TRIGGER, CREATE TYPE,` and `CREATE VIEW`.

   ☒ **A** and **B** are wrong because the `RECOVERY_CATALOG` and `CATALOG_OWNER` roles do not exist. **D** is wrong because it provides the recovery catalog owner with more system privileges than necessary.

Synchronize the Recovery Catalog

5. ☑ **B.** Any manual backups performed outside of RMAN or that were aged out of the target database control file before you create the recovery catalog must be manually registered with the recovery catalog.

☒ **A, C,** and **D** are all steps that occur when you register a database with a recovery catalog.

6. ☑ **B** and **D.** A full resynchronization creates a control file snapshot and synchronizes database structure information as well as information about backups in the target database control file that are not in the recovery catalog. A partial resynchronization compares the target database's control file directly with the control file.

☒ **A** is wrong because RMAN records aged out of the control file can be added to the recovery catalog manually. **C** is wrong because a full resynchronization uses a copy of the control file (a control file snapshot) for its comparison. A partial resynchronization does not.

Create and Use RMAN Stored Scripts

7. ☑ **A.** A local script is available only to the database that was connected when the script was created.

☒ **B** and **C** are wrong because both global and local scripts are stored in the recovery catalog. **D** is wrong because any script operates on one database at a time. **E** is wrong because both local and global scripts are available to any user that authenticates with the recovery catalog.

8. ☑ **A.** Stored scripts, whether they are local or global, must be run within a RUN block as follows:

```
run {execute script full_backup;}
```

☒ **B** is wrong because a script must be enclosed in a RUN block. **C** is wrong because you can include a channel allocation or use the default channel in the RUN command containing the EXECUTE SCRIPT command. **D** is wrong because both local and global scripts apply only to the currently connected target database.

Back Up the Recovery Catalog

9. ☑ **C.** The RESYNC CATALOG command synchronizes the target database's control file information with the recovery catalog database, and the CATALOG START WITH command adds any backup information that is no longer in the target database control file.

☒ **A** is wrong because you do not need to re-create the recovery catalog, you just need to resynchronize it. **B** is wrong because the database itself is already registered with the recovery catalog. **D** is wrong because you do not need to re-create the recovery catalog or reregister the target database.

10. ☑ **B.** When the recovery catalog schema version is less than the RMAN client version, you must use UPGRADE CATALOG.

☒ **A** and **D** are wrong because structural changes to either database means you should back up your control file, but this does not trigger a recovery catalog upgrade. **C** is wrong because you can use RMAN clients that are older than the recovery catalog database version, although some features of the newer RMAN client will not be available, such as flashback database.

Create and Use a Virtual Private Catalog

11. ☑ **D.** To allow access to a virtual private catalog, you must grant the role RECOVERY_ CATALOG_OWNER as a SQL command to each user that will access a virtual private catalog.

☒ **A** is wrong because the SELECT_CATALOG_ROLE allows access to a database's data dictionary and does not control access to RMAN virtual catalogs. **B** and **C** are wrong because these roles do not exist in a default installation of the database.

12. ☑ **D.** To create the virtual catalog, you connect to the base catalog, create the virtual catalog, connect to the target database, register the database, and finally back it up. You need to create the virtual catalog only once, and each target database needs to be registered only once. Subsequent backup operations can occur after connecting to the base catalog and the target database.

☒ **A** is wrong because the base catalog and virtual catalog are on the instance with the service name CATDB2, not the target database DW. **B** is wrong because EXEC CATOWNER.DBMS_ RCVCAT.CREATE_VIRTUAL_CATALOG is only for pre-11g clients and must be run by the virtual catalog owner at a SQL> prompt. **C** is wrong because GRANT CATALOG FOR DATABASE DW TO VPC1 must be run by the base catalog owner and only if the database is already registered in the base catalog.

Configure Backup Settings

13. ☑ **A, E,** and **H.** RMAN backs up the current control file and the SPFILE (if you use one) after a successful backup, when you explicitly back up the current controlfile, and when the structure of the database changes.

☒ **B, C, D, F,** and **G** are wrong. RMAN does not back up the control file under any of these circumstances.

14. ☑ **C, H, I. C** is cannot be backed up because RMAN backs up databases; an instance comprises the Oracle memory structures and cannot be backed up. **H** cannot be backed up because CONTROLFILE is not a valid option; you must use CURRENT CONTROLFILE to back up the control file. **I** cannot be backed up because you should never, ever back up the online redo log files.

☒ **A, B, D, E, F,** and **G** can all be backed up and are therefore incorrect. All other objects listed, the current control file, the SPFILE, the entire database, an individual datafile, an individual tablespace, or one or more archived redo log files can be backed up by RMAN.

15. ☑ **A** and **D.** The SHOW ALL command shows all settings for the connected target; you can use CONFIGURE...CLEAR to reset a configuration value to its default.
☒ **B** is wrong because CONFIGURE...CLEAR resets the configuration setting to its default value. **C** is wrong because SHOW ALL works only when you are connected to a target database. **E** is wrong since SHOW ALL lists all configuration values regardless of whether they have been changed from the default.

Allocate Channels to Use in Backing Up

16. ☑ **C.** You can use CONFIGURE only at the RMAN command prompt to set default values, and it cannot be used within a RUN block.
☒ **A** is wrong because the CONFIGURE command cannot be used within a RUN block. **B** is wrong for the same reason; additionally, any channels allocated within a RUN block override the default channel. **D** is wrong since you can use BACKUP either as a standalone command or within a RUN block.

Configure Backup Optimization

17. ☑ **B.** Backup optimization is not used for backing up individual tablespaces.
☒ **A, C,** and **D** are wrong. Backup optimization is used for all of these commands.

4
Creating RMAN Backups

T

his chapter offers what you've all been waiting for: You'll learn to create backups using Recovery Manager (RMAN). Needless to say, you can create many different types of backups using RMAN and leverage the many features new to Oracle Database 11g to make your backups smaller and less time-consuming.

RMAN supports a number of backup methods that can be used according to your availability needs, the desired size of your recovery window, and the amount of downtime you can endure while the database or a part of the database is involved in a recovery operation. You'll learn more about configuring and using recovery in Chapter 5.

First, you'll learn how to create image file backups—in other words, exact copies of your database's datafiles. Even though you can make copies of your database files manually, RMAN provides a number of added benefits. You'll also get an overview of the other types of RMAN backups: whole database backups, as well as whole database backups that you can use as part of an incremental backup strategy. RMAN has many features that can make an incremental backup run even faster, such as creating a block change tracking file to mark which datafile blocks have changed since the last backup.

Next, you'll learn how to create an archival backup for long-term retention. Business requirements and recent changes to record-keeping and privacy laws demand a retention period for corporate data that is frequently beyond the configured RMAN retention policy. An RMAN archival backup gives you a consistent and simple snapshot of your database at a point in time in the past.

As of Oracle Database 11g, RMAN provides enhancements such as multisection backups for very large database (VLDB) environments. In previous versions of RMAN, a bigfile tablespace took a long time to back up because RMAN could only process the bigfile tablespace serially. In Oracle Database 11g, RMAN can back up large datafiles as a multisection backup, leveraging multiple output devices (multiple channels either to disk or tape) to dramatically reduce the time it takes to back up the datafile, among other advantages. RMAN's alternative compression techniques and encryption methods further reduce backup size and make the backups unavailable to unauthorized parties by using standalone passwords or the database's encryption wallet.

Finally, you'll get a whirlwind tour of RMAN reporting capabilities. As a robust backup tool, RMAN has a wealth of commands and many useful data dictionary views. This makes it easy for you to identify the state and contents of your backups, either on the target database or in the repository itself.

Using RMAN to Create Backups

You'll find very few reasons for not using RMAN as your main tool for managing backups. Following are some of the major features of RMAN, which are either unavailable with traditional backup methods or are limited by significant restrictions using traditional backup methods:

- **Skip unused blocks**   Blocks that have never been written to, such as blocks above the high water mark (HWM) in a table, are not backed up by RMAN when the backup is an RMAN backupset. Traditional backup methods have no way to know which blocks have been used.

- **Backup compression**   In addition to skipping blocks that have never been used, RMAN can also use one of two Oracle-specific binary compression modes to save space on the backup device. Although operating system–specific compression techniques are available with traditional backup methods, the compression algorithms used by RMAN are customized to maximize the compression for the typical kinds of data found in Oracle data blocks. Although a slight increase in CPU time is required during an RMAN compressed backup or recovery operation, the amount of media used for backup can be significantly reduced, as well as network bandwidth reduction if the backup is performed over the network. Multiple CPUs can be configured for an RMAN backup to help alleviate the compression overhead.

- **Open database backups**   Tablespace backups can be performed in RMAN without using the BEGIN/END BACKUP clause with ALTER TABLESPACE. Whether using RMAN or a traditional backup method, however, the database must be in ARCHIVELOG mode.

- **True incremental backups**   For any RMAN incremental backup, unchanged blocks since the last backup will not be written to the backup file. This saves a significant amount of disk space, I/O time, and CPU time. For restore and recovery operations, RMAN supports *incrementally updated backups*. Data blocks from an incremental backup are applied to a previous backup to potentially reduce the amount of time and number of files that need to be accessed to perform a recovery operation. You'll see an example of an incrementally updated backup later in this chapter.

- **Block-level recovery**   To help avoid downtime during a recovery operation, RMAN supports *block-level recovery* for recovery operations that need to restore or repair only a small number of blocks identified as being corrupt during the backup operation. The rest of the tablespace and the objects within the tablespace can remain online while RMAN repairs the damaged blocks. The rows of a table not being repaired by RMAN are even available to applications and users. You'll learn about block-level recovery in Chapter 5.

■ **Multiple I/O channels** During a backup or recovery operation, RMAN can utilize many I/O channels using separate operating system processes, thus performing concurrent I/O. Traditional backup methods, such as a Unix `cp` command or an Oracle `export`, are typically single-threaded operations.

■ **Platform independence** Backups written with RMAN commands are syntactically identical regardless of the hardware or software platform used. In other words, RMAN scripts are platform-independent. The only difference will be the media management channel configuration. If you don't use RMAN, something like a Unix script containing lots of `cp` commands will not run at all if the backup script is migrated to a Windows platform.

■ **Tape manager support** All major enterprise backup systems are supported within RMAN by a third-party media management driver, which is provided by a tape backup vendor.

■ **Cataloging** A record of all RMAN backups is recorded in the target database control file and optionally in a recovery catalog stored in a different database. This makes restore and recovery operations relatively simple compared to manually tracking operating system–level backups using "copy" commands. The benefits and reviewed catalog configuration are discussed in Chapter 3.

■ **Scripting capabilities** RMAN scripts can be saved in a recovery catalog for retrieval during a backup session. The tight integration of the scripting language, the ease of maintaining scripts in RMAN, and the Oracle scheduling facility make RMAN a better choice compared to storing traditional operating system scripts in an operating system directory with the operating system's native scheduling mechanisms.

■ **Encrypted backups** RMAN uses backup encryption integrated into Oracle Database 11g to store encrypted backups. Storing encrypted backups on tape requires the Advanced Security option.

In a few limited cases, a traditional backup method can have an advantage over RMAN. For example, RMAN does not support the backup of password files and other nondatabase files, such as tnsnames.ora, listener.ora, and sqlnet.ora. However, these files are relatively static in nature, and they can be easily backed up and restored using a traditional backup method, such as the Unix cp command.

CERTIFICATION OBJECTIVE 4.01

Create Image File Backups

RMAN supports a number of different backup methods. The choice of method depends on your availability needs, the desired size of your recovery window, and the amount of downtime you can endure while the database (or a part of the database) is involved in a recovery operation.

RMAN stores its backups in one of two formats: backupsets or image copies. This section highlights and defines the differences between the two, and more examples of each backup type are provided later in this chapter.

Creating Backupsets

A *backupset* is an object specific to RMAN; only RMAN can create and read backupsets. As you learned in Chapter 3, a backupset is a set of files called *backup pieces* that can be stored on a file system or on an Automatic Storage Management (ASM) disk. Each backup piece can contain one or more database file backups. All backupsets and pieces are recorded in the RMAN repository, the same as any other RMAN-initiated backup.

By default, any backups to disk default to a backupset backup type:

```
CONFIGURE DEVICE TYPE DISK PARALLELISM 1 BACKUP TYPE TO
BACKUPSET; # default
```

As a result, the following backup command does not need the AS BACKUPSET qualifier, but you can specify it anyway, especially if it's in a global script that could be run in an RMAN session with different defaults:

```
RMAN> backup as backupset format '/u01/hr/backups/userbak.set'
2>        tablespace sysaux;
```

The FORMAT clause can use substitution variables to differentiate backupsets by database, by piece, and so forth. Here are a few sample substitution variable types:

- **%d** Database name
- **%e** Archived log sequence number
- **%f** Absolute file number
- **%F** Combines the DBID, day, month, year, and sequence number, separated by dashes
- **%c** Copy number for multiple copies in a duplexed backup
- **%I** Database identifier (DBID)
- **%n** Database name padded to eight characters
- **%p** Piece number within the backupset
- **%s** Backupset number
- **%t** Backupset timestamp
- **%U** System-generated unique filename (the default)

EXERCISE 4-1

Create a Compressed Backupset

In this exercise, you'll create an RMAN backup to the directory /u06/backup that includes the database name, backupset number, a backupset timestamp, and a piece number within the backupset. You'll create a second RMAN backup using the default backup location and backupset format.

1. Connect to the target database and the recovery catalog on the HR database:

```
[oracle@srv04 ~]$ rman target / catalog rman/rman@rcat

Recovery Manager: Release 11.1.0.6.0 -
        Production on Sat May 3 21:15:51 2008

Copyright (c) 1982, 2007, Oracle.  All rights reserved.

connected to target database: HR (DBID=3318356692)
connected to recovery catalog database

RMAN>
```

2. Run the RMAN backup, and explicitly specify AS COMPRESSED BACKUPSET, even if this is already the default:

```
RMAN> backup as compressed backupset
2>       format '/u06/backup/rman_%d_%s_%t_%p.bkupset'
3>       tablespace users;

Starting backup at 03-MAY-08
using channel ORA_DISK_1
channel ORA_DISK_1: starting compressed full datafile backup set
channel ORA_DISK_1: specifying datafile(s) in backup set
input datafile file number=00004 name=/u01/app/oracle/oradata/
hr/users01.dbf
channel ORA_DISK_1: starting piece 1 at 03-MAY-08
channel ORA_DISK_1: finished piece 1 at 03-MAY-08
piece handle=/u06/backup/rman_HR_2_653777029_1.bkupset
tag=TAG20080503T204349 comment=NONE
channel ORA_DISK_1: backup set complete, elapsed time: 00:00:04
Finished backup at 03-MAY-08

RMAN>
```

3. Run the RMAN backup again, this time backing up the SYSAUX tablespace and using the default location and format:

```
RMAN> backup as compressed backupset tablespace sysaux;

Starting backup at 03-MAY-08
using channel ORA_DISK_1
channel ORA_DISK_1: starting compressed full datafile backup set
channel ORA_DISK_1: specifying datafile(s) in backup set
input datafile file number=00002
name=/u01/app/oracle/oradata/hr/sysaux01.dbf
channel ORA_DISK_1: starting piece 1 at 03-MAY-08
channel ORA_DISK_1: finished piece 1 at 03-MAY-08
piece handle=/u01/app/oracle/flash_recovery_area
   /HR/backupset/2008_05_03/o1_mf_nnndf_TAG20080503T210504_
41t6hb0w_.bkp
tag=TAG20080503T210504 comment=NONE
channel ORA_DISK_1: backup set complete, elapsed time: 00:00:56
Finished backup at 03-MAY-08

RMAN>
```

The `FORMAT` parameter can be provided in two other ways: in the `ALLOCATE` `CHANNEL` and as part of the `CONFIGURE` commands. The default `FORMAT` applies only to the control file autobackup as in this example:

```
CONFIGURE CONTROLFILE AUTOBACKUP FORMAT FOR
    DEVICE TYPE DISK TO '%F'; # default
```

Creating Image Copies

An *image copy* is an exact copy of a tablespace's datafile, an archived redo log file, or a control file. Although you can use an operating system command to perform the copy, using the RMAN command `BACKUP AS COPY` provides the additional benefits of block verification and automatically recording the backup into the control file and the recovery catalog (if you have configured a recovery catalog). Another spin-off benefit to making image copies is that the copies can be used "as is" outside of RMAN if, for some reason, a recovery operation must occur outside of RMAN.

A restriction applies when you're using image copies in that image copies can be written only to disk. This can turn out to be a benefit, however: Although disk space may be at a premium compared to tape storage, restoration time is considerably less because the file used for recovery is already on disk.

You can use a disk image copy in a recovery scenario using two different methods: using an RMAN command or a SQL command. If you are in RMAN, you use the `SWITCH` command. In the next example, you lose the disk containing the tablespace `STAR_SCHEMA` and you want to switch to a backup copy:

```
RMAN> sql "alter tablespace star_schema offline immediate";
RMAN> switch tablespace star_schema to copy;
RMAN> recover tablespace star_schema;
RMAN> sql "alter tablespace star_schema online";
```

Alternatively, at the SQL prompt, you can use the `ALTER DATABASE RENAME` `FILE` command, as long as the tablespace containing the datafile is offline or the database is in `MOUNT` mode.

Finally, note that an image copy of a tablespace or archived redo log file contains all blocks in the tablespace or archived redo log file. An image copy of a datafile can be used as a full or incremental level 0 backup as long as you add the `INCREMENTAL` `LEVEL 0` parameter:

```
RMAN> backup incremental level 0
2> as copy
3> tablespace sysaux;
```

```
Starting backup at 13-NOV-08
allocated channel: ORA_DISK_1
channel ORA_DISK_1: SID=118 device type=DISK
channel ORA_DISK_1: starting datafile copy

input datafile file number=00002
        name=+DATA/dw/datafile/sysaux.257.630244581

output file name=+RECOV/dw/datafile/sysaux.421.670716759
        tag=TAG20081113T221210 RECID=12 STAMP=670716858

channel ORA_DISK_1: datafile copy complete, elapsed time: 00:01:46

Finished backup at 13-NOV-08

RMAN>
```

CERTIFICATION OBJECTIVE 4.02

Create a Whole Database Backup

An RMAN backup can be one of five types:

- A whole database backup
- A full backup
- An incremental level 0 backup
- A differential incremental level 1 backup
- A cumulative incremental level 1 backup

In the following sections you'll learn the differences between these types of backups and how to perform them.

Whole Database Backups

A whole database backup includes a copy of all datafiles in the database plus the control file. You can also include archived redo log files and the server parameter file (SPFILE).

If your default backup device is disk, the following command will back up your database as image files, including all database files, the control file, all archived redo log files, and the SPFILE:

```
RMAN> backup as copy database spfile plus archivelog;
```

Even if CONTROLFILE AUTOBACKUP is OFF, RMAN backs up the current control file whenever datafile #1 is included in the backup. Therefore, backing up the entire database in a whole database backup includes datafile #1 and, as a result, backs up the control file. Additionally, setting CONTROLFILE AUTOBACKUP to ON results in no significant performance hit to any RMAN backup unless disk space is extremely tight and the control file is very large after many RMAN backups and a long control file retention period.

If you add the DELETE INPUT clause to the preceding BACKUP command, RMAN deletes the archived log files from all destinations after they are backed up. If you are using a flash recovery area, this clause is generally unnecessary, as RMAN automatically deletes obsolete files in the flash recovery area when space is running low.

Finally, you can back up a previous backup of a database (either image copies or backupset) to another location (such as tape) by using this command:

```
backup copy of database;
```

Full Backups

A full backup is different from a whole database backup. A full backup can consist of a single datafile or tablespace, while a whole database backup includes all datafiles in a database. For full backups of tablespaces or archived redo log files, RMAN copies all data blocks into a backupset; blocks that have never been used are skipped. For an image copy, all blocks are included whether or not they have been used.

A full backup of an individual database object is a logical subset of a whole database backup. When performing database recovery, RMAN may use a more recent full backup of a tablespace than the most recent backup piece, which RMAN uses from an older backup of a whole database backup. This is because a whole database backup is a snapshot of the entire database. You plug in a datafile and let the automated recovery process resynchronize between data in datafiles, redo log entries, and the control file.

You perform a full backup of an individual database object much like a whole database backup, except that you use the TABLESPACE keyword instead of the

DATABASE keyword in the BACKUP command. This is because you are backing up tablespaces individually.

EXERCISE 4-2

Perform a Full Backup of Two Tablespaces

In this exercise, you'll perform a full backup of the USERS and SYSAUX tablespaces in the same BACKUP command.

1. Connect to RMAN and run the BACKUP command with the tablespaces separated by commas:

```
RMAN> backup tablespace sysaux, users;

Starting backup at 04-MAY-08
using channel ORA_DISK_1
channel ORA_DISK_1: starting full datafile backup set
channel ORA_DISK_1: specifying datafile(s) in backup set
input datafile file number=00002
name=/u01/app/oracle/oradata/hr/sysaux01.dbf
input datafile file number=00004
name=/u01/app/oracle/oradata/hr/users01.dbf
channel ORA_DISK_1: starting piece 1 at 04-MAY-08
channel ORA_DISK_1: finished piece 1 at 04-MAY-08
piece handle=/u01/app/oracle/flash_recovery_area/

HR/backupset/2008_05_04/o1_mf_nnndf_TAG20080504T101253_41vnnjbx_.bkp
tag=TAG20080504T101253 comment=NONE
channel ORA_DISK_1: backup set complete, elapsed time: 00:01:37
Finished backup at 04-MAY-08

RMAN>
```

Note that the control file and SPFILE are not included in this backup unless you have CONTROLFILE AUTOBACKUP set to ON or datafile #1 is included in the backup; by default, it is set to OFF, as in this example.

If you are using Oracle Enterprise Manager Database Control, you can perform an ad-hoc or scheduled full backup of a tablespace using a GUI tablespace, as you can see in Figure 4-1.

A full backup cannot participate in an incremental backup strategy; in other words, a full backup stands alone regardless of other incremental backups you are

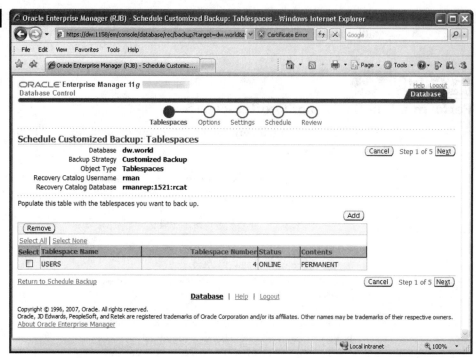

performing for the same objects. You'll see how to set up an incremental backup
strategy in the next section.

Incremental Backups

As mentioned in Chapter 3, an incremental backup can be one of two types: level
0 or level 1. A level 0 incremental backup includes all blocks in the specified
datafiles except for blocks that have never been used. In addition, a level 0 backup
is physically identical to a full backup of the same datafiles, except that a full backup
cannot be used in an incremental backup strategy—it stands alone. A level 1 backup
can be one of two types: either a differential backup that backs up changed blocks
since the last backup at level 0 or 1, or a cumulative backup that backs up all changed
blocks since the last level 0 backup.

You use the following keywords in the RMAN BACKUP command to specify an
incremental level 0 or level 1 backup:

```
INCREMENTAL LEVEL [0|1]
```

You'll learn how to set up an incremental backup strategy for the USERS tablespace in the following sections.

Level 0 Incremental Backups

A level 0 backup includes all blocks in a database object except for blocks that were never used above the HWM. Subsequent level 1 backups use the most recent level 0 backup as the base for comparison when identifying changed blocks.

How often you perform a level 0 backup depends on how much the database object, such as a tablespace, changes between backups. A tablespace containing tables that are completely replaced on a weekly basis would most likely have more frequent level 0 backups than a tablespace containing tables that your applications change infrequently—for example, only 5 percent of the table's rows every week, but the changes might depend on the block distribution of those rows.

In this example, you perform the first level 0 backup of the USERS tablespace in your incremental backup strategy:

```
RMAN> backup incremental level 0 tablespace users;

Starting backup at 04-MAY-08
starting full resync of recovery catalog
full resync complete
using channel ORA_DISK_1
channel ORA_DISK_1: starting incremental level 0 datafile backupset
channel ORA_DISK_1: specifying datafile(s) in backupset
input datafile file number=00004 name=/u01/app/oracle/oradata/hr/users01.dbf
channel ORA_DISK_1: starting piece 1 at 04-MAY-08
channel ORA_DISK_1: finished piece 1 at 04-MAY-08
piece handle=/u01/app/oracle/flash_recovery_area
    /HR/backupset/2008_05_04/o1_mf_nnnd0_TAG20080504T092723_41vkyx2g_.bkp
tag=TAG20080504T092723 comment=NONE
channel ORA_DISK_1: backupset complete, elapsed time: 00:00:02
Finished backup at 04-MAY-08

RMAN>
```

Subsequent level 1 backups will use this backup as the starting point for identifying changed blocks.

Differential Incremental Backups

A *differential* backup is the default type of incremental backup that backs up all changed blocks since the last level 0 or level 1 incremental backup. Again using the USERS tablespace, here's how you perform an incremental backup:

```
RMAN> backup incremental level 1 tablespace users;
Starting backup at 04-MAY-08
starting full resync of recovery catalog
full resync complete
using channel ORA_DISK_1
channel ORA_DISK_1: starting incremental level 1 datafile backupset
channel ORA_DISK_1: specifying datafile(s) in backupset
input datafile file number=00004
name=/u01/app/oracle/oradata/hr/users01.dbf
channel ORA_DISK_1: starting piece 1 at 04-MAY-08
channel ORA_DISK_1: finished piece 1 at 04-MAY-08
piece handle=/u01/app/oracle/flash_recovery_area

/HR/backupset/2008_05_04/o1_mf_nnnd1_TAG20080504T113026_41vs5tcj_.bkp
tag=TAG20080504T113026 comment=NONE
channel ORA_DISK_1: backupset complete, elapsed time: 00:00:03
Finished backup at 04-MAY-08

RMAN>
```

on the ***Differential is the default incremental backup type. Unlike most Oracle***
ⓘob ***commands that allow you to use a keyword that is the default,*** DIFFERENTIAL
can not be specified for the RMAN BACKUP ***command.***

Cumulative Incremental Backups

Cumulative incremental backups back up all changed blocks since the last level 0 incremental backup. You perform a cumulative incremental level 1 backup the same way that you perform a differential level 1 backup, except that you specify the CUMULATIVE keyword, as in this example:

```
RMAN> backup incremental level 1 cumulative tablespace users;

Starting backup at 04-MAY-08
starting full resync of recovery catalog
full resync complete
using channel ORA_DISK_1
channel ORA_DISK_1: starting incremental level 1 datafile backupset
channel ORA_DISK_1: specifying datafile(s) in backupset
input datafile file number=00004
name=/u01/app/oracle/oradata/hr/users01.dbf
channel ORA_DISK_1: starting piece 1 at 04-MAY-08
```

```
channel ORA_DISK_1: finished piece 1 at 04-MAY-08
piece
handle=/u01/app/oracle/flash_recovery_area
/HR/backupset/2008_05_04/o1_mf_nnnd1_TAG20080504T113943_41vsq1oc_.bkp

tag=TAG20080504T113943 comment=NONE
channel ORA_DISK_1: backupset complete, elapsed time: 00:00:03
Finished backup at 04-MAY-08

RMAN>
```

The decision whether to use a cumulative or differential backup is based partly on where you want to spend the CPU cycles and how much disk space is available. Using cumulative backups means that each incremental backup will become progressively larger and take longer until another level 0 incremental backup is performed. This can be beneficial in that only two backupsets will be required during a restore and recovery operation. On the other hand, differential backups record only the changes since the last backup, so each backupset might be smaller or larger than the previous one, with no overlap in data blocks backed up. However, a restore and recovery operation can take longer if you have to restore from several backupsets instead of just two.

CERTIFICATION OBJECTIVE 4.03

Enable Fast Incremental Backup

Another way to improve the performance of incremental backups is to enable *block change tracking*. For a traditional incremental backup, RMAN must inspect every block of the tablespace or datafile to be backed up to see if the block has changed since the last backup. For a very large database, the time it takes to scan the blocks in the database can easily exceed the time it takes to perform the actual backup.

By enabling block change tracking, RMAN knows which blocks have changed within a datafile by using a *change tracking file*. Although a slight overhead is incurred in space usage and maintenance of the tracking file every time a block is changed, the trade-off is well worth it if frequent incremental backups are performed on the database.

Once block change tracking is enabled, RMAN can perform fast incremental backups. In addition, database recovery is faster because fewer changed blocks need to be applied to a restored datafile. The following sections explain how block change tracking works, show you how to enable block change tracking and fast incremental backups, and show you how to monitor how well block change tracking is working in your database.

Understanding Block Change Tracking

Once you create a block change tracking file for your database, the maintenance of the tracking file is automatic and transparent. The size of the tracking file is proportional to the size of your database, the number of instances if you have a Real Application Cluster (RAC) database, and the number of previous backups maintained in the block change tracking file. (Oracle maintains up to eight previous backups in the block change tracking file.) The first incremental level 0 backup reads every block in the datafile, and subsequent incremental level 1 backups use the block change tracking file.

Updates to the block change tracking file occur in parallel with redo generation to the online redo log files. Figure 4-2 shows a committed transaction in the SGA that both generates redo in the online redo log files, and is processed by the CTWR (Change Tracking Writer) process and recorded in the change tracking file.

FIGURE 4-2

Committed transactions and the change tracking file

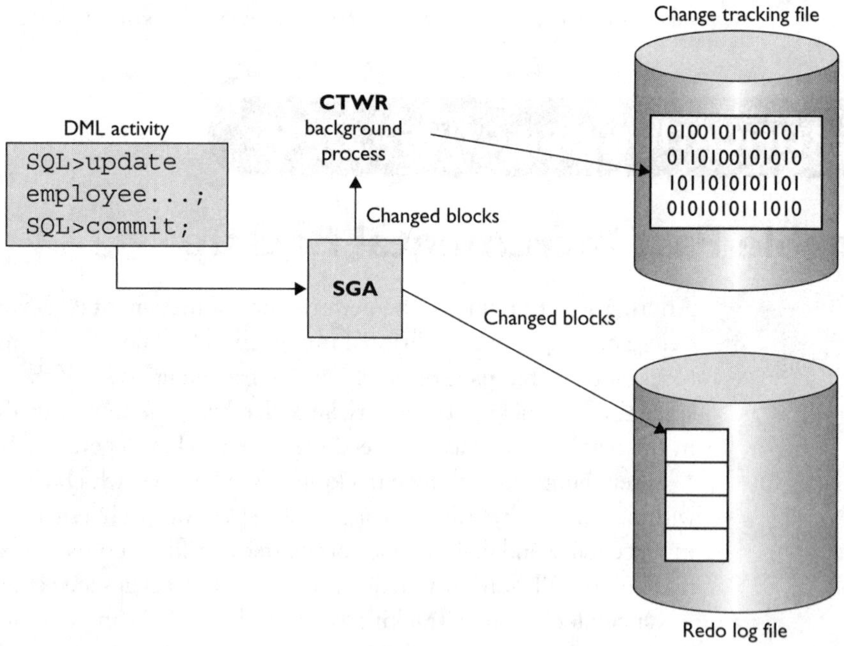

Enabling Fast Incremental Backup

You enable or disable block change tracking with the ALTER DATABASE command. In its simplest form, the following command is used to create and enable block change tracking:

```
alter database enable block change tracking;
```

If you do not specify a filename for the tracking file, Oracle creates it in the location specified by the initialization parameter DB_CREATE_FILE_DEST as an Oracle Managed File (OMF). If you want to explicitly specify the name and location of the tracking file, use the USING FILE clause. This example creates a block change tracking file in the DATA disk group and enables block change tracking:

```
SQL> alter database enable block change tracking
  2       using file '+DATA';
Database altered.
SQL>
```

Since the tracking file now exists in an ASM disk group, you can discover its size and where it is located within the DATA disk group by using the asmcmd utility:

```
[oracle@dw ~]$ asmcmd
ASMCMD> cd data/dw
ASMCMD> ls
CHANGETRACKING/
CONTROLFILE/
DATAFILE/
ONLINELOG/
PARAMETERFILE/
TEMPFILE/
spfiledw.ora
ASMCMD> cd changetracking
ASMCMD> ls -s
Block_Size  Blocks     Bytes      Space    Name
       512   22657   11600384   25165824   ctf.270.632356105
ASMCMD>
```

The next time a level 1 incremental backup is performed after an initial level 0 backup, RMAN will have to use only the contents of the file ctf.270.632356105 (an OMF-named file in the DW/CHANGETRACKING directory of the DATA disk group), to determine which blocks need to be backed up. The space needed for the block change tracking file is approximately 1/30,000 the size of the database.

You turn off block change tracking by using this command:

```
alter database disable block change tracking;
```

This ALTER DATABASE command drops the block change tracking file. If you re-create it later, you will have to create another level 0 incremental backup before RMAN can use the block change tracking file, which minimizes the number of blocks that have to be read for the next level 1 incremental backup.

Finally, you can rename the tracking file by using the same command you use to rename any database file: ALTER DATABASE RENAME. Your database must be in the MOUNT state to rename a tracking file.

EXERCISE 4-3

Relocate the Block Change Tracking File

In this exercise, you'll locate the block change tracking file and move it to another file system on the same server.

1. Find the location of the current block change tracking file:

```
SQL> select filename from v$block_change_tracking;

FILENAME
------------------------------------
/u01/oradata/db_block_trk.chg

SQL>
```

2. Shut down the database and restart it in MOUNT mode:

```
SQL> shutdown immediate
Database closed.
Database dismounted.
ORACLE instance shut down.
SQL> startup mount
ORACLE instance started.

Total System Global Area  636100608 bytes
Fixed Size                  1301784 bytes
Variable Size             473957096 bytes
Database Buffers          155189248 bytes
Redo Buffers                5652480 bytes
```

```
Database mounted.
SQL>
```

3. Relocate the existing block change tracking file to the new location using operating system commands; using SQL*Plus on most platforms, you can execute operating system commands from the SQL> prompt:

```
SQL> ! mv /u01/oradata/db_block_trk.chg /u04/oradata/
db_block_trk.chg
SQL>
```

4. Change the location of the file in the target database control file:

```
SQL> alter database rename file '/u01/oradata/db_block_trk.chg'
  2>    to '/u04/oradata/db_block_trk.chg';

Database altered.

SQL>
```

5. Start the database:

```
SQL> alter database open;

Database altered.

SQL>
```

6. Verify the new location of the block change tracking file:

```
SQL> select filename from v$block_change_tracking;

FILENAME
--------------------------------------
/u04/oradata/db_block_trk.chg

SQL>
```

If you cannot afford to have your database down, even for a few minutes, then the only alternative is to drop and re-create the block change tracking file at a new location while the database is open using the ALTER DATABASE [ENABLE|DISABLE] BLOCK CHANGE TRACKING command.

Monitoring Block Change Tracking

The dynamic performance view V$BLOCK_CHANGE_TRACKING contains the name and size of the block change tracking file plus the status of change tracking:

```
SQL> select filename, status, bytes from v$block_change_tracking;

FILENAME                                          STATUS      BYTES
------------------------------------------------- ---------- ----------
+DATA/dw/changetracking/ctf.270.632356105         ENABLED    11599872
SQL>
```

To see the benefits of block change tracking, you can use the following query on the dynamic performance view V$BACKUP_DATAFILE to calculate the percentage of blocks read and the number of blocks backed up during an incremental level 1 backup:

```
select file#, avg(datafile_blocks) blocks,
  avg(blocks_read) blocks_read,
  avg(blocks_read/datafile_blocks)*100 pct_read,
  avg(blocks) blocks_backed_up
from v$backup_datafile
where used_change_tracking = 'YES'
  and incremental_level = 1
group by file#
order by file#
;
```

The dynamic performance view V$BACKUP_DATAFILE contains one row for each datafile backed up using RMAN. This query further refines the results to pick the backups that used block change tracking during an incremental level 1 backup.

CERTIFICATION OBJECTIVE 4.04

Create Duplex Backup and Back Up Backupsets

RMAN provides a number of options to make multiple copies of your backup simultaneously, to create backups of your existing backupsets, and to skip unnecessary backups of read-only tablespaces. Each of these topics is covered in the following sections along with relevant examples.

Creating Duplexed Backupsets

To make multiple backups of the same backupset simultaneously, you can configure RMAN to make up to four duplexed copies of each backup piece. As with most RMAN commands, you can specify a default value for the COPIES parameter using the CONFIGURE command, as in this example:

```
RMAN> configure datafile backup copies
2>          for device type sbt to 3;

new RMAN configuration parameters:
CONFIGURE DATAFILE BACKUP COPIES FOR DEVICE TYPE 'SBT_TAPE' TO 3;
new RMAN configuration parameters are successfully stored
starting full resync of recovery catalog
full resync complete

RMAN>
```

Duplexing has a few restrictions: You cannot duplex backups to the flash recovery area, and you cannot duplex image copies—only backupsets. For duplexed disk backups, you specify multiple locations for a backup using the FORMAT clause. You can specify multiple locations either in the BACKUP command or when setting default values for device type DISK in the CONFIGURE command.

In this example, you back up the USERS tablespace to two different disk locations simultaneously:

```
RMAN> backup as compressed backupset
2>       device type disk
3>       copies 2
4>       tablespace users
5>       format '/u01/oradata/bkup/%U', '/u04/oradata/bkup/%U';

Starting backup at 05-MAY-08
starting full resync of recovery catalog
full resync complete
allocated channel: ORA_DISK_1
channel ORA_DISK_1: SID=134 device type=DISK
channel ORA_DISK_1: starting compressed full datafile backupset
channel ORA_DISK_1: specifying datafile(s) in backupset
input datafile file number=00004 name=/u01/app/oracle/oradata/
hr/users01.dbf
channel ORA_DISK_1: starting piece 1 at 05-MAY-08
channel ORA_DISK_1: finished piece 1 at 05-MAY-08 with 2 copies
          and tag TAG20080505T215539
```

```
piece handle=/u01/oradata/bkup/0vjfl32r_1_1 comment=NONE
piece handle=/u04/oradata/bkup/0vjfl32r_1_2 comment=NONE
channel ORA_DISK_1: backupset complete, elapsed time: 00:00:09
Finished backup at 05-MAY-08
```

RMAN>

Note that even though you have the same format for each copy of the backupset, RMAN's default format, %U, is a shorthand for %u_%p_%c. As you may remember from the discussion on RMAN substitution variables, %c translates to a copy number in a duplexed backup operation.

EXERCISE 4-4

Configuring Multiple Disk Locations for a Duplexed Disk Backup

In this exercise, you will use the RMAN CONFIGURE command to set the default disk locations for duplexed backups so you don't have to specify FORMAT for each BACKUP operation to device type DISK.

1. Connect to RMAN and show the current RMAN default values:

```
RMAN> show all;

RMAN configuration parameters for database with db_unique_
name HR are:
CONFIGURE RETENTION POLICY TO REDUNDANCY 1; # default
CONFIGURE BACKUP OPTIMIZATION OFF; # default
CONFIGURE DEFAULT DEVICE TYPE TO DISK; # default
CONFIGURE CONTROLFILE AUTOBACKUP OFF; # default
CONFIGURE CONTROLFILE AUTOBACKUP FORMAT FOR
     DEVICE TYPE DISK TO '%F'; # default
CONFIGURE DEVICE TYPE DISK PARALLELISM 1
     BACKUP TYPE TO BACKUPSET; # default
CONFIGURE DATAFILE BACKUP COPIES FOR DEVICE TYPE DISK TO 1; #
default
CONFIGURE ARCHIVELOG BACKUP COPIES FOR
     DEVICE TYPE DISK TO 1; # default
CONFIGURE MAXSETSIZE TO UNLIMITED; # default
CONFIGURE ENCRYPTION FOR DATABASE OFF; # default
CONFIGURE ENCRYPTION ALGORITHM 'AES128'; # default
CONFIGURE COMPRESSION ALGORITHM 'BZIP2'; # default
CONFIGURE ARCHIVELOG DELETION POLICY TO NONE; # default
```

```
CONFIGURE SNAPSHOT CONTROLFILE NAME TO
 '/u01/app/oracle/product/11.1.0/db_1/dbs/snapcf_hr.f'; #
default
RMAN>
```

2. Change the value for the DISK device type to include two backup locations and two copies as the default:

```
RMAN> configure datafile backup copies for device type disk to 2;

starting full resync of recovery catalog
full resync complete
new RMAN configuration parameters:
CONFIGURE DATAFILE BACKUP COPIES FOR DEVICE TYPE DISK TO 2;
new RMAN configuration parameters are successfully stored
starting full resync of recovery catalog
full resync complete

RMAN> configure channel device type disk
2>         format '/u01/oradata/bkup/%U', '/u04/oradata/bkup/%U';

new RMAN configuration parameters:
CONFIGURE CHANNEL DEVICE TYPE DISK FORMAT
        '/u01/oradata/bkup/%U',
        '/u04/oradata/bkup/%U';
new RMAN configuration parameters are successfully stored
released channel: ORA_DISK_1
starting full resync of recovery catalog
full resync complete

RMAN>
```

3. Perform a backup of the USERS tablespace and confirm that RMAN creates two copies of the backupset:

```
RMAN> backup as compressed backupset tablespace users;

Starting backup at 05-MAY-08
allocated channel: ORA_DISK_1
channel ORA_DISK_1: SID=134 device type=DISK
channel ORA_DISK_1: starting compressed full datafile backupset
channel ORA_DISK_1: specifying datafile(s) in backupset
input datafile file number=00004 name=/u01/app/oracle/oradata/hr/
users01.dbf
channel ORA_DISK_1: starting piece 1 at 05-MAY-08
```

```
channel ORA_DISK_1: finished piece 1 at 05-MAY-08
    with 2 copies and tag TAG20080505T223400
piece handle=/u01/oradata/bkup/10jf15ao_1_1 comment=NONE
piece handle=/u04/oradata/bkup/10jf15ao_1_2 comment=NONE
channel ORA_DISK_1: backupset complete, elapsed time: 00:00:08
Finished backup at 05-MAY-08

RMAN>
```

Creating Backups of Backupsets

One option for creating a second copy of a backup is to create a backup of existing backupsets. This is especially useful if you forgot to duplex a previous backup and you don't want to perform a time-consuming backup again. If your backupsets are on disk (you cannot back up existing backupsets that are on tape), you can use the BACKUP . . . BACKUPSET command to copy all backupsets on one disk, to another disk, or to tape. This command copies all existing disk-based backupsets to the default tape device and channel:

```
RMAN> backup device type sbt backupset all;
```

If you want to keep recent backupsets on disk and older backupsets on tape, you can use the COMPLETED and DELETE INPUT options. In the following, example, all backupsets older than two weeks are backed up to tape and deleted from the disk:

```
RMAN> backup device type sbt backupset
2>       completed before 'sysdate-14'
3>       delete input;
```

Backing Up Read-Only Tablespaces

As you might expect, backing up a read-only tablespace needs to happen often enough to satisfy the retention period configured in RMAN. You can force RMAN to skip a read-only tablespace by using the SKIP READONLY option of the BACKUP command.

If you configured RMAN for backup optimization (covered in Chapter 3), RMAN backs up read-only tablespaces only when there are not enough backups of the tablespace to satisfy the retention policy.

Create an Archival Backup for Long-term Retention

Archival backups, new to Oracle Database 11g, give you the flexibility to take a snapshot of the database and retain it indefinitely or for a specific period of time. The following sections explain how archival backups work, how to perform an archival backup, and how to manage archival backups using the CHANGE command.

Understanding Archival Backups

By default, RMAN keeps your backups and archived log files not only to satisfy the configured retention policy, but also to provide a mechanism to restore your database to any point in time between the backup and the present. RMAN uses a combination of full backups, incremental backups, and archived redo log files.

In certain situations, you may want only a snapshot of the database at a certain point in time for archival or regulatory purposes. This causes two complications with the default RMAN configuration: First, your snapshot will most likely fall outside of your retention policy, and you certainly don't want your yearly database snapshot to disappear before the end of the week! Second, you don't want RMAN to maintain one, two, or more years' worth of archived redo log files if you are not going to restore your database to a point in time between the snapshot and the current time.

RMAN addresses the need for a database snapshot by supporting an *archival backup*. If you label a backup as an archival backup, RMAN does not consider the backup to be obsolete using the configured retention policy; instead, RMAN marks an archival backup as obsolete after the amount of time you specify. Alternatively, you can specify that RMAN keep the archival backup indefinitely.

on the *j*ob *You can use an archival backup to migrate a copy of the database to another system for testing purposes without affecting the retention policy of the original database. Once you have created the database on the test system, you can delete the archival backup.*

Performing an Archival Backup

One restriction for archival backups is that you cannot use the flash recovery area to store an archival backup. If you have a flash recovery area configured, you will have to use the FORMAT parameter to specify an alternative disk location for the backup. Additionally, a tape device might be the best option for long-term storage of archival backups.

This example creates an archival backup to be retained for one year using the KEEP UNTIL clause:

```
RMAN> backup as compressed backupset
2>      database format '/u04/oradata/archbak/%U'
3>      tag save1yr
4>      keep until time 'sysdate+365'
5>   ;

Starting backup at 06-MAY-08
starting full resync of recovery catalog
full resync complete
current log archived

using channel ORA_DISK_1
backup will be obsolete on date 06-MAY-09
archived logs required to recover from this backup will be backed up
channel ORA_DISK_1: starting compressed full datafile backupset
channel ORA_DISK_1: specifying datafile(s) in backupset
input datafile file number=00002
name=/u01/app/oracle/oradata/hr/sysaux01.dbf
input datafile file number=00001
name=/u01/app/oracle/oradata/hr/system01.dbf
input datafile file number=00003
name=/u01/app/oracle/oradata/hr/undotbs01.dbf
input datafile file number=00005
name=/u01/app/oracle/oradata/hr/example01.dbf
input datafile file number=00004 name=/u01/app/oracle/oradata/hr/users01.dbf
channel ORA_DISK_1: starting piece 1 at 06-MAY-08
channel ORA_DISK_1: finished piece 1 at 06-MAY-08
        with 2 copies and tag SAVE1YR
piece handle=/u04/oradata/archbak/11jfnj56_1_1 comment=NONE
piece handle=/u04/oradata/archbak/11jfnj56_1_2 comment=NONE
channel ORA_DISK_1: backupset complete, elapsed time: 00:02:56

current log archived
 . . .
```

```
using channel ORA_DISK_1
backup will be obsolete on date 06-MAY-09
archived logs required to recover from this backup will be backed up
channel ORA_DISK_1: starting compressed full datafile backupset
channel ORA_DISK_1: specifying datafile(s) in backupset
including current control file in backupset
channel ORA_DISK_1: starting piece 1 at 06-MAY-08
channel ORA_DISK_1: finished piece 1 at 06-MAY-08
with 2 copies and tag SAVE1YR
piece handle=/u04/oradata/archbak/14jfnjd0_1_1 comment=NONE
piece handle=/u04/oradata/archbak/14jfnjd0_1_2 comment=NONE
channel ORA_DISK_1: backupset complete, elapsed time: 00:00:02
Finished backup at 06-MAY-08

RMAN>
```

Since the HR database has a flash recovery area defined, you use the FORMAT clause to specify a location in which to store the archival backup. Note also that RMAN backs up any archived logs, which would be required to use the backup in a possible future recovery scenario.

Alternatively, you can perform the same backup but retain it indefinitely:

```
 RMAN> backup as compressed backupset
2>       database format '/u04/oradata/archbak/%U'
3>       tag saveforever
4>       keep forever;
 . . .
using channel ORA_DISK_1
backup will never be obsolete
archived logs required to recover from this backup will be backed up
 . . .
```

Managing Archival Backups

In some situations, you might want to change the status of a backup. For example, you might want to change an archival backup's retention period, change an archival backup to a standard backup, or change a consistent backup to an archival backup. As you might expect, you can use the CHANGE command to accomplish this task. Although the CHANGE command has many other uses (such as to change the availability of a backup or to change the priority of failures in the database), the CHANGE command in relation to archival backups is covered here.

This example changes the backup created earlier with the tag SAVEFOREVER to fall under the existing retention policy instead:

```
RMAN> change backup tag 'saveforever' nokeep;

starting full resync of recovery catalog
full resync complete
using channel ORA_DISK_1
keep attributes for the backup are deleted
backupset key=3321 RECID=26 STAMP=654037077
keep attributes for the backup are deleted
backupset key=3344 RECID=27 STAMP=654037106
keep attributes for the backup are deleted
backupset key=3345 RECID=28 STAMP=654037128
keep attributes for the backup are deleted
backupset key=3346 RECID=29 STAMP=654037151

RMAN>
```

Depending on the retention policy and the other older or newer backups for this database, the backup could be deleted the next time RMAN starts. The backup could be retained longer if the configured retention policy needs this backup to fulfill the retention policy.

You can also use the CHANGE command to change all backups of a certain type. For example, if you want to remove the archive flag from all image copies of the database, you use the NOKEEP parameter:

```
change copy of database nokeep;
```

CERTIFICATION OBJECTIVE 4.06

Create a Multisection, Compressed, and Encrypted Backup

In previous versions of RMAN (before Oracle Database 11g), using bigfile tablespaces had one big advantage and one big disadvantage. The big advantage was that you could have a database with a much larger size than in previous versions of Oracle (up to 1022 bigfile tablespaces of 128 terabytes each). The big disadvantage was that backing up a single bigfile tablespace took a long time because RMAN could back up a bigfile tablespace only using a single channel. In general, backing up four 32TB datafiles in parallel took less time than backing up a single 128TB datafile. As a result, some organizations (with a lot of data) were somewhat restricted to how big they could make their bigfile tablespaces.

As of Oracle Database 11g, RMAN solves the problem of backing up large bigfile tablespaces by supporting *multisection backups*. A multisection backup produces a multipiece backupset from a single datafile and uses several channels, to disk or tape, to back up each piece of the datafile in parallel.

This section shows you not only how to create a multisection backup, but also how to compress your backups with new compression algorithms. It also examines how to ensure the privacy of the data in your backup by encrypting backups using two different methods.

Creating a Multisection Backup

Creating a multisection backup is easy, but you must specify the section size with each BACKUP command. In addition, you can run the RMAN VALIDATE command by section. New data dictionary views, both the V$ and RC_ views, help you to identify which backups are multisection and how many blocks are in each section of a multisection backup.

Specifying the Section Size

To create a multisection backup, you add the SECTION SIZE parameter to the BACKUP command. The section size can be specified in kilobytes, megabytes, or gigabytes. Here is the general syntax for specifying a multisection backup:

```
BACKUP <backup options> SECTION SIZE <size> [K|M|G]
```

In this example HR database, the USERS tablespace is approximately 25MB, and we want to back it up with a section size of 10MB:

```
RMAN> backup tablespace users
2>        section size 10m;

Starting backup at 07-MAY-08
starting full resync of recovery catalog
full resync complete
allocated channel: ORA_DISK_1
channel ORA_DISK_1: SID=116 device type=DISK
channel ORA_DISK_1: starting full datafile backupset
channel ORA_DISK_1: specifying datafile(s) in backupset
```

```
input datafile file number=00004
name=/u01/app/oracle/oradata/hr/users01.dbf
backing up blocks 1 through 1280
channel ORA_DISK_1: starting piece 1 at 07-MAY-08
channel ORA_DISK_1: finished piece 1 at 07-MAY-08
piece handle=/u01/oradata/bkup/1cjfq4mm_1_1
     tag=TAG20080507T195357 comment=NONE
channel ORA_DISK_1: backupset complete, elapsed time: 00:00:04
channel ORA_DISK_1: starting full datafile backupset
channel ORA_DISK_1: specifying datafile(s) in backupset
input datafile file number=00004
      name=/u01/app/oracle/oradata/hr/users01.dbf
backing up blocks 1281 through 2560
channel ORA_DISK_1: starting piece 2 at 07-MAY-08
channel ORA_DISK_1: finished piece 2 at 07-MAY-08
piece handle=/u01/oradata/bkup/1cjfq4mm_2_1
     tag=TAG20080507T195357 comment=NONE
channel ORA_DISK_1: backupset complete, elapsed time: 00:00:03
channel ORA_DISK_1: starting full datafile backupset
channel ORA_DISK_1: specifying datafile(s) in backupset
input datafile file number=00004
     name=/u01/app/oracle/oradata/hr/users01.dbf
backing up blocks 2561 through 2912
channel ORA_DISK_1: starting piece 3 at 07-MAY-08
channel ORA_DISK_1: finished piece 3 at 07-MAY-08
piece handle=/u01/oradata/bkup/1cjfq4mm_3_1
     tag=TAG20080507T195357 comment=NONE
channel ORA_DISK_1: backupset complete, elapsed time: 00:00:01
Finished backup at 07-MAY-08
```

```
RMAN>
```

This backup created three backup pieces: the first two of 10MB each, and the third piece approximately 5MB, which is the remainder of the datafile.

on the job

Don't use a high value for parallelism in your multisection backups to back up a large file on a small number of disks. The I/O contention of multiple RMAN threads accessing the same disk will erase any time savings gained by using a high value for parallelism.

Validating a Backup with a Section Size

You can also use the SECTION SIZE parameter with the VALIDATE command. The benefits of parallel operations for datafile block validation are the same as the benefits of using the BACKUP command: It will take you significantly less time to ensure that a datafile's blocks are readable and have valid checksums. This example validates the datafile backed up in the previous section:

```
RMAN> validate tablespace users
2>        section size 10m;

Starting validate at 08-MAY-08
starting full resync of recovery catalog
full resync complete
using channel ORA_DISK_1
channel ORA_DISK_1: starting validation of datafile
channel ORA_DISK_1: specifying datafile(s) for validation
input datafile file number=00004 name=/u01/app/oracle/oradata/hr/users01.dbf
validating blocks 1 through 1280
channel ORA_DISK_1: validation complete, elapsed time: 00:00:01
channel ORA_DISK_1: starting validation of datafile
channel ORA_DISK_1: specifying datafile(s) for validation
input datafile file number=00004 name=/u01/app/oracle/oradata/hr/users01.dbf
validating blocks 1281 through 2560
channel ORA_DISK_1: validation complete, elapsed time: 00:00:01
channel ORA_DISK_1: starting validation of datafile
channel ORA_DISK_1: specifying datafile(s) for validation
input datafile file number=00004 name=/u01/app/oracle/oradata/hr/users01.dbf
validating blocks 2561 through 2912
channel ORA_DISK_1: validation complete, elapsed time: 00:00:01
List of Datafiles
=================
File Status Marked Corrupt Empty Blocks Blocks Examined High SCN
---- ------ -------------- ------------ --------------- --------
4    OK     0              573          2910            1045509
   File Name: /u01/app/oracle/oradata/hr/users01.dbf
   Block Type Blocks Failing Blocks Processed
   ---------- -------------- ----------------
   Data       0              2121
   Index      0              33
   Other      0              183

Finished validate at 08-MAY-08

RMAN>
```

Multisection Data Dictionary Views

The views V$BACKUP_SET and RC_BACKUP_SET have a MULTI_SECTION column that indicates whether the backup is a multisection backup. Similarly, the V$BACKUP_DATAFILE and RC_BACKUP_DATAFILE views have a SECTION_SIZE column that indicates the number of blocks in each piece of a multisection backup.

Remember that the V$ views exist on the target database and the RC_ views exist on the recovery catalog database.

Compressing Backups

In addition to skipping unused blocks during a backup, RMAN can also apply one of two compression methods to the used blocks in a backup when you specify the COMPRESSED parameter: BZIP2 or ZLIB. By default, RMAN uses BZIP2 as follows:

```
CONFIGURE COMPRESSION ALGORITHM 'BZIP2'; # default
```

The ZLIB algorithm is significantly faster than BZIP2 but doesn't compress the backup as much. In addition, it can be used only if you set the COMPATIBLE initialization parameter to 11.1.0 or higher.

The BZIP2 algorithm, as you might expect, creates much smaller backups but requires more CPU time to compress the blocks. If not too many other server processes are demanding CPU resources when your backups run, use ZLIB or BZIP2. On the other hand, if a lot of disk space is available and the network path from the database to your backup location is not congested, it might take less time overall not to use compression.

Regardless of what compression method you use, restoring a compressed backup requires no knowledge of the compression method used during the original backup. RMAN automatically detects the compression method used and decompresses accordingly.

Encrypting Backups

To ensure the security and privacy of your backups, you can encrypt them in one of three ways: via transparent encryption, password encryption, or dual mode encryption. By default, encryption is turned off:

```
CONFIGURE ENCRYPTION FOR DATABASE OFF; # default
CONFIGURE ENCRYPTION ALGORITHM 'AES128'; # default
```

In the following sections, you'll learn how to enable each type of encryption.

Using Transparent Encryption

You can set transparent (wallet-based) encryption as the default RMAN encryption method using the CONFIGURE command as follows:

```
RMAN> configure encryption for database on;

starting full resync of recovery catalog
full resync complete
```

```
new RMAN configuration parameters:
CONFIGURE ENCRYPTION FOR DATABASE ON;
new RMAN configuration parameters are successfully stored
starting full resync of recovery catalog
full resync complete

RMAN>
```

Keep in mind that your database wallet must be open as well. If it is not open, you might think that everything is going as planned—until the encryption process attempts to start. This is shown by the backup failure error message in the following output:

```
RMAN> backup as compressed backupset tablespace users;

Starting backup at 09-MAY-08
allocated channel: ORA_DISK_1
channel ORA_DISK_1: SID=106 device type=DISK
channel ORA_DISK_1: starting compressed full datafile backup set
channel ORA_DISK_1: specifying datafile(s) in backup set
input datafile file number=00004 name=+DATA/dw/datafile/
users.259.632441707
channel ORA_DISK_1: starting piece 1 at 09-MAY-08
RMAN-00571: ===========================================================
RMAN-00569: =========== ERROR MESSAGE STACK FOLLOWS ==========
RMAN-00571: ===========================================================
RMAN-03009: failure of backup command on
ORA_DISK_1 channel at 05/09/2008 20:04:31
ORA-19914: unable to encrypt backup
ORA-28365: wallet is not open

RMAN>
```

Opening the wallet at the SQL> prompt makes everything work a lot more smoothly:

```
SQL> alter system set encryption wallet open
  2     identified by "fre#3dXX0";

System altered.

SQL>
. . .
RMAN> backup as compressed backupset tablespace users;
```

```
Starting backup at 09-MAY-08
using channel ORA_DISK_1
. . .
channel ORA_DISK_1: starting piece 1 at 09-MAY-08
channel ORA_DISK_1: finished piece 1 at 09-MAY-08

piece handle=+RECOV/dw/backupset/2008_05_09/
     nnndf0_tag20080509t201659_0.550.654293845 tag=TAG20080509T
201659
     comment=NONE
channel ORA_DISK_1: backupset complete, elapsed time: 00:00:07
Finished backup at 09-MAY-08

RMAN>
```

As you might expect, even if transparent encryption is not the default, you can turn it on just for the duration of a single backup. As in the previous example, the database wallet must be open. Here is an example:

```
RMAN> set encryption on;
executing command: SET encryption
RMAN> backup as compressed backupset tablespace users;

Starting backup at 09-MAY-08
using channel ORA_DISK_1

. . .
channel ORA_DISK_1: backupset complete, elapsed time: 00:00:04
Finished backup at 09-MAY-08

RMAN> set encryption off;
executing command: SET encryption
RMAN>
```

To restore or recover from an encrypted backup, the database wallet must be open and either the encryption default must be ON or you must use SET ENCRYPTION ON before the recovery operation.

Using Password Encryption

To enable password encryption for a specific backup, use the SET ENCRYPTION command as follows:

```
RMAN> set encryption identified by "F45$Xa98";

executing command: SET encryption
```

```
RMAN> backup as compressed backupset tablespace users;
     . . .
```

Password encryption is inherently less secure and reliable than transparent (wallet-based) encryption, because a password can be lost, forgotten, or intercepted easily. Use password encryption only when backups must be transportable to a different database.

When you want to restore this backup, either to the same database (if wallet-based encryption is off) or to a different database, you must specify the decryption password with SET DECRYPTION:

```
RMAN> set decryption identified by "F45$Xa98";
executing command: SET decryption
RMAN>
```

If you are recovering one or more tablespaces or the entire database from backups that have different passwords, you can conveniently specify all the passwords at once with SET DECRYPTION:

```
RMAN> set decryption identified by "F45$Xa98", "XX407$9!@";

executing command: SET decryption

RMAN>
```

RMAN will try each password in turn for every encrypted backup until it finds a match. RMAN will terminate with an error only if no passwords match any of the passwords in any of the backups.

Using Dual Mode Encryption

You can use both transparent encryption and password encryption at the same time. This is useful if your backup might be used to restore or recover within the same database, and on occasion it can be used to recover another database. When both methods are in effect, you can use either the password or the database wallet to restore the backup. When recovering to a remote database, you must specify the password before recovering, as follows:

```
RMAN> set encryption on;

executing command: SET encryption
```

```
RMAN> set encryption identified by "F45$Xa98";

executing command: SET encryption

RMAN>
```

If you want to use only password-based encryption for a backup, add the ONLY clause to SET ENCRYPTION:

```
RMAN> set encryption identified by "F45$Xa98" only;
```

As a result, even if ENCRYPTION defaults to ON (and therefore uses the wallet), all subsequent backups use password encryption only until you turn off password encryption or exit RMAN altogether.

Report On and Maintain Backups

Once you have successfully completed your backups, you will probably need to find out which backups are available, which backups are obsolete, and which backups need to occur to satisfy your retention policy. RMAN has the LIST and REPORT commands to help you extract this metadata from the recovery catalog or the target database control file.

The LIST command provides basic information about the backupsets, image copies, proxy copies, and stored scripts recorded in the recovery catalog. In contrast, the REPORT command provides a more detailed analysis of the backup information in the recovery catalog. For example, the REPORT NEED BACKUP command lists all datafiles that don't have enough backups to satisfy the database's retention policy. In contrast, the REPORT OBSOLETE command identifies files that are no longer needed to satisfy the database's retention policy, such as extra datafile copies or archived redo log files that are superseded by a more recent datafile backup. If you are low on disk space, you can use DELETE OBSOLETE to remove these files.

Occasionally, you can lose a disk containing backups due to a hardware failure. Also, tapes containing backups can sometimes wear out and are no longer writeable or readable. As a result, you should run the CROSSCHECK command on a regular basis to ensure that the recovery catalog reflects the existence and integrity of these backups. Files that are no longer available for recovery are marked as EXPIRED, and you can remove them with the DELETE EXPIRED command.

The following sections describe each of these commands with numerous examples.

Using the LIST Command

The LIST command displays information about backupsets and image copies in the repository and can also store the contents of scripts stored in the repository catalog. The following example shows a summary of the backups, and then lists the stored script names:

```
RMAN> list backup summary;

starting full resync of recovery catalog
full resync complete

List of Backups
===============
Key      TY LV S Device Type Completion Time #Pieces #Copies
Compressed Tag
-------  -- -- - ----------- --------------- ------- ------- ----
3690     B  F  A DISK        08-MAY-08       1       1       YES

 TAG20080508T234536
3691     B  F  A DISK        08-MAY-08       1       1       YES

 TAG20080508T234536
3692     B  F  A DISK        08-MAY-08       1       1       YES

 TAG20080508T234536
3693     B  F  A DISK        08-MAY-08       1       1       YES

 TAG20080508T234536
3908     B  F  A DISK        09-MAY-08       1       1       YES

 TAG20080509T202532
3928     B  F  A DISK        09-MAY-08       1       1       NO

 TAG20080509T202558

RMAN> list script names;

List of Stored Scripts in Recovery Catalog

    Scripts of Target Database DW

      Script Name
```

```
    Description
    ----------------------------------------------------------
    local_backup_db


Global Scripts


    Script Name
    Description
    ----------------------------------------------------------
    backup_ts

    global_backup_db
RMAN>
```

Another variation on the LIST command is LIST FAILURE, which displays database failures; LIST FAILURE, ADVISE FAILURE, and REPAIR FAILURE are covered in Chapter 13.

Using the REPORT Command

In contrast to the LIST command, the REPORT command performs a more detailed analysis of the information in the recovery catalog, such as which files need more backups to comply with the defined retention policy. The next example changes the retention policy to two copies, and then queries the recovery catalog to see which datafiles don't have two copies:

```
RMAN> configure retention policy to redundancy 2;

old RMAN configuration parameters:
CONFIGURE RETENTION POLICY TO REDUNDANCY 1;
new RMAN configuration parameters:
CONFIGURE RETENTION POLICY TO REDUNDANCY 2;
new RMAN configuration parameters are successfully stored
starting full resync of recovery catalog
full resync complete

RMAN> report need backup;

RMAN retention policy will be applied to the command
RMAN retention policy is set to redundancy 2
```

```
Report of files with less than 2 redundant backups
File #bkps Name
---- ----- -------------------------------------------------------
1    1     +DATA/dw/datafile/system.256.630244579
3    1     +DATA/dw/datafile/undotbs1.258.630244583
5    1     +DATA/dw/datafile/example.265.630244801
6    1     +DATA/dw/datafile/users_crypt.267.630456963
7    1     +DATA/dw/datafile/inet_star.268.632004213
8    1     +DATA/dw/datafile/inet_intl_star.269.632009933
9    1     /u02/oradata/xport_dw.dbf
10   1     +DATA/dw/datafile/dmarts.271.633226419
```

RMAN>

As this report indicates, the datafiles for the USERS and SYSAUX tablespaces have enough backup copies to satisfy the retention policy.

This example finds out what the datafiles looked like back on 8/30/2007, and then queries the current status of the datafiles:

```
RMAN> report schema at time='30-aug-2007';

Report of database schema for database with db_unique_name DW

List of Permanent Datafiles
===========================
File Size(MB) Tablespace          RB segs Datafile Name
---- -------- ------------------- ------- -----------------------------
1    750      SYSTEM              YES
                                          +DATA/dw/datafile/system.256.630244579
2    829      SYSAUX              NO
                                          +DATA/dw/datafile/sysaux.257.630244581
3    60       UNDOTBS1            YES
                                          +DATA/dw/datafile/undotbs1.258.630244583
4    5        USERS               NO
                                          +DATA/dw/datafile/users.259.632441707
5    100      EXAMPLE             NO
                                          +DATA/dw/datafile/example.265.630244801
6    500      USERS_CRYPT         NO
                                          +DATA/dw/datafile/users_crypt.267.630456963

List of Temporary Files
=======================
File Size(MB) Tablespace          Maxsize(MB) Tempfile Name
```

```
---- -------- -------------------- ----------- ------------------------
1    60       TEMP                     32767
                                 +DATA/dw/tempfile/temp.264.630244787


RMAN> report schema;
Report of database schema for database with db_unique_name DW

List of Permanent Datafiles
===========================
File Size(MB) Tablespace           RB segs Datafile Name
---- -------- -------------------- ------- ------------------------
1    750      SYSTEM                   YES
                                 +DATA/dw/datafile/system.256.630244579
2    829      SYSAUX                   NO
                                 +DATA/dw/datafile/sysaux.257.630244581
3    60       UNDOTBS1                 YES
                                 +DATA/dw/datafile/undotbs1.258.630244583
4    5        USERS                    NO
                                 +DATA/dw/datafile/users.259.632441707
5    100      EXAMPLE                  NO
                                 +DATA/dw/datafile/example.265.630244801
6    500      USERS_CRYPT              NO
                                 +DATA/dw/datafile/users_crypt.267.630456963
7    100      INET_STAR                NO
                                 +DATA/dw/datafile/inet_star.268.632004213
8    50       INET_INTL_STAR           NO
                                 +DATA/dw/datafile/inet_intl_star.269.632009933
List of Temporary Files
=======================
File Size(MB) Tablespace           Maxsize(MB) Tempfile Name
---- -------- -------------------- ----------- --------------------
1    60       TEMP                     32767
                                 +DATA/dw/tempfile/temp.264.630244787
RMAN>
```

At some point between 8/30/2007 and today, the tablespaces INET_STAR and INET_INTL_STAR were created.

You can query the recovery catalog using Enterprise Manager Database Control (or Grid Control using Oracle RAC) as well. From the database home page, select the Availability tab, and click the Manage Current Backups link. You can see in Figure 4-3 the current list of backupsets and image copies recorded in the recovery catalog.

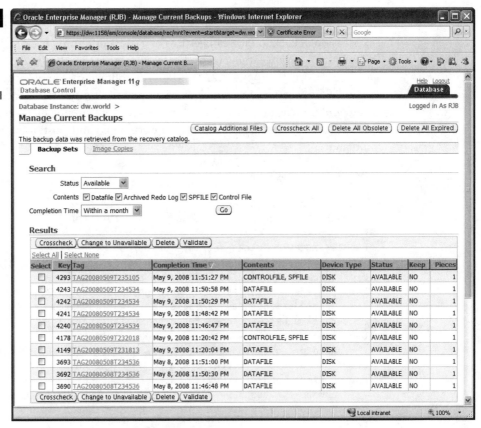

FIGURE 4-3

Querying
the recovery
catalog using EM
Database Control

Using the DELETE Command

Once you have identified which datafiles and archived redo log files are obsolete (as defined by your database's retention policy), you can remove them manually with the DELETE OBSOLETE command. You can remove obsolete files either one at a time or remove all obsolete backups using this command:

```
RMAN> delete noprompt obsolete;
```

Note that if you are using a flash recovery area, RMAN automatically removes obsolete files when the free space in the flash recovery area is low.

Using the CROSSCHECK Command

On occasion, a backup tape can get lost or a disk containing backup files can fail. To keep the recovery catalog up to date, you can use the CROSSCHECK command to mark the missing backups as EXPIRED. In the following example, a backup directory on the /u05 file system has failed. A backup of the USERS tablespace on this file system and the backup are recorded in the recovery catalog. To synchronize the recovery catalog with the backups that are still valid and exist, use the CROSSCHECK command:

```
RMAN> crosscheck backup;

using channel ORA_DISK_1
crosschecked backup piece: found to be 'AVAILABLE'
backup piece
handle=+RECOV/dw/backupset/2008_05_09/
    nnndf0_tag20080509t234534_0.430.654306351 RECID=590 STAMP=654306351
crosschecked backup piece: found to be 'AVAILABLE'
backup piece handle=+RECOV/dw/backupset/2008_05_09/
    nnndf0_tag20080509t234534_0.555.654306439 RECID=591 STAMP=654306439
crosschecked backup piece: found to be 'AVAILABLE'
backup piece handle=+RECOV/dw/backupset/2008_05_09/
    nnndf0_tag20080509t234534_0.558.654306543 RECID=592 STAMP=654306542
crosschecked backup piece: found to be 'AVAILABLE'
backup piece handle=+RECOV/dw/backupset/2008_05_09/
    nnndf0_tag20080509t234534_0.363.654306657 RECID=593 STAMP=654306656
crosschecked backup piece: found to be 'AVAILABLE'
backup piece handle=+RECOV/dw/autobackup/2008_05_09/
    s_654306665.566.654306687 RECID=594 STAMP=654306686
crosschecked backup piece: found to be 'EXPIRED'
backup piece handle=/u05/oradata/rmtbak/jojg18cv_1_1 RECID=595
STAMP=654352823
crosschecked backup piece: found to be 'AVAILABLE'
backup piece handle=+RECOV/dw/autobackup/2008_05_10/
s_654352833.562.654352853 RECID=596 STAMP=654352852
Crosschecked 7 objects

RMAN>
```

RMAN identifies the backup on /u05/oradata/rmtbak as EXPIRED. Once you have marked expired backups as EXPIRED in the recovery catalog with the

CROSSCHECK command, you can remove the entries in the recovery catalog by using the DELETE EXPIRED command:

```
RMAN> delete expired backup;

using channel ORA_DISK_1

List of Backup Pieces
BP Key  BS Key  Pc# Cp# Status       Device Type Piece Name
-------  -------  --- --- -----------  ----------- ----------
4560    4557    1   1   EXPIRED      DISK
                                     /u05/oradata/rmtbak/jojg18cv_1_1

Do you really want to delete the above objects (enter YES or NO)? yes
deleted backup piece
backup piece handle=/u05/oradata/rmtbak/
            jojg18cv_1_1 RECID=595 STAMP=654352823
Deleted 1 EXPIRED objects

RMAN>
```

Note that you don't always have to delete expired backups. If the disk or tape becomes available in the future, you can run CROSSCHECK again. RMAN will find the backup and mark it as AVAILABLE; as a result, it can be used again in a recovery operation.

CERTIFICATION SUMMARY

This chapter dove into the mechanics of performing backups after presenting a thorough introduction to the key features of RMAN: optimized backup compression, true incremental backups, parallel operations, and advanced scripting capabilities. There are very few situations in which a non-RMAN backup method is required or can back up your database quickly while the database is available to users.

The first part of the chapter covered the basics of creating a backupset (the default) or image copies. You can create image copies of database datafiles and archived redo logs using operating system commands. However, RMAN provides a number of advantages when performing an image copy, such as block verification and backupset compression and decompression. When compressing a backup, RMAN provides two different encryption methods depending on your available disk space and CPU contention.

Next, the chapter explained the somewhat subtle distinctions between a whole database backup, a full backup, and an incremental backup. A whole database backup is a snapshot of all datafiles, the control file, and all archived redo log files. In contrast, a full backup is a complete backup of one or more individual database objects and cannot participate in an incremental backup strategy. Incremental backups can be level 0 or level 1. Level 0 backups are logically equivalent to full backups but can be used as the base for level 1 incremental backups, which can be either cumulative or differential.

RMAN has a number of features to make your backups more reliable and take less time to complete. Incremental backups use a block change tracking file to identify which data blocks have changed since the last incremental backup. As a result, RMAN does not have to read all blocks in every datafile to successfully back up only the changed blocks. Duplexed backups decrease the amount of time it takes to make simultaneous multiple copies of datafiles. You can send one copy to a local disk at the same time you send another copy to an offsite disk, all in less time than it takes to make two sequential backups or a local backup, followed by a copy of the backup to an offsite location. To further decrease the time it takes to complete your backups, RMAN can skip backing up a read-only tablespace by using the `SKIP READONLY` option or by configuring backup optimization.

Archival backups, another new RMAN feature as of Oracle Database 11g, are backups that never expire and provide a snapshot of your database for regulatory compliance. Because they provide a snapshot of your database at a point of time in the past with a specific retention time or an indefinite retention time, you keep your recovery area clean of archived redo log files that would otherwise have to remain in your flash recovery area for an equivalent recovery window.

Multisection RMAN backups give you the flexibility to back up and validate backups of very large datafiles in sections. In previous versions, large datafiles (such as those found in bigfile tablespaces) took a prohibitively long amount of time to back up because RMAN could allocate only one thread to back up the datafile sequentially.

To enhance the security of your backups, RMAN can use either password-based or wallet-based encryption, or it can use both at the same time. Wallet-based encryption is the preferred method, but in cases where you must restore your datafiles to another database, providing a strong password keeps the backup secure until you are ready to restore it into a target database.

Finally, you were introduced to two commands used to query the contents of your recovery catalog: the LIST and REPORT commands. The LIST command gives you a high-level view of your backups, including backupsets, image copies, and stored scripts. The REPORT command gives you a more in-depth analysis of your backups, such as identifying missing backups or database objects that need to be backed up again to satisfy your configured retention policy. Once you identify any extra backups, you can use the DELETE command to remove them. You can also use the DELETE command to remove backups from the recovery catalog that have been identified as missing with the CROSSCHECK command.

✓ TWO-MINUTE DRILL

Create Image File Backups

❑ RMAN backups are either backupsets or image backups.

❑ Backupsets can be created only by RMAN and can be read only by RMAN.

❑ The FORMAT clause of the BACKUP command specifies the substitution variables for the destination backup filename.

❑ You can create image copies of datafiles, archived redo log files, and control files.

❑ Image copies can be written only to disk.

❑ You can use the SWITCH command to quickly and easily switch between a datafile and its image copy during a recovery operation.

Create a Whole Database Backup

❑ A whole database backup includes all datafiles plus the control file.

❑ A full backup of a datafile is a logical subset of a whole database backup.

❑ A full backup cannot be used as the basis for an incremental backup strategy.

❑ An incremental backup is level 0 or level 1.

❑ An incremental level 0 backup can be used as the basis for an incremental backup strategy.

❑ Differential backups back up all changed blocks since the last level 0 or level 1 incremental backup.

❑ Cumulative incremental backups back up all changed blocks since the last level 0 backup.

Enable Fast Incremental Backup

❑ Enable fast incremental backup by creating a block change tracking file.

❑ Perform a level 0 incremental backup before configuring RMAN to use a block change tracking file.

❑ The data dictionary view V$BLOCK_CHANGE_TRACKING provides the name and status of the block change tracking file.

Create Duplex Backup and Back Up Backupsets

❑ Duplexed backupsets can significantly reduce the time it takes to create multiple copies of the same backup.

❑ Backups cannot be duplexed to the flash recovery area, and you cannot duplex image copies.

❑ Use the BACKUP . . . BACKUPSET commands to create a copy of an existing RMAN backup to disk or tape.

❑ RMAN will skip the backup of read-only tablespaces if you use SKIP READONLY in the BACKUP command.

❑ If you configure RMAN for backup optimization, RMAN will back up only additional copies of read-only tablespaces to satisfy the configured retention policy.

Create an Archival Backup for Long-term Retention

❑ An archival backup is a snapshot of the database at a certain point in time created to satisfy archival or regulatory purposes.

❑ Archival backups make it easy to migrate a copy of the database to another system without affecting the retention policy of the original database.

❑ To create an archival backup, you specify either the KEEP UNTIL TIME or KEEP FOREVER option in the BACKUP command.

❑ An RMAN archival backup also includes any archived logs required to use the backup in a recovery scenario.

❑ You can use the CHANGE command to change the status of an archival backup.

Create a Multisection, Compressed, and Encrypted Backup

❑ Multisection RMAN backups can significantly reduce the time it takes to back up very large datafiles to multiple destinations.

❑ You can run the VALIDATE command in multisection mode.

❑ The SECTION SIZE parameter determines the size for each section in a multisection backup or validate operation.

❑ The V$BACKUP_SET and RC_BACKUP_SET views contain a MULTI_SECTION column to indicate whether the backup is a multisection backup.

❑ The V$BACKUP_DATAFILE and RC_BACKUP_DATAFILE views contain a SECTION_SIZE column that contains the number of blocks in each piece of a multisection backup.

❑ RMAN can compress backups of used blocks using BZIP2 or ZLIB.

❑ ZLIB is faster but compresses less. BZIP2 is slower but compresses more.

❑ Transparent encryption uses a database wallet to encrypt a backup, and the backup can be restored only to the source database.

❑ Password encryption uses a password to encrypt a backup, and the backup can be restored either to the source database or another database.

❑ You can use both transparent encryption and password encryption on the same backup.

❑ Transparent encryption can be enabled for a single backup using the SET ENCRYPTION command.

Report On and Maintain Backups

❑ The LIST command provides basic information about the availability of backupsets, image copies, proxy copies, and stored scripts.

❑ The REPORT command provides a more detailed analysis of the backup information in the recovery catalog.

❑ You can use the REPORT command to identify obsolete backups.

❑ You can use the REPORT command to identify datafiles that need more backup copies to satisfy the retention policy.

❑ The CROSSCHECK command validates the backup entries in the recovery catalog versus the existence of the actual backups on disk or tape.

❑ The DELETE OBSOLETE command removes obsolete backups from the recovery catalog and the backup location.

❑ You can remove EXPIRED backups with the DELETE EXPIRED command.

SELF TEST

The following questions will help you measure your understanding of the material presented in this chapter. Read all the choices carefully as there might be more than one correct answer. Choose all correct answers for each question.

Create Image File Backups

1. Which of the following is the default substitution variable for the FORMAT clause of the BACKUP command?
   A. %t
   B. %d
   C. %u
   D. %U
   E. %I

2. Which of the following are candidates for RMAN image copies? (Choose two answers.)
   A. Datafiles
   B. Archived redo log files
   C. Online redo log files
   D. Password files

3. The tablespace BI_HR in your database is on a disk that has crashed, but you have an image copy plus all required redo log files in the flash recovery area. Put the following sequence of RMAN commands in the correct order to recover the BI_HR tablespace successfully:
   1. recover tablespace bi_hr;
   2. sql "alter tablespace bi_hr online";
   3. switch tablespace bi_hr to copy;
   4. sql "alter tablespace bi_hr offline immediate";
   A. 4, 3, 2, 1
   B. 4, 3, 1, 2
   C. 3, 4, 1, 2
   D. 4, 1, 3, 2

Create a Whole Database Backup

4. You run the following command to create a whole database backup:
   ```
   RMAN> backup as copy database spfile plus archivelog delete input;
   ```
   What does the DELETE INPUT clause do?
   A. After the backup completes, RMAN deletes the archived log files from all archived log file destinations except for the flash recovery area.
   B. After the backup completes, RMAN deletes the archived log files from the flash recovery area only.
   C. After the backup completes, RMAN deletes the archived log files from the flash recovery area and any other archived log file destinations.
   D. RMAN deletes all obsolete copies of database backups after the backup completes.

5. What is the difference between a full backup and a whole database backup? (Choose the best answer.)
   A. A whole database backup can be used as the basis for an incremental backup strategy but a full database backup cannot.
   B. A full database backup can be used as the basis for an incremental backup strategy but a whole database backup cannot.
   C. A whole database backup can only be an image copy. A full backup can be an image copy or a backupset.
   D. A full backup consists of a backup of one or more datafiles or tablespaces, whereas a whole database backup contains all datafiles, for all tablespaces plus the control file.

6. What is true about a level 0 incremental backup? (Choose all correct answers.)
   A. A level 0 backup includes all blocks in a datafile, including blocks that have never been used.
   B. A level 0 backup includes all blocks in a datafile, except for blocks that have never been used.
   C. A level 0 backup can be used with a level 1 cumulative backup.
   D. A level 0 backup can be used with a level 1 differential backup.
   E. A level 0 backup of a datafile has additional information that differentiates it from a full backup of the same datafile.

7. Identify the true statement regarding incremental and differential backups.
   A. A differential backup is the default type of incremental backup and backs up all changed blocks since the last level 0 or level 1 incremental backup.
   B. A cumulative backup is the default type of incremental backup and backs up all changed blocks since the last level 0 or level 1 incremental backup.

C. A differential backup is the default type of incremental backup and backs up all changed blocks since the last level 0 incremental backup.

D. A cumulative backup is the default type of incremental backup and backs up all changed blocks since the last level 1 incremental backup.

Enable Fast Incremental Backup

8. What method does RMAN use to enable fast incremental backup? (Choose the best answer.)

A. It uses differential incremental level 1 backups.

B. It uses a block change tracking file.

C. It uses duplexed backupsets.

D. It uses whole database backups as the basis for an incremental backup.

9. You create a block change tracking file for your database. What happens if you run the following command? (Choose the best answer.)

```
RMAN> backup incremental level 1 database;
```

A. The command fails because you need to run a level 0 backup first to initialize the block change tracking file.

B. A level 0 incremental backup automatically runs before the level 1 backup so that RMAN initializes the block change tracking file.

C. RMAN generates a warning message indicating that the block change tracking file needs to be initialized.

D. The backup runs successfully but does not use the block change tracking file.

Create Duplex Backup and Back Up Backupsets

10. When you want to create a duplexed backupset, what is the maximum number of copies of each backup piece you can create with one BACKUP command?

A. Two for disk locations and four for tape destinations.

B. A maximum of four.

C. Two for tape locations and four for disk locations.

D. The maximum is limited only by the number of destination disks or tape drives.

11. Which of the following duplexed backups will run successfully? (Choose all correct answers.)

A. An image copy duplexed to four tape drives

B. A backupset duplexed to two tape drives

C. A backupset duplexed to eight NAS disks

D. An image copy duplexed to four disk drives

E. A backupset duplexed to two file systems on different servers

Create an Archival Backup for Long-term Retention

12. Identify the true statements regarding archival backups. (Choose all correct answers.)

A. Archival backups can be retained indefinitely.

B. You can drop an archival backup using the CHANGE . . . DROP command.

C. Archival backups include all archived redo logs from the archival date to the present.

D. Once you create an archival backup, you must either keep it for the retention period specified or drop it.

E. You can use an archival backup to migrate a copy of the database without affecting the retention policy.

F. You can change the retention period of an archival backup once it has been created.

Create a Multisection, Compressed, and Encrypted Backup

13. You have a datafile from the smallfile tablespace USERS that has a size of 90MB and you run the following RMAN command:

```
RMAN> backup tablespace users section size 40m;
```

How many sections does this backup create?

A. The command does not run because multisection backups apply only to bigfile tablespaces.

B. Two sections of 45MB each.

C. Two sections of 40MB each and one section of 10MB.

D. The command does not run because you can only back up the entire database as a multisection backup.

14. Identify the true statement about the dynamic performance and data dictionary views related to multisection backups.

A. The views V$BACKUP_SET and RC_BACKUP_SET have a column named MULTI_SECTION. The views V$BACKUP_DATAFILE and RC_BACKUP_DATAFILE have a column named SECTION_SIZE.

B. The views V$BACKUP_SET and RC_BACKUP_SET have a column named SECTION_SIZE. The views V$BACKUP_DATAFILE and RC_BACKUP_DATAFILE have a column named MULTI_SECTION.

C. The views V$BACKUP_SET and V$BACKUP_DATAFILE have a column named MULTI_SECTION. The views RC_BACKUP_SET and RC_BACKUP_DATAFILE have a column named SECTION_SIZE.

D. The views V$BACKUP_SET and V$BACKUP_DATAFILE have a column named SECTION_SIZE. The views RC_BACKUP_SET and RC_BACKUP_DATAFILE have a column named MULTI_SECTION.

Report On and Maintain Backups

15. Which RMAN command would you use to find out which datafiles need another backup to satisfy the retention policy?

A. REPORT NEED BACKUP

B. LIST NEED BACKUP

C. CROSSCHECK NEED BACKUP

D. CONFIGURE RETENTION POLICY

16. One of your backups to disk is missing, and after you run the CROSSCHECK command, this backup is marked as EXPIRED. Later, you find the backup file on another disk and move it back to its original location. You run the CROSSCHECK command again. What is the status of the backup?

A. The backup is marked as OBSOLETE.

B. The backup is marked as AVAILABLE.

C. The backup is still marked as EXPIRED until the next incremental backup.

D. You cannot change the status of a backup unless it is stored in the flash recovery area.

SELF TEST ANSWERS

Create Image File Backups

1. ☑ **D.** %U is the default and is a system-generated unique filename that is equivalent to %u_%p_%c.
    ☒ **A, B, C,** and **E** are wrong. These choices are valid in the FORMAT command but are not the default.

2. ☑ **A** and **B.** In addition to datafiles and archived redo log files, you can also create image copies of control files.
    ☒ **C** and **D** cannot be backed up as image copies. In fact, they cannot be backed up using RMAN.

3. ☑ **B.** All of these commands can be run at the RMAN prompt and successfully make the BI_HR tablespace once again available to users.
    ☒ **A, C,** and **D** do not correctly recover the tablespace using image copies.

Create a Whole Database Backup

4. ☑ **C.** When the backup completes successfully, RMAN deletes all archived redo log files from all destinations including the flash recovery area.
    ☒ **A** and **B** are wrong because RMAN deletes archived redo log files from all destinations. **D** is wrong because the DELETE INPUT command applies only to archived redo log files that apply to this backup.

5. ☑ **D.** A whole database backup can also include archived redo log files and the SPFILE.
    ☒ **A** and **B** are wrong because either can be the basis for an incremental backup strategy as long as you use the INCREMENTAL LEVEL 0 parameter in the BACKUP command. **C** is wrong because both a whole database backup and a full backup can be image copies or backupsets.

6. ☑ **B, C,** and **D.** A level 0 backup includes all blocks in a datafile, except for blocks that have never been used. It also can be used with both cumulative and incremental level 1 backups.
    ☒ **A** is wrong because a level 0 backup excludes blocks that have never been used. **E** is wrong because a level 0 backup is physically identical to full backup of the same datafile; the differentiation is the metadata stored in the recovery catalog.

7. ☑ **A.** A differential backup is the default and backs up all changed blocks since the last level 0 or level 1 backup. You cannot specify the DIFFERENTIAL keyword, which is the default.
    ☒ **B** is wrong because a cumulative backup is not the default and it backs up only changed blocks since the last level 0 backup. **C** is wrong because differential backups also back up changed blocks from the last level 1 incremental backup. **D** is wrong because a cumulative backup is not the default type of incremental backup and it backs up only changed blocks since the last level 0 backup.

Enable Fast Incremental Backup

8. ☑ **B.** RMAN uses a block change tracking file to indicate which blocks need to be backed up since the last level 0 incremental backup.

☒ **A** is wrong because even though differential incremental backups reduce the backup time, this is not the mechanism for determining which blocks have been changed since the last level 0 backup. **C** and **D** are wrong for the same reason.

9. ☑ **D.** Even though the block change tracking file exists, RMAN does not use it until after you run the first level 0 incremental backup.

☒ **A** is wrong because even though the block change tracking file is not used, the backup still runs successfully. **B** is wrong because RMAN will not automatically run a level 0 backup. **C** is wrong because RMAN uses or does not use the block change tracking file transparently.

Create Duplex Backup and Back Up Backupsets

10. ☑ **B.** RMAN creates a maximum of four copies for disk or tape locations.

☒ **A, C,** and **D** are wrong. There is no differentiation between tape and disk for duplexed backups, and the range is from two to four.

11. ☑ **B** and **E.** Duplexed backups can include only backupsets and cannot reside in the flash recovery area.

☒ **A** and **D** are wrong because you cannot duplex image copies. **C** is wrong since you can duplex only four copies in one backup.

Create an Archival Backup for Long-term Retention

12. ☑ **A, E,** and **F.** Archival backups can be kept for an indefinite period of time or retained for a specific period of time using the KEEP UNTIL clause. In addition, you can use an archival backup to migrate a database, and you can change the retention period as many times as you need to after you create it.

☒ **B** is wrong since the correct clause is CHANGE . . . NOKEEP. **C** is wrong because only the archived redo logs necessary for the snapshot are included in the backup. **D** is wrong because you can easily change the retention period for any archival backup.

Create a Multisection, Compressed, and Encrypted Backup

13. ☑ **C.** RMAN backs up the datafile in multiples of the section size and any remainder resides in the last section.

☒ **A** is wrong because you can use multisection backups for any type of tablespace. **B** is wrong because RMAN does not round up the section size to create equal section sizes in the output.

D is wrong because you can back up either an individual tablespace or the entire database as a multisection backup.

14. ☑ **A.** `SECTION_SIZE` indicates the section size for the backup piece. `MULTI_SECTION` has a value of `YES` or `NO` to indicate if the backup is a multisection backup.

   ☒ **B, C,** and **D** are wrong. Each of these answers has an invalid combination of columns and their associated views.

Report on and Maintain Backups

15. ☑ **A.** The `REPORT NEED BACKUP` command identifies any datafiles that need at least one additional backup to satisfy the configured retention policy.

   ☒ **B** and **C** are syntactically incorrect. **D** defines the retention policy for your database but does not determine which datafiles do not have enough backups to satisfy the retention policy.

16. ☑ **B.** When the `CROSSCHECK` command runs again, it finds the file in its original location and marks it as `AVAILABLE`.

   ☒ **A** is wrong because backups are marked as `OBSOLETE` only when a more recent backup runs and identifies older backups as outside of the retention policy. **C** is wrong because the `CROSSCHECK` command immediately changes the status for any backups that are now available. **D** is wrong because a backup's status is independent of where it is stored.

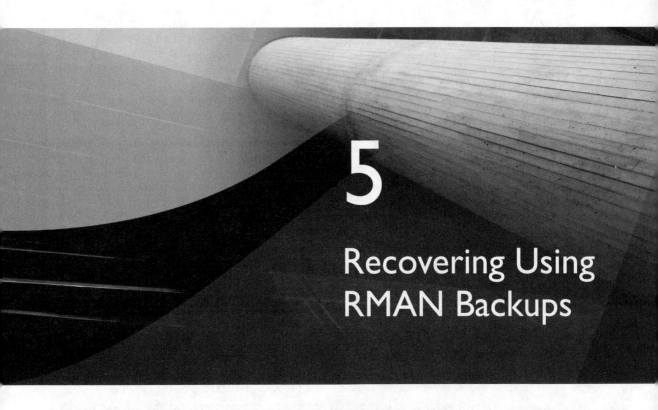

5
Recovering Using RMAN Backups

I n this chapter, you will learn how to use RMAN in a recovery scenario. This is required if you have lost a noncritical datafile, a critical datafile, a control file, or possibly the entire database.

This chapter addresses recovery scenarios for a database running in ARCHIVELOG mode. Of course, if it isn't apparent by now, you should be running in ARCHIVELOG mode, considering all the advantages and the relatively few disadvantages presented in previous chapters. However, if you are not running in ARCHIVELOG mode, your recovery options are also presented as well as those for NOARCHIVELOG mode.

Image copies play an important role in your backup and recovery scenarios. You'll learn how to recover an image copy to make it even faster to recover your database in case of media failure. In addition, you'll see how to switch to an image copy and then switch back.

Once you create your backups, you want to make sure that you can use them to recover your database. You'll learn how to restore a database to a new host either to test your recovery scenarios or move a production database to the new host.

Finally, you'll learn how to perform incomplete recovery and recover your database up to a point in time in the past. This is useful when you have logical corruption in your database, including but not limited to user errors or DBA errors that would merely be re-created with a full recovery. An incomplete recovery also assumes that you can not use other less drastic options, such as using Oracle's flashback table functionality or using SELECT . . . AS OF.

CERTIFICATION OBJECTIVE 5.01

Perform Complete Recovery from a Critical or Noncritical Data File Loss Using RMAN

In the following sections, you'll learn how to use the RESTORE and RECOVER commands for a database running in ARCHIVELOG mode. First, you'll read about the basic functions of RESTORE and RECOVER and how they work. Next, you'll see how to recover both a noncritical and a critical datafile successfully.

Using the RMAN RESTORE and RECOVER Commands

In general, recovering from a database failure is a two-step process: restoring one or more database files from a backup location and applying archived and online redo log files to bring the entire database or individual datafile up to the specified System Change Number (SCN), which is usually the most recent SCN (the last committed transaction).

The RESTORE command is the first step in any recovery process. When you issue a RESTORE command, RMAN retrieves one or more datafiles from disk or tape along with any archived redo log files required during the recovery operation. If your backup files are on tape, you will need to allocate the necessary tape channels as well.

When you issue the RECOVER command, RMAN applies the committed changes in the archived and online redo log files to the restored datafiles. A disaster recovery scenario is called for when most database datafiles are lost or corrupted. The recovery process can be as simple as the following example (command output excluded for clarity):

```
SQL> shutdown immediate;
SQL> startup mount;
[oracle@srv04 ~]$ rman target / catalog rman/rman@rcat
RMAN> restore database;
RMAN> recover database;
RMAN> sql 'alter database open';
```

Using the Database Control to perform a recovery operation is almost as easy. As you can see in Figure 5-1, the steps you perform are straightforward but might not be as easy as typing two or three SQL and RMAN commands.

The recovery process is slightly different, depending on whether you lose a critical or a noncritical datafile. If you lose a critical datafile, you must shut down and start up the database in MOUNT mode before you can recover the database. For a noncritical datafile, you can perform the recovery while users are connected and using other available datafiles.

Performing Complete Recovery of a Noncritical Datafile

If you lose a datafile that is not a part of the SYSTEM or UNDO tablespace, the datafile is considered noncritical (although the users of the lost datafile might disagree with this assessment). When the database is in ARCHIVELOG mode, a corrupted or missing datafile that is not part of the SYSTEM or UNDO tablespace affects only objects in the corrupted or missing datafile.

FIGURE 5-1

Recovering
a database using
the Database
Control

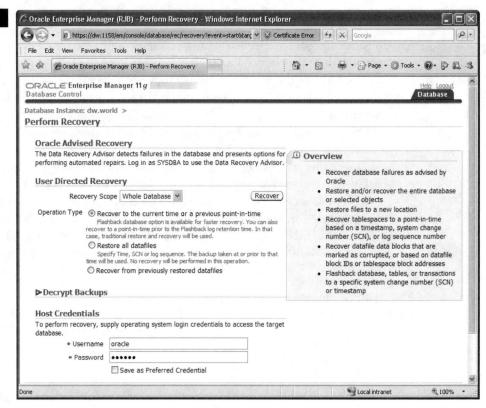

The general steps to recover a datafile from a noncritical tablespace are as follows:

1. If the database is open, take the tablespace containing the corrupted or missing datafile offline with the ALTER TABLESPACE command.

2. Use the RMAN RESTORE command to load the datafile(s) for the tablespace from the backup location.

3. Use the RMAN RECOVER command to apply archived and online redo log files to the restored datafile(s).

4. Bring the tablespace back online.

Because the database is in ARCHIVELOG mode, recovery up to the last committed transaction is possible. In other words, users do not have to re-enter any data for previously committed transactions.

EXERCISE 5-1

Restore and Recover the USERS Tablespace

In this exercise, the datafile for the USERS tablespace was accidentally deleted by the system administrator. Restore and recover the tablespace while the database is still open for access to the other tablespaces.

1. Connect to RMAN and take the USERS tablespace offline:

```
RMAN> sql "alter tablespace users offline immediate";
sql statement: alter tablespace users offline immediate
RMAN>
```

Any users trying to access the tablespace while it is offline will receive a message similar to the following:

```
SQL> select * from sales_data;
                 *
ERROR at line 1:
ORA-00376: file 4 cannot be read at this time
ORA-01110: data file 4: '/u01/app/oracle/oradata/hr/users01.dbf'

SQL>
```

2. Restore the USERS tablespace:

```
RMAN> restore tablespace users;

Starting restore at 24-MAY-08
allocated channel: ORA_DISK_1
channel ORA_DISK_1: SID=129 device type=DISK

channel ORA_DISK_1: starting datafile backup set restore
channel ORA_DISK_1: specifying datafile(s) to restore from backup set
channel ORA_DISK_1: restoring datafile 00004 to
        /u01/app/oracle/oradata/hr/users01.dbf
channel ORA_DISK_1: reading from backup piece
/u01/oradata/bkup/1sjh6l0u_1_1
channel ORA_DISK_1: piece handle=/u01/oradata/bkup/1sjh6l0u_1_1
                             tag=TAG20080524T170221
channel ORA_DISK_1: restored backup piece 1
channel ORA_DISK_1: restore complete, elapsed time: 00:00:15
Finished restore at 24-MAY-08
RMAN>
```

3. Recover the USERS tablespace to apply the archived and online redo log files:

```
RMAN> recover tablespace users;

Starting recover at 24-MAY-08
using channel ORA_DISK_1

starting media recovery
media recovery complete, elapsed time: 00:00:00

Finished recover at 24-MAY-08

RMAN>
```

4. Bring the USERS tablespace back online:

```
RMAN> sql "alter tablespace users online";

sql statement: alter tablespace users online

RMAN>
```

5. Confirm that users can once again access the USERS tablespace:

```
SQL> select * from sales_data;

SALES_ID SALE_DATE TRAN_AMT
-------- --------- --------
     202 15-MAR-08  1402.12
 . . .
```

Performing Complete Recovery of a Critical Datafile

The procedure for recovering a critical datafile is similar to that of a noncritical datafile, except that the database must be shut down and opened in the MOUNT state to perform the recovery operation. If the lost datafile is from the SYSTEM tablespace, the instance will most likely crash or shut down automatically. Here are the steps you use to recover a critical datafile:

1. Shut down the database with SHUTDOWN ABORT if it is not already shut down.

2. Reopen the database with STARTUP MOUNT.

3. Use the RMAN RESTORE command to copy (restore) the datafile(s) for the critical tablespace from the backup location.

4. Use the RMAN RECOVER command to apply any archived or online redo log files.

5. Reopen the database for users with ALTER DATABASE OPEN.

All committed transactions are recovered up until the time of failure, so users will not have to re-enter any data. In the case of the SYSTEM tablespace, you may not have any user transactions but you will not lose any new objects created since the last backup.

CERTIFICATION OBJECTIVE 5.02

Perform Incomplete Recovery Using RMAN

On occasion, you might need to restore a database to a point of time in the past. For example, applications could have made numerous erroneous changes to the database in the last 24 hours, and you may not be able to reverse errors easily with a table flashback, or perhaps you do not have flashback configured for the database.

Using restore points makes it easier to perform point-in-time recovery, whether you're performing incomplete recovery in RMAN or flashback database. After you learn about restore points, you'll perform an incomplete recovery using a restore point.

Creating Restore Points

You can create two types of restore points—either as of a specific time or with an SCN number in the past. Which type you use depends on your environment and which option is the more convenient. If you do not specify either option, Oracle uses the current SCN and assumes you want the restore time to be the current time. Remember that you can retrieve the current SCN from V$DATABASE:

```
SQL> select current_scn from v$database;

CURRENT_SCN
```

```
-----------
  34674668
```

SQL>

To create a restore point for the present time or SCN, use this format of the CREATE RESTORE POINT command:

```
SQL> create restore point good_for_now;

Restore point created.
```

SQL>

To create a restore point for a particular SCN, use the AS OF syntax:

```
SQL> create restore point good_for_now as of scn 34674668;

Restore point created.
```

SQL>

on the **j o b**

Restore points are also useful when you want to use Oracle's flashback technology to flash back a table or the database to a point in time in the past.

Oracle keeps restore points for at least as long as the time specified in the CONTROL_FILE_RECORD_KEEP_TIME initialization parameter. If you explicitly want to keep a restore point longer, use the PRESERVE keyword when you create the restore point:

```
SQL> create restore point good_for_now preserve;

Restore point created.
```

SQL>

As you might expect, you can explicitly remove a restore point with the DROP RESTORE POINT command:

```
SQL> drop restore point good_for_now;
```

```
Restore point dropped.

SQL>
```

Performing Server-Managed Incomplete Recovery

To perform server-managed (RMAN) incomplete recovery (as opposed to user-managed recovery, covered in Chapter 6), use the following steps:

1. Determine the target point for the restore (SCN, time, restore point, or log sequence number).

2. Set the NLS variables at the operating system prompt if you are using time-based incomplete recovery:

   ■ NLS_LANG

   ■ NLS_DATE_FORMAT

3. Stop and restart the database in MOUNT mode.

4. Using an RMAN RUN block, use the SET UNTIL, RESTORE, and RECOVER commands.

5. Optionally, open the database in READ ONLY mode to verify that the restore point was the desired restore point.

6. Open the database using RESETLOGS.

It's important to specify the correct NLS variables so that RMAN will interpret the date strings you provide correctly; here are some sample values:

```
$ export NLS_LANG = american_america.us7ascii
$ export NLS_DATE_FORMAT = "Mon DD YYYY HH24:MI:SS"
```

Also note that opening the database as READ ONLY after your incomplete recovery gives you the opportunity to run another incomplete recovery for an SCN or a time before or after your original SCN, or time. Once you open the database for read/write with RESETLOGS, the current log sequence is set to 1 and any redo information not applied during recovery is discarded. This prevents you from performing another recovery using a redo generated after the SCN or timestamp of your incomplete recovery.

Perform Incomplete Recovery to Restore the USERS Tablespace

In this exercise, you will create a restore point and use it later to recover from the inadvertent deletion of tables and views in the EXAMPLE tablespace.

1. Create a restore point for the current SCN:

```
SQL> create restore point before_disaster_strikes;

Restore point created.

SQL>
```

2. "Accidentally" drop some tables and views in the EXAMPLE tablespace:

```
SQL> drop table hr.job_history;

Table dropped.

SQL> drop view hr.emp_details_view;

View dropped.

SQL>
```

3. Shut down the instance and restart the database in MOUNT mode:

```
SQL> shutdown immediate
Database closed.
Database dismounted.
ORACLE instance shut down.
SQL> startup mount
ORACLE instance started.

Total System Global Area  636100608 bytes
Fixed Size                  1301784 bytes
Variable Size             490734312 bytes
Database Buffers          138412032 bytes
Redo Buffers                5652480 bytes
Database mounted.
SQL>
```

4. At the RMAN prompt, create a RUN block that uses the restore point created earlier to restore and recover the database to the time of the restore point:

```
RMAN> run
2>    {
3>       set until restore point before_disaster_strikes;
4>       restore database;
5>       recover database;
6>    }

executing command: SET until clause
starting full resync of recovery catalog
full resync complete

Starting restore at 25-MAY-08
allocated channel: ORA_DISK_1
channel ORA_DISK_1: SID=151 device type=DISK
channel ORA_DISK_1: starting datafile backup set restore
channel ORA_DISK_1: specifying datafile(s) to restore from backup set
channel ORA_DISK_1: restoring datafile 00001 to
      /u01/app/oracle/oradata/hr/system01.dbf
channel ORA_DISK_1: restoring datafile 00002 to
      /u01/app/oracle/oradata/hr/sysaux01.dbf
channel ORA_DISK_1: restoring datafile 00003 to
      /u01/app/oracle/oradata/hr/undotbs01.dbf
channel ORA_DISK_1: restoring datafile 00004 to
      /u01/app/oracle/oradata/hr/users01.dbf
channel ORA_DISK_1: restoring datafile 00005 to
      /u01/app/oracle/oradata/hr/example01.dbf
channel ORA_DISK_1: reading from backup piece
/u01/oradata/bkup/1ujh9bkl_1_1
channel ORA_DISK_1: piece handle=/u01/oradata/bkup/1ujh9bkl_1_1
                  tag=TAG20080525T174036
channel ORA_DISK_1: restored backup piece 1
channel ORA_DISK_1: restore complete, elapsed time: 00:03:27
Finished restore at 25-MAY-08

Starting recover at 25-MAY-08
using channel ORA_DISK_1

starting media recovery
media recovery complete, elapsed time: 00:00:12

Finished recover at 25-MAY-08

RMAN>
```

5. Open the database with RESETLOGS:

```
SQL> alter database open resetlogs;

Database altered.

SQL>
```

6. Verify the existence of the dropped table:

```
SQL> select * from hr.job_history;
```

EMPLOYEE_ID	START_DAT	END_DATE	JOB_ID	DEPARTMENT_ID
102	13-JAN-93	24-JUL-98	IT_PROG	60
101	21-SEP-89	27-OCT-93	AC_ACCOUNT	110
101	28-OCT-93	15-MAR-97	AC_MGR	110
201	17-FEB-96	19-DEC-99	MK_REP	20
114	24-MAR-98	31-DEC-99	ST_CLERK	50
122	01-JAN-99	31-DEC-99	ST_CLERK	50
200	17-SEP-87	17-JUN-93	AD_ASST	90
176	24-MAR-98	31-DEC-98	SA_REP	80
176	01-JAN-99	31-DEC-99	SA_MAN	80
200	01-JUL-94	31-DEC-98	AC_ACCOUNT	90

```
10 rows selected.

SQL>
```

Note that several less draconian methods are available to restore and recover these tables and views, such as flashback database, restoring and recovering each tablespace while the database is still online, or retrieving the tables from the recycle bin. Each recovery situation must be evaluated separately, balancing these factors:

- The time required to obtain the backup files needed for recovery. If backup files are on a tape offsite, then the time required could be unacceptable.
- The time to restore and recover the entire database once the recovery files are available.
- The time the DBA must spend to perform the recovery.
- The time the users must spend to re-enter lost data.
- The tolerance for database downtime.

Recover Using Incrementally Updated Backups

Using image copies in your backup and recovery strategy significantly reduces the time it takes to restore a datafile or the entire database. Image copies are already in the native Oracle datafile format and do not need to be re-created from a compressed or uncompressed RMAN backupset. RMAN can improve on this even more, because you can incrementally update an image copy using an incremental backup. In the following sections, you'll learn more about how to recover an image copy, and you'll review a sample image copy strategy.

Recovering Image Copies

When you update an image copy with an incremental backup, any recovery scenario that uses the image copy needs to apply only the archived and online redo log files since the last incremental backup. There is no longer any need to perform another full image copy of the datafile or database. The incremental recovery of each datafile is indistinguishable from a full image copy.

If more than one image copy of a datafile exists, RMAN automatically determines which one to use—usually the most recently created or incrementally updated version. If the recovery process for an image copy fails when applying an incremental backup, such as the temporary unavailability of the incremental backup, just restart the recovery process when the incremental backup is available again. RMAN picks up where it left off.

Implementing an Image Copy Strategy

Here is a sample RMAN script to implement an incrementally updated image copy strategy on a daily basis, after you've created the image copy of the entire database:

```
run {
    recover copy of database
       with tag 'inc_upd';
    backup incremental level 1
       for recover of copy
       with tag 'inc_upd'
       database;
}
```

Here's a breakdown of what happens in this RUN block. The first time you run it, there is no level 0 image copy to restore and, similarly, no level 0 incremental backup yet, so you get these messages:

```
Starting recover at 25-MAY-08
using channel ORA_DISK_1
no copy of datafile 1 found to recover
no copy of datafile 2 found to recover
no copy of datafile 3 found to recover
no copy of datafile 4 found to recover
no copy of datafile 5 found to recover
Finished recover at 25-MAY-08

Starting backup at 25-MAY-08
using channel ORA_DISK_1
no parent backup or copy of datafile 2 found
no parent backup or copy of datafile 1 found
no parent backup or copy of datafile 3 found
no parent backup or copy of datafile 5 found
no parent backup or copy of datafile 4 found
channel ORA_DISK_1: starting datafile copy
. . .
```

RMAN automatically creates a level 0 backup whenever a level 1 backup occurs and there is no level 0 backup. The next time you run the script, the level 0 backup exists but no incremental level 0 backup exists yet. So the RECOVER command in the RUN block still generates these messages:

```
Starting recover at 25-MAY-08
using channel ORA_DISK_1
no copy of datafile 1 found to recover
no copy of datafile 2 found to recover
no copy of datafile 3 found to recover
no copy of datafile 4 found to recover
no copy of datafile 5 found to recover
Finished recover at 25-MAY-08

Starting backup at 25-MAY-08
using channel ORA_DISK_1
channel ORA_DISK_1: starting incremental level 1 datafile backup set
. . .
```

On the third and successive invocations of this RUN block, the RECOVER command updates the image copy with the latest level 1 backup, and another level 1 incremental backup occurs. This will be applied the next time this RUN block is executed. As a result, any recovery operation after the third invocation of this script will involve no more than the image copies, one incremental backup, and any archived and online redo logs generated since the last level 1 incremental backup.

on the job

Be sure to use tags with an incrementally updated image copy strategy. Without tags, a more recent, and possibly incorrect, incremental backup would be used to recover the image copies.

CERTIFICATION OBJECTIVE 5.04

Switch to Image Copies for Fast Recovery

Once you've starting making image copies, and even incrementally updating them, you can use them in a restore and recover operation to quickly recover some or all of your database. To recover your database even faster, you can perform a fast switch to image copies. In other words, you can use the image copies directly, skip the restore step, and apply only the recovery step. After the original datafiles are repaired or restored, you can easily switch back with little or no impact to users who are using other datafiles. The database does not need to be shut down unless you are switching to the image copies of the SYSTEM or UNDO tablespace datafiles.

Using the SET NEWNAME command within the RUN block to specify an alternative location for the replacement image copy allows RMAN to make the switch to image copies even easier.

Performing a Fast Switch to Image Copies

When disaster strikes and you lose a single datafile, or even all datafiles, image copies significantly reduce the time required to recover your database. Once you've switched to an image copy, you will most likely want to switch back to the original datafile locations after the media failure has been repaired. Here you'll learn how to switch to an image copy and then switch back.

Switch to an Image Copy

The steps to switch to a datafile copy are very straightforward. This assumes, of course, that you have image copies of the damaged or lost datafile, as well as all archived and online redo log files since the image copy was created. Here are the steps:

1. Take the tablespace(s) containing the missing datafiles offline. You can use one of the dynamic performance views V$RECOVER_FILE, V$DATAFILE_HEADER, or V$TABLESPACE to identify which datafiles need recovery.

2. Use the RMAN SWITCH TO . . . COPY to point to the image copy of the missing datafiles.

3. Recover the datafiles using the RMAN RECOVER command.

4. Bring the tablespace(s) back online.

W a t c h   *The RMAN SWITCH command is equivalent to the SQL command ALTER DATABASE RENAME FILE.*

EXERCISE 5-3

Use the SWITCH Command to Recover a Datafile Quickly

The datafile for the USERS tablespace mysteriously disappears. Users start to complain immediately, reporting this message when they try to create or update a table:

```
ERROR at line 1:
ORA-01116: error in opening database file 4
ORA-01110: data file 4: '/u01/app/oracle/oradata/hr/users01.dbf'
ORA-27041: unable to open file
Linux Error: 2: No such file or directory
Additional information: 3
```

In addition, you see this message in the alert log. This alert should also be visible as an alert on the Enterprise Manager home page:

```
Fri May 30 19:45:13 2008
Checker run found 1 new persistent data failures
```

Find out what datafile number you need to restore, switch to an image copy, and then recover the datafile and bring the tablespace back online:

1. Since you already know that datafile #4 is having problems, query V$TABLESPACE to confirm that the USERS tablespace is the culprit:

```
SQL> select ts#, name
  2  from v$tablespace
  3  where ts# = 4;

     TS# NAME
---------- --------------------
       4 USERS

SQL>
```

The dynamic performance view V$DATAFILE_HEADER shows the error as well but does not always identify the tablespace name:

```
SQL> select file#, status, error, recover, tablespace_name, name
  2  from v$datafile_header
  3  where recover = 'YES'
  4     or (recover is null and error is not null);

     FILE# STATUS  ERROR              REC TABLESPACE_NAME NAME
---------- ------- ------------------ --- --------------- ------
        4 ONLINE  CANNOT OPEN FILE

SQL>
```

2. Take the USERS tablespace offline at the SQL prompt:

```
SQL> alter tablespace users offline immediate;

Tablespace altered.

SQL>
```

Alternatively, you can take the tablespace offline using the RMAN SQL command.

3. Switch to the datafile copy for the USERS tablespace:

```
RMAN> switch tablespace users to copy;

datafile 4 switched to datafile copy
    "/u01/oradata/bkup/data_D-HR_I-3318356692_TS-USERS_FNO-4_37jhmn1m"
```

```
starting full resync of recovery catalog
full resync complete

RMAN>
```

Note that you can use the SWITCH command with either the DATAFILE or TABLESPACE parameter, whichever is easier or more convenient. Note also that you don't need to know where your datafile copy is. RMAN knows where it is and will switch it and update the control file and recovery catalog automatically with the new location.

4. Recover the USERS tablespace using the recent archived and online redo log files:

```
RMAN> recover tablespace users;

Starting recover at 30-MAY-08
using channel ORA_DISK_1

starting media recovery
media recovery complete, elapsed time: 00:00:20

Finished recover at 30-MAY-08

RMAN>
```

5. Finally, bring the USERS tablespace back online:

```
RMAN> sql "alter tablespace users online";

sql statement: alter tablespace users online

RMAN>
```

Alternatively, you can of course bring the tablespace back online using the SQL prompt.

Switch Back to Original Location

Once your database is back up and running after switching to an image copy, you will likely want to switch the datafile back to its original location after the source disk has been repaired. This is especially true if the image copy you switched to resides in the flash recovery area. Flash recovery is used primarily for recovery and storage of multiplexed control files and archived redo log files, and it may reside on a slower disk. To move the tablespace and its associated datafiles back to the original location, follow these steps:

1. Create an image copy of the datafiles in the original location.
2. Take the tablespace offline.
3. Use the `SWITCH TO . . . COPY` command to switch back to the restored (re-created) datafile.
4. Recover the datafiles.
5. Bring the tablespace back online.

Note that you can perform most of these steps while the users are still using the original image copy. The tablespace will once again be unavailable during recovery. This step should be short if not many archived redo log files have been created since the image copy was made in the original location.

EXERCISE 5-4

Use the SWITCH Command after Creating the USERS Tablespace's Datafile in the Original Location

In this exercise, you'll switch the datafile for the USERS tablespace back to its original location after the source disk has been repaired (or you have figured out why datafiles are disappearing from the source disk). The datafile locations for each tablespace are currently as follows:

```
SQL> select file#, df.name, ts#, ts.name
  2  from v$datafile df join v$tablespace ts using(ts#);

    FILE# NAME                                       TS# NAME
---------- ------------------------------------ ---------- ------------
        1 /u01/app/oracle/oradata/h            0 SYSTEM
          r/system01.dbf
        2 /u01/app/oracle/oradata/h            1 SYSAUX
          r/sysaux01.dbf
        3 /u01/app/oracle/oradata/h            2 UNDOTBS1
          r/undotbs01.dbf
        4 /u01/oradata/bkup/data_D-            4 USERS
          HR_I-3318356692_TS-USERS_
          FNO-4_37jhmn1m
        5 /u01/app/oracle/oradata/h            6 EXAMPLE
          r/example01.dbf

SQL>
```

234 Chapter 5: Recovering Using RMAN Backups

1. Create an image copy of the datafile back to the original location:

```
RMAN> backup as copy tablespace users
2>        format '/u01/app/oracle/oradata/hr/users01.dbf';

Starting backup at 30-MAY-08
using channel ORA_DISK_1
channel ORA_DISK_1: starting datafile copy
input datafile file number=00004
   name=/u01/oradata/bkup/data_D-HR_I-3318356692_TS-USERS_FNO-4_37jhmn1m
output file name=/u01/app/oracle/oradata/hr/users01.dbf
tag=TAG20080530T211450 RECID=36 STAMP=656111726
channel ORA_DISK_1: datafile copy complete, elapsed time: 00:00:16
Finished backup at 30-MAY-08

RMAN>
```

Note that you can name the image copy anything you want. In this case, you'll use the original name of the datafile to be consistent with the other datafile names.

2. Take the USERS tablespace offline in preparation for the SWITCH command:

```
RMAN> sql "alter tablespace users offline";

sql statement: alter tablespace users offline
starting full resync of recovery catalog
full resync complete

RMAN>
```

3. Switch to the newly created copy:

```
RMAN> switch tablespace users to copy;

datafile 4 switched to datafile copy
        "/u01/app/oracle/oradata/hr/users01.dbf"
starting full resync of recovery catalog
full resync complete

RMAN>
```

4. Recover the datafile in its new location:

```
RMAN> recover tablespace users;

Starting recover at 30-MAY-08
using channel ORA_DISK_1
```

```
starting media recovery
media recovery complete, elapsed time: 00:00:00

Finished recover at 30-MAY-08

RMAN>
```

5. Bring the USERS tablespace back online:

```
RMAN> sql "alter tablespace users online";

sql statement: alter tablespace users online
starting full resync of recovery catalog
full resync complete

RMAN>
```

6. Confirm that the datafile for the USERS tablespace is back in its original location:

```
SQL> select file#, df.name, ts#, ts.name
  2  from v$datafile df join v$tablespace ts using(ts#)
  3  where ts.name = 'USERS';

     FILE# NAME                             TS# NAME
---------- ------------------------- ---------- -------------
         4 /u01/app/oracle/oradata/h          4 USERS
           r/users01.dbf

SQL>
```

7. Create a new image copy to be ready when or if the datafile disappears again, although you could also use the image copy you just switched from:

```
RMAN> backup as copy tablespace users;

Starting backup at 30-MAY-08
starting full resync of recovery catalog
full resync complete
using channel ORA_DISK_1
channel ORA_DISK_1: starting datafile copy
input datafile file number=00004
name=/u01/app/oracle/oradata/hr/users01.dbf
output file name=/u01/oradata/bkup/
```

```
        data_D-HR_I-3318356692_TS-USERS_FNO-4_39jhn16a
    tag=TAG20080530T220810 RECID=38 STAMP=656114935
    channel ORA_DISK_1: datafile copy complete, elapsed time: 00:00:26
    Finished backup at 30-MAY-08

    RMAN>
```

Using the **RMAN SET NEWNAME** with Fast Switch

One of the many options for the SET command in RMAN is the SET NEWNAME command. Inside of a RUN block, SET NEWNAME makes it easy to specify one or more new datafile destinations in preparation for subsequent RESTORE and SWITCH commands. Here is an RMAN RUN block to specify a new location for the restored datafile of the USERS tablespace:

```
run {
    sql "alter tablespace users offline immediate";
    set newname
        for datafile '/u01/app/oracle/oradata/hr/users01.dbf'
            to '/u06/oradata/users01.dbf';
    restore tablespace users;
    switch datafile all;
    recover tablespace users;
    sql "alter tablespace users online";
}
```

Note that the SWITCH command is used in much the same way as it's used in the preceding section. The difference is that this example restores a datafile from a backup (most likely a backupset) to an alternative location instead of switching to an existing image copy. The result of the SWITCH command, whether in a RUN block or as a standalone command, is to update the control file (and the recovery catalog if you're using one) with the new filenames.

If you did not specify the SET command in the preceding example, RMAN would restore the datafile for the USERS tablespace to its original location, and the SWITCH command would not perform any useful action.

CERTIFICATION OBJECTIVE 5.05

Restore a Database onto a New Host

RMAN can make it easy to restore a database to a new host in a number of ways, and a number of motives exist for restoring a database to a new host. The following sections delve into the reasons you should and should not restore and recover a database to a new host. In addition, you'll learn the steps for preparing the host and performing the actual restore and recovery operation.

Understanding Restoration to a New Host

If you want to perform a disaster recovery test to another host, or you want to move a database permanently to another host, then using the RMAN RESTORE and RECOVER commands is the best method to use. However, using the procedures outlined in the following sections will keep the original database identifier (DBID) and will therefore cause a conflict in the RMAN repository, because the restored database with the same DBID will be considered the current target database. As a result, these procedures should not be used to create a permanent second database—use the RMAN DUPLICATE command for that. The procedures for using DUPLICATE are detailed in Chapter 7.

Preparing the New Host

To prepare the new host to receive the restored and recovered database, follow these steps:

1. Record the DBID of the source database. Use this command to query the DBID:

```
SQL> select dbid from v$database;

      DBID
----------
3318356692

SQL>
```

2. Copy the initialization parameter file from the source database to the new host.

3. Make sure that all source database backups are available to the new host. Do *not* connect to the recovery catalog.

Restoring and Recovering on the New Host

Although a lot of steps are required to restore and recover to the new host, each step is straightforward:

1. Configure environment variables on the new host.
2. Connect to the new target database with NOCATALOG.
3. Set the DBID.
4. Start the instance with NOMOUNT.
5. Restore the SPFILE from backup.
6. Shut down the new instance.
7. Edit the PFILE.
8. Start the instance with NOMOUNT (again).
9. Create an RMAN RUN block to restore the control file.
10. Create an RMAN RUN block to restore and recover the database.
11. Open the database with RESETLOGS.

The following sections offer a brief overview of each step.

1. Configure environment variables on the new host.   Define the environment variable (on Unix or Linux systems) ORACLE_SID:

```
[oracle@srv04]$ export ORACLE_SID=hr
```

2. Connect to the new target database with NOCATALOG.   Connect to the new target database but not the recovery catalog, as in this example:

```
[oracle@srv04]$ rman target /
```

3. Set the DBID.   From within RMAN, set the DBID. You found the DBID earlier by querying V$DATABASE:

```
RMAN> set dbid 3318356692;
```

4. Start the instance in NOMOUNT mode. Start the database in
NOMOUNT mode:

```
RMAN> startup nomount
```

RMAN will return a warning message and use a default parameter file because
the parameter file has not been restored yet.

5. Restore the SPFILE. Within an RMAN RUN block, restore the SPFILE using
a command similar to the following:

```
RMAN> restore spfile to pfile '?/oradata/testrecov/initorcl.ora'
   2         from autobackup;
```

Note that you're restoring the SPFILE to a PFILE, so you can make edits later.

6. Shut down the new instance. Shut down the new instance with either
SHUTDOWN IMMEDIATE or SHUTDOWN ABORT. Since ABORT requires recovery
on restart, IMMEDIATE is the preferable option.

7. Edit the PFILE. Edit the newly created PFILE to change any server-specific
locations for initialization parameters such as these:

- IFILE
- LOG_ARCHIVE_DEST_*
- CONTROL_FILES

8. Start the instance in NOMOUNT mode. Start the instance in NOMOUNT
mode again. You use the edited control file because you don't have the control file
restored yet:

```
SQL> startup force nomount pfile = '?/oradata/testrecov/initorcl.ora';
```

9. Create an RMAN RUN block. Now that the database is using the restored
and edited parameter file, you can execute an RMAN RUN block to restore the
control file and change the restored database to MOUNT mode:

```
run {
    restore controlfile from autobackup;
    alter database mount;
}
```

RMAN will restore the control file to the location specified for CONTROL_FILES in the initialization parameter file. Remember that many commands, such as ALTER DATABASE, work identically at both a SQL> prompt and an RMAN> prompt—convenient but sometimes confusing.

10. Create and run the RMAN recovery script. Create an RMAN RUN block that contains the appropriate SET NEWNAME commands to specify the new locations for each datafile, such as in this example:

```
set newname for datafile 1 to '?/oradata/testrecov/users01.dbf';
```

The script should also include any ALTER DATABASE . . . RENAME commands for the online redo log files:

```
sql "alter database rename file
        ''/u01/app/oracle/oradata/orcl/redo01.log'' to
        ''?/oradata/testrecov/redo01.log'' ";
```

Limit the recovery to the last archived redo log file, because the online redo log files for the new instance are not valid. RMAN will fail if it tries to recover past the last archived redo log file:

```
set until scn 49382031;
```

Finally, restore the database. Then use the SWITCH command to switch the datafile names in the control file to their new names and locations, and then recover the database:

```
restore database;
switch datafile all;
recover database;
```

11. Open the database with RESETLOGS. Finally, open the database with the RESETLOGS option and you can proceed with testing the restored and recovered database:

```
RMAN> alter database open resetlogs;
```

CERTIFICATION OBJECTIVE 5.06

Recover Using a Backup Control File

In rare instances, you may lose all copies of the current control file. This is rare because you should have the control file multiplexed to several locations. Even if you do lose all copies of the current control file, you should have at least one autobackup of the control file from the most recent RMAN backup. In addition, if you are using a recovery catalog, all metadata within your most recent control file resides in the recovery catalog.

The SPFILE is also susceptible to loss if it does not reside on a mirrored external file system or on a mirrored ASM disk group. When RMAN performs a control file autobackup, both the current control file and SPFILE are backed up.

In the following sections, you'll learn how to recover both the control file and the SPFILE if all online versions of either of these files are lost.

Restoring the SPFILE from the Autobackup

To restore the SPFILE from the autobackup, first set the DBID if the instance is not running when the SPFILE is lost:

```
RMAN> set dbid 3318356692;
```

Next, restart the database with a default SPFILE, as you did earlier in this chapter when you restored and recovered a database on a new host:

```
RMAN> startup force nomount;
```

Next, restore the SPFILE from the autobackup to the original location:

```
RMAN> restore spfile from autobackup;
```

Finally, start the database:

```
RMAN> startup force;
```

Restoring the Control File from the Autobackup

Restoring the control file from an autobackup is similar to the steps you use to restore an SPFILE from an autobackup. Here are the sample RMAN commands:

```
RMAN> startup nomount;
RMAN> restore controlfile from autobackup;
```

```
RMAN> alter database mount;
RMAN> recover database;
RMAN> alter database open resetlogs;
```

Note that since there is no control file, you have to open the database with NOMOUNT and then restore the control file. After you mount the database, you must recover the database, because the backup control file contains information about an older version of the database. For the same reason, you must open the database with RESETLOGS.

RMAN restores the control file to all locations specified by the initialization parameter CONTROL_FILES. If one or more of those locations are still not available, you will have to edit the CONTROL_FILES parameter to specify alternative locations or temporarily restore the control file to a different location:

```
RMAN> restore controlfile to '/u06/oradata/rest_cf.dbf' from autobackup;
```

EXERCISE 5-5

Restore the Control File from an Autobackup

In this exercise, all copies of the control file were accidentally deleted by an overly eager system administrator trying to free up disk space. Restore and recover the database with a control file restored from a control file and SPFILE autobackup:

1. Identify the control file locations where all copies of the control file used to reside:

```
SQL> show parameter control_files

NAME                       TYPE        VALUE
------------------------   ---------   ---------------------
control_files              string      /u01/app/oracle/oradata/hr/con
                                       trol01.ctl, /u02/app/oracle/or
                                       adata/hr/control02.ctl, /u03/a
                                       pp/oracle/oradata/hr/control03
                                       .ctl
SQL>
```

2. Shut down the instance (if it is not already down), and reopen it in NOMOUNT mode:

```
SQL> connect / as sysdba
Connected.
SQL> shutdown immediate;
ORA-00210: cannot open the specified control file
ORA-00202: control file: '/u01/app/oracle/oradata/hr/control01.ctl'
ORA-27041: unable to open file
Linux Error: 2: No such file or directory
Additional information: 3
SQL> startup force nomount;
ORACLE instance started.

Total System Global Area  636100608 bytes
Fixed Size                  1301784 bytes
Variable Size             448791272 bytes
Database Buffers          180355072 bytes
Redo Buffers                5652480 bytes
SQL>
```

3. Start RMAN and restore the control file from autobackup to the original locations:

```
[oracle@srv04 ~]$ rman target / catalog rman/rman@rcat

Recovery Manager: Release 11.1.0.6.0 -
          Production on Sat May 31 23:20:20 2008

Copyright (c) 1982, 2007, Oracle.  All rights reserved.

connected to target database: HR (not mounted)
connected to recovery catalog database

RMAN> restore controlfile from autobackup;

Starting restore at 31-MAY-08
allocated channel: ORA_DISK_1
channel ORA_DISK_1: SID=152 device type=DISK

recovery area destination: /u01/app/oracle/flash_recovery_area
database name (or database unique name) used for search: HR
channel ORA_DISK_1: AUTOBACKUP
/u01/app/oracle/flash_recovery_area/HR/autobackup
   /2008_05_31/o1_mf_s_656205340_4448nf6k_.bkp found in the
recovery area
```

```
channel ORA_DISK_1: looking for AUTOBACKUP on day: 20080531
channel ORA_DISK_1: restoring control file from AUTOBACKUP
/u01/app/oracle/flash_recovery_area/HR/autobackup
   /2008_05_31/o1_mf_s_656205340_4448nf6k_.bkp
channel ORA_DISK_1: control file restore from AUTOBACKUP complete
output file name=/u01/app/oracle/oradata/hr/control01.ctl
output file name=/u02/app/oracle/oradata/hr/control02.ctl
output file name=/u03/app/oracle/oradata/hr/control03.ctl
Finished restore at 31-MAY-08

RMAN>
```

A few points are worth noting here. RMAN can connect to the instance even if it is not mounted. In fact, RMAN has to connect to an unmounted database to be able to restore the control file. RMAN finds the control file autobackup in the flash recovery area and writes it to the three control file destinations specified by the CONTROL_FILES initialization parameter.

4. Mount the database, recover the database (to synchronize the datafiles with the restored control file), and open the database with RESETLOGS:

```
RMAN> alter database mount;

database mounted
released channel: ORA_DISK_1

RMAN> recover database;

Starting recover at 31-MAY-08
Starting implicit crosscheck backup at 31-MAY-08
allocated channel: ORA_DISK_1
channel ORA_DISK_1: SID=152 device type=DISK
Crosschecked 11 objects
Finished implicit crosscheck backup at 31-MAY-08

Starting implicit crosscheck copy at 31-MAY-08
using channel ORA_DISK_1
Crosschecked 1 objects
Finished implicit crosscheck copy at 31-MAY-08

searching for all files in the recovery area
cataloging files...
cataloging done

List of Cataloged Files
=========================
```

```
File Name:
/u01/app/oracle/flash_recovery_area/HR/autobackup
        /2008_05_31/o1_mf_s_656205340_4448nf6k_.bkp

using channel ORA_DISK_1

starting media recovery

archived log for thread 1 with sequence 20 is already on disk
as file
        /u01/app/oracle/oradata/hr/redo02.log
archived log file name=/u01/app/oracle/oradata/hr/redo02.log
        thread=1 sequence=20
media recovery complete, elapsed time: 00:00:01
Finished recover at 31-MAY-08

RMAN> alter database open resetlogs;

database opened
new incarnation of database registered in recovery catalog
RPC call appears to have failed to start on channel default
RPC call OK on channel default
starting full resync of recovery catalog
full resync complete

RMAN>
```

CERTIFICATION OBJECTIVE 5.07

Perform Disaster Recovery

Disaster recovery comes in many forms. If you are running your database in NOARCHIVELOG mode, you are more likely to suffer data loss when a datafile, control file, or all database-related files are lost. In other words, running in NOARCHIVELOG mode is a disaster waiting to happen.

If you have good reasons for running in NOARCHIVELOG mode (and there are few good reasons to run in NOARCHIVELOG mode), you can still recover some or most of the data, depending on how recently your backups were made. If you perform incremental backups in NOARCHIVELOG mode, you will be able to restore even more committed user data.

Ideally, your database is running in ARCHIVELOG mode, but you could still lose every database file from the target database. If you have an intact set of datafiles, archived redo log files, and at least one control file autobackup, you can recover all committed transactions up to and including the last archived redo log file.

In the following sections, you'll see how to maximize the recoverability of a database in NOARCHIVELOG mode and learn the steps required to fully recover a database running in ARCHIVELOG mode.

Performing Recovery in NOARCHIVELOG Mode

As mentioned several times in this book, if not several times in this chapter, it is highly recommended that your database be running in ARCHIVELOG mode. If it is not and you lose even one datafile, you must restore the database from the most recent full backup, including all control files and datafiles. While the following procedure is straightforward, the database users must re-enter all changes made since the last backup:

1. Shut down the instance if it's not already down.

2. Using operating system commands, restore all datafiles and control files to their original locations, or new locations if the original locations are no longer available.

3. Update the CONTROL_FILES parameter in the restored initialization parameter file if the restored control file is in a new location.

4. Start the database with STARTUP MOUNT.

5. Use ALTER DATABASE RENAME to change the location of datafiles and online redo log files if the original location is no longer available.

6. Run the RECOVER DATABASE UNTIL CANCEL command to mimic incomplete recovery and reset the online redo log files; specify CANCEL immediately.

7. Open the database with ALTER DATABASE OPEN RESETLOGS.

Using Incremental Backups in NOARCHIVELOG Mode

If you are running your database in NOARCHIVELOG mode, and you make regular incremental backups, you can take level 0 incremental backups and apply level 1 incremental backups to recover your database up to the point in time of your last incremental backup. The incremental backups must be consistent backups—in other words, you performed the backups while the database was in the MOUNT state. In addition, the database must be shut down with NORMAL, IMMEDIATE, or TRANSACTIONAL to ensure that all datafiles and the controlfile (and all multiplexed copies of the control files) have the synchronized System Change Numbers (SCNs).

Use the following RMAN commands to restore and recover the database with all incremental backups:

```
startup force nomount; # if the control file is also lost
restore controlfile;
alter database mount;
restore database;
recover database noredo;
alter database open resetlogs;
```

You need to specify NOREDO in the RECOVER DATABASE command only if the online redo log files are lost. If the current online redo log files contain all changes since the last incremental backup, you don't need to specify NOREDO and all committed transactions from the online redo log files will be applied to the restored datafiles after the incremental backups are applied.

Performing Recovery of the Entire Database

In this scenario, your worst nightmare has come true: You have lost the entire target database, the recovery catalog database, all control files, all online redo log files, and all parameter files. However, all is not lost, because your database was in ARCHIVELOG mode and you have one of your control file autobackups, a backup of all datafiles, along with all archived redo log files created since the last backup. As a result, you can restore the database in much the same way as you restore and recover a database to a new host, as shown earlier in this chapter.

These steps assume that the Oracle database software is already installed on the new host and the directory structure on the new host is the same as the old host. Here are the steps with the relevant commands required:

1. Connect to RMAN without connecting to a recovery catalog using CONNECT TARGET /.

2. Set the DBID for the database using SET DBID.

3. Start the database with STARTUP NOMOUNT. RMAN uses a default SPFILE because it has not been restored yet.

4. Restore the SPFILE with RESTORE SPFILE FROM AUTOBACKUP.

5. Restart with the new SPFILE using `STARTUP FORCE NOMOUNT`.

6. Restore the control file from an autobackup using `RESTORE CONTROLFILE FROM AUTOBACKUP`.

7. Mount the database with `ALTER DATABASE MOUNT`.

8. Restore and recover the database with `RESTORE DATABASE` and `RECOVER DATABASE`.

9. Open the database with `RESETLOGS`.

CERTIFICATION SUMMARY

This chapter started out describing the most basic type of recovery operation for a database in `ARCHIVELOG` mode. For a noncritical datafile, you take the tablespace containing the datafile offline, restore the missing or damaged datafile, and then recover the datafile using archived and online redo log files. For a critical datafile, the procedure is much the same, except that you must shut down the database and start it in `MOUNT` mode before starting the recovery operation.

On some occasions, you'll want to perform an incomplete recovery, typically because you want to roll back the database in time permanently due to numerous erroneous changes to the database that cannot be reversed using Oracle Flashback technology. You learned how to create a restore point as a marker for an SCN or a point in time, and then how to use that restore point later for an incomplete recovery operation.

Image copies should play an important role in your disaster recovery plan. To speed up the recovery process even more, you can apply subsequent incremental backups to an image copy so that any recovery operation using the image copy has to use only the archived and online redo log files to recover the database. You saw a script that you can use to keep your image copies up-to-date with every incremental backup.

Once you create your image copies and keep them updated with incremental updates, you want to be ready to use them. Typically, you will restore a backupset or image copy. An even faster method is to use the image copy in place and apply any recent incremental updates and archived redo log files. You learned how to switch to an image copy, recover the image copy, and how to switch it back to its original location.

When using an RMAN `RUN` block, you can use the `SET NEWNAME` command to specify an alternative location for a datafile during a restore operation. Once RMAN restores the datafile, you use the `SWITCH` command to update the control file and the recovery catalog with the new location for the datafile.

If you are not permanently moving a database to a new host, you can use the RMAN RESTORE and RECOVER commands to create a copy of the database on a new host quickly and easily. You use the original DBID on the copied database and make sure that you don't connect to a recovery catalog with the copied database. Otherwise, you will compromise the integrity of the source database's backup metadata.

Next, you saw the steps required to recover using a backup control file and a backup SPFILE. The procedure is much the same as, and reiterates the importance of, mirroring your control file and ensuring that you configure your RMAN backups with AUTOBACKUP set to ON.

Finally, you saw the high level steps required for recovering from the ultimate disaster: losing all datafiles, control files, and SPFILEs. The procedure is fairly straightforward and minimizes data loss, as long as your database is running in ARCHIVELOG mode. Many, if not all, of the steps required for performing disaster recovery were covered in separate sections earlier in the chapter.

✓ TWO-MINUTE DRILL

Perform Complete Recovery from a Critical or Noncritical Data File Loss Using RMAN

❏ Use RMAN RESTORE and RECOVER for complete recovery from a critical and noncritical data file loss.

❏ Datafiles from the SYSTEM and UNDO tablespaces are critical datafiles.

❏ When restoring and recovering a critical datafile, the database must be in MOUNT mode.

❏ You can completely recover any datafile if the database is in ARCHIVELOG mode.

Perform Incomplete Recovery Using RMAN

❏ You use restore points to recover a database to an SCN or a time in the past.

❏ Use CREATE RESTORE POINT to create a restore point.

❏ You must open the database with RESETLOGS if you perform incomplete recovery.

Recover Using Incrementally Updated Backups

❏ You can recover image copies with more recent incremental level 1 backups.

❏ RMAN automatically determines the best image copy to use if more than one are available.

❏ Use tags with an incrementally updated image copy strategy to ensure that the correct incremental backup updates the image copy.

Switch to Image Copies for Fast Recovery

❏ Using image copies skips the restore step and saves overall recovery time.

❏ Use the RMAN command SWITCH TO . . . COPY to switch to the most recent image copy for a datafile, tablespace, or database.

❏ RMAN automatically applies incremental backups and archived redo log files when you recover with an image copy.

❏ Use the dynamic performance views V$TABLESPACE and V$DATAFILE_HEADER to determine the tablespace and datafile number needing recovery.

❑ After switching to an image copy, you can switch back to an image copy at the original location when it becomes available.

❑ You use the `SET NEWNAME` command in RMAN to identify new locations for restored datafiles.

❑ After restoring one or more datafiles with `RESTORE`, you use the `SWITCH` command to update the control file and recovery catalog with the new datafile locations.

Restore a Database onto a New Host

❑ Restoring a database to a new host is appropriate for disaster recovery testing or permanently moving the database to a new host.

❑ The `DUPLICATE` command is more appropriate if you want to make a permanent copy of the database with a new DBID.

❑ When connecting to the new database, do not connect to a recovery catalog.

❑ The RMAN recovery script uses `SET NEWNAME` to specify new locations for each datafile.

❑ Restore the database to the SCN of the last archived redo log file.

❑ You must open the new database with `RESETLOGS`.

Recover Using a Backup Control File

❑ You can use an RMAN autobackup to restore either an SPFILE or control file when all online copies are lost.

❑ RMAN restores the control file to all locations specified by the initialization parameter `CONTROL_FILES`.

❑ If the SPFILE is lost, RMAN uses a default SPFILE when you start the database with `NOMOUNT`.

❑ Use `RESTORE SPFILE FROM AUTOBACKUP` to restore the SPFILE.

❑ Use `RESTORE CONTROLFILE FROM AUTOBACKUP` to restore the control file.

❑ When restoring a control file from autobackup you must open the database with `RESETLOGS`.

❑ You can optionally restore a copy of the control file to an alternate location.

Perform Disaster Recovery

❏ Data loss is likely to occur if you lose all datafiles and control files while in NOARCHIVELOG mode.

❏ To perform disaster recovery in NOARCHIVELOG mode, use operating system commands to copy the closed database backup files to the original or alternative location.

❏ Use RECOVER DATABASE UNTIL CANCEL to simulate incomplete recovery and to reinitialize the online redo log files.

❏ After the recovery operation is complete, open the database with RESETLOGS.

❏ You can use incremental backups in NOARCHIVELOG mode to minimize data loss.

❏ Specify NOREDO in the RECOVER DATABASE command if all online redo log files are lost.

SELF TEST

The following questions will help you measure your understanding of the material presented in this chapter. Read all the choices carefully because there might be more than one correct answer. Choose all correct answers for each question.

Perform Complete Recovery from a Critical or Noncritical Data File Loss Using RMAN

1. What is the difference between a critical and a noncritical datafile in a recovery scenario?
   A. To recover a critical datafile, only the tablespace containing the critical datafile must be offline.
   B. To recover a noncritical datafile, both the SYSTEM tablespace and the tablespace containing the critical datafile must be offline.
   C. To recover a critical datafile, the database must be in NOMOUNT mode. To recover a noncritical datafile, the database must be in MOUNT mode.
   D. To recover a critical datafile, the database must be in MOUNT mode. To recover a noncritical datafile, the database can be open.

2. Which tablespaces contain critical datafiles that must be recovered when the database is offline?
   A. SYSTEM and SYSAUX
   B. SYSTEM and UNDO
   C. SYSTEM, SYSAUX, and UNDO
   D. SYSTEM and USERS

3. During complete recovery of a noncritical datafile, which of the following steps are not required? (Choose two answers.)
   A. Use the RMAN RESTORE command to load the missing datafiles from backup.
   B. Reopen the database with RESETLOGS.
   C. Shut down the database and reopen in MOUNT mode.
   D. Bring the tablespace containing the missing or damaged datafiles offline before the recovery operation and online after recovery is complete.
   E. Use the RMAN RECOVER command to apply committed transactions from archived and online redo log files.

Perform Incomplete Recovery Using RMAN

4. Which of the following methods can you use to retrieve the current System Change Number (SCN)?

   A. Query the CURRENT_SCN column from V$DATAFILE_HEADER.

   B. Query the CURRENT_SCN column of the V$INSTANCE view.

   C. Query the LAST_SCN column of the V$DATABASE view.

   D. Query the CURRENT_SCN column of the V$DATABASE view.

   E. Start RMAN and connect to the target database; the current SCN and the DBID are displayed.

5. Which of the following CREATE RESTORE POINT commands will preserve the restore point past the time specified by the initialization parameter CONTROL_FILE_RECORD_KEEP_TIME?

   A. CREATE RESTORE POINT SAVE_IT_PAST KEEP

   B. CREATE RESTORE POINT SAVE_IT_PAST AS OF SCN 3988943

   C. CREATE RESTORE POINT SAVE_IT_NOW PRESERVE

   D. CREATE RESTORE POINT SAVE_IT_NOW UNTIL FOREVER

6. Which operating system environment variables should be set when you use RMAN time-based incomplete recovery? (Choose two answers.)

   A. ORACLE_SID

   B. NLS_LANG

   C. ORACLE_BASE

   D. NLS_DATE_FORMAT

   E. NLS_TIME_FORMAT

Recover Using Incrementally Updated Backups

7. You are implementing an incrementally updated backup strategy using the following RMAN script:

```
run {
      recover copy of database
          with tag 'inc_upd';
      backup incremental level 1
          for recover of copy
          with tag 'inc_upd'
          database;
    }
```

How many times do you need to run this script before the image copy is updated with an incremental level 1 backup?

   A. Once

   B. Twice

   C. Three times

   D. At least four times

Switch to Image Copies for Fast Recovery

8. The RMAN `SWITCH` command is equivalent to what SQL command?

   A. `ALTER SYSTEM RENAME FILE`

   B. `ALTER DATABASE ARCHIVELOG`

   C. `ALTER DATABASE OPEN RESETLOGS`

   D. `ALTER SYSTEM SWITCH LOGFILE`

9. You have these two commands within an RMAN `RUN` block:

```
set newname for datafile '/u01/ordata/dw/users04.dbf'
    to '/u06/oradata/dw/users04.dbf';
restore tablespace users;
```

What happens when the `RESTORE` command runs?

   A. The command fails and the RUN block terminates because you need to run a `SWITCH` command first.

   B. The control file is updated with the new location of the datafile.

   C. The latest version of the datafiles for the `USERS` tablespace are restored to the location /u01/oradata/dw.

   D. The latest version of the datafiles for the `USERS` tablespace are restored to the location /u06/oradata/dw.

Restore a Database onto a New Host

10. Which of the following are valid reasons to restore backups of your database to a new host? (Choose all that apply.)

   A. Creating a new node in a RAC environment

   B. Testing your disaster recovery plan

   C. Creating another copy of your database

   D. When the `DUPLICATE` command is not available

   E. Permanently moving your database to a new host

11. When restoring a database to a new host, what is the first command you should run as part of the restoration process?

   A. `STARTUP NOMOUNT`

   B. `SET DBID`

C. `RESTORE SPFILE FROM AUTOBACKUP`

D. `RESTORE CONTROLFILE FROM AUTOBACKUP`

Recover Using a Backup Control File

12. Place the following commands in the correct order for restoring a control file from an RMAN autobackup:

1. `RECOVER DATABASE`
2. `ALTER DATABASE OPEN RESETLOGS`
3. `STARTUP NOMOUNT`
4. `ALTER DATABASE MOUNT`
5. `RESTORE CONTROLFILE FROM AUTOBACKUP`

A. 5, 3, 4, 1, 2

B. 3, 5, 4, 1, 2

C. 3, 5, 4, 2, 1

D. 5, 1, 3, 4, 2

13. When you run the RMAN `RESTORE CONTROLFILE` command, where does RMAN put the previous version of the control file? (Choose the best answer.)

A. To all available locations defined by the `CONTROL_FILES` initialization parameter

B. To the flash recovery area

C. To all locations defined by the `CONTROL_FILES` initialization parameter unless overridden with the `TO '<filename>'` clause

D. To the first location defined by the `CONTROL_FILES` initialization parameter

Perform Disaster Recovery

14. Your database is running in `NOARCHIVELOG` mode, and you perform occasional incremental level 1 backups in `MOUNT` mode. To what point in time can you recover the database if you lose a datafile for the `USERS` tablespace?

A. You can recover the entire database up to the point in time of the last incremental level 1 backup.

B. You can recover the entire database up to the point in time of the last incremental level 0 backup.

C. You can recover the `USERS` tablespace up to the point in time of the last incremental level 1 backup.

D. You can recover the `USERS` tablespace up to the point in time of the last incremental level 0 backup.

SELF TEST ANSWERS

Perform Complete Recovery from a Critical or Noncritical Data File Loss Using RMAN

1. ☑ **D.** When you restore and recover a critical datafile, the entire database must be shut down and reopened in MOUNT mode to open the control file and make the datafile locations available to RMAN.

   ☒ **A** is wrong because the entire database must be offline when recovering a critical datafile. **B** is wrong because recovering a noncritical datafile requires only the tablespace containing the missing or damaged datafile to be offline. **C** is wrong because the database must be in MOUNT mode to recover a critical datafile, and can be in OPEN mode to recover a noncritical datafile.

2. ☑ **B.** The SYSTEM and UNDO tablespaces contain critical datafiles and therefore require the database to be in MOUNT mode during the recovery process.

   ☒ **A, C,** and **D** are wrong because the SYSAUX and USERS tablespaces do not contain critical datafiles.

3. ☑ **B** and **C.** The database does not need to be opened with RESETLOGS because you are not performing incomplete recovery. For a noncritical datafile, only the tablespace containing the missing or damaged datafile needs to be offline.

   ☒ **A, D,** and **E** are wrong. These steps are all required.

Perform Incomplete Recovery Using RMAN

4. ☑ **D.** V$DATABASE contains the most recent SCN in the CURRENT_SCN column.

   ☒ **A** and **B** are wrong because the column CURRENT_SCN does not exist in either V$DATAFILE_HEADER or V$INSTANCE. **C** is wrong because V$DATABASE does not have a column named LAST_SCN. **E** is wrong because when RMAN starts, it shows only the DBID and not the current SCN.

5. ☑ **C.** The keyword PRESERVE keeps the restore point past the time specified by CONTROL_FILE_RECORD_KEEP_TIME.

   ☒ **A** is wrong because the keyword KEEP is not valid for the command. **B** is wrong because PRESERVE was not specified. **D** is wrong because UNTIL FOREVER is not valid for the command.

6. ☑ **B** and **D.** Both NLS_LANG and NLS_DATE_FORMAT must be set so that RMAN will correctly interpret date strings provided during a recovery operation.

   ☒ **A, C,** and **E** are wrong. ORACLE_SID and ORACLE_BASE are required to connect to the correct database and database software, but they are not directly related to RMAN time-based recovery. NLS_TIME_FORMAT is not a valid environment variable.

Recover Using Incrementally Updated Backups

7. ☑ **C.** The first time the script runs, there is no level 0 image copy nor a level 1 incremental backup. The second time the script runs, the level 0 image copy exists but there is no incremental level 1 backup to apply to it. The third and successive time, the first incremental level 1 backup is applied to the image copy.
   ☒ **A, B,** and **D** all specify the wrong number of executions.

Switch to Image Copies for Fast Recovery

8. ☑ **A.** Both the RMAN `SWITCH` and the SQL `ALTER SYSTEM RENAME FILE` commands update the location of the datafile in both the control file and the recovery catalog.
   ☒ **B** is wrong because this command puts the database into `ARCHIVELOG` mode. **C** is wrong because the command is used only after incomplete recovery. **D** is wrong because the command switches online redo log files, not datafile names.

9. ☑ **D.** The `SET NEWNAME` specifies the new location for the datafile, and `RESTORE` puts the backup version of the datafile at the new location.
   ☒ **A** is wrong because the datafile must be restored before the control file can be updated with `SWITCH`. **B** is wrong because only `SWITCH` will update the control file with the new location. **C** is wrong because the `RESTORE` command uses the new location specified with `SET NEWNAME`.

Restore a Database onto a New Host

10. ☑ **B** and **E.** Restoring your database to a new host is appropriate to test your disaster recovery plan or to move your database permanently to a new host since the procedure keeps the existing DBID.
   ☒ **A** is wrong because you don't need to restore copies of datafiles for new nodes in a RAC environment, only a new instance is created. **C** is wrong because the DBID remains the same on the new database, and this will cause conflicts in the recovery catalog. **D** is wrong because the `DUPLICATE` command is always available in RMAN to let you make a second copy of your database along with the required changes to the DBID in the new database.

11. ☑ **B.** The DBID must be set first so that the correct datafiles, SPFILE, and control file are restored from the source database backup location.
   ☒ **A, C,** and **D** are wrong. All of these steps are valid for restoring a database to a new host but must be run after the DBID is set.

Recover Using a Backup Control File

12. ☑ **B.** The specified order is correct. You must open the database with `RESETLOGS` since your restored control file has information about an older version of the database.
   ☒ **A, C,** and **D** specify an incorrect sequence of commands.

13. ☑ C. The command restores the control file from autobackup to all locations defined by the initialization parameter CONTROL_FILES. If any of those locations are unavailable, change the value of CONTROL_FILES or use the TO '<filename>' option.

   ☒ A is wrong because the command fails if any of the locations defined by CONTROL_FILES are not available. B is wrong because the autobackup of the control file will most likely originate from the flash recovery area. D is wrong because RMAN restores the control file to all locations defined by CONTROL_FILES.

Perform Disaster Recovery

14. ☑ A. If you are not running in ARCHIVELOG mode, you must restore the entire database, including control files. You can recover it up to the point in time of the last incremental level 1 backup in MOUNT mode.

   ☒ B is wrong because you can apply incremental level 1 backups to the database, even in NOARCHIVELOG mode. C and D are wrong because you must recover the entire database when you are running in NOARCHIVELOG mode.

6

User-Managed Backup and Recovery

I n Chapter 5 you learned about the intricacies of using RMAN for recovering your database, which Oracle considers a *server-managed recovery* operation. In contrast, using operating system commands and SQL commands to restore and recover your database is known as *user-managed backup and recovery*. In this chapter, the focus is on user-managed backup and recovery, although some of the scenarios presented here will appear to be similar to the scenarios presented in Chapter 5 using the equivalent RMAN commands.

Data loss or corruption usually falls into one of three categories: user error, application error, or media failure. User error occurs when a DBA or system administrator inadvertently deletes or replaces a datafile or other Oracle-related file. Application errors, such as a backup script with a logic error, may back up the wrong file or delete a file that should be kept. Media failure applies to hardware failures that make a datafile either temporarily or permanently unavailable. This includes but is not limited to controller failures, disk failures, and network failures. For all three categories, the procedures for recovery are the same after any hardware problems are resolved.

You'll recall the distinction between the *restore* and *recover* steps when a datafile is lost or damaged. From an industry point of view, bringing your database back online from a disaster is typically known as *recovery*. However, Oracle naming conventions subdivides this process into two steps, restore and recover. In summary, the restore process copies a backup file into place if, for example, a datafile is lost or damaged. Recovery then applies archived and perhaps online redo log information to bring the state of the database back to the point of time of the failure, or to any point before the point of failure.

Another important distinction when considering database failures is *critical* versus *noncritical* failures. For noncritical failures, the database can continue to operate for all or most users. For example, you may lose only one copy of a multiplexed redo log group or a datafile from a tablespace used by only one application. Critical failures prevent the database from running, which occurs with, for example, the loss of a datafile from the SYSTEM tablespace or all control files.

The first part of this chapter shows you how to recover from the loss of one or more datafiles in a temporary tablespace; you can accomplish this without shutting down the database. Similarly, you'll learn how to recover from the loss of a redo log group member or an entire redo log group (a redo log group can have one or more members, each of which is a redo log file).

Next, you'll learn the difference between complete and incomplete recovery and when each method is appropriate for your environment. Incomplete recovery is required when a media failure occurs and one or more archived or online redo log files are not available for the recovery process. In addition, you may perform incomplete recovery when you want to bring the database to a point in time before a user (or another DBA) incorrectly dropped or modified database objects and other less-draconian recovery methods are not available.

Finally, you'll learn how to recover from the loss of one or more control files. Ideally, you have mirrored your control file several times, However, if the worst comes to pass, you can use a backup control file while minimizing or eliminating downtime and data loss.

CERTIFICATION OBJECTIVE 6.01

Recover from a Lost Tempfile

Recovering from the loss of one or more tempfiles is a straightforward process. Remember that a tempfile is identical to a datafile except that it belongs to a temporary tablespace. The impact to a running database is minimal depending on the query mix. In all cases, you can recover the tempfile while the database is up, even if the original file location is not available.

Losing a Tempfile

One of the consequences of losing a tempfile is that any SQL statements that need temporary disk space for sorting (in other words, insufficient memory is available in Oracle's memory space) will fail. If one or all of the datafiles for the TEMP tablespace is deleted at the operating system level, you can create a new tempfile in the same directory as the original one using the ALTER TABLESPACE command. If the original directory location is not available, you can create it in a different location. After that you can drop the original tempfile using a similar ALTER TABLESPACE command.

EXERCISE 6-1

Create a Replacement Tempfile for the TEMP tablespace

In this exercise, the tempfile for the TEMP tablespace was accidentally deleted, so you must create another tempfile to replace it while the database is still running.

1. Identify the name of the tempfile for the TEMP tablespace:

```
SQL> select file#, name from v$tempfile;

     FILE# NAME
---------- ------------------------------------------------
         1 /u01/app/oracle/oradata/hr/temp01.dbf

SQL>
```

2. Create a new tempfile with a different name for the TEMP tablespace:

```
SQL> alter tablespace temp add tempfile
  2      '/u01/app/oracle/oradata/hr/temp02.dbf'
  3      size 25m;

Tablespace altered.

SQL>
```

3. Drop the previous tempfile. This will update only the control file because the original tempfile is missing:

```
SQL> alter tablespace temp drop tempfile
  2      '/u01/app/oracle/oradata/hr/temp01.dbf';

Tablespace altered.

SQL>
```

4. Confirm that the TEMP tablespace contains only the newly created tempfile:

```
SQL> select file#, name from v$tempfile;

     FILE# NAME
---------- ------------------------------------------------
         2 /u01/app/oracle/oradata/hr/temp02.dbf

SQL>
```

Starting a Database Without a Tempfile

Recovering from the loss of a tempfile is even easier if you start the database with a missing tempfile. The database starts, and if the original disk directory location is available, Oracle re-creates all missing tempfiles, as you can see in this excerpt from the alert log:

```
Re-creating tempfile /u01/app/oracle/oradata/hr/temp02.dbf
Re-creating tempfile /u01/app/oracle/oradata/hr/temp03.dbf
```

If the original disk directory location is no longer available, the database still starts, and you can use the steps from the preceding section to re-create the tempfile(s) manually for the TEMP tablespace.

CERTIFICATION OBJECTIVE 6.02

Recover from a Lost Redo Log Group

The loss of a redo log group or a redo log group member can mean data loss and a significant recovery effort. It can also mean no data loss and a minimal recovery effort, depending on the status of the redo log group and whether you lose the entire log group or only a member of a log group. The following sections review how log groups work and how the different log group statuses change as redo is written to the group, how the database switches to the next log group, and how a filled log group is copied to an archive location.

Let's review the types of log group failures and how to recover from each one. In most scenarios, data loss is minimal or nonexistent, especially if you mirror your log groups.

Understanding Log Group Status

A redo log group can have one of six statuses in the view V$LOG, described in Table 6-1.

At any given point in time, the most common statuses are CURRENT, ACTIVE, and INACTIVE. A redo log group is in the UNUSED state after creation, and once it's used it will never return to that state. The CLEARING and CLEARING_CURRENT states exist when you re-create a corrupted log file, which hopefully will not occur very often!

	Log File Status	Status Description
TABLE 6-1 Log File Status in V$LOG	CURRENT	Oracle is writing to this log group, and this group is needed for instance recovery.
	ACTIVE	This log group is needed for instance recovery, but Oracle is not writing to this log group. It may or may not be archived yet.
	INACTIVE	The log group is not needed for instance recovery, may be in use for media recovery, and may or may not be archived.
	UNUSED	The log group has not been used yet.
	CLEARING	The log is being cleared by ALTER DATABASE CLEAR LOGFILE. After being cleared, the status changes to UNUSED.
	CLEARING_CURRENT	An error has occurred during ALTER DATABASE CLEAR LOGFILE.

Our sample database has three redo log file groups, and this query of V$LOG shows the status of each log:

```
SQL> select group#, sequence#, archived, status
  2  from v$log;

    GROUP#  SEQUENCE# ARC STATUS
---------- ---------- --- ----------------
         1         88 NO  CURRENT
         2         86 YES INACTIVE
         3         87 YES INACTIVE
SQL>
```

The two log file groups with a status of INACTIVE have been archived. Depending on the I/O load of the system and other factors, the ARCHIVED status will be NO until the log file has been successfully written to all mandatory archived log file destinations.

Recovering from Log Group Member Failures

If one member of a log group becomes damaged or is lost, the Log Writer (LGWR) process continues to write to the undamaged member and no data loss or interruption in service occurs. However, it is imperative that you correct this problem as soon as possible, because the log group with only one member is now the single point of failure in your database. If it is lost, your recovery efforts will increase and loss of committed transactions is likely.

In this example, the second member of the third redo log file group becomes damaged. These error messages should appear in the alert log. You will see similar messages on the Enterprise Manager Database Control home page if it is configured:

```
Mon Jun 30 11:13:16 2008
Errors in file /u01/app/oracle/diag/rdbms/hr/hr/trace/hr_arc2_5718.trc:
ORA-00313: open failed for members of log group 3 of thread 1
ORA-00312: online log 3 thread 1: '/u06/app/oracle/oradata/hr/redo03.log'
ORA-27046: file size is not a multiple of logical block size
Additional information: 1
```

You can also identify the lost or damaged redo log file member using the V$LOGFILE view:

```
SQL> select group#, status, member from v$logfile;

    GROUP# STATUS  MEMBER
---------- ------- -------------------------------------------
         3         /u01/app/oracle/oradata/hr/redo03.log
         2         /u01/app/oracle/oradata/hr/redo02.log
         1         /u01/app/oracle/oradata/hr/redo01.log
         1         /u06/app/oracle/oradata/hr/redo01.log
         2         /u06/app/oracle/oradata/hr/redo02.log
         3 INVALID /u06/app/oracle/oradata/hr/redo03.log

6 rows selected.
SQL>
```

The solution to this problem is straightforward. Drop the invalid member and add a new member to the group, as in this example:

```
SQL> alter database drop logfile member
  2      '/u06/app/oracle/oradata/hr/redo03.log';

Database altered.

SQL> alter database add logfile member
  2      '/u06/app/oracle/oradata/hr/redo03a.log'
  3      to group 3;

Database altered.

SQL>
```

Note that the redundancy provided by the repaired redo log file group will not be available until the next time this log file group is active. If the destination disk itself is not damaged and the original redo log file is logically corrupted from user error or a rogue process, you can reuse the original redo log file by specifying the REUSE clause as follows:

```
alter database add logfile member
    '/u06/app/oracle/oradata/hr/redo03.log'
    reuse to group 3;
```

Recovering from Loss of an Entire Log Group

The loss of all members of a redo log group may have no effect on the database or may cause loss of committed transactions, which depends on the state of the redo log group. The three possible states of a log file group are INACTIVE, ACTIVE, and CURRENT.

Recovering from a Lost INACTIVE Redo Log Group

The loss of all members of a redo log group marked INACTIVE is the most benign redo log group failure, although you must act quickly before the Oracle database processes need to use the redo log group again. If Oracle needs to use the redo log group before it is repaired, the database halts until the problem is fixed. The group is not needed for crash recovery because it is INACTIVE. Therefore, you can clear the group using the ALTER DATABASE CLEAR LOGFILE command.

A damaged redo log group with a status of INACTIVE may or may not be archived yet. The archival status determines which form of the ALTER DATABASE CLEAR LOGFILE command to use.

Clearing an Archived Inactive Redo Log Group   If a damaged inactive redo log group has been archived, you can identify the group number of the damaged group from the alert log or from the dynamic performance view V$LOGFILE. Remember that you can look at the ARCHIVED column in the dynamic performance view V$LOG to determine whether the log group has been archived yet.

In this example, redo log group #1 is damaged but has been archived. Use the ALTER DATABASE command as follows:

```
SQL> alter database clear logfile group 1;

Database altered.

SQL>
```

If the instance is down, start the database in MOUNT mode and run this command. Otherwise, you can run the command when the database is OPEN. All members of the redo log file group are reinitialized. If any or all of the redo log group members are missing, they are then re-created, provided that the destination directories are available.

The redo log group has been archived. Thus, no data loss will result and all backups in combination with archived redo log files can be used for complete recovery of the database. Until the database reuses the redo log file group, it has a status of UNUSED, as you can see in this query:

```
SQL> select group#, sequence#, archived, status from v$log;

    GROUP#  SEQUENCE# ARC STATUS
---------- ---------- --- ----------------
         1          0 YES UNUSED
         2         98 NO  CURRENT
         3         96 YES INACTIVE

SQL>
```

Clearing a Nonarchived Inactive Redo Log Group   If you have a nonarchived inactive redo log group, you will not lose any committed transactions. However, you must perform a full backup after clearing the redo log group to ensure that you can perform a complete recovery. You will have a gap in archived redo log files. Therefore, you will be able to perform only incomplete recovery up to the System Change Number (SCN) of the last transaction in the archived redo log file created before the missing log file.

To clear the second unarchived log group, start up the database in MOUNT mode (if it is not already up) and use the following command:

```
alter database clear logfile unarchived group 2;
```

Note the UNARCHIVED keyword in this command. It performs the same action that occurs when you cleared an archived redo log group, but this is Oracle's way of forcing you to acknowledge that you will have a gap in your archived redo log files.

After clearing the log file group, perform a full backup using operating system commands (remember, this is user-managed recovery, not system-managed recovery using RMAN). This provides a backup that you can use for complete recovery along with all successive archived redo log files.

A complicating factor to consider when you're clearing a nonarchived inactive redo log group is whether an offline datafile needs the cleared log file group before it can be brought online. In this scenario, you must drop the tablespace containing the offline datafile and re-create it using logical backups or some other method. You cannot recover the datafile and therefore the tablespace containing the datafile, because the redo required to bring the datafile back online is gone. Oracle makes you acknowledge that your datafile is unrecoverable in this scenario as well, and you must use the UNRECOVERABLE DATAFILE keywords when you clear the log file group:

```
alter database clear logfile unarchived group 2 unrecoverable datafile;
```

The final step after clearing the redo log file group and creating a backup is to back up the control file to a specific directory or to the trace file directory:

```
alter database backup controlfile to trace;
```

Recovering from a Lost ACTIVE Redo Log Group

If a damaged redo log group is in the ACTIVE state, Oracle is not currently writing to it but it is needed for instance recovery. Try this command:

```
alter system checkpoint;
```

If it runs successfully, all committed changes are written to the datafiles on disk.

Next, clear the redo log file group as you did with an inactive redo log group, and you will not lose any transactions. In addition, your archived redo log file stream will be intact.

If the checkpoint fails, you must perform an incomplete recovery using Flashback Database. You can also perform an incomplete recovery using all archived and online redo log files up to but not including the damaged redo log group.

Recovering from a Lost CURRENT Redo Log Group

A lost redo log group in the CURRENT state is currently being written to by the LGWR process—or it *was* being written to at the time of failure. The instance will crash, and your only option is to perform incomplete recovery using Flashback Database. Again, you can do likewise with all archived and online redo log files up to but not including the damaged redo log group.

After performing incomplete recovery with the database in MOUNT mode, open the database with RESETLOGS:

```
alter database open resetlogs;
```

If the location for the damaged online redo log file group is available, Oracle will reinitialize the log file group along with all other groups, resetting the log sequence number to 1 and starting a new incarnation. If the location is no longer available, rename the online redo log files and point them to a new location as in this example, before opening the database with RESETLOGS:

```
alter database rename file '/u01/app/oracle/oradata/hr/redo02.log'
   to '/u02/app/oracle/oradata/hr/redo02.log';
alter database rename file '/u06/app/oracle/oradata/hr/redo02.log'
   to '/u07/app/oracle/oradata/hr/redo02.log';
```

When you open the database with RESETLOGS, Oracle re-creates and initializes any missing online redo log files.

CERTIFICATION OBJECTIVE 6.03

Recover from the Loss of the Password File

The loss of an Oracle password file is rather trivial compared to the loss of a datafile, a redo log file, or a control file. It won't cause the database to shut down but will prevent some or all DBAs from connecting to the database when it is not open. Although the password file is relatively easy to re-create, be sure that you make a backup copy of the password file using an operating system copy utility whenever it changes.

In the following sections, you'll get a brief refresher course on how the password file authenticates privileged users; then you'll learn how to re-create the password file when and if it becomes lost or corrupted.

Review of Authentication Methods

You can use two different methods to authenticate a database administrator: operating system (OS) authentication or password file authentication. Which method you use depends on whether you have a secure connection to the server (for remote administration) and whether you want to use OS groups to manage DBA privileges.

If you do not have a secure remote connection, you must use a password file. If you have a secure connection, or you're administering the database locally, you have the option to use OS authentication or a password file. Figure 6-1 identifies the options for a DBA when deciding which method will work the best in a particular environment.

For connecting locally to the server, the main consideration is the convenience of using the same account for both the OS and the Oracle server, versus maintaining a password file. For a remote administrator, the security of the connection is the driving factor when choosing an authentication method. Without a secure connection, a malicious hacker could easily impersonate a user with the same account as that of an administrator on the server itself, and thereby gain full access to the database with OS authentication.

on the
Úo b
When using a password file for authentication, ensure that the password file itself is in a directory location that is accessible only by the OS administrators and the user or group that owns the Oracle software installation.

A user could be a member of the OSDBA or OSOPER group and have an entry in the password file. In this situation, OS authentication takes precedence and the user connects with the group-assigned privileges regardless of the username and password specified.

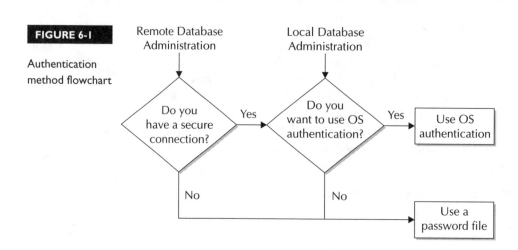

FIGURE 6-1

Authentication
method flowchart

Along with the additional privileges available to the users who connect as SYSDBA or SYSOPER, the default schema is also different for these users when they connect to the database. Users who connect with the SYSDBA or SYSASM privilege connect as the SYS user. The SYSOPER privilege sets the user to PUBLIC:

```
SQL> connect rjb/rjb as sysdba
Connected.
SQL> show user
USER is "SYS"
SQL>
```

Re-creating a Password File

A default installation of the Oracle database using the Oracle Universal Installer with a seed database, or using the Database Creation Assistant, will automatically create a password file. However, on some occasions you might need to re-create a password file if it is accidentally deleted or damaged. The orapwd command will create a password file with a single entry for the SYS user and other options when you run the orapwd command without any options:

```
[oracle@dw ~]$ orapwd
Usage: orapwd file=<fname> password=<password>
    entries=<users> force=<y/n> ignorecase=<y/n> nosysdba=<y/n>

  where
    file - name of password file (required),
    password - password for SYS (optional),
    entries - maximum number of distinct DBA (required),
    force - whether to overwrite existing file (optional),
    ignorecase - passwords are case-insensitive (optional),
    nosysdba - whether to shut out the SYSDBA logon
      (optional Database Vault only).

  There must be no spaces around equal-to (=) characters.

[oracle@dw ~]$
```

The default location for the password file is $ORACLE_HOME/dbs on Unix or Linux, and %ORACLE_HOME%\database on Windows. The name of the password file is the string "orapw" plus the name of the instance in lowercase. For example, the password file for the DW database would be $ORACLE_HOME/dbs/ orapwdw, and for Windows the default is PWD<*sid*>.ora.

Once you've re-created the password file, you will have to grant the SYSDBA, SYSOPER, or SYSASM privileges to database users who previously had those privileges. In addition, if the password you provided in the orapwd command is not the same password that the SYS account uses in the database, this is not a problem. When you connect using CONNECT / AS SYSDBA, you're using operating system authentication. When you connect using CONNECT SYS/<*syspassword*> AS SYSDBA, the password <*syspassword*> is the password for SYS in the database. And just to reiterate, if the database is down or in MOUNT mode, you must use operating system authentication or the password file. Also worth noting again is that operating system authentication takes precedence over password file authentication, so as long as you fulfill the requirements for OS authentication, the password file will not be used for authentication even if it exists.

on the
() o b

As of Oracle Database 11g, database passwords are case-sensitive. To disable case-sensitivity, set the SEC_CASE_SENSITIVE_LOGON initialization parameter to FALSE.

The system initialization parameter REMOTE_LOGIN_PASSWORDFILE controls how the password file is used for the database instance. It has three possible values: NONE, SHARED, and EXCLUSIVE.

If the value is NONE, Oracle ignores any password file that exists. Any privileged users must be authenticated by other means, such as by OS authentication, which is discussed in the next section.

With a value of SHARED, multiple databases can share the same password file. However, only the SYS user is authenticated with the password file and the password for SYS cannot be changed (unless you re-create the password file). As a result, this method is not the most secure, but it does allow a DBA to maintain more than one database with a single SYS account.

on the
() o b

If a shared password file must be used, ensure that the password for SYS is at least eight characters long and includes a combination of uppercase and lowercase alphabetic, numeric, and special characters to fend off a brute-force attack such as a dictionary attack.

A value of EXCLUSIVE binds the password file to one database only, and other database user accounts can exist in the password file. As soon as the password file is created, use this value to maximize the security of SYSDBA, SYSOPER, or SYSASM connections.

The dynamic performance view V$PWFILE_USERS lists all the database users who have SYSDBA, SYSOPER, or SYSASM privileges, as shown here:

```
SQL> select * from v$pwfile_users;

USERNAME                        SYSDB SYSOP SYSAS
------------------------------- ----- ----- -----
SYS                             TRUE  TRUE  FALSE
RJB                             TRUE  FALSE FALSE
```

EXERCISE 6-2

Re-create the Password File after Accidental Deletion

In this exercise, you'll re-create the password file for the HR database using the orapwd command and add the user RJB to the list of users in the SYSDBA group. Additionally, you'll give the user SCOTT the SYSOPER privilege:

1. Create the new password file with 10 entries and the new default password for the SYS account:

```
[oracle@srv04 ~]$ orapwd file=$ORACLE_HOME/dbs/orapwhr \
    password=bigsys entries=10
```

2. Connect as SYS and grant the SYSDBA privilege to the user RJB and the SYSASM privilege to SCOTT:

```
[oracle@srv04 ~]$ sqlplus sys/bigsys as sysdba

SQL*Plus: Release 11.1.0.6.0 - Production on Fri Jul 4
12:32:39 2008

Copyright (c) 1982, 2007, Oracle.  All rights reserved.

Connected to:
Oracle Database 11g Enterprise Edition Release 11.1.0.6.0 -
Production
With the Partitioning, OLAP, Data Mining and Real Application
    Testing options

SQL> grant sysdba to rjb;
```

```
        Grant succeeded.

        SQL> grant sysoper to scott;

        Grant succeeded.

        SQL>
```

3. Confirm that the users RJB and SCOTT have the new privileges:

```
        SQL> select * from v$pwfile_users;

        USERNAME                        SYSDB SYSOP SYSAS
        ------------------------------- ----- ----- -----
        SYS                             TRUE  TRUE  FALSE
        RJB                             TRUE  FALSE FALSE
        SCOTT                           FALSE TRUE  FALSE

        SQL>
```

CERTIFICATION OBJECTIVE 6.04

Perform User-Managed Complete Database Recovery

Recovery falls into one of two general categories: *complete* and *incomplete*. Firstly, if media failure occurs in your database, you will want to use complete recovery to bring your database back up to the state it was in before the media failure. This would include recovery of all committed transactions. Secondly, and in contrast, the database media itself may be intact but a number of changes or logical corruptions to the database have occurred, and these are not easily reversible using logical backups or by users re-entering the correct data to reverse incorrect transactions. In this second scenario, you might consider using incomplete recovery, which is covered later in this chapter.

The following section provides a thorough review and hands-on exercises for complete database recovery when the database is closed (shut down) as well as when the database is open (available to users). You can recover the database when it is open as long as the SYSTEM tablespace is not damaged.

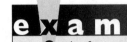

Whether the database is open or closed during complete recovery, you need to perform the same basic steps:

1. Identify files needed for recovery.
2. Restore recovery-related files that can contain both committed and uncommitted transactions.
3. Start up the database in MOUNT mode.
4. Bring datafiles online.
5. Apply archived and online redo log files to roll forward the database; this is also known as *cache recovery*.
6. Open the database to provide high availability.
7. Oracle automatically applies undo blocks to roll back uncommitted changes, which is also known as *transaction recovery*.
8. Open the database as read-write if it was opened as read-only. Undo data is applied for uncommitted transactions even if the database is open as read-only.

For either open or closed database recovery, you can recover the database all at once or recover a single tablespace or datafile at a time. Before you can perform step 3 in the preceding list, you must make sure all archived redo log files needed for complete or incomplete recovery are restored from tape or backup disk; they must also be available when you run the RECOVER command at the SQL> prompt.

Performing Complete Closed Database Recovery

The phrase "closed database recovery" is somewhat of a misnomer if you consider that the database instance may still be available when one or more datafiles become unavailable. This is an advantage, because you can then query the dynamic performance view V$RECOVER_FILE to see which files need media recovery and V$RECOVERY_LOG to see the archived log files needed to recover the restored datafile(s).

If one of the datafiles for the SYSTEM tablespace becomes unavailable or is damaged, the instance crashes or shuts down immediately. Even if the SYSTEM or UNDO tablespace is still available, the instance may still crash. In this scenario, you might be able to surmise which datafiles must be recovered by looking at the alert log or by inspecting the disk file system for missing files and restoring them from backup. If all else fails, you can restore all datafiles from the latest backup and recover the entire database.

Identifying Recovery-related Files

If your database is still running after media failure of one or more datafiles, the dynamic performance view V$RECOVER_FILE contains a list of the datafiles that need recovery.

In this example, a system administrator inadvertently deletes a datafile from disk. If she does not know which one was deleted, you can identify it by using V$RECOVER_FILE:

```
SQL> select file#, error from v$recover_file;

     FILE# ERROR
---------- ----------------------------------------
         7 FILE NOT FOUND

SQL>
```

Joining V$RECOVER_FILE with V$DATAFILE and V$TABLESPACE helps you identify which tablespace is affected:

```
SQL> select file#, d.name d_name, t.name t_name, status, error
  2  from v$recover_file r
  3      join v$datafile d using(file#)
  4      join v$tablespace t using(ts#)
  5  ;

FILE# D_NAME                           T_NAME      STATUS  ERROR
------- -------------------------------  ----------  ------- ----------------
      7 /u01/app/oracle/oradata/h CHGTRK        ONLINE  FILE NOT FOUND
        r/chgtrk02.dbf

SQL>
```

To recover this tablespace successfully, you'll need archived and online redo log files. V$RECOVERY_LOG tells you which archived redo log files you'll need:

```
SQL> select archive_name from v$recovery_log;

ARCHIVE_NAME
```

```
    --------------------------------------------------
    /u01/app/oracle/flash_recovery_area/HR/archivelog
        /2008_07_05/o1_mf_1_120_46zc6k8m_.arc

SQL>
```

In this example, only one archived redo log file is required to recover the CHGTRK tablespace.

Restoring Recovery-related Files

After you have identified the tablespace and datafiles that need recovery, you can shut down the database (if it is not already down) and repair the problem that caused the media failure. (This includes asking the system administrator not to delete your datafiles.) Copy the datafile from the backup location to the original location, if it's available. If the original location is not available, you can copy the backup datafile to an alternative location. Once the database is started in MOUNT mode, rename the datafile as follows, identifying the new location of the datafile in the control file:

```
SQL> alter database rename file
  2      '/u01/app/oracle/oradata/hr/chgtrk02.dbf'
  3      to '/u09/oracle/oradata/hr/chgtrk02.dbf'
  4  ;
```

In addition, ensure that all archived redo log files are available in the default archiving location. If insufficient space is available for all required archived redo log files, you can restore them to a location that offers enough disk space. You can then specify the alternative location when you recover the datafile. After all required datafiles are in their original or new locations, you can bring the datafiles online, as in this example:

```
SQL> alter database datafile
  2      '/u09/oracle/oradata/hr/chgtrk02.dbf' online;
```

Applying Redo Log Files

Now that you have restored the missing or damaged datafiles and have verified that the archived redo log files are in place, you can recover the database to bring all datafiles to the same SCN before you open the database for users. The command for recovering the database is as you might expect: RECOVER. Here it is in an example:

```
SQL> recover automatic database;
```

If you do not use the AUTOMATIC keyword, you are prompted to apply each archived and online redo log file. For complete recovery, you want to use AUTOMATIC so that all archived and online redo log files are applied to the datafiles. You may, however, want to be prompted for each log file in two scenarios: when you want to specify an alternative location for a specific log file, or when you are performing cancel-based (incomplete) recovery, which is discussed later in this chapter. Another keyword available in the RECOVER command is the FROM keyword. This makes it easy to specify an alternative source location for all archived redo log files.

Finally, you can open the database because you have performed these tasks while the database was in MOUNT mode:

```
SQL> alter database open;
```

EXERCISE 6-3

Perform a Complete Database Recovery

In this exercise, you'll create, populate, drop, restore, and recover the CHGTRK tablespace:

1. Create the CHGTRK tablespace:

```
SQL> create tablespace chgtrk
  2      datafile '/u01/app/oracle/oradata/hr/chktrk02.dbf'
  3      size 50m autoextend on next 25m;

Tablespace created.

SQL>
```

2. Back up the tablespace after placing it in BACKUP mode:

```
SQL> alter tablespace chgtrk begin backup;

Tablespace altered.

SQL> ! cp /u01/app/oracle/oradata/hr/chgtrk02.dbf
         /u06/backup/chgtrk02.dbf.bak

SQL> alter tablespace chgtrk end backup;

Tablespace altered.

SQL>
```

Note that the exclamation mark can be used within SQL*Plus to execute operating system commands on Unix platforms.

3. Create a few tables in the CHGTRK tablespace so that the Data Definition Language (DDL) and redo for this tablespace appears in the online redo log files and eventually the archived redo log files. Here's an example:

```
SQL> create table test_recov tablespace chgtrk
  2    as select * from dba_objects;
```

4. Force a log switch and archive the current online redo log file. You could also wait until Oracle generates enough internal redo to create the archived redo log files containing the redo for this tablespace:

```
SQL> alter system archive log current;

System altered.

SQL>
```

5. "Accidentally" drop the datafile for the CHGTRK tablespace:

```
[oracle@srv04 hr]$ rm /u01/app/oracle/oradata/hr/chgtrk02.dbf
```

6. Verify that you can no longer create objects in the CHGTRK tablespace:

```
SQL> create table temp_dba_objects
  2    tablespace chgtrk as select * from dba_objects;
create table temp_dba_objects tablespace chgtrk as select *
from dba_objects

     *
ERROR at line 1:
ORA-01116: error in opening database file 7
ORA-01110: data file 7: '/u01/app/oracle/oradata/hr/chgtrk02
.dbf'
ORA-27041: unable to open file
Linux Error: 2: No such file or directory
Additional information: 3

SQL>
```

7. Shut down the database and restart it in MOUNT mode:

```
SQL> shutdown immediate
Database closed.
Database dismounted.
ORACLE instance shut down.
```

```
SQL> startup mount
ORACLE instance started.

Total System Global Area   636100608 bytes
Fixed Size                   1301784 bytes
Variable Size              503317224 bytes
Database Buffers           125829120 bytes
Redo Buffers                 5652480 bytes
Database mounted.
SQL>
```

8. Use the views V$RECOVER_FILE and V$RECOVERY_LOG to identify the data-files and redo log files required for recovery:

```
SQL> select file#, d.name d_name, t.name t_name, status, error
  2  from v$recover_file r
  3      join v$datafile d using(file#)
  4      join v$tablespace t using(ts#)
  5  ;

  FILE# D_NAME                     T_NAME      STATUS   ERROR
------- -------------------------- ----------- -------- --------
      7 /u01/app/oracle/oradata/h  CHGTRK      ONLINE   FILE NOT
FOUND
        r/chgtrk02.dbf

SQL> select archive_name from v$recovery_log;

ARCHIVE_NAME
---------------------------------------------
/u01/app/oracle/flash_recovery_area/HR/archive
elog/2008_07_05/o1_mf_1_120_46zc6k8m_.arc

SQL>
```

9. The datafile's original location is available, so you don't need to specify a new location with ALTER DATABASE RENAME FILE. Copy the backup of the datafile to its original location:

```
[oracle@srv04 hr]$ cp /u06/backup/chgtrk02.dbf.bak \
>         /u01/app/oracle/oradata/hr/chgtrk02.dbf
[oracle@srv04 hr]$
```

10. Bring the restored datafile online:

```
SQL> alter database datafile
  2      '/u01/app/oracle/oradata/hr/chgtrk02.dbf' online;

Database altered.

SQL>
```

11. Use the RECOVER command and automatically apply any necessary archived redo log files:

```
SQL> recover automatic database;
Media recovery complete.
SQL>
```

12. Open the database:

```
SQL> alter database open;

Database altered.

SQL>
```

Performing Complete Open Database Recovery

In many situations, the database will continue to be available when datafiles for noncritical tablespaces become damaged or otherwise unavailable. Queries against tables in a damaged tablespace will return errors. Any attempt to write to the damaged tablespace will immediately bring the tablespace offline. As with closed database recovery, you need to query V$RECOVER_FILE and V$RECOVERY_LOG to find the files required for recovery.

While the database is open, take all tablespaces with damaged datafiles offline:

```
SQL> alter tablespace chgtrk offline temporary;
```

Specifying TEMPORARY issues a checkpoint for the remaining online datafiles in the tablespace, if any exist. This can save time in the recovery process if the hardware problem with the damaged datafile is temporary, because media recovery might not be necessary.

If the hardware problem is permanent, you can restore the damaged datafile from backup just as you can with complete closed database recovery. The difference with open database recovery lies in the RECOVER command—you recover a tablespace, and not the entire database:

```
SQL> recover automatic tablespace chgtrk;
SQL> alter tablespace chgtrk online;
```

Whether you use complete open or complete closed database recovery depends primarily on whether the database is open, as you might expect. However, if enough datafiles are missing or damaged, the database will not be of much use to most of your users, and the recovery effort will take less time if the database is not open. In addition, if the SYSTEM tablespace is damaged or unavailable, the database instance will crash and you will have to perform complete closed database recovery.

CERTIFICATION OBJECTIVE 6.05

Perform User-Managed Incomplete Database Recovery

Incomplete database recovery follows the same steps used in complete database recovery, except that you apply only the archived and online redo log files up to the desired point in time. As you might expect, incomplete recovery is also known as point-in-time recovery (PITR). You can recover a single tablespace or the entire database up to a specific SCN or point in time.

If you are interested in recovering only a small set of logically isolated tables to a previous point in time, you may be able to perform recovery using Oracle's Flashback Table features. This assumes that you have a large enough undo tablespace containing all of a particular table's transactions back to the desired point in time. Another method you can consider is Oracle's Flashback Database functionality, which can dramatically reduce the recovery time if you have a large enough Flashback recovery area and you have enabled Flashback Database logging.

In other words, consider incomplete database as a last resort. It might restore most of the database to your desired state, but you might lose many important transactions. Thus, Flashback Table may be a better alternative. If you have Flashback logging enabled, Flashback Database may throw out some good transactions with the bad ones. However, the time to recover is dramatically reduced because you do not need to restore backup datafiles before the recovery operation. Additionally, flashing back using the Flashback logs will often take significantly less time than applying archived and redo log files to the restored datafiles.

Following are some typical scenarios for which you must perform incomplete recovery:

- You lose a datafile and a required archive redo log file is missing.
- You are using the database as a test database and you want to rewind the state of the database to a point in time in the past so that you can repeat your tests.
- You want to roll back the database to a point in time before a serious user error.
- The database has corrupt blocks.

The following sections provide some guidelines for the type of incomplete recovery to perform, which usually depends on the type of error that has occurred. In addition, you'll see an example of cancel-based incomplete recovery. Recovery operations discussed prior to this didn't specify a stopping point for redo log file application:

```
SQL> recover automatic database;
```

As you remember from earlier in the chapter, AUTOMATIC does not prompt for each archived or online redo log file. It does, however, apply all archived and online redo logs to the datafiles to bring the database up to the last committed transaction.

Choosing the PITR Method

You have three options when choosing a point-in-time, or incomplete, recovery method:

- Specifying a time at which to stop
- Choosing an SCN at which to stop
- Specifying CANCEL during the recovery process

You would use time-based incomplete recovery if you knew the time of day when the corruption occurred. For example, suppose the data entry department started entering the wrong invoices into the system at 9 A.M., or a power surge from a storm at 11:00 A.M. caused a temporary disk controller failure that wrote random data to data blocks in the Oracle datafiles. Here's an example of time-based recovery:

```
SQL> recover database until time '2008-07-04:11:07:48';
```

SCN-based incomplete recovery works well if your applications save the SCN at critical points in a process flow, or the alert or trace logs indicate a serious error as of a particular SCN. Here's an example of how you would automatically apply all archived redo log files to a restored backup up to SCN 30412:

```
SQL> recover automatic database until change 30412;
```

Finally, you would typically use cancel-based incomplete recovery if you have a gap in the archived redo log files during the recovery process. This allows you to stop the recovery process before the RECOVER command tries to apply the missing archived redo log file. Here is an example:

```
SQL> recover database until cancel;
```

Note that you can use AUTOMATIC with all types of incomplete recovery just as you can with complete recovery. Leaving off AUTOMATIC gives you a little more control during the recovery process. For example, you still want to stop recovery at a particular point in time, but you may want to specify an alternative archived redo log file (from a duplexed archive log file location) for a damaged redo log file in the default location.

Regardless of the incomplete recovery method you use, you must open the database with RESETLOGS to start the log sequence over at 1 with a new database incarnation. Although you can easily recover a database through previous incarnations, it is unlikely you will use the orphaned backups from previous incarnations either because a gap exists in the archived redo log stream or because the data from the orphaned backup is unusable from a business perspective.

Performing User-Managed, Time-based Incomplete Recovery

You perform incomplete recovery much like you would complete recovery. You must have available backups of all datafiles along with all archived redo log files to bring all datafiles up to the desired point in time. Here are the steps:

1. Shut down the database if it is not already down.
2. Restore datafiles from a backup location to the current location.
3. Start up the database in MOUNT mode.
4. Recover the database using the RECOVER command.
5. Open the database with RESETLOGS.

EXERCISE 6-4

Perform Incomplete Time-based Recovery

For this exercise, several critical tables were dropped at 11:05 A.M. You have decided that the best recovery option is to perform time-based incomplete recovery on the entire database. Recover the database as of 11:00 A.M. using the most recent full backup.

1. Shut down the database:

```
SQL> connect / as sysdba
Connected.
SQL> shutdown immediate
Database closed.
Database dismounted.
ORACLE instance shut down.
SQL>
```

2. Copy backups of all datafiles to the current datafile location:

```
[oracle@srv04 ~]$ cd /u06/backup
[oracle@srv04 backup]$ ls
bi06.dbf  chgtrk02.dbf  example01.dbf  sysaux01.dbf
system01.dbf  temp02.dbf  temp03.dbf  undotbs01.dbf
users01.dbf
[oracle@srv04 backup]$ cp *dbf /u01/app/oracle/oradata/hr
[oracle@srv04 backup]$
```

3. Start up the database in MOUNT mode:

```
SQL> startup mount
ORACLE instance started.

Total System Global Area  636100608 bytes
Fixed Size                  1301784 bytes
Variable Size             478151400 bytes
Database Buffers          150994944 bytes
Redo Buffers                5652480 bytes
Database mounted.
SQL>
```

4. Perform a manual time-based incomplete recovery as of 11:00 A.M.:

```
SQL> recover database until time '2008-07-06:11:00:00';
Media recovery complete.
SQL>
```

Notice in this example that you were not prompted to apply any archived redo log files. The recovery operation started shortly after the corruption occurred in the database. So all redo information required to recover the database was present in the online redo log files. You can see this in the alert log with online redo log recoveries only, as shown next:

```
ALTER DATABASE RECOVER  database until time '2008-07-06:11:00:00'
Media Recovery Start
Fast Parallel Media Recovery enabled
Recovery of Online Redo Log: Thread 1 Group 1 Seq 126 Reading mem 0
  Mem# 0: /u01/app/oracle/oradata/hr/redo01.log
  Mem# 1: /u06/app/oracle/oradata/hr/redo01.log
Recovery of Online Redo Log: Thread 1 Group 3 Seq 127 Reading mem 0
  Mem# 0: /u01/app/oracle/oradata/hr/redo03.log
  Mem# 1: /u06/app/oracle/oradata/hr/redo03a.log
Sun Jul 06 11:20:39 2008
Recovery of Online Redo Log: Thread 1 Group 2 Seq 128 Reading mem 0
  Mem# 0: /u01/app/oracle/oradata/hr/redo02.log
  Mem# 1: /u06/app/oracle/oradata/hr/redo02.log
Incomplete Recovery applied until change 5624352 time 07/06/2008
11:00:07
Media Recovery Complete (hr)
Completed: ALTER DATABASE RECOVER  database until time '2008-07-
06:11:00:00'
```

If the recovery process needed archived redo log files (which it didn't), you would see these types of entries in the alter log:

```
ORA-00279: change 5561591 generated at 07/05/2008 11:44:30
   needed for thread 1
ORA-00289: suggestion :
/u01/app/oracle/flash_recovery_area/HR/archivelog/
   2008_07_05/o1_mf_1_120_46zc6k8m_.arc
ORA-00280: change 5561591 for thread 1 is in sequence #120

Specify log: {<RET>=suggested | filename | AUTO | CANCEL}

ORA-00279: change 5564346 generated at 07/05/2008 12:18:09
   needed for thread 1
ORA-00289: suggestion :
/u01/app/oracle/flash_recovery_area/HR/archivelog/
   2008_07_05/o1_mf_1_121_46zc6q4b_.arc
ORA-00280: change 5564346 for thread 1 is in sequence #121

Specify log: {<RET>=suggested | filename | AUTO | CANCEL}
```

5. Finally, open the database with the RESETLOGS option:

```
SQL> alter database open resetlogs;

Database altered.

SQL> archive log list
Database log mode              Archive Mode
Automatic archival             Enabled
Archive destination            USE_DB_RECOVERY_FILE_DEST
Oldest online log sequence     1
Next log sequence to archive   1
Current log sequence           1
SQL>
```

Note the SQL*Plus command ARCHIVE LOG LIST, which shows you that the log sequence number has been reset to 1 and the RESETLOGS operation has created a new database incarnation.

CERTIFICATION OBJECTIVE 6.06

Perform User-Managed and Server-Managed Backups

The types of user-managed backup you can perform are dependent on whether your database is running in ARCHIVELOG mode. This book has stressed the distinct advantages of running your database in ARCHIVELOG mode, with only minor disadvantages. If you are not running in ARCHIVELOG mode, you must shut down the database to perform a backup using operating system commands. If you are using ARCHIVELOG mode, you can put an individual tablespace or the entire database into BEGIN BACKUP mode, copy the datafiles to a backup location, and then take the database out of backup mode with END BACKUP. This can all occur while users are accessing the database, though the response time may decrease a bit while the backup occurs.

In this section, you'll see how a user-managed backup can occur while the database is shut down (typically for a database in NOARCHIVELOG mode), and how it can occur while the database is open. Before you can perform the backup, you need to know which files to back up, which is also covered in this section. Although this objective references server-managed backups using RMAN, these were discussed thoroughly in Chapter 5 and RMAN is not covered here.

Identifying Files for Manual Backup

Whether you're backing up your database in NOARCHIVELOG mode (closed database backup) or in ARCHIVELOG mode (open database backup), you need to identify the files you need to back up. While the database is open, you can query the dynamic performance views V$DATAFILE and V$CONTROLFILE. Here's an example:

```
SQL> select name from v$datafile;

NAME
--------------------------------------------------
/u01/app/oracle/oradata/hr/system01.dbf
/u01/app/oracle/oradata/hr/sysaux01.dbf
/u01/app/oracle/oradata/hr/undotbs01.dbf
/u01/app/oracle/oradata/hr/users01.dbf
/u01/app/oracle/oradata/hr/example01.dbf
/u01/app/oracle/oradata/hr/bi06.dbf
/u01/app/oracle/oradata/hr/chgtrk02.dbf

7 rows selected.

SQL> select name from v$controlfile;

NAME
--------------------------------------------------
/u01/app/oracle/oradata/hr/control01.ctl
/u01/app/oracle/oradata/hr/control02.ctl
/u01/app/oracle/oradata/hr/control03.ctl

SQL>
```

Note that you need to back up only one copy of the control file, because all multiplexed copies are identical. Also, you do not need to back up online redo log files.

Remember that you should never back up the online redo log files. This is very important to remember, because if you restore datafiles for complete recovery, then by restoring old copies of the redo log files you will almost certainly cause loss of committed transactions. If you lose online redo log file groups or an online redo log file group member, follow the steps at the beginning of this chapter!

Backing Up a Database in NOARCHIVELOG Mode

To perform full backup of a database in NOARCHIVELOG mode, start by shutting down the database:

```
SQL> shutdown immediate
Database closed.
Database dismounted.
ORACLE instance shut down.
SQL>
```

Next, use operating system commands to copy the files identified in the dynamic performance views V$DATAFILE and V$CONTROLFILE:

```
SQL> ! cp /u01/app/oracle/oradata/hr/*.dbf /u06/backup
SQL> ! cp /u01/app/oracle/oradata/hr/control01.ctl /u06/backup
SQL>
```

The datafiles are in a consistent state because the database is shut down. In other words, the SCNs for all datafiles are the same. Note that you can run the operating system backup commands within SQL*Plus by using the escape character, !. Finally, restart the database:

```
SQL> startup
ORACLE instance started.

Total System Global Area   636100608 bytes
Fixed Size                   1301784 bytes
Variable Size              490734312 bytes
Database Buffers           138412032 bytes
Redo Buffers                 5652480 bytes
Database mounted.
Database opened.
SQL>
```

Backing Up a Database in ARCHIVELOG Mode

A distinct advantage to using ARCHIVELOG mode is that you can perform online backups (also known as *hot backups*), while the database is available to users. Users could experience a slight decrease in response time, depending on the system load and whether you are backing up the entire database at once or one tablespace at a time. The backup of a given tablespace's datafile could be inconsistent with other datafile backups (in other words, the SCNs are not the same). If you are running your database in ARCHIVELOG mode, the recovery process can use archived and online redo log files to recover all datafiles to the same SCN.

You can back up the entire database while the database is online (with ALTER DATABASE BEGIN BACKUP). Typically you would back up only one tablespace at a time to minimize response time delays for users accessing the database while it is online. In addition, you should perform online backups of tablespaces with frequent Data Manipulation Language (DML) activity more often than tablespaces with low activity, and far more often than read-only tablespaces.

To back up the datafiles for an individual tablespace, you use the data dictionary view DBA_DATA_FILES instead of the dynamic performance view V$DATAFILE. This is because DBA_DATA_FILES associates the tablespace name with its datafiles, as the association between the datafile name and its tablespace might not be obvious by viewing V$DATAFILE. Here is a query against DBA_DATA_FILES:

```
SQL> select tablespace_name, file_name from dba_data_files;

TABLESPACE_NAME   FILE_NAME
----------------  ----------------------------------------------------
USERS             /u01/app/oracle/oradata/hr/users01.dbf
UNDOTBS1          /u01/app/oracle/oradata/hr/undotbs01.dbf
SYSAUX            /u01/app/oracle/oradata/hr/sysaux01.dbf
SYSTEM            /u01/app/oracle/oradata/hr/system01.dbf
EXAMPLE           /u01/app/oracle/oradata/hr/example01.dbf
CHGTRK            /u01/app/oracle/oradata/hr/chgtrk02.dbf
BI                /u01/app/oracle/oradata/hr/bi06.dbf
USERS             /u01/app/oracle/oradata/hr/users02.dbf

8 rows selected.

SQL>
```

Note in this example that the USERS tablespace contains two datafiles and that both must be backed up to perform media recovery successfully for the USERS tablespace. To enable operating system backup of the USERS tablespace's datafiles, put it in backup mode as follows:

```
SQL> alter tablespace users begin backup;

Tablespace altered.

SQL>
```

Next, perform an operating system copy command, much as you did with a full database backup in NOARCHIVELOG mode:

```
SQL> ! cp /u01/app/oracle/oradata/hr/users*.dbf /u06/backup
SQL> ! ls -l /u06/backup/users*.dbf
-rw-r-----  1 oracle oinstall 219291648 Jul  6 12:18
/u06/backup/users01.dbf
-rw-r-----  1 oracle oinstall  20979712 Jul  6 12:18
/u06/backup/users02.dbf
SQL>
```

Finally, terminate backup mode for the USERS tablespace:

```
SQL> alter tablespace users end backup;

Tablespace altered.

SQL>
```

on the job

It is important that you end backup mode for a tablespace. The database will not shut down if any tablespaces are in backup mode, and leaving a tablespace in backup mode continues to generate and retain unnecessary redo after you complete the backup of the tablespace.

CERTIFICATION OBJECTIVE 6.07

Identify the Need for Backup Mode

Backup mode is required for any backup of a tablespace or the entire database because of the nature of a data block: Copying a datafile at the same time that the Oracle Database Writer (DBWR) process is updating the block can cause a *fractured block*. In other words, the header and footer of the block are not consistent at a given SCN.

Oracle provides two solutions for this problem. If you use RMAN to back up your datafiles, RMAN automatically rereads the block over and over until it is consistent. If the block doesn't become consistent after a fixed number of retries, then RMAN determines that the block is permanently corrupted and reports an error.

If you are not using RMAN, you must use `ALTER DATABASE BEGIN BACKUP` or `ALTER TABLESPACE . . . BEGIN BACKUP`. For both of these commands, Oracle generates additional redo for the database or for the individual tablespace, respectively. Each block modified while the datafile is in backup mode is written to the redo log before any changes are applied to the block. In other words, Oracle saves the before image of the block in the redo stream. And, of course, the changes to a block are written to the redo stream as well. During recovery, Oracle can use the copy of the block in the redo stream if the recovery process detects a fractured block.

CERTIFICATION OBJECTIVE 6.08

Back Up and Recover a Control File

Although the control file is one of the smaller files in your database environment, it is critical to the operation of the database because it contains the metadata for all objects in your database. The control file contains datafile locations, online redo log file locations, and so forth. Therefore, it is wise not only to multiplex the control file in several locations but to back it up frequently. In the following sections, you'll learn how to back up the control file while the database is available to users. And when disaster strikes, you'll learn how to recover from the loss of one or more copies of your control file.

Backing Up the Control File in ARCHIVELOG mode

Backing up the control file for a database running in `ARCHIVELOG` mode produces the same end result as the method you use in `NOARCHIVELOG` mode. The only difference is that you can use two different SQL commands to perform the backup. Earlier in the chapter, you learned how to back up the control file when the database is shut down.

on the
job

As you recall from Chapter 5, you can back up the control file with RMAN using the `BACKUP CURRENT CONTROLFILE` *command.*

The first method for backing up a control file in `ARCHIVELOG` mode creates an exact copy of the current control file to a location you specify:

```
SQL> alter database backup controlfile to '/u06/backup/controlfile
.bkup';

Database altered.

SQL> ! ls /u06/backup/control*
/u06/backup/control01.ctl  /u06/backup/controlfile.bkup

SQL>
```

The other method creates an editable script that re-creates the control file. Here is the command:

```
SQL> alter database backup controlfile to trace;

Database altered.

SQL>
```

Oracle creates the script in the location where all trace files reside, which by default for the HR database is $ORACLE_BASE/diag/rdbms/hr/hr/trace. Here is an excerpt from the generated script:

```
. . .
-- The following commands will create a new control file and use it
-- to open the database.
-- Data used by Recovery Manager will be lost.
-- Additional logs may be required for media recovery of offline
-- Use this only if the current versions of all online logs are
-- available.
-- After mounting the created controlfile, the following SQL
-- statement will place the database in the appropriate
-- protection mode:
--  ALTER DATABASE SET STANDBY DATABASE TO MAXIMIZE PERFORMANCE
STARTUP NOMOUNT
CREATE CONTROLFILE REUSE DATABASE "HR" NORESETLOGS  ARCHIVELOG
    MAXLOGFILES 16
    MAXLOGMEMBERS 3
    MAXDATAFILES 100
    MAXINSTANCES 8
    MAXLOGHISTORY 292
```

```
LOGFILE
  GROUP 1 (
    '/u01/app/oracle/oradata/hr/redo01.log',
    '/u06/app/oracle/oradata/hr/redo01.log'
  ) SIZE 50M,
. . .
```

Recovering the Control File

Chapter 5 covered a scenario in which one of your multiplexed control files is lost. The recovery process in this scenario is very straightforward, because you can replace the missing copy by copying one of the multiplexed copies, and then restart the database. However, even if you multiplex your control file in several locations, it is still possible that all copies of the control file can be lost due to a catastrophic failure of all disks containing the control file. In this event, you will have to use a backup copy of the control file created with one of the methods discussed in the preceding section (with hopes that not all backups failed during the hypothetical catastrophic event).

Depending on the status of the online redo log files and the status of the datafiles, you perform slightly different actions. In most cases, you must open the database with RESETLOGS after the recovery operation. Table 6-2 describes the actions you must perform for each combination of online redo log and datafile availability.

| TABLE 6-2

Control File
Recovery
Scenarios	Availability of Online Redo Log Files	Availability of Datafiles	Recovery Procedure
	Available	Current	Recover the database with a restored copy of the control file, applying online redo logs if necessary. Open the database with RESETLOGS.
	Unavailable	Current	Re-create the control file and open the database with RESETLOGS.
	Available	Restored from Backup	Restore a control file from backup, perform complete recovery, and then open the database with RESETLOGS.
	Unavailable	Restored from Backup	Restore a control file from backup, perform incomplete recovery, and then open the database with RESETLOGS.

In each of the scenarios in Table 6-2, you perform the following steps:

1. Shut down the database with SHUTDOWN ABORT (if it has not already crashed).
2. Restore the control file from backup.
3. Start up the database in MOUNT mode.
4. Start database recovery and specify BACKUP CONTROLFILE in the RECOVER command.
5. Open the database with RESETLOGS.

If the following conditions are true, you do not have to open the database with RESETLOGS, and you will not lose any committed transactions:

■ You manually ran CREATE CONTROLFILE or have a backup of the control file created with ALTER DATABASE BACKUP CONTROLFILE TO TRACE.

■ All online redo log files are available.

■ All datafiles are current.

All other scenarios, including using a backup control file with undamaged online redo log files and datafiles, will require opening the database with RESETLOGS.

A RECOVER command using a backup copy of the control file will look like this:

```
SQL> recover database using backup controlfile until cancel;
```

Even if all archived and online redo log files are intact, the RECOVER command will prompt for a missing archived redo log file. This indicates that unarchived changes existed in the online redo log files. In this scenario, you must manually specify the locations of each online redo log file until the RECOVER command finds the required redo information.

EXERCISE 6-5

Recover from the Loss of All Control Files

In this exercise, you'll use a backup copy of the control file to recover from the loss of all online control files.

1. Shut down the database if it has not already crashed after the inadvertent deletion of all online control files:

```
SQL> startup
ORACLE instance started.
```

```
Total System Global Area   636100608 bytes
Fixed Size                   1301784 bytes
Variable Size              490734312 bytes
Database Buffers           138412032 bytes
Redo Buffers                 5652480 bytes
ORA-00205: error in identifying control file, check alert log
for more info

SQL> shutdown abort
ORACLE instance shut down.
SQL>
```

2. All online redo log files and datafiles appear to be intact, along with the disks containing the original copies of the control file. Use operating system copy commands to restore a backup of the control file to the original locations:

```
SQL> ! cp /u06/backup/control01.ctl
/u01/app/oracle/oradata/hr/control01.ctl
SQL> ! cp /u06/backup/control01.ctl
/u01/app/oracle/oradata/hr/control02.ctl
SQL> ! cp /u06/backup/control01.ctl
/u01/app/oracle/oradata/hr/control03.ctl
SQL>
```

3. Open the database in MOUNT mode and perform non-AUTOMATIC recovery so that you can manually specify online redo log files, if so required:

```
SQL> recover database using backup controlfile until cancel;
ORA-00279: change 5625919 generated at 07/06/2008 11:48:28
     needed for thread 1
ORA-00289: suggestion :
/u01/app/oracle/flash_recovery_area/HR/archivelog/
     2008_07_06/o1_mf_1_1_472fxokb_.arc
ORA-00280: change 5625919 for thread 1 is in sequence #1

Specify log: {<RET>=suggested | filename | AUTO | CANCEL}
 . . .
Media recovery complete.
SQL>
```

4. Finally, open the database with RESETLOGS:

```
SQL> alter database open resetlogs;

Database altered.

SQL>
```

CERTIFICATION SUMMARY

This chapter covered user-managed backup and recovery—you did not use system-managed backup and recovery methods, such as RMAN. You performed most of these backup and recovery operations with operating system and SQL*Plus commands while the database was shut down or in MOUNT mode.

The first part of the chapter started with one of the more straightforward recovery techniques: replacing a lost tempfile. The impact to the user is temporary, the database remains open, and you can create another tempfile within minutes of discovering the problem.

Next, you saw a few more complicated scenarios involving redo log file failures. Losing one member of a redo log file group, even if it is active, is easy to repair and does not impact users and their transactions. Recovering from the loss of an entire redo log group is a bit more complicated. This is because loss of committed transactions is possible if the database is currently attempting to write to the lost redo log file group.

The password file is critical to the database in that it controls the authentication of DBAs who want to connect to the database as SYSDBA. It is easy to re-create the password file, but you should back it up using operating system commands whenever you add or remove SYSDBA, SYSOPER, or SYSASM privileges for a DBA.

You can perform some backups while the database is online, either backing up one tablespace at a time or backing up all datafiles in the database. If you are running your database in NOARCHIVELOG mode, the only way you can create a consistent backup without archived redo log files is to perform the backup while the database is shut down. You learned about several user-managed methods to back up and recover your database whether you are in ARCHIVELOG or NOARCHIVELOG mode.

Finally, you saw some techniques that can be used to recover your database with a backup control file if all current copies of the control file are lost or damaged. If you frequently back up your control file (for example, after every structural database change), there is no loss of committed transactions if the data files and online redo log files are intact.

✔ TWO-MINUTE DRILL

Recover from a Lost Tempfile

❑ A tempfile can be recovered while the database is open.

❑ The impact of a lost tempfile is noticed when users attempt to sort large result sets.

❑ When a tempfile is lost, you can re-create it in the original location or specify a new location.

❑ If the database starts without tempfiles, it creates them in the location specified in the control file.

Recover from a Lost Redo Log Group

❑ A redo log group can have six statuses: CURRENT, ACTIVE, INACTIVE, UNUSED, CLEARING, or CLEARING_CURRENT. The most common statuses are CURRENT, ACTIVE, and INACTIVE.

❑ You can use the dynamic performance view V$LOG to query the status of each redo log group.

❑ If one member of a log group becomes damaged or is lost, the LGWR (Log Writer) process continues to write to the undamaged member and no data loss or interruption in service occurs.

❑ The dynamic performance view V$LOGFILE shows the status of each individual member of each log file group.

❑ If the status of a log file group member is INVALID in the view V$LOGFILE, it is damaged or unavailable and must be re-created.

❑ Losing a log file group with a status of INACTIVE will most likely not result in the loss of committed transactions as long as the other member(s) of the log file group remain intact.

❑ Losing an inactive log file group that has not been archived will result in a gap in the archived redo log files and necessitates a full backup after recovering the log file group.

❑ Losing a redo log file group with a status of ACTIVE will not cause the loss of committed transactions if you can successfully perform ALTER SYSTEM CHECKPOINT. If the checkpoint fails, you must perform incomplete recovery.

❑ Losing a redo log file group with a status of CURRENT will crash the instance, and you must perform incomplete recovery.

Recover from the Loss of the Password File

❑ Losing a password file prevents DBAs from connecting to an open or closed instance with the SYSDBA, SYSOPER, or SYSASM privilege.

❑ You must use a password file if you are connecting remotely and the connection is not secure.

❑ Connecting with the SYSDBA or SYSASM privilege connects to the database as the SYS user. The SYSOPER privilege connects as PUBLIC.

❑ You use the `orapwd` command at an operating system prompt to re-create the password file.

❑ The default location for the password file is $ORACLE_HOME/dbs on Unix or Linux, and %ORACLE_HOME%\database on Windows.

❑ The dynamic performance view V$PWFILE_USERS lists all the database users who have SYSDBA, SYSOPER, or SYSASM privileges.

Perform User-Managed Complete Database Recovery

❑ If media failure occurs in your database, you will typically want to use complete recovery to bring your database back up to the state it was in before the media failure, which includes all committed transactions.

❑ For either open or closed database recovery, you can recover the database all at once, a single tablespace at a time, or one datafile at a time.

❑ You can query the dynamic performance view V$RECOVER_FILE to see which files need media recovery and V$RECOVERY_LOG to see the archived log files needed to recover the restored datafile(s) for complete database recovery.

❑ You perform user-managed complete recovery after the database is restarted in MOUNT mode.

❑ All archived redo log files required to recover the restored datafiles must be available in the default location to automate the recovery process with the AUTOMATIC clause of the RECOVER command.

❑ If the archived redo log files required for recovery are in several locations, you can specify these locations manually during the recovery process when you do not specify the AUTOMATIC keyword.

❑ You can perform complete open database recovery on one or more damaged tablespaces by taking the tablespace(s) offline with the ALTER TABLESPACE . . . OFFLINE TEMPORARY command.

❑ To recover a tablespace while it is offline and the rest of the database is online, you use the RECOVER AUTOMATIC TABLESPACE . . . command after restoring the tablespace's datafile(s) from the backup location.

Perform User-Managed Incomplete Database Recovery

❑ For an incomplete database recovery, you follow the same steps used for complete database recovery, except that you apply only the archived and online redo log files up to the desired point in time.

❑ For incomplete recovery, you can specify a time at which to stop or an SCN (System Change Number) at which to stop, or you can specify CANCEL during the recovery process.

❑ You can use time-based incomplete recovery if you know the time of day when the corruption occurred.

❑ SCN-based incomplete recovery works well if your applications save the SCN (and thus a COMMIT point) at critical points in a process flow.

❑ You typically use cancel-based incomplete recovery if you have a gap in the archived redo log files during the recovery process.

❑ Regardless of the incomplete recovery method, you must open the database with RESETLOGS to start the log sequence at 1 with a new database incarnation.

Perform User-Managed and Server-Managed Backups

❑ If you are not running in ARCHIVELOG mode, you must shut down the database to perform a backup using operating system commands.

❑ If you are using ARCHIVELOG mode, you can put an individual tablespace or the entire database into BEGIN BACKUP mode. You can then proceed to copy the datafiles to a backup location. After that, you can take the database out of backup mode with END BACKUP.

❑ While the database is open, you can query the dynamic performance views V$DATAFILE and V$CONTROLFILE to identify the locations of all datafiles and all online controlfile copies.

❑ When you perform a backup with the database closed, the backup is considered consistent because the SCNs for all datafiles match; all files are frozen in time.

❑ To back up the datafiles for an individual tablespace, you use the data dictionary view DBA_DATA_FILES to see the association between tablespaces and datafile names.

❑ The database will not shut down if any tablespaces are in backup mode.

Identify the Need for Backup Mode

❑ Copying a datafile with an operating system command at the same time the Oracle DBWR process is updating the block can cause a *fractured block*.

❑ If you use RMAN to back up your datafiles, RMAN automatically rereads the block over and over until it is consistent.

❑ For ALTER DATABASE BEGIN BACKUP or ALTER TABLESPACE . . . BEGIN BACKUP, Oracle generates additional redo (the before-image of the block) for the database or for the individual tablespace until you take the database or tablespace out of backup mode.

Back Up and Recover a Control File

❑ If you want to back up your control file while the database is open, you can do it with two different SQL commands: ALTER DATABASE BACKUP CONTROLFILE TO <*filename*> and ALTER DATABASE BACKUP CONTROLFILE TO TRACE

❑ ALTER DATABASE BACKUP CONTROLFILE TO <*FILENAME*> creates an exact binary copy of the control file at the specified location.

❑ ALTER DATABASE BACKUP CONTROLFILE TO TRACE creates an editable script that re-creates the control file in the directory $ORACLE_BASE/diag/rdbms/<*database*>/<*instance*>/trace.

❑ Losing all copies of the online control file does not lose any committed transactions if you have a recent backup copy of the control file and both the datafiles and online redo log files are intact.

❑ You do not have to open the database with RESETLOGS after restoring your control file if you manually create the replacement control file using CREATE CONTROLFILE or you use a version of the control file script that you created with ALTER DATABASE BACKUP CONTROLFILE TO TRACE.

SELF TEST

The following questions will help you measure your understanding of the material presented in this chapter. Read all the choices carefully, because there might be more than one correct answer. Choose all correct answers for each question.

Recover from a Lost Tempfile

1. If you lose all of the tempfiles from your temporary tablespace, what is the most likely result noticed by your users?

A. The database becomes unavailable and users cannot connect.

B. The users can't perform SELECT statements.

C. The users cannot add or delete rows in any table.

D. The users can't use ORDER BY or GROUP BY in their queries.

2. Which is the best method for recovering a tempfile? (Choose the best answer.)

A. Drop the TEMP tablespace and re-create it with a datafile in a new location.

B. Add another tempfile to the TEMP tablespace and drop the corrupted or missing tempfile while the database is running.

C. Shut down the database, restore the tempfile from a backup, and recover it using archived and online redo log files.

D. Add another tempfile to the TEMP tablespace and drop the corrupted or missing tempfile after the database has been shut down and restarted in MOUNT mode.

Recover from a Lost Redo Log Group

3. Which of the following is not a valid status for an online redo log group?

A. CURRENT

B. ACTIVE

C. INVALID

D. UNUSED

E. CLEARING

4. What is the difference between the V$LOG and V$LOGFILE views?

A. V$LOG contains the status of all archived redo log files and V$LOGFILE contains the status of all online redo log files.

B. V$LOG contains the status of the online redo log group members and V$LOGFILE contains the status of individual online redo log groups.

C. V$LOG contains the status of all online redo log files and V$LOGFILE contains the status of all archived redo log files.

D. V$LOG contains the status of the online redo log groups and V$LOGFILE contains the status of individual redo log group members.

Recover from the Loss of the Password File

5. Which methods can you use to recover a lost or damaged password file? (Choose all that apply.)

A. Use the orapwd command at an operating system prompt to re-create the password file.

B. Restore the password file from backup, and apply any archived and online redo log files to bring its contents to the present time.

C. Use the orapwd SQL command to re-create the password file.

D. Restore the password file from an operating system backup.

Perform User-Managed Complete Database Recovery

6. You will perform complete closed database recovery. Put the following steps in the correct order.
   1. Open the database to users.
   2. Identify files needed for recovery.
   3. Start up the database in MOUNT mode.
   4. Bring the datafiles online.
   5. Apply archived and online redo log files to roll forward.
   6. Oracle applies undo to roll back uncommitted changes.
   7. Restore recovery-related files containing committed and uncommitted transactions.

   A. 1, 2, 7, 3, 4, 5, 6
   B. 2, 7, 3, 4, 5, 1, 6
   C. 2, 7, 4, 3, 5, 1, 6
   D. 1, 2, 7, 3, 5, 6, 1

7. Inspect the following query against the dynamic performance views V$RECOVER_FILE, V$DATAFILE, and V$TABLESPACE:

```
select file#, d.name d_name, t.name t_name, status, error
from v$recover_file r
    join v$datafile d using(file#)
    join v$tablespace t using(ts#);
```

For what type of backup or recovery related task is this view useful? (Choose the best answer.)

A. It identifies datafiles with errors along with their associated tablespaces.

B. It identifies tablespaces with errors along with all datafiles in the tablespace.

C. It identifies all tablespaces that are offline and have errors.

D. It identifies all tablespaces that are online and have errors.

E. It identifies tablespaces that have datafiles that are in need of a backup.

Perform User-Managed Incomplete Database Recovery

8. You want to perform user-managed, incomplete database recovery. Which of the following methods are not available for incomplete database recovery? (Choose all that apply.)

A. Recovery up to the last commit for a specified table

B. Recovery up to the last available archived redo log file

C. Recovery up to a specified SCN

D. Recovery up to a specified timestamp

E. Recovery until you cancel the recovery option

Perform User-Managed and Server-Managed Backups

9. Which two dynamic performance views can you use to identify files that need to be backed up, regardless of whether you are in ARCHIVELOG mode or NOARCHIVELOG mode?

A. V$DATAFILE and V$LOGFILE

B. V$DATAFILE and V$TEMPFILE

C. V$LOGFILE and V$LOG

D. V$DATAFILE and V$CONTROLFILE

Identify the Need for Backup Mode

10. Which of the following backup methods will alleviate the problem caused by fractured blocks during an online backup? (Choose all correct answers.)

A. Use ALTER DATAFILE BEGIN BACKUP.

B. Use RMAN to back up your datafiles.

C. Perform backups while in RESTRICTED mode.

D. Use ALTER DATABASE BEGIN BACKUP.

E. Use ALTER TABLESPACE BEGIN BACKUP.

Back Up and Recover a Control File

11. Which of the following commands does not back up the current control file?

A. SQL> ALTER DATABASE BACKUP CONTROLFILE TO TRACE;

B. SQL> ALTER SYSTEM BACKUP CURRENT CONTROLFILE;

    C. `RMAN> BACKUP CURRENT CONTROLFILE;`

    D. `SQL> ALTER DATABASE BACKUP CONTROLFILE TO`
       `'/U08/BACKUP/CTL.BAK';`

12. You have lost all online control files. Specify the correct order for the following tasks:

1. Restore the control file from backup or run `CREATE CONTROLFILE`.
2. Start database recovery and specify the keywords `BACKUP CONTROLFILE`.
3. Start up the database in `MOUNT` mode.
4. Open the database with `RESETLOGS`.
5. Shut down the database.

    A. 5, 1, 3, 2, 4

    B. 1, 5, 3, 2, 4

    C. 5, 1, 3, 4, 2

    D. 1, 5, 3, 4, 2

SELF TEST ANSWERS

Recover from a Lost Tempfile

1. ☑ **D.** Temporary tablespaces provide sort space for queries that use ORDER BY and GROUP BY when the sort operation will not fit in memory. Other operations cause sorts as well: SELECT DISTINCT, index creations, and index rebuilds.

   ☒ **A** is wrong because the database remains available for some queries and most DML activity even if the TEMP tablespace is unavailable. **B** is wrong because users can still perform SELECT statements that don't need sorting or the sort operation will fit into memory. **C** is a wrong answer because most DML activity does not require the TEMP tablespace.

2. ☑ **B.** Once the missing tempfile is dropped and a new one added, the TEMP tablespace is automatically available to users.

   ☒ **A** is wrong because dropping the tablespace is not necessary, and you cannot drop the default temporary tablespace. **C** is wrong because you cannot recover a temporary tablespace; there are no permanent objects in a temporary tablespace. **D** is wrong because the database does not need to be shut down to recover a temporary tablespace.

Recover from a Lost Redo Log Group

3. ☑ **C.** The status INVALID is valid only for an online redo log group member, not for the entire group.

   ☒ **A, B, D,** and **E** are valid statuses for an online redo log group.

4. ☑ **D.** V$LOG contains the status of redo log groups, including whether the group is currently being written to. V$LOGFILE contains the status of individual redo log group members.

   ☒ **A, B,** and **C** are wrong. The views V$LOG and V$LOGFILE do not contain information about archived redo log files, although the view V$LOG has a column to indicate whether the redo log file group has been archived or not.

Recover from the Loss of the Password File

5. ☑ **A** and **D.** Either method can be used to recover the password file, but using the orapwd command requires that you re-create the privileged user accounts that need SYSDBA, SYSOPER, and SYSADM privileges.

   ☒ **B** is wrong because you do not apply redo log files to the password file. **C** is wrong because orapwd is valid only at an operating system command prompt.

Perform User-Managed Complete Database Recovery

6. ☑ **B,** Complete closed or open database recovery requires the same steps in this order.
☒ **A, C,** and **D** are not in the correct order.

7. ☑ **A.** The query identifies all datafiles with errors, the tablespace in which they reside, and whether the tablespace is offline or online.
☒ **B** is wrong because the error reporting is at the datafile level. **C** and **D** are wrong because the view shows datafiles with errors (not tablespaces), regardless of whether they are offline or online. **E** is wrong because these views are not indicative of the backup retention policy for the tablespace.

Perform User-Managed Incomplete Database Recovery

8. ☑ **A** and **B.** You cannot perform a recovery using archived and online redo log files to recover the database to a commit point for a table or as of the last archived redo log file.
☒ **C, D,** and **E** are incorrect. All three of these options are available using the RECOVER command when you want to perform incomplete recovery.

Perform User-Managed and Server-Managed Backups

9. ☑ **D.** The view V$DATAFILE contains all datafiles, and V$CONTROLFILE contains a list of all copies of the control file.
☒ **A** is wrong because you do not need to back up the online redo log files. **B** is wrong because you do not need to back up datafiles from temporary tablespaces that do not contain any permanent objects and can be easily recreated if lost. **C** is wrong because online redo log files do not need to be backed up and V$LOG contains information about online redo log file groups, not individual files.

Identify the Need for Backup Mode

10. ☑ **B, D,** and **E.** If you use RMAN to perform online backups, it rereads the block if the SCN in the header and footer do not match. You use ALTER DATABASE BEGIN BACKUP to perform online backups of the entire database all at once. Use ALTER TABLESPACE BEGIN BACKUP to perform a backup of one tablespace at a time.
☒ **A** is wrong because you cannot put an individual datafile into backup mode. **C** is wrong because opening the database in RESTRICTED mode prevents non-SYSDBA users from connecting to the database but does not prevent block fracturing.

Back Up and Recover a Control File

11. ☑ **B.** There is no such command.

☒ **A** creates a text-based file containing two different CREATE CONTROLFILE commands, depending on the availability of your datafiles and online redo log files. **C** is one of many ways that RMAN backs up the control file. **D** creates a binary copy of the control file at the specified location.

12. ☑ **A.** The first step is to shut down the database (with ABORT), and the last step is to open the database with RESETLOGS (if you used a backup control file or you do not have current online redo logs or datafiles).

☒ **B, C,** and **D** are wrong, because all three of these sequences are out of order.

7
Miscellaneous RMAN Features

Chapter 6 took a little detour away from RMAN to cover user-managed recovery techniques. It's important that you know how to make backups outside of RMAN for three reasons:

- The complexity of using RMAN might be overkill for a small read-only database.
- A user-managed backup strategy (including logical backups) can be a fallback for RMAN-created backups in case of a corrupted RMAN backup or bug in RMAN itself (both of which are quite rare).
- You need to know how to perform user-managed backups for the certification exam!

This chapter moves back into the world of RMAN and covers two important RMAN features: creating a duplicate database, and using tablespace point-in-time recovery (TSPITR).

RMAN makes it easy to make a full copy or a subset of a target database. The copied database has a new database ID (DBID) and can thus coexist on the same network as the source database. The copied database can even be on the same host and can use the same RMAN catalog as the source database because it has its own DBID. A copy of a database has many uses, including testing of backup and recovery procedures.

Using TSPITR is another recovery feature of RMAN that is useful for situations in which the damage to the database is local to a small subset of tablespaces or tables, such as a logical corruption of a table or an erroneous TRUNCATE TABLE statement. TSPITR is the ideal tool for the job when other methods such as Flashback Database or Flashback Table are not configured in your database. You could lose other committed transactions as part of the incomplete recovery process.

CERTIFICATION OBJECTIVE 7.01

Creating a Duplicate Database Using RMAN

You can use several methods to create a duplicate database, but they all use RMAN, either directly or indirectly. You use a combination of SQL*Plus and RMAN commands to create a duplicate database, or you use operating system commands if you need more control over the duplication process. Alternatively, you can use Enterprise Manager (also known as Enterprise Manager Database Control, EM for short, or the Grid Control), to automate the process using either a database backup or even a live instance.

The following sections provide an in-depth example of cloning our human resources database (hr) to a test database (hrtest) on the same host (srv04).

Using RMAN to Create a Duplicate Database

Before continuing with the example, it's important to clarify some naming conventions. The *source database* is the database you want to copy. The *duplicate database* is the copy of your source database. The *source instance* is the instance RMAN will use to access the source database, as you might expect. The new instance is called the *auxiliary instance* during the copy operation. After the copy operation is complete, you can call it anything you want because it no longer has any connection to the source database!

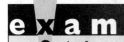

The official Oracle documentation occasionally refers to the source database as the target database, and the exam will do this as well. This is a bit counter-intuitive, but is probably linked to the RMAN command line where the `TARGET` argument references the database you want to back up.

Here are the general steps to follow to create a duplicate database on another host:

1. Create a password file for the auxiliary instance.
2. Ensure network connectivity to the auxiliary instance.
3. Create an initialization parameter file for the auxiliary instance.
4. Start the auxiliary instance in NOMOUNT mode.
5. Start the source database in MOUNT or OPEN mode.
6. Create backups or copy existing backups and archived redo log files to a location accessible by the auxiliary instance unless you are using active database duplication.

7. Allocate auxiliary channels if necessary.

8. Run the RMAN DUPLICATE command.

9. Open the auxiliary instance.

In the scenario that follows, the source and destination server (srv04) already has the Oracle software installed as well as the existing hr database.

Configure the Auxiliary Instance

Some preparation on the destination server is required before you perform the database duplication. First, you must create a password file for the auxiliary instance, because you are going to duplicate from an active database instead of backups. You must also create a password file if your RMAN client runs on another host; however, this scenario runs the RMAN executable on the same host as the destination database. Create the password file with the same SYS password as the source database's password file:

```
[oracle@srv04 ~]$ orapwd file=$ORACLE_HOME/dbs/orapwhrtest \
>    password=sysdbapwd entries=10
[oracle@srv04 ~]$
```

Note that the default location for all database password files is $ORACLE_HOME/dbs.

Establish Network Connectivity

If the source database was on a different host, you would have to ensure network connectivity to the source server. In this scenario, the source and destination are the same and no adjustments to the tnsnames.ora file are necessary. However, because the new instance is open in NOMOUNT mode, the process that registers the instance with the listener has not started yet. Thus you must manually add an entry such as the following and restart the listener:

```
sid_list_listener =
  (sid_list =
    (sid_desc =
      (global_dbname=hrtest.world)
      (sid_name = hrtest)
      (oracle_home=/u01/app/oracle/product/11.1.0/db_1)
    )
  )
```

Create an Initialization Parameter File

The next step is to create an initialization parameter file for the auxiliary instance. Only DB_NAME must be specified; all other parameters are optional, depending on whether you use Oracle Managed Files or you want to specify an alternative location for one or more file destinations. Table 7-1 lists the parameters you can specify in the auxiliary initialization file along with their descriptions and under what circumstances they are required.

TABLE 7-1	Initialization Parameter	Value(s)	Required?
Initialization Parameters for the Auxiliary Instance.	DB_NAME	The name you specify in the DUPLICATE command, which must be unique among databases in the destination ORACLE_HOME.	Yes
	CONTROL_FILES	All control file locations.	Yes, unless you use Oracle-Managed Files (OMF)
	DB_BLOCK_SIZE	The block size for the duplicate database. This size must match the source database.	Yes, if set in the source database.
	DB_FILE_NAME_CONVERT	Pairs of strings for converting datafile and tempfile names.	No
	LOG_FILE_NAME_CONVERT	Pairs of strings to rename online redo log files.	No
	DB_CREATE_FILE_DEST	Location for OMFs.	No
	DB_CREATE_ONLINE_LOG_DEST_*n*	Location for Oracle-managed online redo log files.	No
	DB_RECOVERY_FILE_DEST	Location of the flash recovery area.	No

Note that the DB_FILE_NAME_CONVERT parameter can be specified when you run the DUPLICATE command. Here is the initialization parameter file (inithrtest. ora) for the auxiliary instance created in $ORACLE_HOME/dbs:

```
DB_NAME=hrtest
DB_BLOCK_SIZE=8192
CONTROL_FILES=(/u01/app/oracle/oradata/hrtest/control01.ctl,
               /u01/app/oracle/oradata/hrtest/control02.ctl,
               /u01/app/oracle/oradata/hrtest/control03.ctl)
DB_FILE_NAME_CONVERT=(/u01/app/oracle/oradata/hr/,
               /u01/app/oracle/oradata/hrtest/)
```

```
LOG_FILE_NAME_CONVERT=(/u01/app/oracle/oradata/hr/,
                       /u01/app/oracle/oradata/hrtest/,
                       /u06/app/oracle/oradata/hr/,
                       /u06/app/oracle/oradata/hrtest/)
```

Start the Auxiliary Instance in NOMOUNT Mode and Create an SPFILE

Using the initialization parameter file you just created, start the instance in NOMOUNT mode and create an SPFILE:

```
[oracle@srv04 ~]$ export ORACLE_SID=hrtest
[oracle@srv04 ~]$ sqlplus / as sysdba

SQL*Plus: Release 11.1.0.6.0 - Production on Thu Jul 17 22:08:08 2008

Copyright (c) 1982, 2007, Oracle.  All rights reserved.

Connected to an idle instance.

SQL> startup nomount pfile='$ORACLE_HOME/dbs/inithrtest.ora'
ORACLE instance started.

Total System Global Area  146472960 bytes
Fixed Size                  1298472 bytes
Variable Size              92278744 bytes
Database Buffers           50331648 bytes
Redo Buffers                2564096 bytes
SQL> create spfile from pfile;

File created.

SQL>
```

Note that you are setting the environment variable ORACLE_SID to the new instance name. This has the desired effect of creating any missing instance directories automatically, such as the diagnostic directory structure:

```
[root@srv04 hrtest]# pwd
/u01/app/oracle/diag/rdbms/hrtest/hrtest
[root@srv04 hrtest]# ls
alert  cdump  hm  incident  incpkg  ir  lck  metadata  stage
sweep  trace
[root@srv04 hrtest]#
```

Note also that the newly created SPFILE resides in the default directory $ORACLE_HOME/dbs with other SPFILEs and password files.

Start the Source Database in MOUNT or OPEN Mode

If the source database is not already open, start it in MOUNT or OPEN mode. If you do not want users to access the database during the duplication process, open it in MOUNT mode:

```
[oracle@srv04 ~]$ export ORACLE_SID=hr
[oracle@srv04 ~]$ sqlplus / as sysdba

SQL*Plus: Release 11.1.0.6.0 - Production on Thu Jul 17 22:27:54 2008

Copyright (c) 1982, 2007, Oracle.  All rights reserved.

Connected to an idle instance.

SQL> startup mount
ORACLE instance started.

Total System Global Area  636100608 bytes
Fixed Size                  1301784 bytes
Variable Size             478151400 bytes
Database Buffers          150994944 bytes
Redo Buffers                5652480 bytes
Database mounted.
SQL>
```

Create Backups for the DUPLICATE Command

All datafile backups, including incremental backups and archived redo log files, must be available on a file system accessible by the auxiliary instance. In this scenario, you are performing an active database duplication; therefore, you do not have to create or copy backups for the operation.

Allocate Auxiliary Channels if Necessary

If you are using backups for the duplication process, you need to configure RMAN channels to be used on the auxiliary database instance. The channel on the auxiliary instance restores the backups, so you need to specify the ALLOCATE command in the RUN block, as in this example:

```
RMAN> run
        { allocate auxiliary channel aux0 device type disk;
          allocate auxiliary channel aux1 device type disk;
          . . .
          duplicate target database . . .
        }
```

Even if your device type is DISK, you can allocate multiple channels to enable parallel processing of the backups and therefore reduce the time it takes to perform the copy.

For the purposes of this scenario, the default DISK channel on the auxiliary instance is sufficient. So you will not need to specify any additional channels for the DUPLICATE command.

Run the RMAN DUPLICATE Command

Here is the moment we've all been waiting for: starting RMAN and performing the duplication process. Start the RMAN executable and connect to the source database:

```
[oracle@srv04 ~]$ rman
Recovery Manager: Release 11.1.0.6.0
        - Production on Thu Jul 17 23:00:07 2008

Copyright (c) 1982, 2007, Oracle.  All rights reserved.

RMAN> connect target sys@hr

target database Password:
connected to target database: HR  (DBID=3318356692)

RMAN>
```

Next, connect to the auxiliary instance:

```
RMAN> connect auxiliary sys@hrtest

auxiliary database Password:
connected to auxiliary database: HRTEST (not mounted)

RMAN>
```

Of course, you can put all of the CONNECT statements on the RMAN command line:

```
[oracle@srv04 ~]$ rman target sys/syspw1@hr auxiliary sys/
syspw2@hrtest
```

Finally, run the DUPLICATE command with the ACTIVE DATABASE clause to perform the copy directly from the live datafiles:

```
RMAN> duplicate target database
2>        to hrtest
3>        from active database
4>    ;
```

RMAN conveniently creates a temporary script with all the appropriate SET NEWNAME commands and proceeds to copy the database:

```
Starting Duplicate Db at 18-JUL-08
using target database control file instead of recovery catalog
allocated channel: ORA_AUX_DISK_1
channel ORA_AUX_DISK_1: SID=97 device type=DISK

contents of Memory Script:
{
   set newname for datafile  1 to
 "/u01/app/oracle/oradata/hrtest/system01.dbf";
   set newname for datafile  2 to
 "/u01/app/oracle/oradata/hrtest/sysaux01.dbf";
   set newname for datafile  3 to
 "/u01/app/oracle/oradata/hrtest/undotbs01.dbf";
   set newname for datafile  4 to
 "/u01/app/oracle/oradata/hrtest/users01.dbf";
   set newname for datafile  5 to
 "/u01/app/oracle/oradata/hrtest/example01.dbf";
   set newname for datafile  6 to
 "/u01/app/oracle/oradata/hrtest/bi06.dbf";
   set newname for datafile  7 to
 "/u01/app/oracle/oradata/hrtest/chgtrk02.dbf";
   set newname for datafile  8 to
 "/u01/app/oracle/oradata/hrtest/users02.dbf";
   backup as copy reuse
   datafile  1 auxiliary format
 "/u01/app/oracle/oradata/hrtest/system01.dbf"   datafile
2 auxiliary format
 "/u01/app/oracle/oradata/hrtest/sysaux01.dbf"   datafile
3 auxiliary format
```

```
    "/u01/app/oracle/oradata/hrtest/undotbs01.dbf"   datafile
  4 auxiliary format
    "/u01/app/oracle/oradata/hrtest/users01.dbf"   datafile
  5 auxiliary format
    "/u01/app/oracle/oradata/hrtest/example01.dbf"   datafile
  6 auxiliary format
    "/u01/app/oracle/oradata/hrtest/bi06.dbf"   datafile
  7 auxiliary format
    "/u01/app/oracle/oradata/hrtest/chgtrk02.dbf"   datafile
  8 auxiliary format
    "/u01/app/oracle/oradata/hrtest/users02.dbf"   ;
    sql 'alter system archive log current';
}
executing Memory Script

executing command: SET NEWNAME
executing command: SET NEWNAME
executing command: SET NEWNAME
executing command: SET NEWNAME
executing command: SET NEWNAME
executing command: SET NEWNAME
executing command: SET NEWNAME
executing command: SET NEWNAME

Starting backup at 18-JUL-08
allocated channel: ORA_DISK_1
channel ORA_DISK_1: SID=116 device type=DISK
channel ORA_DISK_1: starting datafile copy
. . .
contents of Memory Script:
{
    Alter clone database open resetlogs;
}
executing Memory Script

database opened
Finished Duplicate Db at 18-JUL-08

RMAN>
```

In summary, here is what the DUPLICATE command does:

- Creates a control file for the duplicate database.
- Restores the target data files to the duplicate database or copies directly from the running database.

- Performs incomplete recovery up to the last archived redo log file.
- Shuts down and restarts the auxiliary instance.
- Opens the auxiliary database with the `RESETLOGS` option.
- Creates the online redo log files.
- Generates a new DBID for the auxiliary database.

Here are some other options available with the `DUPLICATE` command:

- **`SKIP READONLY`** Exclude read-only tablespaces from the copy operation.
- **`SKIP TABLESPACE`** Exclude specific tablespaces, except for `SYSTEM` and `UNDO`.
- **`NOFILENAMECHECK`** Don't check for duplicate filenames between the source and destination databases.
- **`OPEN RESTRICTED`** When the destination database is ready, open it immediately with the `RESTRICTED SESSION` option.

Using Enterprise Manager to Create a Duplicate Database

You can also use Enterprise Manager (EM) to create a duplicate database. You can use three sources to create the duplicate database with EM:

- A running instance
- A staging area common to the source and destination hosts, which is big enough to hold a new backup
- An existing backup of the source database

Behind the scenes, EM uses a combination of SQL commands, operating system commands, and RMAN commands to perform the cloning operation. Whether you use the RMAN methods presented earlier in the chapter or the EM GUI depends on your level of expertise and comfort level with the command line, as well as how many databases you want to clone. If you need to clone several databases, it can take less time to create SQL and RMAN scripts to automate the process versus using EM repeatedly.

In the next scenario, you will use EM to clone a running database. The human resources database HR runs on the server srv04, and you will clone it to run as a third database on the same server, srv04, to create a database called HRTEST2.

From the EM home page for the source database (in this case the hr database), select the Data Movement tab and click the Clone Database link under the Move Database Files column. You will see the screen shown in Figure 7-1.

Select the A Running Database and the Copy Database Files Over Oracle Net radio buttons, and then click the Continue button. In the screen shown in Figure 7-2, specify the username and password for the owner of the Oracle software on the source server, which is typically `oracle`.

Click the Next button. In the screen shown in Figure 7-3, specify the destination Oracle home directory and host (in this case srv04), destination host credentials, and destination database name. Even if the source database is using Automatic Storage Management (ASM) or raw disks for datafile storage, you will use the file system on the destination server for the cloned database.

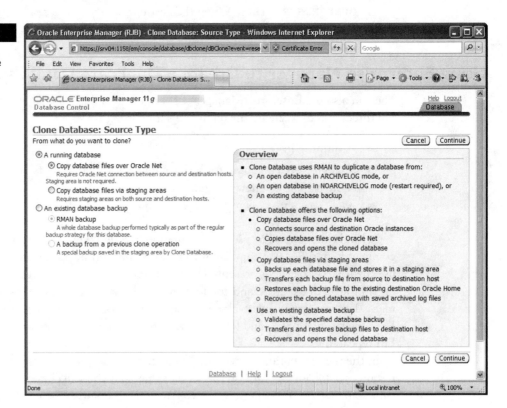

FIGURE 7-1

Selecting clone source type

FIGURE 7-2

Specifying host
credentials for
the source server

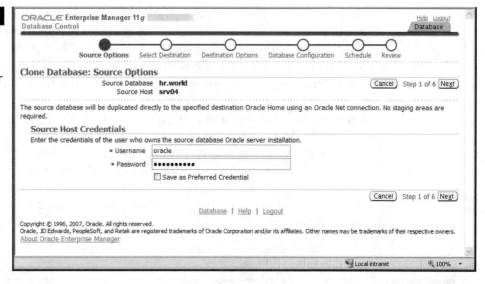

FIGURE 7-3

Specifying
destination
credentials and
database name

Click Next again. The next screen, shown in Figure 7-4, estimates the disk space required for the new database. Select the Use Database Area And Flash Recovery Area radio button to enable the use of Oracle Managed Files (OMF), freeing you from explicitly naming every database object, such as archived redo log files. In addition, you can select the Customize link to refine the destination locations for the database files, control files, and online redo log files.

After you click the Next button, the screen shown in Figure 7-5 appears, where you specify the location of the network files that EM will modify using the new database name. In addition, you specify the passwords for the SYS, SYSMAN, and DBSNMP accounts, as well as optionally registering this database with EM.

Click the Next button to open the Scheduler page shown in Figure 7-6. The cloning process will run as a batch job. You can run it immediately or schedule it to run at a later time.

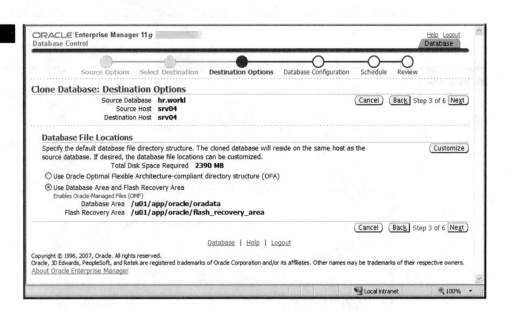

FIGURE 7-4

Specifying and customizing database file locations

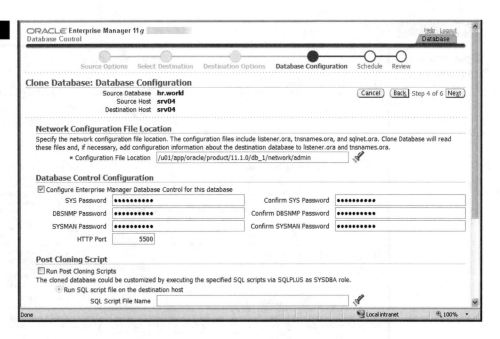

FIGURE 7-5

Specifying network configuration file location and passwords

FIGURE 7-6

Specifying schedule options for a cloning job

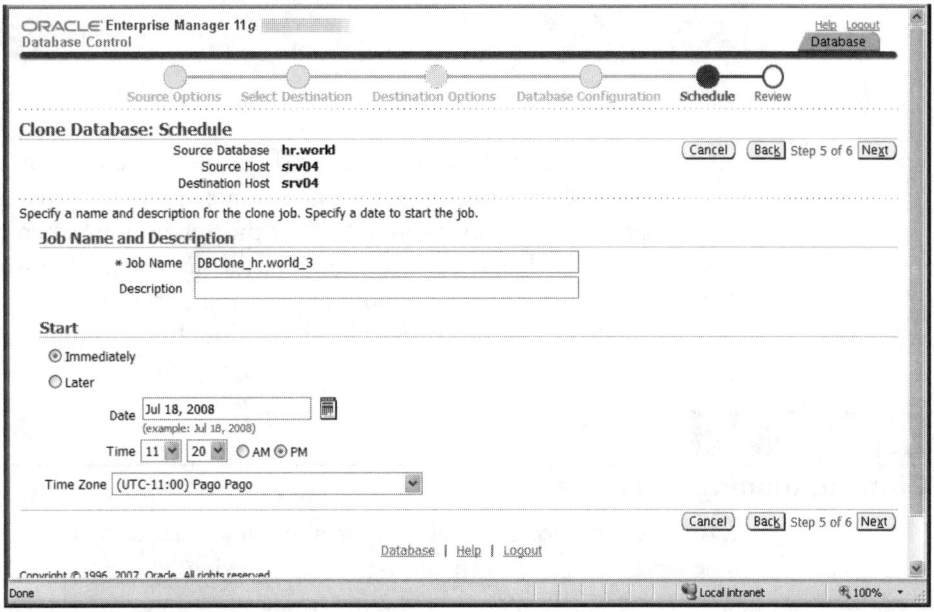

FIGURE 7-7

Clone database
job review page

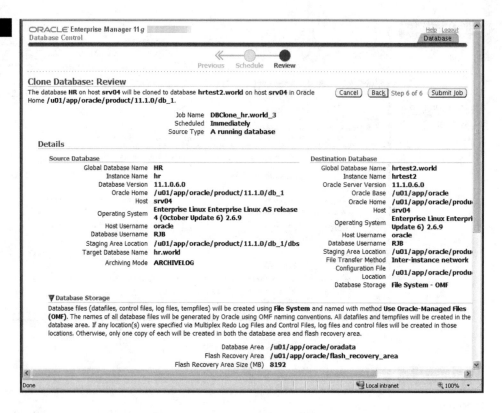

Click Next to open the Review screen shown in Figure 7-7. You can optionally cancel the entire operation or go back one or more pages to correct any options.

If all options are specified correctly, click the Submit Job button to initiate the cloning operation. The next screen confirms the successful submission of the job; click the View Status button to monitor the status of the cloning procedure. When the job completes with no errors, the new database hrtest2 is up and running.

EXERCISE 7-1

Clone a Running Database

In this exercise, clone a database from a running instance to another database on the same server using the instructions provided previously to clone a database using EM.

CERTIFICATION OBJECTIVE 7.02

Using a Duplicate Database

A duplicate database can be used for many things, including the following:

- Test backup and recovery procedures without disrupting the production database.
- Test a database upgrade.
- Test the effect of application upgrades on database performance.
- Generate reports that would otherwise have a detrimental effect on the response time for an online transaction processing (OLTP) production system.
- Export a table from a duplicate database that was inadvertently dropped from the production database, and then import it back into the production database; this assumes that the table is static or read-only.

EXERCISE 7-2

Recover a Dropped Table Using a Cloned Database

In this exercise, you will use the cloned database to recover the table HR.JOB_HISTORY. The SQL> prompt is changed in the following examples on each database using the SET SQLPROMPT command to indicate clearly what commands you execute on each database.

1. "Accidentally" drop the table HR.JOB_HISTORY in the HR database:

```
hr SQL> drop table hr.job_history;

Table dropped.

hr SQL>
```

2. Create the Data Pump transfer directory on the source database, and then grant permissions on the directory object to the user RJB:

```
hrtest SQL> create directory DPXFER as '/tmp/DataPumpXfer';

Directory created.
```

```
hrtest SQL> grant read, write on directory DPXFER to rjb;

Grant succeeded.

hrtest SQL>
```

3. Create the same directory and permissions on the HR database (the destination database). If the databases were on different hosts, ensure that the directory object references a shared file system directory.

4. Run Data Pump export on the database containing the table to be restored (this database was originally the auxiliary database):

```
[oracle@srv04 ~]$ expdp rjb/rjb@hrtest directory=dpxfer  \
        dumpfile=jobhist.dmp tables=hr.job_history

Export: Release 11.1.0.6.0 - Production on Saturday, 19 July, 2008 18:28:29
Copyright (c) 2003, 2007, Oracle.  All rights reserved.

Connected to: Oracle Database 11g Enterprise Edition
        Release 11.1.0.6.0 - Production
With the Partitioning, OLAP, Data Mining and Real
        Application Testing options
Starting "RJB"."SYS_EXPORT_TABLE_01":  rjb/********
   directory=dpxfer dumpfile=jobhist.dmp tables=hr.job_history
Estimate in progress using BLOCKS method...
Processing object type TABLE_EXPORT/TABLE/TABLE_DATA
Total estimation using BLOCKS method: 64 KB
Processing object type TABLE_EXPORT/TABLE/TABLE
Processing object type TABLE_EXPORT/TABLE/GRANT/OWNER_GRANT/OBJECT_GRANT
Processing object type TABLE_EXPORT/TABLE/INDEX/INDEX
Processing object type TABLE_EXPORT/TABLE/CONSTRAINT/CONSTRAINT
Processing object type TABLE_EXPORT/TABLE/INDEX/STATISTICS/INDEX_STATISTICS
Processing object type TABLE_EXPORT/TABLE/COMMENT
Processing object type TABLE_EXPORT/TABLE/CONSTRAINT/REF_CONSTRAINT
Processing object type TABLE_EXPORT/TABLE/STATISTICS/TABLE_STATISTICS
. . exported "HR"."JOB_HISTORY"              7.054 KB     10 rows
Master table "RJB"."SYS_EXPORT_TABLE_01" successfully loaded/unloaded
**********************************************************************
Dump file set for RJB.SYS_EXPORT_TABLE_01 is:
  /tmp/DataPumpXfer/jobhist.dmp
Job "RJB"."SYS_EXPORT_TABLE_01" successfully completed at 18:29:07
[oracle@srv04 ~]$
```

5. Run Data Pump import to restore the table to the source database:

```
[oracle@srv04 ~]$ impdp rjb/rjb@hr directory=dpxfer dumpfile=jobhist.dmp

Import: Release 11.1.0.6.0 - Production on Saturday, 19 July, 2008 18:33:56
Copyright (c) 2003, 2007, Oracle.  All rights reserved.


Connected to: Oracle Database 11g Enterprise Edition
      Release 11.1.0.6.0 - Production
With the Partitioning, OLAP, Data Mining and Real
      Application Testing options
Master table "RJB"."SYS_IMPORT_FULL_01" successfully loaded/unloaded
Starting "RJB"."SYS_IMPORT_FULL_01":  rjb/********@hr
      directory=dpxfer dumpfile=jobhist.dmp
Processing object type TABLE_EXPORT/TABLE/TABLE
Processing object type TABLE_EXPORT/TABLE/TABLE_DATA
. . imported "HR"."JOB_HISTORY"                 7.054 KB       10 rows
Processing object type TABLE_EXPORT/TABLE/GRANT/OWNER_GRANT/OBJECT_GRANT
Processing object type TABLE_EXPORT/TABLE/INDEX/INDEX
Processing object type TABLE_EXPORT/TABLE/CONSTRAINT/CONSTRAINT
Processing object type TABLE_EXPORT/TABLE/INDEX/STATISTICS/INDEX_STATISTICS
Processing object type TABLE_EXPORT/TABLE/COMMENT
Processing object type TABLE_EXPORT/TABLE/CONSTRAINT/REF_CONSTRAINT
Processing object type TABLE_EXPORT/TABLE/STATISTICS/TABLE_STATISTICS
Job "RJB"."SYS_IMPORT_FULL_01" successfully completed at 18:34:56

[oracle@srv04 ~]$
```

6. Confirm that the table has been successfully restored:

```
hr SQL> describe hr.job_history
 Name                                      Null?    Type
 ----------------------------------------- -------- --------------------
 EMPLOYEE_ID                               NOT NULL NUMBER(6)
 START_DATE                                NOT NULL DATE
 END_DATE                                  NOT NULL DATE
 JOB_ID                                    NOT NULL VARCHAR2(10)
 DEPARTMENT_ID                                      NUMBER(4)

hr SQL>
```

Alternatively, you can create a database link from the HR database to the
HRTEST database to restore the table. Again, this method is feasible only if the
table is static or read-only. Note that you can use several other ways to recover the
table, but it's good to have yet another way to recover part or your entire database
when disaster strikes.

CERTIFICATION OBJECTIVE 7.03

Identify the Situations that Require TSPITR

RMAN facilitates automatic TSPITR, making it easy to restore the contents of one or more tablespaces to a previous point in time without affecting other tablespaces or other objects in the database. TSPITR is a useful recovery tool for these scenarios:

- Corruption or deletion of rows in key tables that occurs in a logically-isolated tablespace; in other words, no indexes or parent/child relationships from objects in other tablespaces.

- Incorrect Data Definition Language (DDL) changes the structure of one or more tables in a tablespace, and therefore Flashback Table is not available to recover these tables.

- A table is dropped with the PURGE option.

Flashback Database can perform the task, but this has two drawbacks: First, all objects in the database are rolled back (not just a tablespace you are trying to recover). Second, you must maintain flashback logs to use Flashback Database, whereas a tablespace's TSPITR window extends back to the earliest recoverable backup for the tablespace.

TSPITR is not a cure-all for all tablespace disasters. For example, you cannot use it to recover a dropped tablespace. You also cannot recover a renamed tablespace to a point in time before it was renamed.

Before we delve into an in-depth example in the next section, you should understand the following terminology:

- **Target time**   The point in time or SCN to which the tablespace will be recovered.

- **Recovery set**   The group of datafiles containing the tablespace(s) to be recovered.

- **Auxiliary set**   Other datafiles required to recover the tablespace(s), such as the datafiles for the SYSTEM, UNDO, and TEMP tablespaces.

- **Auxiliary destination**   A temporary location to store the auxiliary set of files, including online and archived redo log files, and a copy of the control file created during the recovery process.

The key to TSPITR is an auxiliary instance to facilitate the recovery process, as covered earlier in this chapter. The auxiliary instance does the work of restoring a backup control file from before the desired point in time, restores the recovery set and the auxiliary set from the target database, and finally recovers the database for the auxiliary instance to the desired point in time. Here is a complete list of steps that RMAN performs during TSPITR:

1. Restores a backup control file to the auxiliary instance
2. Restores the data files for the recovery set to the target database
3. Restores the data files for the auxiliary set to the auxiliary instance
4. Recovers the data files to the desired point in time
5. Exports dictionary metadata for the recovered tablespace to the target database
6. Issues SWITCH commands on the target database to reference the recovered data files in the recovery set
7. Imports dictionary metadata from the auxiliary instance to the target instance so that the target instance can access the recovered objects
8. Opens the auxiliary database with the RESETLOGS option
9. Exports dictionary metadata for the recovery objects to the target database
10. Shuts down the auxiliary instance
11. Imports the dictionary metadata from the auxiliary to the target
12. Deletes all auxiliary files

CERTIFICATION OBJECTIVE 7.04

Perform Automated TSPITR

In the following scenario, your HR database includes a tablespace BI containing a key table SALES_RESULTS_2008Q1. The table is accidentally dropped around 9:58 P.M. on 7/19/2008. You conclude that the table, its indexes, and any related tables all reside in the tablespace BI. So using TSPITR is a viable option for recovering this table.

on the
job

Be sure to select the correct time for TSPITR. Once you recover the tablespace and bring it online, you can no longer use any previous backups unless you are using a recovery catalog.

In the following sections, you'll perform some preliminary steps before the actual recovery operation. First, you'll make sure that no other tablespaces have dependencies on the tablespace to be recovered. In addition, you'll determine whether any other objects will be lost in the target tablespace when it is recovered (any objects created after the desired point in time). Finally, you'll perform automated RMAN TSPITR, the Oracle-recommended option.

Verifying Tablespace Dependencies

Other tablespaces may have objects with dependencies on objects in the tablespace to be recovered. Use the data dictionary view TS_PITR_CHECK to identify any dependencies, as in this example:

```
SQL> select obj1_owner, obj1_name, ts1_name,
  2          obj2_owner, obj2_name, ts2_name
  3  from ts_pitr_check
  4  where (ts1_name = 'BI' and ts2_name != 'BI')
  5     or (ts1_name != 'BI' and ts2_name = 'BI')
  6  ;

no rows selected

SQL>
```

To resolve any issues found, you can either temporarily remove the dependencies or add the tablespace containing objects with dependencies to the recover set. You are better off with the latter, however, to ensure that your tables remain logically consistent with one another.

Identifying Objects Lost after TSPITR

In addition to resolving any dependencies with the tablespace to be recovered, you also need to identify any objects created after the target time that will be lost if you recover the tablespace. You can use the data dictionary view TS_PITR_OBJECTS_TO_BE_DROPPED to determine which objects you will lose after your target recovery time, as in this example:

```
SQL> select owner, name, tablespace_name,
  2      to_char(creation_time, 'yyyy-mm-dd:hh24:mi:ss') create_time
  3  from ts_pitr_objects_to_be_dropped
  4  where tablespace_name = 'BI'
  5    and creation_time >
  6          to_date('2008-07-19:21:55:00','yyyy-mm-dd:hh24:mi:ss')
  7  ;

OWNER         NAME                          TABLESPACE_NAME CREATE_TIME
-----------   ---------------------------   --------------- -------------------
RJB           SALES_RESULTS_2007_TEMP       BI              2008-07-19:22:00:56

SQL>
```

To resolve these issues, you can export individual objects before the recovery operation and then import them after recovery is complete. In this case, you determine that the table SALES_RESULTS_2007_TEMP was a temporary table and you don't need it after the recovery operation.

Performing Automated TSPITR

The most straightforward method for running TSPITR is, not surprisingly, the RMAN fully automated method. In this case, you run two RMAN commands to back up and bring the recovered tablespace (and the table SALES_RESULTS_2008Q1) online. In this example, you will recover the BI tablespace to July 19, 2008, as of 9:55 P.M.:

```
RMAN> connect target /

connected to target database: HR (DBID=3318356692)

RMAN> connect catalog rman/rman@rcat

connected to recovery catalog database

RMAN> recover tablespace bi
2>       until time '2008-07-19:21:55:00'
3>       auxiliary destination '/u01/app/oracle/oradata/auxinst'
4> ;

Starting recover at 2008-07-19:22:01:53
allocated channel: ORA_DISK_1
channel ORA_DISK_1: SID=98 device type=DISK

Creating automatic instance, with SID='vdym'
```

```
initialization parameters used for automatic instance:
db_name=HR
compatible=11.1.0.0.0
db_block_size=8192
. . .
auxiliary instance file /u01/app/oracle/oradata/auxinst
        /TSPITR_HR_VDYM/onlinelog/o1_mf_2_485c3w3y_.log deleted
auxiliary instance file /u01/app/oracle/oradata/auxinst
        /TSPITR_HR_VDYM/onlinelog/o1_mf_3_485c3xr8_.log deleted
Finished recover at 2008-07-19:22:11:50

RMAN>
```

Note that the RMAN RECOVER command cleans up the temporary instance but does not bring the BI tablespace back online. So, back it up and bring it back online:

```
RMAN> backup as compressed backupset tablespace bi;
. . .
RMAN> sql "alter tablespace bi online";

sql statement: alter tablespace bi online
starting full resync of recovery catalog
full resync complete

RMAN>
```

CERTIFICATION SUMMARY

This chapter covered two short but important RMAN topics: creating a duplicate database, and performing tablespace point-in-time recovery (TSPITR). The topics seem unrelated but have one very important thing in common: they both rely on creating an auxiliary instance for performing the requested task. After duplicating a database, RMAN keeps the temporary instance and the database; in contrast, in the case of TSPITR, RMAN drops the auxiliary instance after performing the recovery operation.

Duplicating a database using RMAN is mostly automated except for a few manual setup steps. These steps include tasks such as creating a password file, setting up network connectivity, and creating a text-based initialization parameter file with only a few required parameters, such as DB_NAME. Specifying other initialization parameters is dependent on whether you explicitly specify DB_BLOCK_SIZE in the source database, and how much pathname mapping you need to do to specify locations correctly for datafiles, control files, and online redo log files. Using Enterprise Manager (EM) to duplicate a database is the easier method but may not provide the customization available using RMAN and SQL command line commands.

The second half of the chapter covered TSPITR. A variety of recovery techniques are available to you. Which one you use depends on the type of damage to your database. If the corruption or damage is limited to tables in one tablespace with few or no dependencies to objects in other tablespaces, TSPITR is likely your best option. In addition, the database and all other tablespaces remain available to users during the TSPITR operation.

✓ TWO-MINUTE DRILL

Creating a Duplicate Database Using RMAN

❑ When you duplicate a database, the source database is copied to the duplicate database.

❑ The source database is also known as the target database.

❑ The duplicate database is also known as the auxiliary database.

❑ Preparing to create a duplicate database includes creating a password file, ensuring network connectivity, and creating an initialization parameter file for the auxiliary instance.

❑ At a minimum, you need to specify the DB_NAME in the auxiliary instance's initialization parameter file. You must also specify DB_BLOCK_SIZE if it is set explicitly in the target database.

❑ The initialization parameter DB_FILE_NAME_CONVERT specifies the file system mapping for datafile and tempfile names.

❑ The initialization parameter LOG_FILE_NAME_CONVERT specifies the file system mapping for online redo log files.

❑ The initialization parameter CONTROL_FILES specifies the new names for all control files, unless you are using Oracle Managed Files (OMF) as OMF will name files for you.

❑ The RMAN command for performing database duplication is DUPLICATE TARGET DATABASE.

❑ You can specify FROM ACTIVE DATABASE in the DUPLICATE command to create the copy from an online database instead of from a database backup.

❑ The duplicate database has a new DBID, even if it has the same database name as the source database.

Using a Duplicate Database

❑ A duplicate database can be used to test backup and recovery procedures without affecting the availability of the source database.

❑ You can use a duplicate database to test a database upgrade or test performance of application upgrades.

❑ You can export one or more tables from a duplicate database and import it back into the production database as a secondary recovery method.

Identify the Situations that Require TSPITR

❑ TSPITR is useful when one or more corrupt or missing tables are isolated to a single tablespace and have minimal or no dependencies with objects in other tablespaces.

❑ You can use TSPITR when DDL changes prohibit the use of Flashback Table to recover the objects.

❑ You cannot use TSPITR to recover a dropped tablespace or to recover a renamed tablespace to a point in time before it was renamed.

Perform Automated TSPITR

❑ The target time is the point in time to which the tablespace(s) will be recovered.

❑ The recovery set is the group of datafiles containing the tablespaces to be recovered.

❑ The auxiliary set is a set of other datafiles required to recover the datafiles in the recovery set, such as the SYSTEM tablespace.

❑ The auxiliary destination is a temporary work area used by RMAN to store auxiliary set files, log files, and a copy of the control file.

❑ RMAN drops the auxiliary instance and deletes all auxiliary files at the completion of TSPITR.

❑ You use the data dictionary view TS_PITR_CHECK to discover dependencies between the objects in the tablespace to be recovered and objects in other tablespaces.

❑ You use the data dictionary view TS_PITR_OBJECTS_TO_BE_DROPPED to determine objects you will lose after TSPITR completes.

❑ You perform TSPITR in RMAN using the RECOVER TABLESPACE command with the UNTIL TIME and AUXILIARY DESTINATION clauses.

❑ After TSPITR is complete, you need to back up the recovered tablespace and bring it back online.

SELF TEST

The following questions will help you measure your understanding of the material presented in this chapter. Read all the choices carefully, because there might be more than one correct answer. Choose all correct answers for each question.

Creating a Duplicate Database Using RMAN

1. Identify the correct statement regarding duplicate databases created with RMAN.

A. RMAN copies the source database to the target database and both can have the same name.

B. RMAN creates an auxiliary instance for the duration of the copy operation and drops it after the copy operation is complete.

C. The auxiliary database is the same as the target database.

D. RMAN copies the database from the target to the duplicate database and both can have the same name.

E. The source database must be shut down before you can start up the destination database.

2. To create a duplicate database, put the following steps in the correct order:
1. Start the auxiliary instance as NOMOUNT.
2. Allocate auxiliary channels if necessary.
3. Run the RMAN DUPLICATE command.
4. Create a password file for the auxiliary instance.
5. Ensure network connectivity to the auxiliary instance.
6. Open the auxiliary instance.
7. Start the source database in MOUNT or OPEN mode.
8. Create an initialization parameter file for the auxiliary instance.
9. Create backups or copy existing backups and archived log files to a common location accessible by the auxiliary instance.

A. 5, 4, 8, 1, 7, 9, 3, 2, 6

B. 4, 5, 8, 1, 7, 9, 2, 3, 6

C. 4, 5, 8, 1, 7, 9, 3, 2, 6

D. 5, 4, 1, 8, 7, 9, 2, 3, 6

3. Which of the following clauses is not valid for the RMAN DUPLICATE command?

A. SKIP OFFLINE

B. SKIP READONLY

C. SKIP TABLESPACE

D. NOFILENAMECHECK

E. OPEN RESTRICTED

Using a Duplicate Database

4. Identify reasons for creating a duplicate database. (Choose all correct answers.)

    A. You want to test a new application's performance with no impact to the production database.

    B. You want to perform TSPITR.

    C. You want to test an upgrade from Oracle Database 11g R1 to Oracle Database 11g R2.

    D. You want to test backup and recovery procedures.

Identify the Situations that Require TSPITR

5. You can use TSPITR for which of the following scenarios? (Choose two answers.)

    A. You accidentally drop the USERS tablespace.

    B. You dropped two columns in a table.

    C. You renamed a tablespace and want to recover the tablespace with the old name.

    D. A user deleted most of the rows in a table that does not have any dependencies on objects in other tablespaces.

Perform Automated TSPITR

6. Identify the correct statement regarding TSPITR terminology.

    A. The auxiliary set contains all datafiles for recovery except the SYSTEM and UNDO tablespaces.

    B. The recovery set is the group of datafiles containing the tablespace(s) to be recovered.

    C. The auxiliary destination is the permanent location for the auxiliary instance's datafiles.

    D. The target time is any time after the corrupted tables were modified or tables were accidentally dropped.

7. Identify the data dictionary view you can use to check for object dependencies between tablespaces.

    A. TS_PITR_CHECK

    B. TS_PITR_DEPENDENCY_CHECK

    C. TS_PITR_CHECK_DEPENDENCY

    D. TS_PITR_OBJECTS_TO_BE_DROPPED

8. Identify the steps you must perform manually after using automated TSPITR in RMAN. (Choose all that apply.)

   A. Bring the recovered tablespace(s) online.

   B. Back up the recovered tablespace(s).

   C. Delete the temporary files created in the auxiliary location.

   D. Create a text-based initialization parameter file for the auxiliary instance.

SELF TEST ANSWERS

Creating a Duplicate Database Using RMAN

1. ☑ **D.** You can keep the same name because RMAN creates a new DBID and therefore you can use the same recovery catalog for both databases.

   ☒ **A** is wrong because the target database is the same as the source database. **B** is wrong because RMAN does not drop the auxiliary instance or database after the copy operation is complete. **C** is wrong because the target database is the source database and the auxiliary database is the destination database. **E** is wrong because both databases can be open at the same time, even on the same host and with the same recovery catalog.

2. ☑ **B.** These steps are in the correct order.

   ☒ **A, C,** and **D** are in the wrong order.

3. ☑ **A.** The SKIP OFFLINE option is not valid for the DUPLICATE command.

   ☒ **B** is wrong because the SKIP READONLY clause excludes read-only tablespaces. **C** is wrong because SKIP TABLESPACE excludes one or more tablespaces from the copy operation; you cannot skip the SYSTEM or UNDO tablespaces. **D** is wrong because NOFILENAMECHECK doesn't check for duplicate filenames between the source and destination. **E** is wrong because OPEN RESTRICTED opens the destination database with the RESTRICTED SESSION option.

Using a Duplicate Database

4. ☑ **A, C,** and **D.** These are all valid reasons to create a duplicate database.

   ☒ **B** is incorrect because you cannot use a duplicate database to perform TSPITR.

Identify the Situations that Require TSPITR

5. ☑ **B** and **D.** You can use TSPITR to recover from DDL changes to a table; in addition, you can recover a table that has corrupted or erroneously altered rows. TSPITR is also useful if the table is dropped with the PURGE option and therefore not reclaimable from the recycle bin.

   ☒ **A** is wrong because you cannot use TSPITR for dropped tablespaces. **C** is wrong because you cannot use TSPITR to recover the tablespace with a previous name; in other words, the tablespace was renamed at some point in the past.

Perform Automated TSPITR

6. ☑ **B.** RMAN creates the recovery set and uses it in the auxiliary instance.
   ☒ **A** is wrong because the auxiliary set does include the SYSTEM, UNDO, and TEMP tablespaces, if required. **C** is wrong because the auxiliary set is deleted after the recovery operation is complete. **D** is wrong because the target time is any time before the corruption or deletion of table rows.

7. ☑ **A.** You use the view TS_PITR_CHECK to identify object dependencies between one or more tablespaces and all other tablespaces in the database.
   ☒ **B** and **C** are wrong because there are no such views in the data dictionary. **D** is wrong because TS_PITR_OBJECTS_TO_BE_DROPPED is used to identify other objects that you can lose if you perform TSPITR.

8. ☑ **A** and **B.** These steps must be performed manually after RMAN completes the automated portion of TSPITR.
   ☒ **C** is wrong because RMAN automatically shuts down the auxiliary instance and removes all temporary files used for the recovery operation. **D** is wrong because you need to manually create a text-based initialization parameter file for duplicating a database, but not for TSPITR.

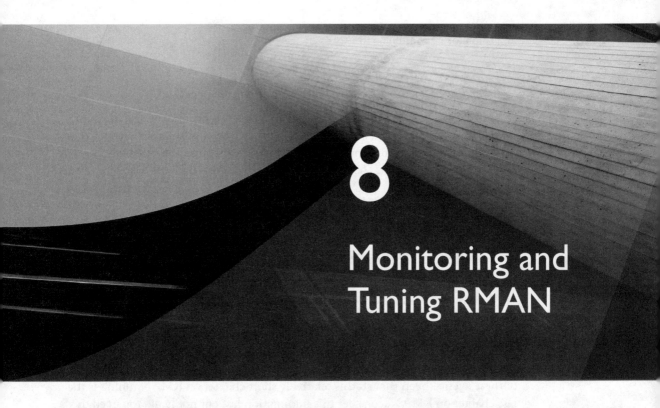

8

Monitoring and Tuning RMAN

T uning RMAN backup and recovery operations is frequently an afterthought. If you run a full backup once a week and incremental backups daily, you might not think you'd need to optimize your backup and recovery operations because they take up only about 4 hours of your time every week. This logic seems to make sense, until the following events occur in your organization:

- Your company expands its offices worldwide, users will be accessing the database at all times of the day and night, and you don't want a backup operation reducing response time.

- New applications increase demand for the tape library system.

- Management demands improvements in the database recovery time to meet service-level agreements (SLAs).

Optimizing your RMAN backup and recovery operations will mitigate the effects of these events. Even though this relatively short chapter on RMAN tuning is the last chapter on RMAN, consider this information last but not least. You need to understand the importance of tuning RMAN and be able to identify bottlenecks in the different phases of an RMAN backup.

First, you'll learn about the dynamic performance views that you can use to monitor an RMAN backup in progress, such as V$SESSION and V$PROCESS. RMAN makes it easy to identify a specific backup job in V$SESSION.

Next, you'll dive into some tuning exercises, using techniques such as multiple channel allocation to improve the performance of your backup operations. You'll also learn where RMAN bottlenecks occur and how to measure a bottleneck with views such as V$BACKUP_SYNC_IO and V$BACKUP_ASYNC_IO. The RMAN BACKUP command itself offers you a lot of flexibility by letting you control the size of each backup piece, determine how many files to put into a backup set, and decrease the load on the system by defining a desired backup duration.

Finally, you'll see some pros and cons of using asynchronous versus synchronous I/O for RMAN tape and disk operations. Ideally, you can use asynchronous I/O to maximize throughput. Even if the tape subsystem or operating system cannot leverage asynchronous I/O, you can still use initialization parameters and RMAN settings to maximize throughput.

Monitoring RMAN Sessions and Jobs

At any given point in time, you may have multiple backup jobs running, each with one or more channels. Each channel utilizes one operating system process. If you want to identify which channel is using the most CPU or I/O resources at the operating system level, you can join the dynamic performance views V$SESSION and V$PROCESS to identify the operating system processes associated with each RMAN channel.

In addition to identifying the processes associated with each RMAN job, you can also determine the progress of a backup or restore operation. You can use the dynamic performance view V$SESSION_LONGOPS to identify how much work an RMAN session has completed and the estimated total amount of work.

Finally, RMAN provides troubleshooting information in a number of ways, above and beyond the command output at the RMAN> prompt, when something goes wrong. You can also enable enhanced debugging to help you and Oracle Support identify the cause of a serious RMAN problem.

In the following sections, you'll be introduced to the dynamic performance views V$SESSION, V$PROCESS, and V$SESSION_LONGOPS that can help you identify and monitor RMAN backup and restore jobs. Also, you'll learn where to look when a backup or restore job fails.

Using V$SESSION and V$PROCESS

The dynamic performance view V$PROCESS contains a row for each operating system process connected to the database instance. V$SESSION contains additional information about each session connected to the database, such as the current SQL command and the Oracle username executing the command. These sessions include RMAN sessions. As a result, you can monitor RMAN sessions using these views as well.

RMAN populates the column V$SESSION.CLIENT_INFO with the string rman and the name of the channel. Remember that each RMAN channel corresponds to a server process, and therefore V$SESSION will have one row for each channel.

To retrieve information from V$SESSION and V$PROCESS about current RMAN sessions, join the views V$SESSION and V$PROCESS on the PADDR and ADDR columns, as you will see in the first exercise.

EXERCISE 8-1

Monitor RMAN Channels

In this exercise, you'll start an RMAN job that uses two or more channels and retrieve the channel names from V$SESSION and V$PROCESS.

1. Create an RMAN job that backs up the USERS tablespace using two disk channels:

```
RMAN> run {
2>          allocate channel ch1 type disk;
3>          allocate channel ch2 type disk;
4>          backup as compressed backupset tablespace users;
5>     }

starting full resync of recovery catalog
full resync complete
released channel: ORA_DISK_1
allocated channel: ch1
channel ch1: SID=130 device type=DISK
starting full resync of recovery catalog
full resync complete

allocated channel: ch2
channel ch2: SID=126 device type=DISK
. . .
Finished Control File and SPFILE Autobackup at 27-JUL-08
released channel: ch1
released channel: ch2

RMAN>
```

2. While the RMAN job is running, join the views V$PROCESS and V$SESSION to retrieve the CLIENT_INFO column contents:

```
SQL> select sid, spid, client_info
  2  from v$process p join v$session s on (p.addr = s.paddr)
  3  where client_info like '%rman%'
  4  ;

     SID SPID                          CLIENT_INFO
---------- ------------------------- -----------------------
     126 25070                         rman channel=ch2
     130 7732                          rman channel=ch1

SQL>
```

Note that RMAN's user processes will still exist in V$SESSION until you exit
RMAN or start another backup operation.

If you have multiple RMAN jobs running, some with two or more channels
allocated, it might be difficult to identify which process corresponds to which RMAN
backup or recovery operation. To facilitate the desired differentiation, you can use the
SET COMMAND ID command within an RMAN RUN block, as in this example:

```
run {
    set command id to 'bkup users';
    backup tablespace users;
    }
```

When this RMAN job runs, the CLIENT_INFO column in V$SESSION contains
the string id=bkup users to help you identify the session for each RMAN job.

EXERCISE 8-2

Monitor Multiple RMAN Jobs

In this exercise, you'll start two RMAN jobs and identify each job in V$SESSION
and V$PROCESS using the SET COMMAND option in RMAN.

1. Create two RMAN jobs (in two different RMAN sessions) that back up the
   USERS and CHGTRK tablespaces and use the SET COMMAND option:

```
/* session 1 */
RMAN> run {
2>          set command id to 'bkup users';
4>          backup as compressed backupset tablespace users;
5>          }
. . .
/* session 2 */
RMAN> run {
2>          set command id to 'bkup chgtrk';
4>          backup as compressed backupset tablespace users;
5>          }
```

2. While the RMAN job is running, join the views V$PROCESS and
   V$SESSION to retrieve the CLIENT_INFO column contents:

```
SQL> select sid, spid, client_info
  2  from v$process p join v$session s on (p.addr = s.paddr)
  3  where client_info like '%id=%';
```

```
        SID SPID                        CLIENT_INFO
---------- -------------------------   -----------------------
        141 19708                      id=bkup users
         94 19714                      id=bkup chgtrk

SQL>
```

Using V$SESSION_LONGOPS

The dynamic performance view V$SESSION_LONGOPS isn't specific to RMAN either. Oracle records any operations that run for more than 6 seconds (in absolute time), including RMAN backup and recovery operations, statistics gathering, and long queries in V$SESSION_LONGOPS.

RMAN populates two different types of rows in V$SESSION_LONGOPS: detail rows and aggregate rows. Detail rows contain information about a single RMAN job step, such as creating a single backup set. Aggregate rows apply to all files referenced in a single RMAN command, such as BACKUP DATABASE. As you might expect, aggregate rows are updated less frequently than detail rows.

The initialization parameter STATISTICS_LEVEL must be set to TYPICAL or ALL before the view V$SESSION_LONGOPS will contain information about long-running RMAN jobs. The default value for STATISTICS_LEVEL is TYPICAL.

This example initiates a full database backup, and while the backup is running, both detail and aggregate rows for active RMAN jobs are shown:

```
SQL> select sid, serial#, opname, context, sofar, totalwork
  2  from v$session_longops
  3  where opname like 'RMAN%'
  4    and sofar <> totalwork
  5  ;
```

```
    SID   SERIAL# OPNAME                           CONTEXT      SOFAR TOTALWORK
------- --------- ------------------------ -------- ---------- ----------
    130     39804 RMAN: aggregate output          7      97557         0
     94     47546 RMAN: aggregate input           7     191692    331808
    155      1196 RMAN: full datafile backup      1     219980    331808
    155      1196 RMAN: full datafile backup      2     121172         0

SQL>
```

The SID and SERIAL# are the same columns you see in V$SESSION. The OPNAME column is a text description of the operation monitored in the row, and for RMAN, it contains the prefix RMAN:. The CONTEXT column contains a value of 7 for aggregate operations, 2 for backup output operations, and 1 for everything else.

The column SOFAR is, as you might expect, a measure of the progress of a step. Its value differs depending on the type of operation:

- For image copies, it is the number of blocks read.
- For backup input rows, it is the number of blocks read from the files being backed up.
- For backup output rows (backup set or image copy), it is the number of blocks written so far to the backup piece.
- For restore operations, it is the number of blocks processed so far to the destination files.
- For proxy copies (copy operations from a media manager to or from disk), it is the number of files that have been copied so far.

The column TOTALWORK has a similar definition, except that it estimates the total amount of work required during the step:

- For image copies, it is the total number of blocks in the file.
- For backup input rows, it is the total number of blocks to be read from all files in the step.
- For backup output rows, it is always zero because RMAN does not know how many blocks will be written into a backup piece until it is done.
- For restore operations, it is the total number of blocks in all files restored in a single job step or aggregate.
- For proxy copies, it is the total number of files to be copied in the job step.

To calculate the progress of an RMAN step as a percent complete, you can divide SOFAR by TOTALWORK as follows and add this expression to the SELECT statement:

```
round(sofar/totalwork*100,1)
```

Leveraging RMAN Error Logs and Messages

When something goes wrong, RMAN debugging information can be found in several places. The following sections show you where you can find debugging information. When you don't have enough information, you can turn on additional debugging output using the RMAN DEBUG command.

Identifying RMAN Message Output

When disaster strikes your RMAN backup and recovery operations, you can find information in many locations, such as the following:

- **RMAN command output**   The interactive output you see when you execute RMAN commands at the RMAN> prompt.
- **User-specified RMAN trace file**   The output saved to a user-specified trace file when you use the rman . . . debug trace command at the operating system prompt.
- **Alert log**   The standard Oracle alert log location defined by the initialization parameter DIAGNOSTIC_DEST or USER_DUMP_DEST.
- **Oracle trace file**   Detailed diagnostic output from Oracle errors generated during RMAN commands, located in DIAGNOSTIC_DEST or USER_DUMP_DEST.
- **Vendor trace files**   The file sbtio.log or other vendor-assigned filenames containing media-management software errors in DIAGNOSTIC_DEST or USER_DUMP_DEST.

RMAN-specific error messages have a prefix with the format RMAN-*nnnn*, and this message can be preceded or followed by ORA-*nnnnn* messages or vendor-specific messages, depending on the type of error.

Using the RMAN DEBUG Command

Turning on RMAN debugging generates a lot of output, so Oracle recommends that you specify a file to contain debugging output. To turn on debugging, you use the debug option on the RMAN executable's command line. Add the `trace` option to specify a file for the debugging output. Here is an example:

```
[oracle@srv04 ~]$ rman target / catalog rman/rman@rcat \
>       debug trace dbg_rman.trc
```

When RMAN starts, debugging information is sent to the specified trace file. Within an RMAN session, you can turn on or turn off debugging using the DEBUG ON or DEBUG OFF command. For example, you might want to trace the errors when backing up one problematic datafile but not the others.

<hr>

EXERCISE 8-3

Debug Part of an RMAN Session

In this exercise, you'll turn on RMAN debugging, back up the USERS and CHGTRK tablespaces, but debug only the backup of the CHGTRK tablespace.

1. Start RMAN with the debug option:

```
[oracle@srv04 ~]$ rman target / catalog rman/rman@rcat \
>           debug trace rman_debug.txt

Recovery Manager: Release 11.1.0.6.0 -
              Production on Tue Jul 29 21:04:52 2008

Copyright (c) 1982, 2007, Oracle.  All rights reserved.

RMAN-06005: connected to target database: HR (DBID=3318356692)
RMAN-06008: connected to recovery catalog database

RMAN>
```

2. Turn off debugging temporarily for the USERS tablespace but turn it back on for the CHGTRK tablespace:

```
RMAN> run {
2>        debug off;
3>        backup tablespace users;
4>        debug on;
5>        backup tablespace chgtrk;
6>        }

Debugging turned off
```

```
Starting backup at 29-JUL-08
using channel ORA_DISK_1
. . .
Finished Control File and SPFILE Autobackup at 29-JUL-08

RMAN-03036: Debugging set to level=9, types=ALL

RMAN-03090: Starting backup at 29-JUL-08
. . .
RMAN-03091: Finished Control File and SPFILE Autobackup at 29-JUL-08

RMAN>
```

3. Verify the size of the trace file:

```
[oracle@srv04 ~]$ ls -l rman_debug.txt
-rw-r--r--  1 oracle oinstall 352932 Jul 29 21:12 rman_debug.txt
[oracle@srv04 ~]$
```

Note that even for a single tablespace backup, the trace file is larger than 350K bytes.

Note that the DEBUG command at the RMAN> command line does not do anything unless you specify debug when starting the RMAN executable at the operating system command line.

CERTIFICATION OBJECTIVE 8.02

Tuning RMAN

You can tune RMAN operations in many ways. You can tune the overall throughput of a backup by using multiple RMAN channels and assigning datafiles to different channels. Each channel is assigned to a single process, so parallel processing can speed the backup process. Conversely, you can multiplex several backup files to the same backup piece. For a particular channel, you can use the MAXPIECESIZE and MAXOPENFILES parameters to maximize throughput to a specific output device. The BACKUP command uses these parameters in addition to FILESPERSET and BACKUP DURATION to optimize your backup operation. You can also use BACKUP DURATION to minimize the effect of the backup on response time if your database must be continuously available and you have to contend with stringent SLAs. Finally, you can also use database initialization parameters to optimize backup and recovery performance, especially for synchronous I/O operations.

If you understand how each tuning method works, you can keep the user response time fast, optimize your hardware and software environment, and potentially delay upgrades when budgets are tight (which is almost always). A throughput *bottleneck* will almost always exist somewhere in your environment. A bottleneck is the slowest step or task during an RMAN backup.

The next section reviews the basic steps that a channel performs during a backup operation. The techniques presented in the following sections will help you identify where the bottleneck is within the channel's tasks and how to minimize its impact on backup and recovery operations.

Identifying Backup and Restore Steps

RMAN backup performs its tasks within a channel in one of three main phases:

1. *Read phase:* The channel reads data blocks into the input buffers.
2. *Copy phase:* The channel copies blocks from the input buffers to the output buffers and performs additional processing, if necessary:

   ■ **Validation**   Check blocks for corruption, which is not CPU-intensive.

   ■ **Compression**   Use BZIP2 or ZLIB to compress the block, which is CPU-intensive.

   ■ **Encryption**   Use an encryption algorithm (transparent, password-protected, or both) to secure the data, which is CPU-intensive.

3. *Write phase:* The channel writes the blocks from the output buffers to the output device (disk or tape).

Using dynamic performance views, you can identify which phase of which channel operation is the bottleneck and address it accordingly.

In some scenarios, you may want to increase the backup time to ensure that the recovery time will be short. Creating image copies and recovering the image copies on a daily or hourly basis will add to the backup time but will dramatically reduce recovery time.

Parallelizing Backup Sets

One of the simplest ways to improve RMAN performance is to allocate multiple channels (either disk or tape). The number of channels you allocate should be no larger than the number of physical devices; allocating two or more channels (and therefore processes) for a single physical device will not improve performance and may even decrease performance. If you're writing to a single Automatic Storage Management (ASM) disk group or a file system striped by the operating system, you can allocate more channels and improve throughput since the logical ASM disk group or striped file system maps to two or more physical disks. You can allocate up to 255 channels, and each channel can read up to 64 datafiles in parallel. Each channel writes to a separate backup copy or image copy.

If the number of datafiles in your database is relatively constant, you can allocate a fixed number of channels and assign each datafile to a specific channel. Here is an example:

```
run {
    allocate channel dc1 device type disk;
    allocate channel dc2 device type disk;
    allocate channel dc3 device type disk;
    backup incremental level 0
      (datafile 1,2,9    channel dc1)
      (datafile 3,8,7    channel dc2)
      (datafile 4,6,7    channel dc3)
      as compressed backupset;
}
```

Note also that you can specify the path name for a datafile instead of the datafile number, as in this example:

```
(datafile '/u01/oradata/users02.dbf' channel dc2)
```

To automate this process further, you can use the CONFIGURE command to increase the parallelism for each device type. Here is the default RMAN configuration for disk device channels:

```
CONFIGURE DEVICE TYPE DISK PARALLELISM 1 BACKUP
    TYPE TO BACKUPSET; # default
```

Understanding RMAN Multiplexing

You can improve RMAN performance and throughput by *multiplexing* backup and recovery operations. Multiplexing enables RMAN to read from multiple files simultaneously and write the data blocks to the same backup piece.

on the **job**

Note that you cannot multiplex image copies.

Using multiplexing as an RMAN tuning method is one way to reduce bottlenecks in backup and recovery operations. The level of multiplexing is primarily controlled by two parameters: FILESPERSET and MAXOPENFILES.

The FILESPERSET parameter of the RMAN BACKUP command determines the number of datafiles to put in each backup set. If a single channel backs up 10 datafiles and the value of FILESPERSET is 4, RMAN will back up only four files per backup set. The parameter FILESPERSET defaults to 64.

The level of multiplexing (the number of input files that are read and written to the same backup piece) is the minimum of MAXOPENFILES and the number of files in each backup set. The default value for MAXOPENFILES is 8. Here is an equation that may make the calculation easier to understand:

```
multiplexing_level =
        min(MAXOPENFILES, min(FILESPERSET, files_per_channel))
```

This example backs up 10 datafiles in one channel, the value for MAXOPENFILES is 12, and the value for FILESPERSET is at the default value of 64. Therefore, the multiplexing level is calculated as follows:

```
multiplexing_level = min(12, min(64, 10)) = 10
```

RMAN allocates a different number and size of disk I/O buffers depending on the level of multiplexing in your RMAN job. Once the level of multiplexing is derived by RMAN using the FILESPERSET and MAXOPENFILES parameters using the aforementioned equation, you can use the information in Table 8-1 to find out how many and what size buffers RMAN needs to perform the backup.

Oracle recommends that the value FILESPERSET should be 8 or less to optimize recovery performance. In other words, putting too many input files into a single backupset will slow down a recovery operation because the RESTORE or RECOVER command will still have to read a large number of unneeded blocks in the backupset when you recover a single datafile.

TABLE 8-1 RMAN Datafile Buffer Sizing

Level of Multiplexing	Size of Input Disk Buffer
<= 4	16 buffers of 1MB each divided among all input files
5–8	A variable number of 512MB buffers to keep total buffer size under 16MB
> 8	Total of 4 buffers of 128KB for each (512KB) for each input file

Tuning RMAN Channels

You can further tune your RMAN backup performance by tuning individual channels with the CONFIGURE CHANNEL and ALLOCATE CHANNEL commands. Each CHANNEL command accepts the following parameters:

- **MAXPIECESIZE** The maximum size of a backup piece.
- **RATE** The number of bytes per second read by RMAN on the channel.
- **MAXOPENFILES** The maximum number of input files that a channel can have open at a given time.

The MAXPIECESIZE parameter is useful when you back up to disk and the underlying operating system limits the size of an individual disk file, or when a tape media manager cannot split a backup piece across multiple tapes.

Note that the RATE parameter doesn't improve performance but throttles performance intentionally to limit the disk bandwidth available to a channel. This is useful when your RMAN backups must occur during periods of peak activity elsewhere in the database.

MAXOPENFILES was reviewed in the preceding section, but it is worth revisiting when you want to optimize the performance of an individual channel. For example, you can use MAXOPENFILES to limit RMAN's use of operating system file handles or buffers.

Tuning the BACKUP Command

Just like the CONFIGURE CHANNEL command, the BACKUP command has parameters that can help you improve performance or limit the computing resources that a channel uses for an RMAN backup. Here are the key tuning parameters for the BACKUP command:

- **MAXPIECESIZE** The maximum size of a backup piece per channel.
- **FILESPERSET** The maximum number of files per backupset.
- **MAXOPENFILES** The maximum number of input files that a channel can have open at a given time.
- **BACKUP DURATION** Decrease or increase the time to complete the backup.

You've seen the parameters MAXPIECESIZE, FILESPERSET, and MAXOPENFILES before. Note that MAXPIECESIZE and MAXOPENFILES have the same purpose as in the CHANNEL commands, except that they apply to all channels in the backup.

BACKUP DURATION specifies an amount of time to complete the backup. You can qualify this option with MINIMIZE TIME to run the backup as fast as possible, or MINIMIZE LOAD to use the entire timeframe specified in the BACKUP DURATION window. In addition, you can use the PARTIAL option, as you might expect, to save a partial backup that was terminated due to time constraints. For example, to limit a full database backup to 2 hours, run it as fast as possible, and save a partial backup, use this command:

```
RMAN> backup duration 2:00 partial database;
```

If the backup does not complete in the specified time frame, the partial backup is still usable in a recovery scenario after a successive BACKUP command finishes the backup and you use the PARTIAL option.

Configuring LARGE_POOL_SIZE

You can adjust the value of the initialization parameter LARGE_POOL_SIZE to improve RMAN backup performance. If you do not set LARGE_POOL_SIZE, the RMAN server processes use memory from the shared pool. This may cause contention with many other processes that use the shared pool. If RMAN's request for memory from the shared pool cannot be fulfilled, RMAN uses memory from the Program Global Area (PGA), writes a message to the alert log, and uses synchronous I/O for this backup. But synchronous I/O can be inefficient; therefore, you can resize the value of the large pool for disk backups using this calculation:

```
additional_large_pool_size = #channels * 16MB
```

If you are backing up to tape, add memory to account for the size of the tape driver buffer (equivalent to the RMAN channel parameter BLKSIZE):

```
additional_large_pool_size = #channels * (16MB + (4 * tape_buffer_size))
```

Note also that RMAN will only use memory from the large pool if DBWR_IO_SLAVES is set to a value greater than zero. You will learn how to set this initialization parameter later in this chapter.

CERTIFICATION OBJECTIVE 8.03

Configure RMAN for Asynchronous I/O

Whether you use synchronous or asynchronous I/O in your RMAN environment depends on several factors. These factors include the type of device you use for backupsets (disk or tape) and whether the output device or host operating system supports synchronous or asynchronous I/O. Even if the host operating system or device does not support native asynchronous I/O, you can configure RMAN to simulate asynchronous I/O using initialization parameters such as DBWR_IO_ SLAVES.

After you review the key differences between asynchronous and synchronous I/O, you will learn how to monitor the performance of each type of I/O using dynamic performance views, identify where the throughput bottleneck is, and adjust RMAN parameters accordingly.

Understanding Asynchronous and Synchronous I/O

When RMAN reads or writes data, the I/O operations are either *synchronous* or *asynchronous*. A synchronous I/O operation limits a server process from performing more than one operation at a time. It must wait for one operation to finish before another can start. As you might expect, an asynchronous operation can initiate an I/O operation and immediately perform other operations including initiating another I/O operation.

You can use initialization parameters to control the type of I/O operations. For tape backups, you can set BACKUP_TAPE_IO_SLAVES to TRUE to configure backups for asynchronous operations. Otherwise, set it to FALSE for synchronous operations. The default is FALSE.

For disk backups, most modern operating systems support native asynchronous I/O. However, if your operating system does not support it, you can still set BACKUP_ TAPE_IO_SLAVES to TRUE and direct Oracle to simulate asynchronous I/O by setting DBWR_IO_SLAVES to a nonzero value. This allocates four backup disk I/O slaves to simulate RMAN asynchronous I/O operations.

Monitoring Asynchronous I/O

To monitor asynchronous I/O operations, you use the dynamic performance view
`V$BACKUP_ASYNC_IO`. The key columns to watch are the following:

- **`IO_COUNT`**   Number of I/Os performed on the file.
- **`LONG_WAITS`**   Number of times the backup or restore process had to tell
  the OS to wait for the I/O to complete.
- **`SHORT_WAIT_TIME_TOTAL`**   Total time, in hundredths of a second, taken
  for nonblocking polling for I/O completion.
- **`LONG_WAIT_TIME_TOTAL`**   Total time, in hundredths of a second, taken
  while blocking waits for I/O completion.

The largest ratio of `LONG_WAITS` to `IO_COUNT` is a likely bottleneck in the
backup process. `SHORT_WAIT_TIME_TOTAL` and `LONG_WAIT_TIME_TOTAL` are also
indicators of a bottleneck if they are nonzero.

This example identifies two input files with nonzero ratios:

```
SQL> select long_waits / io_count waitcountratio, filename
  2  from v$backup_async_io
  3  where long_waits / io_count > 0
  4  order by long_waits / io_count desc
  5  ;

WAITCOUNTRATIO FILENAME
-------------- ----------------------------------------
    .248201439 /u01/oradata/bkup/6bjmt1e3_1_1
            .2 /u01/app/oracle/flash_recovery_area/HR/a
               utobackup/2008_07_31/o1_mf_s_661554862_%
               u_.bkp
SQL>
```

For these two files, you may consider increasing the multiplexing to decrease or
eliminate the wait times when backing them up.

Monitoring Synchronous I/O

The dynamic performance view `V$BACKUP_SYNC_IO` will help you identify
bottlenecks in synchronous I/O operations, as well as the progress of backup jobs.
You use the column `DISCRETE_BYTES_PER_SECOND` to view the I/O rate of the
operation. You then compare that rate to the maximum rate of the output device,

such as a tape drive. If the rate is significantly lower, you can tune the process to improve the throughput of the backup operation by parallelization or increasing the level of multiplexing for the channel.

e x a m

ⓦ a t c h

If you are using synchronous I/O but you have set BACKUP_ DISK_IO_SLAVES to TRUE, then the I/O

performance is monitored in V$BACKUP_ ASYNC_IO.

CERTIFICATION SUMMARY

This chapter provided a short but important list of tips to help you effectively tune your RMAN operations to maximize the throughput of your backup and recovery operations. First, you learned how to monitor the progress of RMAN jobs using the dynamic performance views V$SESSION, V$PROCESS, and V$SESSION_LONGOPS.

When disaster strikes, even if it's a small disaster, you can look in several places to debug backup or recovery problems. If the solution to the problem is not obvious from the command line output, you can use the alert log or standard Oracle trace files. You can create RMAN-specific trace files with the DEBUG option as well. If you are using tape devices, the file sbtio.log can provide clues, along with any other vendor-specific trace or dump files.

After you learned about the steps RMAN performs during a backup or restore operation, you saw several ways to tune your RMAN backups. This included increasing the multiplexing level for one or more channels, tuning the BACKUP command with its command line options, and configuring the LARGE_POOL_SIZE for large RMAN memory buffer requests.

Finally, the chapter compared and contrasted synchronous and asynchronous I/O. Both methods record backup and recovery progress in the dynamic performance views V$BACKUP_SYNC_IO and V$BACKUP_ASYNC_IO, which can help you identify bottlenecks for specific files in the backup.

TWO-MINUTE DRILL

Monitoring RMAN Sessions and Jobs

❑ You can join V$SESSION with V$PROCESS to identify the operating system processes associated with each RMAN channel.

❑ The RMAN command SET COMMAND ID helps you to distinguish processes for different backup jobs in V$SESSION.

❑ Use V$SESSION_LONGOPS to monitor status of RMAN jobs that run for more than 6 seconds.

❑ The view V$SESSION_LONGOPS contains both detail rows and aggregate rows for each RMAN job.

❑ You must set the initialization parameter STATISTICS_LEVEL to TYPICAL or ALL before RMAN will record job status information in V$SESSION_LONGOPS.

❑ RMAN debugging information appears in command line output, RMAN-specific trace files, the alert log, Oracle trace files, and vendor-specific trace files.

❑ Add the debug option to the operating system command line to turn debugging on and optionally specify a file to contain the debugging output.

❑ Use the DEBUG ON or DEBUG OFF command to turn on or turn off RMAN debugging within an RMAN session.

Tuning RMAN

❑ RMAN backup or recovery jobs perform tasks in three main phases: read, copy, and write.

❑ The RMAN copy phase is further broken down into three subphases: validation, compression, and encryption.

❑ Parallelization (allocating multiple channels) can improve backup performance.

❑ You can allocate up to 255 channels per RMAN session, and each channel can read up to 64 datafiles in parallel.

❑ Multiplexing is primarily controlled by the RMAN parameters FILESPERSET and MAXOPENFILES.

❑ You can calculate the level of multiplexing by using this formula:
   min(MAXOPENFILES, min(FILESPERSET, files_per_channel))

❑ You tune RMAN channels by using the MAXPIECESIZE, RATE, and MAXOPENFILES parameters.

❑ You tune the BACKUP command by using the MAXPIECESIZE, FILESPERSET, MAXOPENFILES, and the BACKUP DURATION parameters.

❑ The BACKUP parameter BACKUP DURATION can be set to MINIMIZE TIME to perform the backup as quickly as possible or MINIMIZE LOAD to reduce the I/O demands on the database.

❑ You can configure the initialization parameter LARGE_POOL_SIZE to reduce contention on the shared pool for RMAN backups.

Configure RMAN for Asynchronous I/O

❑ Synchronous backup operations must wait until completion before initiating another I/O request. Asynchronous backup operations do not have to wait.

❑ You set the initialization parameter BACKUP_TAPE_IO_SLAVES to TRUE to configure tape backups for asynchronous operations.

❑ Setting the initialization parameter DBWR_IO_SLAVES allocates four backup disk I/O slave process to simulate RMAN asynchronous I/O operations.

❑ Use the dynamic performance view V$BACKUP_ASYNC_IO to monitor asynchronous RMAN operations.

❑ The ratio of LONG_WAITS to IO_COUNT in V$BACKUP_ASYNC_IO should be as low as possible to reduce or eliminate bottlenecks.

❑ If either the V$BACKUP_ASYNC_IO column SHORT_WAIT_TIME_TOTAL or LONG_WAIT_TIME_TOTAL is not zero, then the associated file should be tuned.

❑ You use the dynamic performance view V$BACKUP_SYNC_IO to identify bottlenecks in synchronous RMAN backup or recovery operations.

❑ The column DISCRETE_BYTES_PER_SECOND in V$BACKUP_SYNC_IO can be compared to the maximum rate of a tape output device to identify opportunities for tuning.

SELF TEST

The following questions will help you measure your understanding of the material presented in this chapter. Read all the choices carefully because there might be more than one correct answer. Choose all correct answers for each question.

Monitoring RMAN Sessions and Jobs

1. Which of the following two dynamic performance views can you use to identify the relationship between Oracle server sessions and RMAN channels?

   A. V$PROCESS and V$SESSION

   B. V$PROCESS and V$BACKUP_SESSION

   C. V$PROCESS and V$BACKUP_ASYNC_IO

   D. V$BACKUP_ASYNC_IO and V$SESSION

   E. V$BACKUP_SYNC_IO and V$BACKUP_ASYNC_IO

2. You create three RMAN sessions to back up three different tablespaces. Your third RMAN session runs this command:

   ```
   run {
           set command id to 'user bkup';
           backup tablespace users;
       }
   ```

   What values does the column V$SESSION.CLIENT_INFO have for this command? Choose all that apply.

   A. rman channel=ORA_DISK_1, id=user bkup

   B. id=user bkup, rman channel=ORA_DISK_1

   C. id=user bkup, cmd=backup tablespace users

   D. id=user bkup

   E. The column CLIENT_INFO is in V$PROCESS, not V$SESSION

3. Identify the location where RMAN message output and troubleshooting information can be found. (Choose all that apply.)

   A. The Oracle server trace file

   B. The RMAN trace file

   C. The view V$PROCESS

   D. The database alert log

   E. RMAN command output

   F. The vendor-specific file sbtio.log

   G. The table SYS.AUDIT$

Tuning RMAN

4. The initialization parameters in your database are set as follows:

   ```
   BACKUP_TAPE_IO_SLAVES = TRUE
   LARGE_POOL_SIZE = 50M
   JAVA_POOL_SIZE = 75M
   PGA_AGGREGATE_TARGET = 20M
   ```

   Identify the correct statements regarding where RMAN allocates the memory buffers for tape backup:

   A. RMAN uses the Java pool in the SGA.

   B. RMAN uses the shared pool in the SGA.

   C. RMAN allocates memory from the large pool in the PGA.

   D. RMAN allocates memory from the large pool in the SGA.

5. Which of the following are bottlenecks that affect RMAN backup and recovery operations? (Choose all that apply.)

   A. Reading data from the database

   B. Writing data to disk

   C. Writing data to tape

   D. Validating data blocks

   E. Using SGA memory buffers versus PGA memory buffers

6. Which RMAN parameter(s) control multiplexing to disk and tape? (Choose the best answer.)

   A. FILESPERSET from the BACKUP command

   B. FILESPERSET from the BACKUP command and MAXOPENFILES from the CONFIGURE command

   C. FILESPERSET from the CONFIGURE command and MAXOPENFILES from the BACKUP command

   D. MAXOPENFILES from the CONFIGURE command

Configure RMAN for Asynchronous I/O

7. Identify the types of rows in V$BACKUP_SYNC_IO during an RMAN backup operation. (Choose all that apply.)

   A. One row for each datafile

   B. One row for each tablespace

   C. One row for each backup piece

   D. One row for each channel

   E. One row for each input or output device type

8. You can use `V$BACKUP_ASYNC_IO` to monitor asynchronous RMAN I/O. What column or columns do you use to determine which file is the bottleneck during a backup?

   A. A large value for `LONG_WAITS` / `IO_COUNT`

   B. A large value for `LONG_WAITS`

   C. A large value for `IO_COUNT`

   D. A large value for `IO_COUNT` / `LONG_WAITS`

9. You set the initialization parameter `BACKUP_TAPE_IO_SLAVES` to `TRUE`. What effect does this have on the type of I/O that the server processes perform for RMAN if you are using tape? (Choose the best answer.)

   A. If `LARGE_POOL_SIZE` is set to a nonzero value, tape I/O is automatically synchronous.

   B. If `LARGE_POOL_SIZE` is set to a nonzero value, tape I/O is automatically asynchronous.

   C. Tape I/O is automatically synchronous.

   D. Tape I/O is automatically asynchronous.

SELF TEST ANSWERS

Monitoring RMAN Sessions and Jobs

1. ☑ **A.** You join the views V$PROCESS and V$SESSION on the ADDR and PADDR columns and select rows where the beginning of the column CLIENT_INFO contains the string RMAN.
   ☒ **B** is wrong because there is no such view V$BACKUP_SESSION. **C, D,** and **E** are wrong because you use V$BACKUP_ASYNC_IO and V$BACKUP_SYNC_IO to monitor performance of RMAN jobs for asynchronous and synchronous I/O, respectively.

2. ☑ **B** and **D.** The view V$SESSION has two rows for each backup process, both of them with the value specified in the RMAN command SET COMMAND ID.
   ☒ **A** is wrong because the values for CLIENT_INFO are in the wrong order. **C** is wrong because the actual RMAN command is not included in CLIENT_INFO. **E** is wrong because CLIENT_INFO is, in fact, in the view V$SESSION.

3. ☑ **A, B, D, E,** and **F.** RMAN debugging information and other message output can be found in the Oracle server trace files, the RMAN trace file, the database alert log, output from the RMAN command itself, and the vendor-specific file sbtio.log (for tape libraries).
   ☒ **C** and **G** are wrong. RMAN does not record any debugging or error information in the view V$PROCESS or in the table SYS.AUDIT$.

Tuning RMAN

4. ☑ **D.** If you set BACKUP_TAPE_IO_SLAVES to TRUE, then RMAN allocates tape buffers from the shared pool unless the initialization parameter LARGE_POOL_SIZE is set, in which case RMAN allocates tape buffers from the large pool.
   ☒ **A, B,** and **C** are incorrect; the parameters JAVA_POOL_SIZE and PGA_AGGREGATE_TARGET have no effect on the location of the RMAN buffers.

5. ☑ **A, B, C,** and **D.** All of these options are potential bottlenecks.
   ☒ **E** is wrong. The location of the RMAN data buffers is not a factor that can cause a bottleneck and reduce RMAN throughput.

6. ☑ **B.** Both FILESPERSET and MAXOPENFILES control the level of multiplexing during an RMAN backup operation.
   ☒ **A** is wrong because MAXOPENFILES in the CONFIGURE command also controls the level of multiplexing, not just FILESPERSET. **C** is wrong because FILESPERSET is not a valid option for the CONFIGURE command and MAXOPENFILES is not a valid option for the BACKUP command. **D** is wrong because MAXOPENFILES of the CONFIGURE command is not the only parameter that controls the level of multiplexing.

Configure RMAN for Asynchronous I/O

7. ☑ **A** and **C.** The view V$BACKUP_SYNC_IO contains a row for each datafile and a row for each backup piece. In addition, V$BACKUP_SYNC_IO contains an aggregate row for all datafiles.
☒ **B** is wrong because the tracking in V$BACKUP_SYNC_IO is at the datafile level. **D** is wrong because individual channels are not tracked in V$BACKUP_SYNC_IO. **E** is wrong because individual devices are not tracked in V$BACKUP_SYNC_IO.

8. ☑ **A.** The file with the largest value for the ratio of LONG_WAITS to IO_COUNT indicates that the file is the bottleneck.
☒ **B** is wrong because a large value for LONG_WAITS doesn't by itself indicate a bottleneck. Similarly, **C** is wrong because a large value for IO_COUNT doesn't by itself indicate a bottleneck. **D** is wrong because a small value for IO_COUNT / LONG_WAITS identifies a bottleneck, not a large value.

9. ☑ **D.** If you set BACKUP_TAPE_IO_SLAVES to TRUE, tape I/O is automatically asynchronous.
☒ **A** and **B** are wrong because LARGE_POOL_SIZE has no effect on whether the I/O is synchronous or asynchronous. **C** is wrong because tape I/O is synchronous if BACKUP_TAPE_IO_SLAVES is set to FALSE.

9
Configuring and Using Flashback

Disaster strikes when you least expect it, and Oracle's flashback features, which are a part of Oracle's Total Recall option, make it easy to recover from logical corruptions such as erroneously dropped tables or incorrect transactions. Most, if not all, of these recovery options are available to database users, freeing up the DBA for other tasks and potentially decreasing the recovery time. Flashback technology makes it easy for you to view the changes from the erroneous operations before you reverse the changes. You can view all data at a point in time, all changes to a row for a particular time period, or all changes within a specific transaction.

Oracle's flashback features are supported by one of three structures in the database: undo data, the flash recovery area, and the recycle bin. The undo data in the undo tablespace, in addition to supporting transaction rollback, supports most of the Flashback Table operations. *Flashback Data Archives* support queries of previous versions of table rows. Flashback Data Archives provide an area in one or more tablespaces outside of the undo tablespace to support a much longer retention period than an undo tablespace can. *Flashback logs*, which reside in the flash recovery area, makes it easy to roll back your entire database to a previous time without performing a traditional restore and recovery operation. The *recycle bin* within each tablespace contains one or more versions of dropped tables and indexes, which can easily be restored by the user as long as there is no space pressure within the tablespace.

This chapter covers Flashback Drop after reviewing the role of the undo tablespace for other database features. Flashback Drop relies on a construct introduced in Oracle Database 10g, the recycle bin. The recycle bin is a data dictionary table that tracks one or more versions of dropped tables and allows you to recover any version of the table to its state immediately before it was dropped.

Next, you'll learn about flashback technologies at the table level. You can query a table to see what a row looked like at a particular time, and depending on how far back in time you need to go, Oracle will use either undo data or a Flashback Data Archive if it is configured. You can also query the contents of a particular row as it changed during a specified time interval, or query changes to all rows for a particular database transaction.

Finally, you'll learn how to use flashback technology at the database level with Flashback Database. Although you don't want to use a sledgehammer on a mosquito, you may have to roll back an entire database to an earlier point in time if the logical corruptions are widespread or the object dependencies make it difficult or impossible to use flashback technologies at the table level.

CERTIFICATION OBJECTIVE 9.01

Restore Dropped Tables from the Recycle Bin

Flashback Drop relies on a construct introduced in Oracle Database 10g, the recycle bin, which behaves much like the recycle bin on a Windows-based computer. If enough room is available in the tablespace, dropped objects can be restored to their original schema with all indexes, triggers, and constraints intact. The following sections explore every aspect of the recycle bin: how to configure it, how to restore dropped tables, how space is managed in the recycle bin, how to bypass the recycle bin, and how to access tables directly in the recycle bin.

Understanding the Recycle Bin

In a nutshell, the recycle bin is a data dictionary table that keeps track of dropped objects. The objects themselves still exist in the same location within the tablespace but they are renamed. They are still listed in data dictionary views such as USER_ TABLES, albeit with new names. The recycle bin supports objects with the same original name. In other words, if you create an EMPLOYEES table and subsequently drop it on three different occasions, all three versions of the EMPLOYEES table will be available in the recycle bin as long as enough space is available in the tablespace.

Even though you can refer to all objects in the recycle bin collectively, each tablespace has its own local recycle bin. Thus, some newer dropped objects may be aged out of the USERS tablespace due to space pressure. However, older dropped objects can remain for a much longer time in the TRAINING tablespace if new objects are not created frequently in that tablespace.

The recycle bin is enabled by default. To turn the recycle bin on and off, you can use the RECYCLEBIN initialization parameter:

```
recyclebin = on
```

You can also enable or disable the recycle bin at the session level using ALTER SESSION:

```
SQL> alter session set recyclebin=off;
```

RECYCLEBIN is a dynamic initialization parameter, so you can change it using ALTER SYSTEM. The change will take effect immediately if you specify SCOPE=MEMORY or SCOPE=BOTH:

```
alter system set recyclebin=off scope=both;
```

Regardless of which method you use to disable the recycle bin, the objects that are already in the bin stay there unless you purge them or they are purged due to space pressure from new objects. Until you re-enable the recycle bin, newly dropped objects will not be recoverable using the recycle bin.

When you drop an object with the recycle bin enabled, the space allocated to the dropped object and all associated objects (such as indexes) is immediately reflected in the data dictionary view DBA_FREE_SPACE. However, the space used by the objects still counts toward a user's quota until the object is explicitly removed from the recycle bin or is forced out by new objects in the tablespace. In addition, the table and its dependent objects are renamed to a system-assigned name using this format:

```
BIN$unique_id$version
```

The *unique_id* portion of the name is a 26-character globally unique name for the object. A table with the same name dropped in a different database will have a different *unique_id*. The *version* portion of the name is the version number of the dropped object, which is assigned by Oracle. The next time a table with the same name is dropped, both the *unique_id* and *version* are the same, but each will have different values for DROPTIME. You will learn how to select which version to recover later in this chapter.

Querying the Recycle Bin

To query the recycle bin, you can use the data dictionary view USER_RECYCLEBIN; RECYCLEBIN is a global synonym for USER_RECYCLEBIN. You can view purged objects for all users using the view DBA_RECYCLEBIN:

```
SQL> select owner, object_name, original_name,
  2      type, ts_name, droptime, can_undrop
  3  from dba_recyclebin;

OWNER        OBJECT_NAME                              ORIGINAL_NAME
------------ ---------------------------------------- ----------------------
TYPE         TS_NAME       DROPTIME                   CAN_UNDROP
---------- ------------ -------------------- ----------
HR           BIN$UmhMiy3i2+zgQKjAYAI1cw==$0   JOB_HISTORY
TABLE        EXAMPLE       2008-07-19:16:38:48 YES

HR           BIN$UmhMiy3h2+zgQKjAYAI1cw==$0   JHIST_EMP_ID_ST_DATE_PK
```

```
INDEX       EXAMPLE      2008-07-19:16:38:48 NO

HR                 BIN$UmhMiy3g2+zgQKjAYAI1cw==$0   JHIST_DEPARTMENT_IX
INDEX       EXAMPLE      2008-07-19:16:38:47 NO

HR                 BIN$UmhMiy3f2+zgQKjAYAI1cw==$0   JHIST_EMPLOYEE_IX
INDEX       EXAMPLE      2008-07-19:16:38:47 NO

HR                 BIN$UmhMiy3e2+zgQKjAYAI1cw==$0   JHIST_JOB_IX
INDEX       EXAMPLE      2008-07-19:16:38:47 NO

BRETT              BIN$U/9fvJKUXOzgQKjAYAIWhw==$0   SYS_C0004004

INDEX       USERS        2008-08-09:10:17:59 NO

BRETT              BIN$U/9fvJKSXOzgQKjAYAIWhw==$0   FAVRE_2_JETS
TABLE       USERS        2008-08-09:10:16:39 YES

7 rows selected.

SQL>
```

Note the column CAN_UNDROP. At first glance, you might think that if the object is in the recycle bin, it can be recovered. Upon closer inspection, you can see that CAN_UNDROP is set to NO for objects such as indexes because you cannot undrop an index. You must undrop the table first, and any associated indexes will be automatically undropped.

The data dictionary view USER_RECYCLEBIN has the same columns as DBA_RECYCLEBIN, except that USER_RECYCLEBIN does not have the OWNER column. This is consistent with all other Oracle data dictionary views that have the USER_, DBA_, and ALL_ prefixes, although in this case no ALL_RECYCLEBIN data dictionary view exists.

EXERCISE 9-1

Move Objects to the Recycle Bin

In this exercise, you'll create and drop the same table twice, and then query the recycle bin to identify the name of the table and its dependent objects in the recycle bin.

1. Create the table VAC_SCHED and insert a row into it:

```
SQL> create table vac_sched
  2  (
  3     emp_no    number,
  4     vac_no    number,
```

```
   5      start_date date,
   6      end_date   date,
   7    primary key(emp_no, vac_no)
   8    );

Table created.

SQL> insert into vac_sched values(4,17,'15-sep-08','30-sep-08');

1 row created.

SQL> commit;

Commit complete.

SQL>
```

2. Drop the table:

```
SQL> drop table vac_sched;

Table dropped.

SQL>
```

3. Create the table again, and insert a row with different values from those in the row you inserted into the first version of the table:

```
SQL> create table vac_sched
   2    (
   3      emp_no      number,
   4      vac_no      number,
   5      start_date date,
   6      end_date   date,
   7    primary key(emp_no, vac_no)
   8    );

Table created.

SQL> insert into vac_sched values(58,2,'21-sep-08','25-sep-08');

1 row created.

SQL> commit;

Commit complete.

SQL>
```

4. Drop the table again:

```
SQL> drop table vac_sched;

Table dropped.

SQL>
```

5. Query the recycle bin and confirm that the table has two different system-assigned names in the recycle bin:

```
SQL> select object_name, original_name, type, droptime
  2  from recyclebin;

OBJECT_NAME                                          ORIGINAL_NAME
-------------------------------------------------- -------------
TYPE       DROPTIME
---------- -------------------
BIN$U/9fvJKbXOzgQKjAYAIWhw==$0                        VAC_SCHED
TABLE      2008-08-09:10:57:56

BIN$U/9fvJKaXOzgQKjAYAIWhw==$0                        SYS_C0013050
INDEX      2008-08-09:10:57:56

BIN$U/9fvJKXXOzgQKjAYAIWhw==$0                        SYS_C0013049
INDEX      2008-08-09:10:56:41

BIN$U/9fvJKYXOzgQKjAYAIWhw==$0                        VAC_SCHED
TABLE      2008-08-09:10:56:41

SQL>
```

Looking closely, you can see that the new names differ by one character in the eighth position of the *unique_id* portion of the name.

As you might expect, you can purge the entire contents of the recycle bin with the PURGE RECYCLEBIN command. If you have the appropriate privileges, you can purge the contents of the recycle bin for all users using the PURGE DBA_RECYCLEBIN command.

Restoring Tables from the Recycle Bin

To restore a table from the recycle bin, you use the FLASHBACK TABLE . . . TO BEFORE DROP command. If you specify the original table name in the command, the most recently dropped version of the table and its dependent objects are restored. If you want to restore a previous version of the same table, you must specify the name of the previous version in the recycle bin, as in this example:

```
SQL> flashback table "BIN$U/9fvJKcXOzgQKjAYAIWhw==$0" to before
drop;

Flashback complete.

SQL>
```

Note that you will always have to put the recycle bin object name in double quotes due to lowercase or special characters in the base-64 string representation of the dropped table.

If you attempt to restore a table that has been re-created since it was dropped, you will receive an error unless you use the RENAME TO clause to give the restored table a new name. Here is an example:

```
SQL> flashback table vac_sched to before drop
  2  rename to old_vac_sched;

Flashback complete.

SQL>
```

When you flashback a table using the RENAME option, the table acquires its original name but the table's dependent objects do not. If you want to keep the original names for the indexes, triggers, and constraints, query the recycle bin before you flashback and rename the other objects after the table is restored.

EXERCISE 9-2

Restore a Table from the Recycle Bin, Keeping the Original Dependent Object Names

This exercise picks up where you left off in Exercise 9-1. Query the recycle bin for the VAC_SCHED table and its dependent objects, restore the most recent version of the table, and rename the dependent objects to their original names.

1. Query the recycle bin and identify the most recently dropped version of VAC_SCHED along with its dependent objects:

```
SQL> select object_name, original_name, type, droptime
  2  from recyclebin
  3  order by droptime desc;
```

```
OBJECT_NAME                                              ORIGINAL_NAME
------------------------------------------------------  -------------
TYPE        DROPTIME
----------  -------------------
BIN$U/9fvJKbXOzgQKjAYAIWhw==$0                           VAC_SCHED
TABLE       2008-08-09:10:57:56

BIN$U/9fvJKaXOzgQKjAYAIWhw==$0                           SYS_C0013050
INDEX       2008-08-09:10:57:56

BIN$U/9fvJKXXOzgQKjAYAIWhw==$0                           SYS_C0013049
INDEX       2008-08-09:10:56:41

BIN$U/9fvJKYXOzgQKjAYAIWhw==$0                           VAC_SCHED
TABLE       2008-08-09:10:56:41

SQL>
```

2. Restore the most recent version of the table:

```
SQL> flashback table vac_sched to before drop;

Flashback complete.

SQL>
```

3. Rename the primary key constraint's index to its original name (the index dropped at the same time as the table):

```
SQL> alter index "BIN$U/9fvJKaXOzgQKjAYAIWhw==$0" rename to
sys_c0013050;

Index altered.

SQL>
```

4. Query the data dictionary view USER_CONSTRAINTS to identify the name of the primary key constraint:

```
SQL> select table_name, constraint_name
  2  from user_constraints
  3  where table_name = 'VAC_SCHED';

TABLE_NAME                       CONSTRAINT_NAME
-------------------------------  -----------------------------
VAC_SCHED                        BIN$U/9fvJKZXOzgQKjAYAIWhw==$0

SQL>
```

5. Rename the constraint to its original name, or at least to a more understandable name if the original name was system-generated:

```
SQL> alter table vac_sched
  2  rename constraint "BIN$U/9fvJKZXOzgQKjAYAIWhw==$0"
  3  to vac_sched_pk;

Table altered.

SQL>
```

Recycle Bin Space Reclamation

In the following sections, you'll learn more about how Oracle manages the space in the recycle bin, how you can manually manage the space, and how you can query the contents of the recycle bin. Both automated and manual recycle bin space management functions can be used.

Automatic Recycle Bin Space Reclamation

The space in the recycle bin, and by extension the space in the tablespace containing the recycle bin, is managed automatically by Oracle. In other words, all dropped objects remain available for recovery in the recycle bin as long as new objects don't need the space occupied by dropped objects.

Older objects in the recycle bin are removed before new objects when free space is low; in the next section, you'll learn you how to remove objects selectively from the recycle bin. If the tablespace is autoextensible (the tablespace has the AUTOEXTEND ON attribute), space from dropped objects is used first. If insufficient space is available for a new object, the tablespace autoextends.

Manual Recycle Bin Space Reclamation

You can manually remove objects from the recycle bin by using the PURGE command. When you purge a table from the recycle bin, the table and all its dependent objects are removed as well. This makes sense, because you would not have much use for a table's index once the table itself is gone!

When you purge a table from the recycle bin, you can use either the recycle bin name of the object or the original name of the object. If you specify the original table name, the oldest version of the table is purged first. Therefore, if you want to purge a more recent version of the table, use the recycle bin object name, as in this example:

```
SQL> show recyclebin;
ORIGINAL NAME      RECYCLEBIN NAME                   OBJECT TYPE  DROP TIME
---------------    -----------------------------     -----------  -----------
SALES_Q4           BIN$U/9fvJKfXOzgQKjAYAIWhw==$0 TABLE          2008-08-10
                                                                 :22:30:28
SALES_Q4           BIN$U/9fvJKeXOzgQKjAYAIWhw==$0 TABLE          2008-08-10
                                                                 :22:28:10
VAC_SCHED          BIN$U/9fvJKYXOzgQKjAYAIWhw==$0 TABLE          2008-08-09
                                                                 :10:56:41
SQL> purge table "BIN$U/9fvJKfXOzgQKjAYAIWhw==$0";

Table purged.

SQL>
```

You can also purge indexes in the recycle bin. This is useful if you want to keep tables in the recycle bin that otherwise might be aged out by new objects. If you need to recover a table from the recycle bin that no longer has its associated index, you can easily re-create it after you have recovered the table itself.

If you need even finer-grained control of which objects you can purge from the recycle bin, you can purge recycle bin objects from a specific tablespace for the current user, as in this example:

```
SQL> purge tablespace users;

Tablespace purged.

SQL>
```

Furthermore, if you want to purge only objects owned by a particular user, and you have the DROP ANY TABLE system privilege, you can drop all recycle bin objects for a specific user, as in this example:

```
SQL> purge tablespace web_orders user inet_us;

Tablespace purged.

SQL>
```

You can drop all objects from the recycle bin from all tablespaces if you have the SYSDBA privilege and you use the command PURGE DBA_RECYCLEBIN.

Bypassing the Recycle Bin

You can explicitly bypass the recycle bin when you drop a table by appending PURGE to the DROP TABLE command. This can be useful if you know that the table is temporary or has been erroneously created, and you will never need to resurrect it. Remember also that a dropped table that remains in the recycle bin still counts toward a user's quota on the tablespace. Oracle's definition of *space pressure*, which drives removal of objects from the recycle bin, includes a user exhausting her disk quota in a tablespace. Therefore, using DROP TABLE . . . PURGE will prevent removal of a user's other objects in the recycle bin even if enough free space exists in the tablespace itself.

Another operation that bypasses the recycle bin is the DROP TABLESPACE command. This makes a lot of sense when you consider that the objects in the recycle bin are still in the tablespace—just renamed. Note that you must include the INCLUDING CONTENTS clause if any non–recycle bin objects exist in the tablespace when you use the DROP TABLESPACE command.

Finally, if you issue the DROP USER . . . CASCADE command, all the user's objects are dropped from all tablespaces and not placed into the recycle bin. Any of the user's objects will be automatically purged if they are already in the recycle bin when you issue the DROP USER command.

Accessing Tables in the Recycle Bin

When an object resides in the recycle bin, you can still use a SELECT statement to access the dropped table. Also, the dropped table still appears in the data dictionary views DBA_TABLES, DBA_OBJECTS, and DBA_SEGMENTS. Other than the very cryptic name of the table in the recycle bin, if the value of the column DROPPED in these views is set to YES, then you know the table is in the recycle bin.

Here is an example of accessing a table in the recycle bin:

```
SQL> show recyclebin
ORIGINAL NAME     RECYCLEBIN NAME                    OBJECT TYPE   DROP TIME
----------------  ---------------------------------  ------------  ----------
JOB_HISTORY       BIN$UmhMiy3i2+zgQKjAYAI1cw==$0 TABLE             2008-07-19
                                                                   :16:38:48
OLD_EMPLOYEES     BIN$VCfmqQB0FfPgQKjAYAJKzg==$0 TABLE             2008-08-10
                                                                   :23:50:57
```

```
SQL> describe "BIN$VCfmqQB0FfPgQKjAYAJKzg==$0"
 Name                                      Null?    Type
 ---------------------------------------- -------- --------------------
 EMPLOYEE_ID                                        NUMBER(6)
 FIRST_NAME                                         VARCHAR2(20)
 LAST_NAME                                 NOT NULL VARCHAR2(25)
 EMAIL                                     NOT NULL VARCHAR2(25)
 PHONE_NUMBER                                       VARCHAR2(20)
 HIRE_DATE                                 NOT NULL DATE
 JOB_ID                                    NOT NULL VARCHAR2(10)
 SALARY                                             NUMBER(8,2)
 COMMISSION_PCT                                     NUMBER(2,2)
 MANAGER_ID                                         NUMBER(6)
 DEPARTMENT_ID                                      NUMBER(4)

SQL> select last_name, first_name, email
  2  from "BIN$VCfmqQB0FfPgQKjAYAJKzg==$0"
  3  where rownum < 10;

LAST_NAME                FIRST_NAME            EMAIL
------------------------ --------------------  -------------------------
King                     Steven                SKING
Kochhar                  Neena                 NKOCHHAR
De Haan                  Lex                   LDEHAAN
Hunold                   Alexander             AHUNOLD
Ernst                    Bruce                 BERNST
Austin                   David                 DAUSTIN
Pataballa                Valli                 VPATABAL
Lorentz                  Diana                 DLORENTZ
Greenberg                Nancy                 NGREENBE

9 rows selected.

SQL>
```

Note that you can also use the AS OF clause in a SELECT query on a table in the recycle bin for flashback queries, which are covered later in this chapter. No other Data Manipulation Language (DML) or Data Definition Language (DDL) operations are allowed on tables in the recycle bin unless you recover them with the FLASHBACK TABLE . . . TO BEFORE DROP command first.

CERTIFICATION OBJECTIVE 9.02

Perform Flashback Query

Flashback query makes it easy to see a row in a table at a particular time. In the following sections, you'll learn how to use Flashback Query to view one or more rows in a table at a time in the past. In addition, you'll see how to use flashback version query to view a single row's contents over a specified time range. Before you dive into any undo-dependent flashback features, however, you need to get familiar with the basic tablespace and initialization parameters that support flashback operations.

Configuring Flashback Parameters

To utilize flashback functionality fully, you need to configure your undo tablespace correctly. Your initialization parameters for the undo tablespace should look something like the following:

```
undo_management = auto
undo_tablespace = undotbs1
undo_retention = 1800
```

The UNDO_RETENTION parameter in this example specifies that the undo tablespace should retain undo data for at least 1800 seconds (30 minutes) as long as enough space exists in the undo tablespace. Setting UNDO_MANAGEMENT to AUTO directs Oracle to subsequently adjust the undo retention based on the size of the undo tablespace. By default, unexpired undos will be overwritten to ensure that DML operations will not fail due to a lack of available space in the undo tablespace.

ⓦatch

The UNDO_RETENTION parameter is ignored if your undo tablespace is a fixed size. In this case, Oracle automatically adjusts UNDO_ RETENTION to give the best retention period based on the tablespace size and the current system load.

To ensure the success of flashback operations or long-running queries at the expense of DML activity, you must specify RETENTION GUARANTEE for the undo tablespace either when you create the tablespace or later with the ALTER TABLESPACE command, as in this example:

```
SQL> alter tablespace undotbs1 retention guarantee;

Tablespace altered.

SQL>
```

You can check the retention status of an undo tablespace by querying the data dictionary view DBA_TABLESPACES, as in this example:

```
SQL> select tablespace_name, retention
  2  from dba_tablespaces
  3  where tablespace_name like 'UNDO%';

TABLESPACE_NAME                 RETENTION
------------------------------- -----------
UNDOTBS1                        GUARANTEE

SQL>
```

When retention guarantee is enabled, the specified minimum undo retention period is guaranteed. As a result, DML activity can fail if long-running queries or flashback operations are using unexpired undo information.

If you need a much longer retention period for a subset of tables in the database, you should use Flashback Data Archive, which is covered later in this chapter.

Using Flashback Query

Flashback Query allows you to query data in one or more tables in a SELECT query as of a time in the past. Any changes to data in a table generates undo (or optionally data in a Flashback Data Archive), which can give you a snapshot of the entire database down to the granularity of a transaction.

Flashback Query uses the AS OF clause to specify the previous point in time as a timestamp or System Change Number (SCN). In the following example, the user HR is cleaning up the EMPLOYEES table and deletes two employees who no longer work for the company:

```
SQL> delete from employees
  2  where employee_id in (195,196);
2 rows deleted.
```

```
SQL> commit;
Commit complete.

SQL>
```

Normally, the user HR will copy these rows to the EMPLOYEES_ARCHIVE table first, but she forgot to do that this time. The user HR doesn't need to put those rows back into the EMPLOYEES table, but she needs to put the two deleted rows into the archive table. Because the user HR knows she deleted the rows less than an hour ago, she can use a relative timestamp value with Flashback Query to retrieve the rows:

```
SQL>  insert into hr.employees_archive
  2       select * from hr.employees
  3           as of timestamp systimestamp - interval '60' minute
  4           where hr.employees.employee_id not in
  5               (select employee_id from hr.employees);

2 rows created.

SQL> commit;
Commit complete.

SQL>
```

We can use this to retrieve the employee records that existed an hour ago but do not exist now because we know that EMPLOYEE_ID is the primary key of the table. Note also that we didn't have to know which records were deleted. We essentially compare the table as it exists now to the table that existed an hour ago, and then insert the records that no longer exist in the original table into the archive table.

on the **Job**   *It is preferable to use the SCN for flashback over a timestamp. SCNs are exact, whereas the timestamp values are stored only every 3 seconds to support flashback operations. As a result, enabling flashback using timestamps may be off by as much as 1.5 seconds.*

Although we could use Flashback Table to get the entire table back and then archive and delete the affected rows, in this case it is much simpler to retrieve the deleted rows and insert them directly into the archive table.

Another variation of Flashback Table is to use Create Table As Select (CTAS) with the subquery being a Flashback Query:

```
SQL> delete from employees where employee_id in (195,196);
2 rows deleted.
```

```
SQL> commit;
Commit complete.

SQL> create table employees_deleted as
  2         select * from employees
  3              as of timestamp systimestamp - interval '60' minute
  4              where employees.employee_id not in
  5                   (select employee_id from employees);
Table created.

SQL> select employee_id, last_name from employees_deleted;

EMPLOYEE_ID LAST_NAME
----------- ------------------------
        195 Jones
        196 Walsh

2 rows selected.
```

This is known as an *out-of-place restore*, which means restoring the table or a subset of the table to a location that differs from the original. This has the advantage of letting you manipulate the missing rows, if necessary, before placing them back in the table. For example, after you review the out-of-place restore, an existing referential integrity constraint may require that you insert a row into a parent table before the restored row can be placed back into the child table.

One of the disadvantages of an out-of-place restore using CTAS is that neither constraints nor indexes are rebuilt automatically.

Using Flashback Version Query

Flashback Version Query is another flashback feature that relies on undo data and provides a finer level of detail than an AS OF query (a Flashback Query). Whereas the Flashback methods presented up to now bring back rows of a table (or an entire table for a particular point in time), Flashback Version Query will return the entire history of a row between two SCNs or timestamps.

For the examples in this and the next sections, the user HR makes a number of changes to the HR.EMPLOYEES and HR.DEPARTMENTS tables:

```
SQL> select dbms_flashback.get_system_change_number from dual;

GET_SYSTEM_CHANGE_NUMBER
------------------------
                27153780
```

```
SQL> update hr.employees set salary = salary*1.2 where employee_id=195;

1 row updated.

SQL> select dbms_flashback.get_system_change_number from dual;

GET_SYSTEM_CHANGE_NUMBER
-----------------------
              27153831

SQL> delete from hr.employees where employee_id = 196;

1 row deleted.

SQL> select dbms_flashback.get_system_change_number from dual;

GET_SYSTEM_CHANGE_NUMBER
-----------------------
              27153862

SQL> insert into hr.departments values (660,'Security', 100, 1700);

1 row created.

SQL> select dbms_flashback.get_system_change_number from dual;

GET_SYSTEM_CHANGE_NUMBER
-----------------------
              27153917

SQL> update hr.employees set manager_id = 100 where employee_id = 195;

1 row updated.

SQL> commit;

Commit complete.

SQL> select dbms_flashback.get_system_change_number from dual;

GET_SYSTEM_CHANGE_NUMBER
-----------------------
              27154008

SQL> update hr.employees set department_id = 660 where employee_id = 195;

1 row updated.
```

```
SQL> select dbms_flashback.get_system_change_number from dual;

GET_SYSTEM_CHANGE_NUMBER
------------------------
              27154044

SQL> commit;

Commit complete.

SQL> select dbms_flashback.get_system_change_number from dual;

GET_SYSTEM_CHANGE_NUMBER
------------------------
              27154069

SQL>
```

The next day, the primary HR account user is out of the office and the other HR department employees want to know which rows and tables were changed. Using Flashback Version Query, the user HR (or any account with the required privileges), can see not only the values of a column at a particular time, but also the entire history of any changes between specified timestamps or SCNs.

A Flashback Version Query uses the VERSIONS BETWEEN clause to specify a range of SCNs or timestamps for analysis of a given table (in this case, the EMPLOYEES table). When VERSIONS BETWEEN is used in a Flashback Version Query, a number of pseudocolumns are available to help identify the SCN and timestamp of the modifications. Also, the transaction ID and the type of operation performed on the row are available. Table 9-1 shows the pseudocolumns available with Flashback Version Query.

TABLE 9-1   Flashback Version Query Pseudocolumns

Pseudocolumn	Description
VERSIONS_START{SCN|TIME}	The starting SCN or timestamp when the change was made to the row.
VERSION_END{SCN|TIME}	The ending SCN or timestamp when the change was no longer valid for the row. If this is NULL, either the row version is still current or the row was deleted.
VERSIONS_XID	The transaction ID of the transaction that created the row version.
VERSIONS_OPERATION	The operation performed on the row (I=Insert, D=Delete, U=Update).

The HR user runs a Flashback Version Query to see the changes to any key columns in HR.EMPLOYEES for the two employees with IDs 195 and 196:

```
SQL> select versions_startscn startscn, versions_endscn endscn,
  2         versions_xid xid, versions_operation oper,
  3         employee_id empid, last_name name, manager_id mgrid, salary sal
  4  from hr.employees
  5  versions between scn 27153780 and 27154069
  6  where employee_id in (195,196);
```

STARTSCN	ENDSCN	XID	OPER	EMPID	NAME	MGRID	SAL
27154046		0500090092230000	U	195	Jones	100	3360
27153964	27154046	0400000044230000	U	195	Jones	100	3360
	27153964			195	Jones	123	2800
27153964		0400000044230000	D	196	Walsh	124	3100
	27153964			196	Walsh	124	3100

```
SQL>
```

The rows are presented with the most recent changes first. Alternatively, the user HR could have filtered the query by TIMESTAMP or displayed the TIMESTAMP values. If required later, either can be used in a Flashback Query or Flashback Table operation. From this output, you can see that one employee was deleted and that another employee received two pay adjustments instead of one. It's also worth noting that some of the transactions contain only one DML command and others have two. In the next section, we'll attempt to correct one or more of these problems using Flashback Transaction.

Some restrictions and caveats do apply when you use Flashback Version Query. First, you can't query these objects with the VERSIONS clause:

- External tables
- Fixed tables (internal Oracle X$ tables)
- Temporary tables
- Views

You would probably not consider querying most of these with the VERSIONS clause, except possibly views. As a result, you can use the VERSIONS clause as part of a view's definition.

Finally, you cannot use the VERSIONS clause across DDL statements that change the structure of the tables in the query. In other words, you can go back in time only up to the first transaction after the last DDL statement on the table, which of course includes creating the table itself!

Use Flashback Transaction

Once you have identified any erroneous or incorrect changes to a table, you can use Flashback Transaction Query to identify any other changes that were made by the transaction containing the inappropriate changes. Once identified, all changes within the transaction can be reversed as a group, typically to maintain referential integrity or the business rules used to process the transaction in the first place.

The following sections provide the details for identifying the Structured Query Language (SQL) needed to reverse an entire transaction or part of the transaction. The data dictionary view FLASHBACK_TRANSACTION_QUERY has all the information you need to identify this SQL. You'll learn how to identify the SQL required using this view and look at how to use the Enterprise Manager (EM) interface to accomplish the same task.

Understanding Flashback Transaction Query

Unlike a Flashback Version Query, a Flashback Transaction Query does not reference the table involved in DML transactions. Instead, you query the data dictionary view FLASHBACK_TRANSACTION_QUERY. The columns of FLASHBACK_TRANSACTION_QUERY are summarized in Table 9-2.

The table FLASHBACK_TRANSACTION_QUERY contains all changes to the database, including DDL operations. This makes sense, because Oracle uses tables and indexes to manage the data dictionary and space allocation. Thus, a DDL operation shows up in FLASHBACK_TRANSACTION_QUERY as a series of space management and metadata maintenance operations.

Dropped tables and users show up in FLASHBACK_TRANSACTION_QUERY as well. However, they no longer exist, so object numbers show up instead of table names and user ID numbers replace the usernames.

TABLE 9-2	FLASHBACK_TRANSACTION_QUERY Columns

Column Name	Description
XID	Transaction ID number
START_SCN	SCN for the first DML in the transaction
START_TIMESTAMP	Timestamp of the first DML in the transaction
COMMIT_SCN	SCN when the transaction was committed
COMMIT_TIMESTAMP	Timestamp when the transaction was committed
LOGON_USER	User who owned the transaction
UNDO_CHANGE#	Undo SCN
OPERATION	DML operation performed: DELETE, INSERT, UPDATE, BEGIN, or UNKNOWN
TABLE_NAME	Table changed by DML
TABLE_OWNER	Owner of the table changed by DML
ROW_ID	ROWID of the row modified by DML
UNDO_SQL	SQL statement to undo the DML operation

Undo space is not unlimited; thus you may have only partial transactions in FLASHBACK_TRANSACTION_QUERY. In this situation, the value of the OPERATION column contains UNKNOWN for any DML that is no longer in the undo tablespace for the selected transaction.

Flashback Transaction Query Prerequisites

Before you can use Flashback Transaction Query, you must enable additional logging to the redo log stream. The redo log stream is the same data that Log Miner uses, except with a different interface. Obviously, the redo log stream data is in addition to the information recorded in the undo tablespace. Both enhanced redo and undo information are required for Flashback Transaction Query.

First, enable logging of columns and primary key (PK) values referenced in DML changes, using these ALTER DATABASE commands:

```
SQL> alter database add supplemental log data;

Database altered.
```

```
SQL> alter database add supplemental log data (primary key) columns;

Database altered.

SQL>
```

Next, grant the appropriate permissions on the DBMS_FLASHBACK package, as well as give the SELECT ANY TRANSACTION privilege to the users who will be using Flashback Transaction Query:

```
SQL> grant execute on dbms_flashback to hr;

Grant succeeded.

SQL> grant select any transaction to hr;

Grant succeeded.

SQL>
```

Using Flashback Transaction Query

To investigate the changes that were made to the EMPLOYEES table, you can query the view FLASHBACK_TRANSACTION_QUERY with the oldest transaction from the Flashback Version Query shown earlier in this chapter:

```
SQL> select start_scn, commit_scn, logon_user,
  2      operation, table_name, undo_sql
  3  from flashback_transaction_query
  4  where xid = hextoraw('0400000044230000');

 START_SCN COMMIT_SCN LOGON_USER   OPERATION    TABLE_NAME
---------- ---------- ------------ ------------ ---------------
UNDO_SQL
-------------------------------------------------------------------------
  27153828   27153964 HR              UPDATE      EMPLOYEES
update "HR"."EMPLOYEES" set "MANAGER_ID" = '123' where ROWID = 'AAARAIAA
FAAAABXABf';

  27153828   27153964 HR              INSERT      DEPARTMENTS
delete from "HR"."DEPARTMENTS" where ROWID = 'AAARADAAFAAAAA4AAA';
```

```
   27153828    27153964 HR              DELETE       EMPLOYEES
insert into "HR"."EMPLOYEES"("EMPLOYEE_ID","FIRST_NAME","LAST_NAME","EMA
IL","PHONE_NUMBER","HIRE_DATE","JOB_ID","SALARY","COMMISSION_PCT","MANAG
ER_ID","DEPARTMENT_ID") values ('196','Alana','Walsh','AWALSH','650.507.
9811',TO_DATE('24-APR-98', 'DD-MON-RR'),'SH_CLERK','3100',NULL,'124','50
');

   27153828    27153964 HR              UPDATE       EMPLOYEES
update "HR"."EMPLOYEES" set "SALARY" = '2800' where ROWID = 'AAARAIAAFAA
AABXABf';

   27153828    27153964 HR              BEGIN

SQL>
```

This confirms what we already expected—that another user in the HR department made the deletion and salary update—pointing out the usefulness of assigning separate user accounts for each member of the HR department. The UNDO_SQL column contains the actual SQL code that can be used to reverse the effect of the transaction. Note, to the contrary, that in this example, this is the first transaction to occur between the SCNs of interest. If other transactions made further updates to the same columns, you might want to review the other updates before running the SQL code in the UNDO_SQL column.

Using EM with Flashback Transaction Query

Enterprise Manager (EM) provides an easy way to browse the contents of the FLASHBACK_TRANSACTION_QUERY view and optionally reverse some or all of the changes you see in that view. EM provides an easy-to-use GUI as the front end for the procedure DBMS_FLASHBACK.TRANSACTION_BACKOUT. From the EM home page, select the Schema tab and click the Tables link. In the Search boxes, select the HR schema and the table EMPLOYEES. After clicking the Go button, you will see the results shown in Figure 9-1.

FIGURE 9-1

EM table
search results

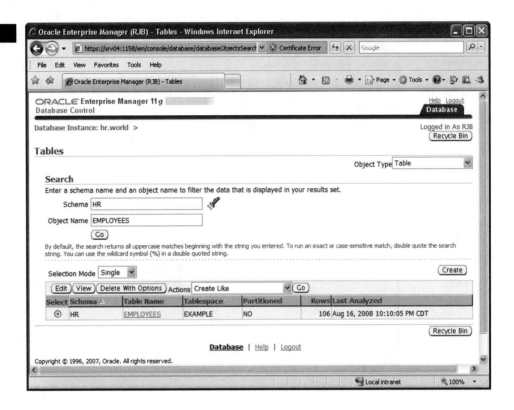

Next, select Flashback Transaction from the Actions drop-down menu and click the Go button. In Figure 9-2, you see step 1 of the Flashback Transaction wizard, where you enter the beginning and ending SCNs from the Flashback Version Query earlier in the chapter. You also have the option to show all transactions for the table or a timestamp range. Once you identify the range, you can further filter the results by using a WHERE clause at the bottom of the page.

FIGURE 9-2

Specifying
SCN range
for Flashback
Transaction
Query

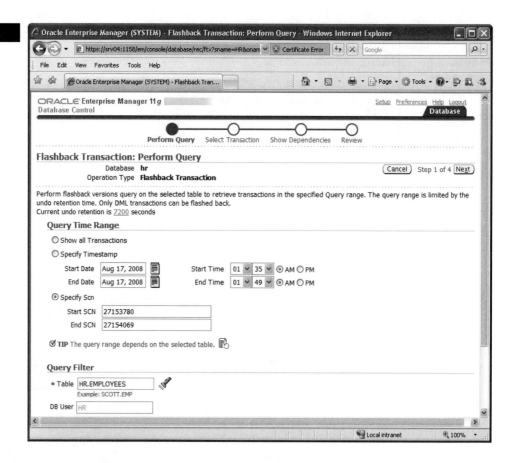

Click the Next button. You see the page in Figure 9-3 identifying the only
transactions in the range you specified. Select the radio button next to the most
recent transaction.

FIGURE 9-3

Identifying
transaction
to view in EM

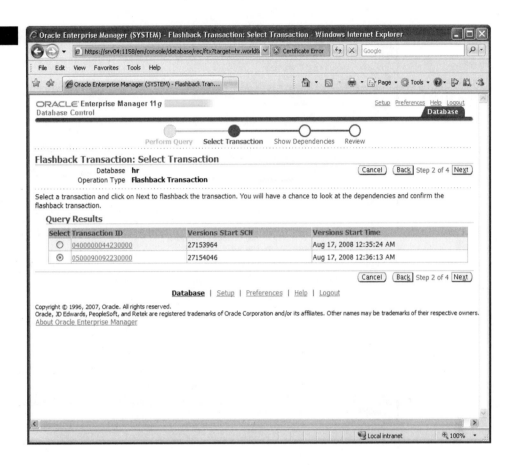

Click the Next button to proceed to the next step. After a short wait, you will
see the page shown in Figure 9-4—the Review screen, where you can back out the
transaction.

FIGURE 9-4

Flashback
Transaction
Review screen

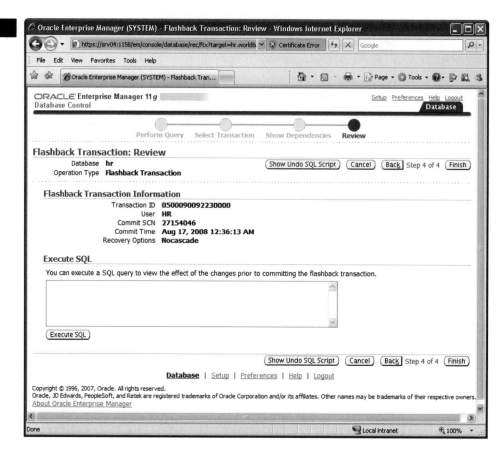

Click the Show Undo SQL Script button in Figure 9-4 and you'll see the page in Figure 9-5 that shows the SQL that EM will perform to roll back the selected transaction.

Choosing Transaction Back-out Options

Note in Figure 9-5 that the transaction rollback will use the NOCASCADE option as the default. In other words, the transaction will back out the transaction expecting no dependent transactions. If any dependent transactions exist, EM will offer

FIGURE 9-5

Flashback
Transaction SQL

the three other options when it runs the procedure DBMS_FLASHBACK
.TRANSACTION_BACKOUT. Here is a summary of all four backout options:

- **CASCADE** Back out all transactions and their dependent transactions.
- **NOCASCADE** Back out only the specified transaction, if possible.
- **NOCASCADE_FORCE** Back out the specified transactions, ignoring dependent transactions.
- **NONCONFLICT_ONLY** Back out changes to nonconflicting rows of the specified transaction only.

Note that using NONCONFLICT_ONLY leaves the database in a consistent state but the specified transactions are no longer atomic.

CERTIFICATION OBJECTIVE 9.04

Perform Flashback Table Operations

Oracle's Flashback Table feature restores the state of rows in a table as of a point of time in the past. It also restores the table's indexes, triggers, and constraints, while the database is online. This increases the overall availability of the database. In the following sections, you'll learn more about when to use Flashback Table and how to configure your environment for Flashback Table. You'll also see some real-world scenarios for which you might use Flashback Table.

Understanding Flashback Table

A table can be restored as of a timestamp or an SCN. Flashback Table is preferable to other Flashback methods if the scope of user errors is small and limited to one or very few tables. It's also the most straightforward if you know that you want to restore the table to a point in the past unconditionally. For recovering the state of a larger number of tables, Flashback Database may be a better choice. Flashback Table cannot be used on a standby database and cannot reconstruct all DDL operations, such as adding and dropping columns. Since Flashback Table uses the undo tablespace, your window of recovery is relatively limited compared to other recovery methods, such as RMAN-based recovery or Flashback Database.

Flashback Table is performed in-place, while the database is online, rolling back changes to the table and all its dependent objects, such as indexes. If the table has other tables as dependent objects, you can specify more than one table in the FLASHBACK TABLE command. Whether you specify one or many tables in a Flashback Table operation, the operation is considered to be a single transaction. All changes are successful or they are rolled back as in a traditional transaction.

Nonsystem users can perform the flashback as long as they have the appropriate privileges. You'll learn how to configure all aspects of using Flashback Table in the next section.

Configuring Flashback Table

To perform Flashback Table, a user must have the FLASHBACK ANY TABLE privilege
or the FLASHBACK object privilege on a specific table:

```
SQL> grant flashback any table to m_phelps;

Grant succeeded.

SQL>
```

As is true with all schema objects, a user does not need additional privileges to
flashback her own tables. However, to use Flashback Table on a table or tables, you
must enable *row movement* on the table before performing the flashback operation.
Row movement need not be in effect when the user error occurs. Row movement is
also required to support Oracle's segment shrink functionality. This is because row
movement will change the ROWID of a table row. Do not enable row movement if
your applications depend on the ROWID being the same for a given row until the
row is deleted.

Using Flashback Table

Before using Flashback Table, you must consider a few restrictions. First, even with
the appropriate privileges, you cannot perform Flashback Table on system tables,
fixed (X$) tables, or remote tables.

In addition, Flashback Table operations cannot span DDL operations, such as adding
or dropping a column. This is true with all flashback features except for Flashback
Database. However, you can flashback a table to a point in time before an index on the
table was dropped, although the index will not be re-created during the Flashback Table
operation.

Finally, any statistics gathered for the tables in the FLASHBACK TABLE command
are not flashed back. As a result, it is a good practice to gather new statistics on the
tables immediately after the Flashback Table operation is complete.

Use Flashback Table on a Table

In this exercise, you will use Flashback Table to recover from accidental deletion of all rows from the EMPLOYEES table.

1. Enable row movement for several tables. You can safely enable row movement because none of your applications reference your tables by ROWID:

```
SQL> alter table employees enable row movement;
Table altered.
SQL> alter table departments enable row movement;
Table altered.
SQL> alter table jobs enable row movement;
Table altered.
```

2. "Inadvertently" delete all the rows in the EMPLOYEES table:

```
SQL> delete from hr.employees
  2  /
107 rows deleted.

SQL> commit
  2  ;
Commit complete.
```

3. The HR user can bring back the entire table quickly without calling the DBA. This is because the undo tablespace is large enough and the HR user notices the problem within the retention period:

```
SQL> flashback table employees
  2       to timestamp systimestamp - interval '15' minute;
Flashback complete.

SQL> select count(*) from employees;
  COUNT(*)
----------
       107
```

If the accidental deletions were not noticed right away, and changes were made to dependent tables in the meantime, you can include the dependent tables in the Flashback Table operation as well:

```
SQL>  flashback table employees, departments
  2        to timestamp systimestamp - interval '15' minute;
Flashback complete.
```

Set Up and Use a Flashback Data Archive

Regulations such as Sarbanes-Oxley (2002) and the Health Insurance Portability and Accountability Act of 1996 (HIPAA) require strict control and tracking requirements for customer and patient data. Retaining a historical record of all changes to rows in critical tables is error prone and requires custom applications or database triggers to maintain repositories for the historical changes. Every time you create a new application or update a table in an application that requires historical tracking, you must make changes to your tracking application as well. You can use Flashback Data Archive to save historical changes automatically to all key tables for as long as regulatory agencies or your stakeholders require.

Understanding Flashback Data Archive

Flashback Data Archive is implemented natively in Oracle (as opposed to an application layer using triggers or a set of PL/SQL packages). In a nutshell, you create one or more repository areas (one of which can be the default), assign a default retention period for objects in the repository, and then mark the appropriate tables for tracking.

A Flashback Data Archive acts much like an undo tablespace. However, a Flashback Data Archive records only UPDATE and DELETE statements but not INSERT statements. In addition, undo data is typically retained for a period of hours or days for all objects. Rows in Flashback Data Archives can span years or even decades. Flashback Data Archives have a much narrower focus as well, recording only historical changes to table rows. Oracle uses data in an undo tablespace for read-consistency in long-running transactions and to roll back uncommitted transactions.

You can access data in a Flashback Data Archive just as you do with Flashback Query using the AS OF clause in a SELECT statement. Flashback Version Query and Flashback Transaction Query can also use the data in a Flashback Data Archive. In the following sections, you'll learn how to create a Flashback Data Archive, assign permissions to users and objects, and query historical data in a Flashback Data Archive.

Creating an Archive

You can create one or several Flashback Data Archives in existing tablespaces using the CREATE FLASHBACK ARCHIVE command. However, Oracle best practices recommend that you use dedicated tablespaces. All archives must have a default retention period using the RETENTION clause and can optionally be identified as the default archive using the DEFAULT keyword. The disk quota in an archive is limited by the disk space within the tablespace, unless you assign a maximum amount of disk space in the archive using the QUOTA keyword.

In this example, you first create a dedicated tablespace for your Flashback Data Archive:

```
SQL> create tablespace fbda1
  2  datafile '+data' size 10g;

Tablespace created.
SQL>
```

Next, you create three Flashback Data Archives: one for the ES department with no quota limit and a ten-year retention period, a second one for the finance department with a 500MB limit and a seven-year retention period, and a third for all other users in the USERS4 tablespace as the default with a 250MB limit and a two-year retention period:

```
SQL> create flashback archive fb_es
  2  tablespace fbda1 retention 10 year;

Flashback archive created.

SQL> create flashback archive fb_fi
  2  tablespace fbda1 quota 500m
  3  retention 7 year;

Flashback archive created.
```

```
SQL> create flashback archive default fb_dflt
  2  tablespace users4 quota 250m
  3  retention 2 year;

Flashback archive created.

SQL>
```

You cannot specify more than one tablespace in the CREATE FLASHBACK ARCHIVE command. You must use the ALTER FLASHBACK ARCHIVE command to add a tablespace, as you'll see later in this chapter, in the section "Managing Flashback Data Archives."

Depending on your business requirements, you can enable and disable Flashback Data Archive on a table at will. For example, you might want to drop a column to a table being tracked by Flashback Data Archive. However, no DDL statements are allowed on tables being tracked using Flashback Data Archive except for adding columns. Once you disable Flashback Data Archive for a table, the historical data for the table is lost even if you immediately re-enable it for the table.

Using Flashback Data Archive Data Dictionary Views

Two new data dictionary views support Flashback Data Archives: DBA_FLASHBACK_ ARCHIVE and DBA_FLASHBACK_ARCHIVE_TS. DBA_FLASHBACK_ARCHIVE lists the archives, and DBA_FLASHBACK_ARCHIVE_TS displays the tablespace-to-archive mapping:

```
SQL> select flashback_archive_name, flashback_archive#,
  2       retention_in_days, status
  3  from dba_flashback_archive;

FLASHBACK_AR FLASHBACK_ARCHIVE# RETENTION_IN_DAYS STATUS
------------ ------------------ ----------------- -------
FB_ES                         1              3650
FB_FI                         2              2555
FB_DFLT                       3               730 DEFAULT

SQL> select * from dba_flashback_archive_ts;

FLASHBACK_AR FLASHBACK_ARCHIVE# TABLESPACE QUOTA_IN_M
------------ ------------------ ---------- ----------
FB_ES                         1 FBDA1
FB_FI                         2 FBDA1      500
FB_DFLT                       3 USERS4     250

SQL>
```

The view DBA_FLASHBACK_ARCHIVE_TABLES tracks the tables enabled for flashback archiving. We'll show you the contents of this view later in this chapter after enabling a table for flashback archiving.

Assigning Flashback Data Archive Permissions

A user must have the FLASHBACK ARCHIVE ADMINISTER system privilege to create or modify Flashback Data Archives, and the FLASHBACK ARCHIVE object privilege to enable tracking on a table. Once enabled, a user doesn't need any specific permissions to use the AS OF clause in a SELECT statement other than the SELECT permission on the table itself.

The FLASHBACK ARCHIVE ADMINISTER privilege also includes privileges for adding and removing tablespaces from an archive, dropping an archive, and performing an ad hoc purge of history data.

Managing Flashback Data Archives

You can easily add another tablespace to an existing archive. Use the ALTER FLASHBACK ARCHIVE command like the following to add the USERS3 tablespace to the FB_DFLT archive with a quota of 400MB:

```
SQL> alter flashback archive fb_dflt
  2  add tablespace users3 quota 400m;

Flashback archive altered.

SQL>
```

You can purge archive data with the purge clause. In this example, you want to purge all rows in the FB_DFLT archive before January 1, 2005:

```
SQL> alter flashback archive fb_dflt
  2  purge before timestamp
  3  to_timestamp('2005-01-01 00:00:00', 'YYYY-MM-DD HH24:MI:SS');
```

Assigning a Table to a Flashback Data Archive

You assign a table to an archive either at table creation using the standard CREATE TABLE syntax with the addition of the FLASHBACK ARCHIVE clause, or later with the ALTER TABLE command as in this example:

```
SQL> alter table hr.employees flashback archive fb_es;

Table altered.
```

Note that in the previous command that specified a particular archive for the HR.EMPLOYEES table, if you did not specify an archive, Oracle assigns `FB_DFLT`. You can review the tables that use Flashback Data Archive by querying the data dictionary view `DBA_FLASHBACK_ARCHIVE_TABLES`:

```
SQL> select * from dba_flashback_archive_tables;

TABLE_NAME            OWNER_NAME FLASHBACK_AR ARCHIVE_TABLE_NAME
--------------------- ---------- ------------ --------------------
EMPLOYEES             HR         FB_ES        SYS_FBA_HIST_70313

SQL>
```

Querying Flashback Data Archives

Querying the historical data for a table in a Flashback Data Archive is as easy as using the `AS OF` clause in a table when you are using DML activity stored in an undo tablespace. In fact, users will not know whether they are retrieving historical data from the undo tablespace or from a Flashback Data Archive.

In this scenario, much like in the scenarios earlier in this chapter, one of the employees in the HR department deletes an employee row in the EMPLOYEES table and forgets to archive it to the EMPLOYEE_HISTORY table first. With Flashback Data Archives enabled for the EMPLOYEES table, the HR employee can rely on the `FB_ES` archive to satisfy any queries on employees no longer in the EMPLOYEES table. This is a `DELETE` statement from three weeks ago:

```
SQL> delete from employees where employee_id = 169;

1 row deleted.

SQL> commit;

Commit complete.

SQL>
```

The HR employee needs to find the hire date for employee 169. She retrieves the historical information from the EMPLOYEES table with the `AS OF` clause specifying a time four weeks ago:

```
SQL> select employee_id, last_name, hire_date
  2  from employees
  3  as of timestamp (systimestamp - interval '28' day)
  4  where employee_id = 169;
```

```
EMPLOYEE_ID LAST_NAME                        HIRE_DATE
----------- ------------------------         ---------
        169 Bloom                            23-MAR-98

SQL>
```

It is completely transparent to the user whether Oracle is using an undo tablespace or a Flashback Data Archive for a query containing AS OF.

Configure, Monitor Flashback Database and Perform Flashback Database Operations

As you might expect, Oracle's Flashback Database feature uses the FLASHBACK DATABASE command to return the database to a past time or SCN, providing a fast alternative to performing incomplete database recovery. In the following sections, you'll learn how to configure Flashback Database, you'll step through a simple example, and you'll learn how to monitor a Flashback Database. In addition, you'll review some of the finer points, such as how to exclude one or more tablespaces from a Flashback Database operation and how to use guaranteed restore points.

Understanding Flashback Database

You can use Flashback Database to bring your entire database quickly to a previous point in time. When you enable Flashback Database, the before images of modified blocks are saved in the flash recovery area as Flashback Database logs. When a logical corruption occurs that requires a recovery to a time in the past, the Flashback Database logs restore the data blocks' before images, and then the archived and online redo logs roll forward to the desired flashback time. This process is typically much faster than performing a traditional restore and recovery operation, because the database's datafiles do not need to be restored.

When Flashback Database is enabled, the before image data is saved in a buffer that is appropriately named the *flashback buffer*. Then it uses the Recovery Writer (RVWR) background process to save the before image information from the flashback buffer to the Flashback Database logs in the flash recovery area. The logs in the flash recovery area are reused in a circular fashion. How far back you can rewind the database depends on the amount of space in your flash recovery area and the guaranteed restore points you have configured. You'll learn more about guaranteed restore points later in this section.

Configuring Flashback Database

To use Flashback Database, you must configure the flash recovery area (see Chapter 2 for more information on configuring the flash recovery area using the parameters DB_RECOVERY_FILE_DEST and DB_RECOVERY_FILE_DEST_SIZE). Configuring the size of the flash recovery area correctly ensures that enough space exists for Flashback Database logs in addition to all the other information in the flash recovery area, such as archived redo log files and RMAN backups. You set the initialization parameter DB_FLASHBACK_RETENTION_TARGET to an upper limit (in minutes) for your usable recovery window. This parameter is a target and not a guarantee. You will use guaranteed restore points to ensure the retention of Flashback Database logs in the flash recovery area.

Here is the typical sequence of commands you will use to enable Flashback Database:

```
shutdown immediate;
startup mount exclusive;
alter database archivelog;
/* if you are not already in ARCHIVELOG mode */
alter system set db_flashback_retention_target=2880;
alter database flashback on;
alter database open;
```

In this example, the target retention time for Flashback logs is 2880 minutes (2 days).

Using Flashback Database

The most straightforward scenario for using Flashback Database is to restore the entire database to a specific timestamp. However, many scenarios are not this clear. In the following sections, you'll learn how to use Flashback Database with an SCN or a guaranteed restore point. You'll also learn how to exclude one or more tablespaces from the Flashback Database operation, and you'll see some dynamic performance views that can help you monitor the ability to meet your retention target.

Performing Flashback Database

You can use the FLASHBACK DATABASE command from RMAN or from the SQL> prompt. Some subtle syntactical differences exist between the two versions. The RMAN version offers you some additional granularity options, such as flashing back to a particular log sequence number and thread (instance). Here's an example:

```
RMAN> flashback database to sequence=307 thread=2;
```

We'll use the SQL version of the FLASHBACK DATABASE command in the rest of this section. The basic syntax for the SQL FLASHBACK DATABASE command is as follows:

```
flashback [standby] database [database]
{ to {scn | timestamp} expr
| to before {scn | timestamp } expr
| to restore point expr
}
```

You can use either the TO SCN or TO TIMESTAMP clause to set the point to which the entire database should be flashed back, which is in addition to a guaranteed restore point. You can flash back TO BEFORE a critical point, such as a transaction that produced an unintended consequence for multiple tables. Use the ORA_ROWSCN pseudocolumn for a particular table row to see the SCNs of the most recent changes to the row:

```
SQL> select ora_rowscn, last_name, first_name
  2  from employees
  3  where employee_id = 102;

ORA_ROWSCN LAST_NAME                        FIRST_NAME
---------- ------------------------         --------------------
  27247532 De Haan                          Lex

SQL>
```

With the database open for more than an hour, verify that the flashback data is available and then flash it back—you will lose all transactions that occurred during that time:

```
shutdown;
startup mount exclusive;
flashback database to timestamp sysdate-(1/24);
```

When you execute the FLASHBACK DATABASE command, Oracle checks to make sure all required archived and online redo log files are available. If the logs are available, the online datafiles are reverted to the time, SCN, or guaranteed restore point specified.

If there is not enough data online in the archive logs and the flashback area, you will need to use traditional database recovery methods to recover the data. For example, you might need to use a file system recovery method followed by rolling the data forward.

Once the flashback has completed, you must open the database using the RESETLOGS option to have write access to the database:

```
alter database open resetlogs;
```

To turn off the flashback database option, execute the ALTER DATABASE FLASHBACK OFF command when the database is mounted but not open:

```
startup mount exclusive;
alter database flashback off;
alter database open;
```

Excluding Tablespaces from Flashback Database

By default, all tablespaces will participate in a Flashback Database operation unless you change the FLASHBACK attribute to OFF at the time the tablespace is created or later using the ALTER TABLESPACE command. Here's an example:

```
SQL> alter tablespace example flashback off;

Tablespace altered.

SQL>
```

To re-enable Flashback Database on this tablespace, you use ALTER TABLESPACE EXAMPLE FLASHBACK ON, as you'd expect, but the database must be shut down and reopened in MOUNT mode.

When you need to use Flashback Database, offline all tablespaces with the FLASHBACK attribute set to OFF. When the database is back up, you can use other point-in-time recovery methods to recover the offline datafiles and eventually bring them back online.

Using Guaranteed Restore Points

A *guaranteed restore point* is similar to a regular restore point in that it can be used as an alias for an SCN during a recovery operation. A guaranteed restore point is different in that it is not aged out of the control file and must be explicitly dropped.

Not surprisingly, guaranteed restore points are useful for Flashback Database operations. Creating a guaranteed restore point when you have flashback logging enabled ensures that flashback logs are retained in the flash recovery area so that the database can be rolled back to any point after the creation of the guaranteed restore point.

Here is an example of a guaranteed restore point created before a major application upgrade:

```
SQL> create restore point before_app_upgr
  2       guarantee flashback database;

Restore point created.

SQL>
```

Here is how you would use this guaranteed restore point:

```
SQL> flashback database to restore point before_app_upgr;
```

To use guaranteed restore points, you must also enable these prerequisites:

- The COMPATIBLE initialization parameter must be 10.2 or higher.
- The database must be running in ARCHIVELOG mode.
- You must have archived redo log files available starting from the time of the first guaranteed restore point.
- You must have a flash recovery area configured.

on the **Ọob** *Keep in mind that guaranteed restore points will likely cause space pressure in the flash recovery area over time because Oracle will retain any flashback logs in the flash recovery area after the first guaranteed restore point.*

Monitoring Flashback Database

You can use several dynamic performance views to monitor the space usage of the flash recovery area to ensure that you can meet the retention target for possible Flashback Database operations.

You can determine how far back you can flashback the database by querying the V$FLASHBACK_DATABASE_LOG view. The amount of flashback data retained in the database is controlled by the initialization parameter and the size of the flash recovery area. The following listing shows the available columns in V$FLASHBACK_ DATABASE_LOG and sample contents:

```
SQL> describe V$FLASHBACK_DATABASE_LOG

Name                                         Null?    Type
-------------------------------------------- -------- -------
OLDEST_FLASHBACK_SCN                                  NUMBER
OLDEST_FLASHBACK_TIME                                 DATE
RETENTION_TARGET                                      NUMBER
FLASHBACK_SIZE                                        NUMBER
ESTIMATED_FLASHBACK_SIZE                              NUMBER


SQL> select * from V$FLASHBACK_DATABASE_LOG;

OLDEST_FLASHBACK_SCN OLDEST_FL RETENTION_TARGET FLASHBACK_SIZE
-------------------- --------- ---------------- --------------
ESTIMATED_FLASHBACK_SIZE
------------------------
             5903482 12-AUG-08             1440        8192000
                95224008
```

You can verify the database's flashback status by querying V$DATABASE. The FLASHBACK_ON column will have a value of YES if the flashback has been enabled for the database:

```
select current_scn, flashback_on from V$DATABASE;

CURRENT_SCN FLA
----------- ---
    5910734 YES
```

Finally, you can use the view V$FLASHBACK_DATABASE_STAT to monitor the rate at which flashback data is generated on an hour-by-hour basis:

```
SQL> select to_char(begin_time,'dd-mon-yy hh24:mi') begin_time,
  2         to_char(end_time,'dd-mon-yy hh24:mi') end_time,
  3         flashback_data, db_data, redo_data,
  4         estimated_flashback_size est_fb_sz
  5  from v$flashback_database_stat;

BEGIN_TIME      END_TIME        FLASHBCK_DATA   DB_DATA   REDO_DATA
EST_FB_SZ
--------------- --------------- ------------- --------- ---------- -----
```

```
17-aug-08 16:28 17-aug-08 17:13      12738560   18407424     7079424
95224008

SQL>
```

FLASHBACK_DATA is the number of bytes of flashback data written during the interval. REDO_DATA is the number of bytes of redo written during the same period. DB_DATA is the number of bytes in all data blocks written. The column ESTIMATED_FLASHBACK_SIZE (abbreviated to EST_FB_SZ) contains the same value as ESTIMATED_FLASHBACK_SIZE in V$FLASHBACK_DATABASE_LOG.

CERTIFICATION SUMMARY

The beginning of the chapter reviewed the Flashback Drop feature that uses a recycle bin construct supported in every tablespace. It behaves much like the recycle bin on a Windows-based computer. If enough room is available in the tablespace, dropped objects can be restored to their original schema with all indexes, triggers, and constraints intact. The recycle bin uses a data dictionary table that keeps track of dropped objects. You can restore one or more versions of a dropped table from the recycle bin as long as the recycle bin is enabled and space pressure in the tablespace has not purged the dropped table from the tablespace.

Next, you learned the basics of Flashback Query and how it can view one or more rows of a table at a time in the past. To use Flashback Query, you must first properly configure automatic undo management, and then size the undo tablespace to accommodate undo retention of undo data as far back as needed. Undo retention must accommodate DML transactions, query read consistency, and support Flashback Query to the desired point of time in the past.

Flashback Transaction is similar to Flashback Query, except Flashback Transaction uses the data dictionary view FLASHBACK_TRANSACTION_QUERY to contain information about past transactions on one or more tables. To support Flashback Transaction, you must enable supplemental logging for all table columns and the primary key column, somewhat increasing the amount of data that the Log Writer (LGWR) process writes to the redo log files. Flashback Transaction leverages Log Miner technology to retrieve the details on previous transactions. Once you've identified the changes made within a transaction, you can use Enterprise Manager or the UNDO_SQL column in FLASHBACK_TRANSACTION_QUERY to reverse part or all of the transaction. This depends on your tolerance for atomicity and other subsequent transactions in the database.

Flashback Table is another technology that lets you rewind the state of one table or a group of tables to a time in the past. Like many flashback features, Flashback Table relies on data in the undo tablespace and is subject to the configured retention policy.

Flashback Data Archive provides a way to preserve the history of selected tables over a much longer period of time than is supported by the undo tablespace. To configure and use Flashback Data Archive, you create one or more repository areas (one of which can be the default), assign a default retention period for objects in the repository, and then mark the appropriate tables for tracking. Once changes start recording in the Flashback Data Archive, you can use the familiar AS OF clause in the SELECT statement to view previous versions of rows in a table.

Finally, you learned how to configure and use Flashback Database to roll back the entire database to a time in the past. After you configure the flash recovery area to retain the before images of changed data blocks (flashback logs), you can recover the database to a specific timestamp or SCN as long as the required flashback logs are still in the flash recovery area. You can use guaranteed restore points to ensure that the database can be rolled back to the guaranteed restore point or any SCN or timestamp since you created the guaranteed restore point.

✓ TWO-MINUTE DRILL

Restore Dropped Tables from the Recycle Bin

❏ Flashback Drop uses the recycle bin to recover dropped tables.

❏ The recycle bin is a data dictionary table that keeps track of dropped objects.

❏ You can restore the current or previous versions of dropped tables from the recycle bin.

❏ When you drop an object with the recycle bin enabled, the space allocated to the dropped object and all associated objects (such as indexes) is immediately reflected in the data dictionary view DBA_FREE_SPACE.

❏ When a table is dropped, the table and its dependent objects are renamed to a system-assigned name using the format BIN$unique_id$version.

❏ To query the recycle bin, you can use the data dictionary view USER_RECYCLEBIN. RECYCLEBIN is a global synonym for USER_RECYCLEBIN.

❏ The data dictionary view USER_RECYCLEBIN has the same columns as DBA_RECYCLEBIN, except that USER_RECYCLEBIN does not have the OWNER column.

❏ To restore a table from the recycle bin, you use the FLASHBACK TABLE . . . TO BEFORE DROP command.

❏ If you attempt to restore a table that has been re-created since it was dropped, you will receive an error unless you use the RENAME TO clause to give the restored table a new name.

❏ The space in the recycle bin, and by extension the space in the tablespace containing the recycle bin, is managed automatically by Oracle.

❏ All dropped objects remain available for recovery in the recycle bin as long as new objects don't need the space occupied by dropped objects.

❏ You can use the PURGE command to remove tables manually from the recycle bin.

❏ When an object resides in the recycle bin, you can still use a SELECT statement to access the dropped table. The dropped table still appears in the data dictionary views DBA_TABLES, DBA_OBJECTS, and DBA_SEGMENTS.

Perform Flashback Query

❑ Flashback query enables you to view one or more rows in a table at a time in the past.

❑ To ensure the success of flashback operations or long-running queries at the expense of DML activity, you must specify RETENTION GUARANTEE for the undo tablespace.

❑ You can check the retention status of an undo tablespace by querying the data dictionary view DBA_TABLESPACES.

❑ Flashback Query uses the AS OF clause to specify the previous point in time as a timestamp or SCN.

❑ Flashback Version Query, another flashback feature that relies on undo data, provides a finer level of detail than an AS OF query (a Flashback Query).

❑ A Flashback Version Query uses the VERSIONS BETWEEN clause to specify a range of SCNs or timestamps for analysis of a given table.

Use Flashback Transaction

❑ The data dictionary view FLASHBACK_TRANSACTION_QUERY has all the information you need to identify the SQL required to reverse a transaction.

❑ Before you can use Flashback Transaction Query, you must enable additional logging to the redo log stream. This is the same data that Log Miner uses although using a different interface.

❑ You must grant permissions on the DBMS_FLASHBACK package, as well as the SELECT ANY TRANSACTION privilege to the users who will be using Flashback Transaction Query.

❑ The UNDO_SQL column of FLASHBACK_TRANSACTION_QUERY contains the actual SQL code that can be used to reverse the effect of the transaction.

❑ Enterprise Manager (EM) provides an easy-to-use GUI as the front end for the procedure DBMS_FLASHBACK.TRANSACTION_BACKOUT.

❑ The four transaction backout options are CASCADE, NOCASCADE, NOCASCADE_ FORCE, and NONCONFLICT_ONLY.

Perform Flashback Table Operations

❑ Oracle's Flashback Table feature not only restores the state of rows in a table as of a point of time in the past, but also restores the table's indexes, triggers, and constraints while the database is online.

❑ Flashback Table is preferable to other flashback methods if the scope of user errors is small and limited to one or very few tables.

❑ Flashback Table is performed in place while the database is online, rolling back changes to the table and all its dependent objects, such as indexes.

❑ To perform Flashback Table, a user must have the FLASHBACK ANY TABLE privilege or the FLASHBACK object privilege on a specific table.

❑ To use Flashback Table on a table or tables, you must enable row movement on the table before performing the Flashback operation, although row movement need not be in effect when the user error occurs.

❑ Flashback Table operations cannot span DDL operations, such as adding or dropping a column.

Set Up and Use a Flashback Data Archive

❑ A Flashback Data Archive retains historical data for one or more tables for a specified retention period.

❑ To enable a Flashback Data Archive, you create one or more repository areas (one of which can be the default), assign a default retention period for objects in the repository, and then mark the appropriate tables for tracking.

❑ A Flashback Data Archive acts much like an undo tablespace. However, a Flashback Data Archive records only UPDATE and DELETE statements but not INSERT statements.

❑ You can access data in a Flashback Data Archive just as you do with Flashback Query using the AS OF clause in a SELECT statement.

❑ You create one or several Flashback Data Archives in existing tablespaces using the CREATE FLASHBACK ARCHIVE command.

❑ The data dictionary views supporting Flashback Data Archives are DBA_FLASHBACK_ARCHIVE and DBA_FLASHBACK_ARCHIVE_TS.

❑ The view DBA_FLASHBACK_ARCHIVE_TABLES tracks the tables enabled for flashback archiving.

❏ A user must have the FLASHBACK ARCHIVE ADMINISTER system privilege to create or modify Flashback Data Archives.

❏ You assign a table to an archive either at table creation using the standard CREATE TABLE syntax with the addition of the FLASHBACK ARCHIVE clause, or later with the ALTER TABLE command.

Configure, Monitor Flashback Database and Perform Flashback Database Operations

❏ Flashback Database uses the FLASHBACK DATABASE command to return the database to a past time or SCN, providing a fast alternative to performing incomplete database recovery.

❏ When you enable Flashback Database, the before images of modified blocks are saved in the flash recovery area as Flashback Database logs.

❏ The logs in the flash recovery area are reused in a circular fashion.

❏ Configuring the size of the flash recovery area correctly ensures that enough space is available for Flashback Database logs in addition to all the other information in the flash recovery area.

❏ You set the initialization parameter DB_FLASHBACK_RETENTION_TARGET to an upper limit (in minutes) for your usable recovery window; this is a target, not a guarantee.

❏ You can use the FLASHBACK DATABASE command from RMAN or from the SQL> prompt.

❏ You can use either the TO SCN or TO TIMESTAMP clause to set the point to which the entire database should be flashed back, in addition to a guaranteed restore point.

❏ You can use the ORA_ROWSCN pseudocolumn for a given table row to see the SCNs of the most recent changes to a table's row.

❏ If not enough data exists in the archive logs and the flashback area, you will need to use traditional database recovery methods to recover the data.

❏ To turn off the flashback database option, execute the ALTER DATABASE FLASHBACK OFF command when the database is mounted but not open.

❏ By default, all tablespaces will participate in a Flashback Database operation unless you change the FLASHBACK attribute to OFF at the time the tablespace is created, or later using the ALTER TABLESPACE command.

❑ A guaranteed restore point is similar to a regular restore point in that it can be used as an alias for an SCN during a recovery operation.

❑ A guaranteed restore point is different in that it is not aged out of the control file and must be explicitly dropped.

❑ Creating a guaranteed restore point when you have flashback logging enabled ensures that flashback logs are retained in the flash recovery area so that the database can be rolled back to any point after the creation of the guaranteed restore point.

❑ You can determine how far back you can flashback the database by querying the V$FLASHBACK_DATABASE_LOG view.

❑ You can use the view V$FLASHBACK_DATABASE_STAT to monitor the rate at which flashback data is generated on an hour-by-hour basis.

SELF TEST

The following questions will help you measure your understanding of the material presented in this chapter. Read all the choices carefully, because there might be more than one correct answer. Choose all correct answers for each question.

Restore Dropped Tables from the Recycle Bin

1. Which of the following statements is true about the recycle bin?
   A. When you drop an object, the space allocated by the object is not immediately reflected in DBA_FREE_SPACE and counts against the user's quota.
   B. When you drop an object, the space allocated by the object is immediately reflected in DBA_FREE_SPACE and does not count against the user's quota.
   C. When you drop an object, the space allocated by the object is immediately reflected in DBA_FREE_SPACE but still counts against the user's quota.
   D. When you drop an object, the space allocated by the object is not immediately reflected in DBA_FREE_SPACE and does not count against the user's quota.

2. The column CAN_UNDROP is set to YES for an object in the view DBA_RECYCLEBIN. Which of the following is true for this object? (Choose all that apply.)
   A. The object is a table.
   B. The object can be undropped by the user who owns the object.
   C. The object can be undropped only by a user with DBA privileges.
   D. The object does not have any dependent objects in the recycle bin.
   E. No existing object with the same name exists outside of the recycle bin.

Perform Flashback Query

3. Which of the following parameters directly affect the behavior and proper functioning of Flashback Table? (Choose all that apply.)
   A. DB_RECOVERY_FILE_DEST
   B. UNDO_MANAGEMENT
   C. DB_RECOVERY_FILE_DEST_SIZE
   D. UNDO_TABLESPACE
   E. UNDO_RETENTION

4. When using the VERSIONS BETWEEN clause for Flashback Version Query, what can't you use to restrict the number of rows returned by the query?

A. A timestamp

B. An SCN

C. A WHERE clause on any column in the table

D. A guaranteed restore point

Use Flashback Transaction

5. Which of the following columns is not in the data dictionary view FLASHBACK_TRANSACTION_QUERY?

A. UNDO_SQL

B. XID

C. OPERATION

D. ORA_ROWSCN

6. What happens to the rows in FLASHBACK_TRANSACTION_QUERY when part of the transaction is no longer available in the undo tablespace?

A. The user ID number replaces the user name in the LOGON_USER column.

B. The OPERATION column contains the value UNKNOWN.

C. The object number replaces the table name in the TABLE_NAME column.

D. The OPERATION column contains the value UNAVAILABLE.

E. All rows for the transaction are no longer available in FLASHBACK_TRANSACTION_QUERY.

Perform Flashback Table Operations

7. What methods can you use in the AS OF clause of a Flashback Table operation to specify the time in the past to which you want to recover the table? (Choose all that apply.)

A. A timestamp

B. A filter condition in the WHERE clause

C. An SCN

D. A restore point

E. A guaranteed restore point

8. You create the table VAC_SCHED on Monday with a primary key index; the SCN right after table creation was 5680123. On Wednesday, you drop the index. On Thursday, you accidentally delete most of the rows in the database. On Friday, you execute this command:

```
SQL> FLASHBACK TABLE VAC_SCHED TO SCN 5680123;
```

You have set guaranteed undo retention to 1 week. What is the result of running this command?

   A. The table is recovered to SCN 5680123 without the index.

   B. The table is recovered using the data in the undo tablespace and the index is re-created using the dropped index in the recycle bin.

   C. The table is recovered and all rows deleted on Thursday are restoring using archived and online redo log files.

   D. The command fails because FLASHBACK TABLE cannot recover a table before a change to a dependent object.

Set Up and Use a Flashback Data Archive

9. Identify the true statement about Flashback Data Archives.

   A. You can specify more than one default Flashback Data Archive.

   B. If you do not specify a RETENTION clause for a Flashback Data Archive, you must specify it when assigning a table to the Flashback Data Archive.

   C. The QUOTA parameter is required when creating a Flashback Data Archive to limit the amount of space used in the tablespace.

   D. A Flashback Data Archive can exist in multiple tablespaces including undo tablespaces and temporary tablespaces.

10. Which of the following data dictionary views contains a list of the tables using a Flashback Data Archive?

   A. DBA_FLASHBACK_ARCHIVE_TABLES

   B. DBA_FLASHBACK_ARCHIVE

   C. DBA_FLASHBACK_ARCHIVE_TS

   D. DBA_FLASHBACK_DATA_ARCHIVE_TABLES

Configure, Monitor Flashback Database and Perform Flashback Database Operations

11. Which of the following initialization parameters is not required to configure Flashback Database operations?

    A. DB_RECOVERY_FILE_DEST_SIZE

    B. UNDO_RETENTION

    C. DB_FLASHBACK_RETENTION_TARGET

    D. DB_RECOVERY_FILE_DEST

12. What is the difference between a regular restore point and a guaranteed restore point? (Choose all that apply.)

    A. A regular restore point does not require that a flash recovery area be configured.

    B. A guaranteed restore point can be used only with Flashback Database.

    C. A guaranteed restore point cannot be dropped.

    D. A guaranteed restore point will never be aged out of the control file.

    E. You must have flashback logging enabled to use guaranteed restore points.

SELF TEST ANSWERS

Restore Dropped Tables from the Recycle Bin

1. ☑ **C.** A dropped object's space is immediately reflected in DBA_FREE_SPACE but still counts against the user's quota until it is purged from the recycle bin.
   ☒ **A, B,** and **D** are incorrect. All three reflect incorrect statements about free space management and quota management for objects in the recycle bin.

2. ☑ **A** and **B.** Table objects in the recycle bin can be undropped, and they can be undropped by the original owner or a user with DBA privileges.
   ☒ **C** is wrong because an object in the recycle bin can be undropped by the owner or a user with DBA privileges; the view DBA_RECYCLEBIN has an OWNER column to indicate which user dropped the object. **D** is wrong because a table in the recycle bin may or may not have dependent objects in the recycle bin. **E** is wrong because there may or may not be an object with the same original name as an object in the recycle bin.

Perform Flashback Query

3. ☑ **B, D,** and **E.** For Flashback Query, Flashback Table, Flashback Transaction Query, and Flashback Version Query, you must have automatic undo management configured, an undo tablespace defined, and an undo retention value to specify how long undo data is retained in the undo tablespace.
   ☒ **A** and **C** are wrong. The parameters DB_RECOVERY_FILE_DEST and DB_RECOVERY_FILE_DEST_SIZE are used to configure Flashback Data Archive retention, but not Flashback Query.

4. ☑ **D.** Guaranteed restore points are used only in recovery scenarios such as Flashback Database.
   ☒ **A, B,** and **C** can be used and are therefore wrong. You can restrict the results of a Flashback Version Query by SCN or timestamp. You can further filter the rows by using a WHERE clause on the table columns.

Use Flashback Transaction

5. ☑ **D.** ORA_ROWSCN is a pseudocolumn that is available for all tables and contains the last SCN that modified or created the row.
   ☒ **A, B,** and **C** are wrong. UNDO_SQL is the SQL you can use to reverse the change to the row, XID is the transaction ID, and OPERATION is the DML operation performed.

6. ☑ **B.** The OPERATION column in FLASHBACK_TRANSACTION_QUERY contains UNKNOWN for data no longer in the undo tablespace.

☒ **A** is wrong because the user ID replaces the user name in the LOGON_USER column when the user no longer exists. **C** is wrong because the object number replaces the table name in the TABLE_NAME column when the table no longer exists. **D** is wrong because the OPERATION column contains UNKNOWN, not UNAVAILABLE, when the information is no longer available in the undo tablespace. **E** is wrong because part of a transaction might still be available in the undo tablespace.

Perform Flashback Table Operations

7. ☑ **A, C, D,** and **E.** You can use the AS OF clause with the TIMESTAMP or SCN qualifier to specify a time to which you want to recover the table. In addition, you can specify a restore point or a guaranteed restore point for Flashback Table. Guaranteed restore points are also useful in Flashback Database operations to ensure that flashback logs are maintained in the flash recovery area at least a far back as the earliest guaranteed restore point.

☒ **B** is wrong because you cannot use a WHERE clause to specify the time in the past for the FLASHBACK TABLE operation.

8. ☑ **A.** The table is recovered to its original state right after creation with no rows and without the index.

☒ **B** is wrong because FLASHBACK TABLE does not leverage the recycle bin. **C** is wrong because the table is recovered as of the SCN, but not rolled forward. **D** is wrong because a dropped index does not affect the recoverability of a table; however, a change to the structure of the table itself prevents a flashback operation to before the DDL change to the table.

Set Up and Use a Flashback Data Archive

9. ☑ **B.** You must either specify a default retention period for the Flashback Data Archive itself or specify a retention period when adding the table to the archive.

☒ **A** is wrong because you can have several Flashback Data Archives. **C** is wrong because the QUOTA parameter is needed only if you want to limit the amount of space used by the Flashback Data Archive in the tablespace; otherwise it can grow to use all available space in the tablespace. **D** is wrong because you can create Flashback Data Archives only in permanent, non-undo tablespaces.

10. ☑ **A.** DBA_FLASHBACK_ARCHIVE_TABLES contains a list of tables currently using a Flashback Data Archive.

☒ **B** is wrong because DBA_FLASHBACK_ARCHIVE contains a list of the archives, but not the tables within. **C** is wrong because DBA_FLASHBACK_ARCHIVE_TS contains the archive to tablespace mapping. **D** is wrong because DBA_FLASHBACK_DATA_ARCHIVE_TABLES is not a valid data dictionary view.

Configure, Monitor Flashback Database and Perform Flashback Database Operations

11. ☑ **B.** The initialization parameter UNDO_RETENTION is required for other Flashback features, but not for Flashback Database.

☒ **A, C,** and **D** are wrong. The parameters DB_RECOVERY_FILE_DEST_SIZE and DB_RECOVERY_FILE_DEST are required to define the location and size of the Flash Recovery area, and DB_FLASHBACK_RETENTION_TARGET is needed to define a desired upper limit for the Flashback Database recovery window.

12. ☑ **A** and **D.** A regular restore point does not require a flash recovery area, and it can be aged out of the control file; a guaranteed restore point will never be aged out of the control file unless it is explicitly dropped.

☒ **B** is wrong because a guaranteed restore point can be referenced for other flashback features, not just Flashback Database. **C** is wrong because you can explicitly drop any type of restore point. **E** is wrong because you can define guaranteed restore points without flashback logging enabled; however, you must still have a flash recovery area enabled.

10
Memory Management Techniques

W

ith any computing resource, memory is finite and is usually the most expensive computing resource in your environment. On your database servers, Oracle could be competing for memory resources with other non-database applications (although Oracle recommends dedicating servers for database functions). In any case, once you know how much memory Oracle can use, you must decide how to divide the memory among the Oracle processes and functions. You might be able to completely automate Oracle memory management, but you will likely encounter situations in which you'll need to tweak some of your memory settings manually.

This chapter starts out with a review of the Oracle memory structures. (See Chapter 1 for an in-depth explanation of physical storage structures, memory structures, and background processes.) Oracle has many levels of memory automation; you can choose a "one-size-fits-all" approach, tune all memory yourself, or set up something in between. You can completely automate the total amount of memory using Automatic Memory Management (AMM), and Oracle will automatically adjust the memory allocation between the System Global Area (SGA) and the instance Program Global Area (PGA) automatically. If you want to have slightly more control over the total size of the SGA, you can use Automatic Shared Memory Management (ASMM) to set a target and maximum size for the SGA only, and Oracle will still automatically tune each SGA component. Understanding which SGA components can be automatically tuned and which must be manually tuned is key to passing the memory management questions on the exam.

Finally, the chapter wraps up with PGA memory management. You'll learn how to automatically and manually allocate and tune the PGA memory allocation and how to monitor the performance of the instance PGA.

CERTIFICATION OBJECTIVE 10.01

Implement Automatic Memory Management

Oracle recommends that you configure a new database using AMM, and then monitor the database to see how well Oracle can manage the total memory allocation. You can switch your database to ASMM at a later time to exercise more control over the total size of the SGA, but still let Oracle manage the memory allocation for individual components of the SGA.

First, you'll get a brief refresher on Oracle memory structures and the relationship between the memory structures within the SGA and the PGA. Next, you'll learn how to configure AMM and learn about the dependencies between the various memory initialization parameters. Even with AMM enabled, you can still set a related memory initialization parameter to a lower bound to prevent Oracle from auto-tuning the parameter to a low or zero value. You'll also see how to exercise a little more control over memory allocation by enabling ASMM. Regardless of your level of memory automation, you'll need to know the dynamic performance views you can use to monitor how well Oracle is utilizing memory.

Understanding Oracle Memory Structures

Oracle uses the server's physical memory to hold many things for an Oracle instance:

- The Oracle executable code itself
- Session information
- Individual processes associated with the database
- Information shared between processes (such as locks on database objects)

In addition, the memory structures contain user and data dictionary SQL statements, along with cached information that is eventually permanently stored on disk, such as data blocks from database segments and information about completed transactions in the database. The data area allocated for an Oracle instance is called the *System Global Area (SGA)*. The Oracle executables reside in the software code area. In addition, an area called the *Program Global Area (PGA)* is private to each server and background process; one PGA is allocated for each user session or server process. The sum of memory for each private PGA area must be less than or equal to the server level PGA maximum limit.

Figure 10-1 (repeated from Chapter 1 for your convenience) shows the components of these Oracle memory structures.

System Global Area

The SGA is a group of memory structures for an Oracle instance that are shared by the users of the database instance. When an Oracle instance is started, memory is allocated for the SGA based on the values specified in the initialization parameter file or hard-coded in the Oracle software depending on the automation level you've chosen.

FIGURE 10-1

Oracle logical
memory
structures

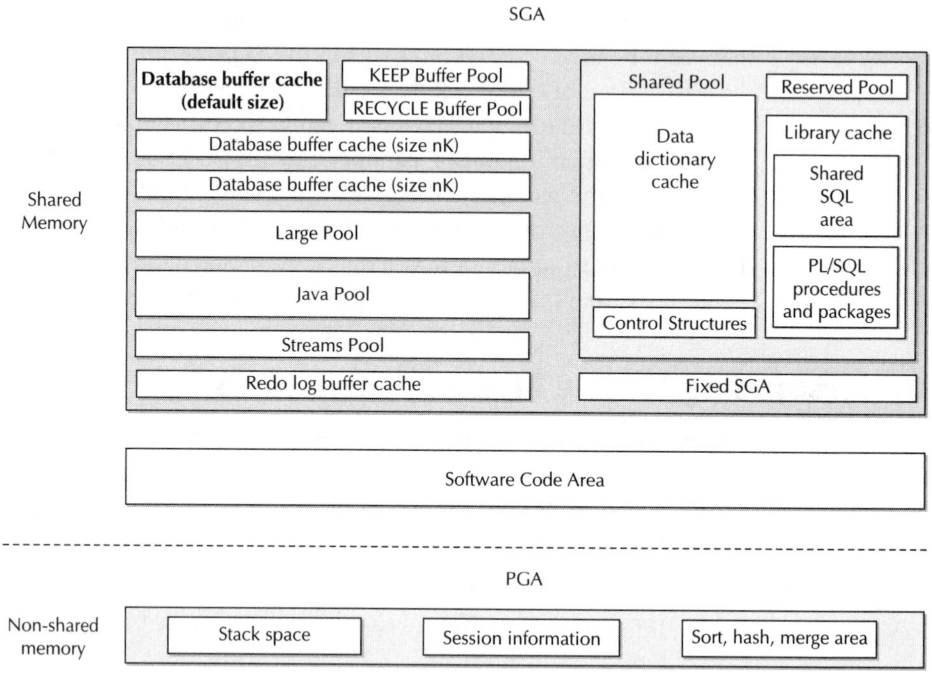

Memory in the SGA is allocated in units of *granules*. A granule can be either 4MB or 16MB, depending on the total size of the SGA. If the SGA is less than or equal to 128MB, a granule is 4MB; otherwise, it is 16MB. The next few sections cover the highlights of how Oracle uses each section in the SGA.

Buffer Caches   The database *buffer cache* holds blocks of data from disk that have been recently read to satisfy a SELECT statement or that contain modified blocks that have been changed or added from a Data Manipulation Language (DML) statement. Oracle allows for tablespaces with up to five different block sizes (one block size for the default, and up to four others). Each block size requires its own buffer cache.

Oracle can use two additional caches with the same block size as the default block size: the KEEP buffer pool and the RECYCLE buffer pool. Both of these pools allocate memory independently of other caches in the SGA.

When a table is created, you can specify the pool where the table's data blocks will reside by using the BUFFER_POOL KEEP or BUFFER_POOL RECYCLE clause in the STORAGE clause. For tables that you use frequently throughout the day, it would be advantageous to place the tables into the KEEP buffer pool to minimize the I/O needed to retrieve blocks in the table.

Shared Pool   The *shared pool* contains two major subcaches: the library cache and the data dictionary cache. The *library cache* holds information about SQL and PL/SQL statements that are run against the database. In the library cache, because it is shared by all users, many different database users can potentially share the same SQL statement.

Along with the SQL statement itself, the execution plan of the SQL statement is stored in the library cache. The second time an identical SQL statement is run, by the same user or a different user, the execution plan is already computed, improving the execution time of the query or DML statement. If the library cache is sized too small, then frequently used execution plans can be flushed out of the cache, requiring just as frequent reloads of SQL statements into the library cache.

The *data dictionary* is a collection of database tables, owned by the SYS and SYSTEM schemas, that contain the metadata about the database, its structures, and the privileges and roles of database users. The *data dictionary cache* holds the most frequently requested rows from the data dictionary tables, except for table and column descriptions unless they are frequently accessed. Data blocks from tables in the data dictionary are used continually to assist in processing user queries and other DML commands.

If the data dictionary cache is too small, requests for information from the data dictionary will cause extra I/O to occur; these I/O-bound data dictionary requests are called *recursive calls* and should be avoided by sizing the data dictionary cache correctly.

Redo Log Buffer   The *redo log buffer* holds the most recent changes to the data blocks in the datafiles. When the redo log buffer is one-third full, or every 3 seconds, or when a log switch occurs (a log switch can be forced), Oracle writes redo log records to the redo log files. The Log Writer (LGWR) process will write the redo log records to the redo log files when 1MB of redo is stored in the redo log buffer. The entries in the redo log buffer, once written to the redo log files, are critical to database recovery if the instance crashes before the changed data blocks are written from the buffer cache to the datafiles. A user's committed transaction is not considered complete until the redo log entries and the transaction's System Change Number (SCN) have been successfully written to the redo log files.

Large Pool The *large pool* is an optional area of the SGA. It is used for transactions that interact with more than one database, message buffers for processes performing parallel queries, and RMAN parallel backup and restore operations. As the name implies, the large pool makes available large blocks of memory for operations that need to allocate large blocks of memory at a time.

Java Pool The *Java pool* is used by the Oracle JVM (Java Virtual Machine) for all Java code and data within a user session. Storing Java code and data in the Java pool is analogous to SQL and PL/SQL code cached in the shared pool, except the Java pool is not subdivided as much as the shared pool.

Streams Pool The *streams pool* holds data and control structures to support the Oracle Streams feature of Oracle Enterprise Edition. Oracle Streams manages the sharing of data and events in a distributed environment.

Program Global Area

The PGA is an area of memory allocating dynamic sections of itself, privately for one set of connection processes. Each set of connection processes is a connection or session into a database. A session can originate as a single user connection from one user, or as a shared connection as part of a pool from an application or a web server. The configuration of the PGA depends on the connection configuration of the Oracle database: either *shared server* or *dedicated*.

In a shared server configuration, multiple users share a connection to the database, minimizing memory usage on the server, but potentially affecting response time for user requests. In a shared server environment, the SGA holds the persistent session information for a user instead of the PGA.

Shared server environments are ideal for a large number of simultaneous connections to the database with infrequent or short-lived requests. In a dedicated server environment, each user process gets its own connection to the database; the PGA contains the session memory for this configuration. The PGA also includes a sort area that is used whenever a user request requires a sort, bitmap merge, or hash join operation.

Software Code Area

Software code areas store the Oracle executable files that are running as part of an Oracle instance. These code areas are static in nature and change only when a new release of the software is installed. Typically, the Oracle software code areas are located in a privileged memory area separate from other user programs.

Oracle software code is strictly read-only and can be installed either shared or nonshared. Installing Oracle software code as sharable saves memory when multiple Oracle instances are running on the same server and at the same software release level.

Configuring Automatic Memory Management

A good starting point for a new database installation is to use Automatic Memory Management. Using AMM, Oracle takes your memory target and automatically balances SGA and PGA memory based on the current workload. You use two initialization parameters to control AMM, MEMORY_TARGET and MEMORY_MAX_ TARGET. You use MEMORY_TARGET to dynamically set the combined SGA and PGA memory usage. By now you should be very familiar with the ALTER SYSTEM command used to change MEMORY_TARGET (unless MEMORY_MAX_TARGET is exceeded):

```
SQL> alter system set memory_target = 500m;
```

The parameter MEMORY_MAX_TARGET, in contrast, is an upper bound for MEMORY_ TARGET and is not dynamic. You set MEMORY_MAX_TARGET as a static parameter to ensure that you cannot set MEMORY_TARGET too high while the database is running. If MEMORY_MAX_TARGET is not set at instance startup, it is set to the value of MEMORY_TARGET.

Table 10-1 details the effects of setting other initialization parameters when MEMORY_TARGET is set to a nonzero value. This table will be referenced again later in the chapter.

TABLE 10-1   Dependencies for a Nonzero MEMORY_TARGET

When MEMORY_TARGET > 0 and these parameters are set...	The behavior is...
Both SGA_TARGET and PGA_AGGREGATE_ TARGET set	SGA_TARGET and PGA_AGGREGATE_TARGET are minimum values for SGA and PGA; MEMORY_TARGET ranges from SGA_TARGET + PGA_AGGREGATE_TARGET to MEMORY_ MAX_TARGET
SGA_TARGET is set, but PGA_AGGREGATE_ TARGET is NOT set	Both parameters are still auto-tuned, but PGA_AGGREGATE_ TARGET starts out at MEMORY_TARGET – SGA_TARGET
SGA_TARGET is NOT set, but PGA_ AGGREGATE_TARGET is set	Both parameters are still auto-tuned, but SGA_TARGET starts out at MIN(MEMORY_TARGET-PGA_AGGREGATE_TARGET, SGA_MAX_SIZE)
Both SGA_TARGET and PGA_AGGREGATE_ TARGET are NOT set	Both SGA_TARGET and PGA_AGGREGATE_TARGET are auto-tuned, with 60% for SGA and 40% for PGA

exam

The exam very specifically gives you scenarios combining various initialization parameters such as MEMORY_TARGET and SGA_TARGET set to zero and nonzero values, and then asks you what *the effect is on instance memory and other initialization parameters. You'll have to memorize the contents of Tables 10-1 and 10-2 to answer those questions!*

Table 10-2 details the effects and behavior of other related initialization parameters when MEMORY_TARGET is not set, or explicitly set to zero.

To enable automatic memory management, you can use the current values for SGA_TARGET and PGA_AGGREGATE_TARGET to calculate the desired value for MEMORY_TARGET. Follow these steps:

1. Use the SQL*Plus command SHOW PARAMETER TARGET to determine the current SGA and PGA targets.

2. Find the maximum PGA allocated from V$PGASTAT using the PGA statistic 'maximum PGA allocated'.

3. Calculate MEMORY_TARGET by adding the SGA target value to the maximum of the PGA target and the maximum PGA allocated since the instance was started.

4. Set the MEMORY_MAX_TARGET in the SPFILE to a value at least as high as MEMORY_TARGET in step 3.

5. Restart the instance.

6. Set MEMORY_TARGET in both the running instance and the SPFILE to the value calculated in step 3, and set both SGA_TARGET and PGA_AGGREGATE_TARGET to zero if you don't want a minimum value for those parameters.

TABLE 10-2	Dependencies for a Zero MEMORY_TARGET

When MEMORY_TARGET = 0 (or not set) and these parameters are set...	The behavior is...
SGA_TARGET is set	Oracle auto-tunes SGA components, and PGA is auto-tuned whether or not it is explicitly set
SGA_TARGET is NOT set	Some SGA components must be explicitly specified, and PGA is auto-tuned

EXERCISE 10-1

Enable Automatic Memory Management

In this exercise, you have upgraded your database from Oracle 10g to 11g and want to enable automatic memory management:

1. Use the SQL*Plus command SHOW PARAMETER TARGET to determine the current SGA and PGA targets:

```
SQL> show parameter target

NAME                              TYPE          VALUE
--------------------------------- ----------    ------------
archive_lag_target                integer       0
db_flashback_retention_target     integer       2880
fast_start_io_target              integer       0
fast_start_mttr_target            integer       0
memory_max_target                 big integer   0
memory_target                     big integer   0
pga_aggregate_target              big integer   156M
sga_target                        big integer   452M
SQL>
```

2. Find the maximum PGA allocated from V$PGASTAT:

```
SQL> select value from v$pgastat where name='maximum PGA allocated';

    VALUE
----------
 221533184

SQL>
```

Since the value from V$PGASTAT is higher that the PGA target value, you will use 222M in the next step.

3. Calculate MEMORY_TARGET by adding the current SGA target value to the larger of the PGA target and the maximum PGA allocated since the instance was started:

```
SQL> /* MEMORY_TARGET = 452M + 222M = 674M */
SQL> /* Run this command after restart: */
SQL> /* alter system set memory_target = 674m; */
```

4. Set the MEMORY_MAX_TARGET in the SPFILE to a value at least as high as your calculation for MEMORY_TARGET in step 3 (adding 100MB in this case):

```
SQL> /* MEMORY_TARGET =  452M + 222M + 100M = 774M */
SQL> alter system set memory_max_target = 774m scope=spfile;

System altered.

SQL>
```

5. Restart the instance.

```
SQL> shutdown immediate;
SQL> startup;
```

You need to shut down the instance, since MEMORY_MAX_TARGET is not a dynamic parameter.

6. Set MEMORY_TARGET in both the running instance and the SPFILE to the value calculated in step 3, and set both SGA_TARGET and PGA_AGGREGATE_TARGET to zero if you don't want a minimum value for those parameters:

```
SQL> alter system set memory_target = 674m;

System altered.

SQL> alter system set sga_target = 0;

System altered.

SQL> alter system set pga_aggregate_target = 0;

System altered.

SQL>
```

Monitoring Automatic Memory Management

As with most, if not all, features of Oracle Database, you can monitor the feature using either Enterprise Manager (EM) or dynamic performance views. To monitor Automatic Memory Management (AMM), start at the EM home page, select the Server tab, and then click the Memory Advisors link under Database Configuration. You'll see the screen shown in Figure 10-2.

FIGURE 10-2

Monitoring
AMM using EM

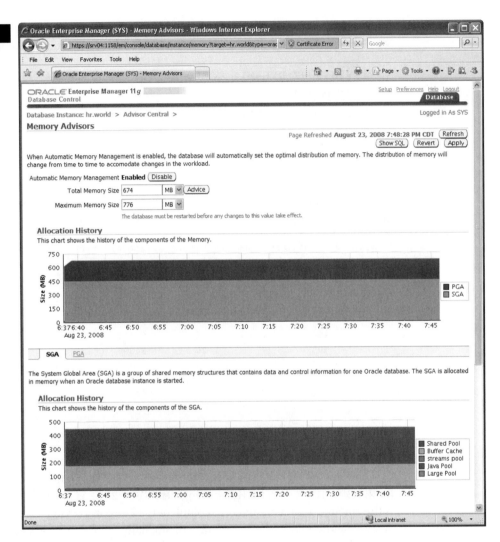

You can see the total memory allocated as the sum of the SGA and PGA allocation. At the bottom of the screen, you can see the SGA memory allocation by SGA components. This screen also provides the option to switch back and forth between SGA and PGA.

Alternatively, you can go straight to the source and use dynamic performance views to see the status of memory components and look for tuning advice:

- ■ **V$MEMORY_DYNAMIC_COMPONENTS**   Current status of all memory components.
- ■ **V$MEMORY_RESIZE_OPS**   A circular buffer of the last 800 memory sizing requests.
- ■ **V$MEMORY_TARGET_ADVICE**   Tuning advice for the MEMORY_TARGET initialization parameter.

In this example, the V$MEMORY_TARGET_ADVICE view is queried to compare the effects of changing the MEMORY_TARGET initialization parameter:

```
SQL> select * from v$memory_target_advice order by memory_size;

MEMORY_SIZE MEMORY_SIZE_FACTOR ESTD_DB_TIME ESTD_DB_TIME_FACTOR    VERSION
----------- ------------------ ------------ ------------------- ----------
        202                .5        93688              1.1091          0
        303               .75        91390              1.0819          0
        404                 1        84472                   1          0
        505              1.25        84396               .9991          0
        606               1.5        84396               .9991          0
        707              1.75        84396               .9991          0
        808                 2        84396               .9991          0

7 rows selected.

SQL>
```

The value of 1 for the column MEMORY_SIZE_FACTOR reflects the current value for MEMORY_SIZE, and for this instance, MEMORY_SIZE is 404MB. EST_DB_TIME is the amount of time required to complete the current workload. In this scenario, decreasing the MEMORY_SIZE value will gradually increase the amount of time required to complete the current workload. Increasing the amount of memory by about 100MB will noticeably improve the performance of the instance. However, any increases beyond 100MB given the current workload will not have much effect on performance.

CERTIFICATION OBJECTIVE 10.02

Manually Configure SGA Parameters

If you want to exercise more control over memory allocation for the SGA (PGA memory tuning is covered later in this chapter), you can switch from completely AMM to Automatic Shared Memory Management (ASMM). Enabling ASMM is as easy as setting SGA_TARGET to the desired value. Even after enabling ASMM, you can still control the minimum size of the components within the SGA controlled by SGA_TARGET. In addition, you will still need to tune some initialization parameters manually.

Understanding Automatic Shared Memory Management

Using ASSM helps you simplify SGA memory management if you want a fixed amount of memory allocated to the SGA. You will likely experience less memory-related errors when components such as the buffer cache can expand during heavy online transaction processing (OLTP) activity; or, conversely, if the large pool can expand at the expense of the buffer cache during non-peak hours when OLTP activity is low and RMAN backups require more memory in the large pool.

The adjustments to the automatically tuned parameters are saved across shutdowns if you are using an SPFILE. Therefore, you don't have to wait for Oracle to relearn the optimal parameters every time you restart the instance.

ASMM uses the Memory Manager (MMAN) background process to coordinate changes in memory size. Every few minutes, MMAN checks the size of each component and makes adjustments when one component needs more memory and another component is not using its allocation fully.

TABLE 10-3	Auto-tuned SGA Parameters

SGA Component	Initialization Parameter
Shared pool	`SHARED_POOL_SIZE`
Large pool	`LARGE_POOL_SIZE`
Java pool	`JAVA_POOL_SIZE`
Buffer cache	`DB_CACHE_SIZE`
Streams pool	`STREAMS_POOL_SIZE`

Switching to ASMM

If you are switching to ASMM, you are either switching from completely manual shared memory management or from AMM; the procedure is slightly different for each scenario. In both cases, the value of SGA_TARGET is set to the desired SGA size.

Switching from Manual Memory Management to ASMM

If you are using manual SGA memory management, your SGA-related parameters should already be set to somewhat reasonable values. Use the sum of the values in the VALUE column of the V$SGA dynamic performance view, less the memory identified by CURRENT_SIZE in the dynamic performance view V$SGA_DYNAMIC_FREE_MEMORY, which is currently not in use. Use the result of this calculation to set SGA_TARGET.

To maximize Oracle's automatic tuning, set the initialization parameters in Table 10-3 to zero using ALTER SYSTEM commands.

You can also leave any of these parameters with a nonzero value, and Oracle will ensure that the memory allocated for that memory area does not fall below that value. For example, you may want to ensure that the size of the shared pool does not fall below 128MB for a poorly designed application that will fail unless the shared pool is at least 128MB. But keep in mind that this prevents other SGA components from using the memory allocated for the shared pool. You should have to use this feature rarely or never, but when you do, use it with caution.

EXERCISE 10-2

Enable Automatic Shared Memory Management

In this exercise, you'll switch from manual memory management to ASMM.

1. Using this query, calculate a value for SGA_TARGET based on the current values:

```
SQL> select
  2      (
  3          (select sum(value) from v$sga) -
```

```
  4          (select current_size from v$sga_dynamic_free_memory)
  5      ) sga_target
  6  from dual;

SGA_TARGET
----------
 422670336

SQL>
```

In other words, calculate the total memory currently allocated to SGA components, less the amount of unused memory within the allocation.

2. Use this value to set the value of SGA_TARGET (remember that this new value must be less than SGA_MAX_SIZE):

```
SQL> alter system set sga_target=422670336;
```

3. Set the initialization parameters in Table 10-3 to zero:

```
SQL> alter system set SHARED_POOL_SIZE = 0;
SQL> alter system set LARGE_POOL_SIZE = 0;
SQL> alter system set JAVA_POOL_SIZE = 0;
SQL> alter system set DB_CACHE_SIZE = 0;
SQL> alter system set STREAMS_POOL_SIZE = 0;
```

Switching from AMM to ASMM

Switching from AMM to ASMM is even easier than switching from manual memory management to ASMM. First, set the value of MEMORY_TARGET to zero:

```
SQL> alter system set memory_target = 0;
```

After you issue this command, Oracle automatically sets SGA_TARGET based on the current SGA memory usage. As you did when converting from manual memory management to ASMM, set the initialization parameters in Table 10-3 to zero to maximize Oracle's ability to auto-tune those parameters.

Disabling ASMM

You can dynamically disable ASMM by setting SGA_TARGET to zero:

```
SQL> alter system set sga_target = 0;
```

All of the initialization parameters in Table 10-3 are set to their current auto-tuned value. Note that the current values will most likely be different from any minimum values assigned to those parameters in the SPFILE.

Identifying ASMM Manually Tuned Parameters

When you use ASMM, only the parameters in Table 10-3 are auto-tuned. The following SGA parameters, however, must be manually tuned:

- `DB_KEEP_CACHE_SIZE`
- `DB_RECYCLE_CACHE_SIZE`
- `DB_nK_CACHE_SIZE` (where n = 2, 4, 8, 16, or 32)
- `LOG_BUFFER`

When you set these parameters manually, the memory allocated to these parameters is subtracted from the memory specified by `SGA_TARGET`.

Modifying the SGA_TARGET Parameter

Because `SGA_TARGET` is a dynamic parameter, you can adjust its size as long as it is not greater than `SGA_MAX_SIZE`. `SGA_MAX_SIZE` is analogous to the parameters `MEMORY_MAX_TARGET` and `MEMORY_TARGET` in that it provides an upper limit to the value of `SGA_TARGET`.

When you increase the value of `SGA_TARGET`, the additional memory is distributed among the other memory components that are currently being auto-tuned. Similarly, reducing the value of `SGA_TARGET` proportionally reduces the memory from the memory components that are auto-tuned.

Modifying Auto-Tuned Parameters

As mentioned, the parameters in Table 10-3 can be manually adjusted even if you set `SGA_TARGET` to auto-tune these parameters. At instance startup, any nonzero values for these parameters sets a lower limit for the memory allocated to the component. When the instance is running, you can change the values of these parameters as well. However, the memory allocated to the component is not changed unless the value you specify with `ALTER SYSTEM` is greater than the amount of memory currently allocated to the component. For example, if `SHARED_POOL_SIZE` is set to 300MB, and the current auto-tune value is 400MB, then setting `SHARED_POOL_SIZE` to 500MB will automatically allocate another 100MB from the other auto-tuned components.

On the other hand, if `SHARED_POOL_SIZE` is set to 300MB, and the current auto-tune value is 400MB, then setting `SHARED_POOL_SIZE` to 350MB will not change the memory allocated to the shared pool. The amount of memory allocated to the shared pool, however, cannot fall below 350MB when Oracle auto-tunes all SGA components.

Tuning SGA Components

Ideally, all of the SGA should fit into physical memory and should not be swapped out to disk as virtual memory. You can set the initialization parameter LOCK_SGA on some operating systems to TRUE to ensure that the SGA will always be in physical memory. Unfortunately, you cannot use AMM or ASMM with the LOCK_SGA parameter.

Your tuning goal, when manually tuning the SGA buffer cache, is to have a high buffer cache hit ratio. In other words, requested blocks are already in the buffer cache instead of on disk.

A high hit ratio might not necessarily be an indication of a well-tuned system. For example, a query running 100 times per second may request the same small set of data blocks over and over, artificially raising the hit ratio. In this case, application tuning (or user education) is in order.

Similarly, a low hit ratio may not mean a poorly tuned system. Large full table scans, where the table is larger than the buffer cache, might be necessary because the optimizer determines it will take less time than using an index. However, a full table scan will not take advantage of blocks that might already be in the buffer cache for the table that is being scanned.

CERTIFICATION OBJECTIVE 10.03

Configure Automatic PGA Memory Management

PGA memory (the total instance PGA memory and the PGA memory allocated to each user or background process) is automatically managed along with SGA memory when you use AMM. If you need further control of PGA memory, you can use the initialization parameter PGA_AGGREGATE_TARGET to set a desired upper limit for PGA memory used by all server and background processes.

Understanding the components of the PGA will help you understand how to set PGA_AGGREGATE_TARGET. You also need to understand which dynamic performance views will help you see how efficiently the PGA is using memory.

Understanding PGA Components

As mentioned at the beginning of this chapter, the PGA is a memory region containing data and control information for server and background processes. This memory is dedicated to the server or background process. In other words, it is not shared with any other server or background process. The total of all PGA memory allocated to all server and background processes is known as the instance or aggregate PGA.

If you have configured shared servers for your database connections, the connection information is located in the SGA in either the shared pool or the large pool. This makes sense because the SGA is a shared area. PGA memory contains the following components:

■ **Private SQL area**   Bind information and run-time memory structures for each session's execution of the same SQL statement (in the library cache).

■ **Cursor and SQL area**   Named cursors created by Oracle Call Interface (OCI) or Pro*C applications.

■ **Work area**   Memory to support memory-intensive operators such as ORDER BY, GROUP BY, hash joins, bitmap operations and bulk loads.

■ **Session memory**   Session variables such as logon information; if you are using shared servers, session memory is shared in the shared pool or large pool.

Configuring PGA Memory Management

Automatic PGA memory management is enabled by default and behaves similarly whether you are using AMM or not. PGA_AGGREGATE_TARGET is either derived by AMM or you set it explicitly. Oracle then automatically manages the work areas for all sessions within the PGA depending on the workload. Initialization parameters such as SORT_AREA_SIZE and HASH_AREA_SIZE, which were the subject of frequent tuning headaches in previous versions of Oracle, are deprecated in Oracle Database 11g and are retained for backward compatibility. When automatic PGA memory management is enabled, these parameters are ignored if set but are calculated and show up in dynamic performance views such as V$PARAMETER:

```
SQL> show parameter area_size

NAME                                     TYPE        VALUE
---------------------------------------- ----------- ---------------
bitmap_merge_area_size                   integer     1048576
create_bitmap_area_size                  integer     8388608
hash_area_size                           integer     131072
sort_area_size                           integer     65536
```

```
workarea_size_policy                          string     AUTO
SQL>
```

When you create a new instance or until you have run representative workloads, you do not have any statistics available to precisely size the PGA using PGA_AGGREGATE_TARGET. Therefore, as a starting point, you must first determine how much server memory to allocate to Oracle. A typical value for a single instance, leaving memory for the operating system and assuming no other applications on the server, is 80 percent of physical memory.

From the memory allocated to Oracle, you can divide the memory between the SGA and PGA depending on the type of database applications you will run on the server:

- **Online Transaction Processing (OLTP)**   PGA can be as low as 20 percent of available memory.
- **Decision Support Systems (DSS) running memory-intensive queries**   PGA can range from 50 to 70 percent of available memory, with 50 percent as a good starting point.

Managing PGA Memory

Because PGA_AGGREGATE_TARGET is not a hard upper bound, Oracle may allocate more memory to the PGA during a typical workload. Thus, you should monitor PGA memory usage using dynamic performance views and, of course, the PGA Memory Advisor via the EM web interface.

The dynamic performance view V$PGA_STAT provides an overview of all PGA memory, as you can see from this query:

```
SQL> select * from v$pgastat;

NAME                                                VALUE UNIT
------------------------------------------------ ---------- -------
aggregate PGA target parameter                  176160768 bytes
aggregate PGA auto target                        72585216 bytes
global memory bound                              35231744 bytes
total PGA inuse                                  95510528 bytes
total PGA allocated                             184295424 bytes
maximum PGA allocated                           499208192 bytes
```

```
total freeable PGA memory                    13041664 bytes
process count                                      43
max processes count                                51
PGA memory freed back to OS                2656108544 bytes
total PGA used for auto workareas                   0 bytes
maximum PGA used for auto workareas           7198720 bytes
total PGA used for manual workareas                 0 bytes
maximum PGA used for manual workareas          271360 bytes
over allocation count                             229
bytes processed                            4525369344 bytes
extra bytes read/written                            0 bytes
cache hit percentage                              100 percent
recompute count (total)                          8001

19 rows selected.

SQL>
```

The value for `cache hit percentage` is the first place to look, which ideally is 100 percent if all work areas for all processes received all the memory they need. The value for `cache hit percentage` is calculated using `extra bytes read/ written`. This value is the number of extra bytes that were read or written using multiple passes because the work areas did not have enough memory.

You can monitor an individual session's PGA memory using `V$PROCESS` and these columns:

- **PGA_USED_MEM**   PGA memory currently in use by the process.
- **PGA_ALLOC_MEM**   Memory allocated for the process, including memory not yet released to the operating system.
- **PGA_MAX_MEM**   Maximum PGA memory ever used by the process.

For a quick overview of PGA memory usage and tuning recommendations, start from the EM home page, click the Server tab, and then click the Memory Advisors link under the Database Configuration heading. On the Memory Advisors page, click the PGA tab, and you'll see the page shown in Figure 10-3.

As you can see, all the statistics on this page are derived from dynamic performance views such as `V$PGASTAT`.

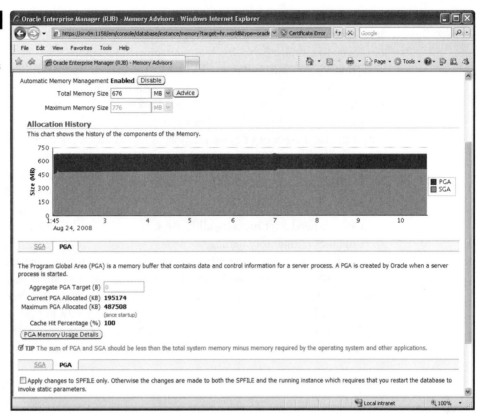

FIGURE 10-3

Viewing PGA memory statistics and tuning advice using EM

CERTIFICATION SUMMARY

The chapter started with a brief refresher of Oracle memory structures. Even though this topic was covered thoroughly in Chapter 1, a reiteration of the Oracle memory structures is extremely helpful when considering how Oracle automatically manages and tunes memory and allocates the right amount of memory to the SGA and PGA from the total memory available.

The next topic, Automatic Memory Management, is the "set it and forget it" feature of Oracle Database 11g that can greatly simplify memory management. After you set the total amount of memory that Oracle can use for the SGA and PGA using the MEMORY_TARGET parameter, Oracle automatically adjusts the total size of the SGA and PGA (and the structures within the SGA and PGA) to accommodate changing workloads, such as OLTP during the day, DSS queries in the evening, and backup operations overnight. Setting the memory target is only half of the story. You also need to monitor how Oracle is managing the memory. You saw the dynamic performance views as well as the EM pages you can use to monitor memory usage.

Allowing Oracle to completely manage all memory works in many environments, but there are always exceptions to the rule. Therefore, you may want to exercise a bit more control over SGA memory using the parameter `SGA_TARGET`. Even when the total amount of SGA memory is fixed and Oracle dynamically changes the memory usage of areas within the SGA, you can still set minimum values for several initialization parameters depending on your application requirements. You learned how to switch from either AMM or manual SGA management to ASMM. Furthermore, when ASMM does not provide the performance or fine-grained control you need over memory allocation, you can disable ASMM and revert back to manual SGA memory management.

The chapter wrapped up with a discussion of PGA memory management. Whether you are using AMM, ASMM, or manual SGA memory management, PGA memory management is automated using the parameter `PGA_AGGREGATE_TARGET`. Using AMM sets `PGA_AGGREGATE_TARGET` automatically. For ASMM and manual SGA memory management, you set `PGA_AGGREGATE_TARGET` manually and monitor PGA memory usage using dynamic performance views and EM.

TWO-MINUTE DRILL

Implement Automatic Memory Management

❏ The System Global Area (SGA) is shared by all server and background processes.

❏ The Program Global Area (PGA) is private to each server and background process unless you are using shared servers for user session connections.

❏ The software code area contains the Oracle executable files that run as part of an Oracle instance.

❏ You configure AMM by setting the parameter MEMORY_TARGET.

❏ MEMORY_MAX_TARGET is an upper bound for MEMORY_TARGET. The former is not a dynamic parameter.

❏ When MEMORY_TARGET is set and both SGA_TARGET and PGA_AGGREGATE_ TARGET are set, then SGA_TARGET and PGA_AGGREGATE_TARGET are used as minimum values.

❏ When MEMORY_TARGET is set and neither SGA_TARGET nor PGA_AGGREGATE_ TARGET are set, then SGA_TARGET is set to 60 percent and PGA_AGGREGATE_ TARGET is set to 40 percent.

Manually Configure SGA Parameters

❏ You can set MEMORY_TARGET to zero and SGA_TARGET to a nonzero value to exercise more control over SGA memory.

❏ Adjustments to automatically tuned SGA parameters are saved across instance restarts.

❏ ASMM uses the MMAN background process to coordinate changes in memory size.

❏ The five auto-tuned ASMM initialization parameters are SHARED_POOL_ SIZE, LARGE_POOL_SIZE, JAVA_POOL_SIZE, DB_CACHE_SIZE, and STREAMS_POOL_SIZE.

❏ The manually tuned ASMM initialization parameters are DB_KEEP_CACHE_ SIZE, DB_RECYCLE_CACHE_SIZE, DB_*n*K_CACHE_SIZE, and LOG_BUFFER.

❑ You can easily disable ASMM by setting SGA_TARGET to zero, but then the current auto-tuned ASMM initialization parameters are set to their current values.

❑ The static parameter SGA_MAX_SIZE is the upper limit for the value of SGA_TARGET.

Configure Automatic PGA Memory Management

❑ The parameter PGA_AGGREGATE_TARGET sets an upper limit for memory used by all server and background processes and enables auto-tuning of PGA memory.

❑ PGA memory areas include private SQL areas, named cursors, work areas for sorting operations, and session-specific memory variables.

❑ For OLTP systems, PGA memory can be as low as 20 percent of the memory allocated for Oracle.

❑ For DSS systems, PGA memory can be as high as 70 percent of the memory allocated for Oracle.

❑ The dynamic performance view V$PGASTAT contains a complete overview of PGA memory usage since instance startup.

❑ The columns PGA_USED_MEM, PGA_ALLOC_MEM, and PGA_MAX_MEM in the dynamic performance view V$PROCESS detail the PGA memory usage for an individual process.

SELF TEST

The following questions will help you measure your understanding of the material presented in this chapter. Read all the choices carefully, because there might be more than one correct answer. Choose all correct answers for each question.

Implement Automatic Memory Management

1. Identify the true statement about Automatic Memory Management (AMM).
   A. MEMORY_TARGET must be less than MEMORY_MAX_TARGET, and MEMORY_TARGET is a dynamic parameter.
   B. MEMORY_TARGET enables AMM, and it is a static parameter.
   C. MEMORY_MAX_TARGET enables AMM, and it is a static parameter.
   D. MEMORY_MAX_TARGET enables AMM, and it is a dynamic parameter.

2. You set your initialization parameters as follows:

   ```
   MEMORY_MAX_TARGET = 1G
   MEMORY_TARGET = 750M
   SGA_TARGET = 300M
   PGA_AGGREGATE_TARGET = 200M
   ```

   How does the value of MEMORY_TARGET vary in this instance?
   A. MEMORY_TARGET ranges from 500M to 750M.
   B. MEMORY_TARGET ranges from 500M to 1G.
   C. MEMORY_TARGET ranges from 300M to 1G.
   D. MEMORY_TARGET ranges from 300M to 750M.
   E. You cannot set SGA_TARGET and PGA_AGGREGATE_TARGET when you set MEMORY_TARGET

3. You set your initialization parameters as follows:

   ```
   MEMORY_TARGET = 750M
   SGA_TARGET = 300M
   ```

   You do not set PGA_AGGREGATE_TARGET. How do the values of SGA_TARGET and PGA_AGGREGATE_TARGET vary in the running instance?
   A. Both parameters are auto-tuned, but PGA_AGGREGATE_TARGET starts out at MEMORY_TARGET – SGA_TARGET.
   B. Only SGA_TARGET is auto-tuned, and PGA_AGGREGATE_TARGET is fixed at MEMORY_TARGET – SGA_TARGET.

    C. Both parameters are auto-tuned, but `PGA_AGGREGATE_TARGET` starts out at 40 percent of available memory by default.

    D. `SGA_TARGET` is fixed at 300M, and `PGA_AGGREGATE_TARGET` starts out at `MEMORY_TARGET` – `SGA_TARGET`.

Manually Configure SGA Parameters

4. Which of the following initialization parameters control Automatic Shared Memory Management (ASSM)?

    A. `SGA_MAX_SIZE`

    B. `MEMORY_TARGET`

    C. `MEMORY_MAX_TARGET`

    D. `SGA_TARGET`

    E. `SGA_MAX_TARGET`

5. Which of the following parameters can you set to zero to maximize the auto-tuning capabilities of ASMM? (Choose all that apply.)

    A. `LOG_BUFFER`

    B. `STREAMS_POOL_SIZE`

    C. `DB_CACHE_SIZE`

    D. `SHARED_POOL_SIZE`

    E. `DB_8K_CACHE_SIZE`

6. You want to switch from AMM to ASMM. What is the correct statement you need to run? (Choose the best answer.)

    A. `alter system set memory_max_target = 0;`

    B. `alter system set memory_target = 0;`

    C. `alter system set sga_target = 500m;`

    D. `alter system set sga_max_size = 750m;`

Configure Automatic PGA Memory Management

7. Your instance is configured for shared servers. Which of the following memory areas reside in private PGA memory? (Choose all that apply.)

    A. Session bind information

    B. Session memory

    C. Log buffers

D. OCI named cursors

E. Bitmap join work areas

8. Your server's physical memory is 8GB and no other applications or Oracle instances are running on the server. For a new Oracle instance running a decision support system, what is a good starting point for setting `PGA_AGGREGATE_TARGET`?

A. 3.2GB

B. 1.6GB

C. 4.48GB

D. 6.4GB

SELF TEST ANSWERS

Implement Automatic Memory Management

1. ☑ **D.** MEMORY_TARGET enables AMM; it is a dynamic parameter and cannot be more than MEMORY_MAX_TARGET.
   ☒ **A, B,** and **C** are incorrect.

2. ☑ **B.** When you set MEMORY_TARGET, SGA_TARGET, and PGA_AGGREGATE_TARGET, then SGA_TARGET and PGA_AGGREGATE_TARGET are minimum values for the SGA and PGA—and MEMORY_TARGET can range from the sum of SGA_TARGET + PGA_AGGREGATE_TARGET to MEMORY_MAX_TARGET.
   ☒ **A** is wrong because MEMORY_TARGET can be increased up to MEMORY_MAX_TARGET while the instance is running. **C** is wrong because the sum of SGA_TARGET + PGA_AGGREGATE_TARGET is a starting value for MEMORY_TARGET. **D** is wrong because the sum of SGA_TARGET + PGA_AGGREGATE_TARGET is a starting value for MEMORY_TARGET, and MEMORY_TARGET can be set as high as the value of MEMORY_MAX_TARGET. **E** is wrong because you can set SGA_TARGET and PGA_AGGREGATE_TARGET as minimum values in conjunction with MEMORY_TARGET.

3. ☑ **A.** SGA_TARGET starts out with a minimum value of 300M, PGA_AGGREGATE_TARGET starts out at MEMORY_TARGET – SGA_TARGET, and both parameters are auto-tuned.
   ☒ **B** is wrong because both parameters are auto-tuned when MEMORY_TARGET is set. **C** is wrong because PGA_AGGREGATE_TARGET starts out at MEMORY_TARGET – SGA_TARGET. **D** is wrong because SGA_TARGET has a minimum value of 300M.

Manually Configure SGA Parameters

4. ☑ **D.** You set SGA_TARGET to enable ASSM, and you can still control the minimum values for auto-tuned parameters controlled by SGA_TARGET.
   ☒ **A** is wrong because SGA_MAX_SIZE is the upper limit for the dynamic parameter SGA_TARGET. **B** is wrong because MEMORY_TARGET controls AMM, not ASSM. **C** is wrong because MEMORY_MAX_TARGET is the upper limit for the value of MEMORY_TARGET. **E** is wrong because there is no such parameter SGA_MAX_TARGET.

5. ☑ **B, C,** and **D.** In addition to STREAMS_POOL_SIZE, DB_CACHE_SIZE, and SHARED_POOL_SIZE, ASSM auto-tunes LARGE_POOL_SIZE and JAVA_POOL_SIZE.
   ☒ **A** and **E** are wrong. LOG_BUFFER and all DB_nK_CACHE_SIZE parameters are not auto-tuned by ASSM.

6. ☑ **B.** When you set MEMORY_TARGET to zero, Oracle automatically sets SGA_TARGET based on current SGA memory usage and enables ASSM.

☓ **A** is wrong because MEMORY_MAX_TARGET is not a dynamic parameter and does not disable AMM. **C** is wrong because setting SGA_TARGET while AMM is enabled only sets a minimum value for the SGA while AMM is enabled. **D** is wrong because SGA_MAX_SIZE only sets a maximum value for SGA_TARGET and does not disable AMM.

Configure Automatic PGA Memory Management

7. ☑ **A, D,** and **E.** Bind information, run-time memory structures, named cursors, and work areas are always in PGA memory.

☓ **B** and **C** are wrong. Session memory is in the PGA only in a dedicated server configuration. Log buffers are always in the SGA.

8. ☑ **A.** Oracle memory is typically 80 percent of the server memory, with 50 percent of the remaining memory as a good starting point for PGA_AGGREGATE_TARGET in a DSS system. Therefore, PGA_AGGREGATE_TARGET = 0.50 * (8GB * 0.80) = 3.2GB.

☓ **B, C,** and **D** are wrong because these are all incorrect starting points for PGA_AGGREGATE_TARGET. For OLTP systems, PGA can be as low as 20 percent, but not for DSS applications. Even for DSS applications, PGA can be as high as 70 percent but should start out at 50 percent of memory available to Oracle.

11
Using Database Tuning Advisors

F rom a tuning perspective, every system has a performance bottleneck that may move from component to component over a time period of days or even weeks The goal of performance design is to make sure that the physical limitations of the applications and the associated hardware—I/O throughput rates, memory sizes, query performance, and so on—do not impact performance of the business of the company. If the application performance limits the business process it is supposed to be supporting, the application must be tuned. During the design process, the limits of the application environment—including the hardware and the design of the application's interactions with the database—must be evaluated. No environment provides infinite computing capacity, so every environment is destined to fail at some performance point. In the process of designing the application, you should strive to have your performance needs amply served by the performance capabilities of the environment.

Performance tuning is the final step in a four-step process: planning, implementing, and monitoring must precede it. If you tune only for the sake of tuning, you are failing to address the full cycle of activity and will likely never resolve the underlying flaws that caused the performance problem. Tuning activities can be further subdivided into three parts: performance planning, instance tuning, and SQL tuning. Once you are at the SQL tuning step, you can use the tools presented in this chapter: the SQL Tuning Advisor, the SQL Access Advisor, and Database Replay.

SQL Tuning Advisor, the most granular of the tuning tools, takes one or more SQL statements as input, analyzes all access paths, and generates advice or recommendations to improve the SQL statements. The recommendations may include new indexes, a restructured SQL statement, or the creation of a SQL profile. Within a maintenance window, Oracle automatically runs the SQL Tuning Advisor on high-load statements identified and recorded in the Automatic Workload Repository (AWR).

The SQL Access Advisor, in contrast, takes a much wider view of a tuning operation. It takes all SQL statements within a workload, such as all SQL run by an application within a specified period, and recommends indexes, materialized views, and partitioning schemes to improve the overall performance of the application. Tuning SQL statements individually may be counterproductive. Tuning a single SQL statement in the workload may improve performance at the expense of other SQL statements, and vice versa.

Finally, Database Replay makes it easy to capture a workload in one configuration and replay it one time or several times on another configuration. For example, you may want to compare the performance difference of a given workload on your production system to the performance of the same workload on a server with multiple CPUs and a later release of the operating system or database software. After replaying the workload on the new configuration, Database Replay generates a Workload Replay report that identifies differences in execution times, result sets, and error conditions.

CERTIFICATION OBJECTIVE 11.01

Use the SQL Tuning Advisor

The SQL Tuning Advisor analyzes one or more SQL statements sequentially, examining statistics, and potentially recommends creating a SQL profile, new indexes, materialized views, or a revised SQL statement. You can run the SQL Tuning Advisor manually; however, it is run automatically during every maintenance window on the most resource-intensive SQL statements identified within the production workload. Optionally, you can specify that the analysis performed during the maintenance window automatically implements recommended SQL profiles.

Overview of SQL Tuning Advisor

Whether the SQL Tuning Advisor runs automatically or you run it manually on one or more SQL statements, it performs the same types of analyses:

- **Statistics Analysis**   Check for stale or missing statistics, and recommend refreshing or creating them.
- **SQL Profiling**   Collect auxiliary statistics on a SQL statement along with partial execution statistics and store them in a SQL Profile.
- **Access Paths**   Analyze the impact of creating new indexes, materialized views, and partitioning.
- **Structure Analysis**   Restructure the SQL statements to see if better execution plans are generated.

From the preceding list, you can configure the Automatic SQL Tuning task to automatically implement SQL Profiles if the performance improvement improves by a factor of three. All other recommendations, and SQL Profile recommendations for minimal performance improvements, must be implemented manually after reviewing the Automatic SQL Tuning Report.

Note that SQL Tuning Advisor considers each SQL statement individually. If it recommends an index for a SELECT statement, it may help the performance of the query but may dramatically reduce the performance of DML activity against the table in a heavily OLTP environment. Thus, the SQL Access Advisor, discussed later in this chapter, may be a better analysis tool to analyze all operations against one or more tables in a workload.

Using SQL Tuning Advisor

The SQL Tuning Advisor can use a number of sources for its analysis. If you are experiencing a significant slowdown in database performance, you can run SQL Tuning Advisor on the top SQL statements currently running. In addition, you can specify a single SQL statement or a set of SQL statements. This is specified as a SQL Tuning Set as input to SQL Tuning Advisor. Finally, you can retrieve historical SQL statements from AWR snapshots.

The following sections show you how to configure SQL Tuning Advisor and view its recommendations using EM. Finally, you'll see how to perform the same tasks using the PL/SQL packages DBMS_AUTO_TASK_ADMIN and DBMS_SQLTUNE.

Configuring SQL Tuning Advisor

You can set SQL Tuning Advisor options in Enterprise Manager. Oracle recommends using EM to run the SQL Tuning Advisor due to the relative complexity of using the DBMS_SQLTUNE PL/SQL packages; however, you'll see how to use DBMS_SQLTUNE later in this chapter for those occasions where you need more precise control over the tuning process.

From the EM home page, select the Server tab. Near the bottom of the page, click on the Advisor Central link. Under the Advisors heading, click on the SQL Advisors link. You will see the SQL Advisors page shown in Figure 11-1.

Next, click on the SQL Tuning Advisor link. On the page in Figure 11-2, you can specify the options for a manual invocation of the SQL Tuning Advisor. In this example, you specify a 30-minute time limit for the job, to be run immediately, with only limited analysis of each SQL statement. Using the limited analysis option does not generate any SQL profile recommendations. Unless they already exist on your system, one or more SQL Tuning sets must be created before you can submit this job.

FIGURE 11-1

EM SQL
Advisors page

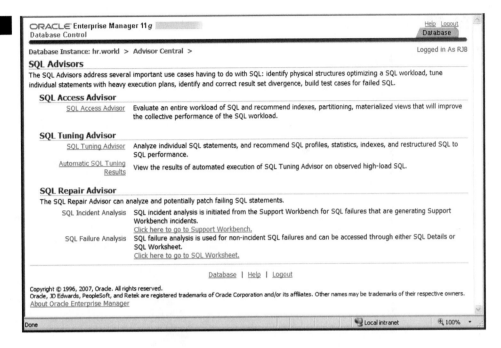

When you click on one of the links in the Overview section of the page shown in Figure 11-2 (Top Activity, Historical SQL, or SQL Tuning Sets), you can create data sources that will create a SQL Tuning Set that you can use as input to the SQL Tuning Advisor. When you click on the Top link in Figure 11-2, you see the Top Activity page shown in Figure 11-3.

At the bottom of the page, you see the Top SQL activity for the selected time period, which in this example is from 12:55 P.M. to 1:00 P.M. The top SQL includes the execution of a PL/SQL package, an UPDATE statement, and an INSERT statement. Clicking on the Select All link adds all three of these statements to a SQL Tuning Set that you can use on the SQL Tuning Advisor page shown in Figure 11-2. After clicking on the Select All link, click on the Go button next to the Schedule SQL Tuning Advisor action in the drop down menu. You will see the page shown in Figure 11-4 with a SQL Tuning Set created from the SQL statements you selected on the previous page.

Running SQL Tuning Advisor

In the page shown in Figure 11-4, you schedule a comprehensive analysis of the selected SQL statements. You also want to run the job immediately. Clicking on the Submit button submits the job for processing. Figure 11-5 shows the job in progress.

Viewing SQL Tuning Advisor Recommendations

After the job submitted in Figure 11-4 completes, you see the results of the analysis. You can also access the results from the Advisor Central page as you can see in Figure 11-6.

FIGURE 11-3

EM Top
Activity page

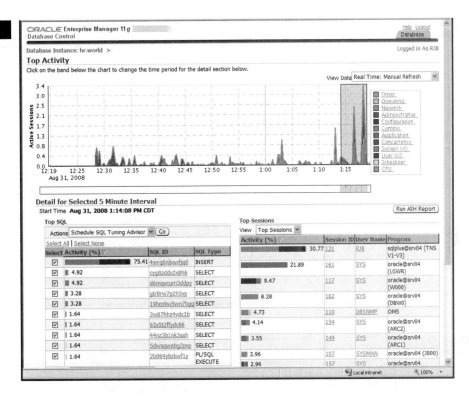

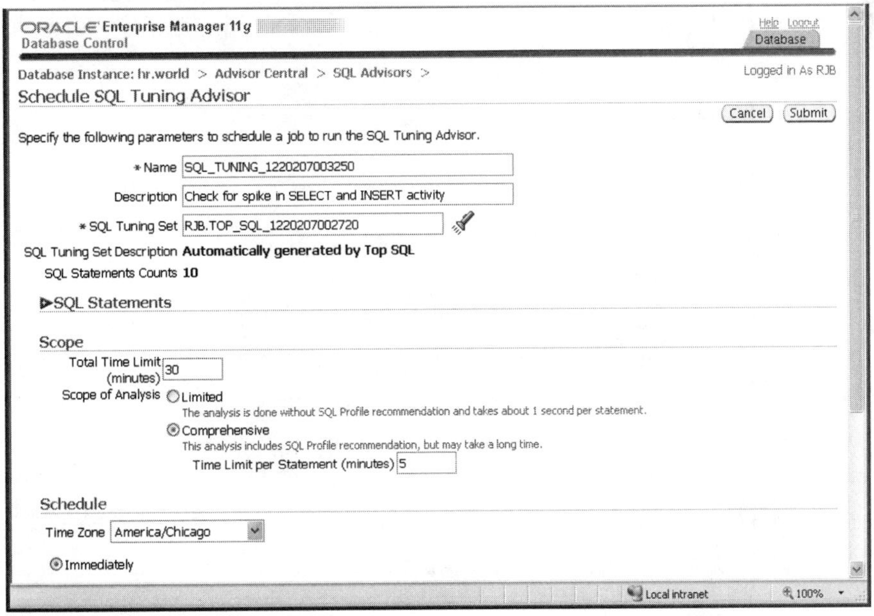

FIGURE 11-4

Schedule SQL
Tuning Advisor
with SQL tuning
set

FIGURE 11-5

SQL Tuning
Advisor job
progress

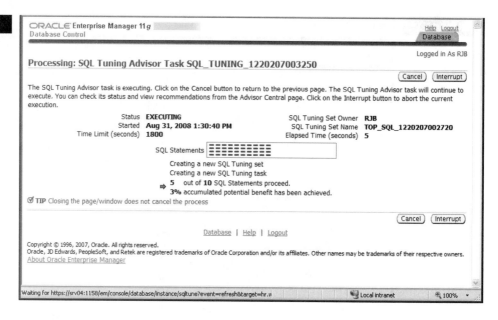

FIGURE 11-5

SQL Tuning
Advisor job
progress

FIGURE 11-6

Advisor Central
task results

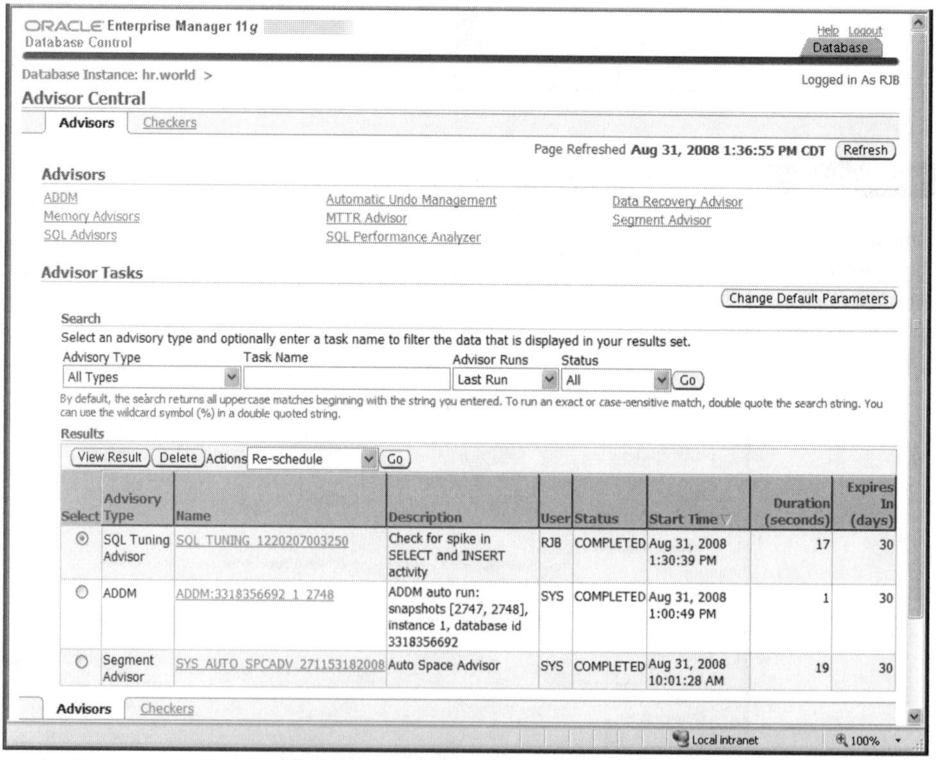

Clicking on the SQL Tuning Advisor task name or selecting the radio button next to the task and clicking View Result, you see the results of the analysis as shown in Figure 11-7.

Note that the results include recommendations for user SQL (e.g., RJB) and for system accounts (e.g., SYSMAN and DBSNMP). Each SQL statement has one or more types of recommendation, including statistics gathering, creating a SQL profile, creating an index, or revising the SQL statement itself. You can easily implement the SQL Profile recommendation by clicking on the Implement All Profiles button.

Selecting the radio button for the fourth SQL statement shown in Figure 11-7, you can see a detailed explanation of all recommendations for this SQL statement in Figure 11-8.

In the page shown in Figure 11-8, you are advised to implement one of the recommendations, such as saving a SQL profile for future executions or creating an index on one of the tables in the SQL query.

FIGURE 11-7

SQL Tuning Advisor recommendations summary

ORACLE Enterprise Manager 11*g*
Database Control

Help Logout
Database

Database Instance: hr.world > Advisor Central >

Logged in As RJB

SQL Tuning Results:SQL_TUNING_1220207003250

Page Refreshed Aug 31, 2008 1:39:53 PM CDT (Refresh)

Status **COMPLETED**	Tuning Set Owner **RJB**
Started **Aug 31, 2008 1:30:39 PM**	Tuning Set Name **TOP_SQL_1220207002720**
Completed **Aug 31, 2008 1:30:56 PM**	Time Limit (seconds) **1800**
	Running Time (seconds) **17**

Recommendations

(View) (Implement All Profiles)

Select	SQL Text	Parsing Schema	SQL ID	Statistics	SQL Profile	Index	Restructure SQL	Miscellaneous	Error
⦿	BEGIN EMD_NOTIFICATION.QUEUE_READY(:1, :2, :3); END;	SYSMAN	2b064ybzkwf1y					✓	
○	insert into object_analysis select * from object_analysis	RJB	4wrq6nbvwfjq0	✓					
○	SELECT COUNT(1) FROM MGMT_VERSIONS WHERE COMPONENT_NAME = UPPER(:B2) AND COMPONENT_MODE = :B1	SYSMAN	5dwsqwabg2pxy						
○	SELECT x.STATE_GUID, x.PAF_JOB_STATUS, x.JOB_STATUS, y.INSTANCE_GUID FROM (...	SYSMAN	44nz3b1nk3sxh		✓	✓		✓	
○	select FUNCTION_NAME, SMALL_READ_MBPS, SMALL_WRITE_MBPS, LARGE_READ_MBPS, LARGE_WRITE_MBPS, SMALL_RE...	DBSNMP	cyg8zddx2x8h6		✓				
○	select distinct object_id from object_analysis	RJB	d6mqvcum3ddpy	✓					
○	select CONSUMER_GROUP_NAME, CPU_CONSUMED_TIME, CPU_WAIT_TIME, IO_REQUESTS, IO_MEGABYTES from V$RSRCM...	DBSNMP	19hm9w5wn7hgg		✓				
○	SELECT event#, sql_id, sql_plan_hash_value, sql_opcode, session_id, session_serial#, module, action,...	DBSNMP	gtr8rw7p2h5xy		✓			✓	
○	select composite_target_name, composite_target_type, composite_target_guid, member_target_name, memb...	SYSMAN	62x5t2ffydc86				✓		
○	select distinct edition_name from object_analysis	RJB	3w87hhz4vdc1b	✓					

(View) (Implement All Profiles)

Local intranet   🔍 100% ▾

FIGURE 11-8

SQL Tuning
Advisor detailed
recommendations

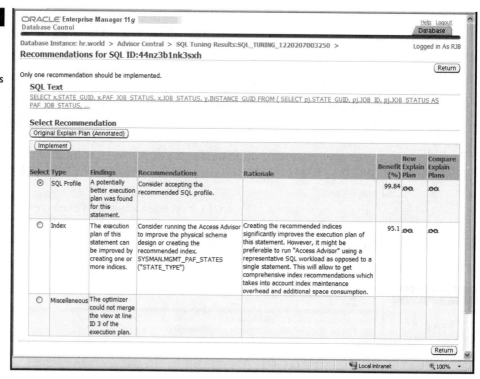

Using DBMS_SQLTUNE

If you need to have more control over your tuning tasks or want to run a specific set of tuning tasks repeatedly, you can use the DBMS_SQLTUNE PL/SQL package to create, run, and monitor a SQL Tuning Advisor job.

For a basic analysis of a SQL statement, you will use the following procedures within DBMS_SQLTUNE:

- **CREATE_TUNING_TASK** Create a tuning task for a SQL statement or a SQL Tuning Set.

- **EXECUTE_TUNING_TASK** Execute a tuning task created with CREATE_ TUNING_TASK.

- **REPORT_TUNING_TASK** Show the results and recommendations from the SQL Tuning Advisor.

In addition, you can use the following data dictionary views to query the name and status of tuning jobs:

- **DBA_ADVISOR_LOG** Task names, status, and execution statistics for all tasks.
- **DBA_/USER_ADVISOR_TASKS** More detailed information about advisor tasks, such as advisor name, user-specified description, and execution type for the current user.
- **V$ADVISOR_PROGRESS** More detailed information about the completion status and time remaining for an advisor task.

EXERCISE 11-1

Run SQL Tuning Advisor for a SQL Statement

In this exercise, you will use DBMS_SQLTUNE to generate recommendations for one of the SQL statements shown in Figure 11-7.

1. Within an anonymous PL/SQL block, define a tuning task for a SQL statement:

```
SQL> declare
  2      tune_task_name  varchar2(30);
  3      bad_sql_stmt    clob;
  4  begin
  5      bad_sql_stmt := 'select distinct object_id from object_analysis';
  6      tune_task_name := dbms_sqltune.create_tuning_task
  7        (sql_text     => bad_sql_stmt,
  8         user_name    => 'RJB',
  9         scope        => 'COMPREHENSIVE',
 10         time_limit   => 60,
 11         task_name    => 'rjb_sql_tuning_task',
 12         description  => 'See what is wrong with the SELECT'
 13        );
 14  end;
 15  /

PL/SQL procedure successfully completed.

SQL>
```

Notice that the values provided to DBMS_SQLTUNE.CREATE_TUNING_TASK correspond to the values provided to EM in Figure 11-4, except that in this case you are specifying a SQL statement explicitly instead of creating a tuning set from a 5-minute interval.

2. Use the SET_TUNING_TASK_PARAMETER procedure to change the time limit to 30 minutes instead of 60 minutes as you originally specified when you set up the task:

```
SQL> begin
  2      dbms_sqltune.set_tuning_task_parameter
  3          (task_name   => 'rjb_sql_tuning_task',
  4           parameter   => 'TIME_LIMIT', value => 30
  5          );
  6   end;
  7   /

PL/SQL procedure successfully completed.

SQL>
```

3. Initiate the tuning task using the EXECUTE_TUNING_TASK procedure:

```
SQL> begin
  2      dbms_sqltune.execute_tuning_task
  3          (task_name => 'rjb_sql_tuning_task');
  4   end;
  5   /

PL/SQL procedure successfully completed.

SQL>
```

4. Query the status of the task by joining DBA_ADVISOR_TASKS and V$ADVISOR_PROGRESS:

```
SQL> select task_name, status, sofar, totalwork
  2  from dba_advisor_tasks
  3     join v$advisor_progress using(task_id)
  4  where task_name = 'rjb_sql_tuning_task'
  5  ;
```

TASK_NAME	STATUS	SOFAR	TOTALWORK
rjb_sql_tuning_task	COMPLETED	1	1

```
SQL>
```

5. Retrieve the recommendations from the tuning task:

```
SQL> select
     dbms_sqltune.report_tuning_task('rjb_sql_tuning_task') from dual;

DBMS_SQLTUNE.REPORT_TUNING_TASK('RJB_SQL_TUNING_TASK')
----------------------------------------------------------------
GENERAL INFORMATION SECTION
----------------------------------------------------------------
Tuning Task Name    : rjb_sql_tuning_task

       Tuning Task Owner  : RJB
       Workload Type      : Single SQL Statement
       Scope              : COMPREHENSIVE
       Time Limit(seconds): 30
       Completion Status  : COMPLETED
       Started at         : 08/31/2008 17:16:22
       Completed at       : 08/31/2008 17:16:36

       DBMS_SQLTUNE.REPORT_TUNING_TASK('RJB_SQL_TUNING_TASK')
       ----------------------------------------------------------------
       Schema Name: RJB
       SQL ID     : 1487f89dbsn5s
       SQL Text   : select distinct object_id from object_analysis


       ----------------------------------------------------------------
       FINDINGS SECTION (1 finding)
       ----------------------------------------------------------------


       1- Statistics Finding
       ---------------------
         Table "RJB"."OBJECT_ANALYSIS" was not analyzed.

       DBMS_SQLTUNE.REPORT_TUNING_TASK('RJB_SQL_TUNING_TASK')
       ----------------------------------------------------------------


         Recommendation
         --------------
         - Consider collecting optimizer statistics for this table.
           execute dbms_stats.gather_table_stats(ownname => 'RJB',
       tabname =>
                   'OBJECT_ANALYSIS', estimate_percent =>
                   DBMS_STATS.AUTO_SAMPLE_SIZE, method_opt =>
                       'FOR ALL COLUMNS SIZE AUTO');
```

```
    Rationale
    ---------
       The optimizer requires up-to-date statistics for the table in
    order to
       select a good execution plan.
```

Note the dramatic increase in ease of use using EM versus the PL/SQL procedures. A SQL tuning set using DBMS_SQLTUNE was not even loaded. CREATE_SQLSET, DBMS_SQLTUNE.LOAD_SQLSET, and so forth. That would have added yet another layer of complexity to this exercise.

CERTIFICATION OBJECTIVE 11.02

Use the SQL Access Advisor to Tune a Workload

At first glance, the SQL Access Advisor appears to perform the same function as the SQL Tuning Advisor. However, there are some key differences that will be detailed in the following sections, such as how the analysis is performed and the types of recommendations generated.

Understanding the SQL Access Advisor

The SQL Access Advisor performs an analysis of overall SQL performance using a workload specification. The workload specification can be one of the following:

- A single SQL statement
- A SQL tuning set
- Current SQL cache contents
- Statistics
- A schema name

Recommendations from SQL Access Advisor include new indexes, materialized views, and partitioning. Another SQL Access Advisor procedure, TUNE_MVIEW recommends changes to materialized views to support fast refresh and query rewrite.

Using the SQL Access Advisor with EM

As with the SQL Tuning Advisor and the DBMS_SQLTUNE package, you can use EM for running the SQL Access Advisor instead of using the DBMS_ADVISOR package directly. The four steps to create a set of recommendations are as follows:

1. Create a task
2. Define the workload
3. Generate the recommendations
4. Review and implement the recommendations

If you are using EM to run the SQL Access Advisor, step 1 is performed automatically.

From the Advisor Central page shown in Figure 11-1, click on the SQL Access Advisor link. You will see the page shown in Figure 11-9 where you can perform one of two tasks: (1) verify that existing structures such as indexes and materialized views are being used, or (2) recommend new structures. In other words, you may be able to drop existing indexes if they are not used for SELECT statements.

For this example, you want to find new access structures so you would select the second radio button. If you select the Inherit Options checkbox, you can choose a template that may fit your environment, such as OLTP or data warehousing. When you click on the Continue button, you will see the first step of the wizard shown in Figure 11-10.

For the source of the tuning activity, you can select one of three sources: (1) recent SQL from the cache, (2) an existing SQL Tuning set (such as the SQL Tuning set created in the SQL Tuning Advisor example earlier in this chapter), or (3) a set of schemas and tables within those schemas. In this example, you want to analyze all current and recent SQL activity. Therefore click on the corresponding radio button and then click on the Next button.

FIGURE 11-9

SQL Access
Advisor options

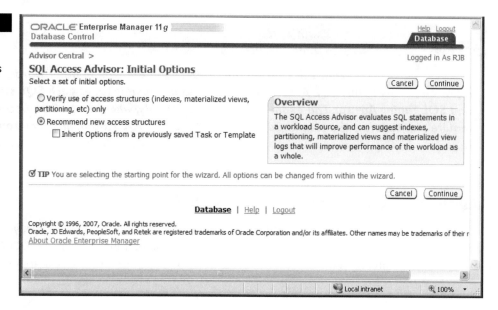

FIGURE 11-10

Specify SQL
Access Advisor
workload source

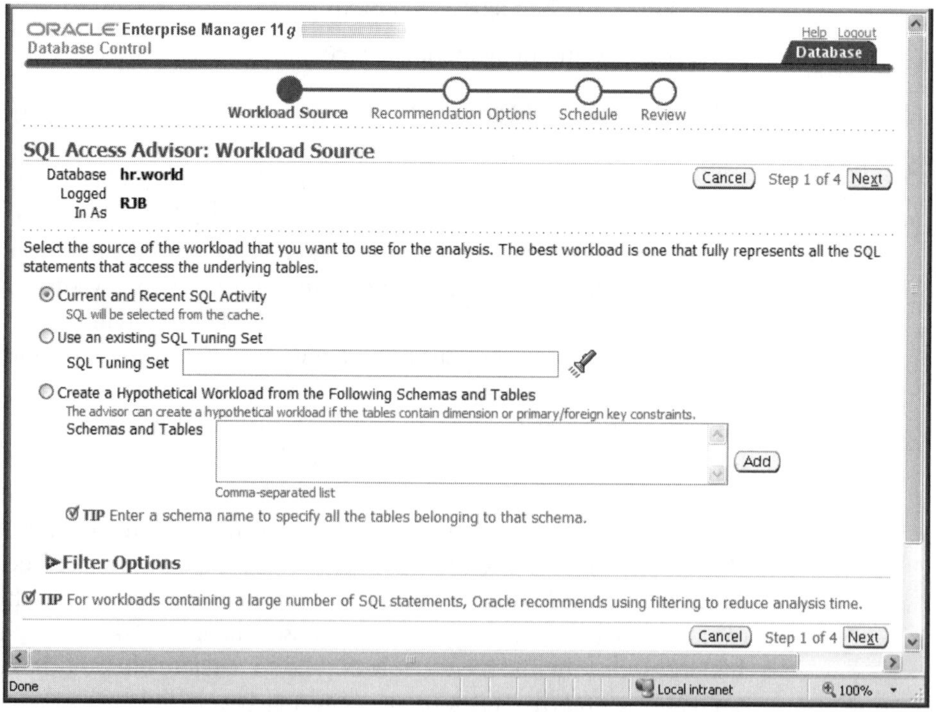

The next page, shown in Figure 11-11, lets you select which types of access structures that SQL Access Advisor should recommend: (1) indexes, (2) materialized views, and (3) partitioning. In addition, you can direct the SQL Access Advisor to perform a limited analysis on just the high-cost statements, or perform a relatively time-consuming analysis on all relationships between the tables in the specified workload. The Advanced Options section lets you further refine the analysis based on disk space limitations as well as specifying alternate locations for recommended indexes and materialized views. Select the Indexes and Materialized Views check boxes and the Comprehensive radio button. Finally, click on the Next button.

The next page, shown in Figure 11-12 specifies the scheduling options for the tuning task. As you can see, EM will automatically create the task for you. Other options on this page include how much logging the SQL Access Advisor generates, how long the task will remain in the database, the total time allotted to this task, and when to start the task.

FIGURE 11-11	

Specifying SQL Access Advisor recommendation options

FIGURE 11-12

Specifying SQL Access Advisor scheduling options

FIGURE 11-12 Specifying SQL Access Advisor scheduling options

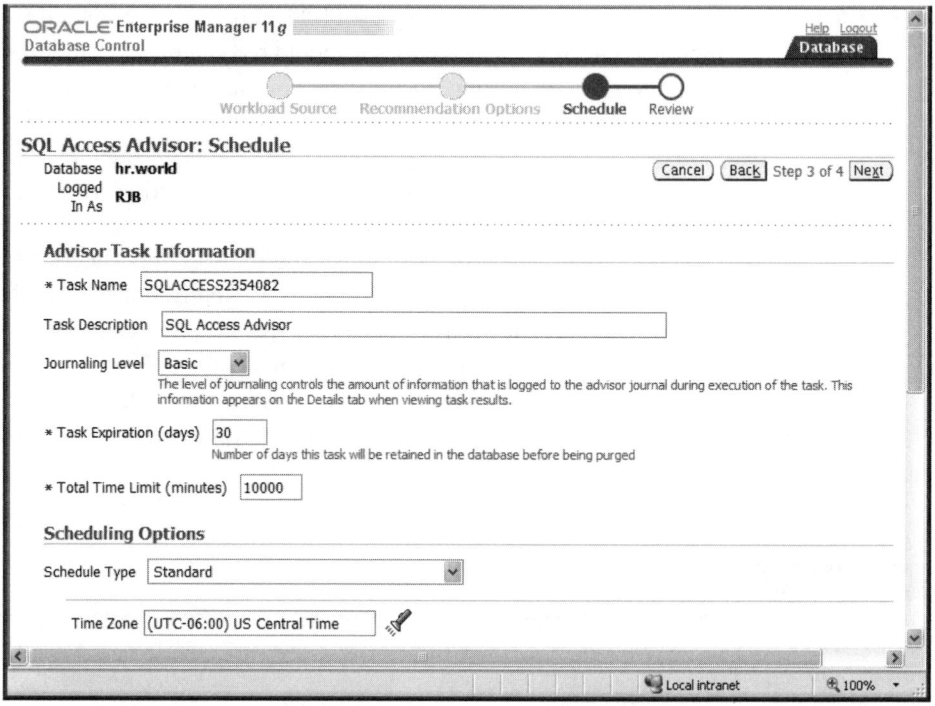

In the page shown in Figure 11-12, accept the default options and click on the Next button to proceed to step 4 of the wizard, as you can see in Figure 11-13. Step 4 summarizes the options you have chosen and gives you a chance to revise the options before submitting the job.

Note the Show SQL button in Figure 11-13. You can use the SQL code to better understand what goes on "under the hood". You can also use the SQL code as the basis of a scripted tuning job that can be incorporated into a batch job, which includes other SQL commands or processes that you cannot easily perform repeatedly within EM. Clicking on the Show SQL button in this example produces the following SQL code:

```
DECLARE

taskname varchar2(30) := 'SQLACCESS2354082';
task_desc varchar2(256) := 'SQL Access Advisor';
task_or_template varchar2(30) := 'SQLACCESS_EMTASK';
task_id number := 0;
```

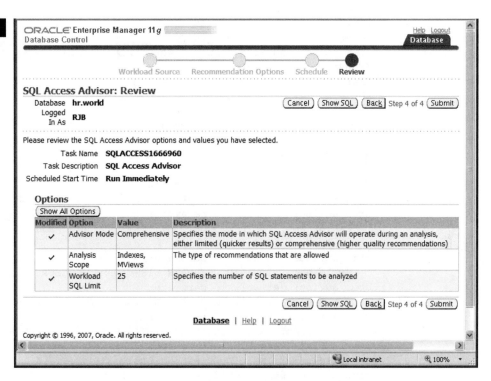

FIGURE 11-13

Reviewing SQL
Access Advisor
options

```
wkld_name varchar2(30) := 'SQLACCESS2354082_wkld';
saved_rows number := 0;
failed_rows number := 0;
num_found number;
hypo_schema varchar2(512);

BEGIN
/* Create Task */
dbms_advisor.create_task(DBMS_ADVISOR.SQLACCESS_ADVISOR,task_id,
        taskname,task_desc,task_or_template);
/* Reset Task */
dbms_advisor.reset_task(taskname);
/* Delete Previous Workload Task Link */
select count(*) into num_found
   from user_advisor_sqla_wk_map
   where task_name = taskname and workload_name = wkld_name;
IF num_found > 0 THEN
dbms_advisor.delete_sqlwkld_ref(taskname,wkld_name);
END IF;
```

```
/* Delete Previous Workload */
select count(*) into num_found
   from user_advisor_sqlw_sum where workload_name = wkld_name;
IF num_found > 0 THEN
dbms_advisor.delete_sqlwkld(wkld_name);
END IF;
/* Create Workload */
dbms_advisor.create_sqlwkld(wkld_name,null);
/* Link Workload to Task */
dbms_advisor.add_sqlwkld_ref(taskname,wkld_name);
/* Set Workload Parameters */
dbms_advisor.set_sqlwkld_parameter
   (wkld_name,'VALID_ACTION_LIST',DBMS_ADVISOR.ADVISOR_UNUSED);
dbms_advisor.set_sqlwkld_parameter
   (wkld_name,'VALID_MODULE_LIST',DBMS_ADVISOR.ADVISOR_UNUSED);
. . .
dbms_advisor.set_sqlwkld_parameter
   (wkld_name,'INVALID_USERNAME_LIST',DBMS_ADVISOR.ADVISOR_UNUSED);
dbms_advisor.set_sqlwkld_parameter
   (wkld_name,'INVALID_MODULE_LIST',DBMS_ADVISOR.ADVISOR_UNUSED);
dbms_advisor.set_sqlwkld_parameter
   (wkld_name,'VALID_SQLSTRING_LIST',DBMS_ADVISOR.ADVISOR_UNUSED);
dbms_advisor.set_sqlwkld_parameter
   (wkld_name,'INVALID_SQLSTRING_LIST','"@!"');
dbms_advisor.set_sqlwkld_parameter(wkld_name,'JOURNALING','4');
dbms_advisor.set_sqlwkld_parameter(wkld_name,'DAYS_TO_EXPIRE','30');
dbms_advisor.import_sqlwkld_sqlcache
   (wkld_name,'REPLACE',2,saved_rows,failed_rows);
/* Set Task Parameters */
dbms_advisor.set_task_parameter
   (taskname,'ANALYSIS_SCOPE','INDEX,MVIEW');
dbms_advisor.set_task_parameter
   (taskname,'RANKING_MEASURE','PRIORITY,OPTIMIZER_COST');
. . .
dbms_advisor.set_task_parameter(taskname,'DAYS_TO_EXPIRE','30');
/* Execute Task */
dbms_advisor.execute_task(taskname);
END;
```

Click on the Submit button shown in Figure 11-13 to start the analysis. From the Advisor Central page, you can monitor the progress of the job. When the job completes, select the job and click on the View Result button. The page in Figure 11-14 shows a summary of the improvements you can make if you implement the recommendations in the second tab. The SQL Statements tab shows you the statements analyzed and gives

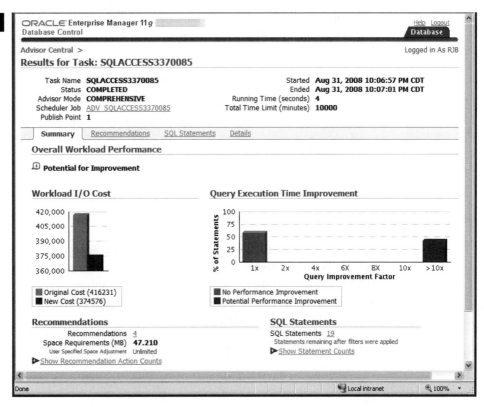

FIGURE 11-14

SQL Access
Advisor
recommendation
summary

you the option to implement the recommendations. The Details tab recaps the options you chose to run this analysis. In this particular analysis, almost half of the recent SQL statements may benefit dramatically if the recommendations are implemented.

Using the SQL Access Advisor with DBMS_ADVISOR

As you can see in the sample SQL in the previous section, using the SQL Access Advisor via the DBMS_ADVISOR package can get quite complex, and using EM is an easier way to run most day to day analyses.

On the contrary, the procedure DBMS_ADVISOR.QUICK_TUNE is straightforward and takes as input a single SQL statement to tune. As a result, it performs much like the SQL Tuning Advisor but can perform a much more in-depth analysis, producing more recommendations than the SQL Tuning Advisor, such as materialized view recommendations.

To run the procedure, create an anonymous PL/SQL block and specify the advisor name, a task name, and the SQL statement, as in this example:

```
SQL> begin
  2       dbms_advisor.quick_tune
  3       (dbms_advisor.sqlaccess_advisor,
  4        'second_rjb_tuning_task',
  5        'select distinct object_id from object_analysis'
  6       );
  7  end;
  8  /

PL/SQL procedure successfully completed.

SQL>
```

The results of the tuning effort reside in the data dictionary view USER_ADVISOR_ACTIONS but the output is not very readable. Therefore, you can use the procedure CREATE_FILE to create the script you can use to implement the recommendations generated by the QUICK_TUNE procedure. First, create a directory object to point to a file system directory to hold the script:

```
SQL> create directory tune_scripts as '/u06/tune_scripts';

Directory created.

SQL>
```

Next, use CREATE_FILE to create the script containing the implementation recommendations:

```
SQL> begin
  2       dbms_advisor.create_file
  3         (dbms_advisor.get_task_script('second_rjb_tuning_task'),
  4          'TUNE_SCRIPTS',
  5          'tune_fts.sql'
  6         );
  7  end;
  8  /

PL/SQL procedure successfully completed.

SQL>
```

In this example, the file tune_fts.sql looks like this:

```
Rem   SQL Access Advisor: Version 11.1.0.6.0 - Production
Rem
Rem   Username:          RJB
Rem   Task:              second_rjb_tuning_task
Rem   Execution date:
Rem

CREATE MATERIALIZED VIEW LOG ON
    "RJB"."OBJECT_ANALYSIS"
    WITH ROWID, SEQUENCE("OBJECT_ID")
    INCLUDING NEW VALUES;

CREATE MATERIALIZED VIEW "RJB"."MV$$_0BDC0000"
    REFRESH FAST WITH ROWID
    ENABLE QUERY REWRITE
    AS SELECT RJB.OBJECT_ANALYSIS.OBJECT_ID C1, COUNT(*) M1
    FROM RJB.OBJECT_ANALYSIS
    GROUP BY RJB.OBJECT_ANALYSIS.OBJECT_ID;

begin
    dbms_stats.gather_table_stats
        ('"RJB"','"MV$$_0BDC0000"',NULL,dbms_stats.auto_sample_size);
end;
/
```

The recommendations include creating a materialized view log, creating a materialized view that can be used for query rewrite, and collecting statistics on the materialized view.

CERTIFICATION OBJECTIVE 11.03

Understand Database Replay

Changes occur in your software and hardware environment, whether it be upgrades to operating system software, database software, or increasing the number of CPUs. Less desirable changes may also occur: due to budgetary constraints, the server hosting your database may soon be part of a consolidation effort and new applications will be added to the server. In any case, you need to measure the impact of these changes. Database Replay will help to assess the change in performance on a test system by capturing the workload on the production server, and then replaying the workload on the test system. This way you can resolve performance problems and ensure that the new production environment will still run your database applications with the same results as the old production system.

Using Database Replay consists of four main steps:

1. Workload capture
2. Workload preprocessing
3. Workload replay
4. Analysis and reporting

Database Replay Workload Capture

The first step of the Database Replay process is to capture the workload. Depending on your environment, you may only need to capture a couple of hours or even a day or two. This depends on the mix of applications in your environment and what time during the day they run.

Included in the capture process are all external database calls from clients; database background activities and internal scheduler jobs are not captured. The client requests are recorded in platform-independent binary files that can be replayed on a database that is installed on a completely different hardware or software platform. As of Oracle Database 11g Release 2, you can even capture client requests on an Oracle Database 10g database and replay them on an Oracle Database 11g Release 2 platform to test a database software upgrade. Each recorded client request contains the following information:

- SQL text
- Bind values
- Transaction information

The transaction information includes timestamps as well. This gives you the option to replay the workload faster, slower, or at the same rate as the original workload. In any case, the timestamps ensure that a client request is replayed in the same chronological order relative to all other recorded requests.

Certain client requests are not captured in a workload. These requests include the following:

- Direct path load operations using SQL*Loader
- Oracle Streams operations
- Advanced Replication streams

- Non-PL/SQL-based Advanced Queuing operations
- Flashback queries
- Oracle Call Interface object navigations
- Non-SQL-based object access
- Distributed transactions
- Remote DESCRIBE and COMMIT commands

Any distributed transactions will still be captured but will be replayed as if they were originally run as local transactions.

The recording process itself incurs minimal overhead on the production system. However, depending on how long you are capturing, you need to ensure that there is enough disk space to hold the captured workload. If you run out of disk space during a capture session, the capture stops.

Be sure to shut down and restart the database instance before starting the capture operation. This ensures that all active transactions complete or roll back before capture begins. Note that ongoing transactions will be captured but not played back correctly because only part of each ongoing transaction will be played back in the target system. You can begin and end the capture process using the PL/SQL package DBMS_WORKLOAD_CAPTURE, as in these code snippets:

```
/* shut down and restart database */
begin
   dbms_workload_capture.start_capture
      ('Data Warehouse Migration','REP_CAP_DIR');
   /* initiate workload */
. . .
   dbms_workload_capture.finish_capture;
end;
```

Database Replay Workload Preprocessing

After the capture operation is complete, the captured information must be preprocessed by transforming the captured data into replay files that can be easily replayed on the target system. The preprocessing step only needs to happen once for each capture operation. Once preprocessed, it can be replayed over and over on one or more target systems. The preprocessing step makes sense even if you're going to replay it only once. You want the replay clients to efficiently send their requests to the new server without delays due to preprocessing the capture data on the fly.

As with nearly every database operation, you can use EM or a PL/SQL package to perform the preprocessing step. After moving the capture files to a location accessible to the replay system, you can use PL/SQL to process the capture files located in the directory object REP_CAP_DIR as follows:

```
begin
   dbms_workload_replay.process_capture (capture_dir => 'REP_
CAP_DIR');
end;
```

Database Replay Workload Replay

During the replay phase, the preprocessed workload executes on the target system using the same timing, concurrency, and transaction dependencies as on the source system. You can, however, "speed up" or "slow down" one or more client requests depending on the requirements of the new environment.

Database Replay uses one or more replay clients to re-create all client requests. You may only need one replay client, or you may need more replay clients than the original number of clients on the source database. Oracle provides a calibration tool that you run against a captured workload to calculate the number of replay clients you will need to ensure that the workload is played back at the desired rate.

Before running the first replay, you must perform some prerequisite checks:

- Ensure that the target system has access to the replay directory.
- Remap references to other production systems via database links, external .tables, directory objects, URLs, and E-mail notifications.
- Remap connection strings to the replay system from the production system.

Failure to remap all references to the production system will certainly cause disruption and unnecessary load on the production system.

By default, the order of all COMMIT statements are preserved, which is usually the best option to prevent data divergence. However, if most or all of the transactions are independent, you can turn off the preservation of COMMIT order to run the replay faster.

You use the PL/SQL package DBMS_WORKLOAD_REPLAY to initialize and start the replay process, as in this example:

```
begin
   dbms_workload_replay.initialize_replay
      ('Data Warehouse Migration','REP_CAP_DIR');
   dbms_workload_replay.start_replay;
end;
```

In addition, you can pause and resume the replay using the PAUSE_REPLAY and RESUME_REPLAY procedures, or terminate the replay early by using CANCEL_REPLAY.

Database Replay Analysis and Reporting

Database Replay generates a report detailing actual results of the replay, including all exception conditions such as data divergence due to incorrect or out of sync DML statements or SQL queries. Also, included in the report are detailed time-based statistics such as total DB time and average session time. You can also use AWR reports to perform a detailed comparison between the captured workload and the replayed workload.

You can use the PL/SQL package DBMS_WORKLOAD_REPLAY to retrieve and generate a report, as in this example:

```
declare
   capture_dir_id        number;
   curr_replay_id        number;
   replay_report         clob;
begin
   /* retrieve pointer to all captured sessions  */
   /* in the replay directory                    */
   capture_dir_id :=
      dbms_workload_replay.get_replay_info(dir => 'REP_CAP_DIR');
   /* get latest replay session id */
   select max(id) into curr_replay_id
   from dba_workload_replays
   where capture_id = capture_dir_id;
   /* generate the report */
   replay_report :=
      dbms_workload_replay.report
         (replay_id => curr_replay_id,
          format => dbms_workload_replay.type_text);
end;
```

Note that you may have more than one report in the replay directory if you have performed the replay more than once. The SELECT statement in the PL/SQL block ensures that you retrieve the latest report. You can use DELETE_REPLAY_INFO to delete a report in the replay directory.

CERTIFICATION SUMMARY

This chapter gave you a whirlwind tour of SQL tuning, starting out with the SQL Tuning Advisor. You can run it manually but in a default installation of Oracle Database 11g, the SQL Tuning Advisor is run automatically during the maintenance window. This is run on the most resource-intensive SQL captured during normal database operations, whether it be data warehouse queries, on-line customer orders, or a mix of both. You can also run the SQL Tuning Advisor manually against one or more specified SQL statements that are currently consuming more resources than you would expect. Whether you run SQL Tuning Advisor manually or as part of the maintenance window, each SQL statement is considered individually with no dependencies on any other SQL statements within the SQL Tuning Advisor job—or any other objects in the database. The SQL Tuning Advisor recommends indexes, statistics collection, and even restructuring the SQL statement itself in order to produce a better execution plan.

Next, the chapter provided an in-depth look at the SQL Access Advisor. It shares some features of the SQL Tuning Advisor in that you can specify a single SQL statement as input. Typically, you will specify a SQL tuning set, an entire schema name, or the current SQL cache contents as input, providing an analysis considering all SQL statements in the set as a whole. This ensures that the improvements made to one SQL statement do not result in dramatically decreased performance of other SQL statements in the set. Recommendations from the SQL Access Advisor include creating new indexes, materialized views, and partitions.

Finally, an overview of Database Replay was given. Although Database Replay is not a tuning tool per se, it can be used to compare performance between a production system and a new system. The new system can involve improved hardware, updated operating system software, or even a new version of the database. Database Replay can help identify bottlenecks before moving a production system, thus ensuring a smooth upgrade.

TWO-MINUTE DRILL

Use the SQL Tuning Advisor

❑ SQL Tuning Advisor performs statistics analysis, SQL Profile analysis, access path analysis, and structure analysis.

❑ SQL Tuning Advisor can automatically implement SQL Profiles.

❑ SQL Tuning Advisor tunes each SQL statement individually.

❑ You can specify a SQL Tuning Set, a workload, recent SQL activity, or a single SQL statement as input to the SQL Tuning Advisor.

❑ You use the DBMS_SQLTUNE PL/SQL package to run the SQL Tuning Advisor as an alternative to using Enterprise Manager.

❑ You use the views DBA_ADVISOR_LOG, DBA_ADVISOR_TASKS, and V$ADVISOR_PROGRESS to monitor the progress and review the results of a SQL Tuning Advisor session.

Use the SQL Access Advisor to Tune a Workload

❑ The SQL Access Advisor analyzes a workload as a whole.

❑ A SQL Access Advisor workload can consist of a single SQL statement, a SQL Tuning Set, the current SQL cache contents, existing statistics, or a schema name.

❑ Recommendations from SQL Access Advisor include new indexes, materialized views, and partitioning.

❑ The four steps comprising a SQL Access Advisor session are: (1) creating the task, (2) defining the workload, (3) generating the recommendations, and (4) reviewing and implementing the recommendations.

❑ You can either review usage of existing structures or recommend new structures in a SQL Access Advisor session.

❑ The procedure DBMS_ADVISOR.QUICK_TUNE automatically creates a task and analyzes a single SQL statement.

❑ The results from a SQL Access Advisor tuning session are recorded in DBA/USER_ADVISOR_ACTION. However, you can use DBMS_ADVISOR_CREATE_FILE to create a more readable report.

Understand Database Replay

❑ Database Replay can help to assess the change in performance on a test system by capturing the workload on a production server, and replaying the workload on a test system.

❑ Database Replay consists of four steps: (1) workload capture, (2) workload preprocessing, (3) workload replay, and (4) analysis and reporting.

❑ Each recorded client request contains the SQL text, bind values, and transaction information, including a timestamp.

❑ Client requests such as SQL*Loader operations, Oracle Streams, flashback queries, distributed transactions, and remote DESCRIBE or COMMIT commands are not included in the capture operation.

❑ The production system should be shut down and restarted before initiating the capture operation.

❑ You use the DBMS_WORKLOAD_CAPTURE.START_CAPTURE procedure to initiate the capture operation.

❑ Captured replay information needs to be processed only once for any number of target environments, and for any number of replays on the target system.

❑ You use the DBMS_WORKLOAD_REPLAY.PROCESS_CAPTURE to process a captured workload before replaying it.

❑ Before replaying a workload, you need to remap references to the production system.

❑ By default, the order of all COMMIT statements is preserved in a replay.

❑ You initialize a workload replay by using DBMS_WORKLOAD_REPLAY .INITIALIZE_REPLAY.

❑ You start a workload replay by using DBMS_WORKLOAD_REPLAY.START_ REPLAY.

❑ You can generate a report from a replay by retrieving the desired replay within a replay directory, and running DBMS_WORKLOAD_REPLAY.REPORT.

SELF TEST

The following questions will help you measure your understanding of the material presented in this chapter. Read all the choices carefully, because there might be more than one correct answer. Choose all correct answers for each question.

Use the SQL Tuning Advisor

1. The SQL Tuning Advisor performs all but which of the following analyses? (Choose the best answer.)

   A. Structure analysis

   B. SQL Profile analysis

   C. Access paths

   D. Changes to materialized views

   E. Statistics analysis

2. Which of the following can you use as input for the SQL Tuning Advisor? (Choose all that apply.)

   A. A single SQL statement provided by a user

   B. An existing SQL Tuning Set (STS)

   C. A preprocessed Database Replay workload

   D. A schema name

   E. A SQL statement identified in EM as using excessive resources

3. Which of the following procedures will run a SQL Tuning Advisor job against a SQL Tuning Set? (Choose the best answer.)

   A. `DBMS_QUICKTUNE.EXECUTE_TUNING_TASK`

   B. `DBMS_SQLTUNE.EXECUTE_TUNING_TASK`

   C. `DBMS_SQLTUNE.RUN_TUNING_TASK`

   D. `DBMS_ADVISOR.EXECUTE_TUNING_TASK`

Use the SQL Access Advisor to Tune a Workload

4. Which of the following can you use as input for the SQL Access Advisor? (Choose all that apply.)

   A. A single SQL statement provided by a user

   B. An existing SQL Tuning Set (STS)

   C. A preprocessed Database Replay workload

   D. A schema name

   E. Current SQL cache contents

5. Which of the following changes can the SQL Access Advisor recommend? (Choose two answers.)

    A. Restructuring one or more SQL statements.

    B. Gathering statistics for selected SQL statements.

    C. Adding a materialized view log.

    D. Enabling query rewrite.

6. Which of the following procedures will run a SQL Access Advisor job against a single SQL statement? (Choose the best answer.)

    A. `DBMS_QUICKTUNE.EXECUTE_TUNING_TASK`

    B. `DBMS_ADVISOR.EXECUTE_TUNING_TASK`

    C. `DBMS_SQLTUNE.RUN_TUNING_TASK`

    D. `DBMS_ADVISOR.QUICK_TUNE`

    E. SQL Access Advisor requires a workload, AWR snapshot, or STS, and cannot analyze a single SQL statement.

Understand Database Replay

7. You want to remap your database links so that they do not reference production database objects. Within which Database Replay step do you perform the remapping? (Choose the best answer.)

    A. During the workload replay step

    B. During the workload preprocessing step

    C. During the workload capture step

    D. Before the workload capture starts

    E. You do not need to remap, since it happens automatically

8. Which of the following database client operations are captured during Database Replay? (Choose all that apply.)

    A. A flashback query

    B. Distributed transactions

    C. Oracle Streams operations

    D. A `CREATE TABLE` statement

    E. A transaction started before capturing begins

SELF TEST ANSWERS

Use the SQL Tuning Advisor

1. ☑ **D.** Only the SQL Access Advisor recommends changes to materialized views including creating materialized view logs.
    ☒ **A, B, C,** and **E** are wrong. The SQL Tuning Advisor performs statistics analysis, SQL Profiling, access paths, and structure analysis.

2. ☑ **A, B,** and **E.** SQL Tuning Advisor can use currently running SQL statements, a single statement provided by any user, an existing SQL Tuning Set, or historical SQL statements from AWR snapshots.
    ☒ **C** is wrong because you cannot use Database Replay workloads to specify SQL for SQL Tuning Advisor. **D** is wrong because you cannot specify a schema or table names, you can only specify SQL statements.

3. ☑ **B.** `DBMS_SQLTUNE.EXECUTE_TUNING_TASK` runs a SQL Tuning Advisor task created with `DBMS_SQLTUNE.CREATE_TUNING_TASK`.
    ☒ **A, C,** and **D** are not valid packages or procedures.

Use the SQL Access Advisor to Tune a Workload

4. ☑ **A, B, D,** and **E.** In addition to a single SQL statement (using `QUICK_TUNE`), an existing STS, a schema name, and current SQL cache contents, SQL Access Advisor also uses statistics to analyze overall SQL performance.
    ☒ **C** is wrong because you cannot use the captured Database Replay information as a source for SQL Access Advisor.

5. ☑ **C** and **D.** The SQL Access Advisor recommends materialized views, materialized view logs, and enabling query rewrite. In addition, SQL Access Advisor will also recommend new indexes or partitions.
    ☒ **A** and **B** are wrong. SQL Tuning Advisor recommends SQL statement restructuring and statistics gathering, not SQL Access Advisor.

6. ☑ **D.** `DBMS_ADVISOR.QUICKTUNE` runs an analysis on a single SQL statement. You provide the name of the tuning task, which the procedure automatically creates, along with the SQL to be tuned.
    ☒ **A, B,** and **C** are wrong because these procedures do not exist. **E** is wrong because SQL Access Advisor can run an analysis on a single SQL statement, just as SQL Tuning Advisor can.

Understand Database Replay

7. ☑ **A.** The database links, external tables, directory objects, and connection string remappings need to occur during the workload capture step immediately before replay is initiated.
    ☒ **B, C,** and **D** are wrong because you do not perform the remapping during these steps. **E** is wrong because you need to perform the remapping manually.

8. ☑ **B, D,** and **E.** Most SQL statements are captured, including the SQL statement's text, bind values, and transaction information. Distributed transactions are captured but replayed as local transactions. Even transactions started before capturing begins are captured, but may cause data divergence during replay. Thus, Oracle recommends restarting the instance before initiating capture.
    ☒ **A** and **C** are wrong. In addition to flashback queries and Oracle Streams operations, OCI object navigations, non-SQL based object access, SQL*Loader operations, and remote COMMIT and DESCRIBE commands are not captured.

12
Disk Space and Resource Management

Y our two most valuable database resources are disk space and CPU time. With careful management of both, you can most likely delay upgrade costs for new disk drives or additional CPUs. In some cases, both these resources go hand in hand: (1) you will save CPU cycles if your disk allocation operations succeed the first time or (2) you are able to recover gracefully from low disk space scenarios.

Oracle provides several tools to help you manage disk space and other resources such as CPU time, idle time, and the number of concurrent connections. First, this chapter will cover Resumable Space Allocation, which enables you to suspend and resume large or long-running database operations that temporarily run out of space. Instead of a long-running job failing and requiring the user to start over after the disk space problem is corrected, the long-running job is suspended. After you take corrective action by providing more disk space for the long-running job, the suspended job automatically resumes.

Next, the chapter will cover another disk-related time-saving feature: transportable tablespaces. You can use this feature to quickly copy one or more tablespaces from one database to another without using the much more time consuming export/import method from previous versions of Oracle. An extension to transportable tablespaces, transportable databases, makes it easy to create a new database and move all non-SYSTEM tablespaces to the new database.

Oracle's segment shrink functionality will also be covered. Over time, heavy DML activity on a table or index may lead to fragmented free space below the high water mark (HWM). Segment shrink compacts the data blocks, leading to better OLTP performance because fewer blocks need to be in the cache for a given set of rows. Full table scans also benefit from segment shrink for the same reason: fewer blocks need to be read to perform the full table scan. This benefits decision support and data warehouse systems.

Finally, the Oracle Database Resource Manager will be covered. You will always have contention among many different concurrent users throughout the day, and you may want to allocate your database resources differently depending on the time of day and which users are using those resources. In one case, you might want to give one user a higher priority over another; the user with a lower priority, however, may need more resources overall. In another scenario, you may want to limit the number of concurrent sessions during the day but not at night. Resource Manager can provide this flexibility and control.

CERTIFICATION OBJECTIVE 12.01

Manage Resumable Space Allocation

Resumable space allocation avoids headaches and saves time by suspending, instead of terminating, a large database operation requiring more disk space than is currently available. While the operation is suspended, you can allocate more disk space on the destination tablespace or increase the quota for the user. Once the low space condition is addressed, the large database operation automatically picks up where it left off.

The following sections first explore the details of resumable space allocation, such as the types of statements that can be resumed. In addition, you will learn how to configure Resumable Space Allocation in your database. Finally, no discussion of resumable space allocation would be complete without an example and an exercise.

Understanding Resumable Space Allocation

As you might expect, the statements that resume are known as resumable statements. The suspended statement, if it is part of a transaction, also suspends the transaction. When disk space becomes available and the suspended statement resumes, the transaction can be committed or rolled back whether or not any statements in the transactions were suspended. The following conditions can trigger resumable space allocation:

- Out of disk space in a permanent or temporary tablespace
- Maximum extents reached on a tablespace
- User space quota exceeded

You can also control how long a statement can be suspended. The default time interval is two hours, at which point the statement fails and returns an error message to the user or application as if the statement was not suspended at all.

There are four general categories of commands that can be resumable: (1) SELECT statements, (2) DML commands, (3) SQL*Loader operations, and (4) DDL statements that allocate disk space.

Resumable SELECT Statements   SELECT statements are resumable only when they run out of space in a temporary tablespace, which typically means that the SELECT statement performs a sort operation such as ORDER BY, DISTINCT, or UNION. SELECT statements issued via an application using Oracle Call Interface (OCI) are also candidates for suspension when you run out of sort space.

Resumable DML Commands   As you might expect, DML commands such as INSERT, UPDATE, and DELETE may cause an out of space condition. For example, a DELETE may cause an out of space condition in the undo tablespace. As with resumable SELECT statements, the DML may come from OCI calls or even PL/SQL programs. In addition, INSERT INTO . . . SELECT from internal or external tables are resumable.

Resumable SQL*Loader Operations   SQL*Loader import operations may cause an out of space condition. On the SQL*Loader command line (using the command sqlldr), you can set the RESUMABLE parameter to TRUE. Once you set RESUMABLE to TRUE, you can assign a name to the resumable operation with the RESUMABLE_NAME parameter, as well as set the resumable timeout with RESUMABLE_ TIMEOUT. RESUMABLE, RESUMABLE_NAME, and RESUMABLE_TIMEOUT will be covered later in this chapter in the context of the ALTER SESSION command.

Resumable DDL Commands   All DDL commands that allocate disk space for new or existing segments are resumable:

- CREATE TABLE . . . AS SELECT (CTAS)
- CREATE INDEX
- ALTER TABLE . . . [MOVE | SPLIT] PARTITION
- ALTER INDEX . . . REBUILD
- ALTER INDEX . . . [REBUILD | SPLIT] PARTITION
- CREATE MATERIALIZED VIEW

Configuring Resumable Space Allocation

Enabling and disabling Resumable Space Allocation is easy to do, and does not consume any significant resources unless you use it. It can be enabled at the instance level using the RESUMABLE_TIMEOUT initialization parameter, or by an ALTER SESSION command.

If you set the initialization parameter `RESUMABLE_TIMEOUT` to a non-zero value, Resumable Space Allocation is enabled. The value you specify for the initialization parameter specifies how long the suspended operation will wait for more resources to be allocated before terminating the operation. Since this is a dynamic parameter, you can change it on the fly without a database restart:

```
SQL> alter system set resumable_timeout = 7200;
```

By default, the value is 0, which means that Resumable Space Allocation is disabled. If it is enabled at the system level, then all sessions can take advantage of Resumable Space Allocation. If you need more fine-grained control of which users can enable Resumable Space Allocation, then you grant the `RESUMABLE` system privilege:

```
SQL> grant resumable to rjb;

Grant succeeded.

SQL>
```

Once a user has the `RESUMABLE` privilege, she can enable it at will using the `ALTER SESSION` command, as in this example:

```
SQL> alter session enable resumable;
```

The default resumable timeout value is 7200 seconds (two hours), unless the `RESUMABLE_TIMEOUT` parameter is set to a non-zero value or you override it with `ALTER SESSION`:

```
SQL> alter session enable resumable timeout 10000;
```

To make it easy to identify your resumable statement in the data dictionary views `DBA_RESUMABLE` and `USER_RESUMABLE`, you can enable Resumable Space Allocation with the `NAME` parameter:

```
SQL> alter session enable resumable name 'Create Big Index';
```

When you query `DBA_RESUMABLE` or `USER_RESUMABLE`, you see the status of the session along with the current SQL statement executing for the sessions with Resumable Space Alocation enabled:

```
SQL> select user_id, session_id, status, name, sql_text
  2  from dba_resumable;
```

```
USER_ID SESSION_ID STATUS      NAME                       SQL_TEXT
---------- ---------- ---------- -------------------- --------------------
      88        133 NORMAL      Create Big Index           create index ie_cust_
                                                           last on customer
                                                           (last_name)
```

SQL>

As you might expect, you can disable Resumable Space Allocation with ALTER
SESSION:

```
SQL> alter session disable resumable;
```

You can further automate enabling Resumable Space Allocation for specific
users by creating a LOGON trigger that will enable Resumable Space Allocation,
assign a name to the session (most likely containing the user name or other easily
identifiable keywords), and set the resumable timeout specific for that user.

Using Resumable Space Allocation

In practice, the DBA or a user can register a trigger for the AFTER SUSPEND system
event. This trigger is fired immediately after a qualifying resumable statement
suspends. The code in the trigger can perform different actions depending on which
user's resumable statement was suspended, the reason for the suspension, or the time
of day. For example, a user running a month-end query may run out of undo space
and you want to let the query complete if at all possible. Therefore, you may want
to increase the timeout value and send an email to the DBA and to the user that
undo space is low and that the statement is temporarily suspended. For all other
types of resumable statements in this scenario, you will abort the statement and
send an email. Here is the basic structure of a PL/SQL trigger to handle resumable
statements:

```
create or replace trigger resumable_notify
    after suspend on database  -- fired when resumable space event
occurs
declare
    -- variables, if required
begin
    -- check DBA_RESUMABLE for user ID, type of
    -- object, then send e-mail
    dbms_resumable.space_error_info(. . .);
    if object_type = 'TABLE' and object_owner = 'HR' then
```

```
            -- give DBA 2 hours to resolve
            dbms_resumable.set_timeout(7200);
            utl_mail.send ('jsmith_hr@example.com', . . . );
        else - terminate all other suspended statements
            dbms_resumable.abort(. . .);
        end if;
    end;
```

EXERCISE 12-1

Configure Resumable Space Allocation for the HR User

In this exercise, detect and correct a space problem for the HR user.

1. Grant the RESUMABLE privilege to HR:

   ```
   SQL> grant resumable to hr;

   Grant succeeded.

   SQL>
   ```

2. Create a tablespace for the HR user and allocate all space in the tablespace using any preferred method:

   ```
   SQL> create tablespace users9 datafile '+DATA' size 10m
   autoextend off;
   SQL> connect hr/hr
   SQL> create table . . .
   SQL> create table . . .
   ```

3. Once the tablespace is full, attempt to create a new table:

   ```
   SQL> create table employee_search as select * from employees;
   create table employee_search as select * from employees
                                                          *
   ERROR at line 1:
   ORA-01658: unable to create INITIAL extent for segment in
   tablespace USERS9

   SQL>
   ```

4. Enable Resumable Space Allocation in the HR session for 3600 seconds (60 minutes):

```
SQL> alter session enable resumable timeout 3600;

Session altered.

SQL>
```

5. As the HR user, retry the CREATE TABLE statement in step 3. The statement does not terminate with an error but appears to hang. The alert log reflects the statement suspension:

```
Sun Sep 21 21:50:30 2008
statement in resumable session 'User HR(82),
      Session 145, Instance 1' was suspended due to
   ORA-01658: unable to create INITIAL extent for segment
      in tablespace USERS9
```

As part of the Automatic Diagnostic Repository (ADR), the message also appears in XML format in the directory $ORACLE_BASE/DIAG/RDBMS/DW/ DW/LOG.XML:

```
<msg time='2008-09-21T21:50:30.068-05:00'
    org_id='oracle' comp_id='rdbms'
 client_id='' type='UNKNOWN' level='16'
 module='SQL*Plus' pid='27121'>
 <txt>statement in resumable session &apos;User HR(82),
     Session 145, Instance 1&apos; was suspended due to
 </txt>
</msg>
<msg time='2008-09-21T21:50:30.071-05:00'
    org_id='oracle' comp_id='rdbms'
 client_id='' type='UNKNOWN' level='16'
 module='SQL*Plus' pid='27121'>
 <txt>    ORA-01658: unable to create INITIAL extent
               for segment in tablespace USERS9
 </txt>
</msg>
```

The suspended statement and the out of space condition also appear on the EM home page in the Alert section, as you can see in Figure 12-1.

FIGURE 12-1

Details of suspended statement on EM home page

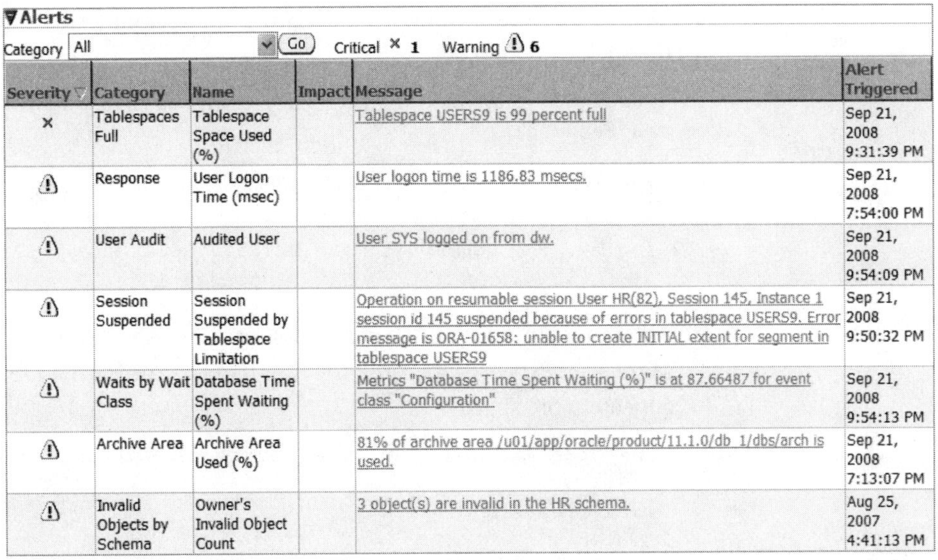

Alerts

Category: All | Go | Critical × 1 | Warning 6

Severity	Category	Name	Impact	Message	Alert Triggered
×	Tablespaces Full	Tablespace Space Used (%)		Tablespace USERS9 is 99 percent full	Sep 21, 2008 9:31:39 PM
⚠	Response	User Logon Time (msec)		User logon time is 1186.83 msecs.	Sep 21, 2008 7:54:00 PM
⚠	User Audit	Audited User		User SYS logged on from dw.	Sep 21, 2008 9:54:09 PM
⚠	Session Suspended	Session Suspended by Tablespace Limitation		Operation on resumable session User HR(82), Session 145, Instance 1 session id 145 suspended because of errors in tablespace USERS9. Error message is ORA-01658: unable to create INITIAL extent for segment in tablespace USERS9	Sep 21, 2008 9:50:32 PM
⚠	Waits by Wait Class	Database Time Spent Waiting (%)		Metrics "Database Time Spent Waiting (%)" is at 87.66487 for event class "Configuration"	Sep 21, 2008 9:54:13 PM
⚠	Archive Area	Archive Area Used (%)		81% of archive area /u01/app/oracle/product/11.1.0/db_1/dbs/arch is used.	Sep 21, 2008 7:13:07 PM
⚠	Invalid Objects by Schema	Owner's Invalid Object Count		3 object(s) are invalid in the HR schema.	Aug 25, 2007 4:41:13 PM

6. Query the data dictionary view DBA_RESUMABLE for additional details about the suspended statement:

```
SQL> select user_id, instance_id, status, name, error_msg
  2  from dba_resumable;

   USER_ID INSTANCE_ID STATUS    NAME                 ERROR_MSG
---------- ----------- --------- -------------------- --------------------
        82           1 SUSPENDED User HR(82), Session ORA-01658: unable to
                                  145, Instance 1      create INITIAL extent
                                                       for segment in
                                                       tablespace USERS9
```

7. As the DBA, allocate another 100MB for the USERS9 tablespace:

```
SQL> alter tablespace users9
  2     add datafile '+DATA'
  3     size 100m;

Tablespace altered.

SQL>
```

The alert log indicates that the resumable statement for HR has resumed:

```
Sun Sep 21 22:06:59 2008
statement in resumable session
    'User HR(82), Session 145, Instance 1' was resumed
```

8. Query DBA_RESUMABLE again to confirm the completion status of the resumable operation:

```
SQL> select user_id, instance_id, status, name, error_msg
  2  from dba_resumable;

   USER_ID INSTANCE_ID STATUS    NAME                 ERROR_MSG
---------- ----------- --------- -------------------- --------------------
        82           1 NORMAL    User HR(82), Session
                                 145, Instance 1
```

9. The statement for the HR user completes successfully, although not as quickly as the user expected, because the user had to wait for the DBA to manually allocate more space:

```
SQL> create table employee_search as select * from employees;

Table created.

SQL>
```

To notify the user that a problem was averted (and explain why the CREATE TABLE took so long), you can create a trigger for the AFTER SUSPEND event as described earlier in this chapter that includes sending the details of the suspend and resume operations via email.

CERTIFICATION OBJECTIVE 12.02

Describe the Concepts of Transportable Tablespaces and Databases

There are many ways to move data from one database to another, such as database links, Data Pump Export/Import, and transportable tablespaces. For large volumes of data, using transportable tablespaces is by far the fastest method. In a nutshell, you export just the metadata for the objects in the tablespace using Data Pump, copy the datafiles comprising the tablespace to the destination database, and import the tablespace's metadata into the destination database.

The following sections further investigate some of the restrictions of transportable tablespaces such as platform limitations. Even platforms with different hardware architectures are candidates for transportable tablespaces. In addition, you will learn how to transport a tablespace using both EM and SQL commands. RMAN is required to transport a tablespace in some scenarios. Finally, a brief overview of how to transport an entire database will be given.

Configuring Transportable Tablespaces

Transporting tablespaces has many uses, such as quickly distributing data from a data warehouse to data marts in other databases, or perhaps being used to converting an entire database from one platform to another. When transporting between platforms, both the source and destination platforms must be on Oracle's list of supported platforms. Most likely, your source and destination platforms will be supported. For example, virtually all hardware platforms based on either 32-bit or 64-bit Intel architecture are supported, along with Solaris, Mac OS, and AIX on proprietary hardware.

The following sections step through the compatibility requirements as well as any additional steps you need to perform for some hardware platforms. Once the compatibility and configuration steps are complete, you will step through an example using both EM and SQL.

Determining Compatibility Requirements

Oracle Database feature compatibility is controlled by the COMPATIBLE initialization parameter, which enables or disables the use of certain features in the database. For the purposes of discussing transportable tablespaces, these are features that require a specific file format on disk. For example, if you want to upgrade to Oracle Database 11g from Oracle Database 10gR2, you may want to set COMPATIBLE to 10.0.0 for a short time. Thus you can downgrade to version 10gR2 if you encounter problems in production, without requiring a restore and recover from backup because the datafile formats for version 11g are not usable on version 10gR2. Even though you may have tested the upgrade on a backup server, some problems with a new release do not appear until a week after you go live with the new release in production!

When you create a transportable tablespace set, Oracle determines the minimum compatibility level of the target database and stores this value in the metadata for the transportable tablespace set. As of Oracle Database 11g, you can always transport a tablespace to another database with the same or higher compatibility level, regardless of the target platform.

TABLE 12-1	Operation Type	Source Database Minimum Compatibility Release Number	Target Database Minimum Compatibility Release Number
	Source and target database on same platform	8.0	8.0
Minimum Compatibility Settings for Transportable Tablespace Scenarios	Source database has different database block size than target database	9.0	9.0
	Source and target database are on different platforms	10.0	10.0

on the
Ĵob

Regardless of the similarities or differences in hardware platforms between the source and target database, both databases must be using the same character set.

Table 12-1 shows the minimum compatibility settings for the source and target database depending on the differences in block size and hardware platforms.

In other words, even if you are running Oracle Database 11g with COMPATIBLE set to 11.0.0, you can transport a tablespace from a database on a different platform that has COMPATIBLE set to 10.0.0.

Determining Endian Requirements

Oracle's transportable tablespace feature, although available for nearly every platform that Oracle Database runs on, requires an extra step depending on the underlying hardware platform. On Intel-based hardware, pairs of bytes in numeric or string values are reversed. For example, the value 2 is stored as 0x0200. This byte ordering is known as *little-endian* because the least significant byte is first. In contrast, a *big-endian* system stores bytes in order of most significant to least significant byte. Therefore, on a big-endian hardware platform, such as Sun SPARC, the value 2 is stored as 0x0002. Understandably, a conversion must be done on column data transported between platforms with different endian formats.

To determine the endian formats of all supported platforms, you can query the dynamic performance view V$TRANSPORTABLE_PLATFORM, as in this example:

```
SQL> select platform_id, platform_name, endian_format
  2  from v$transportable_platform;

PLATFORM_ID PLATFORM_NAME                                       ENDIAN_FORMAT
----------- --------------------------------------------------- ------
          1 Solaris[tm] OE (32-bit)                             Big
          2 Solaris[tm] OE (64-bit)                             Big
          7 Microsoft Windows IA (32-bit)                       Little
         10 Linux IA (32-bit)                                   Little
          6 AIX-Based Systems (64-bit)                          Big
          3 HP-UX (64-bit)                                      Big
          5 HP Tru64 UNIX                                       Little
          4 HP-UX IA (64-bit)                                   Big
         11 Linux IA (64-bit)                                   Little
         15 HP Open VMS                                         Little
          8 Microsoft Windows IA (64-bit)                       Little
          9 IBM zSeries Based Linux                             Big
         13 Linux 64-bit for AMD                                Little
         16 Apple Mac OS                                         Big
         12 Microsoft Windows 64-bit for AMD                    Little
         17 Solaris Operating System (x86)                      Little
         18 IBM Power Based Linux                               Big
         19 HP IA Open VMS                                      Little
         20 Solaris Operating System (AMD64)                    Little

19 rows selected.

SQL>
```

This query also shows you all supported platforms for transportable tablespaces. If the value of ENDIAN_FORMAT is different then you must use RMAN commands at the source or target database to convert the datafiles to the target database's endian format. The required RMAN commands will be discussed later in this chapter. To determine the endian format of your platform, you can join V$DATABASE to V$TRANSPORTABLE_PLATFORM:

```
SQL> select platform_name my_platform,
  2         endian_format my_endian_format
  3  from v$transportable_platform
  4     join v$database using(platform_name)
  5  ;
```

```
MY_PLATFORM                    MY_ENDIAN_FORMAT
------------------------       --------------------
Linux IA (32-bit)              Little

SQL>
```

Transporting Tablespaces

Whether you use SQL commands or EM to transport a tablespace, the general steps are the same. EM does provide some automation to the process that streamlines the procedure and helps to avoid errors. However, as with most EM-based tools, EM does not cover every possible option available at the SQL> command line. Here are the steps:

1. Make tablespace(s) read-only on the source database.
2. Use Data Pump Export to extract tablespace metadata from the source database.
3. If target does not have the same endian format, convert the tablespace contents.
4. Transfer tablespace datafiles and metadata dump file from source to target.
5. Use Data Pump Import to import tablespace metadata into the target tablespace.
6. Make tablespace(s) read-write on both source and target databases.

The following two sections give you an overview of using EM to transport a tablespace and then provide the SQL version of the same operation.

Using EM to Transport a Tablespace

To transport a tablespace using EM, start at the EM home page, and select the Data Movement tab. Under the Move Database Files section, click on the Transportable Tablespaces link and you'll see the page shown in Figure 12-2.

In this step, you'll generate a transportable tablespace set containing the tablespace XPORT_DW in the DW database, and then transport it to the HR database. Ensure that the Generate radio button is selected and that you have provided the hostname credentials for the oracle user (the Linux Oracle user). Click on the Continue button. On the page shown in Figure 12-3, add the XPORT_DW tablespace to the list.

In addition, you can check that all objects in the tablespace are self-contained. In other words, there are no dependencies on objects in other tablespaces. You can take it a step further and check for the reverse condition in that there are no objects in other tablespaces dependent on the tablespace you are transporting.

FIGURE 12-2

Transport
Tablespaces start
page

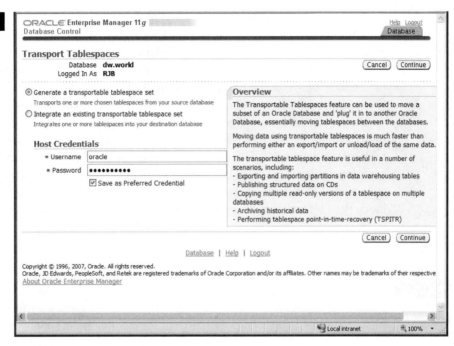

FIGURE 12-3

Selecting
tablespaces for
transport

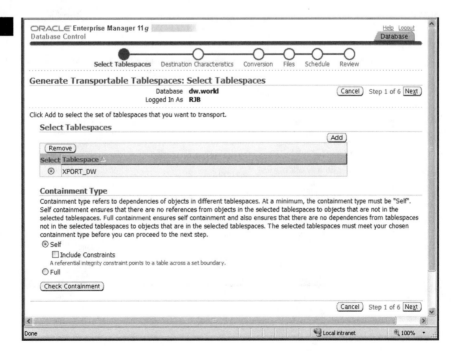

When you click on the Next button, EM checks for dependencies between XPORT_DW tablespace and other tablespaces in the database. On the page shown in Figure 12-4, you specify the destination platform, which is the same for the source and target databases (in this case, both are Linux Intel Architecture 32-bit). If the target database has a different endian format, then EM will convert the tablespace. Select the appropriate options for your environment and click on the Next button.

On the page shown in Figure 12-5, you specify the directory where you want to save the dump file containing the tablespace's metadata, as well as a copy of the tablespace's datafile(s). This location should be accessible by the target database, meaning the location could be on a Network File Server or some similar shared storage area. If it is not, then you will have to use another utility such as FTP to move the files later. In this example, the directory /Temp is accessible by both servers.

FIGURE 12-4

Specifying destination database characteristics

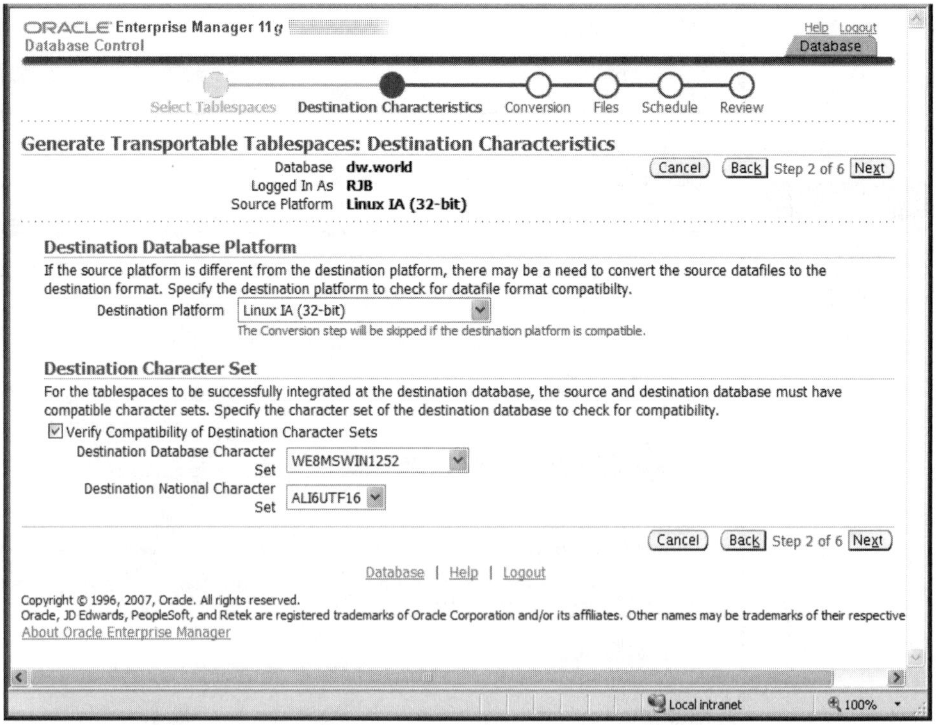

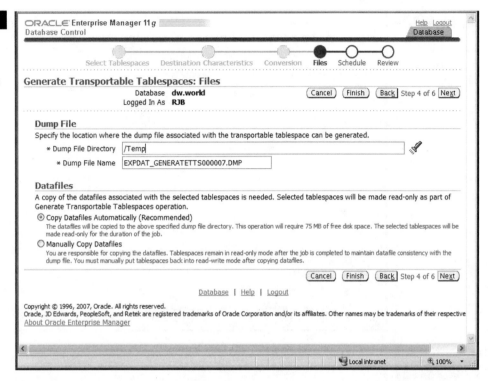

FIGURE 12-5

Specifying
transportable
tablespace dump
file location

Click on the Next button shown in Figure 12-5 and you will schedule a job to transport the tablespace as shown in Figure 12-6.

Figure 12-7 shows the final step in the first half of the transport process, which will give you the opportunity to review the settings you specified before you submit the job.

When you click on the Submit Job button shown in Figure 12-7, EM submits the job to process the transportable tablespace export. EM generates a confirmation page, and you can monitor the progress of the job with the link provided.

After the job completes successfully, you can perform the transportable tablespace import on the destination database. On the page shown in Figure 12-8, you have logged in to EM on the destination database (shown as the HR.WORLD database in Figure 12-8), and you are at the same page as shown in Figure 12-2, except that you will specify Integrate (import) instead of Generate (export).

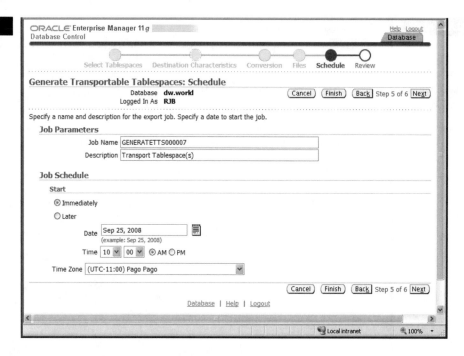

FIGURE 12-6

Scheduling transportable tablespace job

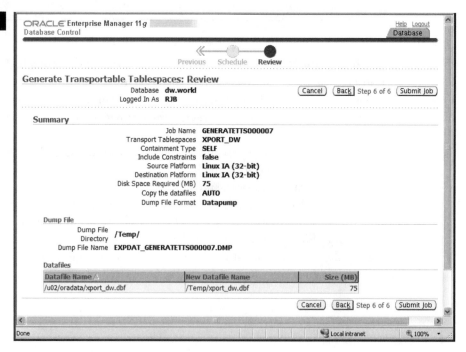

FIGURE 12-7

Review transportable tablespace job settings

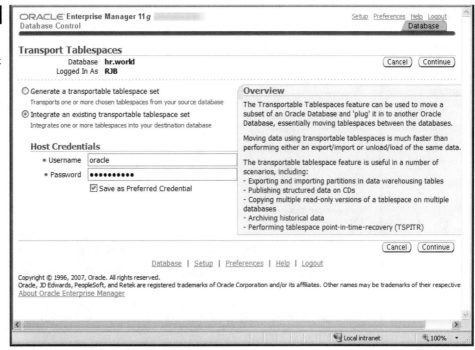

FIGURE 12-8

Transport tablespace import home page

Clicking on the Continue button in Figure 12-8, you see the page shown in Figure 12-9 where you can specify the dump file name and the datafile name you specified in Figure 12-5. When you click the Next button, EM reads the dump file and datafile(s).

On the next page, shown in Figure 12-10, you can change or accept the value EM chooses for the new datafile destination. In addition, you can leave the new datafile in place. After specifying the desired options, click on the Next button.

On the page shown in Figure 12-11, you can optionally remap objects from one schema to another. In other words, if both the source and destination database have an HR schema with identically named tables, you can remap the imported HR objects to the HR_IMPORT user instead and work out the differences after the import has completed.

After you click on the Next button in Figure 12-11, you see the job scheduling page shown in Figure 12-12. Click on the Next button.

FIGURE 12-9

Transport
tablespace dump
file and datafile
locations

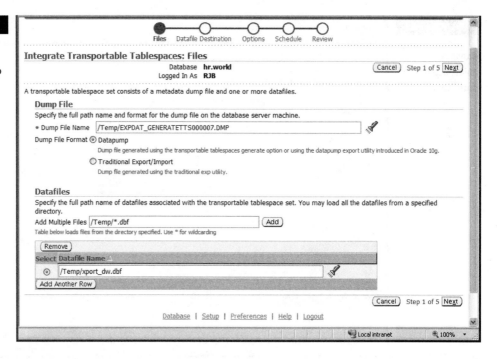

FIGURE 12-10

Specifying
alternate location
for imported
tablespace

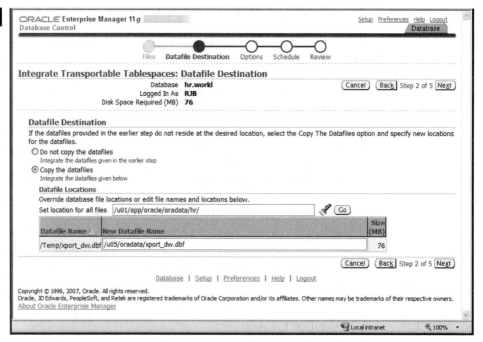

FIGURE 12-11

Specifying schema
remapping during
tablespace import

FIGURE 12-12

Scheduling
transportable
tablespace import
processing

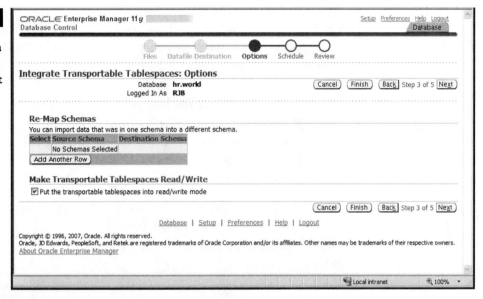

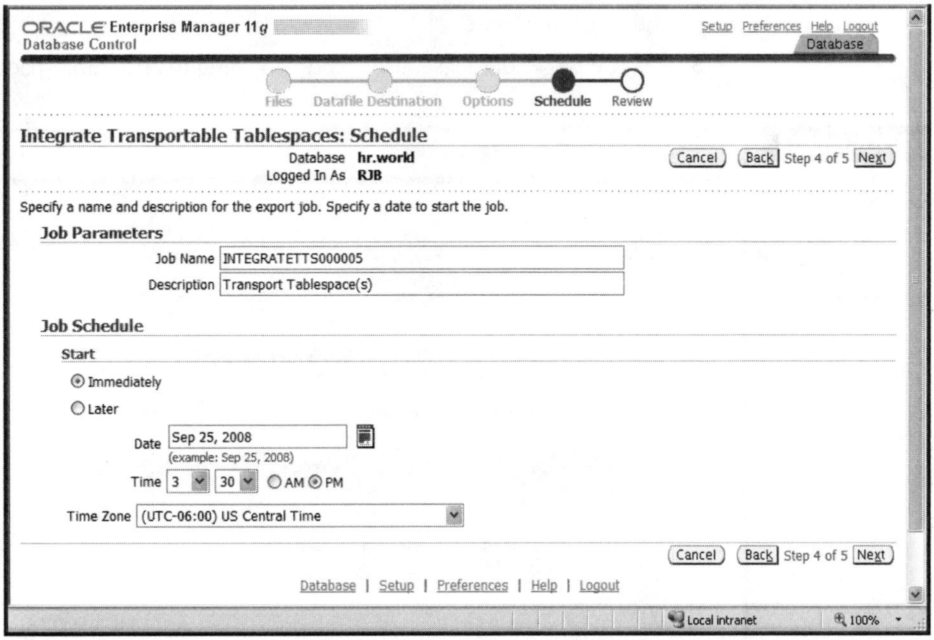

On the page shown in Figure 12-13, you get one more opportunity to review the import job. When you are satisfied with the parameters click on Submit Job. You can monitor the progress of the tablespace import, as you can see in Figure 12-14. When the job completes, the tablespace XPORT_DW is ready to use.

Using SQL to Transport a Tablespace

You can use SQL commands and PL/SQL packages to perform the transportable tablespace operation. You use the expdp and impdp utilities along with DBMS_FILE_TRANSFER PL/SQL package to copy tablespaces from one database to another. Here are the high-level steps:

1. Set up the directory objects on the source and target databases for the dump file sets and the tablespace datafiles (one-time setup).

2. Check for tablespace self-consistency with DBMS_TTS.TRANSPORT_SET_CHECK.

3. Use expdp to create the metadata for the XPORT_DW tablespace.

4. Use DBMS_FILE_TRANSFER to copy the dump file set(s) and datafile(s) to the target database.

5. On the target database, use impdp to "plug in" the tablespace.

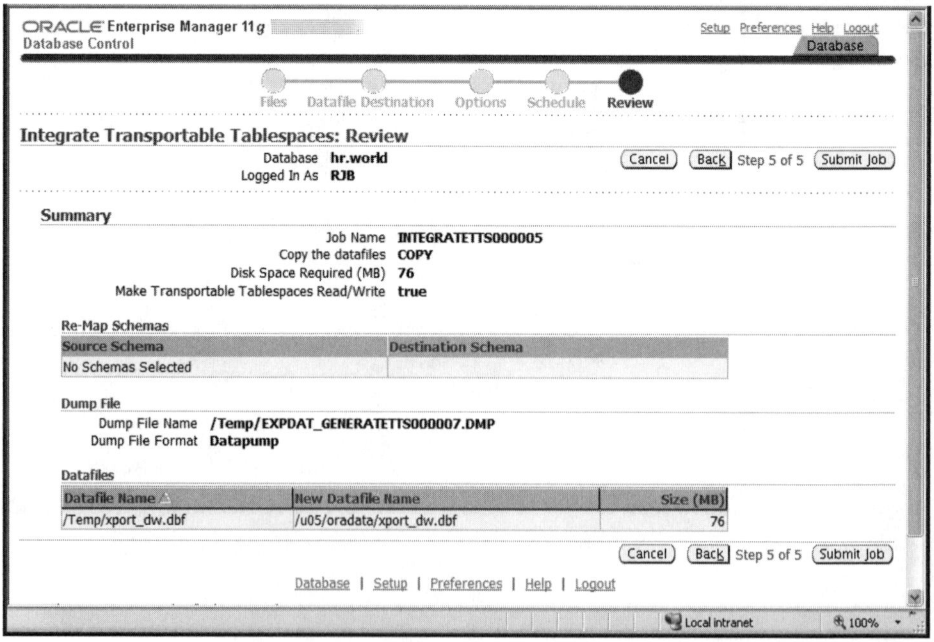

FIGURE 12-13

Reviewing transportable tablespace job parameters

FIGURE 12-14	

Monitoring transportable tablespace import job

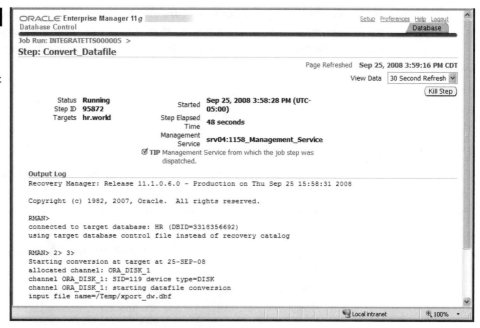

EXERCISE 12-2

Transport a Tablespace Using SQL and PL/SQL

In this exercise, use SQL and the DBMS_FILE_TRANSFER procedure to transport the XPORT_DW tablespace from the DW database on server dw, to the HR database on server srv04.

1. Set up the directory objects on the source and target databases for the dump file sets and the tablespace datafiles (one-time setup).

   On the dw source database you need to create the directory objects that will hold the dump file set as well as a directory object pointing to the location where the datafile for the XPORT_DW tablespace is stored. Below are the SQL commands on the DW database. The file system directory /Temp is common to all servers:

   ```
   SQL> create directory src_dpump_dir as '/Temp';
   Directory created.
   SQL> create directory src_dbf_dir as '/u02/oradata';
   Directory created.
   ```

If the source or target tablespace are stored in an ASM disk group then to make a copy you must use ftp with the /sys/asm virtual directory in the XML DB repository, DBMS_FILE_TRANSFER, or the cp command in the asmcmd utility.

On the HR destination database you will execute similar commands as you can see here:

```
SQL> create directory dest_dpump_dir as '/Temp';
Directory created.
SQL> create directory dest_dbf_dir as '/u05/oradata';
Directory created.
```

These directory objects are persistent, and you may use them in the future for other Data Pump or file-transfer operations.

2. Check for tablespace self-consistency with DBMS_TTS.TRANSPORT_SET_CHECK.

Before transporting the XPORT_DW tablespace, you should check to make sure that all objects in the tablespace are self-contained with the procedure DBMS_TTS.TRANSPORT_SET_CHECK, as follows:

```
SQL> exec dbms_tts.transport_set_check('xport_dw', TRUE);
PL/SQL procedure successfully completed.
SQL> select * from transport_set_violations;
no rows selected
SQL>
```

Not finding any rows in TRANSPORT_SET_VIOLATIONS means that the tablespace has no external dependent objects or any objects owned by SYS. This view is re-created every time you run DBMS_TTS.TRANSPORT_SET_CHECK.

3. Use expdp to create the metadata for the XPORT_DW tablespace.

On the DW database, you will run the expdp command to export the metadata associated with the XPORT_DW tablespace after making the XPORT_DW tablespace read-only:

```
SQL> alter tablespace XPORT_DW read only;
Tablespace altered.
SQL>
```

To run expdp, you open an operating system command prompt and perform the metadata export as follows:

```
[oracle@dw ~]$ expdp rjb/rjb dumpfile=EXPDAT_GENERATETTS000007.DMP \
> directory=src_dpump_dir transport_tablespaces=xport_dw

Export: Release 11.1.0.6.0 -
         Production on Thursday, 25 September, 2008 12:38:16

Copyright (c) 2003, 2007, Oracle.  All rights reserved.


Connected to: Oracle Database 11g Enterprise Edition Release 11.1.0.6.0
   - Production   With the Partitioning, OLAP,
   Data Mining and Real Application Testing options
Starting "RJB"."SYS_EXPORT_TRANSPORTABLE_01":  rjb/********
dumpfile=EXPDAT_GENERATETTS000007.DMP directory=src_dpump_dir
transport_tablespaces=xport_dw
Processing object type TRANSPORTABLE_EXPORT/PLUGTS_BLK
Processing object type TRANSPORTABLE_EXPORT/TABLE
Processing object type TRANSPORTABLE_EXPORT/TABLE_STATISTICS
Processing object type TRANSPORTABLE_EXPORT/POST_INSTANCE/PLUGTS_BLK
Master table "RJB"."SYS_EXPORT_TRANSPORTABLE_01" successfully
loaded/unloaded
************************************************************************
Dump file set for RJB.SYS_EXPORT_TRANSPORTABLE_01 is:
  /Temp/
************************************************************************
Datafiles required for transportable tablespace XPORT_DW:
  /u02/oradata/xport_dw.dbf
Job "RJB"."SYS_EXPORT_TRANSPORTABLE_01" successfully completed at
12:41:07

[oracle@dw ~]$
```

4. Use DBMS_FILE_TRANSFER to copy the dump file set(s) and datafile(s) to the target database.

   In this step, you will copy the tablespace's datafile to the remote database using DBMS_FILE_TRANSFER as follows (although you could use the /Temp directory for this step as well):

```
SQL> begin
  2     dbms_file_transfer.put_file
  3         ('src_dbf_dir','xport_dw.dbf',
  4          'dest_dbf_dir','xport_dw.dbf',
  5          'hr');
  6  end;
  7  /
PL/SQL procedure successfully completed.
SQL>
```

If the tablespace was created using OMF, you will have to use the value of DB_FILE_CREATE_DEST and some detective work, or use the dynamic performance views V$DATAFILE and V$TABLESPACE to track down the actual subdirectory and datafile name on the host operating system.

5. On the target database, use impdp to "plug in" the tablespace.
   In the final step, you will run impdp on the target database to read the metadatafile and "plug in" the tablespace datafile. Here is the output from this operation:

```
[oracle@srv04 ~]$ impdp rjb/rjb directory=dest_dpump_dir \
>   dumpfile=EXPDAT_GENERATETTS000007.DMP \
>   transport_datafiles=/u05/oradata/xport_dw.dbf

Import: Release 11.1.0.6.0
        - Production on Thursday, 25 September, 2008 17:10:00

Copyright (c) 2003, 2007, Oracle.  All rights reserved.

Connected to: Oracle Database 11g Enterprise Edition Release
11.1.0.6.0
        - Production
With the Partitioning, OLAP, Data Mining
        and Real Application Testing options
Master table "RJB"."SYS_IMPORT_TRANSPORTABLE_01"
        successfully loaded/unloaded
Starting "RJB"."SYS_IMPORT_TRANSPORTABLE_01":  rjb/********
directory=dest_dpump_dir dumpfile=EXPDAT_GENERATETTS000007.DMP
transport_datafiles=/u05/oradata/xport_dw.dbf
Processing object type TRANSPORTABLE_EXPORT/PLUGTS_BLK
Processing object type TRANSPORTABLE_EXPORT/TABLE
Processing object type TRANSPORTABLE_EXPORT/TABLE_STATISTICS
Processing object type TRANSPORTABLE_EXPORT/POST_INSTANCE/PLUGTS_BLK
Job "RJB"."SYS_IMPORT_TRANSPORTABLE_01" successfully completed at
17:10:53

[oracle@srv04 ~]$ sqlplus / as sysdba

SQL*Plus: Release 11.1.0.6.0 - Production on Thu Sep 25 17:11:10
2008

Copyright (c) 1982, 2007, Oracle.  All rights reserved.

Connected to:
Oracle Database 11g Enterprise Edition Release 11.1.0.6.0
        - Production
```

```
With the Partitioning, OLAP, Data Mining
    and Real Application Testing options

SQL> select * from v$tablespace;

    TS# NAME                                INC BIG FLA ENC
---------- ------------------------------ --- --- --- ---
      0 SYSTEM                              YES NO  YES
      1 SYSAUX                              YES NO  YES
      2 UNDOTBS1                            YES NO  YES
      4 USERS                               YES NO  YES
      3 TEMP                                NO  NO  YES
      6 EXAMPLE                             YES NO  YES
      9 BI                                  YES NO  YES
     10 CHGTRK                              YES NO  YES
     11 XPORT_DW                            YES NO  YES

9 rows selected.

SQL> alter tablespace xport_dw read write;

Tablespace altered.

SQL>
```

Note that you must change the tablespace from READ ONLY back to READ WRITE. When a tablespace is transported to another database, by default the copy of the tablespace is online but read-only. Also, don't forget to change the source tablespace back to READ WRITE after the completion of the tablespace transport if you made it read-only during a non-RMAN tablespace transport operation.

CERTIFICATION OBJECTIVE 12.03

Reclaim Wasted Space from Tables and Indexes by Using the Segment Shrink Functionality

Frequent inserts, updates, and deletes on a table may over time leave the space within a table fragmented. Oracle can perform *segment shrink* on a table or index to reduce this fragmentation. Shrinking the segment makes the free space in the segment available to other segments in the tablespace with the potential to improve future DML operations on the segment. This is because fewer blocks may need to be retrieved for the DML operation after the segment shrink. Full table scans will also benefit from a segment shrink operation on a table because the table occupies fewer blocks after the shrink operation.

Segment shrink is very similar to online table redefinition in that space in a table is reclaimed. However, segment shrink can be performed in place without the additional space requirements of online table redefinition.

To determine which segments will benefit from segment shrink, you can invoke *Segment Advisor* to perform growth trend analysis on specified segments. In the following sections, you will invoke Segment Advisor on some candidate segments that may be vulnerable to fragmentation using both SQL command-line tools as well as EM.

Understanding Segment Shrink

To reclaim unused space in a segment, Oracle's segment shrink feature performs two different tasks: (1) compacting the data rows, and (2) moving the high water mark (HWM). Figure 12-15 shows a table segment before and after a shrink operation.

The first phase of the segment shrink is compaction, which moves data rows to as far left in the segment as possible, in order to maximize the number of rows retrieved per block. However, since a full table scan reads all blocks up to the HWM, you

FIGURE 12-15

Table segment before and after segment shrink

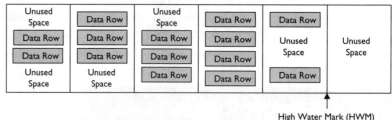

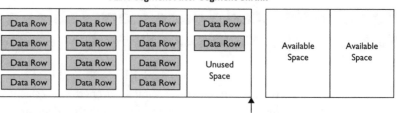

can relocate the HWM as far left as possible in the segment to improve the performance of full table scans as well. The reason Oracle divides the segment shrink operation into two parts is because relocating the HWM can potentially block a user's DML operations, but the shrink-only operation does not. As a result, you can perform compaction during the day with minimal impact on response time for user DML. You can then run the shrink operation at night when DML activity is low. You will see how to initiate one or both phases of a segment shrink operation later in this chapter.

There are many other benefits to a segment shrink operation. When you shrink an index, the index tree is more compact, and therefore fewer I/Os are required to look up a ROWID in the index. Note also that indexes for tables that are shrunk are maintained, and therefore don't need to be rebuilt after a shrink operation. In addition, since the HWM is relocated after a shrink operation, more free space is available for other objects in the tablespace.

Here is a list of candidates for segment shrink:

- Heap- (standard) and index-organized tables
- Indexes
- Partitioned and sub-partitioned tables
- Materialized views and materialized view logs

There are, as you'd expect, a few restrictions to segment shrink operations. First, the tablespace containing the objects to be shrunk must be managed with Automatic Segment Space Management (ASSM), and not freelists. There is no compelling reason since Oracle Database 10g to use freelist-based space management, so this should not be a problem. There are a few objects that cannot be shrunk:

- Clustered tables
- Tables with LONG columns
- Tables with on-commit or ROWID-based materialized views
- Index-organized table (IOT) mapping tables
- Tables containing function-based indexes

Most of these restrictions should have a minimal impact to your environment. For example, you should have converted any LONG columns to CLOB or BLOB columns long ago.

Automating Segment Advisor

Oracle's Segment Advisor can identify candidates for segment shrink, which can run either manually or on a schedule as part of the Automatic Segment Advisor job. Whether it runs manually or automatically, the first phase of Automatic Segment Advisor's analysis uses growth statistics and data sampling stored in the Automatic Workload Repository to determine which objects need further analysis. In addition, Automatic Segment Advisor focuses on tablespaces that have exceeded a critical or warning space threshold since the last analysis.

After performing the analysis on the candidate objects identified in the first phase, the Automatic Segment Advisor can recommend segments (tables or indexes) that are candidates for segment shrink. Once it has made recommendations, you can run segment shrink for a single table or for an entire tablespace.

The Automatic Segment Advisor runs as a scheduler job in the default maintenance window. The total scheduled window time is four hours every weeknight and on weekends for 20 hours a day. Although you cannot specify what objects and tablespaces are analyzed by the Automatic Segment Advisor, you can change when it runs and how many resources it consumes when it runs. Figure 12-16 shows the configuration page for the Automatic Segment Advisor, statistics gathering, and automatic SQL tuning jobs.

Shrinking Segments

You can perform advisor tasks and segment shrink operations using a series of SQL commands on a single segment, or alternatively, use the EM interface to perform the same task. The following sections show you both methods. You can use either method on a selected object, or an object already identified by the Automatic Segment Advisor.

Using SQL to Shrink Segments

Before you can shrink a segment, you must also enable row movement on the table or index. Some applications or operations, such as the table's indexes, rely on ROWID values to access the table rows. Therefore you must make sure that the segment you

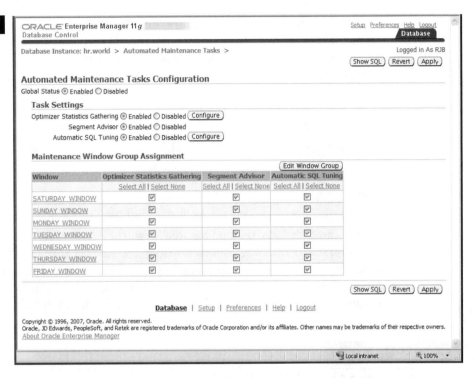

FIGURE 12-16

Configuring automated maintenance tasks

may shrink will not require ROWIDs to be the same for a given row. As you might expect, you enable row movement with ALTER TABLE as follows:

```
SQL> alter table employees enable row movement;
```

The easy part of shrinking a segment is the actual command to shrink the segment. Here is an example:

```
SQL> alter table employees shrink space compact;
```

The COMPACT clause is optional. If you specify COMPACT, only the compaction step occurs, and the HWM stays in place until you run the same ALTER TABLE command again without the COMPACT keyword.

The exam will require that you understand the purpose of the COMPACT keyword. Unlike most Oracle SQL **commands, adding the COMPACT keyword actually performs fewer actions rather than more actions!**

To initiate Segment Advisor on a specific table or on an entire tablespace, you use the PL/SQL package DBMS_ADVISOR. This package is used for other advisors as well, including the SQL Access Advisor and the Undo Advisor. Here are the PL/SQL procedures within DBMS_ADVISOR that you use to perform an analysis:

- **CREATE_TASK**   Create a new task in the advisor repository.
- **CREATE_OBJECT**   Specify a database object for analysis.
- **SET_TASK_PARAMETER**   Set the parameters for the analysis.
- **EXECUTE_TASK**   Perform the analysis.

The results of the analysis produce one or more recommendations, which are not implemented automatically. After Segment Advisor has been invoked to give recommendations, the findings from Segment Advisor are available in the DBA_ADVISOR_FINDINGS data dictionary view. To show the potential benefits of shrinking segments when Segment Advisor recommends a shrink operation, the view DBA_ADVISOR_RECOMMENDATIONS provides the recommended shrink operation along with the potential savings for the operation in bytes.

EXERCISE 12-3

Perform Segment Analysis and Shrink Operations

In this exercise, you will manually run Segment Advisor to analyze a table, and then run the recommendations from the analysis, which will usually include a segment shrink.

1. Add a new text column to the table HR.EMPLOYEES and enable row movement because you will most likely be shrinking the segment later in this exercise:

```
SQL> alter table hr.employees add (work_record varchar2(4000));
Table altered.
SQL> alter table hr.employees enable row movement;
Table altered.
```

2. Perform DML on the HR.EMPLOYEES table, first inserting 100 rows with large values for WORK_RECORD and then updating those rows with small values.

3. Use an anonymous PL/SQL block to set up and initiate a Segment Advisor job, run it and then retrieve the value of the TASK_ID variable:

```
-- begin Segment Advisor analysis for HR.EMPLOYEES
--   rev. 1.1  RJB    07/28/2008
--
-- SQL*Plus variable to retrieve the task number from Segment Advisor
variable task_id number
```

```
-- PL/SQL block follows
declare
    name varchar2(100);
    descr varchar2(500);
    obj_id number;
begin
    name := ''; -- unique name generated from create_task
    descr := 'Check HR.EMPLOYEE table';
    dbms_advisor.create_task
        ('Segment Advisor', :task_id, name, descr, NULL);
    dbms_advisor.create_object
        (name, 'TABLE', 'HR', 'EMPLOYEES', NULL, NULL, obj_id);
    dbms_advisor.set_task_parameter(name, 'RECOMMEND_ALL', 'TRUE');
    dbms_advisor.execute_task(name);
end;

PL/SQL procedure successfully completed.

SQL> print task_id

   TASK_ID
----------
       384
SQL>
```

The procedure DBMS_ADVISOR.CREATE_TASK specifies the type of advisor. In this case it is Segment Advisor. The procedure will return a unique task ID and an automatically generated name to the calling program. You will assign your own description to the task.

Within the task, identified by the uniquely generated name returned from the previous procedure, identify the object to be analyzed with DBMS_ADVISOR.CREATE_OBJECT. Depending on the type of object, the second through the sixth arguments vary. For tables, you only need to specify the schema name and the table name.

Using DBMS_ADVISOR.SET_TASK_PARAMETER, tell Segment Advisor to give all possible recommendations about the table. If you want to turn off recommendations for this task, you would specify FALSE instead of TRUE for the last parameter.

Finally, initiate the Segment Advisor task with the DBMS_ADVISOR.EXECUTE_TASK procedure. Once it is done, you display the identifier for the task (from the variable TASK_ID) so that you can query the results in the appropriate data dictionary views later.

4. Using the task number from the previous step, query DBA_ADVISOR_FINDINGS to see what you can do to improve the space utilization of the HR.EMPLOYEES table:

```
SQL> select owner, task_id, task_name, type,
  2        message, more_info from dba_advisor_findings
  3        where task_id = 384;

OWNER       TASK_ID TASK_NAME  TYPE
---------- ------- --------- ------------
RJB            384 TASK_00003 INFORMATION


MESSAGE
-------------------------------------------------
Perform shrink, estimated savings is 107602 bytes.


MORE_INFO
------------------------------------------------------------------
Allocated Space:262144: Used Space:153011: Reclaimable Space :107602:
```

The results are fairly self-explanatory. You can perform a segment shrink operation on the table to reclaim space from numerous insert, delete, and update operations on the HR.EMPLOYEES table. Because the WORK_RECORD column was added to the HR.EMPLOYEES table after the table was already populated, you may have created some chained rows in the table. In addition, since the WORK_RECORD column can be up to 4000 bytes long, updates or deletes of rows with big WORK_RECORD columns may create blocks in the table with free space that can be reclaimed.

5. Query the data dictionary view DBA_ADVISOR_RECOMMENDATIONS using the same TASK_ID to see the summary of recommendations:

```
SQL> select owner, task_id, task_name, command, attr1
  2        from dba_advisor_actions where task_id = 384;

OWNER       TASK_ID TASK_NAME  COMMAND
---------- ------- --------- ----------------
RJB            384 TASK_00003 SHRINK SPACE


ATTR1
-------------------------------------------------------------
alter table HR.EMPLOYEES shrink space

1 row selected.

SQL>
```

6. Implement the recommendation:

```
SQL> alter table HR.EMPLOYEES shrink space;
Table altered.
```

As mentioned earlier, the shrink operation does not require extra disk space and does not prevent access to the table during the operation, except for a very short period of time at the end of the process to free the unused space. All indexes are maintained on the table during the operation.

Using EM to Shrink Segments

To run Segment Advisor from EM, start at the home page and click on the Advisor Central link at the bottom of the page. On the Advisors tab, click on the Segment Advisor link. On the page shown in Figure 12-17, select the Schema Objects radio button because you are going to analyze the HR.EMPLOYEES table.

FIGURE 12-17

Segment Advisor: select object type for analysis

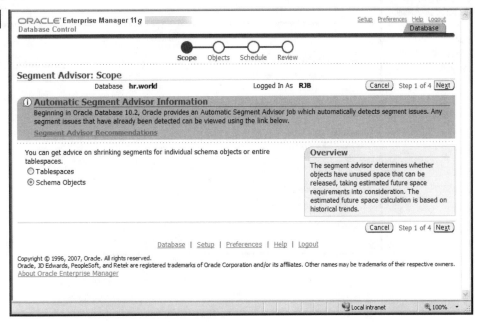

Click on the Next button. On the page shown in Figure 12-18, specify the table HR.EMPLOYEES for analysis. Click on the Submit button to initiate the analysis task.

On the Advisor Central page, you can monitor the progress of the job. You can see the job in progress in Figure 12-19. When the job is completed, click on the job name link to see the results of the analysis.

Figure 12-20 shows the results of the analysis. As you might expect, the Segment Advisor task recommends that you shrink the table. Clicking on the Shrink button will perform the shrink.

As mentioned earlier in the chapter, the Automatic Segment Advisor will generate recommendations as well. In Figure 12-21, Segment Advisor provides four recommendations.

Clicking on the Recommendations link shown in Figure 12-22, you see the individual recommendations for the SYSAUX tablespace, which includes shrinking four tables because they have a relatively significant amount of reclaimable space.

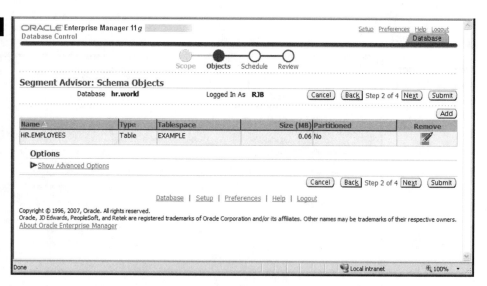

FIGURE 12-18

Segment Advisor: select objects for analysis

FIGURE 12-19

Segment Advisor:
monitor job
progress

FIGURE 12-20

Segment Advisor:
analysis results

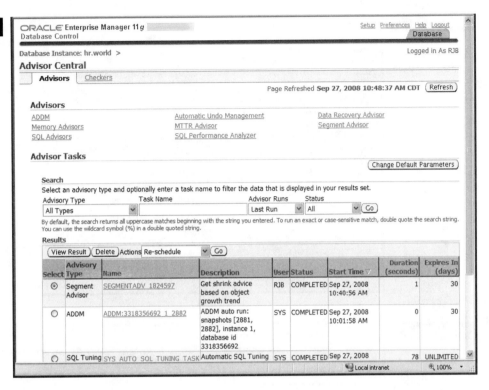

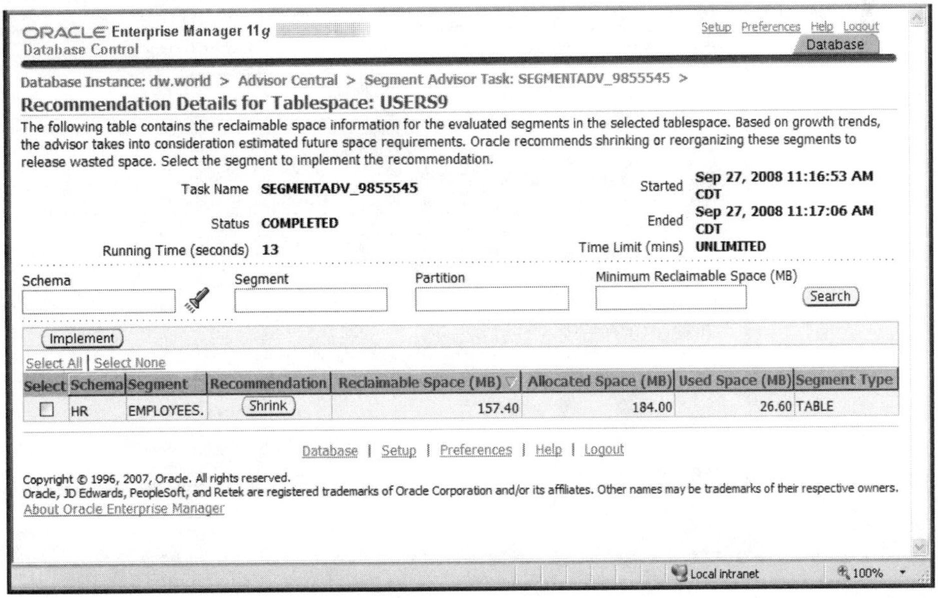

FIGURE 12-21

Automatic
Segment Advisor:
recommendations
summary

FIGURE 12-22

Automatic
Segment Advisor:
SYSAUX
recommendations

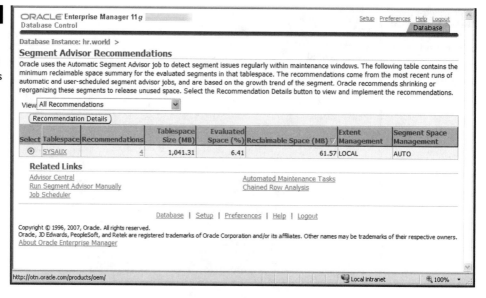

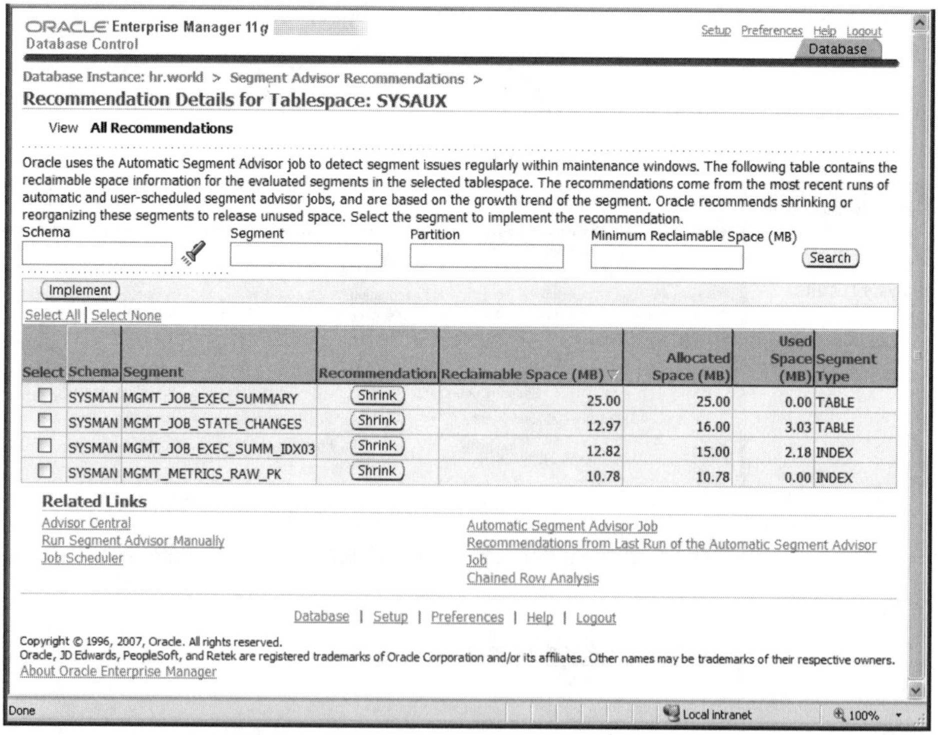

CERTIFICATION OBJECTIVE 12.04

Understand the Database Resource Manager

Your database server has a limited number and amount of resources, and usually there are many users competing for those resources. Controlling allocation to your database resources using the underlying operating system is not desirable for two reasons: first, the operating system software has little or no visibility to the users and groups within the database. Secondly, context switching within the operating system between database processes can cause excessive and unnecessary overhead. Instead, you can use Database Resource Manager to control the distribution of resources among database sessions in a more efficient and fine-grained way than the operating system can.

The following sections give you an overview of Resource Manager terminology, including consumer groups, resource plans, and resource plan directives. Next, you will find an explaination on the types of resources that Resource Manager can control.

Understanding Resource Manager Terminology

Understanding the three basic constructs of Resource Manager is required, not only for the purposes of the certification exam, but to effectively use Resource Manager "out of the box." The three basic constructs are resource consumer groups, resource plans (and subplans), and resource plan directives.

First, you need *resource consumer groups* to identify groups of users or sessions that have similar resource needs. For example, you have system administrators that most likely need as many resources (CPU and disk space) as possible when fixing a critical problem. In contrast, you have batch job users that can wait longer for the results of a query, and therefore will consume less resources if there are other users, such as users in an OLTP group, that need near instantaneous response time when querying a customer's order history.

Second, you need a *resource plan* that assigns various resources at specific percentages or relative priority to a resource group. You can have as many resource plans as you want but only one resource plan can be active at a time. A resource plan can also have a *subplan* that further subdivides resource allocation within a plan. Resource plans prioritize resources by using up to eight *levels*, with level 1 at the highest priority and level 8 at the lowest priority. The consumer groups at level 1 must have their resource requests satisfied before groups in lower levels.

Within the resource plan are *resource plan directives* which associate consumer groups with a resource plan and specify how the resources are divided among the consumer groups or subplans. For example, you may have a resource plan called WEEKDAY that manages three consumer groups: (1) OLTP, (2) REPORTING, and (3) OTHER_GROUPS. Any user or process not explicitly defined in a consumer group within the resource plan is in OTHER_GROUPS by default. The WEEKDAY plan has three directives:

- OLTP gets up to 70% of CPU resources
- REPORTING gets up to 20% of CPU resources
- OTHER_GROUPS gets up to 10% of CPU resources

Note that if the only users requesting resources are in the REPORTING group, they can get more than 20% of the resources until any OLTP or OTHER_GROUPS users request CPU resources.

Figure 12-23 shows an entity-relationship (E-R) diagram containing users, resource consumer groups, resource plans, and resource plan directives.

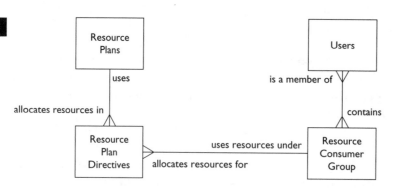

FIGURE 12-23

Resource Manager component relationships

Understanding Resource Manager Allocation Methods

Resource Manager can allocate resources based on one or more of these units of measure:

- **CPU usage**   Divide CPU usage among consumer groups.
- **Degree of parallelism**   Control the maximum degree of parallelism allowed for members of the resource group.
- **Number of active sessions**   Limit the number of active sessions for users in the resource group. New users are queued until a current session finishes.
- **Undo space**   Control the amount of space in the UNDO tablespace generated by DML statements. Exceeding the quota blocks new DML until other users within the consumer group release space. The user can, however, run SELECT statements until enough undo becomes available.
- **CPU time limit**   Maximum CPU usage. Resource Manager estimates execution time using the optimizer and does not start execution of the statement unless it is under the time limit.
- **Idle time limit**   Limit the maximum amount of time that a session is idle.

In addition, Resource Manager can automatically switch a session or process from one consumer group to another based on criteria such as using a certain amount of CPU time or undo space. For example, a session that uses over 100 seconds of CPU can be switched to another consumer group with a lower priority while still allowing the session to continue running. The session's owner is not aware of the consumer group switch other than possibly noticing a slight delay in returning the results of the operation.

CERTIFICATION OBJECTIVE 12.05

Create and Use Database Resource Manager Components

Now that you have a solid understanding of Resource Manager terminology and the types of resources you can control and allocate, it's time to get your hands dirty and see how Resource Manager works using both EM and PL/SQL procedures.

First, a thorough understanding of the default resource plan provided by Oracle, and how each database user uses the default resource plan will be given. Next, you will be shown how to create a new resource plan, create a new consumer group, assign users to the consumer group, then activate the resource plan. Finally, you'll be given several monitoring tools to see how your resources are being used, including several data dictionary views.

The PL/SQL package DBMS_RESOURCE_MANAGER has everything you need to view, create, maintain, and use Resource Manager components. Where appropriate, you'll be given the PL/SQL equivalent of EM pages when exercising Resource Manager.

Understanding DEFAULT_PLAN

Oracle provides a default plan, appropriately named DEFAULT_PLAN, when you create a database. To view this plan, start at the EM home page, click on the Server tab, then click on the Plans link under Resource Manager. You'll see the page shown in Figure 12-24.

Click on the DEFAULT_PLAN link, and you'll see the page shown in Figure 12-25.

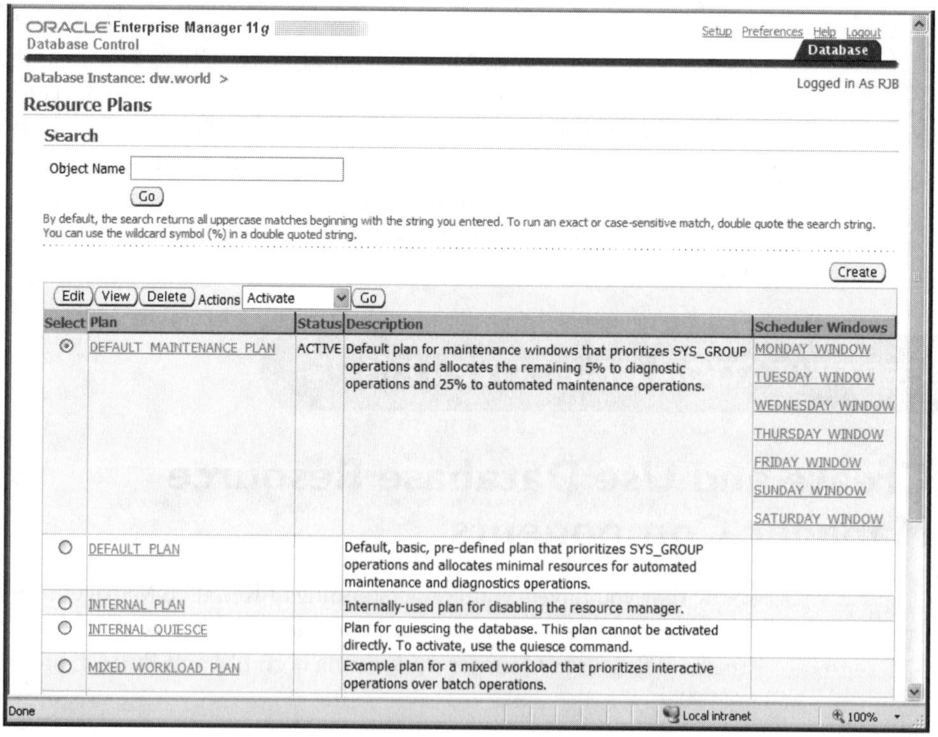

FIGURE 12-24	
EM Resource Plans	

FIGURE 12-24

EM Resource Plans

FIGURE 12-25

Details of the
DEFAULT_PLAN
plan

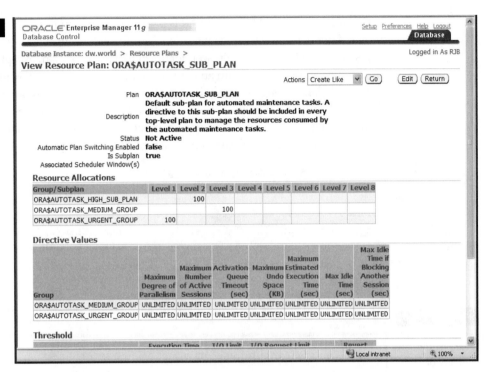

The plan DEFAULT_PLAN contains four groups or subplans. In short, members of
the SYS_GROUP (such as SYS and SYSTEM) get up to 100 percent of the resources
they need when requested. All other consumer groups get a certain percentage of
what the Level 1 group (SYS_GROUP) does not use. Here is a brief explanation of the
groups or subplans within this plan:

- **SYS_GROUP** Administrative users, such as SYS and SYSTEM that usually
  need all available resources for urgent maintenance tasks.

- **ORA$AUTOTASK_SUB_PLAN** A subplan for all automated background tasks,
  using 5 percent of what SYS_GROUP does not use.

- **ORA$DIAGNOSTICS** Routine diagnostics and database analysis, using
  5 percent of what SYS_GROUP does not use.

- **OTHER_GROUPS** All other users that do not fall into the other groups, such
  as OLTP users, batch users, and so forth, using 90 percent of what SYS_GROUP
  does not use.

Since ORA$AUTOTASK_SUB_PLAN is a sub-plan, you can return to the previous page and query its directives, as you can see in Figure 12-26.

As mentioned earlier, a sub-plan is identical to a resource plan, except that it can further allocate resources within an existing plan. Therefore, you could use a sub-plan as a top-level plan, as long as it includes OTHER_GROUPS. However, sub-plans are almost always used only as sub-plans, as the example in Figure 12-26 indicates.

To find out which plan is active (remember, only one resource plan can be active at a time), query the initialization parameter RESOURCE_MANAGER_PLAN:

```
SQL> show parameter resource_manager_plan

NAME                                 TYPE          VALUE
------------------------------------ -----------   ------------------------------
resource_manager_plan                string        SCHEDULER[0x2C0E]:DEFAULT_MAIN
                                                    TENANCE_PLAN
SQL>
```

FIGURE 12-26

Querying the contents of a sub-plan

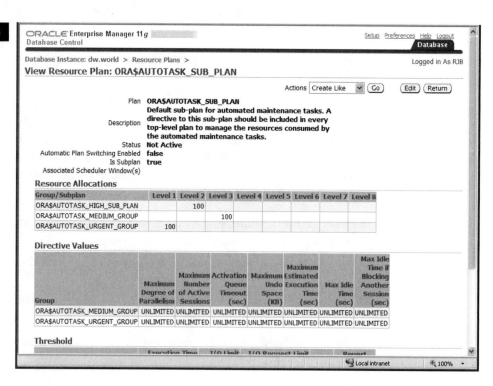

Note that switching between resource plans is done by a scheduler process. As a result, if you want to manually control the current resource plan, you will have to disable the switch via the scheduler process. If you do not set a value for the RESOURCE_MANAGER_PLAN parameter, resource management is not performed in the instance.

You can use the PL/SQL packages CREATE_PLAN, UPDATE_PLAN, and DELETE_PLAN to create, update, and delete resource plans. Some of these procedures will be used in an exercise later in the chapter.

Creating a New Resource Plan

If you are using EM, you can create a new plan from the Resource Plans page by clicking on the Create button on the page shown in Figure 12-24. Figure 12-27 shows you the details of creating a plan using EM.

The PL/SQL equivalent is as follows:

```
execute DBMS_RESOURCE_MANAGER.CREATE_PLAN -
    (Plan => 'DEVELOPERS', -
     Comment => 'Developers, in Development database');
```

FIGURE 12-27	
Creating a resource plan using EM	

Note that before you use any Resource Manager commands, you must create a "pending area" for your work. To create a pending area, use the CREATE_PENDING_AREA procedure of the DBMS_RESOURCE_MANAGER package. When you have completed your changes, use the VALIDATE_PENDING_AREA procedure to check the validity of the new set of plans, subplans, and directives. You can then either submit the changes (via SUBMIT_PENDING_AREA) or clear the changes (via CLEAR_PENDING_AREA). The procedures that manage the pending area do not have any input variables. So, a sample creation of a pending area uses the following syntax:

```
execute DBMS_RESOURCE_MANAGER.CREATE_PENDING_AREA();
```

If the pending area is not created, you will receive an error message when you try to create a resource plan. If you are using EM, the pending area is created for you automatically.

Creating and Assigning Consumer Groups

Figure 12-28 shows you how to create consumer groups and assign users to the group. You can create the group and add users on the same page.

FIGURE 12-28

Creating a resource consumer group

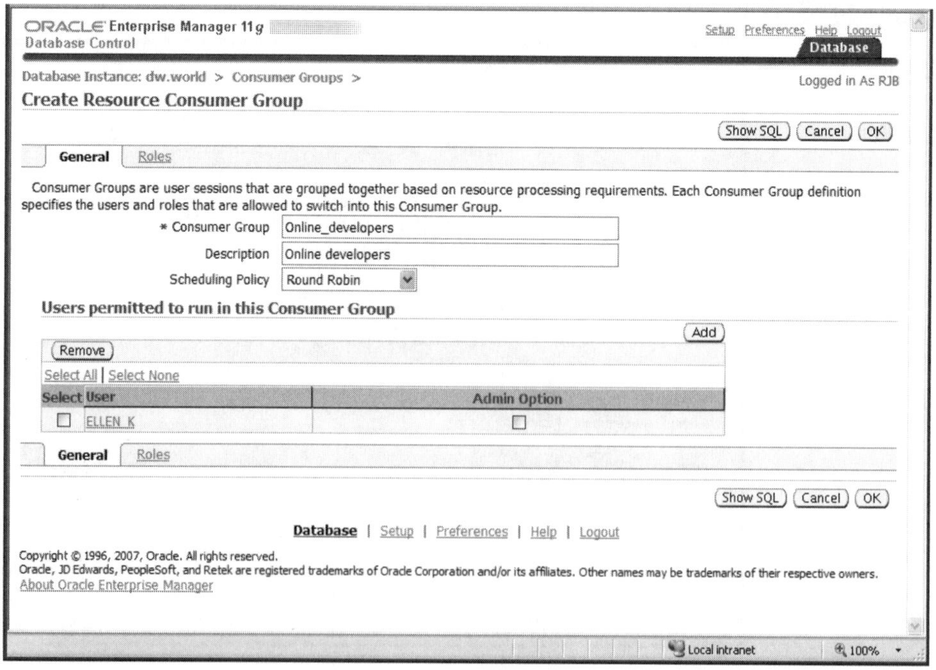

The equivalent PL/SQL procedure looks like this:

```
execute DBMS_RESOURCE_MANAGER.CREATE_CONSUMER_GROUP -
  (Consumer_Group => 'Online_developers', -
   Comment => 'Online developers');
execute dbms_resource_manager.set_initial_consumer_group -
    ('ELLEN_K', 'Online_developers');
```

Understanding Resource Allocation Methods

Creating or modifying directives within a plan is straightforward using EM. If you click on the Edit button shown in Figure 12-25, you can change the resource allocations for groups within the plan. Figure 12-29 shows you the page where you can edit the DEFAULT_PLAN resource plan. Note that you can use the tabs on this page to define resource plan directives for parallelism, undo space usage, idle time, and so forth.

FIGURE 12-29

Editing a resource plan using EM

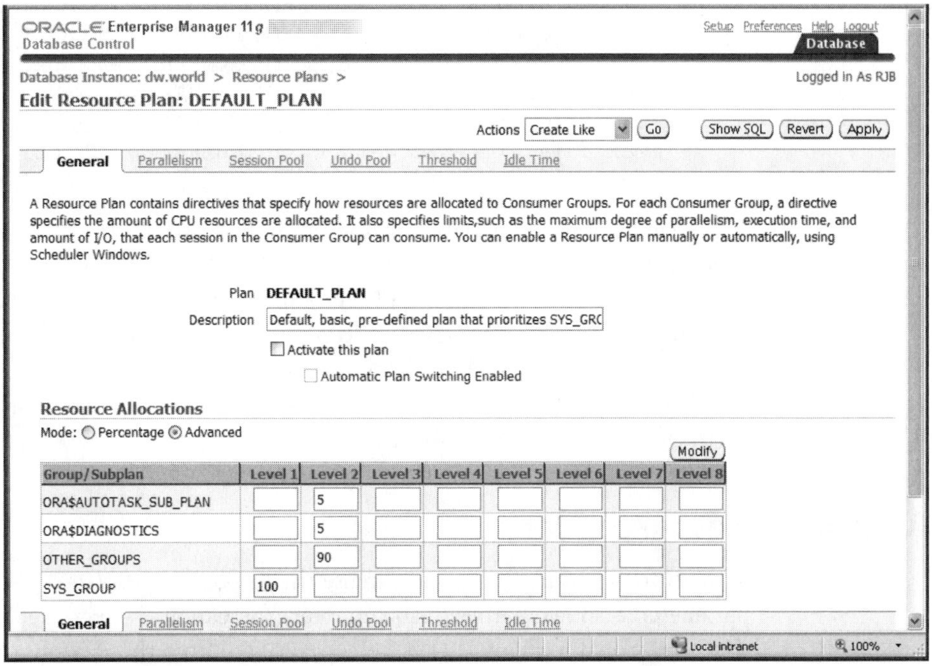

To assign directives to a plan using PL/SQL, use the CREATE_PLAN_DIRECTIVE procedure of the DBMS_RESOURCE_MANAGER package. The syntax for the CREATE_PLAN_DIRECTIVE procedure is shown in the following listing:

```
CREATE_PLAN_DIRECTIVE
    (plan                        IN VARCHAR2,
     group_or_subplan            IN VARCHAR2,
     comment                     IN VARCHAR2,
     cpu_p1                      IN NUMBER    DEFAULT NULL,
     cpu_p2                      IN NUMBER    DEFAULT NULL,
     cpu_p3                      IN NUMBER    DEFAULT NULL,
     cpu_p4                      IN NUMBER    DEFAULT NULL,
     cpu_p5                      IN NUMBER    DEFAULT NULL,
     cpu_p6                      IN NUMBER    DEFAULT NULL,
     cpu_p7                      IN NUMBER    DEFAULT NULL,
     cpu_p8                      IN NUMBER    DEFAULT NULL,
     active_sess_pool_p1         IN NUMBER    DEFAULT UNLIMITED,
     queueing_p1                 IN NUMBER    DEFAULT UNLIMITED,
     parallel_degree_limit_p1    IN NUMBER    DEFAULT NULL,
     switch_group                IN VARCHAR2  DEFAULT NULL,
     switch_time                 IN NUMBER    DEFAULT UNLIMITED,
     switch_estimate             IN BOOLEAN   DEFAULT FALSE,
     max_est_exec_time           IN NUMBER    DEFAULT UNLIMITED,
     undo_pool                   IN NUMBER    DEFAULT UNLIMITED,
     max_idle_time               IN NUMBER    DEFAULT NULL,
     max_idle_time_blocker       IN NUMBER    DEFAULT NULL,
     switch_time_in_call         IN NUMBER    DEFAULT NULL);
```

The multiple CPU variables in the CREATE_PLAN_DIRECTIVE procedure support the creation of multiple levels of CPU allocation. For example, you could allocate 75 percent of all your CPU resources (level 1) to your online users. Of the remaining CPU resources (level 2), you could allocate 50 percent to a second set of users. You could split the remaining 50 percent of resources available at level 2 to multiple groups at a third level. The CREATE_PLAN_DIRECTIVE procedure supports up to eight levels of CPU allocation.

Activating Resource Plans

To activate a resource plan, you can use the RESOURCE_MANAGER_PLAN initialization parameter as shown earlier in the chapter. You can also select the desired plan from the page shown in Figure 12-24, select Activate from the Actions dropdown menu, and click on the Go button.

EXERCISE 12-4

Create and Use a New Resource Manager Plan

In this exercise you will create a new resource plan, consumer group, and directives within the resource plan.

1. Create a pending area for your resource manager session:

```
execute DBMS_RESOURCE_MANAGER.CREATE_PENDING_AREA();
```

If the pending area is not created, you will receive an error message when you try to create a resource plan.

2. Create a plan called DEVELOPERS. By default, the CPU allocation method will use the "emphasis" method, allocating CPU resources based on percentage:

```
execute DBMS_RESOURCE_MANAGER.CREATE_PLAN -
    (Plan => 'DEVELOPERS', -
    Comment => 'Developers, in Development database');
```

3. Create two new consumer groups, ONLINE_DEVELOPERS and BATCH_DEVELOPERS:

```
execute DBMS_RESOURCE_MANAGER.CREATE_CONSUMER_GROUP -
  (Consumer_Group => 'Online_developers', -
  Comment => 'Online developers');

execute DBMS_RESOURCE_MANAGER.CREATE_CONSUMER_GROUP -
  (Consumer_Group => 'Batch_developers', -
  Comment => 'Batch developers');
```

4. Assign the user ELLEN_K to the ONLINE_DEVELOPERS group, and JOHNDOE to the BATCH_DEVELOPERS group:

```
execute dbms_resource_manager.set_initial_consumer_group -
    ('ELLEN_K', 'Online_developers');

execute dbms_resource_manager.set_initial_consumer_group -
    ('JOHNDOE', 'Batch_developers');
```

5. Create two plan directives to allocate 75 percent of CPU resources to the ONLINE_DEVELOPERS group and 25 percent to the BATCH_DEVELOPERS group. In addition, limit parallelism to 12 for ONLINE_DEVELOPERS and to 6 for BATCH_DEVELOPERS:

```
execute DBMS_RESOURCE_MANAGER.CREATE_PLAN_DIRECTIVE -
 (Plan => 'DEVELOPERS', -
  Group_or_subplan => 'ONLINE_DEVELOPERS', -
  Comment => 'online developers', -
  Cpu_p1 => 75, -
  Cpu_p2=> 0, -
  Parallel_degree_limit_p1 => 12);

execute DBMS_RESOURCE_MANAGER.CREATE_PLAN_DIRECTIVE -
 (Plan => 'DEVELOPERS', -
  Group_or_subplan => 'BATCH_DEVELOPERS', -
  Comment => 'Batch developers', -
  Cpu_p1 => 25, -
  Cpu_p2 => 0, -
  Parallel_degree_limit_p1 => 6);
```

6. Validate and submit the pending area:

```
SQL> execute DBMS_RESOURCE_MANAGER.VALIDATE_PENDING_AREA();
BEGIN DBMS_RESOURCE_MANAGER.VALIDATE_PENDING_AREA(); END;

*
ERROR at line 1:
ORA-29382: validation of pending area failed
ORA-29377: consumer group OTHER_GROUPS is not part of top-
plan DEVELOPERS
ORA-06512: at "SYS.DBMS_RMIN", line 434
ORA-06512: at "SYS.DBMS_RESOURCE_MANAGER", line 696
ORA-06512: at line 1

SQL>
```

Remember that your plan must include OTHER_GROUPS so that users other
than those in the consumer groups assigned to the DEVELOPERS plan will have
some resources available when the plan is activated. Therefore, create one
more plan directive for the DEVELOPERS plan that includes OTHER_GROUPS:

```
execute DBMS_RESOURCE_MANAGER.CREATE_PLAN_DIRECTIVE -
 (Plan => 'DEVELOPERS', -
  Group_or_subplan => 'OTHER_GROUPS', -
  Comment => 'Everyone Else', -
  Cpu_p1 => 0, -
  Cpu_p2 => 100, -
  Parallel_degree_limit_p1 => 6);
```

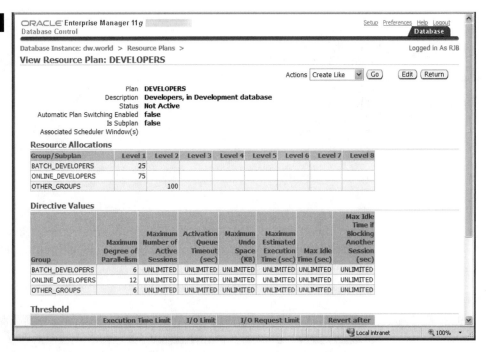

FIGURE 12-30

Validated and
submitted
resource plan
with directives

7. Revalidate the pending area and submit:

   ```
   execute DBMS_RESOURCE_MANAGER.VALIDATE_PENDING_AREA();
   execute DBMS_RESOURCE_MANAGER.SUBMIT_PENDING_AREA();
   ```

8. Navigate to the EM page where you can view plans and plan directives.
   The page should look something like the page shown in Figure 12-30.

Understanding Resource Manager Views

Table 12-2 contains the data dictionary views relevant to resource management.
  For example, to see the status and characteristics of each plan, query
DBA_RSRC_PLANS:

```
SQL> select plan, status, num_plan_directives, mandatory
  2  from dba_rsrc_plans;
```

```
PLAN                           STATUS     NUM_PLAN_DIRECTIVES MANDATORY
------------------------------ ---------- ------------------- ---------
MIXED_WORKLOAD_PLAN                                         6 NO
ORA$AUTOTASK_SUB_PLAN                                       3 YES
ORA$AUTOTASK_HIGH_SUB_PLAN                                  4 YES
DEVELOPERS                                                  3 NO
DEFAULT_PLAN                                                4 YES
INTERNAL_QUIESCE                                            2 YES
INTERNAL_PLAN                                               1 YES
DEFAULT_MAINTENANCE_PLAN                                    4 YES

8 rows selected.

SQL>
```

The column STATUS is PENDING if the plan has not yet been validated and successfully submitted. Otherwise, it is NULL. The column MANDATORY is YES if the plan cannot be dropped.

TABLE 12-2	Data Dictionary View	Description
Resource Manager Data Dictionary Views	DBA_RSRC_PLANS	Resource plans and status of each plan
	DBA_RSRC_PLAN_DIRECTIVES	Resource plan directives
	DBA_RSRC_CONSUMER_GROUPS	Resource plan consumer groups
	DBA_RSRC_CONSUMER_GROUP_PRIVS	Consumer group users and role assignments
	DBA_RSRC_GROUP_MAPPINGS	Consumer group mapping between session attributes and consumer groups
	DBA_RSRC_MAPPING_PRIORITY	Resource mapping priority
	DBA_USERS	The column INITIAL_RSRC_CONSUMER_GROUP contains, as you might expect, the user's initial consumer group, if any
	DBA_RSRC_MANAGER_SYSTEM_PRIVS	Users granted privileges on the DBMS_RESOURCE_MANAGER package

Monitoring Resource Manager

You can monitor Resource Manager using EM or dynamic performance views. From the EM home page, select the Server tab, then click on the Statistics link under the Resource Manager heading. You will see the page shown in Figure 12-31, where you can query CPU, I/O, waits, and queued sessions broken down by resource consumer group.

Three dynamic performance views give you Resource Manager statistics:

- **V$RSRC_CONSUMER_GROUP**   CPU utilization by consumer group
- **V$SYSSTAT**   CPU usage for all sessions
- **V$SESSTAT**   CPU usage by session

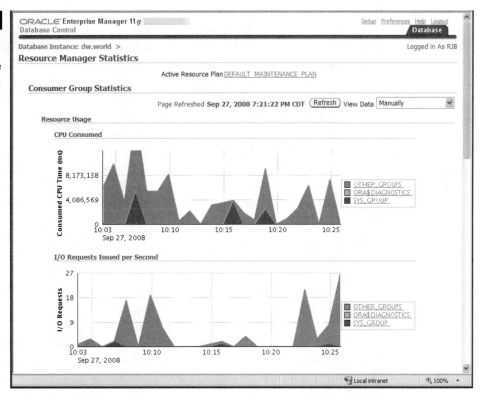

FIGURE 12-31

Using EM to retrieve Resource Manager statistics

CERTIFICATION SUMMARY

This chapter started with a discussion of resumable space allocation. Resumable space allocation can be a big time-saver. Jobs that run out of disk space after 95 percent completion will suspend and not terminate. If, within a specific time period, the DBA allocates or frees up more disk space, the long-running job will automatically resume and finish. Resumable space allocation is triggered for out of disk space conditions in permanent or temporary tablespaces as well as a user exceeding his or her quota.

Continuing the theme of moving or processing large amounts of data in the shortest possible time, transportable tablespaces were introduced. In a fraction of the time it would take to restore and recover a backup of your database to another database, you can export the metadata for one or more tablespaces, copy the tablespace(s) to the new database, then import the metadata to "plug-in" the tablespace. Only a couple of caveats apply to transportable tablespaces: (1) database compatibility level, and (2) platform endian formats. If the target platform has a different endian format, you must use RMAN either at the source database or at the target database to change the endian formats of the data by intelligently "flipping" pairs of bytes in the data blocks.

Next, you learned how to save disk space and potentially reduce I/O time for your table and index segments by using segment shrink. Segment shrink moves data rows as far left (closer to the beginning of the segment) as possible, thus reusing unused space in the segment. Optionally, segment shrink will also relocate the HWM of the segment, freeing up space for other objects in the tablespace. Before you perform a segment shrink, you need to know which segments need shrinking! As a result, you can run the Segment Advisor manually on segments you suspect are using space inefficiently, or you can use the results from Automatic Segment Advisor to identify segments or entire tablespaces that may benefit from a shrink operation. You can use either the EM interface or SQL commands to analyze and shrink segments.

Finally, a whirlwind, yet in-depth tour of using the Database Resource Manager to control resource allocation among the many different types of database users you typically have in your database was given. These users include OLTP users, DSS users, maintenance jobs, and system users. The different components of Resource Manager along with how they are interrelated were presented. The default resource plans may be sufficient for some environments, but eventually you'll want to control how many resources a particular user or group is using in relation to all other users.

This will become evident the first time a user runs an ad-hoc query that runs for 20 minutes while the web site is selling merchandise at a time such as the busiest shopping day of the year. Database Resource Manager provides efficiencies in consumer group switching and fine-grained resource management not available at the operating system level. The Resource Manager discussion was closed by presenting an in-depth exercise that created a plan, added users to two consumer groups, registered the consumer groups with the plan, and defined directives in the plan based on CPU usage and the level of parallelism.

✓ # TWO-MINUTE DRILL

Manage Resumable Space Allocation

❑ Resumable space allocation suspends instead of terminating large database operations which require more disk space than is currently available.

❑ Once a low space condition is addressed, the large database operation automatically picks up where it left off.

❑ Conditions such as out of disk space or quota exceeded can trigger resumable space allocation.

❑ There are four general categories of commands that can be resumable: (1) SELECT statements, (2) DML commands, (3) SQL*Loader operations, and (4) DDL statements that allocate disk space.

❑ All DDL commands that allocate disk space for new or existing segments are resumable, such as CREATE TABLE, CREATE INDEX, and CREATE MATERIALIZED VIEW.

❑ Resumable space allocation can be enabled at the instance level using the RESUMABLE_TIMEOUT initialization parameter or by an ALTER SESSION command.

❑ Setting RESUMABLE_TIMEOUT to 0 disables resumable space allocation.

❑ The default resumable timeout value is 7200 seconds (two hours).

❑ To make it easy to identify your resumable statement in the data dictionary views DBA_RESUMABLE and USER_RESUMABLE, you can enable Resumable Space Allocation with the NAME parameter.

❑ The DBA or a user can register a trigger for the AFTER SUSPEND system event which is fired immediately after a qualifying resumable statement suspends.

Describe the Concepts of Transportable Tablespaces and Databases

❑ When transporting between platforms, both the source and destination platforms must be on Oracle's list of supported platforms.

❑ Oracle Database feature compatibility is controlled by the COMPATIBLE initialization parameter.

❑ When you create a transportable tablespace set, Oracle determines the minimum compatibility level of the target database and stores this value in the metadata for the transportable tablespace set.

❑ A conversion process must be peformed for data columns transported between platforms with different endian formats.

❑ To determine the endian formats of all supported platforms, you can query the dynamic performance view V\$TRANSPORTABLE_PLATFORM.

❑ When transporting a tablespace, the source tablespace must be read-only during the copy process, and changed to read-write after import to the target database.

❑ You use expdp, impdp, and the DBMS_FILE_TRANSFER PL/SQL package to copy metadata and the tablespace's datafiles from one database to another.

Reclaim Wasted Space from Tables and Indexes by Using the Segment Shrink Functionality

❑ Shrinking the segment makes the free space in the segment available to other segments in the tablespace.

❑ Segment shrink has the potential to improve future DML operations on the segment because fewer blocks may need to be retrieved for the DML operation after the segment shrink.

❑ Segment shrink is similar to online table redefinition in that space in a table is reclaimed, but can be performed in place without the additional space requirements of online table redefinition.

❑ Segment shrink has two phases: compacting the data rows and moving the high water mark (HWM).

❑ Moving the HWM is optional or can be delayed to reduce any impact on concurrent DML operations on the segment.

❑ A shrink operation is executed internally as a series of INSERT and DELETE operations; no DML triggers are executed during a shrink.

❑ Segment shrink cannot be used on clustered tables, tables with LONG columns, IOT mapping tables, tables with ROWID-based or on-commit materialized views, and tables containing function based indexes.

❑ Oracle's Segment Advisor, run either manually or on a schedule as part of the Automatic Segment Advisor job, can identify candidates for segment shrink.

❏ Automatic Segment Advisor can recommend segments (tables or indexes) that are candidates for segment shrink.

❏ You cannot specify what objects and tablespaces are analyzed by the Automatic Segment Advisor, you can change when it runs and how many resources it consumes when it runs.

❏ The COMPACT clause of the ALTER TABLE . . . SHRINK SPACE command only performs the compaction step, and the HWM stays in place until you run the same ALTER TABLE command again without the COMPACT keyword.

❏ Before you can shrink a segment, you must also enable row movement on the table or index.

❏ To initiate Segment Advisor on a specific table or on an entire tablespace, you use the PL/SQL package DBMS_ADVISOR.

❏ The findings from Segment Advisor are available in the DBA_ADVISOR_ FINDINGS data dictionary view.

Understand the Database Resource Manager

❏ Using the operating system for resource management is not desirable because context switching within the operating system between database processes can cause excessive and unnecessary overhead.

❏ The three basic constructs of Resource Manager are resource consumer groups, resource plans (and subplans), and resource plan directives.

❏ *Resource consumer groups* to identify groups of users or sessions that have similar resource needs.

❏ A *resource plan* assigns various resources at specific percentages or relative priority to a resource group.

❏ Within the resource plan are *resource plan directives* which associate consumer groups with a resource plan, and specify how the resources are divided among the consumer groups or subplans.

❏ Resource Manager can allocate resources based on CPU usage, degree of parallelism, number of active sessions, undo space, CPU time limit, and idle time limit.

❏ Resource Manager can automatically switch a session or process from one consumer group to another based on criteria such as using a certain amount of CPU time or undo space.

Create and Use Database Resource Manager Components

❏ The PL/SQL package DBMS_RESOURCE_MANAGER has everything you need to view, create, maintain, and use Resource Manager components.

❏ Oracle provides a default plan named DEFAULT_PLAN when you create a database.

❏ A sub-plan is identical to a resource plan, except that it can further allocate resources within an existing plan.

❏ Only one resource plan can be active at a time.

❏ To find out which plan is active, query the initialization parameter RESOURCE_MANAGER_PLAN.

❏ You can use the PL/SQL packages CREATE_PLAN, UPDATE_PLAN, and DELETE_PLAN to create, update, and delete resource plans.

❏ To create a pending area, use the CREATE_PENDING_AREA procedure of the DBMS_RESOURCE_MANAGER package.

❏ Use DBMS_RESOURCE_MANAGER.CREATE_CONSUMER_GROUP to create a new consumer group.

❏ To assign directives to a plan using PL/SQL, use the CREATE_PLAN_DIRECTIVE procedure of the DBMS_RESOURCE_MANAGER package.

❏ To create a pending area for your resource manager session, use DBMS_RESOURCE_MANAGER.CREATE_PENDING_AREA().

❏ To create a new Resource Manager plan, use DBMS_RESOURCE_MANAGER.CREATE_PLAN.

❏ To create a consumer group, use DBMS_RESOURCE_MANAGER.CREATE_CONSUMER_GROUP.

❏ To create plan directives within a plan, use DBMS_RESOURCE_MANAGER.CREATE_PLAN_DIRECTIVE, specifying the plan name, the group affected by the directive, along with CPU, parallelism, and undo space usage limits.

❏ You must validate the pending area with DBMS_RESOURCE_MANAGER.VALIDATE_PENDING_AREA() before submitting the pending area with DBMS_RESOURCE_MANAGER.SUBMIT_PENDING_AREA().

❏ The data dictionary view DBA_RSRC_PLAN shows you all plans in the database plus the status and the permanence of each plan.

❏ The primary dynamic performance view for monitoring Resource Manager is V$RSRC_CONSUMER_GROUP.

SELF TEST

The following questions will help you measure your understanding of the material presented in this chapter. Read all the choices carefully, because there might be more than one correct answer. Choose all correct answers for each question.

Manage Resumable Space Allocation

1. Which of the following commands is not a candidate for resumable space allocation?

    A. `CREATE INDEX . . . ON . . .`

    B. `SELECT . . . ORDER BY`

    C. `$ sqlldr`

    D. `CREATE TABLE . . . (COL1, COL2. . .);`

    E. `DELETE FROM . . .`

2. A user with the `RESUMABLE` privilege executes the following command:

```
SQL> alter session enable resumable;
```

The value for the initialization parameter `RESUMABLE_TIMEOUT` is 3600.
What is the timeout value for resumable statements?

    A. The `ALTER SESSION` command fails because it does not specify a value for `TIMEOUT`

    B. 7200

    C. 3600

    D. 10000

    E. The `ALTER SESSION` command fails because it does not specify a value for `NAME`

Describe the Concepts of Transportable Tablespaces and Databases

3. You are running Oracle Database 11g with the `COMPATIBLE` initialization parameter set to 11.0.0. What is the minimal compatibility level for transporting a tablespace from a database on a different platform?

    A. 8.0

    B. 10.0

    C. 9.0

    D. 11.0

    E. All of the above

4. When transporting a tablespace, what is the purpose of DBMS_TTS.TRANSPORT_SET_CHECK? (Choose the best answer)

 A. It ensures that the COMPATIBILITY level is high enough for the transport operation

 B. It compares the endian level for the source and target databases and runs RMAN to convert the datafiles before transportation

 C. It validates that the metadata for the tablespace does not have any naming conflicts with the target database schemas

 D. It checks for tablespace self-consistency

Reclaim Wasted Space from Tables and Indexes by Using the Segment Shrink Functionality

5. Which of the following commands will shrink space in a table or index segment and relocate the HWM?

 A. `alter table employees shrink space compact hwm;`

 B. `alter table employees shrink space hwm;`

 C. `alter table employees shrink space compact;`

 D. `alter table employees shrink space;`

 E. `alter table employees shrink space cascade;`

6. Which of the following objects are not candidates for segment shrink? (Choose all that apply.)

 A. Clustered tables

 B. Tables with function-based indexes

 C. Index-organized tables

 D. Tables with fast-refreshable materialized views.

 E. Tables with CLOB columns

Understand the Database Resource Manager

7. Identify the correct statement about Database Resource Manager components. (Choose the best answer)

 A. Multiple resource plans can be active at once, but only one can be active for a specific user.

 B. The resource consumer group OTHER_GROUPS is optional in a resource plan.

 C. Resource consumer groups identify groups of users with similar resource needs, and a user can belong to more than one consumer group.

 D. Resource consumer groups identify groups of users with similar resource needs, and a user can belong to only one consumer group.

Create and Use Database Resource Manager Components

8. Which of the following resources cannot be allocated by Resource Manager? (Choose all that apply.)

   A. Network bandwidth

   B. CPU usage

   C. Degree of parallelism

   D. Undo space usage

   E. Temporary tablespace usage

9. You attempt to validate the Resource Manager pending area with DBMS_RESOURCE_MANAGER. VALIDATE_PENDING_AREA(). However, you get this error message:

   ```
   ORA-29382: validation of pending area failed
   ORA-29377: consumer group OTHER_GROUPS is not part of top-plan OLTP_NIGHT
   ```

   How can you fix this problem? (Choose the best answer.)

   A. Create a new pending area, and add OTHER_GROUPS as the first consumer group in the plan OLTP_NIGHT.

   B. The consumer group OTHER_GROUPS was mistakenly added to a sub-plan, therefore you must remove it from all sub-plans.

   C. You must drop the consumer group OTHER_GROUPS before creating this plan.

   D. Add the consumer group OTHER_GROUPS to the plan OLTP_NIGHT, and then revalidate.

10. What is the value of the STATUS column in the data dictionary view DBA_RSRC_PLANS for a plan that is in the pending area but has failed validation?

    A. NULL

    B. PENDING

    C. UNKNOWN

    D. INVALID

SELF TEST ANSWERS

Manage Resumable Space Allocation

1. ☑ **D.** A CREATE TABLE statement cannot cause a low disk space situation unless you use CREATE TABLE AS SELECT or the SYSTEM tablespace runs out of room in the data dictionary.
☒ **A, B, C,** and **E** are incorrect. CREATE INDEX allocates space in a tablespace, and therefore it can trigger resumable space allocation. A SELECT statement can trigger resumable space allocation if it runs out of sort space in the TEMP tablespace for ORDER BY, GROUP BY, or DISTINCT clauses. SQL*Loader operations are resumable as long as you use the RESUMABLE parameter. Finally, a DELETE statement may cause a low space condition in the UNDO tablespace.

2. ☑ **C.** If you do not specify a value for the timeout with ALTER SESSION, it defaults to either 7200 seconds (two hours) or the value of the initialization parameter RESUMABLE_TIMEOUT (in this case 3600) if it is non-zero.
☒ **A, B, D** and **E** are wrong. The TIMEOUT and NAME keywords are optional in ALTER SESSION ENABLE RESUMABLE. The default of 7200 only applies if RESUMABLE_TIMEOUT is not set or is zero.

Describe the Concepts of Transportable Tablespaces and Databases

3. ☑ **B.** If the source and target databases are on different platforms, both the source and target must have a compatibility level of at least 10.0.
☒ **A, C, D,** and **E** are wrong. For transporting between identical platforms, you only need COMPATIBLE=8.0. For transporting between databases with different block sizes, you only need COMPATIBLE=9.0.

4. ☑ **D.** DBMS_TTS.TRANSPORT_SET_CHECK checks to ensure that there are no objects in the tablespace to be transported that have dependencies on objects in other tablespaces in the source database.
☒ **A, B,** and **C** are not valid uses for DBMS_TTS.TRANSPORT_SET_CHECK.

Reclaim Wasted Space from Tables and Indexes by Using the Segment Shrink Functionality

5. ☑ **D.** SHRINK SPACE both compacts the data and moves the HWM. While the HWM is being moved, DML operations on the table are blocked.
☒ **A, B,** and **E** are syntactically incorrect. C is wrong because COMPACT only performs the shrink operation but does not move the HWM after shrinking the segment.

6. ☑ **A and B.** Clustered tables and tables with function-based indexes are not shrinkable. In addition, you cannot shrink tables with LONG columns, IOT mapping tables, or tables with on-commit or ROWID-based materialized views

   ☒ **C, D,** and **E** are wrong. In addition to IOTs and tables with fast-refreshable materialized views, you can shrink partitioned tables, sub-partitioned tables, and of course heap-based tables (the default table type).

Understand the Database Resource Manager

7. ☑ **C.** Users can belong to more than one consumer group. Resource Manager uses the plan directive mapping the most restrictive consumer group within the plan.

   ☒ **A** is wrong because only one resource plan can be active at any given time. **B** is wrong because OTHER_GROUPS must be specified at the top level of a plan to allocate resources for any user that is not a member of other consumer groups in the plan. **D** is wrong because users can belong to more than one consumer group.

Create and Use Database Resource Manager Components

8. ☑ **A and E.** The Database Resource Manager cannot allocate or control network bandwidth or temporary tablespace usage.

   ☒ **B, C,** and **D** are all resources under the control of Resource Manager.

9. ☑ **D.** You can add OTHER_GROUPS to the resource plan, and immediately retry the validation step.

   ☒ **A** is wrong because you do not need to create a new pending area nor do you have to add OTHER_GROUPS first. **B** is wrong because OTHER_GROUPS, as well as any consumer group, can belong to any plan or sub-plan. **C** is wrong because you cannot drop OTHER_GROUPS; it is required for all plans whose groups do not cover all users in the database.

10. ☑ **B.** Until the plan has been successfully validated and submitted, the STATUS column contains the value PENDING.

    ☒ **A, C,** and **D** are incorrect. The only valid values for the STATUS column are NULL and PENDING.

13
Configuring Database Diagnostics

W hen you have to deal with database errors or even a database that is completely down, you don't want to spend extra time documenting one or more database error conditions for Oracle Support. This chapter first gives you a brief overview of how Oracle reports problems with the database, and how it categorizes errors into problems and incidents.

Next, this chapter will step through a few examples of packaging all the necessary information using Support Workbench via the EM interface and sending it to Oracle Support as a service request. The Service Request can be submitted with a few clicks, but it can be customized before submittal either to remove confidential or proprietary information, or to add extra data or information to help Oracle Support solve the issue.

In addition, the Health Monitor framework provides both proactive and reactive tools to deal with database errors. The DBA can run a proactive health check manually using EM or PL/SQL packages. In contrast, the Health Monitor can run diagnostic checks in response to critical database errors.

Finally, the chapter will switch from reporting, managing, and submitting service requests for database problems and incidents, to recovering individual blocks after you have identified the problem. RMAN supports detection and recovery of individual blocks using the DB_BLOCK_CHECKING initialization parameter and the RMAN RECOVER . . . BLOCK command. RMAN also makes it easy to identify failures and implement repairs using the Data Recovery Advisor.

CERTIFICATION OBJECTIVE 13.01

Set Up Automatic Diagnostic Repository

The key to the Automatic Diagnostic Repository (ADR) is the first word: automatic. ADR is an always-on facility that captures errors in trace and dump files the first and any successive times they occur. Thus the "diagnostic" part of the Oracle feature name. The third part, "repository," is a location on disk that stores the diagnostic information on disk and comes with a tool that makes it easy to query the repository even when the database is unavailable.

The following sections provide more details about the structure of the repository, how to retrieve information from the repository, and how to find the diagnostic information you're looking for in the repository using initialization parameters and data dictionary views. In addition, you'll see how to easily and quickly package the diagnostic information from the ADR and send it to Oracle support for problem resolution.

Understanding the ADR

The ADR is a file-based repository of diagnostic and other non-critical information for all products in your environment. Each database instance and Automatic Storage Management (ASM) instance has its own directory structure called an *ADR home* within a top-level directory known as the *ADR base*. In a Real Application Cluster (RAC) environment, each instance has its own subdirectory, which not only makes it easy to view diagnostics for an individual instance, but also makes it easy for the diagnostic tools to analyze data across instances for cluster-wide problems.

The ADR base directory is also known as the ADR root directory. The location for the ADR base is set depending on the values of initialization parameters and environment variables. If the initialization parameter DIAGNOSTIC_DEST is set, the ADR base directory is set to this value, and all other file locations are set relative to this location. If DIAGNOSTIC_DEST is not set, then DIAGNOSTIC_DEST is set to the environment variable ORACLE_BASE. If ORACLE_BASE is not set, DIAGNOSTIC_DEST is set to the value $ORACLE_HOME/log. Figure 13-1 shows the ADR directory structure for the DW database.

For the database in Figure 13-1, the initialization parameter DIAGNOSTIC_DEST is not set, so Oracle sets DIAGNOSTIC_DEST to the value of the environment variable ORACLE_BASE, which in this case is /u01/app/oracle:

```
[oracle@dw ~]$ echo $ORACLE_BASE
/u01/app/oracle
[oracle@dw ~]$ echo $ORACLE_HOME
/u01/app/oracle/product/11.1.0/db_1
[oracle@dw ~]$
```

If ORACLE_BASE were not set, the location for the ADR would be /u01/app/oracle/product/11.1.0/db_1/log.

You can retrieve the values for each diagnostic directory using the dynamic performance view V$DIAG_INFO, as in this example:

```
SQL> select * from v$diag_info;

INST_ID NAME                             VALUE
------- ------------------------------   ----------------------------------------
      1 Diag Enabled                     TRUE
      1 ADR Base                         /u01/app/oracle
      1 ADR Home                         /u01/app/oracle/diag/rdbms/dw/dw
      1 Diag Trace                       /u01/app/oracle/diag/rdbms/dw/dw/trace
```

```
1 Diag Alert              /u01/app/oracle/diag/rdbms/dw/dw/alert
1 Diag Incident           /u01/app/oracle/diag/rdbms/dw/dw/incident
1 Diag Cdump              /u01/app/oracle/diag/rdbms/dw/dw/cdump
1 Health Monitor          /u01/app/oracle/diag/rdbms/dw/dw/hm
1 Default Trace File      /u01/app/oracle/diag/rdbms/dw/dw/trace/
                          dw_ora_12771.trc
1 Active Problem Count     0
1 Active Incident Count    0

11 rows selected.

SQL>
```

FIGURE 13-1

ADR directory
structure for the
DW database

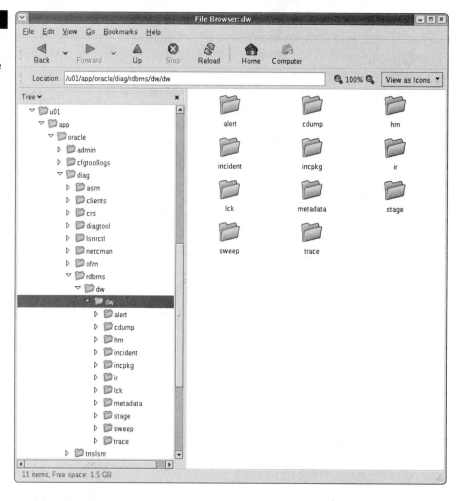

TABLE 13-1	Diagnostic Data Type	Location Within the ADR
ADR Diagnostic Information Directory Locations	Foreground process trace files	`ADR_HOME/trace`
	Background process trace files	`ADR_HOME/trace`
	Alert log	`ADR_HOME/alert` (XML format) `ADR_HOME/trace` (plaintext format)
	Core dumps	`ADR_HOME/cdump`
	Incident dumps	`ADR_HOME/incident/incdir_n`

Note the column `INST_ID`. In a RAC environment, this value differentiates the value of each directory by node. For example, if `DW` were the cluster name, and the cluster contained three instances `DW1`, `DW2`, and `DW3`, the value for the second instance's diagnostic trace directory would be as follows:

```
INST_ID NAME                            VALUE
-------- ------------------------------- ----------------------------------------
      2 Diag Trace                      /u01/app/oracle/diag/rdbms/dw/dw2/trace
```

Compared to previous releases of Oracle, the diagnostic information is more partitioned. In other words, all non-incident traces are stored in the `trace` subdirectory, all core dumps are in the `cdump` directory, and all incident dumps are stored as individual directories within the `incident` subdirectory. Table 13-1 show the ADR location for each type of diagnostic data.

Note the differentiation between trace and dump files. Trace files contain continuous output to diagnose a problem with a running process. A dump file is a one-time diagnostic output file resulting from an incident. Similarly, a core dump is a one-time platform-specific binary memory dump. Note also that there is no initialization parameter or environment variable named `ADR_HOME`. You can determine the value of `ADR_HOME` from the row in `V$DIAG_INFO` containing the name `ADR Home`:

```
      1 ADR Home                        /u01/app/oracle/diag/rdbms/dw/dw
```

Using the ADRCI Tool

The ADR Command Interpreter (ADRCI) tool makes it easy to query the contents of the ADR. You can use the tool in command mode, or create scripts to run in batch mode. You can use ADRCI even when the database is down—remember that the ADR is completely file-system based. In addition to querying the contents of the ADR with ADRCI, you can also package incident and problem information into a compressed ZIP file that you can send to Oracle support.

Note that ADRCI does not require a login or any other authorization. The contents of the ADR are protected only by operating system permissions on the directory containing the ADR file structures. For a default installation of Oracle Database 11g, this means that the ADR has the same permissions as the ORACLE_BASE directory and its subdirectories. You can alter the permissions further if you wish, but you must make sure that the user owning the Oracle processes (usually the oracle user) has full read-write access to the ADR.

When you start ADRCI, you see the current ADR base directory. Type help for a list of commands:

```
[oracle@dw ~]$ adrci

ADRCI: Release 11.1.0.6.0 - Beta on Sat Oct 11 09:45:57 2008
Copyright (c) 1982, 2007, Oracle.  All rights reserved.
ADR base = "/u01/app/oracle"
adrci> help
 HELP [topic]
    Available Topics:
        CREATE REPORT
        ECHO
        EXIT
        HELP
        HOST
        IPS
        PURGE
        RUN
        SET BASE
        SET BROWSER
        SET CONTROL
        SET ECHO
        SET EDITOR
        SET HOMES | HOME | HOMEPATH
        SET TERMOUT
        SHOW ALERT
        SHOW BASE
        SHOW CONTROL
        SHOW HM_RUN
        SHOW HOMES | HOME | HOMEPATH
        SHOW INCDIR
        SHOW INCIDENT
        SHOW PROBLEM
        SHOW REPORT
        SHOW TRACEFILE
        SPOOL
```

```
There are other commands intended to be used directly by Oracle, type
"help extended" to see the list
adrci>
```

Even when there are no incidents or problems to view, you can perform more mundane tasks such as viewing the alert log from ADRCI:

```
adrci> show alert

Choose the alert log from the following homes to view:

1: diag/rdbms/hr/hr
2: diag/rdbms/hrtest/hrtest
3: diag/rdbms/hrtest2/hrtest2
4: diag/rdbms/tspitr_hr_yith/yith
5: diag/rdbms/tspitr_hr_vdym/vdym
6: diag/asm/+asm/+ASM
7: diag/clients/user_oracle/host_512396801_11
8: diag/clients/user_unknown/host_411310321_11
9: diag/tnslsnr/srv04/listener
Q: to quit
Please select option: 1

2008-07-18 16:13:12.361000 -05:00
Starting ORACLE instance (normal)
LICENSE_MAX_SESSION = 0
LICENSE_SESSIONS_WARNING = 0
Shared memory segment for instance monitoring created
Picked latch-free SCN scheme 2
Using LOG_ARCHIVE_DEST_1 parameter default value as
/u01/app/oracle/product/11.1.0/db_1/dbs/arch
Using LOG_ARCHIVE_DEST_10 parameter default value as
USE_DB_RECOVERY_FILE_DEST
Autotune of undo retention is turned on.
IMODE=BR
ILAT =18
LICENSE_MAX_USERS = 0
SYS auditing is disabled
Starting up ORACLE RDBMS Version: 11.1.0.6.0.
. . .
Please select option: q
adrci>
```

Notice that the ADRCI tool tracks all ADR home directories within the ADR root directory. Therefore, you must select which database, ASM, or listener directory you want to view with ADRCI.

FIGURE 13-2

Viewing Alert Log
Contents from
EM

Of course, you can perform the same task from EM. From the bottom of the EM home page, click the Alert Log Contents link. Then select the number of lines at the end of the alert log that you want to see, and click Go. You'll see the page shown in Figure 13-2.

CERTIFICATION OBJECTIVE 13.02

Using Support Workbench

The Support Workbench is accessible through the EM interface, which walks you through all aspects of problem detection, documentation, and resolution. The tools available through the Support Workbench enable you to view details on problems and incidents, run health checks on your database (either reactively or proactively), generate additional diagnostic data for service requests, and run advisors to help you resolve the problem or incident. Support Workbench also facilitates the packaging of all necessary diagnostic and supporting data for submittal to Oracle support using the MetaLink service. Once the service request has been submitted, you can track its status through the resolution cycle and close it when your problem is resolved.

The following sections first explain the distinction among the various events that occur in your database: (1) alerts, (2) problems, and (3) incidents. Next, an overview of how you submit a service request using the quick packaging method will be given. While you are working with Oracle support on the problem, you can run your own health checks and other advisors to help solve the problem. Finally, some advanced packaging options that permit you to add extra information to your service request, such as sample SQL statements and table data, to help Oracle support solve your problem will be described. Conversely, you can edit the package before you submit it to Oracle support to remove proprietary or confidential information.

Understanding Alerts, Problems, and Incidents

Although the alert log (either text format or XML format) contains all alerts for the instance, you see the alerts at the warning and critical levels on the EM home page. The dreaded ORA-00600 error messages are noted on the EM home page. In the next example, you try using a feature that worked in previous versions of Oracle Database but which causes an ORA-00600 message in Oracle Database 11g Release 1:

```
SQL> alter user hr identified by values '';
alter user hr identified by values ''
*
ERROR at line 1:
ORA-00600: internal error code, arguments: [kzsviver:1],
        [], [], [], [], [], [], []
SQL>
```

The alert log shows the error as well:

```
Sat Oct 11 21:08:51 2008
Errors in file /u01/app/oracle/diag/rdbms/hr/hr/trace/hr_ora_
11217.trc
    (incident=80705):
ORA-00600: internal error code, arguments: [kzsviver:1],
        [], [], [], [], [], [], []
Incident details in:
/u01/app/oracle/diag/rdbms/hr/hr/incident/incdir_80705
        /hr_ora_11217_i80705.trc
Sat Oct 11 21:10:16 2008
Trace dumping is performing id=[cdmp_20081011211016]
Sat Oct 11 21:10:17 2008
Sweep Incident[80705]: completed
```

In Figure 13-3, you see both of these types of alerts near the bottom of the page, including the ORA-00600 error that you inadvertently triggered!

A *problem*, defined by the Support Workbench framework, is a critical error in the database, such as the internal error ORA-00600 or some other serious event such as running out of memory in the shared pool or an operating system exception. An *incident* is a single occurrence of a problem. Each problem has a *problem key*, which is a text string that contains the error code and optionally other problem characteristics. A problem may have one or many incidents. Each incident is identified by a numeric incident ID and is stored in its own subdirectory of the ADR (ADR_HOME/incident/incdir_n). When an incident occurs, the database performs the following steps:

1. Adds an entry to the alert log (both text and XML-based).

2. Sends an incident alert to EM.

3. Sends an alert via e-mail to administrator(s) (if configured).

4. Gathers trace files and other incident information.

FIGURE 13-3

Viewing error alerts in EM

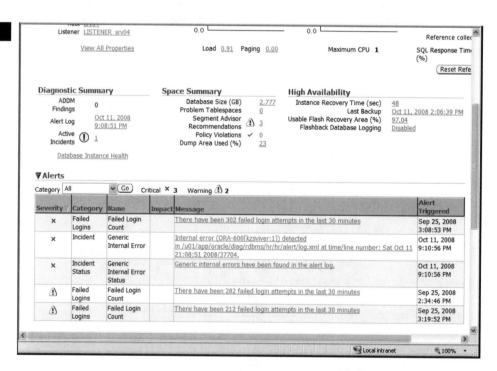

5. Tags all incident information with the incident ID.

6. Creates an incident directory under ADR_HOME for the incident and stores incident information and trace files in the directory.

Managing Service Requests

After Oracle automatically collects incident information and notifies you, you will use Support Workbench as an end-to-end tool to manage the problem. The typical steps you use in Support Workbench are as follows:

1. View critical errors on the EM home page (or via an e-mail message).

2. View the problem details.

3. Gather additional diagnostics and health checks.

4. Create an Oracle Service Request (SR).

5. Package necessary information and send to Oracle support.

6. Track the SR and implement repairs suggested by Oracle and the advisor framework tools.

7. Close the incident(s).

The following sections give you an overview of creating an SR, implementing repairs, and optionally including additional information in the SR using custom packaging.

Creating and Tracking an SR

When an ORA-00600 or any other, less serious error has occurred, you can package the incident details and send them to Oracle support. On the page shown in Figure 13-3, click the message link of the incident, and then click View Problem Details. You see the page in Figure 13-4.

From this page, you can perform a number of actions. You can create a MetaLink service request, research the MetaLink knowledge base, or run additional checkers and diagnostics. You can quickly create a package of all incident information by clicking the Quick Package link. On the page shown in Figure 13-5, you start the process of creating a new package and submitting an SR right after package creation. You supply your MetaLink credentials and Customer Service Identifier (CSI).

When you click Next, EM creates the package. You see the page in Figure 13-6.

On the next page, shown in Figure 13-7, you can review the manifest that Oracle creates for the incident. It shows the summary of the problem and the location of the file containing the manifest.

FIGURE 13-4

Viewing problem
details

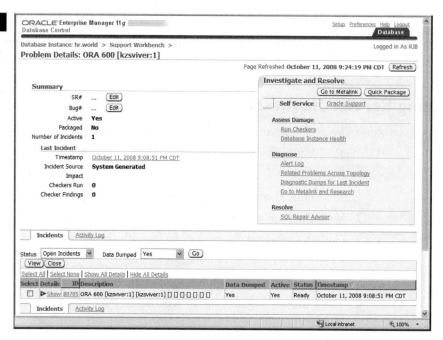

FIGURE 13-5

Quick packaging
an incident: step 1

FIGURE 13-6

Quick packaging
an incident: step 2

FIGURE 13-7

Quick packaging
an incident: step 3

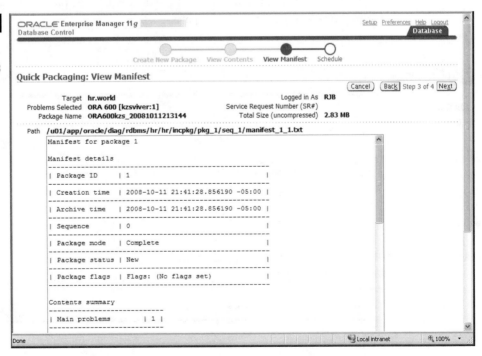

The final step of the quick packaging process, shown in Figure 13-8, gives you the option to submit the package immediately or at a later time. Typically, you will submit the service request right away, but you may want to submit it later if you think you can solve the problem yourself before users start complaining!

After the package has been submitted to Oracle support, you can view the status of the incident resolution on the Problem Details page shown in Figure 13-4.

Implementing Repairs

On the Problem Details page, you can also attempt to use an Oracle Advisor to implement repairs. The advisor available on the page shown in Figure 13-4 is the SQL Repair Advisor. Also available in your toolbox is the Data Recovery Advisor. Due to the nature of the problem in Figure 13-4, Support Workbench has determined that the problem is with a SQL statement, not a data corruption problem, and therefore has not recommended the Data Recovery Advisor this time. Figure 13-9 shows the Incident Analysis page where you can submit the SQL Repair Advisor job.

After the SQL Repair Advisor runs, you can immediately view the results of the job from Advisor Central or return to the database home page and click the Advisor Central link at the bottom of the page.

FIGURE 13-8

Quick packaging
an incident: step 4

FIGURE 13-9

Using SQL Repair Advisor to analyze a failed SQL statement

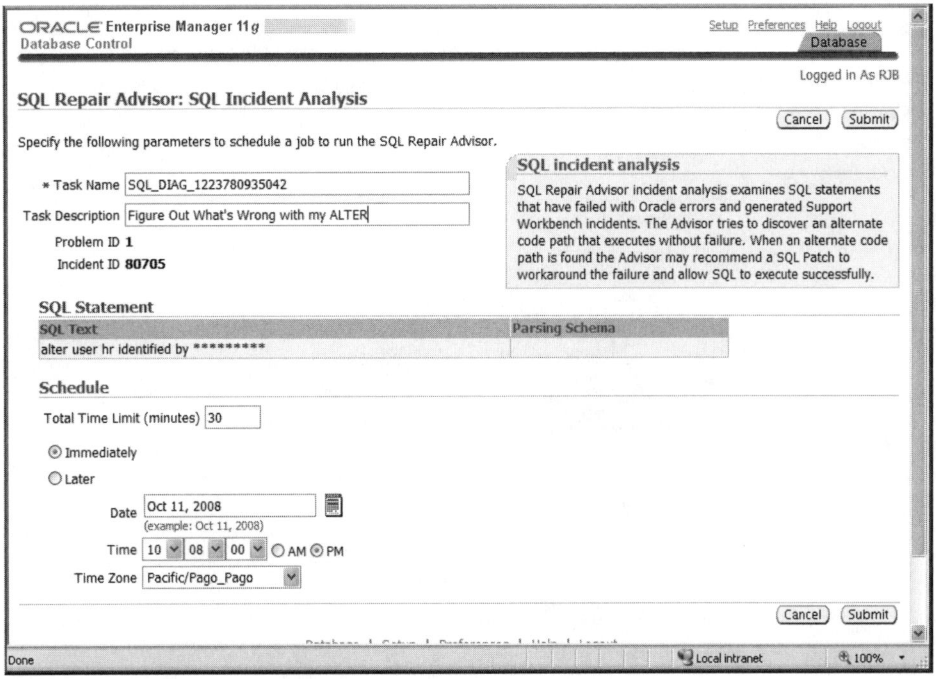

Using Custom Packaging

Custom packaging gives you more flexibility and more control over the contents of an incident package. Unlike quick packaging, custom packaging enables you to

- Add or remove problems or incidents from the package.
- Add, edit, or remove trace files from the package.
- Add or remove external files (Word documents, export dumps, and so on).
- Add other diagnostic information such as SQL test cases.
- Remove sensitive information or other unnecessary information to reduce the size of the package.

To initiate custom packaging, start from the Support Workbench home page shown in Figure 13-10, select the incident(s) you want to package, and then click Package.

As you can see in Figure 13-11, you can create an entirely new package for this incident or even start with an existing package. In the example in Figure 13-11, you selected the package you created during quick packaging when you realized that you needed to add additional documentation and trace files to the incident package before sending it to Oracle support.

FIGURE 13-10

Initiating custom
packaging from
the Support
Workbench

FIGURE 13-11

Using an existing
package for
custom packaging

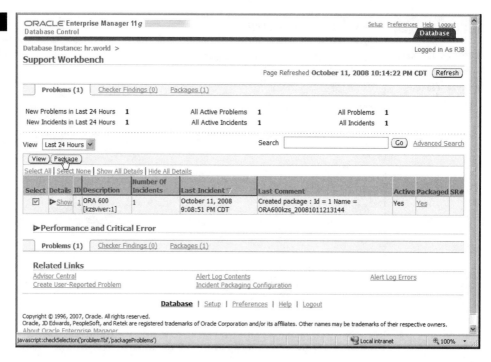

On the page shown in Figure 13-12, you can see the types of information you can add or remove from the package, such as additional external files, other problems, or other dumps. Once the package is completed, you can generate the new upload file and submit it to Oracle support.

Using the Health Monitor

You can use the Oracle Health Monitor framework to proactively or reactively assess the health of your database. Health Monitor checks the status of various database components, including the following:

- Datafiles
- Memory
- Transaction integrity
- Metadata
- Process usage

FIGURE 13-12
Adding or removing information from a custom package

You can run health checks using EM via the Support Workbench, or you can manually run a health check using the DBMS_HM PL/SQL package. Some checks can be run only when the database is open. Other checks are available when the instance is running but the database is in NOMOUNT mode. You can list the checks available and whether they are available in offline or online mode by querying the dynamic performance view V$HM_CHECK:

```
SQL> select id, name, offline_capable from v$hm_check;

        ID NAME                                            OFFLINE_CAPABLE
---------- ----------------------------------------------- ----------------
         0                                                 N
         1 HM Test Check                                   Y
         2 DB Structure Integrity Check                    Y
         3 Data Block Integrity Check                      Y
         4 Redo Integrity Check                            Y
         5 Logical Block Check                             N
        10 Transaction Integrity Check                     N
        11 Undo Segment Integrity Check                    N
        12 All Control Files Check                         Y
        13 CF Member Check                                 Y
        14 All Datafiles Check                             Y
        15 Single Datafile Check                           Y
        16 Log Group Check                                 Y
        17 Log Group Member Check                          Y
        18 Archived Log Check                              Y
        19 Redo Revalidation Check                         Y
        20 IO Revalidation Check                           Y
        21 Block IO Revalidation Check                     Y
        22 Txn Revalidation Check                          N
        23 Failure Simulation Check                        Y
        24 Dictionary Integrity Check                      N

21 rows selected.

SQL>
```

You can view the results of a health check from EM, the ADRCI tool discussed earlier in this chapter, the DBMS_HM package, or the dynamic performance view V$HM_RUN.

From the EM Support Workbench page, click the Run Checkers link to run additional diagnostics. On the page shown in Figure 13-13, you see the health checks recommended for the selected incident. Even if no specific checkers are recommended, you can still run one of the available checkers to, for instance, check the integrity of the redo log stream and the core dictionary objects.

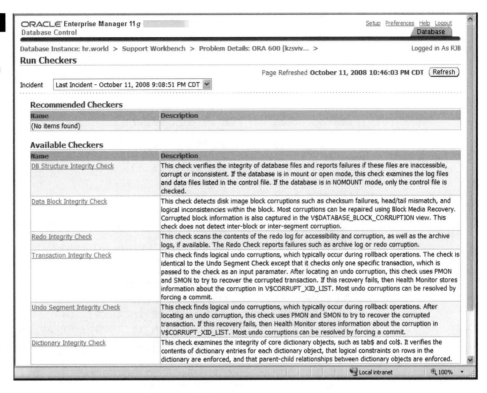

FIGURE 13-13

Run Checkers recommendation page

You can view the results of health checks from the ADRCI tool with the `show hm_run` command. In the following examples, you retrieve the results of a health monitor run first in text format, then you generate a health monitor report in XML format:

```
adrci> show hm_run -p "run_id=36961"

************************************************************
HM RUN RECORD 1607
************************************************************


        RUN_ID                  36961
        RUN_NAME                HM_RUN_36961
        CHECK_NAME              DB Structure Integrity Check
        NAME_ID                 2
        MODE                    2
        START_TIME              2008-09-25 09:37:20.403101 -05:00
        RESUME_TIME             <NULL>
        END_TIME                2008-09-25 09:37:20.658541 -05:00
        MODIFIED_TIME           2008-09-25 09:37:20.658541 -05:00
        TIMEOUT                 0
```

```
FLAGS                    0
STATUS                   5
SRC_INCIDENT_ID          0
NUM_INCIDENTS            0
ERR_NUMBER              0
REPORT_FILE             <NULL>

adrci> create report hm_run hm_run_36961

adrci> show report hm_run hm_run_36961

<?xml version="1.0" encoding="US-ASCII"?>
<HM-REPORT REPORT_ID="HM_RUN_36961">
    <TITLE>HM Report: HM_RUN_36961</TITLE>
    <RUN_INFO>
        <CHECK_NAME>DB Structure Integrity Check</CHECK_NAME>
        <RUN_ID>36961</RUN_ID>
        <RUN_NAME>HM_RUN_36961</RUN_NAME>
        <RUN_MODE>REACTIVE</RUN_MODE>
        <RUN_STATUS>COMPLETED</RUN_STATUS>
        <RUN_ERROR_NUM>0</RUN_ERROR_NUM>
        <SOURCE_INCIDENT_ID>0</SOURCE_INCIDENT_ID>
        <NUM_INCIDENTS_CREATED>0</NUM_INCIDENTS_CREATED>
        <RUN_START_TIME>2008-09-25 09:37:20.403101 -05:00</RUN_START_
TIME>
        <RUN_END_TIME>2008-09-25 09:37:20.658541 -05:00</RUN_END_TIME>
    </RUN_INFO>
    <RUN_PARAMETERS/>
    <RUN-FINDINGS/>
</HM-REPORT>
adrci>
```

CERTIFICATION OBJECTIVE 13.03

Perform Block Media Recovery

Many of the errors you will encounter will be related to bad blocks in your database datafiles, either because of media failures, server memory errors, or logical corruption caused by Oracle errors. Once you've identified these problems using the diagnostic methods provided earlier in this chapter, you can use the tools in the following sections to fix the problems.

As with nearly every Oracle feature, you can adjust the level of control and monitoring that Oracle performs; data block checking is no exception. Regardless of the settings you'll learn about shortly, Oracle always performs the following checks on a data block when it is read or written to a datafile:

- Block version (matches the version of the database)
- Data block address (DBA) in the cache is the same as the DBA value in the block buffer
- Block checksum is correct

You can repair a corrupt block by either recovering the block, dropping the object containing the bad block, or both. The following sections tell you more about block corruption, how to control the amount of overhead Oracle will use to ensure the integrity of blocks, and how to fix a corrupted block.

Understanding Block Corruption

When Oracle detects a corrupted block, it registers an ORA-01578 error in the alert log and on the EM home page. Included in the error message are the absolute file number and block number of the bad block. In addition, the session reading or writing the bad block sees the same error message. Here is an example of a block corruption error message:

```
ORA-01578: ORACLE data block corrupted (file # 6, block # 403)
ORA-01110: data file 6: '/u09/oradata/ord/oe_trans01.dbf'
```

Most often, corruption is caused by operating system or disk hardware failures such as faulty I/O hardware or firmware, operating system caching problems, memory or paging problems, or errors caused by disk repair utilities.

Using the DB_BLOCK_CHECKING Parameter

The initialization parameter DB_BLOCK_CHECKING controls how thoroughly Oracle checks the integrity of every data block that is read or written. The level of checking you enable depends on the level of failure tolerable in your environment (which is usually very low!) balanced against the overhead required to perform the continuous block checks. The possible values for DB_BLOCK_CHECKING are as follows:

- **OFF or FALSE**   No block checking is performed.
- **LOW**   Basic block checks are performed after blocks are changed in memory or read from disk, including inter-instance block transfers in RAC environments.

- ■ **MEDIUM** Includes all LOW checks plus block checking for all non-IOT (index-organized table) blocks.
- ■ **FULL or TRUE** Includes all LOW and MEDIUM checks plus checks for index blocks.

If you can tolerate the performance overhead, Oracle recommends using FULL. The default value is OFF, even though FULL block checking for the SYSTEM tablespace is always enabled. The overhead for block checking ranges from 1 percent to 10 percent, but is closer to 10 percent in an OLTP environment.

Using Block Media Recovery

If you discover only a small handful of blocks to recover in a database from the aforementioned health checks or results discovered in the alert log, RMAN can perform *block media recovery* rather than a full datafile recovery. Block media recovery minimizes redo log application time, and drastically reduces the amount of I/O required to recover only the block or blocks in question. While block media recovery is in progress, the affected datafiles can remain online and available to users.

Block media recovery is only available from within the RMAN application.

In addition to the block verification performed by Oracle as defined by the DB_BLOCK_CHECKING initialization parameter, an RMAN BACKUP or BACKUP VALIDATE command can add corrupted blocks to the dynamic performance view V$DATABASE_BLOCK_CORRUPTION. In addition, the SQL commands ANALYZE TABLE and ANALYZE INDEX can uncover corrupted blocks.

You'll need to know the advantages and disadvantages of block media recovery; as you might expect, there are many more advantages than disadvantages. In addition to touting the benefits of RMAN block media recovery, the prerequisites for block media recovery as well as provide some real-world examples will be defined.

Advantages of Block Media Recovery

Recovering one or a small number of blocks using RMAN has some obvious and some not-so-obvious advantages. First, recovering one block using a recent backup and archived and online redo log files will almost certainly take much less time than restoring and recovering one or more datafiles. In addition, during block media recovery, the entire datafile remains online and available during the recovery process; only the blocks being recovered are unavailable. Therefore, only one table, index, or other database object remains unavailable during block media recovery.

When you use the RMAN RECOVER . . . BLOCK command, RMAN first searches the flashback logs for a good copy of the corrupted block (if Flashback Database is enabled). Otherwise, RMAN uses the latest level 0 or full backup, restores the bad blocks, and performs media recovery on the bad blocks using the redo stream. Note that RMAN cannot use incremental level 1 backups for block media recovery.

You can use the dynamic performance view V$DATABASE_BLOCK_CORRUPTION to view the bad blocks in the database. This view contains blocks that are both physically and logically corrupted. Here are the tools or commands that can populate this view when they find bad blocks:

- RMAN backup commands
- ANALYZE
- dbv operating system utility
- SQL queries that try to access a corrupted block

Prerequisites for Using Block Recovery

Before you can use block media recovery, your database must fulfill a few prerequisites. First, the target database must be in ARCHIVELOG mode. Unless your database is for testing or is a read-only database, your database should be in ARCHIVELOG mode for maximum recoverability anyway!

Second, the backups of datafiles with bad blocks must be full backups or level 0 incremental backups. RMAN cannot use level 1 incremental backups for block recovery. Thus, you must have all archived redo log files since the last full backup or level 0 incremental backup.

Alternatively, you can use flashback logs in the flash recovery area for uncorrupt versions of bad blocks. Therefore, you must have Flashback Database enabled. If an uncorrupt version of a bad block is available in the flash recovery area, RMAN will use that block and perform media recovery on the block using archived and online redo log files. Unless the number of bad blocks is large, recovering a block from the flashback logs will certainly be faster than starting with a level 0 incremental or full backup.

Using the **RMAN RECOVER . . . BLOCK** Command

You can use the RMAN RECOVER . . . BLOCK command in response to an alert or other notification of a bad block. Typically, block corruption is reported in the following locations:

- Output from the RMAN LIST FAILURE, VALIDATE, or BACKUP . . . VALIDATE commands
- The V$DATABASE_BLOCK_CORRUPTION dynamic performance view

- Error messages during a SQL*Plus or other client session
- The alert log or user trace files
- Results from the SQL commands ANALYZE TABLE or ANALYZE INDEX
- Results from the DBVERIFY command-line utility (dbv)

To recover one or more data blocks, RMAN must know the datafile number and block number within the datafile. As mentioned previously, this information is available in a user trace file, as in the following example:

```
ORA-01578: ORACLE data block corrupted (file # 6, block # 403)
ORA-01110: data file 6: '/u09/oradata/ord/oe_trans01.dbf'
```

In addition, the block will appear in the view V$DATABASE_BLOCK_CORRUPTION; the columns FILE# and BLOCK# provide the information needed to execute the RECOVER command. The column CORRUPTION_TYPE identifies the type of corruption in the block, such as FRACTURED, CHECKSUM, or CORRUPT. Fixing the block is easily accomplished in RMAN:

```
RMAN> recover datafile 6 block 403;

Starting recover at 04-SEP-07
using channel ORA_DISK_1

starting media recovery
media recovery complete, elapsed time: 00:00:01

Finished recover at 04-SEP-07

RMAN>
```

A corrupted block must be restored completely. In other words, all redo operations up to the latest SCN against the data block must be applied before the block can be considered usable again.

If all bad blocks are recorded in V$DATABASE_BLOCK_CORRUPTION, you can easily recover all of them at once. Using the following command, RMAN will recover all physically corrupted blocks in V$DATABASE_BLOCK_CORRUPTION:

```
RMAN> recover corruption list;
```

After RMAN recovers the blocks, they are removed from V$DATABASE_BLOCK_ CORRUPTION.

Using the Data Recovery Advisor

The Data Recovery Advisor is part of the Oracle advisor framework and automatically gathers information about a failure when an error is encountered. If you run the Data Recovery Advisor proactively, you are often able to detect and repair a failure before a user query or backup operation detects it. The Date Recovery Advisor can detect relatively small errors such as corrupted blocks. At the other end of the spectrum, it will detect errors that would otherwise prevent successful startup of the database, such as missing online redo log files. Your database may continue running for a short amount of time without online redo log files, but it will not start the next time you shut down and restart. Data Recovery Advisor will catch this error proactively.

Identifying Failures

As with most advisors and Oracle features, you can use either EM or command-line tools to run the Data Recovery Advisor, show the errors, and repair the failures. From the EM home page, click the Advisor Central link at the bottom of the page. From the Advisor Central page, click the Data Recovery Advisor link. If there are outstanding errors, you will see them on this page. The errors are recorded reactively from error events in the database, or as a result of proactively running a health check. Figure 13-14 shows a current data failure in the HR database.

FIGURE 13-14 Viewing data failures using EM

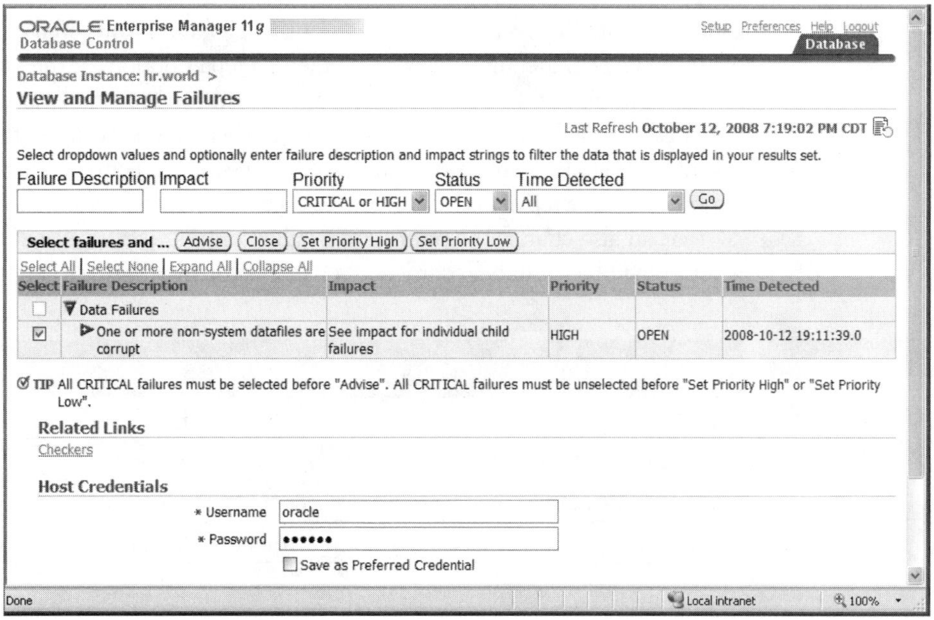

Once the Data Recovery Advisor has identified a failure, you can review the details of the failure using the EM or RMAN interface. From RMAN, you can use the LIST FAILURE, ADVISE FAILURE, REPAIR FAILURE, and CHANGE FAILURE commands. Table 13-2 summarizes the purpose of these commands.

The LIST FAILURE command has a number of options, depending on what types of errors you want to see:

- *Failure#*   List an individual failure's details (by failure number).
- **ALL**   List all failures.
- **CRITICAL**   List failures that make the database unavailable.
- **HIGH**   List serious failures that make parts of the database unavailable, such as a missing datafile.
- **LOW**   List intermittent or lower-priority failures that can wait until more serious problems are fixed. For example, this can include corrupted blocks in infrequently used tablespaces.
- **CLOSED**   List only closed failures.

For example, LIST FAILURE 2097 will list the details for a failure with an identifier of 2097. Also, LIST FAILURE ALL lists all open failures of any priority.

Implementing Repairs

Once the Data Recovery Advisor has identified a failure, you can use the RMAN ADVISE FAILURE command to recommend a repair option for the specified failure. RMAN will suggest a repair and create a script with the recommended repair. If the repair is acceptable (in terms of downtime or other factors), you can then run the REPAIR FAILURE (within the same RMAN session) to perform the recommended action. After the repair action completes successfully, the failure is automatically closed.

You can also change the priority of a failure using CHANGE FAILURE. For example, a corrupted block will be recorded as a HIGH failure, but if it is in an infrequently used

TABLE 13-2	RMAN Command	Description
RMAN Failure Advisory and Repair Commands	LIST FAILURE	List failures recorded by the Data Recovery Advisor
	ADVISE FAILURE	Show recommended repair option
	REPAIR FAILURE	Repair and close failure using RMAN's recommendations
	CHANGE FAILURE	Change the status or close a failure

tablespace, then you can change its priority to LOW so that you only see other more serious failures in the LIST FAILURE command. However, you cannot change the priority of a CRITICAL failure. You can only change the priority of a failure from HIGH to LOW, or vice versa. Here is how you can change the priority of failure number 307 from HIGH to LOW:

```
RMAN> change failure 307 priority low;
```

EXERCISE 13-1

Use Data Recovery Advisor

In this exercise, you'll simulate a serious data failure, query the failure, and repair the failure using RMAN.

1. Create a tablespace XPORT_DW in your database and create one or more tables within the tablespace.

2. At the operating system level, overwrite or delete the datafile for the XPORT_DW tablespace:

```
[oracle@srv04 ~]$ cat /var/log/messages > /u05/oradata/xport_
dw.dbf
```

3. Attempt to access tables within the tablespace from SQL*Plus:

```
SQL> select count(*) from order_hist_xport;
select count(*) from order_hist_xport
                     *
ERROR at line 1:
ORA-00376: file 10 cannot be read at this time
ORA-01110: data file 10: '/u05/oradata/xport_dw.dbf'

SQL>
```

4. From RMAN, query all open failures and list the details for the failures found:

```
RMAN> list failure;

List of Database Failures
=========================

Failure ID Priority Status    Time Detected Summary
---------- -------- --------- ------------- -------
1345       HIGH     OPEN      12-OCT-08     One or more non-system
                                            datafiles are corrupt
```

```
RMAN> list failure 1345 detail;

List of Database Failures
=========================

Failure ID Priority Status    Time Detected Summary
---------- -------- --------- ------------- -------
1345       HIGH     OPEN      12-OCT-08     One or more non-system
                                            datafiles are corrupt
   Impact: See impact for individual child failures
   List of child failures for parent failure ID 1345
   Failure ID Priority Status    Time Detected Summary
   ---------- -------- --------- ------------- -------
   37305      HIGH     OPEN      12-OCT-08     Datafile 10:
                                        '/u05/oradata/xport_dw.dbf' is corrupt
      Impact: Some objects in tablespace XPORT_DW might be unavailable

RMAN>
```

You can see similar information in EM. Navigate to the Data Recovery Advisor page shown in Figure 13-14, and expand the Failure description. Figure 13-15 shows the failure details

FIGURE 13-15

View and Manage Failures details

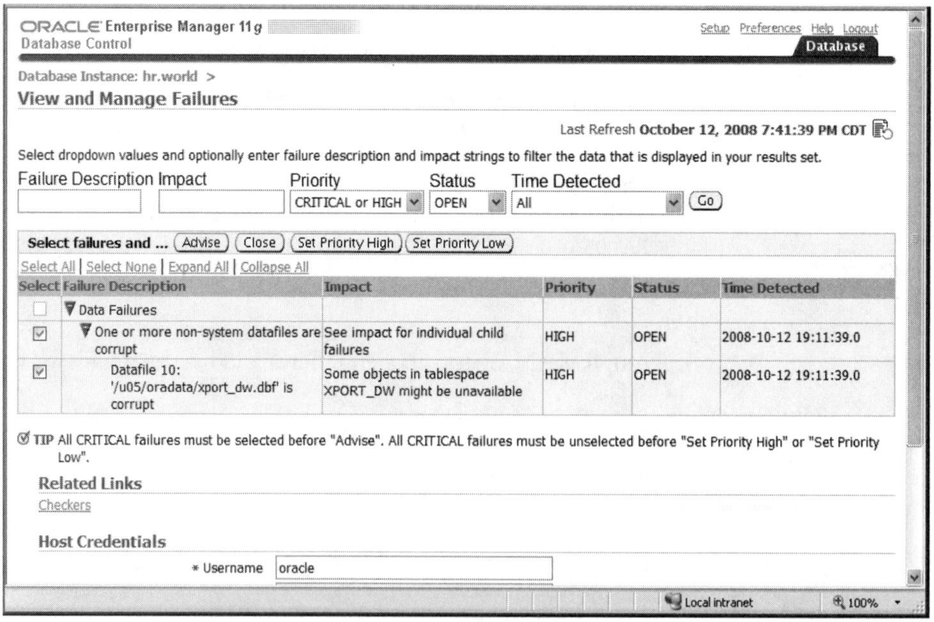

5. Return to RMAN and run the ADVISE FAILURE command:

```
RMAN> advise failure;

List of Database Failures
=========================

Failure ID Priority Status    Time Detected Summary
---------- -------- --------- ------------- -------
1345       HIGH     OPEN      12-OCT-08     One or more non-system
                                            datafiles are corrupt
   Impact: See impact for individual child failures
   List of child failures for parent failure ID 1345
   Failure ID Priority Status    Time Detected Summary
   ---------- -------- --------- ------------- -------
   37305      HIGH     OPEN      12-OCT-08     Datafile 10:
                                 '/u05/oradata/xport_dw.dbf' is corrupt
      Impact: Some objects in tablespace XPORT_DW might be unavailable

analyzing automatic repair options; this may take some time
allocated channel: ORA_DISK_1
channel ORA_DISK_1: SID=110 device type=DISK
analyzing automatic repair options complete

Mandatory Manual Actions
========================
no manual actions available

Optional Manual Actions
========================
no manual actions available

Automated Repair Options
========================
Option Repair Description
------ ------------------
1      Restore and recover datafile 10
   Strategy: The repair includes complete media recovery with no data loss
   Repair script: /u01/app/oracle/diag/rdbms/hr/hr/hm/reco_2543193427.hm

RMAN>
```

Clicking the Advise button shown on the page in Figure 13-15 gives you the same advice, as you might expect. Figure 13-16 shows the RMAN script that OEM will execute to recover from the media failure.

OEM Recovery
Advisor
recommended
actions

6. Run the tablespace recovery in RMAN using the recommendations in /u01/
   app/oracle/diag/rdbms/hr/hr/hm/reco_2543193427.hm, which not
   coincidentally are the same recommendations you see in Figure 13-16:

```
RMAN> sql 'alter database datafile 10 offline';

sql statement: alter database datafile 10 offline

RMAN> restore datafile 10;

Starting restore at 12-OCT-08
using channel ORA_DISK_1

channel ORA_DISK_1: starting datafile backup set restore
channel ORA_DISK_1: specifying datafile(s) to restore from backup set
channel ORA_DISK_1: restoring datafile 00010 to /u05/oradata/xport_dw.dbf
channel ORA_DISK_1: reading from backup piece /u01/oradata/bkup/7ajssndf_1_1
channel ORA_DISK_1: piece handle=/u01/oradata/bkup/7ajssndf_1_1
                    tag=TAG20081011T135702
channel ORA_DISK_1: restored backup piece 1
channel ORA_DISK_1: restore complete, elapsed time: 00:00:17
Finished restore at 12-OCT-08

RMAN> recover datafile 10;
```

```
Starting recover at 12-OCT-08
using channel ORA_DISK_1

starting media recovery

archived log for thread 1 with sequence 181 is already on disk as file
/u01/app/oracle/flash_recovery_area/HR/archivelog/2008_10_11/
               o1_mf_1_181_4h1xrq46_.arc
. . .
archived log file
name=/u01/app/oracle/flash_recovery_area/HR/archivelog/2008_10_12
                    /o1_mf_1_192_4h4sbpnp_.arc thread=1 sequence=192
media recovery complete, elapsed time: 00:00:46
Finished recover at 12-OCT-08

RMAN>
```

   7. Verify that the failure has been completed and closed:

```
RMAN> list failure;

no failures found that match specification

RMAN>
```

Data Recovery Advisor Views

There are several dynamic performance views you can use to retrieve information about failures detected by the Data Recovery Advisor:

- ■ **V$IR_FAILURE**   All failures, including closed failures.
- ■ **V$IR_MANUAL_CHECKLIST**   Listing of manual advice.
- ■ **V$IR_REPAIR**   Listing of repairs.
- ■ **V$IR_REPAIR_SET**   Cross reference of failure and advise identifier numbers.

For example, to retrieve the information for the failure in Exercise 13-1, query V$IR_FAILURE as follows:

```
SQL> select failure_id, parent_id, description, status
  2   from v$ir_failure
  3   where failure_id = 37305;
```

```
FAILURE_ID  PARENT_ID DESCRIPTION                     STATUS
----------  --------- ------------------------------- ------------
     37305       1345 Datafile 10: '/u05/oradata/xpo  CLOSED
                      rt_dw.dbf' is corrupt

SQL>
```

CERTIFICATION SUMMARY

This chapter started with an overview of the Automatic Diagnostic Repository (ADR). ADR is an always-on facility that captures errors in trace and dump files the first and any successive times that they occur. It makes your life easier when an error does occur because it happens without DBA intervention. In addition to facilities within EM, you can use the ADRCI command-line tool to query the contents of ADR when either the database or EM is down (or sometimes both!).

Once ADR has identified one or more problems, you can leverage the information in ADR by using the Support Workbench interface in EM. The tools available through the Support Workbench enable you to view details on problems and incidents, run health checks on your database (either reactively or proactively), generate additional diagnostic data for service requests, and run advisors to help you resolve the problem or incident. It also steps you through packaging all relevant information into a service request (SR) for Oracle support when you cannot solve the problem yourself. The Support Workbench makes it easy to analyze a problem and perform further analyses on the problem, potential causes, and solutions. You also learned the differences and similarities between alerts, problems, and incidents.

Next, one of the tools that is both proactive and reactive, which was the Health Monitor was discussed. The Checkers page in EM (available in several EM pages) lets you proactively run 24 different types of health checks, such as the Redo Integrity Check, Transaction Integrity Check, and Data Dictionary Integrity Check.

One of the more common problems you will encounter in your database is block corruption. You can control how thoroughly Oracle checks each data block as it is read and written using the DB_BLOCK_CHECKING initialization parameter. The trade-off is spending more CPU time on the front end to proactively detect problems versus relaxing the block checks and potentially discovering the problem later when you cannot afford the time to fix it.

The chapter closed with one of the RMAN-based repair tools, the Data Recovery Advisor. Using the RMAN command-line or EM interface, you can query all failures (open or closed) with a status of CRITICAL, HIGH, or LOW. Once a failure has been identified, you can use the advice from the Data Recovery Advisor (frequently in the form of an RMAN script) to repair the problem.

TWO-MINUTE DRILL

Set Up Automatic Diagnostic Repository

❑ ADR is an always-on facility that captures errors in trace and dump files the first and any subsequent times they occur.

❑ ADR uses a location on disk to store the diagnostic information and comes with a tool that makes it easy to query the repository even when the database is unavailable.

❑ Each database instance or Automatic Storage Management (ASM) instance has its own directory structure called an *ADR home* within a top-level directory known as the *ADR base*.

❑ The ADR base directory is also known as the ADR root directory.

❑ If the initialization parameter `DIAGNOSTIC_DEST` is set, the ADR base directory is set to this value and all other file locations are set relative to this location.

❑ If `DIAGNOSTIC_DEST` is not set, then `DIAGNOSTIC_DEST` is set to the environment variable `ORACLE_BASE`.

❑ If `ORACLE_BASE` is not set, `DIAGNOSTIC_DEST` is set to the value `$ORACLE_HOME/log`.

❑ The ADR diagnostic information is partitioned. All non-incident traces are stored in the `trace` subdirectory, all core dumps are stored in the `cdump` directory, and all incident dumps are stored as individual directories within the `incident` subdirectory.

❑ The ADR Command Interpreter (ADRCI) tool makes it easy to query the contents of the ADR. You can use ADRCI even when the database is down.

❑ ADRCI does not require a login or any other authorization. The contents of the ADR are protected only by operating system permissions on the directory containing the ADR file structures.

Using Support Workbench

❑ The Support Workbench, accessible through the EM interface, walks you through all aspects of problem detection, documentation, and resolution.

❑ Support Workbench also facilitates the packaging of all necessary diagnostic and supporting data for submittal to Oracle support using the MetaLink service.

❑ A *problem*, as defined by the Support Workbench framework, is a critical error in the database: for example, the internal error ORA-00600 or some other serious event such as running out of memory in the shared pool, or perhaps an operating system exception.

❑ An *incident* is a single occurrence of a problem.

❑ Each problem has a *problem key*, which is a text string that contains the error code and optionally other problem characteristics.

❑ Custom packaging within the Support Workbench framework gives you more flexibility and more control over the contents of an incident package.

❑ Health Monitor checks the status of various database components, including datafiles, memory, transaction integrity, metadata and process usage.

❑ You can run health checks using EM via the Support Workbench, or you can manually run a health check using the DBMS_HM PL/SQL package.

Perform Block Media Recovery

❑ When Oracle detects a corrupted block, it registers an ORA-01578 error in the alert log and on the EM home page.

❑ The initialization parameter DB_BLOCK_CHECKING controls how thoroughly Oracle checks the integrity of every data block that is read or written.

❑ If you discover only a small handful of blocks to recover in a database from the aforementioned health checks or results discovered in the alert log, then RMAN can perform *block media recovery* rather than a full datafile recovery.

❑ When you use the RMAN RECOVER . . . BLOCK command, RMAN first searches the flashback logs for a good copy of the corrupted block (if Flashback Database is enabled).

❑ You can use the dynamic performance view V$DATABASE_BLOCK_CORRUPTION to view the bad blocks in the database.

❑ The target database must be in ARCHIVELOG mode to use RMAN block recovery.

❑ Alternatively, you can use flashback logs in the flash recovery area for uncorrupt versions of bad blocks.

❑ The Data Recovery Advisor is part of the Oracle advisor framework and automatically gathers information about a failure when an error is encountered.

❑ Once the Data Recovery Advisor has identified a failure, you can review the details of the failure using the EM or RMAN interface.

❑ Once the Data Recovery Advisor has identified a failure, you can use the RMAN ADVISE FAILURE command to recommend a repair option for the specified failure.

SELF TEST

The following questions will help you measure your understanding of the material presented in this chapter. Read all the choices carefully, because there might be more than one correct answer. Choose all correct answers for each question.

Set Up Automatic Diagnostic Repository

1. The value of the initialization parameter DIAGNOSTIC_DEST is NULL, the environment variable ORACLE_HOME is set to /u01/app/oracle/product/11.1.0/db_1, and the value of the environment variable ORACLE_BASE is set to /u01/app/oracle. At startup, what value is assigned by Oracle to DIAGNOSTIC_DEST?
   A. /u01/app/oracle/diag
   B. /u01/app/oracle/log
   C. /u01/app/oracle/product/11.1.0/db_1/log
   D. /u01/app/oracle

2. Which of the following tasks can you accomplish using the adrci command-line tool?
   A. Package incident information into a ZIP file to send to Oracle support.
   B. View diagnostic data within ADR.
   C. Perform a health check on the database while it is running.
   D. Run recommended fixes from the most recent health check on the database.

3. Which of the following directory locations is not available in V$DIAG_INFO? (Choose the best answer.)
   A. Diagnostic trace files
   B. Diagnostic incident files
   C. Diagnostic problem files
   D. Active Problem Count

Using Support Workbench

4. You can use the EM Support Workbench for which of the following tasks? (Choose all correct answers.)
   A. Run recommended repairs.
   B. Manually run a health check.
   C. Close problems and incidents.
   D. Generate additional SQL test cases to help Oracle support solve the problem.
   E. View problems and incidents.

5. Which of the following tasks can you only perform with the EM Support Workbench custom packaging feature?

   A. You can specify an SR associated with the package.

   B. You can customize the package name and description.

   C. You can specify a date and time to upload the package.

   D. You can add or remove external files from a package.

6. Which of the following advisors can you run from the EM Support Workbench Incident Details page? (Choose two answers.)

   A. The SQL Repair Advisor

   B. The Data Recovery Advisor

   C. The SQL Tuning Advisor

   D. The Disk Repair Advisor

Perform Block Media Recovery

7. Which of the following basic consistency checks are performed by Oracle when a block is written or read? (Choose all correct answers.)

   A. Block checksum

   B. Data Block Address in cache matches the address on disk

   C. Block version

   D. The data block is below the HWM when reading or updating a block

8. What are some of the prerequisites for using block media recovery? (Choose all that apply.)

   A. Flashback Database must be enabled.

   B. The database must be in ARCHIVELOG mode.

   C. The last level 1 backup must be available.

   D. DB_BLOCK_CHECKING must be set to LOW, MEDIUM, or FULL.

   E. All archived redo logs since the last full backup must be available.

9. You can use the RMAN CHANGE FAILURE command to change the priority of which types of failures? (Choose all that apply.)

   A. OPEN

   B. HIGH

   C. CRITICAL

   D. LOW

   E. CLOSED

SELF TEST ANSWERS

Set Up Automatic Diagnostic Repository

1. ☑ **D.** The ADR root directory (also known as the ADR base) is set by the parameter DIAGNOSTIC_DEST. If it is not set, Oracle sets DIAGNOSTIC_DEST to the environment variable ORACLE_BASE. If ORACLE_BASE is not set, then the ADR root directory is set to $ORACLE_HOME/log.
   ☒ **A, B,** and **C** are wrong. All three locations are not assigned, given the values of DIAGNOSTIC_DEST, ORACLE_BASE, and ORACLE_HOME.

2. ☑ **A** and **B.** The adrci command-line tool allows you to view diagnostic information in the ADR root directory in addition to packaging both problem and incident information for Oracle support.
   ☒ **C** and **D** are wrong. The adrci command-line tool cannot initiate health checks nor run fixes recommended by other Oracle diagnostic tools.

3. ☑ **C.** The view V$DIAG_INFO does not specify a directory for problems, only incidents. Each incident is labeled with a text string representing the problem identifier.
   ☒ **A, B,** and **D** are listed in V$DIAG_INFO with the operating system–specific path name.

Using Support Workbench

4. ☑ **B, C, D,** and **E.** You can use the Support Workbench for viewing problems and incidents, manually running health checks, generating additional dumps and test cases for Oracle support, creating and tracking a service request to Oracle support, collecting all data related to a problem and packaging it, and closing the problem when it has been resolved.
   ☒ **A** is wrong. The EM support workbench cannot run recommended repairs. However, you can initiate advisors that recommend repairs.

5. ☑ **D.** You can add or remove external files from a package only with the custom packaging method.
   ☒ **A, B,** and **C** are wrong because these tasks can be accomplished using the quick packaging method.

6. ☑ **A** and **B.** You can run either the Data Recovery Advisor or the SQL Repair Advisor from the Incident Details page.
   ☒ **C** and **D** are wrong. You cannot initiate the SQL Tuning Advisor from the EM Support Workbench. There is no such advisor as the Disk Repair Advisor.

Perform Block Media Recovery

7. ☑ **A, B,** and **C.** Oracle performs all of these checks regardless of the setting of DB_BLOCK_CHECKING.

   ☒ **D** is wrong because Oracle does not check if a block is below the high water mark (HWM) when updating or reading a block.

8. ☑ **A, B,** and **E.** To use RMAN's block recovery feature, the database must be in ARCHIVELOG mode, the backups of data files must be full backups or level 0 backups, and archived log files must be available since the last full or level 0 backup. In addition, if Flashback Database is enabled, then RMAN can look for uncorrupted versions of blocks in the flashback logs.

   ☒ **C** is wrong because RMAN cannot use level 1 backups for block recovery. **D** is wrong because DB_BLOCK_CHECKING does not have to be enabled at all to use block recovery.

9. ☑ **B** and **D.** You can change the priority of a HIGH failure to LOW, and vice versa.

   ☒ **A** is wrong because OPEN is not a failure status. **C** is wrong because you cannot change the priority of a CRITICAL failure. **E** is wrong because you cannot change the priority of a CLOSED failure.

14

Using the
Scheduler for
Task Automation

O n many occasions, you, as a database administrator, or your users will need to automate scheduling and running jobs of many kinds—for example, performing maintenance work such as database backups, data loading and validation routines, generating reports, collecting optimizer statistics, or executing business processes. The Scheduler facility can be used to schedule tasks to be run at some point in the future.

The Scheduler can be coupled with the Resource Manager. It can activate Resource Manager plans and run jobs with priorities assigned to various Resource Manager consumer groups.

In earlier releases of the database, job scheduling capabilities were provided through the DBMS_JOB facility. This facility is still supported for backward compatibility, but it is not nearly as versatile as the Scheduler.

In this chapter, you'll learn how to leverage some of the advanced Scheduler capabilities, such as job chains and job prioritization. Job chains are more than just one job running after another. In other words, the success of job A in the chain can trigger job B, or the failure of job A can trigger job C instead. Job prioritization uses job classes and the Resource Manager to provide more resources for one job over another. For example, one class of database users can be allocated a higher percentage of resources, such as CPU time, when more than one class of users is competing for the same resources.

CERTIFICATION OBJECTIVE 14.01

Create a Job, Program, and Schedule

Oracle provides a simple to use, yet advanced scheduling capability to permit application users, developers, and DBAs to run periodic tasks at a specific time. As a DBA, you may want to schedule a nightly backup without using less granular operating system scheduling capabilities. Developers may schedule summary reports to be run on the last day of the month, in the early morning hours, after receiving the last sales receipts for the day, and so on. Oracle Scheduler provides these capabilities and more.

To use and maintain Oracle Scheduler effectively, you need to understand its architecture, including its components—jobs, programs, schedules, job classes, and windows.

Understanding the Scheduler Architecture

The *data dictionary* includes a table that is a storage point for all Scheduler jobs. You can query the table through the DBA_SCHEDULER_JOBS view. The job coordinator process, CJQ0, monitors this table, and when necessary launches job slaves, the Jnnn processes, to run the jobs. The CJQ0 process is launched automatically when a job is due; it is deactivated after a sustained period of Scheduler inactivity. The Jnnn processes are launched on demand, though the maximum number is limited by the JOB_QUEUE_PROCESSES instance parameter; this defaults to 0, but if that value is used, the Scheduler will not function.

The job coordinator picks up jobs from the job queue table and passes them to slaves for execution. It also launches and terminates the slaves according to demand. To see the processes currently running, query the V$PROCESS view. In a Unix/Linux instance, the processes will be separate operating system processes, and in a Windows instance they are threads in the ORACLE.EXE image.

An advanced feature of the Scheduler is to associate it with the Resource Manager. Certain jobs might need to be run with certain priorities, and this can be achieved by linking a job to a Resource Manager consumer group (see Chapter 12 for more information on resource management). It is also possible to use the Scheduler to activate a Resource Manager plan, rather than having to change the RESOURCE_MANAGER_ PLAN instance parameter manually. The Scheduler can be configured and monitored with an API—the DBMS_SCHEDULER PACKAGE—or through Database Control. Figure 14-1 shows the Scheduler home page, with links at the bottom to other scheduler objects such as jobs, programs, and windows.

Jobs

A *job* specifies what to do and when to do it. The *what* can be a single SQL statement, a PL/SQL block, a PL/SQL stored procedure, a Java stored procedure, an external procedure, or any executable file stored in the server's file system—either a binary executable or a shell script. The *when* specifies the timestamp at which to launch the job and a repeat interval for future runs.

You can choose from among several options when creating a job, as you can see from looking at the DBMS_SCHEDULE.CREATE_JOB procedure. This procedure is

FIGURE 14-1

Oracle
Scheduler page

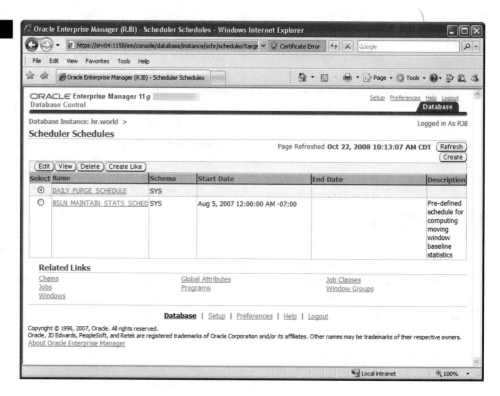

FIGURE 14-1   Oracle Scheduler page

overloaded because it has no less than six forms. Here is a part of the output for the first form of CREATE_JOB from a DESCRIBE of the DBMS_SCHEDULER package:

```
PROCEDURE CREATE_JOB
 Argument Name              Type                      In/Out    Default?
 ----------------------     ----------------------    ------    ---------
 JOB_NAME                   VARCHAR2                   IN
 JOB_TYPE                   VARCHAR2                   IN
 JOB_ACTION                 VARCHAR2                   IN
 NUMBER_OF_ARGUMENTS        BINARY_INTEGER             IN        DEFAULT
 START_DATE                 TIMESTAMP WITH TIME ZONE   IN        DEFAULT
 REPEAT_INTERVAL            VARCHAR2                   IN        DEFAULT
 END_DATE                   TIMESTAMP WITH TIME ZONE   IN        DEFAULT
 JOB_CLASS                  VARCHAR2                   IN        DEFAULT
 ENABLED                    BOOLEAN                    IN        DEFAULT
 AUTO_DROP                  BOOLEAN                    IN        DEFAULT
 COMMENTS                   VARCHAR2                   IN        DEFAULT
```

All forms of the CREATE_JOB procedure must specify a JOB_NAME. This must be unique within the schema in which the job is created.

Next, taking the first form of the procedure, the JOB_TYPE must be one of the following: PLSQL_BLOCK, STORED_PROCEDURE, or EXECUTABLE. If JOB_TYPE is PLSQL_BLOCK, then JOB_ACTION can be either a single SQL statement or a PL/SQL block. If the JOB_TYPE is STORED_PROCEDURE, then JOB_ACTION must name a stored procedure, which can be PL/SQL, Java, or an external procedure written in C. If the JOB_TYPE is EXECUTABLE, then the JOB_ACTION can be anything that could be run from an operating system command-line prompt: a command, an executable binary file, or a shell script or batch file. The NUMBER_OF_ARGUMENTS parameter states how many arguments the JOB_ACTION should take.

The first form of the procedure continues with details of when and how frequently to run the job. The first execution will be on the START_DATE; the INTERVAL defines a repeat frequency, such as daily, until END_DATE. JOB_CLASS has to do with priorities and integration of the Scheduler with the Resource Manager. The ENABLED argument determines whether the job can actually be run. Perhaps surprisingly, this defaults to FALSE. If a job is not created with this argument set to TRUE, it cannot be run (either manually or through a schedule) without enabling it first. Finally, AUTO_DROP controls whether to drop the job definition after the END_DATE. This defaults to TRUE. If a job is created with no scheduling information, it will be run as soon as it is enabled, and then dropped immediately if AUTO_DROP is on TRUE, which is the default.

The third form of the CREATE_JOB procedure has the job details (the JOB_TYPE, JOB_ACTION, and NUMBER_OF_ARGUMENTS) replaced with a PROGRAM_NAME that points to a program, which will provide these details. The fourth form has the scheduling details (START_DATE, REPEAT_INTERVAL, and END_DATE) replaced with a SCHEDULE_NAME that points to a schedule, which will manage the timing of the runs. The second, and briefest, form of the procedure uses both a program and a schedule.

Programs

Programs provide a layer of abstraction between the job and the action it will perform. They are created with the DBMS_SCHEDULER.CREATE_PROGRAM procedure:

```
PROCEDURE CREATE_PROGRAM
Argument Name            Type                In/Out Default?
--------------------     ------------------- ------ --------
PROGRAM_NAME             VARCHAR2            IN
PROGRAM_TYPE             VARCHAR2            IN
PROGRAM_ACTION           VARCHAR2            IN
NUMBER_OF_ARGUMENTS      BINARY_INTEGER      IN     DEFAULT
```

```
ENABLED                 BOOLEAN              IN     DEFAULT
COMMENTS                VARCHAR2             IN     DEFAULT
```

By pulling the *what* of a job out of the job definition itself and defining it in a program, it becomes possible to reference the same program in different jobs and thus to associate it with different schedules and job classes, without having to define it many times. Note that (as for a job) a program must be ENABLED before it can be used.

Schedules

A *schedule* is a specification for when and how frequently a job should run. It is created with the DBMS_SCHEDULER.CREATE_SCHEDULE procedure:

```
PROCEDURE CREATE_SCHEDULE
Argument Name        Type                         In/Out Default?
----------------     ------------------------     ------ --------
SCHEDULE_NAME        VARCHAR2                     IN
START_DATE           TIMESTAMP WITH TIME ZONE     IN     DEFAULT
REPEAT_INTERVAL      VARCHAR2                     IN
END_DATE             TIMESTAMP WITH TIME ZONE     IN     DEFAULT
COMMENTS             VARCHAR2                     IN     DEFAULT
```

The START_DATE defaults to the current date and time. This is the time that any jobs associated with this schedule will run. The REPEAT_INTERVAL specifies how frequently the job should run, until the END_DATE. Schedules without an END_DATE will run forever.

The REPEAT_INTERVAL argument can take a wide variety of calendaring expressions. These consist of up to three elements: a frequency, an interval, and possibly several specifiers. The frequency may be one of these values:

```
YEARLY
MONTHLY
WEEKLY
DAILY
HOURLY
MINUTELY
SECONDLY
```

The specifiers can be one of these values:

```
BYMONTH
BYWEEKNO
BYYEARDAY
BYMONTHDAY
BYHOUR
```

```
BYMINUTE
BYSECOND
```

Using these elements of a REPEAT_INTERVAL makes it possible to set up schedules that should satisfy any requirement. For example,

```
repeat_interval=>'freq=hourly; interval=12'
```

will run the job every 12 hours, starting at the START_DATE. The next example,

```
repeat_interval=>'freq=yearly; bymonth=jan,apr,jul,oct; bymonthday=2'
```

will run the job on the second day of each of the named four months, starting as early in the day as resources permit. A final example,

```
repeat_interval=>'freq=weekly; interval=2; byday=mon; byhour=6; byminute=10'
```

will run the job at 6:10 A.M. on alternate Mondays.

on the
() o b
One schedule can be applied to many jobs; one program can be invoked by many jobs.

Job Classes

A *job class* is used to associate one or more jobs with a Resource Manager consumer group, and also to control logging levels. Classes are created with the DBMS_SCHEDULER.CREATE_JOB_CLASS procedure:

```
PROCEDURE CREATE_JOB_CLASS
Argument Name              Type              In/Out Default?
------------------------   ----------------  ------ --------
JOB_CLASS_NAME             VARCHAR2          IN
RESOURCE_CONSUMER_GROUP    VARCHAR2          IN     DEFAULT
SERVICE                    VARCHAR2          IN     DEFAULT
LOGGING_LEVEL              BINARY_INTEGER    IN     DEFAULT
LOG_HISTORY                BINARY_INTEGER    IN     DEFAULT
COMMENTS                   VARCHAR2          IN     DEFAULT
```

The JOB_CLASS_NAME is the name to be referenced by the JOB_CLASS argument of the CREATE_JOB procedure. The RESOURCE_CONSUMER_GROUP nominates the group whose resource allocations should be applied to the running job, as determined by the Resource Manager plan in effect whenever the job happens to run. The SERVICE has significance only in a Real Application Cluster (RAC) database: you can restrict the job to run only on an instance with a particular service name. The details of logging can also be specified per class.

Windows

A *schedule* specifies exactly when a job should be launched. *Windows* extend the concept of schedules by giving Oracle more freedom to decide when to run the job. A window opens at a certain time and closes after a certain duration: jobs specified to run in a window may be launched, at Oracle's discretion, at any time during the window. The window itself can open repeatedly according to a schedule. Use of windows is of particular value when combined with classes and the Resource Manager: Oracle can schedule jobs to run within a window according to their relative priorities. Windows also activate Resource Manager plans.

Windows are created with the DBMS_SCHEDULER.CREATE_WINDOW procedure:

```
PROCEDURE CREATE_WINDOW
Argument Name            Type                         In/Out Default?
------------------       -------------------------    ------ --------
WINDOW_NAME              VARCHAR2                      IN
RESOURCE_PLAN            VARCHAR2                      IN
START_DATE               TIMESTAMP WITH TIME ZONE IN       DEFAULT
REPEAT_INTERVAL          VARCHAR2                      IN
END_DATE                 TIMESTAMP WITH TIME ZONE IN       DEFAULT
DURATION                 INTERVAL DAY TO SECOND        IN
WINDOW_PRIORITY          VARCHAR2                      IN       DEFAULT
COMMENTS                 VARCHAR2                      IN       DEFAULT
```

The RESOURCE_PLAN nominates the Resource Manager plan that will be activated when the window opens. The window will open on the START_DATE and reopen according to the REPEAT_INTERVAL until the END_DATE. The procedure is overloaded; a second form lets you nominate a precreated schedule rather than specifying the schedule here with these three arguments.

The DURATION is an INTERVAL DAY TO SECOND datatype. This will allow a time span to be specified in days, hours, minutes, and seconds. The basic syntax for an INTERVAL DAY TO SECOND column is

```
'<days> <hours>:<minutes>:<seconds>'
```

Note that that a space appears between the days and the hours, and colons between the hours, minutes, and seconds. So this

```
'1 2:3:4'
```

specifies a time gap of one day, two hours, three minutes, and four seconds.

The PRIORITY argument is intended to manage circumstances where windows overlap and has two possible values: LOW (the default) or HIGH. Only one window can be in effect at a time, and it will be the window with the higher priority. If two or more overlapping windows have the same priority, the window that opened first will take priority.

Windows share the same namespace as schedules. It is therefore impossible to create a window with the same name as a schedule, but this does mean that wherever you can refer to a schedule, you can also refer to a window. Note that a job can be created to run at any time within a named window, rather than at the precise times specified by a schedule. The window itself will open and close according to a schedule—either a schedule defined within the window or a precreated schedule object.

Privileges

All Scheduler *privileges* are granted and revoked with the usual GRANT and REVOKE syntax. A number of Scheduler-related privileges can be used:

- CREATE JOB
- CREATE ANY JOB
- EXECUTE ANY PROGRAM
- EXECUTE ANY CLASS
- MANAGE SCHEDULER
- EXECUTE ON <JOB, PROGRAM, OR CLASS>
- ALTER ON <JOB, PROGRAM, OR SCHEDULE>
- ALL ON <JOB, PROGRAM, SCHEDULE, OR CLASS>

Before a user can create any jobs, schedules, or programs, he or she must be granted the CREATE JOB privilege; this includes the ability to create and use his or her own programs and schedules. To create jobs in other schemes, the user will need the CREATE ANY JOB privilege. To use Scheduler objects in other schemas, you need the EXECUTE privilege on them. The MANAGE SCHEDULER privilege is needed to create job classes and windows and to force windows to open or close irrespective of their schedules.

The ready-made role SCHEDULER_ADMIN includes the first five privileges just listed. It is granted to SYSTEM with ADMIN by default.

CERTIFICATION OBJECTIVE 14.02

Use a Time-based or Event-based Schedule for Executing Scheduler Jobs

You can base the execution of a Scheduler job either on a specific time or an event. For example, you may want to run a backup job at 1:00 A.M. every morning. Alternatively, other jobs may be dependent on a specific event, such as receiving an accounts-receivable file from the accounting department, or the order entry department completing their manual order corrections for the day.

Creating and Scheduling Time-based Jobs

To create and schedule a time-based job with one procedure call, use the CREATE_ JOB procedure. Here's an example:

```
begin
   dbms_scheduler.create_job(
      job_name=>'system.inc_backup',
      job_type=>'executable',
      job_action=>'/home/usr/dba/rman/whole_inc.sh',
      start_date=>trunc(sysdate)+23/24,
      repeat_interval=>'freq=weekly;byday=mon,tue,wed,thu,fri;byhour=23',
      comments=>'launch weekday incremental backup script');
end;
```

This will create a job that will call a Unix shell script at 11:00 every weekday evening, starting today. The job is created in the SYSTEM schema. The operating system permissions on the script will have to be set such that the Oracle owner can run it. When you specify the START_DATE parameter, the scheduler initiates the job as close to this date and time as possible.

EXERCISE 14-1

Creating a Job with the Scheduler API

Use the DBMS_SCHEDULER package to create a job, and confirm that it is working.

1. Connect to your database as a user with the CREATE JOB privilege.

2. Create a table to store times, and set your date format to show the date and time:

```
SQL> create table times (c1 date);
SQL> alter session set nls_date_format='dd-mm-yy hh24:mi:ss';
```

3. Create a job to insert the current time into the table every minute:

```
SQL> begin
  2        dbms_scheduler.create_job(
  3        job_name=>'savedate',
  4        job_type=>'plsql_block',
  5        job_action=>'insert into times values(sysdate);',
  6        start_date=>sysdate,
  7        repeat_interval=>'freq=minutely;interval=1',
  8        enabled=>true,
  9        auto_drop=>false);
 10  end;
 11  /
PL/SQL procedure successfully completed.
```

4. Query the job table to see that the job is scheduled:

```
SQL> select job_name,enabled,
  2     to_char(next_run_date,'dd-mm-yy hh24:mi:ss'),run_count
  3  from user_scheduler_jobs;
JOB_NAME                    ENABL TO_CHAR(NEXT_RUN_  RUN_COUNT
--------------------------- ----- ------------------ ----------
SAVEDATE                    TRUE  15-10-08 14:58:03          2
```

5. Query the times table to demonstrate that the inserts are occurring:

```
SQL> select * from times;
```

6. Disable the job:

```
SQL> exec dbms_scheduler.disable('savedate');
```

7. Re-run the queries from steps 4 and 5 to confirm that the job is disabled and that no more inserts are occurring.

8. Drop the job:

```
SQL> exec dbms_scheduler.drop_job('savedate');
```

Creating and Scheduling Event-based Jobs

Event-based jobs still use the START_DATE parameter; however, the job's initiation also depends on an event specified by the EVENT_CONDITION and QUEUE_SPEC parameters, as in this example:

```
begin
   dbms_scheduler.create_job (
      job_name         => proc_ar_job,
      program_name     => ar_prog,
      start_date       => systimestamp,
      event_condition  => 'tab.user_data.event_name = ''AR_FILE_
ARRIVAL''',
      queue_spec       => 'ar_event_q',
      enabled          => TRUE,
      comments         => 'AR job after monthly receipts received'
end;
```

The EVENT_CONDITION parameter uses syntax from Advanced Queueing (AQ) that checks periodically for an event name AR_FILE_ARRIVAL. The QUEUE_SPEC parameter contains the name of the queue whose events will trigger the event-based job.

Using Programs and Schedules

Programs and schedules let you reuse Scheduler components for similar tasks. Rather than defining each job as a self-contained entity, you create programs and schedules, each of which can be used by many jobs.

The job created in Exercise 14-1 could be split up into a job, a program, and a schedule. To do this through Database Control, from the database home page select the Server tab. Then in the Oracle Scheduler section click the Programs link, click the Create button, and enter the code you want executed, as shown in Figure 14-2. This can be as long and complicated as you want (bearing in mind that the datatype for PROGRAM_ACTION is VARCHAR2 and so is limited to 4KB).

on the job

Keep your JOB_ACTIONs and PROGRAM_ACTIONs as short as possible, preferably using just one statement. Do all the work in a procedure invoked by that statement. This will be far easier to maintain than having a large amount of SQL or PL/SQL in your job and program definitions.

FIGURE 14-2

Creating a
Scheduler
program using
Enterprise
Manager

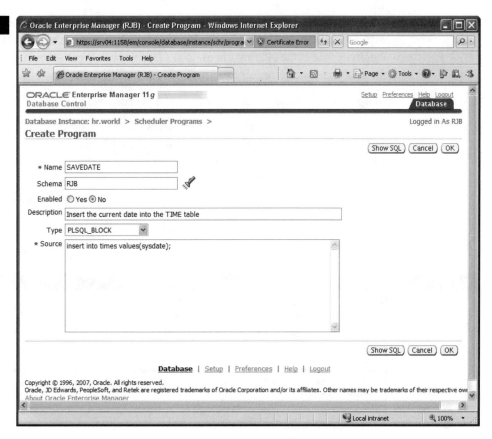

As with most Enterprise Manager (EM) tasks, you can click the Show SQL button to see what code EM will run to perform the specified action:

```
BEGIN
DBMS_SCHEDULER.CREATE_PROGRAM(
program_name=>'"RJB"."SAVEDATE"',
program_action=>'insert into times values(sysdate);',
program_type=>'PLSQL_BLOCK',
number_of_arguments=>0,
comments=>'Insert the current date into the TIME table',
enabled=>FALSE);
END;
```

If you create a program with the CREATE_PROGRAM procedure, then (just as with jobs) the program will be disabled by default. Change this default either by specifying the ENABLED argument as TRUE when you create the program, or by using the ENABLE procedure subsequently:

```
SQL> exec dbms_scheduler.enable('program1');
```

To create a schedule, click the Schedules link from the Oracle Scheduler section, and click Create to view the page shown in Figure 14-3. This GUI does not give access to some of the more complicated interval possibilities, such as every third Tuesday, which would be

```
'freq=weekly;interval=3;byday=tue'
```

but it gives access to all that will usually be required.

FIGURE 14-3

Creating a schedule with EM

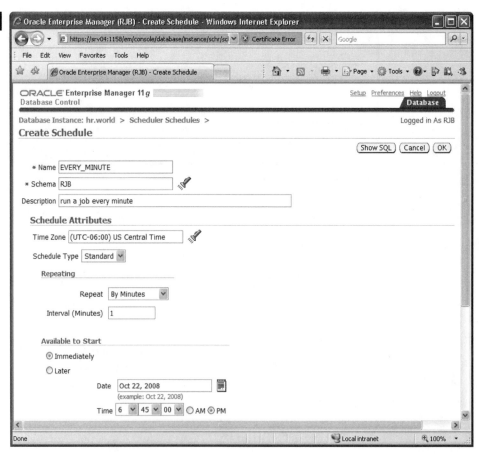

FIGURE 14-4

Creating a job
with EM

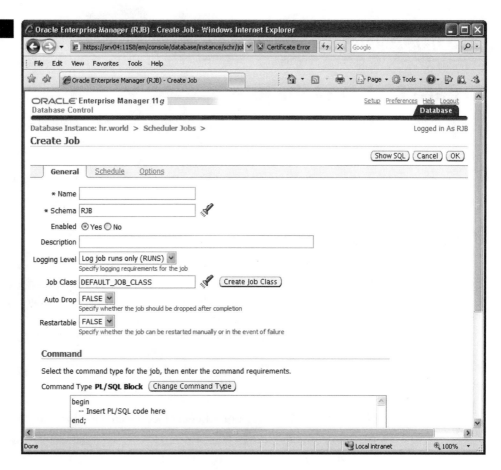

To create a job, click the Jobs link from the Oracle Scheduler section. The initial
window (shown in Figure 14-4) assumes that the job is a PL/SQL block. Clicking the
Change Command Type button will let you select your program type. The Schedule
tab lets you tie the job to a precreated schedule, rather than defining the schedule
within the job.

on the
job

***Programs share the same namespace as jobs; you cannot have a program with
the same name as a job. The same is true for schedules and windows.***

It is also possible to run a job independently of a schedule, by using the RUN_JOB
procedure:

```
SQL> exec dbms_scheduler.run_job('savedate');
```

Create Lightweight Jobs

A *lightweight job* shares many characteristics with a standard job discussed earlier, except that a lightweight job is ideal for running many short-duration jobs that run frequently. A few restrictions to lightweight jobs are discussed in the following sections; these restrictions are offset by the performance improvement due to the low overhead of a lightweight job.

Understanding Lightweight Jobs

If you need to submit hundreds or even tens of jobs every second, a lightweight job is the best way to reduce overhead. For a regular job, Oracle creates a database object containing the metadata for the job, modifies several database tables, and generates redo. In contrast, a lightweight job (also known as a persistent lightweight job) has very small disk space and run-time data requirements. A lightweight job is created using a predefined job template, which can be a program or a stored procedure. Other characteristics of lightweight jobs that distinguish them from regular jobs are as follows:

- Lightweight jobs are not schema objects as regular jobs are.
- Create and drop times for lightweight jobs are significantly less than those of regular jobs since new schema objects are not required.
- Lightweight jobs have a small disk footprint for job metadata and runtime data.
- Session creation time is significantly lower than that for regular jobs.
- Lightweight jobs can be load balanced in a RAC environment because of the small footprint on disk.

You can create a job template to use with lightweight jobs by using DBMS_ SCHEDULER.CREATE_PROGRAM, as described earlier in this chapter. The job template used for lightweight jobs is stored as a program whose type must be PLSQL_ BLOCK or STORED_PROCEDURE. When you create a lightweight job, you specify a JOB_STYLE of LIGHTWEIGHT. By default, the JOB_STYLE is REGULAR.

Lightweight jobs have a few drawbacks, as you might expect. You cannot set privileges on lightweight jobs—they inherit privileges from the template's program. In addition, because the lightweight job uses a template, you cannot create a fully self-contained lightweight job. Finally, you must use a PL/SQL command to create a lightweight job—this is not available through the EM interface.

Using Lightweight Jobs

To create a lightweight job, you create the template once using CREATE_PROGRAM, and then you can run the lightweight job as often as necessary using CREATE_JOB.

EXERCISE 14-2

Create and Run a Lightweight Job

In this exercise, you'll create a small table that you will populate with a lightweight job. Create a template for the lightweight job and then run it once.

1. Create a table to hold the current status of the DUAL table; if the DUAL table has one row, the status is 1; otherwise it is 2:

```
SQL> create table check_dual_status
  2       (status_timestamp      timestamp,
  3        status_code           number(2)
  4       );

Table created.

SQL>
```

2. Create a program using a PL/SQL program that will be the template for the lightweight job:

```
SQL> begin
  2       dbms_scheduler.create_program(
  3           program_name => 'rjb.dual_check',
  4           program_action =>
  5              'begin
  6                   insert into rjb.check_dual_status
  7                   values (systimestamp,
  8                           decode((select count(*) from dual),1,1,2));
  9               end;',
 10           program_type => 'PLSQL_BLOCK',
 11           enabled => true);
 12  end;
 13  /

PL/SQL procedure successfully completed.

SQL>
```

3. Check the status of the job in DBA_SCHEDULER_PROGRAMS:

```
SQL> select owner, program_name, program_type, enabled, max_runs
  2  from dba_scheduler_programs
  3  where owner = 'RJB';

OWNER            PROGRAM_NAME          PROGRAM_TYPE       ENABL  MAX_RUNS
---------------  --------------------  -----------------  -----  ----------
RJB              DUAL_CHECK            PLSQL_BLOCK        TRUE

SQL>
```

4. Use the DUAL_CHECK program name as a template to create and run a light-weight job once:

```
SQL> begin
  2      dbms_scheduler.create_job (
  3          job_name => 'lightweight_job_1',
  4          program_name => 'RJB.DUAL_CHECK',
  5          job_style => 'LIGHTWEIGHT',
  6          comments => 'Check if DUAL has extra rows'
  7      );
  8  end;
  9  /

PL/SQL procedure successfully completed.

SQL>
```

5. Check the contents of the table CHECK_DUAL_STATUS:

```
SQL> select * from check_dual_status;

STATUS_TIMESTAMP                     STATUS_CODE
-----------------------------------  -----------
25-OCT-08 10.13.14.056332 PM                   1

SQL>
```

Use Job Chains to Perform a Series of Related Tasks

In our increasingly complex environments, scheduler jobs may have one or more dependencies. In other words, you may want to run job A, and if job A succeeds, you can run job B. If job A does not succeed, you may want to run job C instead. As a result, regardless of whether job B or job C ran successfully, you may run job D. This is an example of a job chain. A *job chain* is a database object that contains a named series of programs linked together for a combined objective, such as processing the daily Internet and phone orders, sending order confirmation e-mails to the Internet customers, and then sending shipping requests to the warehouse.

Understanding Job Chains

Each part of a chain of programs is called a *step*. Though not required, after one or more initial steps, successive steps are conditional upon the success or failure of the initial steps. Therefore, creating chains without conditions somewhat defeats the purpose of using a chain. You use DBMS_SCHEDULER to create all chain objects and initiate the chain of events. Here are the steps you use for creating and executing a chain:

1. Create the chain using the CREATE_CHAIN procedure.
2. Create one or more chain steps using DEFINE_CHAIN_STEP or DEFINE_CHAIN_EVENT_STEP.
3. Define chain rules using DEFINE_CHAIN_RULE.
4. Enable the chain using the ENABLE procedure.
5. Create a job using CREATE_JOB with a JOB_TYPE of CHAIN.

Creating Chain Objects

You create a chain object with CREATE_CHAIN. To create a chain without any steps or rules, you need to specify only the chain name. Here is an example of creating an empty chain with a description:

```
dbms_scheduler.create_chain(
    chain_name => 'RJB.PROC_DAILY_ORDERS',
    comments => 'Process Daily Internet and Phone Orders');
```

You can also use EM to create a chain. Figure 14-5 shows how to create a chain called `PROC_DAILY_ORDERS`. You can add the chain steps and rules when you create the chain, or you can modify the chain later to add or remove steps or rules.

Defining Chain Steps

You create a chain step with `DEFINE_CHAIN_STEP`. Each chain step has a name within the chain and references one of the following:

- A program
- Another chain (this is known as *nesting* a chain)
- An event

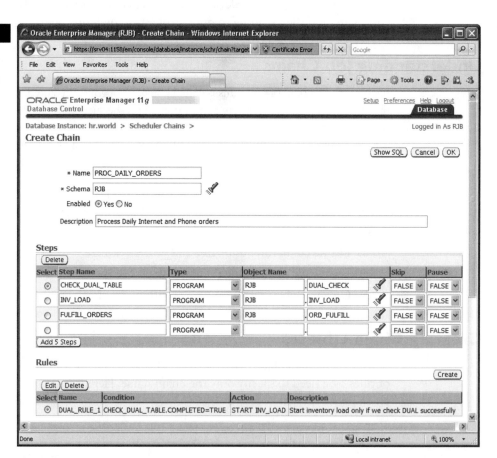

FIGURE 14-5

Creating a Scheduler chain

If one of your steps waits for an event, you use a DEFINE_CHAIN_EVENT_STEP that references an event that must be triggered before the chain step will be executed. For example, you may want to delay a step in a chain until you receive an inventory file from the mainframe system.

In this example, you add two chain steps to the PROC_DAILY_ORDERS chain to check the status of the DUAL table before proceeding to the order processing steps:

```
dbms_scheduler.define_chain_step(
    chain_name => 'RJB.PROC_DAILY_ORDERS',
    step_name => 'CHECK_DUAL_TABLE',
    program_name => 'RJB.DUAL_CHECK');

dbms_scheduler.define_chain_step(
    chain_name => 'RJB.PROC_DAILY_ORDERS',
    step_name => 'INV_LOAD',
    program_name => 'RJB.INV_LOAD');
```

Defining Chain Rules

Chain rules, created with DEFINE_CHAIN_RULE, define dependencies between steps and when steps run. Each chain rule has a *condition* and an *action*. The condition uses syntax very similar to a WHERE clause in a SELECT statement. Typically, you specify a condition based on the success or failure of one or more previous steps in the chain. After evaluating the condition, the chain rule will then perform one of the following actions:

- Run another step.
- Stop a step.
- End execution of the chain.

Continuing the example from the preceding section, this rule will run the step CREATE_SUCCESS_REPORT only if the step CHECK_DUAL_TABLE completes successfully:

```
dbms_scheduler.define_chain_rule(
    chain_name => 'RJB.PROC_DAILY_ORDERS',
    rule_name => 'PROC_ORD_RULE_1',
    condition => 'CHECK_DUAL_TABLE.COMPLETED=TRUE',
    action => 'START INV_LOAD',
    comments => 'Don''t start inventory load until checking DUAL');
```

Starting the Chain

Two steps are used to start a chain: first, you must enable it with the ENABLE procedure. When you create a chain, it is always created in a disabled state. Second, you create a job with a JOB_TYPE of CHAIN. The job schedule can be either event-based or time-based.

In the following example, the chain created previously is enabled, and then a job is created to run daily at 11 P.M.:

```
dbms_scheduler.enable('PROC_DAILY_ORDERS');
dbms_scheduler.create_job(
   job_name => 'daily_orders_proc_job',
   job_type => 'CHAIN',
   job_action => 'PROC_DAILY_ORDERS',
   repeat_interval => 'freq=daily;byhour=23',
   enabled => TRUE);
```

To run a job chain immediately, you can use either RUN_JOB or RUN_CHAIN. If you use RUN_CHAIN, you can start the chain at any step in the chain. For example, you may want to start the chain PROC_DAILY_ORDERS at the INV_LOAD steps right away:

```
dbms_scheduler.run_chain(
   chain_name => 'PROC_DAILY_ORDERS',
   job_name => 'Start inventory load right now',
   start_steps => 'INV_LOAD');
```

Monitoring Job Chains

You can use a number of data dictionary views to query the structure of a chain and monitor the progress of a running chain. As with most data dictionary views, DBA, ALL, and USERS versions can be used:

- *_SCHEDULER_CHAINS
- *_SCHEDULER_CHAIN_RULES
- *_SCHEDULER_CHAIN_STEPS
- *_SCHEDULER_RUNNING_CHAINS

Here is an example of a query on the DBA_SCHEDULER_CHAINS data dictionary view:

```
SQL> select owner, chain_name, enabled, comments
  2  from dba_scheduler_chains;

OWNER                    CHAIN_NAME               ENABL COMMENTS
------------------------ ------------------------ ----- --------------------
RJB                      PROC_DAILY_ORDERS        TRUE  Process Daily Intern
                                                        et and Phone Orders

SQL>
```

CERTIFICATION OBJECTIVE 14.05

Create Windows and Job Classes

Using Scheduler windows and job classes, you can adjust how your jobs run. You might, for example, want a job to run only during a certain window, and if it does not complete, it should pick up where it left off when the window is open again. You can use *job classes* to assign one or more jobs to a resource consumer group and therefore load balance your limited resources when jobs must compete with online users and other jobs. In the following sections, you'll learn how to create job classes and windows with EM and DBMS_SCHEDULER, and then you'll explore some of the preconfigured jobs.

Creating Windows

To create a new window, click the Server tab from the EM home page. Under the Oracle Scheduler heading, click the Windows link. You will see the existing set of windows shown in Figure 14-6. Note that the windows WEEKNIGHT_WINDOW and WEEKEND_WINDOW are retained from previous releases of Oracle Database for backward compatibility.

When you click the Create button, you see the window shown in Figure 14-7, where you can set the resource plan and priority associated with the window.

FIGURE 14-6

Viewing
Scheduler
windows with EM

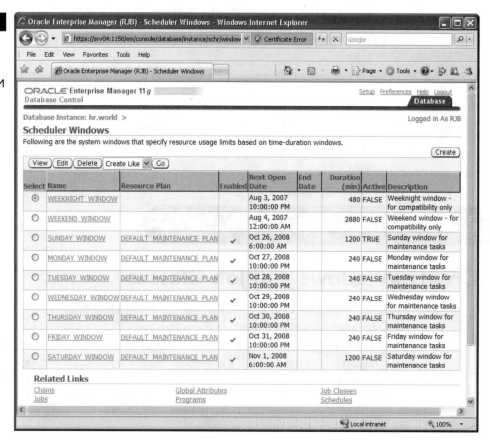

The equivalent PL/SQL (Procedural Language/Structured Query Language) used to create the window looks like this:

```
BEGIN
    DBMS_SCHEDULER.CREATE_WINDOW(
    window_name=>'"NOON_WINDOW"',
    resource_plan=>'DEFAULT_MAINTENANCE_PLAN',
    start_date=>systimestamp at time zone 'America/Chicago',
    duration=>numtodsinterval(60, 'minute'),
    repeat_interval=>null,
    end_date=>null,
    window_priority=>'LOW',
    comments=>'Stuff running over the lunch hour');
END;
```

FIGURE 14-7

Creating a
Scheduler
window

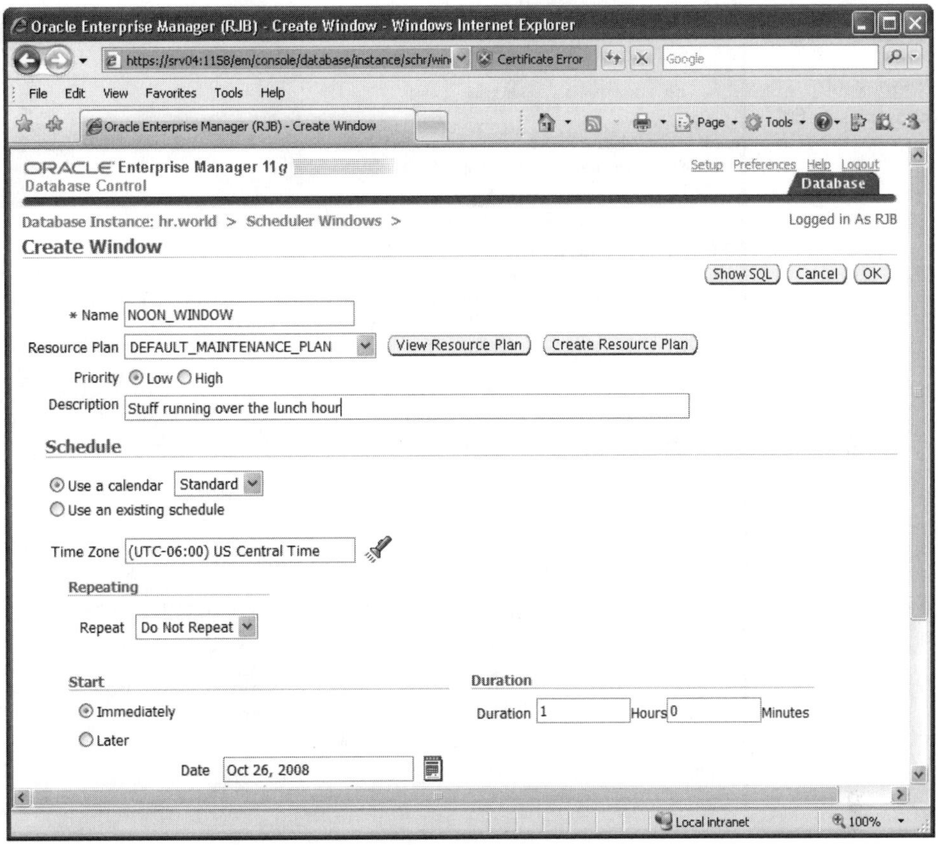

Creating Job Classes

You can view and create job classes in EM using steps similar to creating a window. To create a new job class, click the Server tab from the EM home page. Under the Oracle Scheduler heading, click the Job Classes link. You will see the page shown in Figure 14-8. Note that all jobs that do not specify a job class are assigned the job class DEFAULT_JOB_CLASS by the Scheduler.

To create a new job class, click the Create button. You will see the page shown in Figure 14-9.

FIGURE 14-8

Viewing job
classes using EM

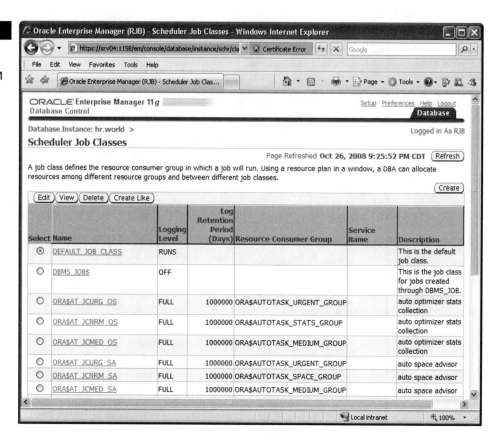

Note that you can assign the resource consumer group to this class. A many-to-one
relationship exists between classes and resource groups, where many classes can use
the same resource consumer group. Here is the SQL that creates the new job class:

```
BEGIN
    sys.dbms_scheduler.create_job_class(
    logging_level => DBMS_SCHEDULER.LOGGING_RUNS,
    log_history => 60,
    resource_consumer_group => 'LOW_GROUP',
    comments => 'Jobs for DSS and DW in here',
    job_class_name => '"DSS JOBS"');
END;
```

FIGURE 14-9

Creating a new
job class

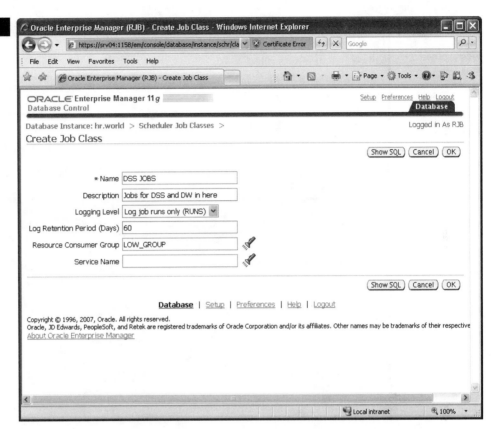

Preconfigured Jobs

Several jobs are configured by default, such as MGMT_STATS_CONFIG_JOB and
MGMT_CONFIG_JOB. To see the details for these jobs, select the Server tab from the
EM home page and click Jobs. You'll see the page shown in Figure 14-10.

In Figure 14-10, you can see that the MGMT_STATS_CONFIG_JOB runs
at a specific time every morning, and the MGMT_CONFIG_JOB runs in the
MAINTENANCE_WINDOW_GROUP.

What happens if a window closes before a job that is run in the window has
completed? The default behavior is that the job will continue until it finishes, but

FIGURE 14-10

Viewing the
preconfigured
jobs

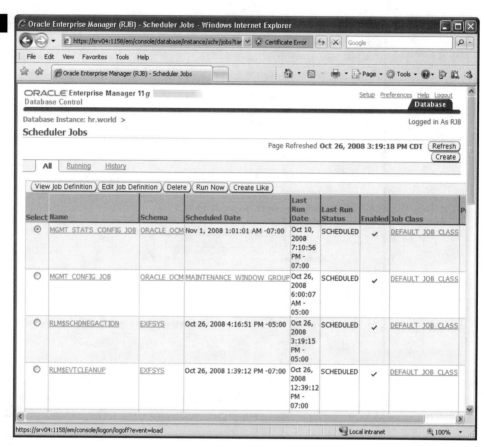

this can be overridden by setting an attribute. This query shows all the Scheduler
jobs in the database, including the attribute STOP_ON_WINDOW_CLOSE:

```
SQL> select owner, job_name, stop_on_window_close, job_priority
  2  from dba_scheduler_jobs;
```

OWNER	JOB_NAME	STOP_ON_WINDOW_CLOSE	JOB_PRIORITY
SYS	XMLDB_NFS_CLEANUP_JOB	FALSE	3
SYS	FGR$AUTOPURGE_JOB	FALSE	3
SYS	BSLN_MAINTAIN_STATS_JOB	FALSE	3
SYS	DRA_REEVALUATE_OPEN_FAILURES	FALSE	3
SYS	HM_CREATE_OFFLINE_DICTIONARY	FALSE	3

```
SYS                   ORA$AUTOTASK_CLEAN            FALSE         3
SYS                   PURGE_LOG                     FALSE         3
ORACLE_OCM            MGMT_STATS_CONFIG_JOB         FALSE         3
ORACLE_OCM            MGMT_CONFIG_JOB               FALSE         3
EXFSYS                RLM$SCHDNEGACTION             FALSE         3
EXFSYS                RLM$EVTCLEANUP                FALSE         3
RJB                   ADV_SEGMENTADV_8648285        FALSE         3
. . .
RJB                   LIGHTWEIGHT_JOB_1             FALSE

21 rows selected.

SQL>
```

To change this attribute, use the SET_ATTRIBUTE procedure:

```
dbms_scheduler.set_attribute(
    name=>'lightweight_job_1',
    attribute=>'stop_on_window_close',
    value=>'true');
```

This will cause the LIGHTWEIGHT_JOB_1 job to abort if it has not finished by the time its window closes.

CERTIFICATION OBJECTIVE 14.06

Use Advanced Scheduler Concepts to Prioritize Jobs

Most likely, you will have many different jobs running within any given window. Within each window, you may have several different classes of jobs running, and each class may have its own priority. As discussed earlier in the chapter, job classes categorize jobs. When you assign a job class to a resource consumer group, the resource plan currently in effect divides the available resources to each job class.

Jobs are prioritized at two levels: the class level and the job level. For jobs at different class levels, resource plans dictate the job priority. Within a class, however, you can assign a job priority. The job with the higher job priority starts first. You saw how to create job classes and windows earlier in the chapter.

Using Classes, Windows, and the Resource Manager

The more advanced capabilities of the Scheduler let you integrate it with the Resource Manager to control and prioritize jobs. These are the relevant components:

- **Job classes**   Jobs can be assigned a class and a class can be linked to a Resource Manager consumer group. Classes also control the logging level for their jobs.
- **Consumer groups**   Resource Manager consumer groups are restricted in the resources they can use, such as CPU usage or the number of active sessions.
- **Resource plans**   A Resource Manager plan defines how to apportion resources to groups. Only one plan is active in the instance at any one time.
- **Windows**   A window is a defined (probably recurring) period of time during which certain jobs will run and a certain plan will be active.
- **Window groups**   Windows can be combined into window groups for ease of administration.

Prioritizing jobs within a window is accomplished at two different levels. On the first level, within a class, jobs can be given different priorities by the Scheduler. However, the Resource Manager will not distinguish between them because all jobs in a class are in the same consumer group. On the second level, if jobs in different classes are scheduled within the same window, the Resource Manager will assign resources to each class according to the consumer groups for that class.

Using Job Classes

You can create a class with database control, or through the API. Here's an example:

```
dbms_scheduler.create_job_class(
    job_class_name=>'daily_reports',
    resource_consumer_group=>'dss',
    logging_level=>dbms_scheduler.logging_full);
```

Then you can assign the jobs to the class, either at job creation time by specifying the JOB_CLASS attribute, or by modifying the job later. To assign a job to a class with the API, you must use the SET_ATTRIBUTE procedure. To put the job REPORTS_JOB into the class just created, use:

```
dbms_scheduler.set_attribute(
    name=>'reports_job',
    attribute=>'job_class',
    value=>'daily_reports');
```

If several jobs are in the one class, you can prioritize them with more SET_ ATTRIBUTE calls:

```
dbms_scheduler.set_attribute(
    name=>'reports_job',
    attribute=>'job_priority',
    value=>2);
```

If several jobs in the same class are scheduled to be executed at the same time, the job priority determines the order in which jobs from that class are picked up for execution by the job coordinator process. The job priority can be a value from 1 through 5, with 1 being the first to be picked up for job execution (the highest priority). The default for all jobs is 3. This could be critical if, for instance, the class's consumer group has an active session pool that is smaller than the number of jobs. So those jobs with the highest priority will run first and the other jobs are queued.

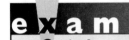

It is not possible to assign priorities by any means other than the SET_ATTRIBUTE procedure of the API.

Logging levels are also controlled by the job's class using three options:

- **DBMS_SCHEDULER.LOGGING_OFF** No logging is done for any jobs in this class.

- **DBMS_SCHEDULER.LOGGING_RUNS** Information is written to the job log regarding each run of each job in the class, including when the run was started and whether the job ran successfully.

- **DBMS_SCHEDULER.LOGGING_FULL** In addition to logging information about the job runs, the log will also record management operations on the class, such as creating new jobs.

To view logging information, query the DBA_SCHEDULER_JOB_LOG view:

```
SQL> select job_name,log_date,status from dba_scheduler_job_log;
JOB_NAME      LOG_DATE                          STATUS
------------- --------------------------------- -----------
PURGE_LOG     16-OCT-08 13-00-03                SUCCEEDED
TEST_JOB      16-OCT-08 11-00-00                FAILED
NIGHT_INCR    16-OCT-08 01-00-13                SUCCEEDED
NIGHT_ARCH    16-OCT-08 01-00-00                SUCCEEDED
```

More detailed information is written to the DBA_SCHEDULER_JOB_RUN_ DETAILS view, including the job's run duration and any error code it returned.

Logging information is cleared by the automatically created PURGE_LOG job. By default, this runs daily and removes all logging information more than 30 days old.

Using Windows

You can create windows either through Database Control or with the CREATE_WINDOW procedure. Here's an example:

```
dbms_scheduler.create_window(
    window_name=>'daily_reporting_window',
    resource_plan=>'night_plan',
    schedule=>'weekday_nights',
    duration=>'0 08:00:00',
    window_priority=>'low',
    comments=>'for running regular reports');
```

This window activates a Resource Manager plan called NIGHT_PLAN. This might be a plan that gives priority to the Decision Support Systems (DSS) consumer groups over the online transaction processing (OLTP) group, for example. It opens according to the schedule WEEKDAY_NIGHTS, which might be Monday through Friday at 20:00 (8 P.M.). The window will remain open for eight hours; the DURATION argument accepts an INTERVAL DAY TO SECOND value, as does the REPEAT_INTERVAL for a schedule. Setting the priority to LOW means that if this window overlaps with another window, the other window will be allowed to impose its Resource Manager plan. This would be the case if you created a different window for your end-of-month processing and the end-of-month happened to be on a week day, for example. You could give the end-of-month window HIGH priority to ensure that the end-of-month Resource Manager plan, which could give top priority to the BATCH group, processes key management reports first.

exam

Watch

Even if a job has priority 1 within its class, it might still run after a job with priority 5 in another class—if the second job's class is in a consumer group with a higher Resource Manager priority.

CERTIFICATION SUMMARY

This chapter started with a brief overview of the Oracle Scheduler architecture along with the data dictionary views and processes used to manage Scheduler objects. It covered the basics of the Scheduler components: jobs, programs, schedules, job classes, and windows.

Once the basics were out of the way, you learned about a couple of different ways to schedule a job, which are time-based or event-based. In other words, you can schedule a job for a specific time, or you can schedule a job dependent on an internal or external event. A specific type of job, called a lightweight job, makes it easy to create a large number of jobs that run in a short amount of time using a minimal amount of overhead. Job chains make a DBA's job easier by creating a series of jobs that can be initiated as a unit. The success or failure of each job within the job chain can conditionally execute other jobs within the chain.

The last part of the chapter delved into some of the more advanced features of the Oracle Scheduler—windows and job classes. Job windows extend the concept of schedules by giving Oracle more flexibility when running a job. A running job may be restricted to running in a single occurrence of a window, or it may suspend at the end of the window and pick up where it left off the next time the window is open. Job classes further refine job priorities and resource usage by associating one or more jobs with a Resource Manager consumer group.

✓ TWO-MINUTE DRILL

Create a Job, Program, and Schedule

- ❏ The data dictionary table DBA_SCHEDULER_JOBS stores information about all jobs associated with a schedule.

- ❏ The CJQ0 job coordinator process monitors the DBA_SCHEDULER_JOBS table, and when necessary, launches job slaves (Jnnn processes) to run Scheduler jobs.

- ❏ A job specifies what to do and when to do it. The *what* can be a single SQL statement, a PL/SQL block, a PL/SQL stored procedure, a Java stored procedure, an external procedure, or any executable file stored in the server's file system.

- ❏ Programs provide a layer of abstraction between the job and the action it will perform, and are created with the DBMS_SCHEDULER.CREATE_PROGRAM procedure.

- ❏ A schedule is a specification for when and how frequently a job should run.

- ❏ A job class is used to associate one or more jobs with a Resource Manager consumer group and also to control logging levels.

- ❏ Windows extend the concept of schedules by giving Oracle more freedom on deciding when to run a job.

- ❏ A window opens at a certain time and closes after a specified duration. So jobs specified to run in a window may be launched, at Oracle's discretion, at any time during the window.

Use a Time-based or Event-based Schedule for Executing Scheduler Jobs

- ❏ You can base the execution of a Scheduler job either on a specific time or an event.

- ❏ To create and schedule a time-based job with one procedure call, use the CREATE_JOB procedure.

- ❏ Event-based jobs still use the START_DATE parameter; however, the job's initiation also depends on an event specified by the EVENT_CONDITION and QUEUE_SPEC parameters.

❑ Programs and schedules let you reuse Scheduler components for similar tasks.

❑ You can run a job independently of a schedule by using the RUN_JOB procedure.

Create Lightweight Jobs

❑ A lightweight job has many of the same characteristics of a standard job, except that a lightweight job is ideal for running many short-duration jobs that run frequently.

❑ If you need to submit hundreds or even tens of jobs every second, a lightweight job is the best way to reduce overhead.

❑ Lightweight jobs have a small disk footprint for job metadata and runtime data.

❑ You cannot set privileges on lightweight jobs because they inherit privileges from the template's program.

Use Job Chains to Perform a Series of Related Tasks

❑ A job chain is a database object that contains a named series of programs linked together for a combined objective.

❑ Each part of a chain of programs is called a step.

❑ You create a chain using the CREATE_CHAIN procedure.

❑ You create a chain step with DEFINE_CHAIN_STEP procedure.

❑ Chain rules, created with DEFINE_CHAIN_RULE, define dependencies between steps and when steps run.

❑ You must enable a job chain with the ENABLE procedure.

❑ To run a job chain, create a job with a JOB_TYPE of CHAIN.

Create Windows and Job Classes

❑ You create a new window with the CREATE_WINDOW procedure.

❑ When you create a new window, you can optionally assign a resource plan and priority.

❑ You create a new job class using the CREATE_JOB_CLASS procedure.

❑ The job class DEFAULT_JOB_CLASS is assigned to a job when a job does not have an explicit class assignment.

❑ If a window closes before a running job has completed, the job will run to completion unless you set the attribute STOP_ON_WINDOW_CLOSE to TRUE.

Use Advanced Scheduler Concepts to Prioritize Jobs

❏ Prioritizing jobs within a window occurs at two levels: within a class by a priority level or between classes by resource consumer group.

❏ Logging levels are controlled by the job's class.

❏ You create a job class with the CREATE_JOB_CLASS procedure.

❏ If several jobs in the same class are scheduled to be executed at the same time, the job priority determines the order in which jobs from that class are picked up for execution by the job coordinator process.

❏ You create a window with the CREATE_WINDOW procedure.

❏ You assign either LOW or HIGH priority to a window to prioritize window attributes when windows overlap.

❏ When windows overlap and they have the same priority, the window opened earlier stays open.

SELF TEST

The following questions will help you measure your understanding of the material presented in this chapter. Read all the choices carefully, because there might be more than one correct answer. Choose all correct answers for each question.

Create a Job, Program, and Schedule

1. When a job is due to run, what process will run it? (Choose the best answer.)

    A. A CJQ*n* process

    B. A J*nnn* process

    C. A server process

    D. A background process

2. Which of the following is a requirement if the Scheduler is to work? (Choose the best answer.)

    A. The instance parameter `JOB_QUEUE_PROCESSES` must be set.

    B. A Resource Manager plan must be enabled.

    C. A schedule must have been created.

    D. All of the above.

    E. None of the above.

3. A Scheduler job can be which of the following types? (Choose all that apply.)

    A. Anonymous PL/SQL block

    B. Executable operating system file

    C. External C procedure

    D. Java stored procedure

    E. Operating system command

    F. Operating system shell script (Unix) or batch file (Windows)

    G. PL/SQL stored procedure

4. You create a job with this syntax:

```
begin
   dbms_scheduler.create_job(
   job_name=>'j1',
   program_name=>'p1',
   schedule_name=>'s1',
   job_class=>'c1');
end;
```

You find that it is not running when expected. What might be a reason for this? (Choose the best answer.)

A. The schedule is associated with a window, which has not opened.

B. The job has not been enabled.

C. The class is part of Resource Manager consumer group with low priority.

D. The permissions on the job are not correct.

5. What are the possible priority levels of a job within a class? (Choose the best answer.)

A. 1 to 5

B. 1 to 999

C. HIGH or LOW

D. Depends on the Resource Manager plan in effect

6. A preconfigured job called MGMT_STATS_CONFIG_JOB is set up to gather optimizer statistics. This job is scheduled to run in both the THURSDAY_WINDOW and the SUNDAY_WINDOW. What will happen if it fails to complete before the window closes? (Choose the best answer.)

A. It will continue to run to completion.

B. It will terminate and continue the next time either window opens.

C. It will terminate and restart the next time either window opens.

D. The behavior will vary depending on whether it was running in the THURSDAY_WINDOW window or the SUNDAY_WINDOW window.

Use a Time-based or Event-based Schedule for Executing Scheduler Jobs

7. You want a job to run every 30 minutes. Which of the following possibilities for the REPEAT_INTERVAL argument are correct syntactically and will achieve this result? (Choose two answers.)

A. `'freq=minutely;interval=30'`

B. `'freq=hourly;interval=1/2'`

C. `'0 00:30:00'`

D. `'freq=minutely;byminute=30'`

E. `'freq=byminute;interval=30'`

8. You create a job class, and you set the LOGGING_LEVEL argument to LOGGING_RUNS. What will be the result? (Choose the best answer.)

A. A log entry will be created for each run of each job in the class, but no information will be included on whether the job was successful.

B. A log entry will be created for each run of each job in the class, plus information on whether the job was successful.

    C. A single log entry will be created for the class whenever it is run.

    D. You cannot set logging per class, only per job.

Create Lightweight Jobs

  9. Which of the following is a prerequisite for using lightweight jobs? (Choose the best answer.)

    A. You must define a schedule specifically for lightweight jobs.

    B. You must have a job template that is a PL/SQL block or a stored procedure.

    C. You must specify a REPEAT_INTERVAL.

    D. You must have a job template that is of type EXECUTABLE to improve performance.

Use Job Chains to Perform a Series of Related Tasks

 10. You create a chain rule for an existing job chain. What types of actions can be performed by the rule after evaluating the condition? (Choose all that apply.)

    A. Terminate the chain execution.

    B. Run another program.

    C. Stop a different step in the chain.

    D. Restart the job from the beginning.

    E. Run another step.

Create Windows and Job Classes

 11. Which of the following statements are correct regarding how Scheduler components can be used together? (Choose all that apply.)

    A. A schedule can be used by many jobs.

    B. A job can use many programs.

    C. A class can have many programs.

    D. Job priorities can be set within a class.

    E. Consumer groups control priorities within a class.

    F. A Resource Manager plan can be activated by a schedule.

 12. Which view will tell you about jobs configured with the Scheduler? (Choose the best answer.)

    A. DBA_JOBS

    B. DBA_SCHEDULER

    C. DBA_SCHEDULED_JOBS

    D. DBA_SCHEDULER_JOBS

Use Advanced Scheduler Concepts to Prioritize Jobs

13. If two windows are overlapping and have equal priority, which window(s) will be open? (Choose the best answer.)

    A. Both windows will be open.

    B. Windows cannot overlap.

    C. Whichever window opened first will remain open; the other will remain closed.

    D. Whichever window opened first will be closed, and the other will open.

14. How long will Scheduler logging records be visible in the DBA_SCHEDULER_JOB_LOG view? (Choose the best answer.)

    A. They will remain until the PURGE_LOG job is run.

    B. By default, they will be kept for 30 days.

    C. By default, they will be kept for 1 day.

    D. By default, the view will be cleared every 30 days.

SELF TEST ANSWERS

Create a Job, Program, and Schedule

1. ☑ **B.** Jobs are run by a job slave process called J*nnn*. The CJQ0 process is the job queue coordinator, which passes the jobs to the slave for execution.
    ☒ **A** is wrong because the CJQ0 process coordinates the J*nnn* processes but does not run the job itself. **C** and **D** are wrong because they are not specific enough.

2. ☑ **A.** The only requirement for the Scheduler to function is that at least one job slave process must be created with the JOB_QUEUE_PROCESSES parameter.
    ☒ **B, C, D,** and **E** are wrong. Resource Manager plans and schedules are optional.

3. ☑ **A, B, C, D, E, F,** and **G.** All the answers are correct.
    ☒ The Scheduler job can be any job that you can run manually.

4. ☑ **B.** As written, the procedure call will not enable the job, so it won't run at all.
    ☒ **A** is wrong since the job will run when the window is open. **C** is wrong because even with low priority, the job will still start. **D** is wrong because you will know right away if the permissions are not correct by the output from the CREATE_JOB procedure.

5. ☑ **A.** Within a class, jobs can have a priority of 1 to 5.
    ☒ **B** is wrong because the range is 1 to 5. **C** is a wrong answer because HIGH and LOW apply to overlapping windows, not jobs within a class. **D** is wrong because the priority range is not dependent on the Resource Manager plan.

6. ☑ **C.** The MGMT_STATS_CONFIG_JOB is configured to stop when its window closes. At the next window, it will start again.
    ☒ **A** is wrong because the job stops at the end of the window unconditionally. **B** is wrong because the job will restart not continue. **D** is wrong because the behavior is not defined within the window itself.

Use a Time-based or Event-based Schedule for Executing Scheduler Jobs

7. ☑ **A** and **B.** Either is the correct syntax to set a half-hour repeat interval.
    ☒ **C** is wrong because it is the format for a DURATION. **D** and **E** are syntactically incorrect.

8. ☑ **B.** With logging set to LOGGING_RUNS, you will get records of each run of each job, including its success or failure. The other possible logging levels are NONE, in which case no logging at all will occur, or FULL, which records details for each run and also administrative actions, such as enabling or disabling jobs.
    ☒ **A** is wrong because LOGGING_RUNS includes a success or failure status. **C** is a wrong answer because a log entry exists for each run in each job. **D** is wrong because LOGGING_RUNS is set per the job's class, not per job.

Create Lightweight Jobs

9. ☑ **B.** Lightweight jobs must specify a template that has a program with a PL/SQL block or a stored procedure.

☒ **A** is wrong because you do not need a schedule. **C** is a wrong answer because you do not have to repeat the lightweight job. **D** is wrong because the program template must be of type PL/SQL or a stored procedure; lightweight jobs run faster due to the low overhead of creating and dropping the job, not because of the type of job template.

Use Job Chains to Perform a Series of Related Tasks

10. ☑ **A, C,** and **E.** Within a chain rule, you can terminate the chain execution, stop another step in progress, or transfer control to another step.

☒ **B** and **D** are incorrect; after the condition is evaluated, the chain rule cannot run another program directly or restart the job.

Create Windows and Job Classes

11. ☑ **A** and **D.** One job can use only one schedule, but one schedule can be used by many jobs. Job priorities can be set at both the class level and the job level.

☒ **B** is wrong because a job can reference only one program. **C** is a wrong answer because a job class associates one or more jobs with a Resource Manager consumer group as well as controls logging levels. **E** is wrong because consumer groups cannot specify a priority level. **F** is wrong because Resource Manager plans can be activated only from windows or a job class.

12. ☑ **D.** The DBA_SCHEDULER_JOBS view externalizes the data dictionary jobs table, with one row per scheduled job.

☒ **A** is wrong because DBA_JOBS has information about jobs but not about associated schedules, if any. **B** is wrong because no DBA_SCHEDULER view exists. **C** is a wrong answer because no view DBA_SCHEDULED_JOBS exists.

Use Advanced Scheduler Concepts to Prioritize Jobs

13. ☑ **C.** If two windows overlap and have equal priority, the window that opened earlier will be the open window.

☒ **A** is wrong because only one window can be open at a time. **B** is a wrong answer because two overlapping windows can exist, but they cannot be open at the same time. **D** is wrong because a window with higher priority will close an already open window with a lower priority.

14. ☑ **B.** By default, the PURGE_LOG job runs daily and keeps log records for 30 days.

☒ **A** is wrong because the PURGE_LOG job runs automatically on a daily basis. **C** is wrong because the default is 30 days, not 1 day. **D** is wrong because the last 30 days of log records are kept and only older records are cleared.

15
Database
Globalization

Ｔhe Oracle database has many capabilities grouped under the term *globalization* that will assist a DBA who must consider users of different nationalities. Globalization was known as National Language Support, or NLS, in earlier releases (you will still see the NLS acronym in several views and parameters), but globalization is more than linguistics: it is a comprehensive set of facilities for managing databases that must cover a wide range of languages, time zones, and cultural variations.

This chapter covers the theoretical and the practical. First, Oracle's character set capabilities, which include language and territory settings will be covered. You'll go over the various initialization parameters that, not surprisingly, begin with NLS. You'll see how to choose a character set, and how to change it later on. In the second part of the chapter, you'll learn how Oracle sorts character strings differently, depending on the character set and its internal representation. Finally, you'll solve the riddle of time zones and how you can make sure your timestamp values are recorded correctly when your client sessions are in North America, the application server is in Germany, and the database server is in Australia.

CERTIFICATION OBJECTIVE 15.01

Customize Language-Dependent Behavior for the Database and Individual Sessions

Large database systems, and many small ones too, will usually have a user community that is distributed geographically, temporally, and linguistically. Consider a database hosted in Johannesburg, South Africa, with end users scattered throughout sub-Saharan Africa. Different users will be expecting data to be presented to them in Portuguese, French, and English, at least. They will be in three different time zones. They will have different standards for the formats of dates and numbers. The situation becomes even more complex when the application is running in a three-tier environment: you may have a database in one location, several geographically distributed application servers, and users further distributed from the application servers.

It is possible for a lazy DBA to ignore globalization completely. Typically, such a DBA will take United States defaults for everything—and then let the programmers sort it out. But this is putting an enormous amount of work onto the programmers, and they may not wish to do it either. The result is an application that works but is detested by a portion of its users. But there is more to this than keeping people happy: there may well be financial implications too. Consider two competing e-commerce sites, both trying to sell goods all over the world. One has taken the trouble to translate everything into languages applicable to each customer; the other insists that all customers use American English. Which one is going to receive the most orders? Furthermore, dates and monetary formats can cause dreadful confusion when different countries have different standards. Such problems can be ignored or resolved programmatically, but a good DBA will attempt to resolve them through the facilities provided as standard within the database.

Globalization Capabilities

Globalization is a lot more than language support, though languages are certainly a major part of it. Globalization also covers aspects of data presentation, calendars, dates, and much more. Perhaps the most important aspect is how data is actually stored in the database: the character set used.

Character Sets

The data stored in a database must be coded into a character set. A *character set* is a defined encoding scheme for representing characters as a sequence of bits. Some products use the character sets provided by the host operating system. For example, Microsoft Word does not have its own character sets; it uses those provided by the Windows operating system. Other products provide their own character sets and are thus independent of whatever is provided by the host operating system. Oracle products fall into the latter group; they ship with their own character sets, which is one reason why Oracle applications are the same on all platforms, and why clients and servers can be on different platforms.

A character set consists of a defined number of distinct characters. The number of characters that a character set can represent is limited by the number of bits the character set uses for each character. A single-byte character set will use only one byte per character: eight bits, though some single-byte character sets restrict this even further by using only seven of the eight bits. A multibyte character set uses one, two, or even three bytes for each character. The variations here are whether the character set is fixed-width (for example, always using two bytes per character) or variable width (where some characters will be represented by one byte, other characters by two or more).

How many characters are actually needed? Well, as a bare minimum, you need upper- and lowercase letters, the digits 0 through 9, a few punctuation marks, and some special characters to mark the end of a line, or a page break, for instance. A seven-bit character set can represent a total of 128 (2^7) characters. It is simply not possible to get more than that number of different bit patterns if you have only seven bits to play with. Seven-bit character sets are just barely functional for modern computer systems, but they are usually inadequate. They provide the characters just named, but very little else. If you need to do simple things like using box drawing characters, or printing a name that includes a letter with an accent, you may find that you can't do it with a seven-bit character set. Anything more advanced, such as storing and displaying data in Arabic or Chinese script, will be totally out of the question. Unfortunately, Oracle's default character sets are seven-bit ASCII or seven-bit EBCDIC, depending on the platform; even such widely used languages as French and Spanish cannot be written correctly in these character sets. This is a historical anomaly, dating back to the days when these character sets were pretty much the only ones in use. Eight-bit character sets can represent 256 (2^8) different characters. These will typically be adequate for any Western European language-based system, though perhaps not for some Eastern European languages, and definitely not for many Asian languages. For these more complex linguistic environments, it is necessary to use a multibyte character set.

Unicode character sets deserve a special mention. The Unicode standards are an international standard for character encoding, which is intended to include every character that will ever be required by any computer system. Currently, Unicode has defined more than thirty-two thousand characters. And for completeness, the acronym ASCII is for American Standard Code for Information Interchange, and EBCDIC is Extended Binary Coded Decimal Interchange Code. EBCDIC was developed by IBM (International Business Machines) and is not usually used outside the IBM environment. More acronyms to note are ISO, for the International Standards Organization, and ANSI, for the American National Standards Institute.

Oracle Database 11g ships with more than 250 character sets. Table 15-1 includes just a few examples.

Language Support

The number of languages supported by Oracle depends on the platform, release, and patch level of the product. To determine the range available on any one installation, query the view V$NLS_VALID_VALUES, as follows:

TABLE 15-1   Sample Oracle Database 11g Character Sets

Encoding Scheme	Example Character Sets
Single-byte seven-bit	US7ASCII. This is the default for Oracle on non-IBM systems. YUG7ASCII. Seven-bit Yugoslavian, a character set suitable for the languages used in much of the Balkans.
Single-byte eight-bit	WE8ISO8859P15. A Western European eight-bit ISO standard character set, which includes the Euro symbol (unlike WE8ISO8859P1). WE8DEC. Developed by Digital Equipment Corporation, widely used in the DEC (or Compaq) environment in Europe. I8EBCDIC1144. An EBCDIC character set specifically developed for Italian.
Fixed-width multibyte	AL16UTF16. This is a Unicode two-byte character set, and the only fixed-width Unicode character set supported by 10g.
Varying-width	UTF8. A Unicode character set, where characters may be from one to four bytes. UTF8 is a standard on Unix systems.
Varying-width multibyte	JA16SJIS. Shift-JIS, a Japanese character set, where a shift-out control code is used to indicate that the following bytes are double-byte characters. A shift-in code switches back to single-byte characters. ZHT16CCDC. A traditional Chinese character set, where the most significant bit of the byte is used to indicate whether the byte is a single character or part of a multibyte character. AL32UTF8. A Unicode varying-width character set.

```
SQL> select * from v$nls_valid_values where
parameter='LANGUAGE';

PARAMETER            VALUE                ISDEP
-------------------- -------------------- -----
LANGUAGE             AMERICAN             FALSE
LANGUAGE             GERMAN               FALSE
LANGUAGE             FRENCH               FALSE
LANGUAGE             CANADIAN FRENCH      FALSE
LANGUAGE             SPANISH              FALSE
. . .
LANGUAGE             ALBANIAN             FALSE
LANGUAGE             BELARUSIAN           FALSE
LANGUAGE             IRISH                FALSE
67 rows selected.
SQL>
```

The language used will determine the language for error messages and also set defaults for date language and sort orders. The defaults are shown here:

Initialization Parameter	Default	Purpose
NLS_LANGUAGE	AMERICAN	Language for messages
NLS_DATE_LANGUAGE	AMERICAN	Used for day and month names
NLS_SORT	BINARY	Linguistic sort sequence

The default sort order—binary—is poor. Binary sorting may be acceptable for a seven-bit character set, but for character sets of eight bits or more the results are often inappropriate. For example, the ASCII value of a lowercase letter *a* is 97, and a lowercase letter *z* is 122. So a binary sort will place *a* before *z*, which is fine. But consider diacritic variations: a lowercase letter *a* with an umlaut, *ä*, is 132, which is way beyond *z*; so the binary sort order will produce "a,z,ä"—which is wrong in any language. The German sort order would give "a,ä,z"—which is correct. For example, consider some names from the German language:

```
SQL> alter session set nls_language = 'AMERICAN';

Session altered.

SQL> select * from names order by name;

NAME
---------------
Kohl
Kunst
Köhler

SQL> alter session set nls_language = 'GERMAN';

Session altered.

SQL> select * from names order by name;

NAME
---------------
Kohl
Köhler
Kunst

SQL> alter session set nls_language = 'AMERICAN';
```

Oracle provides many possible sort orders; there should always be one that will fit your requirements. Again, query V$NLS_VALID_VALUES to see what is available:

```
SQL> select * from v$nls_valid_values where parameter='SORT';

PARAMETER            VALUE                  ISDEP
-------------------- ---------------------- -----
SORT                 BINARY                 FALSE
SORT                 WEST_EUROPEAN          FALSE
SORT                 XWEST_EUROPEAN         FALSE
SORT                 GERMAN                 FALSE
SORT                 XGERMAN                FALSE
SORT                 DANISH                 FALSE
SORT                 XDANISH                FALSE
SORT                 SPANISH                FALSE
SORT                 XSPANISH               FALSE
SORT                 GERMAN_DIN             FALSE
. . .
SORT                 SCHINESE_STROKE_M      FALSE
SORT                 GBK                    FALSE
SORT                 SCHINESE_RADICAL_M     FALSE
SORT                 JAPANESE_M             FALSE
SORT                 KOREAN_M               FALSE

87 rows selected.

SQL>
```

Territory Support

The territory selected sets a number of globalization defaults. To determine the territories your database supports, again query V$NLS_VALID_VALUES:

```
SQL> select * from v$nls_valid_values where
parameter='TERRITORY';

PARAMETER            VALUE                  ISDEP
-------------------- ---------------------- -----
TERRITORY            AMERICA                FALSE
TERRITORY            UNITED KINGDOM         FALSE
TERRITORY            GERMANY                FALSE
TERRITORY            FRANCE                 FALSE
TERRITORY            CANADA                 FALSE
TERRITORY            SPAIN                  FALSE
```

```
TERRITORY               ITALY                  FALSE
TERRITORY               THE NETHERLANDS        FALSE
TERRITORY               SWEDEN                 FALSE
TERRITORY               NORWAY                 FALSE
  . . .
TERRITORY               BELARUS                FALSE

98 rows selected.

SQL>
```

The territory selection sets defaults for day and week numbering, credit and debit symbols, date formats, decimal and group numeric separators, and currency symbols. Some of these can have profound effects on the way your application software will behave.

For example, in the U.S. the decimal separator is a point (.), but in Germany and many other countries it is a comma (,). Consider a number such as "10,001". Is this ten thousand and one, or ten and one thousandth? You certainly need to know. Of equal importance is day of the week numbering. In the U.S., Sunday is day 1 and Saturday is day 7, but in Germany (and indeed in most of Europe) Monday (or Montag, to take the example further) is day 1 and Sunday (Sonnabend) is day 7. If your software includes procedures that will run according to the day number, the results may be disastrous if you do not consider this. The example that follows demonstrates some other territory-related differences in time settings:

```
SQL> alter session set nls_territory = 'AMERICA';

Session altered.

SQL> select systimestamp from dual;

SYSTIMESTAMP
-------------------------------------------------------------
18-OCT-08 03.11.47.811642 PM -05:00

SQL> alter session set nls_territory = 'GERMANY';

Session altered.

SQL> select systimestamp from dual;
```

```
SYSTIMESTAMP
-------------------------------------------------------------------
18.10.08 15:12:20,709876 -05:00

SQL>
```

Here are the defaults for territory-related settings:

Variable	Default / Purpose
NLS_TERRITORY	AMERICA / Geographical location
NLS_CURRENCY	$ / Local currency symbol
NLS_DUAL_CURRENCY	$ / A secondary currency symbol for the territory
NLS_ISO_CURRENCY	AMERICA / Indicates the ISO territory currency symbol
NLS_DATE_FORMAT	DD-MM-RR / Format used for columns of data type DATE
NLS_NUMERIC_CHARACTERS	., / Decimal and group delimiters
NLS_TIMESTAMP_FORMAT	DD-MM-RRHH.MI.SSXFF AM / Format used for columns of data type TIMESTAMP
NLS_TIMESTAMP_TZ_FORMAT	DD-MM-RRHH.MI.SSXFF AM TZR / Format used for columns of data type TIMESTAMP WITH LOCAL TIMEZONE

Other NLS Settings

Apart from the language- and territory-related settings just described, there are a few more advanced settings that are less likely to cause problems:

Variable	Default / Purpose
NLS_CALENDAR	Gregorian / Allows use of alternative calendar systems
NLS_COMP	BINARY / The alternative of ANSI compares letters using their NLS value, not the numeric equivalent
NLS_LENGTH_SEMANTICS	BYTE / Allows one to manipulate multibyte characters as complete characters rather than bytes
NLS_NCHAR_CONV_EXCP	FALSE / Limits error messages generated when converting between VARCHAR2 and NVARCHAR

This example illustrates switching to the Japanese imperial calendar (which counts the years from the ascension of Emperor Akihito to the throne), with an associated effect on the date display:

```
SQL> alter session set nls_calendar = 'Japanese Imperial';

Session altered.

SQL> alter session set nls_date_format = 'dd-mm-yyyy';

Session altered.

SQL> select sysdate from dual;

SYSDATE
----------
18-10-0020

SQL> alter session set nls_calendar = 'Gregorian';

Session altered.

SQL> select sysdate from dual;

SYSDATE
----------
18-OCT-08

SQL>
```

Using Globalization Support Features

Globalization can be specified at any and all of five levels:

- The database
- The instance
- The client environment
- The session
- The statement

The levels are listed in ascending order of priority. Thus, instance settings take precedence over database settings, and so on. An individual statement can control its own globalization characteristics, thus overriding everything else.

e x a m

w a t c h

Remember the precedence of the various points where globalization settings can be specified. On the server side, instance settings take precedence over

database settings, but all the server settings can be overridden on the client side: first by the environment, then at the session and statement levels.

Choosing a Character Set

At database creation time, choice of character set is one of the two most important decisions you make. When you create a database, two settings are vital to get right at creation time; everything else can be changed later. These two are the DB_BLOCK_SIZE parameter, which can never be changed, and the database character set, which it may be possible but not necessarily practicable to change. The difficulty with the DB_BLOCK_SIZE is that this parameter is used as the block size for the SYSTEM tablespace. You can't change that without recreating the data dictionary: in other words, creating a new database. The database character set is used to store all the data in columns of type VARCHAR2, CLOB, CHAR, and LONG (although still supported, you should not be using LONG datatypes unless you need them for backward compatibility). If you change it, you may well destroy all the data in your existing columns of these types.

It is therefore vital to select, at creation time, a character set that will fulfill all your needs, present and future. For example, if you are going to have data in French or Spanish, a Western European character set is needed. If you are going have data in Russian or Czech, you should choose an Eastern European character set. But what if you may have both Eastern and Western European languages? Furthermore, what if you anticipate a need for Korean or Thai as well? Oracle provides two solutions to the problem: the National Character Set, and the use of Unicode.

The National Character Set was introduced with release 8.0 of the database. This is a second character set, specified at database creation time, which is used for columns of data types NVARCHAR2, NCLOB, and NCHAR. So if the DBA anticipated that most of her information would be in English but that some would be Japanese, she could select a Western European character set for the database character set, and a Kanji character set as the National Character Set. With release 9*i*, the rules changed: from then on, the National Character Set can only be Unicode. This should not lead to any drop in functionality, because the promise of Unicode is that it can encode any character. Two types of Unicode are supported as the National Character Set: AL16UTF16 and UTF8. AL16UTF16 is a fixed-width, two-byte character set, and UTF8 is a variable-width character set. The choice between the two is a matter of space efficiency and performance, related to the type of data you anticipate storing in the NVARCHAR2 and NCLOB columns.

It may very well be that the majority of the data could in fact be represented in one byte, and only a few characters would need multiple bytes. In that case, AL16UTF16 will nearly double the storage requirements—quite unnecessarily, because one of the two bytes per character will be packed with zeros. This not only wastes space but also impacts on disk I/O. UTF8 will save a lot of space. But if the majority of the data cannot be coded in one byte, then UTF8 becomes much less efficient because the multibyte characters must be assembled, at run time, from a number of single bytes, with a consequent performance hit. Also, UTF8 will often need three or even four bytes to store a character that AL16UTF16 can encode in two.

The second possibility for a fully multilingual database is to use Unicode as the actual database character set. The supported options are UTF8 and AL32UTF8, which are both variable-width multibyte character sets.

on the
job

A Unicode database may make life simpler for developers, because they do not have to worry about which columns to read and write, but there can be performance implications.

The only limitation on the database character set is that it must have either US7ASCII or EBCDIC as a subset. This is because the database character set is used to store SQL and PL/SQL source code, which is written in these characters.

Both the database character set and the National Character Set are specified in the CREATE DATABASE command. The defaults are US7ASCII and AL16UTF16. If you create a database using the Database Creation Assistant (DBCA), DBCA will provide a default for the database character set, which it will pick up from the character set of the host operating system where you are running DBCA. This may be more appropriate than the seven-bit Oracle default, but remember that your clients may be using terminals with a different operating system from the database server.

Changing Character Sets

There are many occasions when DBAs have wished that they could change the database character set. Typically, this is because the database was created using the default of US7ASCII, and later on a need arises for storing information using characters not included in that character set, such as a French name. Prior to release 9*i* there was no supported technique for changing the character set. From 9*i* onward, there is a supported technique, but there is no guarantee that it will work. It is your responsibility as DBA to carry out thorough checks that the change will not damage the data. The problem is simply that a change of character set does not reformat the data currently in the datafiles, but it will change the way the data is presented. For example, if you were to convert from a Western European character set to an Eastern European character set, many of the letters with the accents common in Western languages would then be interpreted as Cyrillic characters, with disastrous results.

There are two tools provided to assist with deciding on a character set change: the Database Character Set Scanner and the Language and Character Set File Scanner. These are independently executable utilities, `csscan` and `lcsscan` on Unix, `csscan.exe` and `lcsscan.exe` on Windows.

The Database Character Set Scanner will log on to the database and make a pass through the datafiles, generating a report of possible problems. For example,

```
csscan system/systempassword full=y tochar=utf8
```

This command will connect to the database as user `SYSTEM` and scan through all the datafiles to check if conversion to UTF8 would cause any problems. A typical problem when going to UTF8 is that a character that was encoded in one byte in the original character set will require two bytes in UTF8, so the data might not fit in the column after the change. The scanner will produce a comprehensive report listing every row that will have problems with the new character set. You must then take appropriate action to fix the problems before the conversion, if possible.

on the **ɉob** *You must run the `csminst.sql` script to prepare the database for running the character set scanner.*

The Language and Character Set File Scanner is a utility that will attempt to identify the language and character set used for a text file. It will function on plain text only; if you want to use it on, for example, a word processing document, you will have to remove all the control codes first. This scanner may be useful if you have to upload data into your database and do not know what the data is. The tool scans the file and applies a set of heuristics to make an intelligent guess about the language and character set of the data.

Having determined whether it is possible to change the character set without damage, execute the command `ALTER DATABASE CHARACTER SET` to make the change. The equivalent command to change the National Character Set is `ALTER DATABASE NATIONAL CHARACTER SET`. The only limitation with this command is that the target character set must be a superset of the original character set, but that does not guarantee that there will be no corruptions. That is the DBA's responsibility.

Globalization Within the Database

The database's globalization settings are fixed at creation time, according to the instance parameter settings in effect when the `CREATE DATABASE` command was issued and the character set was specified. They are visible in the view `NLS_DATABASE_PARAMETERS` as follows:

```
SQL> select * from nls_database_parameters;

PARAMETER                      VALUE
------------------------------ --------------------------------------
NLS_LANGUAGE                   AMERICAN
NLS_TERRITORY                  AMERICA
NLS_CURRENCY                   $
NLS_ISO_CURRENCY               AMERICA
NLS_NUMERIC_CHARACTERS         .,
NLS_CHARACTERSET               WE8MSWIN1252
NLS_CALENDAR                   GREGORIAN
NLS_DATE_FORMAT                DD-MON-RR
NLS_DATE_LANGUAGE              AMERICAN
NLS_SORT                       BINARY
NLS_TIME_FORMAT                HH.MI.SSXFF AM
NLS_TIMESTAMP_FORMAT           DD-MON-RR HH.MI.SSXFF AM
NLS_TIME_TZ_FORMAT             HH.MI.SSXFF AM TZR
NLS_TIMESTAMP_TZ_FORMAT        DD-MON-RR HH.MI.SSXFF AM TZR
NLS_DUAL_CURRENCY              $
NLS_COMP                       BINARY
NLS_LENGTH_SEMANTICS           BYTE
NLS_NCHAR_CONV_EXCP            FALSE
NLS_NCHAR_CHARACTERSET         AL16UTF16
NLS_RDBMS_VERSION              11.1.0.6.0

20 rows selected.


SQL>
```

Globalization at the Instance Level

Instance parameter settings will override the database settings. In a RAC environment, it is possible for different instances to have different settings, so that, for example, European and U.S. users could each log on to the database through an instance configured appropriately to their different needs. The settings currently in effect are exposed in the view NLS_INSTANCE_PARAMETERS, which has the same rows as NLS_DATABASE_PARAMETERS except for three rows to do with character sets and RDBMS version that do not apply to an instance.

The globalization instance parameters can be changed like any others, but as they are all static, it is necessary to restart the instance before any changes come into effect.

Client-Side Environment Settings

When an Oracle user process starts, it inspects the environment within which it is running to pick up globalization defaults. This mechanism means that it is possible for users who desire different globalization settings to configure their terminals appropriately to their needs, and then Oracle will pick up and apply the settings automatically, without the programmers or the DBA having to take any action. This feature should be used with care, as it can cause confusion because it means that the application software may be running in an environment that the programmers had not anticipated. The internal implementation of this is that the user process reads the environment variables and then generates a series of ALTER SESSION commands to implement them.

The key environment variable is NLS_LANG. The full specification for this is a language, a territory, and a character set. To use French as spoken in Canada with a Western European character set, an end user could set it to

```
NLS_LANG=FRENCH_CANADA.WEISO8859P1
```

and then, no matter what the database and instance globalization are set to, his user process will then display messages and format data according to Canadian French standards. When the user sends data to the server, he will enter it using Canadian French conventions, but the server will then store it in the database according to the database globalization settings. The three elements (language, territory, and character set) of NLS_LANG are all optional.

on the job

The DBA has absolutely no control over what end users do with the NLS_ LANG environment variable. If the application is globalization sensitive, the developers should take this into account and control globalization within the session instead.

The conversion between server-side and client-side globalization settings is done by Oracle Net. In terms of the OSI seven-layer model, any required conversion is a layer 6 (presentation layer) function that is accomplished by Oracle Net's Two-Task Common layer. Some conversion is perfectly straightforward and should always succeed. This is the case with formatting numbers, for instance. Other conversions are problematic. If the client and the server are using different character sets, it may not be possible for data to be converted. An extreme case would be a client process using a multibyte character set intended for an Oriental language, and a database created with US7ASCII. There is no way that the data entered on the client can be stored correctly in the much more limited character set available within the database, and data loss and corruption are inevitable.

EXERCISE 15-1

Make Globalization and Client Environment Settings

This exercise will demonstrate how you, acting as an end user, can customize your environment in order to affect your Oracle sessions.

1. From an operating system prompt, set the NLS_LANG variable to Hungarian, and also adjust the date display from the default. Using Windows,

```
C:\>set NLS_LANG=Hungarian
C:\>set NLS_DATE_FORMAT=Day dd Month yyyy
```

or on Unix,

```
$ export NLS_LANG=Hungarian
$ export NLS_DATE_FORMAT='Day dd Month yyyy'
```

2. From the same operating system session, launch SQL*Plus and connect as user SYSTEM.

3. Display the current date with

```
SQL> select sysdate from dual;
SYSDATE
---------------------------
Szombat   18 Okt\uffffber    2008

SQL>
```

Note the problem with the display of one character in the month name. This is an example of a character used in Eastern European languages that cannot be displayed correctly by a Western European character set.

Session-Level Globalization Settings

Once connected, users can issue ALTER SESSION commands to set up their globalization preferences. Normally this would be done programmatically, perhaps by use of a logon trigger. The application will determine who the user is and configure the environment accordingly. An alternative to ALTER SESSION is the supplied package DBMS_SESSION. The following examples will each have the same effect:

```
SQL> alter session set nls_date_format='dd.mm.yyyy';
Session altered.
SQL> execute dbms_session.set_nls('nls_date_format','''dd.
mm.yyyy''');
PL/SQL procedure successfully completed.
```

Specifications at the session level take precedence over the server-side database and instance settings and will also override any attempt made by the user to configure his session with environment variables. The globalization settings currently in effect for your session are shown in the V$NLS_PARAMETERS view. The same information, with the exception of the character sets, is shown in the NLS_SESSION_PARAMETERS view.

EXERCISE 15-2

Control Globalization Within the Session

For this exercise, it is assumed that you have completed Exercise 15-1 and that you are working in the same SQL*Plus session. You will demonstrate how European and U.S. standards can cause confusion.

1. Confirm that your NLS_LANG environment variable is set to a European language. On Windows,

```
SQL> host echo %NLS_LANG%
```

or on Unix,

```
SQL> ! echo $NLS_LANG
```

```
Hungarian
```

```
SQL>
```

2. Set your date display to show the day number:

```
SQL> alter session set nls_date_format='D';
Session altered.
SQL>
```

3. Display the number of today's day:

```
SQL> select sysdate from dual;

S
-
6

SQL>
```

4. Change your territory to the U.S., and again set the date display format:

```
SQL> alter session set nls_territory=AMERICA;
SQL> alter session set nls_date_format='D';
```

5. Issue the query from Step 3 again, and note that the day number has changed with the shift of environment from Europe to America.

```
SQL> select sysdate from dual;

S
-
7

SQL>
```

Statement Globalization Settings

The tightest level of control over globalization is to manage it programmatically, within each SQL statement. This entails using NLS parameters in SQL functions. Here is an example:

```
SQL> select
  2  to_char(hire_date,'Day dd, Month YYYY',
                         'NLS_DATE_LANGUAGE=DUTCH'),
  3  to_char(hire_date,'Day dd, Month YYYY',
                         'NLS_DATE_LANGUAGE=GERMAN')
  4  from hr.employees;
```

```
TO_CHAR(HIRE_DATE,'DAYDD,MON  TO_CHAR(HIRE_DATE,'DAYDD,MONT
----------------------------  ----------------------------
Woensdag   17, Juni       1987 Mittwoch   17, Juni       1987
Donderdag  21, September  1989 Donnerstag 21, September  1989
Woensdag   13, Januari    1993 Mittwoch   13, Januar     1993
Woensdag   03, Januari    1990 Mittwoch   03, Januar     1990
Dinsdag    21, Mei        1991 Dienstag   21, Mai        1991
Woensdag   25, Juni       1997 Mittwoch   25, Juni       1997
Donderdag  05, Februari   1998 Donnerstag 05, Februar    1998
Zondag     07, Februari   1999 Sonntag    07, Februar    1999

. . .
Dinsdag    07, Juni       1994 Dienstag   07, Juni       1994
Dinsdag    07, Juni       1994 Dienstag   07, Juni       1994
Dinsdag    07, Juni       1994 Dienstag   07, Juni       1994

105 rows selected.

SQL>
```

The SQL functions to consider are the typecasting functions that convert between data types. Depending on the function, various parameters may be used.

Function	Globalization Parameters
TO_DATE	NLS_DATE_LANGUAGE
	NLS_CALENDAR
TO_NUMBER	NLS_NUMERIC_CHARACTERS
	NLS_CURRENCY
	NLS_DUAL_CURRENCY
	NLS_ISO_CURRENCY
	NLS_CALENDAR
TO_CHAR, TO_NCHAR	NLS_DATE_LANGUAGE
	NLS_NUMERIC_CHARACTERS
	NLS_CURRENCY
	NLS_DUAL_CURRENCY
	NLS_ISO_CURRENCY
	NLS_CALENDAR

Numbers, dates, and times can have a wide range of format masks applied for display. Within numbers, these masks allow embedding group and decimal separators, and the various currency symbols; dates can be formatted as virtually any combination of text and numbers; times can be shown with or without time zone indicators and as AM/PM or twenty-four hours.

CERTIFICATION OBJECTIVE 15.02

Work with Database and NLS Character Sets

Once you have your NLS settings in place, you need to understand how they are used when sorting or searching. Depending on the language, the results of a sort on a name or address in the database will return the results in a different order.

Even with Oracle's robust support for character sets, there are occasions where you might want to create a customized globalization environment for a database, or tweak an existing locale. One of the following sections gives you a brief introduction to the Oracle Locale Builder.

The chapter will wrap up with a discussion of time zones, and how Oracle supports them using initialization parameters at both the session and database levels, much like NLS parameters.

Linguistic Sorting and Selection

Oracle's default sort order is binary. The strings to be sorted are read from left to right, and each character is reduced to its numeric ASCII (or EBCDIC) value. The sort is done in one pass. This may be suitable for American English, but it will give incorrect results for other languages. Obvious problems are diacritics such as *ä* or *à* and diphthongs like *æ*, but there are also more subtle matters. For example, in traditional Spanish, *ch* is a character in its own right that comes after *c*; thus the correct order is "Cerveze, Cordoba, Chavez." To sort this correctly, the database must inspect the following character as well as the current character, if the current character is a *c*.

on the job

As a general rule, it is safe to assume that Oracle can handle just about any linguistic problem, but that you as DBA may not be competent to understand it. You will need an expert in whatever languages you are working in to advise.

Linguistic sorting means that rather than replacing each character with its numeric equivalent, Oracle will replace each character with a numeric value that reflects its correct position in the sequence appropriate to the language in use. There are some variations here, depending on the complexity of the environment.

A monolingual sort makes two passes through the strings being compared. The first pass is based on the "major" value of each character. The major value is derived by removing diacritic and case differences. In effect, each letter is considered as uppercase with no accents. Then a second comparison is made, using the "minor" values, which are case and diacritic sensitive. Monolingual sorts are much better than binary but are still not always adequate. For French, for example, Oracle provides the monolingual FRENCH sort order, and the multilingual FRENCH_M, which may be better if the data is not exclusively French.

A technique that may remove confusion is to use Oracle's case- and diacritic-insensitive sort options. For example, you may wish to consider these variations on a Scottish name as equivalent:

MacKay
Mackay
MACKAY

To retrieve all three with one query, first set the NLS_SORT parameter to GENERIC_BASELETTER as follows:

```
SQL> alter session set nls_sort=generic_baseletter;

Session altered.

SQL> alter session set nls_comp=ansi;

Session altered.


SQL> select * from names where name = 'MACKAY';


NAME
--------------
MacKay
Mackay
MACKAY
```

```
SQL> select * from names order by name;

NAME
---------------
Kohl
Kunst
Macdonald
MacDonald
MACDONALD
MACKAY
MacKay
Mackay

9 rows selected.

SQL>
```

This will ignore case and diacritic variations. Then set the `NLS_COMP` parameter away from the default of `BINARY` to `ANSI`. This instructs Oracle to compare values using the `NLS_SORT` rules, not the numeric value of the character. The `GENERIC_BASELETTER` sort order will also "correct" what may appear to some as incorrect ordering. A more complex example would require equating "McKay" with "MacKay"; that would require the Locale Builder.

Similarly, all the sort orders can be suffixed with _AI or _CI for accent-insensitive and case-insensitive sorting. For example,

```
SQL> alter session set nls_sort=FRENCH_CI;
```

will ignore upper- and lowercase variations but will still handle accented characters according to French standards.

The Locale Builder

The globalization support provided as standard by Oracle Database 11*g* is phenomenal, but there may be circumstances that it cannot handle. The Locale Builder is a graphical tool that can create a customized globalization environment, by generating definitions for languages, territories, character sets, and linguistic sorting.

As an example, Oracle does not provide out-of-the-box support for Afrikaans; you could create a customized globalization to fill this gap, which might combine elements of Dutch and English standards with customizations common in Southern Africa such as ignoring the punctuation marks or spaces in names like O'Hara or Du Toit. To launch the Locale Builder, run

```
$ORACLE_HOME/nls/lbuilder/lbuilder.bat
```

on Unix, or

```
%ORACLE_HOME%\nls\lbuilder\lbuilder
```

on Windows. You'll see the application window shown in Figure 15-1.

FIGURE 15-1   Creating a locale with the Locale Builder

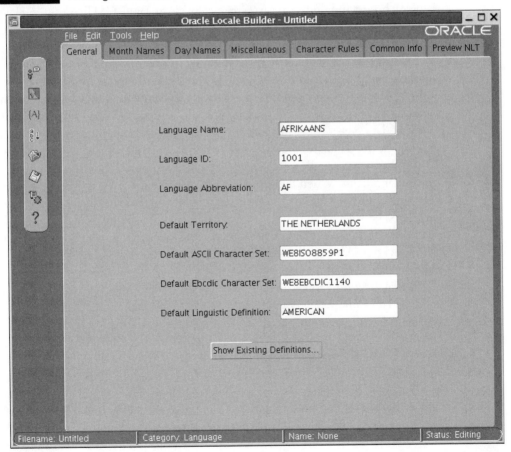

Using Time Zones

Businesses, and therefore databases, must work across time zones. From release 9*i* onward, the Oracle environment can be made time zone aware. This is done by specifying a time zone in which the database operates, and then using the TIMESTAMP WITH TIME ZONE and TIMESTAMP WITH LOCAL TIME ZONE data types. The former will be not be normalized to the database time zone when it is stored, but it will have a time zone indicator to show the zone to which it refers. The latter is normalized to the database time zone on storage but is subsequently converted to the client time zone on retrieval. The usual DATE and TIMESTAMP data types are always normalized to the database time zone on storage and displayed unchanged when selected.

As an example of when time zone processing is important, consider an e-mail database hosted in London, set to Greenwich Mean Time, GMT. A user in Harare (which is two hours ahead of GMT) sends an e-mail at his local time of 15:00; the mail is addressed to two recipients, one in Paris (Central European Time, CET: one hour ahead of GMT with daylight saving time in effect in the Northern hemisphere summer) and the other in Bogotá (which is five hours behind GMT). How do you ensure that the recipients and the sender will all see the mail as having been sent correctly according their local time zone? If the column denoting when the mail was sent is of data type TIMESTAMP WITH LOCAL TIME ZONE, then when the mail is received by the database, the time will be normalized to GMT: it will be saved as 13:00. Then when the Bogotá user retrieves it, the time will be adjusted to 08:00 by his user process. When the Paris user retrieves the mail, she will see it as having been sent at either 14:00 or 15:00, depending on whether the date it was sent was in the period between March and October when daylight saving time is in effect. It is possible to do this type of work programmatically, but it requires a great deal of work as well as knowledge of all time zones and any local quirks for daylight saving. The database can do it all for you.

The database time zone can be set at creation time in the CREATE DATABASE command and adjusted later with ALTER DATABASE SET TIME_ZONE=. If not set, it defaults to the time zone picked up from the host operating system at the time of creation. The client time zone defaults to that of the client operating system, or it can be set with the environment variable ORA_STDZ. Within a session, the time zone can be set with ALTER SESSION SET TIME_ZONE=. Time zones can always be specified by full name, by abbreviated name, or as a fixed offset, in hours and minutes, from GMT. The last option cannot take account of daylight saving time adjustments. The list of supported time zones is displayed in V$TIMEZONE_NAMES.

EXERCISE 15-3

Make Time Zone Adjustments

Confirm and adjust your current time zone, using appropriate data types. Test the results using appropriate formatting masks.

1. Using SQL*Plus, connect to your instance as user SYSTEM.

2. Identify the database time zone with this query:

```
SQL> select property_value from database_properties
  2  where property_name = 'DBTIMEZONE';


PROPERTY_VALUE
-----------------------------------------------
00:00


SQL>
```

3. Create a table as follows:

```
SQL> create table times
        (date_std date,
          date_tz timestamp with time zone,
          date_ltz timestamp with local time zone);
```

4. View the list of supported time zones with this query:

```
SQL> select * from v$timezone_names;
```

5. Adjust your session time zone to something other than the database time zone, for example,

```
SQL> alter session set time_zone='Pacific/Tahiti';
```

6. Set your timestamp with time zone format to twenty-four-hour clock, with abbreviated time zone names with daylight saving variations.

```
SQL> alter session
  2    set nls_timestamp_tz_format='YYYY-MM-DD HH24:MI:SS TZD';
```

7. Set your timestamp format to twenty-four-hour clock.

```
SQL> alter session set nls_timestamp_format='YYYY-MM-DD HH24:
MI:SS';
```

8. Set your date format to twenty-four-hour clock.

```
SQL> alter session set nls_date_format='YYYY-MM-DD HH24:MI:SS';
```

9. Insert a row into the table created in Step 3.

```
SQL> insert into times values('2008-10-26 15:00:00',
  2       '2008-10-26 15:00:00','2008-10-26 15:00:00');
```

10. Display the times.

```
SQL> select * from times;

DATE_STD              DATE_TZ                     DATE_LTZ
------------------    -------------------------   --------------
-----------
2008-10-26 15:00:00  2008-10-26 15:00:00 TAHT   2008-10-26
15:00:00

SQL>
```

Note that all times read 15:00.

11. Switch your session to the database time zone.

```
SQL> alter session set time_zone=DBTIMEZONE;
```

12. Repeat the query from Step 10, and note that the TIMESTAMP WITH
LOCAL TIMEZONE has been adjusted to reflect that your session is now in
a different zone:

```
SQL>  select * from times;

DATE_STD              DATE_TZ                     DATE_LTZ
------------------    -------------------------   --------------
-----------
2008-10-26 15:00:00  2008-10-26 15:00:00 TAHT   2008-10-27
01:00:00

SQL>
```

CERTIFICATION SUMMARY

Globalization capabilities allow you as DBA to customize the Oracle environment to
take account of national language and culture variations. This is virtually essential
in the modern world, where a database must present data in a variety of formats to

suit a range of end users. Globalization parameters can be set at any of five levels: the database, the instance, the client environment, the session, and the statement.

The globalization settings will influence, among other things, the languages for messages, sort orders, date formats, calendars, names of days and months, and numeric formats. Of vital importance is the choice of character sets, of which there are two. The database character set is used for VARCHAR2, CLOB, CHAR, and LONG columns; the National Character Set is used for NVARCHAR2, NCLOB, and NCHAR columns.

A related topic is time zones. These can now be specified for the database and per session, without ambiguity, if appropriate data types are used.

✓ TWO-MINUTE DRILL

Customize Language-Dependent Behavior for the Database and Individual Sessions

- ❑ Globalization covers aspects of data presentation, calendars, dates, and much more.

- ❑ A *character set* is a defined encoding scheme for representing characters as a sequence of bits.

- ❑ The number of characters that a character set can represent is limited by the number of bits the character set uses for each character.

- ❑ The Unicode standards are an international standard for character encoding, which is intended to include every character that will ever be required by any computer system.

- ❑ The number of languages supported by Oracle depends on the platform, release, and patch level of the product.

- ❑ The language used will determine the language for error messages and also set defaults for date language and sort orders.

- ❑ Binary sorting may be acceptable for a seven-bit character set, but for character sets of eight bits or more the results are often inappropriate.

- ❑ Query V$NLS_VALID_VALUES to see the available sort orders.

- ❑ To determine the territories your database supports, again query V$NLS_VAL-ID_VALUES using a PARAMETER value of TERRITORY.

- ❑ Globalization can be specified at any and all of five levels.

- ❑ The database character set is used to store all the data in columns of type VARCHAR2, CLOB, CHAR, and LONG.

- ❑ Two types of Unicode are supported as the National Character Set: AL16UTF16 and UTF8.

- ❑ There are two tools provided to assist with deciding on character set change: the Database Character Set Scanner and the Language and Character Set File Scanner.

- ❑ Instance globalization parameter settings will override the database settings.

❑ The key client-side environment variable is `NLS_LANG`. The full specification for this is a language, a territory, and a character set.

❑ The tightest level of control over globalization is to manage it programmatically, within each SQL statement.

Work with Database and NLS Character Sets

❑ Oracle's default sort order is binary.

❑ Linguistic sorting means that rather than replacing each character with its numeric equivalent, Oracle will replace each character with a numeric value that reflects its correct position in the sequence appropriate to the language in use.

❑ The Locale Builder is a graphical tool that can create a customized globalization environment, by generating definitions for languages, territories, character sets, and linguistic sorting.

❑ Applications are made time-zone aware by specifying a time zone in which the database operates, and then using the `TIMESTAMP WITH TIME ZONE` and `TIMESTAMP WITH LOCAL TIME ZONE` data types.

❑ The usual `DATE` and `TIMESTAMP` data types are always normalized to the database time zone on storage and displayed unchanged when selected.

❑ The database time zone can be set at creation time in the `CREATE DATABASE` command and adjusted later with `ALTER DATABASE SET TIME_ZONE`.

SELF TEST

The following questions will help you measure your understanding of the material presented in this chapter. Read all the choices carefully, because there might be more than one correct answer. Choose all correct answers for each question.

Customize Language-Dependent Behavior for the Database and Individual Sessions

1. Your database was created with US7ASCII as the database character set, and you later find that this is inadequate. What can you do? (Choose the best answer.)

    A. Re-create the database.

    B. Issue an `alter database character set...` command.

    C. Issue an `alter system character set...` command.

    D. Generate a `create controlfile...` command, edit it to specify a different character set, and re-create the controlfile.

2. What are the options for the National Character Set?

    A. None. It must be AL16UTF16.

    B. It can be any Unicode character set.

    C. It can be either AL16UTF16 or UTF8.

    D. It can be any character set you require.

3. Match each character set with a type:

Character Set	Type
1. AL16UTF16	a. Seven-bit single-byte
2. US7ASCII	b. Eight-bit single-byte
3. UTF8	c. Fixed-width multibyte
4. WE8ISO8859P15	d. Variable-width

    A. 1-c; 2-b; 3-d; 4-a

    B. 1-d; 2-a; 3-c; 4-b

    C. 1-c; 2-d; 3-b; 4-a

    D. 1-c; 2-a; 3-d; 4-b

4. Which statements are correct about the TIMESTAMP WITH LOCAL TIME ZONE data type? (Choose two answers.)

   A. Data is saved with a local time zone indicator.

   B. Data is normalized to the database time zone when it is saved.

   C. On retrieval, data is normalized to the retrieving client's time zone.

   D. On retrieval, data is normalized to the time zone of the client that entered it.

5. Globalization can be set at various levels. Put these in order of precedence, lowest first:

   A. Client environment

   B. Database settings

   C. Instance parameters

   D. Session parameters

   E. Statements

6. The NLS_LANGUAGE and NLS_TERRITORY parameters set defaults for a number of other globalization parameters. Which of the following are controlled by NLS_LANGUAGE? (Choose two.)

   A. NLS_DATE_LANGUAGE

   B. NLS_DATE_FORMAT

   C. NLS_NUMERIC_CHARACTERS

   D. NLS_SORT

Work with Database and NLS Character Sets

7. Choose the best description of the Character Set Scanner tool:

   A. It scans character sets to assess their suitability for a particular language.

   B. It scans files to determine the language and character set of the data in them.

   C. It scans datafiles to determine whether the character set can be changed.

   D. It reports on problems a character set change would cause.

8. If the database and the user process are using different character sets, how does data get converted?

   A. Data is not converted, which is why there may be corruptions if the character sets are incompatible.

   B. On data entry, the instance converts data to the database character set. On retrieval, the user process converts to the client character set.

   C. Oracle Net will convert, in both directions.

   D. It depends on various NLS parameters.

9. The database is set to GMT. A client in Buenos Aires (three hours behind GMT) executes these statements at 10:00:00 local time:

```
create table times(c1 timestamp,
c2 timestamp with local time zone);
insert into times values(to_timestamp('10:00:00'),
  to_timestamp('10:00:00'));
commit;
```

A client in Nairobi (three hours ahead of GMT) executes these statements at 18:00:00 local time:

```
alter session set nls_timestamp_format='hh24:mi:ss';
select * from times;
```

What will the Nairobi user see for the columns c1 and c2?

A. 10:00:00 and 16:00:00

B. 13:00:00 and 16:00:00

C. 13:00:00 and 10:00:00

D. 10:00:00 and 13:00:00

10. Study the result of this query:

```
SQL> select * from dates;
C1
--------
06-04-08
```

C1 is a date-type column. How could you determine what the date returned actually means? (Choose two answers.)

A. Query NLS_DATABASE_PARAMETERS.

B. Query NLS_INSTANCE_PARAMETERS.

C. Query NLS_SESSION_PARAMETERS.

D. Set your NLS_DATE_FORMAT to a known value, and rerun the query.

E. Change the query to use TO_CHAR with an NLS parameter.

11. How can you prevent users from causing confusion with, for instance, date and time formats by setting local globalization environment variables?

A. You can't; the users have control over this.

B. Write logon triggers to set the session environment.

C. Set instance globalization parameters to override client-side settings.

D. Configure Oracle Net to convert all data sent to and from the database appropriately.

12. Which view will tell you what languages can be supported by your installation? (Choose the best answer.)

    A. `NLS_DATABASE_PARAMETERS`

    B. `NLS_INSTANCE_PARAMETERS`

    C. `V$NLS_VALID_VALUES`

    D. `V$NLS_LANGUAGES`

13. You want to make the order in which sorted names are returned independent of whether the names include accented characters, upper- and lowercase characters, punctuation marks, or spaces. How can you do this? (Choose the best answer.)

    A. Set the sort order to `GENERIC_BASELETTER`, which will ignore such variations.

    B. Use the `_AI` and `_CI` versions of any of the supported sort orders.

    C. Use the Locale Builder to design a custom sort order.

    D. This cannot be done.

SELF TEST ANSWERS

Customize Language-Dependent Behavior for the Database and Individual Sessions

1. ☑ **B.** Use this command, but test with the character set scanner first.
   ☒ **A** is wrong because you do not need to recreate the database to change the database character set. **C** is wrong because ALTER SYSTEM cannot be used to change the character set. **D** is wrong because changing the character set in the control file will not convert the database character set.

2. ☑ **C.** Either of these Unicode sets is currently allowed.
   ☒ All other answers are wrong because the only two options are AL16UTF16 or UTF8.

3. ☑ **D.** 1-c; 2-a; 3-d; 4-b
   ☒ **A, B,** and **C** are all incorrect.

4. ☑ **B and C.** This is the data type that fully normalizes times to and from the database.
   ☒ **A and D.** Timestamp values are not saved with the time zone indicator, nor is it normalized when retrieved.

5. ☑ The correct order is **B, C, A, D, E.** Instance parameters override the database parameters, and then on the client side environment variables can be overridden by ALTER SESSION commands, and then by individual statements.
   ☒ All other orders are incorrect.

6. ☑ **A and D.** NLS_DATE_LANGUAGE and NLS_SORT are the two parameters controlled by the NLS_LANGUAGE.
   ☒ **B and C** are wrong. NLS_DATE_FORMAT and NLS_NUMERIC_CHARACTERS are controlled by NLS_TERRITORY.

Work with Database and NLS Character Sets

7. ☑ **D.** It will, for instance, report if a changed encoding would prevent data from fitting into an existing column.
   ☒ **A, B,** and **C** are incorrect descriptions.

8. ☑ **C.** Oracle Net will do the best conversion possible.
   ☒ **A, B,** and **D** are incorrect conversion scenarios.

9. ☑ **B.** The database will normalize the time 10:00:00 from the local time zone at the point of entry, GMT+3, to the database time zone, GMT. Thus both times are saved as 13:00:00 GMT. For retrieval, the timestamp column will be displayed as saved, 13:00:00, but the timestamp with local time zone column will adjust the time to that of the time zone of the client retrieving the data, which is GMT+3.
   ☒ **A, C,** and **D** are incorrect.

10. ☑ **C** and **D.** NLS_SESSION_PARAMETERS will show the format used so that you can interpret the output of the query correctly, or you could set the format to a sensible value and re-run the query.
   ☒ **A, B,** and **E** are wrong. You must query the session-specific version of the view to interpret the output correctly.

11. ☑ **B.** The best option is to write logon triggers, which will prevent any possible confusion caused by the client configuration.
   ☒ **A** is wrong because you can control the local settings with a logon trigger (unless the user explicitly overrides them). **C** is wrong because client-side settings can override instance settings. **D** is wrong because you cannot configure Oracle Net to perform a specific conversion.

12. ☑ **C.** The view V$NLS_VALID_VALUES will show you the full range of supported languages, as well as all other globalization options.
   ☒ **A** is wrong because NLS_DATABASE_PARAMETERS shows the permanent values for each database NLS-related initialization parameter. **B** is wrong because NLS_INSTANCE_ PARAMETERS shows the changed NLS values since instance startup. **D** is wrong because there is no such view as V$NLS_LANGUAGES.

13. ☑ **C.** To remove punctuation marks and spaces as well, you will need to create your own variation with the Locale Builder.
   ☒ **A, B,** and **D** are wrong. Setting the sort order to GENERIC_BASELETTER or using the _AI or _CI versions of the sort orders does not remove punctuation marks and spaces.

A

About the CD

T he CD-ROM included with this book comes complete with MasterExam and the electronic version of the book. The software is easy to install on any Windows 2000/ XP/Vista computer and must be installed to access the MasterExam feature. You may, however, browse the electronic book directly from the CD without installation. To register for a second bonus MasterExam, simply click the Online Training link on the Main Page and follow the directions to the free online registration.

System Requirements

Software requires Windows 2000 or higher, Internet Explorer 6.0 or above, and 20MB of hard disk space for full installation. The electronic book requires Adobe Acrobat Reader.

Installing and Running MasterExam

If your computer CD-ROM drive is configured to auto run, the CD-ROM will automatically start up upon inserting the disk. From the opening screen you may install MasterExam by pressing the MasterExam button. This will begin the installation process and create a program group named "LearnKey." To run MasterExam use Start | All Programs | LearnKey | MasterExam. If the auto run feature did not launch your CD, browse to the CD and click on the LaunchTraining.exe icon.

MasterExam

MasterExam provides you with a simulation of the actual exam. The number of questions, the type of questions, and the time allowed are intended to be an accurate representation of the exam environment. You have the option to take an open book exam, including hints, references, and answers; a closed book exam; or the timed MasterExam simulation.

When you launch MasterExam, a digital clock display will appear in the bottom right-hand corner of your screen. The clock will continue to count down to zero unless you choose to end the exam before the time expires.

Electronic Book

The entire contents of the Study Guide are provided in PDF. Adobe's Acrobat Reader has been included on the CD.

Help

A help file is provided through the help button on the main page in the lower left-hand corner. An individual help feature is also available through MasterExam.

Removing Installation(s)

MasterExam is installed to your hard drive. For best results, use the Start | All Programs | LearnKey | Uninstall option to remove MasterExam.

Technical Support

For questions regarding the technical content of the electronic book or MasterExam, please visit www.mhprofessional.com or email customer.service@mcgraw-hill.com. For customers outside the 50 United States, email international_cs@mcgraw-hill.com.

LearnKey Technical Support

For technical problems with the software (installation, operation, removing installations), please visit www.learnkey.com, email techsupport@learnkey.com, or call toll free at 800-482-8244.

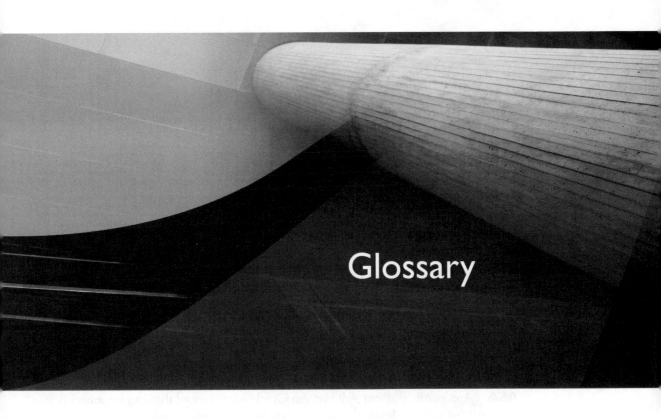

Glossary

A

ACID   Atomicity, Consistency, Isolation, and Durability. Four characteristics that a relational database must be able to maintain for transactions.

ADDM   Automatic Database Diagnostic Monitor. A tool that generates performance tuning reports based on snapshots in the Automatic Workload Repository (AWR).

ADR   Automatic Diagnostic Repository. The default location for the alert log, trace files, and other information useful for fault finding. An always-on facility that captures errors in trace and dump files the first and any subsequent times they occur.

ADRCI   The Automatic Diagnostic Repository (ADR) command-line interface accessed using the `adrci` command.

AES   Advanced Encryption Standard. A widely used data encryption method.

AL16UTF16   A Unicode fixed-width, 2-byte character set, commonly specified for the NLS character set used for NVARCHAR2, NCHAR, and NCLOB data types.

alias   In Oracle Net, a pointer to a connect string. An alias must be resolved to the address of a listener and the name of a service or instance.

ANSI   American National Standards Institute. A U.S. body that defines a number of standards relevant to computing.

API   Application programming interface. A defined method for manipulating data—for example, a set of PL/SQL procedures in a package written to perform a related set of tasks.

ARBn   Background processes that perform extent movement between disks in an Automatic Storage Management (ASM) disk group.

ASA   Automatic Segment Advisor. An Oracle advisory tool that can recommend segments (tables or indexes) that are candidates for segment shrink.

ASCII   American Standard Code for Information Interchange. A standard (with many variations) for coding letters and other characters as bytes.

ASH   Active Session History. A category of information in the AWR that records details of session activity.

ASM   Automatic Storage Management. A logical volume manager (LVM) provided with the Oracle database.

asmcmd   A command-line utility used to query and maintain objects in an ASM disk group.

ASSM   Automatic Segment Space Management. The method of managing space within segments by use of bitmaps.

attribute   One element of a tuple (aka a column or field).

AWR   Automatic Workload Repository. A set of tables in the SYSAUX tablespace, populated with tuning data gathered by the MMON process.

B

background process   A process that is part of the instance that is launched at startup.

BFILE   A large object data type that is stored as an operating system file. The value in the table column is a pointer to the file.

bind variable   A value passed from a user process to a SQL statement at statement execution time.

BLOB   Binary Large Object. A LOB data type for binary data such as photographs and video clips.

block   The unit of storage into which datafiles are formatted. The size can be 2KB, 4KB, 8KB, 16KB, 32KB, or 64KB. Some platforms will not permit all these sizes.

BMR   Block media recovery. An RMAN feature that recovers individual blocks instead of entire database objects to save time during recovery.

C

CET   Central European Time. A time zone used in much of Europe (though not Great Britain) that is one hour ahead of UTC, with daylight savings time in effect during the summer months.

character set   The encoding system for representing data within bytes. Different character sets can store different characters and may not be suitable for all languages. Unicode character sets can store any character.

check constraint   A simple rule enforced by the database that restricts values that can be entered into a column.

checkpoint   An event that forces the DBW*n* (database writer) process to write all dirty buffers from the database buffer cache to the datafiles.

CKPT   The checkpoint process. The background process responsible for recording the current redo byte address—the point at which the DBW*n* has written changed data blocks to disk—and for signaling checkpoints, which force DBW*n* to write all changed blocks to disk immediately.

client-server architecture   A processing paradigm in which the application is divided into client software that interacts with the user and server software that interacts with the data.

CLOB   Character Large Object. A LOB data type for character data, such as text documents stored in the database character set.

cluster   A hardware environment in which more than one computer shares access to storage. A Real Application Cluster (RAC) database consists of several instances on several computers opening one database on a shared storage device.

column   An element of a row: tables are two-dimensional structures, divided horizontally into rows and vertically into columns.

`commit`   To make a change to data permanent.

complete recovery   Following a restore of damaged database files, a complete recovery applies all redos to bring the database up to date with no loss of data.

connect identifier   An Oracle Net alias.

connect role   A preseeded role retained only for backward compatibility. Oracle now adopts a minimal security policy at installation and database creation, allowing administrators better control over database security.

connect string   The database connection details needed to establish a session: the address of the listener and the service or instance name.

consistent backup   A backup made while the database is closed.

constraint   A mechanism for enforcing rules on data: a column value must be unique or may contain only certain values. A primary key constraint specifies that the column must be both unique and not null.

control file   The file containing pointers to the rest of the database, critical sequence information, and the RMAN repository.

CPU   Central processing unit. The chip that provides the processing capability of a computer, such as an Intel Pentium or a Sun SPARC.

CTWR   Change Tracking Writer. The optional background process that records the addresses of changed blocks to enable fast incremental backups.

D

data blocks   The units into which datafiles are formatted, made up of one of more operating system blocks.

data dictionary   The tables and views owned by SYS in the SYSTEM tablespace that define the database and the objects within it.

data dictionary views   Views on the data dictionary tables that let the DBA query the state of the database.

Data Guard   A facility whereby a copy of the production database is created and updated (possibly in real time), with all changes applied to the production database.

Data Pump   A facility for transferring large amounts of data at high speed into, out of, or between databases.

database buffer cache   An area of memory in the System Global Area (SGA) used for working on blocks copied from datafiles.

database link   A connection from one database to another, based on a username and password and a connect string.

Database Replay   An Oracle monitoring feature that can help to assess the change in performance on a test system by capturing the workload on a production server and replaying the workload on a test system.

datafile   The disk-based structure for storing data.

DBA   Database administrator. The person responsible for creating and managing Oracle databases—this could be you.

DBA role   A preseeded role in the database provided for backward compatibility that includes all the privileges needed to manage a database, except the privilege needed to start up or shut down.

DBCA   The Database Configuration Assistant. A GUI tool for creating, modifying, and dropping instances and databases.

DBID   Database identifier. A unique number for each individual database, visible in the DBID column of the V$DATABASE dynamic performance view.

DBMS   Database management system. This is often used interchangeably with RDBMS.

DBNEWID   A command-line utility (usually nid) that can change the value of DBID for a database.

DBWn or DBWR   The database writer. The background process responsible for writing changed blocks from the database buffer cache to the datafiles. An instance can have up to 20 database writer processes, DBW0 through DBW9 and DBWa through DBWj.

DDL   Data Definition Language. The subset of SQL commands that change object definitions within the data dictionary: CREATE, ALTER, DROP, and TRUNCATE.

deadlock   A situation in which two sessions block each other, such that neither can do anything. Deadlocks are detected and resolved automatically by the DIA0 background process.

DHCP   Dynamic Host Configuration Protocol. The standard for configuring the network characteristics of a computer, such as its IP address, in a changing environment where computers can be moved from one location to another.

DIA0   The diagnosability process that detects hang and deadlock situations.

DIAG   The diagnosability process that generates diagnostic dumps.

direct path   A method of I/O on datafiles that bypasses the database buffer cache.

directory object   An Oracle directory: a object within the database that points to an operating system directory.

dirty buffer   A buffer in the database buffer cache that contains a copy of a data block that has been updated and not yet written back to the datafile.

DML   Data Manipulation Language. The subset of SQL commands that change data within the database: INSERT, UPDATE, DELETE, and MERGE.

DM*nn*   Data Pump Master process. The process that controls a data pump job—one will be launched for each job that is running.

DNS   Domain Name Service. The TCP mechanism for resolving network names into IP addresses. Runs on a machine called a DNS server.

domain   The set of values an attribute is allowed to have. Terminology: tables have rows, and rows have columns with values; or, relations have tuples, and tuples have attributes with values taken from their domain.

DSS   Decision Support System. A database, such as a data warehouse, optimized for running queries with high I/O activity on large chunks of data, as opposed to online transaction processing (OLTP) work that accesses small chunks of data at a time.

DW*nn*   Data Pump Worker process. One or more of these will be launched for each data pump job that is running.

E

easy connect   A method of establishing a session against a database by specifying the address on the listener and the service name, without using an Oracle Net alias.

EBCDIC   Extended Binary Coded Decimal Interchange Code. A standard developed by IBM for coding letters and other characters in bytes.

environment variable   A variable set in the operating system shell that can be used by application software and by shell scripts.

equijoin   A join condition using an equality operator.

F

fast incremental backup   An incremental backup that uses a block change tracking file to identify only changed blocks since the last backup.

FGA   Fine-grained auditing. A facility for tracking user access to data, based on the rows that are seen or manipulated.

flash recovery area   A location on a file system or an Automatic Storage Management (ASM) disk group for all recovery-related files.

Flashback Data Archive   A database container object that retains historical data for one or more database objects for a specified retention period.

Flashback Database   A flashback feature that recovers the entire database to a point of time in the past using Flashback Database logs.

Flashback Database logs   Changed database blocks that are stored in the flash recovery area and used for Flashback Database.

Flashback drop   A flashback feature that makes it easy to recover dropped tables if they are still in a tablespace's recycle bin.

Flashback Query   A flashback feature that enables you to view one or more rows in a table at a time in the past.

Flashback Table   A Flashback Query that recovers a single table and its associated objects to a point in time that has passed.

fractured block   A database block that is simultaneously being read by an operating system copy command and modified by the DBWR process.

full backup   A backup containing all blocks of the files backed up, not only those blocks changed since the last backup.

G

GMT Greenwich Mean Time. Now referred to in the United States as UTC, which is the time zone of the meridian through the Greenwich Observatory in London.

grid computing An architecture for which the delivery of a service to end users is not tied to certain server resources but can be provided from anywhere in a pool of resources, linking multiple low-cost, independently capable machines into a single, far more powerful grouped virtual platform.

GUI Graphical user interface. A layer of an application that lets users work with applications using a graphically driven screen interface, using both keyboard and mouse. The X Window System and Microsoft Windows are both GUI applications that provide GUI-driven access to other GUI applications.

H

HTTP Hypertext Transfer Protocol. The protocol that enables the World Wide Web (both invented at the European Organization for Nuclear Research in 1989). This layered protocol runs over TCP/IP.

HWM High water mark. The last block of a segment that has ever been used—blocks above this are part of the segment but are not yet formatted for use.

I

IBM International Business Machines. A well-known computer hardware, software, and services company.

image copy A Recovery Manager (RMAN) bit-for-bit copy of a file.

inconsistent backup A backup made while the database is open.

incremental backup A backup containing only blocks that have been changed since the last backup was made.

instance recovery The automatic repair of damage caused by a disorderly shutdown of the database, either from a crash or from running SHUTDOWN ABORT.

I/O   Input/output. The activity of reading from or writing to disks—often the slowest point of a data processing operation because it's the slowest piece of hardware when compared with CPU and RAM.

IOT   Index-organized table. A table type in which the data rows are stored in the leaf blocks of an index segment. The table is effectively an index.

IP   Internet Protocol. Together with the Transmission Control Protocol, TCP, TCP/IP is the de facto standard communication protocol used for client-server communication over a network.

IPC   Inter-Process Communications protocol. The platform-specific protocol provided by your OS vendor and used for processes running on the same machine to communicate with each other.

ISO   International Organization for Standardization. A group that defines many standards, including SQL.

J

job   A row in a scheduler table that specifies what to do and when to do it. The "what" can be a single SQL statement, a PL/SQL block, a PL/SQL stored procedure, a Java stored procedure, an external procedure, or any executable file stored in the server's file system.

job chain   A database object that contains a named series of programs linked together for a combined objective.

job class   A scheduler object that is used to associate one or more jobs with a Resource Manager consumer group and to control logging levels.

join   The process of connecting rows in different tables based on common column values.

JVM   Java Virtual Machine. The runtime environment needed for running code written in Java. Oracle provides a JVM that executes within the database, and another is provided by your operating system, which runs in the operating system.

L

large pool   A memory structure within the System Global Area (SGA) used by certain processes, principally shared server processes and parallel execution servers.

LDAP   Lightweight Directory Access Protocol. The TCP implementation of the X25 directory standard, used by the Oracle Internet Directory for name resolution, security, and authentication. LDAP is also used by other software vendors, including Microsoft and IBM.

level 0 incremental backup   A full RMAN backup that can be used as the basis for an incremental backup strategy.

level 1 cumulative incremental backup   An RMAN backup of all changed blocks since the last level 0 incremental backup.

level 1 differential incremental backup   An RMAN backup of all changed blocks since the last level 0 or level 1 incremental backup.

LGWR   Log Writer. The background process responsible for flushing change vectors from the log buffer in memory out to the online redo log files on disk.

library cache   A memory structure within the shared pool that is used for caching SQL statements parsed into their executable form.

lightweight job   A scheduler job that has many of the same characteristics of a standard job, except that a lightweight job is ideal for running many short-duration jobs that run frequently.

listener   A server-side process that listens for database connection requests from user processes and launches dedicated server processes to establish sessions. The sessions become the connections between the user process and the database unless shared servers are in use, in which case a dispatcher process is used to share time to shared server processes.

LOB   Large object. A data structure that contains a large amount of binary or character data, such as an image or a document. LOBs (Oracle supports several types) are defined as columns of a table but can be either physically stored in a separate segment or stored within the table itself.

Locale Builder   A graphical tool that can create a customized globalization environment by generating definitions for languages, territories, character sets, and linguistic sorting.

log switch   The action of closing one online logfile group and opening another (triggered by the LGWR process filling the first group), and then causing the now offline log file to be archived.

logical backup   A backup that reads a set of database rows and writes them to a file in the operating system or to another tablespace.

LRU   Least Recently Used. An algorithm in which LRU lists manage access to data structures that are used infrequently.

LVM   Logical Volume Manager. A layer of software that groups physical storage areas (one or more disk partitions) all into groups or volumes. A single volume is then accessed to manage data on one or more underlying physical disks.

M

MMAN   The Memory Manager background process, which monitors and reassigns memory allocations in the SGA for automatically tunable SGA components.

MML   Media Management Layer. Software that lets RMAN make use of automated tape libraries and other SBT (System Backup to Tape) devices.

MMNL   Manageability Monitor Light. The background process responsible for flushing Active Session History (ASH) data to the Automatic Workload Repository (AWR)—if the Manageability Monitor (MMON) is not doing this with the necessary frequency.

MMON   The Manageability Monitor. A background process that is responsible for gathering performance monitoring information and raising alerts.

mounted database   A condition in which the instance has opened the database controlfile, the online redo logfiles, and the datafiles.

MTBF   Mean Time Between Failures. A measure of the average length of running time for a database between unplanned shutdowns.

MTS   Multithreaded server. Since release 9*i*, renamed Shared Server. This is the technique whereby a large number of sessions can share a small pool of server processes, rather than requiring one dedicated server process each. Dedicated server processes can often be the most efficient for anything other than the most extreme types of production environments.

MTTR   Mean Time To Recover. The average time it takes to make the database available for normal use after a failure.

multiplexing   To maintain multiple copies of files (particularly controlfiles and redo log files). Previous versions of Oracle have used the terms *multiplexing* to describe controlfile duplication and *duplexing* to describe log file member duplications.

N

namespace   A logical grouping of objects within which no two objects may have the same name.

NCLOB   National Character Large Object. A LOB data type for character data, such as text documents that are stored in the alternative national database character set.

NLS   National Language Support. The capability of Oracle Database to support many linguistic, geographical, and cultural environments—now usually referred to as *globalization*.

node   A computer attached to a network.

Null   The absence of a value, indicating that the value is not known, missing, or inapplicable. Null values are used in databases to save space and to avoid continually having to program zeros and space characters into empty columns in tables.

O

OC4J   Oracle Containers for J2EE. The control structure provided by the Oracle Internet Application Server for running Java programs.

OCA   Oracle Certified Associate.

OCI   Oracle Call Interface. An API published as a set of C libraries that programmers can use to write user processes that will use an Oracle database.

OCP   Oracle Certified Professional. The qualification you are working toward at the moment.

offline backup   A backup made while the database is closed (completely shut down).

OLAP   Online Analytical Processing. Selection-intensive work involving running very large and intensive queries against a (usually) large database. Oracle provides OLAP capabilities as an option, in addition to the standard query facilities.

OLTP   Online Transaction Processing. A pattern of activity within a database typified by a large number of small, short transactions as well as small queries.

online backup   A backup made while the database is open.

online redo log   The files to which change vectors are streamed by the Log Writer (LGWR), recording all changes made to a database, ensuring complete recoverability.

ORACLE_BASE   The root directory into which all Oracle products are installed.

ORACLE_HOME   The root directory of any one particular Oracle product, within the ORACLE_BASE.

Oracle Net   Oracle's proprietary communications protocol, layered on top of an industry-standard protocol such as TCP/IP.

OS   Operating system. Typically, in the Oracle environment, this will be a version of Unix (perhaps Linux) or Microsoft Windows.

P

parallelization   An RMAN backup technique that allocates multiple channels, improving backup performance by executing partitioned chunks of I/O in parallel.

parse   To verify syntax and convert SQL statements into a form suitable for execution.

PFILE   A text-based file containing initialization parameters and initial values that are set when an Oracle instance starts.

PGA   Program Global Area. The variable-sized block of memory used to maintain the state of a database session. PGAs are private to the session and controlled by the session's server process.

physical backup   A backup of the files that constitute the database.

PL/SQL   Procedural Language/Structured Query Language. Oracle's proprietary programming language, which combines procedural constructs, such as flow control and user interface capabilities, with SQL.

PMON   The process monitor. The background process responsible for monitoring the state of user sessions against an instance.

primary key   The column (or combination of columns), whose value(s) can be used to identify each row in a table.

program   A scheduler object that provides a layer of abstraction between the job and the action it will perform; it is created with the DBMS_SCHEDULER.CREATE_PROGRAM procedure.

R

RAC   Real Application Clusters. Oracle's clustering technology that allows several instances running on different machines to open the same database files with the objectives of scalability, performance, and fault tolerance.

RAID   Redundant Array of Inexpensive Disks. Technique for enhancing performance and/or fault tolerance by using a volume manager to present a number of physical disks to the operating system as a single logical disk.

RAM   Random Access Memory. The chips that make up the real memory in your computer hardware, versus the virtual memory presented to software by the operating system. RAM is the second fastest piece of hardware in your computer other than your CPU.

raw device   An unformatted disk or disk partition.

RBAL   Rebalance process. A background process in an Automatic Storage Management (ASM) instance that coordinates disk activity for disk groups. In an RDBMS instance, RBAL performs opening and closing of the disks in the disk group.

RDBMS   Relational Database Management System. This term is often used interchangeably with DBMS.

recovery catalog   Tables in a database schema that contain metadata and other backup information for RMAN backups of one or more databases.

recovery window   An RMAN time period that defines how far back in time the database can be recovered.

referential integrity   Rules defined in a relational database between primary and foreign keys, where the primary key must exist in a table for a row to exist on a subset table (in the foreign key) and defines one-to-many relationships.

relation   A two-dimensional structure consisting of tuples with attributes (aka a table).

resource consumer groups   Groups of users or sessions that have similar resource needs.

Resource Manager   An Oracle feature that can allocate resources based on CPU usage, degree of parallelism, number of active sessions, undo space, CPU time limit, and idle time limit.

resource plan   A set of rules in Resource Manager that assign various resources at specific percentages or relative priorities to a resource group.

resource plan directives   Rules within Resource Manager that associate consumer groups with a resource plan and specify how the resources are divided among the consumer groups or subplans.

restore point   A database object containing either a System Change Number (SCN) or a time in the past used to recover the database to the SCN or timestamp.

Resumable Space Allocation   An Oracle feature that suspends instead of terminating large database operations that require more disk space than is currently available. A suspended operation can be restarted from where it stopped at a later point in time, when the space issues have been resolved. It saves time.

retention policy   The number of copies of all objects that RMAN will retain for recovery purposes.

RMAN   Recovery Manager. Oracle's backup and recovery tool.

ROWID   The unique identifier of every row in the database, which is used as a pointer to the physical location of the row from logical objects such as tables and indexes. The rowid data type is proprietary to Oracle Corporation and is not part of the SQL standard, and it is not recommended for direct storage into tables because the values can change.

RVWR   The Recovery Writer background process is an optional process responsible for flushing the flashback buffer to the flashback logs.

S

SBT   System backup to tape. An RMAN term for a tape device.

schedule   A specification for when and how frequently a job should run.

schema   The objects owned by a database user; synonymous with a user from a physical perspective. A schema is a user that is used to store tables and indexes. Users are created to access that schema user as multiple application users of that centrally managed schema.

SCN   System Change Number. The continually incrementing number used to track the sequence and exact time of all events within a database.

segment   A database object within a schema that stores data.

segment shrink   A database operation that makes the free space in the segment available to other segments in the tablespace by compacting the data blocks in a segment.

sequence   A database object within a schema that can generate consecutive numbers.

service name   A logical name registered by an instance with a listener, which can be specified by a user process when it issues a connect request. A service name will be mapped onto a System Identifier (SID) by the listener when it establishes a session.

session   A user process (application) connected through a server process that is connected to the instance.

SGA   System Global Area. The block of shared memory that contains the memory structures that make up an Oracle instance.

SID   1. System identifier. The name of an instance that must be unique on the computer on which the instance is running. Users can request a connection to a named SID or to a logical service and let the listener choose an appropriate SID. 2. Session identifier. The number used to uniquely identify a session that is logged on to an Oracle instance.

SMON   The System Monitor. The background process responsible for opening a database and monitoring the instance.

SPFILE   The server parameter file. The file containing the parameters used to build an instance in memory. This is a binary form of the parameter file. A text form of the parameter file is called the PFILE.

SQL   Structured Query Language. An international standard language for extracting data from and manipulating data in relational databases.

SQL Tuning Advisor   An Oracle advisor that performs statistics analysis, SQL Profile analysis, access path analysis, and structure analysis.

synonym   A pointer (named reference) to a database object, typically used to avoid fully qualified names for schema objects.

SYSASM   A system privilege in an ASM instance that facilitates the separation of database administration and storage administration.

SYSDBA   The privilege that lets a user connect with operating system or password file authentication and create, start up, and shut down a database.

SYSOPER   The privilege that lets a user connect with operating system or password file authentication and start up and shut down (but not create) a database.

SYSTEM   A preseeded schema used for database administration purposes.

T

table   A logical two-dimensional data storage structure, consisting of rows and columns.

tablespace   The logical structure that abstracts logical data storage in tables from physical data storage in datafiles.

TCP   Transmission Control Protocol. Together with the Internet Protocol, IP, TCP/IP is the de facto standard communication protocol used for client-server communication over a network.

TCPS   TCP with SSL. The secure sockets version of TCP.

tempfile   The physical storage that makes up a temporary tablespace that is used for storing temporary segments.

TNS   Transparent Network Substrate. The heart of Oracle Net, a proprietary layered protocol running on top of whatever underlying network transport protocol you choose to use—probably TCP/IP.

transaction   A logical unit of work, which will complete in total or not at all.

TSPITR   Tablespace Point In Time Recovery. A recovery method that is ideal for recovering a set of objects isolated to a single tablespace.

tuple   A one-dimensional structure consisting of attributes (aka a row).

U

UGA   User Global Area. The part of the Program Global Area (PGA) that is stored in the System Global Area (SGA) for sessions running through shared servers.

UI   User interface. The layer of an application that communicates with end users; nowadays, the UI is frequently graphical—a GUI.

URL   Uniform Resource Locator. A standard for specifying the location of an object on the Internet (a web site name you type into your browser), consisting of a protocol, a host name and domain, an IP port number, a path and filename, and a series of parameters.

user managed recovery   Recovery using tools or commands outside of RMAN, used to recover a database or tablespace.

UTC   Coordinated Universal Time, previously known as Greenwich Mean Time (GMT). UTC is the global standard time zone. All other time zones relate to it as offsets, which are ahead of or behind UTC.

V

virtual private catalog   A logical partitioning of an RMAN catalog to facilitate separation of duties among several DBAs.

W

whole database backup   A database backup that includes all datafiles plus the control file.

window   A scheduler construct that extends the concept of schedules by giving Oracle more freedom on deciding when to run a job within a specific start and begin time—for a single day or every day of the week.

X

X   As in the X Window System, the standard GUI environment used on most non–Microsoft Windows computers.

XML   Extensible Markup Language. A standard for data interchange using documents, in which the format of the data is defined by tags within the document.

INDEX

U

V

Are You Oracle Certified?

GET YOUR FREE SUBSCRIPTION
TO *ORACLE MAGAZINE*

Oracle Magazine is essential gear for today's information technology professionals. Stay informed and increase your productivity with every issue of *Oracle Magazine*. Inside each free bimonthly issue you'll get:

- Up-to-date information on Oracle Database, Oracle Application Server, Web development, enterprise grid computing, database technology, and business trends
- Third-party news and announcements
- Technical articles on Oracle and partner products, technologies, and operating environments
- Development and administration tips
- Real-world customer stories

If there are other Oracle users at your location who would like to receive their own subscription to *Oracle Magazine*, please photocopy this form and pass it along.

Three easy ways to subscribe:

① Web
Visit our Web site at **oracle.com/oraclemagazine**
You'll find a subscription form there, plus much more

② Fax
Complete the questionnaire on the back of this card and fax the questionnaire side only to **+1.847.763.9638**

③ Mail
Complete the questionnaire on the back of this card and mail it to **P.O. Box 1263, Skokie, IL 60076-8263**

ORACLE®

Want your own FREE subscription?

To receive a free subscription to *Oracle Magazine*, you must fill out the entire card, sign it, and date it (incomplete cards cannot be processed or acknowledged). You can also fax your application to +1.847.763.9638. **Or subscribe at our Web site at oracle.com/oraclemagazine**

O **Yes, please send me a FREE subscription** *Oracle Magazine*.　　O No.

O From time to time, Oracle Publishing allows our partners exclusive access to our e-mail addresses for special promotions and announcements. To be included in this program, please check this circle. If you do not wish to be included, you will only receive notices about your subscription via e-mail.

O Oracle Publishing allows sharing of our postal mailing list with selected third parties. If you prefer your mailing address not to be included in this program, please check this circle.

If at any time you would like to be removed from either mailing list, please contact Customer Service at +1.847.763.9635 or send an e-mail to oracle@halldata.com. If you opt in to the sharing of information, Oracle may also provide you with e-mail related to Oracle products, services, and events. If you want to completely unsubscribe from any e-mail communication from Oracle, please send an e-mail to: unsubscribe@oracle-mail.com with the following in the subject line: REMOVE [your e-mail address]. For complete information on Oracle Publishing's privacy practices, please visit oracle.com/html/privacy/html

X

signature (required)　　　　　　　　　　　　　　　date

name　　　　　　　　　　　　　　　　title

company　　　　　　　　　　　　　　e-mail address

street/p.o. box

city/state/zip or postal code　　　　telephone

country　　　　　　　　　　　　　　fax

Would you like to receive your free subscription in digital format instead of print if it becomes available? O Yes　O No

YOU MUST ANSWER ALL 10 QUESTIONS BELOW.

① WHAT IS THE PRIMARY BUSINESS ACTIVITY OF YOUR FIRM AT THIS LOCATION? (check one only)
- ☐ 01 Aerospace and Defense Manufacturing
- ☐ 02 Application Service Provider
- ☐ 03 Automotive Manufacturing
- ☐ 04 Chemicals
- ☐ 05 Media and Entertainment
- ☐ 06 Construction/Engineering
- ☐ 07 Consumer Sector/Consumer Packaged Goods
- ☐ 08 Education
- ☐ 09 Financial Services/Insurance
- ☐ 10 Health Care
- ☐ 11 High Technology Manufacturing, OEM
- ☐ 12 Industrial Manufacturing
- ☐ 13 Independent Software Vendor
- ☐ 14 Life Sciences (biotech, pharmaceuticals)
- ☐ 15 Natural Resources
- ☐ 16 Oil and Gas
- ☐ 17 Professional Services
- ☐ 18 Public Sector (government)
- ☐ 19 Research
- ☐ 20 Retail/Wholesale/Distribution
- ☐ 21 Systems Integrator, VAR/VAD
- ☐ 22 Telecommunications
- ☐ 23 Travel and Transportation
- ☐ 24 Utilities (electric, gas, sanitation, water)
- ☐ 98 Other Business and Services _____

② WHICH OF THE FOLLOWING BEST DESCRIBES YOUR PRIMARY JOB FUNCTION? (check one only)

CORPORATE MANAGEMENT/STAFF
- ☐ 01 Executive Management (President, Chair, CEO, CFO, Owner, Partner, Principal)
- ☐ 02 Finance/Administrative Management (VP/Director/ Manager/Controller, Purchasing, Administration)
- ☐ 03 Sales/Marketing Management (VP/Director/Manager)
- ☐ 04 Computer Systems/Operations Management (CIO/VP/Director/Manager MIS/IS/IT, Ops)

IS/IT STAFF
- ☐ 05 Application Development/Programming Management
- ☐ 06 Application Development/Programming Staff
- ☐ 07 Consulting
- ☐ 08 DBA/Systems Administrator
- ☐ 09 Education/Training
- ☐ 10 Technical Support Director/Manager
- ☐ 11 Other Technical Management/Staff
- ☐ 98 Other

③ WHAT IS YOUR CURRENT PRIMARY OPERATING PLATFORM (check all that apply)
- ☐ 01 Digital Equipment Corp UNIX/VAX/VMS
- ☐ 02 HP UNIX
- ☐ 03 IBM AIX
- ☐ 04 IBM UNIX
- ☐ 05 Linux (Red Hat)
- ☐ 06 Linux (SUSE)
- ☐ 07 Linux (Oracle Enterprise)
- ☐ 08 Linux (other)
- ☐ 09 Macintosh
- ☐ 10 MVS
- ☐ 11 Netware
- ☐ 12 Network Computing
- ☐ 13 SCO UNIX
- ☐ 14 Sun Solaris/SunOS
- ☐ 15 Windows
- ☐ 16 Other UNIX
- ☐ 98 Other
- 99 ☐ None of the Above

④ DO YOU EVALUATE, SPECIFY, RECOMMEND, OR AUTHORIZE THE PURCHASE OF ANY OF THE FOLLOWING? (check all that apply)
- ☐ 01 Hardware
- ☐ 02 Business Applications (ERP, CRM, etc.)
- ☐ 03 Application Development Tools
- ☐ 04 Database Products
- ☐ 05 Internet or Intranet Products
- ☐ 06 Other Software
- ☐ 07 Middleware Products
- 99 ☐ None of the Above

⑤ IN YOUR JOB, DO YOU USE OR PLAN TO PURCHASE ANY OF THE FOLLOWING PRODUCTS? (check all that apply)

SOFTWARE
- ☐ 01 CAD/CAE/CAM
- ☐ 02 Collaboration Software
- ☐ 03 Communications
- ☐ 04 Database Management
- ☐ 05 File Management
- ☐ 06 Finance
- ☐ 07 Java
- ☐ 08 Multimedia Authoring
- ☐ 09 Networking
- ☐ 10 Programming
- ☐ 11 Project Management
- ☐ 12 Scientific and Engineering
- ☐ 13 Systems Management
- ☐ 14 Workflow

HARDWARE
- ☐ 15 Macintosh
- ☐ 16 Mainframe
- ☐ 17 Massively Parallel Processing
- ☐ 18 Minicomputer
- ☐ 19 Intel x86(32)
- ☐ 20 Intel x86(64)
- ☐ 21 Network Computer
- ☐ 22 Symmetric Multiprocessing
- ☐ 23 Workstation Services

SERVICES
- ☐ 24 Consulting
- ☐ 25 Education/Training
- ☐ 26 Maintenance
- ☐ 27 Online Database
- ☐ 28 Support
- ☐ 29 Technology-Based Training
- ☐ 30 Other
- 99 ☐ None of the Above

⑥ WHAT IS YOUR COMPANY'S SIZE? (check one only)
- ☐ 01 More than 25,000 Employees
- ☐ 02 10,001 to 25,000 Employees
- ☐ 03 5,001 to 10,000 Employees
- ☐ 04 1,001 to 5,000 Employees
- ☐ 05 101 to 1,000 Employees
- ☐ 06 Fewer than 100 Employees

⑦ DURING THE NEXT 12 MONTHS, HOW MUCH DO YOU ANTICIPATE YOUR ORGANIZATION WILL SPEND ON COMPUTER HARDWARE, SOFTWARE, PERIPHERALS, AND SERVICES FOR YOUR LOCATION? (check one only)
- ☐ 01 Less than $10,000
- ☐ 02 $10,000 to $49,999
- ☐ 03 $50,000 to $99,999
- ☐ 04 $100,000 to $499,999
- ☐ 05 $500,000 to $999,999
- ☐ 06 $1,000,000 and Over

⑧ WHAT IS YOUR COMPANY'S YEARLY SALES REVENUE? (check one only)
- ☐ 01 $500, 000, 000 and above
- ☐ 02 $100, 000, 000 to $500, 000, 000
- ☐ 03 $50, 000, 000 to $100, 000, 000
- ☐ 04 $5, 000, 000 to $50, 000, 000
- ☐ 05 $1, 000, 000 to $5, 000, 000

⑨ WHAT LANGUAGES AND FRAMEWORKS DO YOU USE? (check all that apply)
- ☐ 01 Ajax
- ☐ 02 C
- ☐ 03 C++
- ☐ 04 C#
- ☐ 05 Hibernate
- ☐ 06 J++/J#
- ☐ 07 Java
- ☐ 08 JSP
- ☐ 09 .NET
- ☐ 10 Perl
- ☐ 11 PHP
- ☐ 12 PL/SQL
- ☐ 13 Python
- ☐ 14 Ruby/Rails
- ☐ 15 Spring
- ☐ 16 Struts
- ☐ 17 SQL
- ☐ 18 Visual Basic
- ☐ 98 Other

⑩ WHAT ORACLE PRODUCTS ARE IN USE AT YOUR SITE? (check all that apply)

ORACLE DATABASE
- ☐ 01 Oracle Database 11*g*
- ☐ 02 Oracle Database 10*g*
- ☐ 03 Oracle9*i* Database
- ☐ 04 Oracle Embedded Database (Oracle Lite, Times Ten, Berkeley DB)
- ☐ 05 Other Oracle Database Release

ORACLE FUSION MIDDLEWARE
- ☐ 06 Oracle Application Server
- ☐ 07 Oracle Portal
- ☐ 08 Oracle Enterprise Manager
- ☐ 09 Oracle BPEL Process Manager
- ☐ 10 Oracle Identity Management
- ☐ 11 Oracle SOA Suite
- ☐ 12 Oracle Data Hubs

ORACLE DEVELOPMENT TOOLS
- ☐ 13 Oracle JDeveloper
- ☐ 14 Oracle Forms
- ☐ 15 Oracle Reports
- ☐ 16 Oracle Designer
- ☐ 17 Oracle Discoverer
- ☐ 18 Oracle BI Beans
- ☐ 19 Oracle Warehouse Builder
- ☐ 20 Oracle WebCenter
- ☐ 21 Oracle Application Express

ORACLE APPLICATIONS
- ☐ 22 Oracle E-Business Suite
- ☐ 23 PeopleSoft Enterprise
- ☐ 24 JD Edwards EnterpriseOne
- ☐ 25 JD Edwards World
- ☐ 26 Oracle Fusion
- ☐ 27 Hyperion
- ☐ 28 Siebel CRM

ORACLE SERVICES
- ☐ 28 Oracle E-Business Suite On Demand
- ☐ 29 Oracle Technology On Demand
- ☐ 30 Siebel CRM On Demand
- ☐ 31 Oracle Consulting
- ☐ 32 Oracle Education
- ☐ 33 Oracle Support
- ☐ 98 Other
- 99 ☐ None of the Above

08014Q4